THE WHOLE-WORLD WINE CATALOG

William I. Kaufman has written or edited more than a hundred books on gastronomy, travel, television, and other subjects. (Among these books are *Cooking in a Castle, The Coffee Cookbook, Champagne, The Pocket Travel Guide to the West Indies, Your Career in Television,* and *The Executive Diet Book*.) As a photographer he has worked in seventy countries, and his photographs have been seen in twenty one-man shows. In 1971 he was producer, film director, photographer, and publicist for the Danny Kaye UNICEF tour, which began in Asia and concluded in Europe. The same year, Mr. Kaufman received the Christopher Award, "recognizing individuals who have used their talents constructively in the hope that they and others will continue to produce high quality works that promote sound values," and in 1974 the French Republic made him a Chevalier de l'Ordre du Mérite Agricole.

CONTENTS

THE WHOLE-WORLD WINE CATALOG

William I. Kaufman

PENGUIN BOOKS

This book is dedicated to two men—one young and starting his career in wine and one whose passing has left an unalterable void in the ranks of that confrérie of men and women who have devoted their lives and their love to the cultivation and perpetuation of the wine tradition.

The young man is my son, Lazare. He has chosen wine as his profession and his life, and having just reached the enviable age of twenty-one, has already devoted several important years to planning a future that will have meaning. His recipe for success seems to possess several secret ingredients, for he has shown an enormous capacity and ability to work with intelligence, diligence, stability, and persistence. Taking advantage of his long summer holiday from the Lycée Francais, Lazare managed to start his career as a *commis* (assistant) at the Royal Champagne restaurant-hotel. Under the excellent tutelege of the famous Champagne sommelier Monsieur Odile, he was trained well enough to continue his studies with the president of all the sommeliers of France, Monsieur Louis Le Bail, and entered the service at the Plaza Athenée in Paris each summer thereafter, passing from *commis* to *stagiare* (probationer) to *demi-chef sommelier* (sub-head wine steward) and finally receiving his certificate as *chef sommelier* (wine steward), all within a period of five summers, a remarkable feat under any circumstances. Lazare is thus the first American, and the youngest person of any nation, ever to hold the coveted title of "Sommelier de Paris." And he continued to submerge himself in the study of wine as a student at the IPC in Bordeaux. He is a pupil of the great oenologist Dr. Emile Peynaud at the University of Bordeaux II and received his certificate from that university as a qualified "wine taster and analyst of wines." He has done well to lay the groundwork for his goal as a wine expert through hard work and the determination to choose his own path in life in the face of stiff competition.

In half-dedicating this book to Lazare, I hope that he will try to emulate the integrity and valor of the second person who inspired this volume.

I first met Comte Robert-Jean de Voguë while I was living in the Champagne region, writing and making photographs for my beautiful book *Champagne*. Aside from our mutual love for the land of Champagne and the wine of Champagne, we were both collectors of hats. In his entryway the Comte had a small tree that was literally blanketed with hats. He adored collecting them wherever he went in his travels, as I do. To elucidate on the Comte's many military and civil decorations, to speak of his unique contributions to the wine trade, would detract from the projection of the great human qualities that were so much a part of a man for whom I had great respect even though I found myself in his company too few times.

Comte de Voguë epitomized the qualities of refinement, gentility, spirit, an acute sense of business, and a profound love for his fellow man. He was a noble tycoon with the heart of a cleric who loved and shepherded his flock. His legendary social consciousness and his role as the leader of the Resistance in Épernay during World War II led to his arrest and comdemnation to death in 1944, but he remained dauntless. He was still under the death sentence when he was liberated by British paratroopers in 1945.

As head of the House of Moët & Chandon he shall be remembered as the architect of its expansion and shall be revered as an enlightened employer who instituted labor practices that have set the standard for many other enterprises.

The world has lost an important manifestation of what a man can and ought to be, and this dedication is an acknowledgment of that sad fact—small acknowledgment to say the least—but the only one I have to offer in humility and respect.

ACKNOWLEDGMENTS

To say that I have written this book would be presumptuous, so I have chosen the term "edited by" to indicate my function regarding this work.

By the time the manuscript came to completion, I almost felt that I had not only created the idea and served as its editor, but also I had a sense of the fact that I was an explorer returning home from his quest. Each label had become a precious object with a life of its own.

The extraordinary effort has been worth it, however, and I can take leave of my task with the certainty that *The Whole-World Wine Catalog* will bring pleasure to you as you indulge in the fun of learning about these wines, some of which may be unfamiliar to you.

I am grateful to all the producers and importers of wines, all the people at the California Wine Institute, and all the personnel of the various wine commissions who were so cooperative and kind in according me their assistance and their permission to use their printed materials.

Should you own or represent a vineyard that is not manifest here, the omission has not been for lack of trying on my part. I literally contacted everyone in the world associated with the wine trade.

If you are a consumer and lover of wine and find that I missed noting a favorite that you would like to recommend, please do so. Members of the wine trade and consumers alike may write me care of my publishers: Mr. William I. Kaufman, *The Whole-World Wine Catalog,* Viking Penguin Inc., 625 Madison Avenue, New York, New York 10022, U.S.A.

I want particularly to take this opportunity to thank Frank Johnson, whose expertise added so much to this book when I called upon him to edit the editor in the closing days when deadlines were upon us with terrifying proximity.

And most of all I must add a word of gratitude to my assistant, Lucia Vail, without whose mind and typewriting hand there would never have been the organized chaos from which this very challenging volume has emerged.

In vino veritas!

Penguin Books Ltd, Harmondsworth, Middlesex, England
Penguin Books, 625 Madison Avenue, New York, New York 10022, U.S.A.
Penguin Books Australia Ltd, Ringwood, Victoria, Australia
Penguin Books Canada Limited, 2801 John Street Markham, Ontario, Canada L3R 1B4
Penguin Books (N.Z.) Ltd, 182–190 Wairau Road, Auckland 10, New Zealand

First published 1978

Copyright © William I. Kaufman, 1978
All rights reserved

LIBRARY OF CONGRESS CATALOGING IN PUBLICATION DATA
Kaufman, William Irving, 1922—
    The whole-world wine catalog.
    1. Wine and wine making—Catalogs.   2. Wine labels—Catalogs.   I. Title.
TP548.K328   641.2'2   77-25349
ISBN 0 14 046.277 5

Printed in the United States of America by
Georgian Web Offset, Garden City, New York
Set in VIP Helvetica Light

This catalog is for all who enjoy a glass of wine, whether it be made from citrus fruit, spilled from a jug, or poured carefully and tenderly from a rare bottle of Claret. My purpose in creating it was to make it possible for you to walk into any wine shop and have a personal idea of what you are buying and why you are buying it. If you are seeking a new experience in wine, this catalog will point the way.

Many may turn up their noses and challenge the fact that I have included a "pop wine" in close proximity to some of the great classics of the world, but this is a fun book and wine drinking is supposed to be a joyful experience. It has always been that for me, and it is a pleasure I want to share with my readers.

New discoveries should be as important to the wine buff as a rare stamp or coin is to a collector of those items. That is why I have tried to make this book as informative as it can be, and it is my wish that through this catalog you will become daring and try some of the specialties on your wine seller's shelves that you may never have tasted before.

As a food and wine writer and photographer, I have often found myself in unusual corners of the globe where new food tastes have been like the discoveries of fresh, beautiful blossoms in a garden. The same is true of wines. When the wine card is presented, why not take the challenge of picking something unknown to your palate. When I am alone or with new-made foreign friends, I always search for regional wines that I haven't tasted. (Sometimes I may not even know their names.) When I am fortunate enough to have a wine steward, I remember the advice of my old friend Charles Colin, who spent most of his life as chef sommelier at the Hostellerie de la Poste in Avallon, France. Monsieur Colin, whose following included the world's greatest gastronomes, said, "Never be afraid to ask the sommelier to suggest something. Use a sommelier's knowledge. Offer him a challenge when you sit down to dine. Be frank. Ask him to recommend the unusual. Tell him what your financial limit is. Selecting a regional wine that suits the meal but also suits your purse is the real test of a sommelier's skill. Let him test it in your behalf." That's what I do and what I am encouraging you to do. You'll enjoy your meal all the more for calling upon his expertise.

The same principle applies to your dealings with your local wine shop. If you're not sure of what you want, ask your wine seller. Challenge him to choose the best in the house that comes within the range of your purse and your palate. His main interest is to please you and keep you happy as his customer. If he suggests a wine and it turns out to be the wrong wine for you, tell him so. If you taste the wine and find it unpleasing, put the cork back on and return it. He'll appreciate your raising the standards of his stock. Don't forget to sample some of his personal selections—the ones that carry his own label and neckband. Here are some local selections from my own "shop around the corner" that tell you what to look for at your wine seller's.

The information on the label should look something like this—

If you read through this wine catalog before you purchase your next bottle of wine, you will get an idea of the type of wine you want. You may see names and details of wines you have never tasted but that you would like to taste in future. Why not make a list?

If you are planning a dinner party, it might be more interesting to select some wines that neither you nor your friends have ever tried. Buy a single bottle of each of your selections and have a tasting before your meal. It will pique the appetite. Or go a step further and tape black artpaper around each bottle so that the labels are hidden. See whose guesses come closest to being accurate. Laughter always adds the right atmosphere to any social evening.

This catalog contains plenty of solid basic information, but is is far from a definitive work in the true sense of the word. It is a book that contains a wide assortment of wine insignias from every part of the winegrowing world. It will provide the kind of knowledge you need to broaden the base from which you make your personal choices.

The comments written here have, for the most part, been composed by the producers themselves. Each one has assiduously attempted to give you a truthful, objective, and informed opinion about his wine. It is altogether possible that, for a variety of reasons, many of these wines are not available in your wine shop. Some may be missing because the size of the vineyard does not warrant wide distribution; others may have to remain in their region because they do not "travel well" in the hold of a ship or an airplane. But do keep in mind that though a stamp collector may not be able to acquire all the stamps in his catalog, he still takes pleasure in seeing the rare, new, and difficult-to-obtain specimens that may lie outside his reach. That is the rationale that I have used in putting this catalog together.

I cannot tell you what a good time I have had collecting this unique compendium of wine labels, observing closely the exquisite good taste of a Mouton-Rothschild artwork, the rococo elaboration of an old German wine insignia, or the simple modern details of a California design. Each label was fascinating as almost four thousand of them came rolling in, but I was especially enthralled by new discoveries—the possibility of tasting different and unknown wines or savoring the production of the Canadian vineyards that lay so close to our own borders. I became involved in the history of Mead and the traditional methods of producing Port—all played an essential role in making the many hours that went into this collection exciting as well as gratifying and pleasurable.

Pleasure is what I hope will be a key factor in stimulating you to use *The Whole-World Wine Catalog* again and again, for a lifetime in which you will always know the joy of wine.

The character of a wine—its taste and aftertaste—is influenced by and depends upon the variety of grape used in its making. Varieties with unusually strong flavors, like the Tokay or Concord, make wines as unmistakably distinct as the grapes themselves. One of the easiest ways to learn about wine is to become familiar with the characteristics of the individual grapes. It is a great deal simpler to categorize and recognize grape varieties than it is to memorize the names of several hundred regions and several thousand vineyards.

Using this method of identifying grape varieties as the basis of your course of study, you will quickly gather the wine know-how you need to make pleasing selections for your own palate, and you will be overjoyed at the relative ease with which you make good choices once you are able to distinguish a Riesling from a Chardonnay or a Gamay from a Cabernet Sauvignon.

The following list is far from complete, but it does cover most of the outstanding and widely used grapes of wine producers around the world.

Baco Noir   This red hybrid grape produces a wine of dark color with great acidity.

Barbera   A common grape in the Piedmont region of Italy, it produces a dark, tannic, and fresh red wine. The Barbera is used to produce a good California varietal.

Blauer Burgunder   A noble red wine is made from this grape. Rich in body and dry, it is mild and spicy and often possesses a velvety elegance.

Blaufraenkish   This grape produces a dry, fruity red wine with a light- to ruby-color. It reaches its peak on full maturity.

Cabernet Sauvignon   The famous Claret wines of Bordeaux, principally the Médoc and St.-Émilion regions, receive their flavor and character from this grape. The grapes produce a wine that has a bouquet of freshly crushed grape flowers that blends admirably with the extractive materials of oak wood. A favorite of California winegrowers, who sometimes call it simply *Cabernet,* this grape also produces excellent wines for growers in Australia and South Africa.

California White Riesling   This grape is also known in California as *Johannisberg Riesling.* A dry wine, good but not equal to the full-bodied and crisp, balanced German wines.

Carignane   This grape is of Spanish origin but has been growing in the South of France since about the twelfth century. It still grows widely both there and in Algeria. The wines are of medium acidity and color. They have good quality but are without distinction.

Catawba   Henry Wadsworth Longfellow called the wine of this grape "dulcet, delicious and dreamy." The wine is fruity and spicy.

Charbono   This grape is a California hybrid used to produce a Chianti-type wine.

Chardonnay   This variety has many close relatives. It has long been confused with the Pinto Blanc. However, it is a distinct and well-marked variety known as the "Queen of Burgundy" because it is responsible for the character of their greatest white wines. The Chardonnay is exceedingly popular in California, where the wines of these grapes are crisp and fruity in flavor and possess a distinctive bouquet.

Chasselas   A table grape in France, Chasselas is used in Switzerland and Alsace for ordinary white wine. California wine producers use it for blending.

Chelois   This is a hybrid that produces a slightly foxy, dry red wine.

Concord   A native of the United States, this grape is popular for its sweetness and most often used for ceremonial and holiday wines.

Delaware   This delicate sweet pink grape is often used for red and white wines. It produces a full-bodied clean white wine.

De Chaunac   Rich, heavy, dark red wine is produced from de Chaunac.

Diana   This native hybrid is grown in New York State and in the Sandusky region of Ohio.

Dolcetto   From the Piedmont region of Italy, the Dolcetto produces a strong, rounded, flavorful dry red wine.

Doradillo   This grape is often used for the production of Sherry.

Dutchess   A hybrid of the Concord and Delaware grapes, it produces a delightful white wine.

Elvira   In the eastern United States the Elvira is often used in the making of "Champagne" and good still wine.

Emerald Riesling   This cross between a Muscadelle of California and a white Riesling produces a pleasant, medium-dry wine.

Folle Blanche   Produced in California for its earthy taste, this grape makes a light, pale-greenish white wine.

Franken Riesling   This is the California name used most often for Sylvaner.

Freisa   Another grape from the Piedmont region of Italy, it produces a dry red wine that softens with age. Slightly sweet.

French Colombard   This grape is used a great deal in California Champagne.

Frontignac   The name of this grape, which was first grown in North Africa, is a variation of "Frontignan," a village near Montpellier in Southern France that is famous for its Muscat wine.

Veltliner   This type of grape yields a mild, distinctive white wine with a delicate bouquet.

Fumé Blanc   See **Sauvignon Blanc.**

Furmint   Also called *Imperial Tokay,* this grape produces a dry table wine or sweet dessert wine in America.

Gamay   Due to the granite in the hills of Beaujolais, the Gamay produces excellent wine there; but in other areas of France, the product of these grapes is inferior. In California, however, the Gamay is highly regarded and results in very good wine.

Gamay California   There are two: Napa Valley Gamay, which is a fuller, more flavored wine; and California Gamay Beaujolais, a fruity, light wine more typical of its French cousin. Drink it while it is young.

Gewürztraminer   A favorite grape of Alsace, the Gewürztraminer is a choice Traminer. A wonderful, elegant, dry white wine of flowery bouquet comes from these grapes, which also grow well in California.

Green Hungarian   A popular California grape producing a pleasant, easy-to-drink, fruity, light white wine.

Grenache   This grape of Spanish origin is principally used in the making of both rosé and Port wines. It lacks sufficient color for dry red table wines and is often combined with Hermitage. The softness of the Grenache blends well with the stronger Hermitage character and produces a Burgundy-type wine. Fragrant, fruity rosés are produced with the Grenache in California.

Grignolino   A Piedmontese grape variety that produces a dry, light-bodied red wine, Grignolino joins Cabernet and Pinot Noir on the list of California favorites.

Grüner Veltliner   The typical wine made from this grape is effervescent and highly palatable. It is spicy and fruity, with a pleasant heartiness.

Hermitage   As far as can be determined, this grape originated in Persia, but it is now one of the main varieties grown in the Rhône Valley of France. It is known there as the *Syrah* or, in some local areas, the *Serine.* It produces a full-bodied wine with a fine dark color and a bouquet reminiscent of violets, which gives it a highly unique flavor.

Ives   This is a native black grape, very popular with the winegrowers of Ohio.

Muscat   Of North African origin, the Muscat grape is grown all over the world. With the exception of Alsace, the wines it produces are sweet. The grape is also known as *Muscat of Alexandria, Moscato,* and *Muskat-Ottonel.*

Müller-Thurgau   This important German grape is a cross between Riesling and Sylvaner. Ripening early, Müller-Thurgau produces a mild wine with an effervescent flavor and a distinct bouquet of Muscatel.

Nebbiolo   This grape is best known for producing the big Italian wine called Barolo, famous for its scent and flavor.

Neuburger   A full-bodied, mostly mild wine with a particularly fine aroma is produced from Neuburger.

Niagara   These grapes produce a foxy, sweet white wine.

Palomino   This is the world's greatest Sherry grape. It produces a light amber wine, medium-bodied and pleasantly dry. Its characteristics contribute to the nutty flavor and refined aroma expected in fine Sherry.

Petite Sirah   An increasingly desirable California varietal, originally from the Rhône Valley in France. The wine from this grape covers a large range, from light and fruity to rich and full-bodied, depending on the location of the vineyard. It is sometimes spelled *Petite Syrah.*

Pinot Gris   Known as *Tokay* in Alsace and Switzerland and as *Ruländer* in Germany, the grape produces a fine wine with a scented aroma and rich flavor.

Pinot Noir   This red jewel produces the finest wines of Burgundy and Champagne. The white wines are made by pressing before fermentation. It is dominant in all fine Champagne. It is also used in Germany and Eastern Europe for those purposes. In California, its name on a label is a sign of the best quality possible.

Portugieser   This grape, contrary to the sound of its name, comes from Germany. Its wine is the most commonly consumed red wine in that country.

Prosecco   In the Veneto region of Italy, this grape produces fragrant and clear wines that are still or sparkling.

Rhine Riesling   See **Riesling.**

Riesling   This is the finest and best-known white-wine grape grown in Germany.

When planted in suitable locations, this top-quality grape yields an outstanding wine, characterized by its delicate bouquet. This grape is also grown extensively in the United States.

Ruby Cabernet   Not equal to the Cabernet Sauvignon, this grape produces a light and pleasant wine. Nevertheless, take warning: do not confuse it with Cabernet Sauvignon or you will be disappointed.

Ruländer   A very important wine-producing grape in Germany, although it originated in Burgundy, the Ruländer wines are full-bodied and pleasantly fruity.

St. Laurent   A fine grape producing a high-quality wine with excellent bouquet and a deep red color.

Sangiovese   The main grape of Chianti.

Sauvignon Blanc   Famous for its use in producing the dry white wines of Graves and other regions of France, this grape also produces dry white wines of good character in the Livermore and Santa Clara valleys of California.

Scuppernong   The first grape variety developed in America, Scuppernong most often is used in the making of white wines.

Semillon   The Sauternes and white wines of Barsac and Graves in France obtain their character from the Semillon grape. Sauternes rely on the *pourriture noble* (see page 9) produced on these grapes for their luscious sweet wine.

Spätburgunder   What Riesling is to German white wine, this grape is to the finest German red wine. Originating in Burgundy, it has become indigenous to Germany. Typical Spätburgunder is velvety and fruity.

Sylvaner   Famous in Germany and Alsace, as well as in other parts of the world, the typical Sylvaner tastes mild and fruity. Some winegrowers prefer the *Silvaner* spelling.

Teroldego   In the Trentino region of Italy, the Teroldego grape produces a big, red, full-bodied quality wine with a bitter, nutty aftertaste.

Tokay   A dry table wine or sweet dessert wine is produced from this grape, which is also called *Aszu* and *Szamorondi*.

Tollinger   This grape produces a light wine with a very fresh taste. Its original home was in the Tyrol.

Traminer   Easily recognizable by its own pronounced bouquet, this wine has a deep golden color and a spicy and aromatic fruity flavor.

Trebbiano   A full-bodied round white wine is made from this grape, which is called *Ugni Blanc* in the South of France and *Trebbiano* in central Italy.

Ugni Blanc   See **Trebbiano**.

Verdicchio   A delightful pale straw color and full white wine is produced from this well-known grape.

Weisser Burgunder   A top-quality wine producer, these grapes yield wines that are characterized by their special bouquet and robustness. They are best when aged.

Welschriesling   See **Riesling**.

Zierfandler or **Rotgipfler**   These two grapes are customarily blended before reaching the market and produce wines of outstanding quality with a superior bouquet and a full body that reach their peak when well aged.

Zinfandel   This California varietal is best grown in the northern parts of the state, in the regions of Sonoma, Napa, and Santa Cruz. Red, fruity, with a good aroma, Zinfandels are best when consumed young.

THE LANGUAGE OF WINE AND WINE LABELS

Acidity   An indication of the tartness or sharpness to the taste; the presence of agreeable fruit acids. It should be clearly distinguished from sourness.

Aging   Maturation of the wine. When the wine is first placed in casks and stored in the producer's cellars, aging is very active. It continues at a much slower pace once it is in the bottle.

American Wine   Ordinarily used to designate U.S. wines other than those grown in California. Most such wines are made from characteristically flavored native American grapes. The term is also used to differentiate wines grown in the United States from wines of the same names grown in France, Italy, and other foreign countries. In this usage, *U.S. Wine* rather than American Wine is sometimes preferred, for *U.S. Wine* clearly embraces both California wines and wines of other states. Referring to these wines as "domestic" is discouraged because the term suggests cheapness and inferior quality to many people.

Amontillado   Dry type of Sherry.

Amoroso   Medium-dry type of Sherry.

Aperitif   A French word from the medieval Latin *aperire*, "to open." It refers to wine and other drinks taken before meals to stimulate the appetite. In the strictest sense, it applies to vermouths and any wines flavored with herbs and other aromatic substances; in general usage, any wine served before a meal may be referred to as an aperitif.

Appellation D'Origine or **Appellation Contrôlée**   Term appears on labels of fine French wines. Signifies origin and right to use the name it bears as guaranteed by French law.

Appleness   A frequent characteristic of fine white wine.

Argols   The tartrate deposited by wines during aging.

Aroma   The pleasant and desirable odors that contribute so much to the enjoyment of a wine. Aroma is derived wholly or in part from the grape and in most cases is indicative of the grape variety used in producing the wine. Aroma is determined by the palate during tasting; in contrast, bouquet is determined by the sense of smell before tasting the wine.

Aromatic   The delectable qualities from volatile essences.

Astringency   The quality that causes the mouth to pucker. The degree of astringency in a wine depends primarily upon the amount of tannin it has absorbed from the skins and seeds of the grapes. Moderate astringency is a desirable quality in many red wines and is demanded by many consumers, but it is not to be confused with dryness. Never call an astringent wine "sour."

Balance   Denotes complete harmony in the principal constituents of the wine. Excessive amounts of any one constituent can cause disharmony of palate impression. Wines so constituted are described as "poorly balanced" or "unbalanced."

Baumé   A measure of the sugar content of the grape. One Baumé is equal to approximately 1.75% of sugar content.

Baumé Hydrometer   The instrument for measuring the Baumé.

Beloe Vino   Red wine (Russian).

Bianco   White (Italian).

Big Wine   A tasting term to express body and apparent fruitiness.

Bijelo   White (Yugoslavian).

Binning   Bottle aging of newly bottled wines, usually in bins, before release for sale.

Biser   Sparkling (Yugoslavian).

Bitter   Excessive tannin from stems, stalks, or seeds during crushing for fermentation; too long in wood.

Bjalo Vino   White wine (Bulgarian).

Blanco   White (Spanish).

Blending   The art of combining two or more wines, selected for compatibility and balance, to result in a wine that is as consistent as possible from vintage to vintage. A side effect of skillful blending is the production of a wine that is more appealing than any of the constituents would have been on their own.

Blume   Bouquet, aroma (German).

Body   The consistency ("thickness") of a wine as detected by its feel in the mouth. The body of a wine is attributable to the presence of nonsugar solids, which vary from wine to wine and district to district. It is detected by the receptors sensitive to viscosity and possibly salinity. Thus, wines can be described as "thin," "medium-bodied," or "full-bodied."

Bouquet   That part of the fragrance of the wine that originates from fermentation and aging, as distinguished from *aroma,* the fragrance of the grape in the wine. The fragrance to the nose, before tasting.

Brilliant   A wine of remarkably high clarity.

Bronze   The amber hue apparent around the rim of a glass of aged red wine.

Brut   The epitome of dryness, which means that little or no "dosage" has been added to the wine.

California Wine   Wine produced 100% in California, from grapes grown within that state. Under existing federal and state wine laws, no wine may be labeled or advertised as California wine unless it conforms to strict California standards. In contrast, New York State wines may be made from 75% of grapes grown within the state and must be finished in the state. They may contain up to 25% of grapes from other regions and still be labeled after the local region. The same is true of wine produced in Ohio.

Cantina Solidale   A winegrowing cooperative (Italian).

Casa Vinicola   A wine firm (Italian).

Cepa   A grape or wine variety (Spanish).

Cépage   Grape variety (French).

Chablis   A dry white wine originally made from Pinot Chardonnay grapes grown in any of the vineyards in the Chablis region of France.

Cherveno Vino   Red wine (Bulgarian).

Character   The wine's "personality," as revealed by the sense of taste and smell; the combination of vinosity, balance, and style.

Charnu   A wine of full body (French).

Château-Bottled   Wine bottled at the château, estate, or vineyard where grapes for its production are grown.

Chianti   A very popular dry red wine produced in Tuscany, Italy, and in California.

Claret   A term for red Bordeaux wines; particularly used in England.

Classico   Best of the region (Italian).

Clean   A well-made wine, well-stored, with no alien tastes.

Climat   Vineyard (French).

Clos   A vineyard (French). It formerly meant and, in some cases, still signifies an enclosure, fence, or wall.

Cloudy   An imperfect wine containing sediment.

Coarse   A young wine lacking breed and without finesse.

Commune   Parish (French).

Condition   A wine's clarity or soundness.

Consorzio   Legally recognized growers' association (Italian).

Controlled Fermentation   The most common method is refrigeration, the aim of which is to speed up or slow down the process as needed.

Corky   Indicating an off-taste from a bad cork.

Crémant   Half-sparkling (French).

Crno   Red (Yugoslavian).

Cru   A vineyard or growth (French).

Cuvée   General term meaning blending or vatting. When applied to Champagne, the term indicates the first pressing from freshly gathered grapes.

Cuveno Vino   Selected wine (Yugoslavian).

Decant   To transfer wine from its original bottle or container for the purpose of drawing the bright wine away from the sediment or crust.

Delicate   A light wine, usually white, young and fresh.

Demi-Sec   Half-dry. A term used to describe a fairly sweet Champagne.

Denominacion de Origen   Similar to Appellation Contrôlée (Italian).

Dolce   Very sweet (Italian).

Domaine   Bottled on the property where the wine is made (French).

Dosage   The addition of sugared wine to another wine in order to make it conform to established standards of dryness. Used only for Champagne and sparkling wines.

Doux   Sweet (French).

Dry   Opposite of *sweet;* free of sugar. Fermentation converts the natural sugar of the grape into wine alcohol and carbon dioxide gas. A wine becomes dry when all this sugar has been consumed by fermentation. Dryness should not be confused with astringency, acidity, tartness, or sourness. It simply means lacking in sweetness. The wines that uninformed individuals are apt to call "sour" are dry or tart, especially made with these flavor characteristics to blend with the flavors of main-course dishes.

Dulce   Sweet (Spanish).

Earthy   Some vineyards translate their soil noticeably in the wine.

Eigenbaugewachs   From the vineyards of the producer (Austrian).

Elegant   A flattering term for an outstanding wine.

Emborellado   Estate-bottled (Spanish).

Epitrapezio   Table wine (Greek).

Espumoso   Sparkling (Spanish).

Fermentation   The chemical process whereby sugars are broken down into alcohol, carbon dioxide gas, and other by-products.

Fine   Fining, the process of clearing young wines by adding beaten egg, lactic acid, heavy gelatin, isinglass, etc. Clarifying the wine.

Finish   The very last impression of the tasting mouthful.

Fino   Denoting the qualities of dryness and lightness in Sherry.

Flat   Lacking acidity; in Champagne, without effervescence.

Flinty   Often used to describe wine that is dry, clean, sharp.

Flor   A selected yeast culture that, under suitable conditions, grows on the surface of wine and produces the flavor characteristic in Sherries so named.

Fortified   Wines whose natural alcoholic strength is increased by the addition of Brandy.

Foxiness   An unpleasant characteristic of some native eastern American grape species.

Fruity   With pronounced flavor and/or fragrance of the constituent grape.

Full   A full-bodied wine's alcoholicity and viscosity.

Generic   Wine-type names that stand for definite characteristics. Generic names were originally of geographic origin and were applied to the names of wines grown in specific Old World viticultural districts. As centuries passed and these wines increased in fame, their names came to designate *any* wine with similar characteristics, wherever it was grown. Burgundy, Champagne, Bordeaux, Port, Rhine Wine, Sauterne, and Sherry are the best-known generic or semi-generic wine types of geographic origin. Vermouth is an example of a generic name without geographic significance.

Grand Crus   A top growth (French).

Green   Disagreeable acidity.

Heavy   A wine that is full-bodied but lacking in finesse.

Hock   A dry white table wine usually made with Riesling grapes in which, as with other white wines, the fermentation takes place after the skins have been separated. This preserves the delicate flavor which is characteristic of the wine. Hock was originally produced at Hochheim, Germany.

Imbottigliato nel Origine   Estate-bottled (Italian).

Iskriashto Vino   Sparkling wine (Bulgarian).

Label   The "credentials" of a wine.

Light   Lacking body to an extent, but still pleasant.

Lozia   Vineyards (Bulgarian).

Lozova Prachka   Variety of wine (Bulgarian).

Madeira   A rich, dry fortified wine of the Sherry class originally made on the island of Madeira from white grapes to which additional sugar has been added for sweetening.

Maderise   Past its prime with an acquired brownish color.

Medium   As applied to Sherry, it means slightly sweet, in the middle range between dry and sweet.

Mellow   Soft in taste; term used to describe *vino rosso* red dinner wines. Also sometimes used to designate well-matured Sherries and other wines containing some sweetness.

Messo in Bottiglia   Estate-bottled (Italian).

Metallic   A hint of bitterness, a hard finish.

Mise en Bouteille   When these words appear on a label, they are followed by an indication of where the wine was bottled. Any one of the following expressions means that the wine has been produced, aged, and bottled in the same estate: *Mis en bouteille au Château; Mise de la Propriété; Mis en bouteille par le Propriétaire; Mise du Domaine; Mis en bouteille au Domaine* (French).

Moldy   An unpleasant taste that permeates the wine from fungus on grapes or from musty casks.

Moselle   A dry white wine with aromatic flavor produced in the Moselle region in Germany.

Muscatel   A rich, spicy fortified wine made from the Muscat grape.

Must   The mixture of grape juice, skins, and seeds that ferment to form wine. Sometimes used to signify the juice without the skins and seeds.

Négociant   A wine merchant who purchases wine from the grower and places it in his own cellars for aging and sale (French).

Noble   A quality of aroma that shows the aristocratic lineage of the grape variety.

Noble Rot   See **Pourriture Noble.**

Nonvintage   Wines blended from several vintages in order to obtain a wine of higher quality. The purpose of this blending is to maintain consistency of quality and taste from year to year, without change in color, character, bouquet, and so on.

Nose   Refers merely to the qualities of bouquet and aroma.

Nutty   Term denoting the characteristic flavor of Sherry.

Oinos Erythros   Red wine (Greek).

Oinos Lefkos   White wine (Greek).

Oloroso   A medium-type Sherry, darker and richer than Amontillado.

Originalabfüllung   Estate-Bottled (Austrian).

Oxidation   The effect of air on wine. The character of a wine can be substantially altered in proportion to its exposure to air.

Palaion   Old wine (Greek).

Palomino   A white grape with a thick yellowish skin that is the traditional grape used for the making of Sherry in Spain and in other countries as well.

Pétillant   A wine that is slightly bubbly.

Pinot   Dry, fresh, straw-colored white table wines slightly fuller than Riesling or any white Hock. Grapes or wine originally from Burgundy.

Piquant   A young wine of certain captivating bouquet and taste.

Poljoprivredne Zadruge   Made in———cooperative (Yugoslavian).

Pourriture Noble   A state of overripeness that concentrates the sugar content of grapes. For some sweet wines, especially Sauternes, this is considered highly desirable.

Prirodno   Natural (Yugoslavian).

Punjeno U.   Bottled at   (Yugoslavian).

4 Anos   Bottled when four years old (Spanish).

Récolte   Vintage (French).

Red Wines   Any wines that have the slightest red coloring, obtained from the pigment found on the inside of the grape skin.

Reserva   Mature fine-quality wine (Spanish).

Rich   A wine having a generous bouquet, flavor, and fullness of body.

Ried   Vineyard (Austrian).

Riesling   A dry white table wine of light body and pale color. Also used to refer to grape varieties that have small greenish-yellow berries and are used in the production of dry and sweet wine of low acidity.

Riserva   Better-quality wine (Italian).

Room Temperature   The temperature at which red wines are usually served, between 60 and 65 degrees F. Older and greater red wines are better at room temperature. Other red wines (particularly young ones) are often preferred slightly cool. Wine is never brought to room temperature by abrupt "warming," which would spoil it, but it is left to stand for a few hours in the dining room.

Rosso   Red (Italian).

Rotwein   Red wine (German).

Rounded   A wine with all the vinous elements well-balanced.

Rosé   Pink wine; a very pale red wine obtained by removing the grape skins as soon as the required amount of color has been attained.

Rough   Insufficient age.

Ruby   A Port of very deep red color, usually quite young, as opposed to one that has been aged for some time in wood and has become *tawny*, which means pale in color through repeated finings.

Ruzica   Rosé (Yugoslavian).

Sack   The Old English spelling of the Spanish *seco*, which became the generic term used to denote the drier fortified wines, as opposed to *mountain*, which were sweet. The term fell into disuse during the last century. Today it forms part of a trademarked brand fabricated by a large Sherry shipper.

Sauterne   A medium-to-sweet light table wine first produced at Sauternes in the Gironde, France.

Schaumwein   Sparkling wine (German).

Sec   Dry; also used to denote a medium-sweet Champagne (French).

Secco   Dry (Italian).

Seco   Dry (Spanish).

Sediment   Deposit that results from aging in the bottle. Sediment does not harm the wine in any way. It is very often an indication that the wine is a great and old one. A bottle showing sediment should be left to rest upright until the sediment has dropped to the bottom of the bottle. It should then either be decanted or poured so carefully that only clear wine can pass into the glass.

Sekt   Sparkling Champagne (German).

Shampanskoe   Champagne (Russian).

Silky   The satin-smoothness of some dessert wines.

Sladko Vino   Sweet wine (Bulgarian).

Slatko   Sweet (Yugoslavian).

Soft   A loose term suggesting low acidity.

Solera   The Spanish system of progressively blending Sherries in tiers of small casks in order to blend wines of the same type but varying ages.

Sound   Well-made wine with no defects.

Spumante   Sparkling (Italian).

Stolovoe Vino   Table wine (Russian).

Stravecchio   Old, ripe (Italian).

Strugure   Grape (Romanian).

Suho   Dry (Yugoslavian).

Suho Vino   Dry wine (Yugoslavian).

Table Wine   The "right" name for all still wines the alcohol content of which does not exceed 14% by volume. Most table wines are dry, as are most dinner wines, but it is incorrect to call *all* of them "dry." Formerly this practice was much in vogue, but it has been discontinued in recent days when many dinner wines, such as Sauterne, are actually semi-sweet or sweet; others, such as Sherry and other dessert wines, are nearly dry. Table, or dinner, wine is the proper term because most wines of this class add to the taste and enjoyment of the meal. It is a term that guides the consumer in selecting wines that are suitable as adjuncts to good food. The class includes those wines sometimes referred to as *light wines* or *natural wines*.

Tafelwein   Table wine (German).

Tannin   A complex organic constituent that imparts astringency, particularly in red wines.

Tart   Possessing agreeable acidity. In wine, tartness reflects the content of agreeable fruit acids.

Tawny   The quality of paleness or golden tinge that Port acquires when matured in wood. The loss of red color results from repeated finings. Such wines are frequently called *Tawny Ports*.

Tenementi   Estate (Italian).

Tinto   Red (Spanish).

Ullage   The amount of airspace above the wine in a bottle or above the liquid in a cask that is no longer full.

Varietal   When a wine is named for the principal variety of grape used in its production, it is said to have a varietal name. U.S. federal regulations require that a varietal wine derive at least 51% of its volume, characteristic flavor, and aroma from the grape variety for which it is named. Cabernet Sauvignon, Chardonnay, and Zinfandel are some of the varietal names that apply here.

Vendange Tardive   Wine from late-picked grapes (French). Possible indication of more strength or sweetness.

Venemmia   Vintage (Italian).

Vie   Vine (Romanian).

Viile   Vineyard (Romanian).

Vin Alb   White wine (Romanian).

Vin Blanc   White wine (French).

Vin de Masa   Table wine (Romanian).

Vin Doux   Sweet wine (French).

Vin Mousseaux   Sparkling wine (French).

Vin Nature   Natural, unsweetened wine (French).

Vin Ordinaire   Ordinary cheap wine (French).

Vin Rosé   A pink wine (French).

Vin Rosu   Red wine (Romanian).

Vin Rouge   Red wine (French).

Vin Sec   Dry wine (French).

Vin Superioare   Superior wine (Romanian).

Vina or **Vinedo**   Vineyard (Spanish).

Vini da Banco   Ordinary wine (Italian).

Vino de Cosecha Propria   Wine produced by the vineyard owner (Spanish).

Vino Liquoroso   Very sweet wine (Italian).

Vino Ordinario   Ordinary wine (Italian).

Vintage   A vintage year is one in which the grapes have reached full maturity; particularly applicable in Europe, where growing conditions vary greatly from year to year. Less applicable in regions such as California, where grapes reach maturity every year. May also signify the gathering of grapes and their fermentation into wine; also, the crop of grapes or wine of one season. A vintage wine produced in the United States is one labeled with the year in which at least 95% of its grapes were gathered and crushed and the juice therefrom fermented.

Visokokvalitetno   High quality (Yugoslavian).

Weeper   A wine leaking from its cork or capsule.

Weisswein   White wine (German).

Weinkellerei   Wine celler (German).

Winzergenossenschaft   Winegrowers' cooperative (German).

Woody   The characteristic odor of wet oak is apparent in wine that has been aged too long or has been allowed to come in contact with faulty wood. The term is used when this characteristic is excessive.

Xiros   Dry (Greek).

Prior to the discovery of paper, wine was identified in two ways: by the vessel in which it was contained and by a seal that was placed upon the vessel. In order to show the progression of the wine label from a simple hand-drawn insignia to a very complex printed art form I have selected the history of one such label, that of Château Filhot, as a symbol of all wine-label development.

Château Filhot is a property in the village of Sauternes; the vineyards of the château can be traced back to the fourteenth century. The village itself was built near an ancient Roman way, traces of which can still be found along the woods of Filhot. Developed by the family of Pope Clement V, who built the castle of Villandraut near Sauternes, the vineyards became a battlefield in the fifteenth century during the Hundred Years' War. Following the French victory at that time, there was some confusion as to which properties belonged to the crown and which to the rich burgesses of Bordeaux. In histories of the sixteenth and seventeenth centuries the property is again mentioned, as south of the village of Sauternes was occupied by the *Cru du Roy à Sauternes*. A lawyer certified to the excellence of the area's wine in 1672, but the vineyard was ill-fated and was destroyed by mold in 1708. Marked by an old tower, which is the current site of the cellars of Château Filhot, the property was listed as *Pinau du Roy* (cellar of the king).

The name Filhot derives from that of the family Jacques de Filhot, whose name appears in the archives as a burgess of Bordeaux, an avid supporter of King Louis XIV during the first years of his reign. Jacques' son bought the noble house of Verdolet at Sauternes, and his grandson replanted the vineyard in grapes for the making of white wines, developing it into the most important and famed vineyard of Sauternes at that time. His seal, *Vin de Filhot Sauternes,* appeared in this form.

The de Filhot family raised the name Sauternes to prominence wherever white wines were cherished. The last de Filhot mentioned in the archives of the Gironde was president of the Parliament of Bordeaux. He ordered that only the best grapes, enriched by the *pourriture noble,* be harvested for the making of his Sauternes wines. President de Filhot began the construction of present-day Château Filhot and purchased the neighboring property of Coutet at Barsac, thus giving birth to a confusion that has existed ever since, for Coutet and Filhot have similar labels even though the vineyards no longer belong to the same family. In 1807 President de Filhot's daughter, Josephine, married the Marquis de Lur-Saluces, and at her death in 1815 the property stayed in the family of her husband. Known at the time as the third-most-important growth of the Graves de Sauternes, the Clos Filhot label disappeared and was listed in the 1855 Classification among the *deuxième crus.* But the then Marquis de Lur-Saluces, Romain Bertrand, son of Josephine de Filhot de Lur-Saluces, rebuilt the Château Filhot and the vineyards that surrounded it. He also bought the adjacent vineyard of Pineau, upon which the modern-day cellars have been rebuilt. Sold under the names Vin de Sauternes and Château Sauternes, Marquis Romain Bertrand de Lur-Saluces' wine became world-famous in the second part of the nineteenth century. His label looked as you see it here.

The blight of phylloxera and the political crises at the end of the nineteenth century caused the family management to concentrate on other vineyards that required attention. The vineyards of Pinau were completely destroyed, and the vineyards of Filhot were partially ruined. Recognizing the blemish that had fallen upon the name Sauternes, and anxious to restore it to its former fame, the name Château Filhot reappeared on labels shortly after 1900; but the production of the wine was greatly reduced.

In 1935 the Comtesse Durieu de Lacarelle, born Thérèse de Lur-Saluces, came to her brother's aid and prevailed upon her husband to purchase the family property of Château Filhot in her name. In return, her brother accorded to her and her heirs the right to use her maiden name, Lur-Saluces. The son of Comtesse Thérèse, Louis de Lacarelle, revivified the vineyard in 1968; after two centuries, the name Filhot reappeared on the label of the property.

Château Filhot was inherited by the daughter of Louis, Victoire Durieu de Lacarelle, present owner of the vineyards and wife of Comte Pierre de Vaucelles, former ambassador of France. Since 1973 Château Filhot has been under the direction of her son, Henri de Vaucelles, and his wife, Sophie de Sigalas, who maintain the long tradition of this ancient wine of quality.

Behind every wine label lies a similar history of personal and political events that blended to influence the shape, color, and design of these small, informative, and often very beautiful and artistic bearers of facts, the interpretation of which can mean the difference between your pleasure or your disappointment in the wines you have chosen to buy.

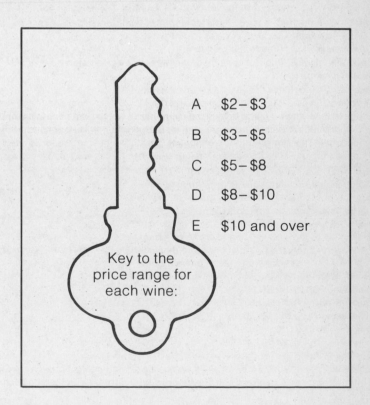

A $2 – $3

B $3 – $5

C $5 – $8

D $8 – $10

E $10 and over

Key to the price range for each wine:

Virtually every combination of climate and soil in the world is to be found in California; as a result, almost every known grape and wine type finds an ideal home in one or more of California's wine districts. Often grapes from more than one district are used to produce a wine, while wines from more than one district are sometimes blended to achieve a desired taste and character. Here are the nine best-known producing areas in California, from north to south:

Sonoma–Mendocino   District; directly north of San Francisco
Napa–Solano   District; northeast of San Francisco
Lodi–Sacramento   District; northeast of San Francisco
Livermore Valley–Alameda   District; east of San Francisco
Modesto–Ripon–Escalon   District; southeast of San Francisco
Santa Clara–Santa Cruz–San Benito   District; south of San Francisco
Monterey County   South of San Francisco
Fresno–San Joaquin–Kern   District; extending through the southern part of San Joaquin Valley
Cucamonga   District, though labeled as a single entity, includes the winegrowing regions of Los Angeles County, the Cucamonga–Ontario area, and the San Diego region

A study of the temperature and moisture of these districts and areas within the districts explains why each is used for growing the varieties in question. The coastal region is generally cooler than the others; its grapes, often grown on hillsides without irrigation, develop the higher fruit acidity favored in traditional European table wines. The interior valleys have warmer sunshine to ripen their grapes to the high sugar content desired for dessert wines.

Altitude and soil may also influence the composition of the grapes. These factors vary from vineyard to vineyard and from district to district; in California, however, they play a less important part than the climate or the variety of grape. All California grapes, with the exception of a few hundred acres in cultivation, come from the Old World's greatest wine-grape family—the *Vitis vinifera*. These grapes thrive in the mild weather and excellent soil of California. There is sometimes a close resemblance between California and European wines made from the same grape varieties and grown under similar conditions because, oddly enough, geographically and geologically, California districts and European wine regions are often very much alike.

California wines can be placed in five categories: appetizer wines, red dinner wines, white dinner wines, dessert wines, and sparkling wines. The first of these categories, *appetizer wines,* as their name indicates, are enjoyed before the meal. They are:

Sherry,   The most popular appetizer wine, often made from the Palomino grape. Sherry has a characteristic nutty flavor obtained either by aging at warm temperatures or by coming into contact with a special strain of yeast, called "flor," during the aging process. Its color ranges from pale gold to dark amber, and it is either dry, medium-dry, or sweet. The sweet is also called "Cream Sherry." Some similar sweet-tasting dessert wines are *Madeira* and *Marsala.*
Vermouth   Wine flavored with herbs or other aromatic substances. The two principle types are dry (pale) and sweet (dark).
Special Natural Wines   Made from private formulas in which pure natural flavors (rather than synthetic flavorings) such as herbs or fruit flavors are added to the wine. These are sometimes labeled "aperitif wines." They often bear unique names. *May Wine,* traditional in spring or early summer, secures its flavor from woodruff, a sweet-scented herb. *Retsina* is made from white wine to which resin is added during fermentation.

The second category, *red dinner wines,* sometimes called "table wines," are usually dry and are suitable accompaniments to the main course. "Dry" means that most or all of the grape sugar has been fermented out; thus the opposite of dry is "sweet" (not "wet"). Most desirable dinner wines are dry. Some reds are soft and mellow, while others may impart a robust astringency that results from tannin, the substance that makes your mouth slightly puckery when you drink tea. Most red dinner wines fall into two general types, Burgundy and Claret, but there are also some lesser reds and some semi-sweet red dinner wines known as *Vino Rossos.*

Burgundy   The name is used to describe generous, full-bodied, dry red dinner wines with a pronounced flavor, body, and bouquet and a deep red color. California Burgundy is made from a number of different grape varieties, including Gamay, Petite Sirah, Pinot Noir, Carignane, and Zinfandel. Each has its own distinctive flavor and aroma, but the main characteristics of California Burgundy are velvety soft body and deep, rich bouquet.
Claret   The name applies to any dry, pleasantly tart, light or medium-bodied dinner wine of ruby-red color. Clarets are made from one or more of a number of grape varieties:

California Zinfandel   A fruity and aromatic wine that is widely grown.
California Cabernet Sauvignon   Stronger in flavor and taste than other Clarets and the California production can be fuller in body and deeper in color than Burgundy. When young, it may be astringent; when aged, it achieves a velvety richness.
Ruby Cabernet   A blend of Cabernet Sauvignon and Carignane, which produces a wine of brilliant deep-ruby color with fruity aroma. Its full name is used to avoid confusion with its Cabernet parent.
Merlot   A varietal wine. It has a Cabernet-like aroma and flavor and a deep-ruby color.
Barbera   Far heavier-bodied and more tart than most California Burgundy. It is made from and has the distinct flavor and aroma of the Barbera grape.
Charbono   Made from the Charbono grape, it is also heavy-bodied.
Grignolino   A light dinner wine named for the grape from which it is made. It has a decided orange-red color and is made more like rosé. The lighter blends are sometimes labeled rosés.
Chianti   May resemble either Burgundy or Claret in body and flavor, but unlike them, it has a strong, tart flavor. Chianti is usually fruity and ruby-red.
Vino Rosso   This is a general term applied to red dinner wines that are also known as "mellow red wines." Often labeled with Italian names even though they come from California, to indicate that they are "family wines," they are usually slightly sweet to semi-sweet, medium- to heavy-bodied, ruby-red, and softer in flavor than Chianti or other red dinner wines.

Concord, Ives, Norton   Red dinner wines with their own characteristic flavor and aroma, plus the tartness of corresponding grapes grown in the East. Ives and Norton are usually dry; the Concord ranges from semi-sweet to very sweet and is classed as dessert wine.
Rosé Wines   These range from dry to slightly sweet and are singularly fruity-flavored, light-bodied, and made from Cabernet, Gamay, Grenache, Grignolino, or Zinfandel grapes.

The third category, *white California dinner wines,* range from extremely dry and tart to sweet and full-bodied. Their color ranges from pale straw to deep gold, and their alcoholic content from 10 to 14 percent. The most popular California white dinner wine is Chablis.

Chablis   Dry, with a fruity flavor and a delicate pale-gold color. It is fuller-bodied than Rhine Wine. Chablis is made from such white grape varieties as the aristocratic Chardonnay and Pinot Blanc. It can also be produced from Burger, Golden Chasselas, Green Hungarian, and several other varieties such as Chenin Blanc, French Colombard, Pinot Blanc, Folle Blanche. Chablis-type wines are named for their respective grapes, and each has a distinct flavor and aroma, e.g., *Chardonnay, Pinot Chardonnay. Chenin Blanc* comes from a grape that also produces a wine labeled *White Pinot.*
Rhine Wine   A generic name applied to any light-bodied white, pale-gold, or slightly green-gold dinner wine. The wine can range from tart to semi-sweet in flavor. Originally, Rhine Wine was made from a few special varieties, notably the Rieslings, but in the United States wines of many other grapes are classed as Rhine Wine. Often these wines are packaged in extra-tall, easy-to-recognize tapered bottles. Rhine Wine made from Riesling grapes is called *Riesling* and has the particular flavor and aroma that is characteristic of Rieslings. *Moselle,* another name for certain Rhine wines, has no significance in California production; this wine is called *Hock* in England and Australia.
Johannisberg Riesling   This is sometimes called *White Riesling* and is produced from the grape of the same name. Also available from California are *Grey Riesling, Franken Riesling* (Sylvaner grapes) *Traminer, Gewürztraminer,* and *Emerald Riesling* wines, all made from the corresponding grapes. It is interesting to note that the Emerald Riesling grape was developed in California as a cross between Johannisberg Riesling grapes and Muscadelle varieties.
Sauterne   California Sauternes are golden-hued, fragrant, full-bodied white dinner wines ranging from dry to sweet. California Sauterne is drier than wines of this name produced in France. *Fumé Blanc* and *Sauvignon Blanc,* both of which are predominantly the product of the Sauvignon grape, as well

as *Semillon,* are Sauterne-type wines named for the grapes from which they are pressed. They naturally retain the characteristic of their respective varieties.

Other white California dinner wines are made from Muscat grapes. They are often referred to very simply as "sweet white wine" although *Light Muscat* can vary from nearly dry to sweet. Light Muscat is sometimes labeled with a specific variety name, such as *Muscat Canelli* or *Muscat de Frontignan.* Both are synonyms for *Muscat Blanc.*

In the fourth wine category, *California dessert wines* are sweet and full-bodied. They can be served with the final course of the meal or as refreshments any time of day or night. Ranging from medium-sweet to sweet and from pale gold to red, their alcoholic content is 18 to 21 percent. In addition to Cream Sherry, three distinct types lead the popularity polls: Port, Muscatel, and Tokay.

Port Port may be made from Carignane, Petite Sirah, Tinta Cao, Tinta Madeira, and Zinfandel grapes.

Muscatel This is a rich, flavorful, sweet dessert wine with the unmistakable flavor and aroma of Muscat grapes. Its color ranges from golden or dark amber to red. Most Muscatel is made from a golden grape called Muscat of Alexandria, but several other varieties are used in California. They make for varying flavor. *Red Muscatel* and *Black Muscatel* (a much darker red) are produced from the Muscat Hamburg or Black Muscat grape. *Muscat de Frontignan* and *Muscat Canelli,* made from Muscat Blanc grapes, are also very pleasant dessert wines.

Tokay Amber-colored, with a slight nutty or Sherry-like flavor, Tokay is actually a blend of dessert wines, usually Angelica, Port, and Sherry. California Tokay is not to be confused with Tokay wines from Hungary or with the Flame Tokay grape, which may or may not be used in U.S. production.

Other sweet California wines suitable for serving with dessert are *Angelica,* a very sweet white wine; and *Kosher wines,* which are equally sweet. The word "Kosher" applies to any wine that has been produced under rabbinical supervision and is so certified.

The fifth category of California wines, *sparkling wines,* are those wines that have been made effervescent through a second fermentation in closed containers. Sparkling wine can be red, pink, or white. The most popular types are California Champagne, Sparkling Burgundy, and Cold Duck.

Champagne Traditionally made from Chardonnay, Pinot Noir, or Pinot Blanc; but in America the wine is made from Burger, Emerald Riesling, Folle Blanche, French Colombard, Green Hungarian, St.-Émilion, Sauvignon Vert, Catawba, Delaware, Elvira, and other grapes.

Pink Champagne This results from letting the grape skins remain with the juice just long enough to obtain the desired hue.

Sparkling Burgundy This is usually semi-sweet or sweet red wine made effervescent by a secondary fermentation in closed containers. Barbera, Carignane, Mondeuse, Petite Sirah, and Pinot Noir are the grapes most often used for its production.

Cold Duck This is produced by blending white Champagne and Sparkling Burgundy, sometimes with an addition of a little Concord grape wine. It is ruby-red and can be semi-sweet or sweet.

Other sparkling wines are *Sparkling Muscat,* a Muscat-grape-flavored, Champagne-like wine that is also called *Moscato Spumante. Sparkling Rosé* is similar to Pink Champagne and is often made from the same grapes used to produce rosé dinner wines. *Crackling wines* are less effervescent than Champagne-type wines and are often referred to as "*Pétillant*" or "*frizzante.*" U.S. law requires such wines to be made by a natural second fermentation within the bottle or other closed container.

HOW TO READ A CALIFORNIA WINE LABEL

In California wine labels may be for a *generic* wine or a *varietal* wine.

VARIETAL

PETITE SIRAH This means that a minimum 51% (although it is usually a much higher percentage) of the wine came exclusively from the Petite Sirah grape.

PRODUCED & BOTTLED BY This means that at least 75% of the wine was fermented by the named winery.

ALCOHOL 12% BY VOLUME This simply states that the wine contains 12% alcohol by volume, although federal regulations allow up to 1.5% variation. Table wines legally may contain from 10% to 14% alcohol by volume. Sherry wines may range from 17% to 21%; other dessert wines, such as Port, Muscatel, Tokay, and Angelica, from 18% to 21%; and special natural wines that contain fruit or other flavorings, with unique names coined by their makers, are permitted a maximum of 21% with no specific minimum alcoholic content.

CALIFORNIA By state regulation, wines bearing the appellation *California,* or a geographical subdivision thereof, must be made of grapes grown only in California.

ESTATE BOTTLED This is a term used to designate wines produced from grapes grown in vineyards either owned or controlled by the wine maker and in the vicinity of the winery.

THE YEAR 19— This means that at least 95% of the wine was made from grapes grown and crushed in that year. Because the climate in California's wine country is so consistently favorable for wine growing, vintage dating per se is used by some wineries primarily as a guide to the age of the wines in the bottle.

BACK LABELS These labels are not required. Their only limitation is that all information thereon must be truthful. They are just an extra touch added by the vintner.

GENERIC

Many wineries produce generic wines, such as Burgundy, Chablis, Claret, and Rhine. They are made from blends of grapes to yield a wine comparable to the Old World counterparts from which they derived their names. They are consistent in taste. The name of the winery is your best assurance of quality in selecting generic wines.

PRODUCED & BOTTLED BY Same as varietal information
ALCOHOL 12.5% BY VOLUME Same as varietal information
CALIFORNIA Same as varietal information
HEARTY BURGUNDY Characteristics approximately those of French Burgundy wine

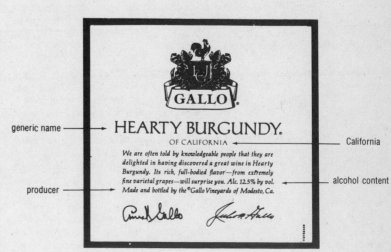

producer: Alexander Valley Vineyards
classification: White varietal table wine
grape variety: Johannisberg Riesling (100%)
district: Sonoma County—Alexander Valley
city or village: Healdsburg

The estate-bottled 1975 Johannisberg Riesling was made from selected grapes picked in late September at 22 degrees sugar and immediately crushed and pressed. The juice was allowed to settle for two days, then the sediment was racked off. The wine fermented for three months at 47 degrees F. This prolonged cold fermentation produced a wine with pronounced varietal character and a small amount of residual sugar.

Clear light yellow color and an intense bouquet with Riesling character. The wine is complex with slight residual sugar and a lingering aftertaste.   **price range:** B

producer: Alexander Valley Winery (Johnson's)
classification:V White varietal table wine
grape variety: Chenin Blanc (100%)
district: Sonoma County—Alexander Valley
city or village: Healdsburg

Family-owned vineyards and winery.
Light straw color and a strong, fruity varietal bouquet.   **price range:** A

producer: Alexander Valley Winery (Johnson's)
classification: Rosé varietal table wine
grape variety: Pinot Noir (100%)
district: Sonoma County—Alexander Valley
city or village: Healdsburg

Family-owned vineyards and winery.
Dark rose color and a fruity bouquet. The flavor is unmistakably Pinot Noir.
price range: A

producer: Almadén Vineyards
classification: White sparkling wine
district: North Coast Counties
Bottle-fermented dry Champagne.
price range: B

producer: Almadén Vineyards
classification: White varietal table wine
grape variety: Chenin Blanc
district: Monterey County

Golden color and a fresh, flowery bouquet. The wine is fruity, medium dry, and medium-bodied.   **price range:** A

producer: Almadén Vineyards
classification: Red varietal table wine
grape variety: Cabernet Sauvignon (100%)
district: San Benito County
city or village: Paicines

Deep ruby color and a fruity, complex bouquet. A very soft Cabernet Sauvignon.
price range: B

producer: Almadén Vineyards
classification: White varietal table wine
grape variety: Gewürztraminer
district: San Benito County

Pale gold color and a very spicy, fragrant bouquet. The wine is medium-bodied and medium dry, with good resemblance to an Alsatian Gewürztraminer.   **price range:** B

producer: Almadén Vineyards
classification: White sparkling wine
grape variety: Pinot Chardonnay
district: San Benito County
city or village: Paicines

"Blanc de Blancs" Champagne, bottle-fermented.

Pale golden color and a fruity bouquet. The wine is dry and full-bodied.
price range: C

producer: Almadén Vineyards
classification: Red varietal table
grape variety: Petite Sirah
district: North Coast Counties

Deep purple-red color and a full, spicy bouquet suggesting currants. The wine is very full-bodied and soft.   **price range:** A

producer: Almadén Vineyards
classification: White varietal table wine
grape variety: Johannisberg Riesling (100%)
district: North Coast Counties—San Benito County
city or village: Paicines

Pale gold color and a flowery bouquet. The wine is dry and delicate to the taste.
price range: A

producer: Almadén Vineyards
classification: White varietal table wine
grape variety: Pinot Chardonnay (100%)
district: North Coast Counties—San Benito County
city or village: Paicines

Golden color and a complex, very fragrant bouquet. The wine is dry and full-bodied.   **price range:** B

producer: Almadén Vineyards
classification: White table wine
grape variety: Semillon
district: North Coast Counties
Dry Sauterne.

Pale gold color and a very fragrant, aromatic, and fruity bouquet. The wine is dry and medium-bodied.   **price range:** A

producer: Almadén Vineyards
classification: White varietal table wine
grape variety: Sylvaner
district: North Coast Counties

Delicate, clean bouquet; the wine is dry and delicate.   **price range:** A

Many wine-jug stoppers of the fifteenth century were made in the shape of a man's head, and the headgear denoted the quality of the wine. The best wine had a king's head and crown; the poorest, no hat at all.

producer: Almadén Vineyards
classification: White table wine
grape variety: Sauvignon Blanc, Semillon
district: North Coast Counties
Golden color and a fruity bouquet. The wine is full and dry. **price range:** A

producer: Almadén Vineyards
classification: Red varietal table wine
grape variety: Pinot Noir (100%)
district: San Benito County
city or village: Paicines
Deep red color and a fruity bouquet with a violet fragrance. The wine is soft, full, and dry. **price range:** B

producer: Almadén Vineyards
classification: Red table wine
district: North Coast Counties
"Mountain Red Chianti."
Berrylike bouquet; the wine is dry, tart, and robust. **price range:** A

producer: Almadén Vineyards
classification: Red varietal table wine
grape variety: Gamay Beaujolais (100%)

district: San Benito/Monterey counties
Light red color and a very fragrant, fruity bouquet. The wine is dry and medium-bodied. **price range:** B

producer: Almadén Vineyards
classification: White varietal table wine
grape variety: Chenin Blanc
district: North Coast Counties
Flowery bouquet; the wine is medium-bodied and semi-dry. **price range:** A

producer: Almadén Vineyards
classification: White varietal table wine
grape variety: Johannisberg Riesling
district: San Benito County
Flowery bouquet; the wine is very dry and delicate. **price range:** A

producer: Almadén Vineyards
classification: Fortified wine
grape variety: Tinta Madeira
Ruby Port.
Ruby-red color and a rich, fruity bouquet. The wine is full-bodied and sweet.
price range: A

producer: Almadén Vineyards
classification: Fortified wine
Solera Sherry.
Amber color and a very nutty bouquet. The wine is dry and full-bodied.
price range: A

producer: Almadén Vineyards
classification: Red varietal table wine
grape variety: Zinfandel
district: Monterey County
Garnet-red color and a fruity bouquet with a berrylike fragrance. The wine is dry and medium-bodied. **price range:** A

producer: Almadén Vineyards
classification: White varietal table wine
grape variety: Pinot Chardonnay
district: North Coast Counties
Fresh, fragrant bouquet; the wine is full-bodied and quite dry to the taste.
price range: A

producer: Almadén Vineyards
classification: Red varietal table wine
grape variety: Cabernet Sauvignon
district: North Coast Counties

Deep ruby-red color and a very fruity, complex bouquet. The wine is dry and medium- to full-bodied. **price range:** A

producer: Almadén Vineyards
classification: White varietal table wine
grape variety: Pinot Blanc
district: North Coast Counties
Fruity, flowery bouquet; the wine is full-bodied and quite dry. **price range:** A

producer: André Champagne Cellars (Gallo Winery)
classification: White sparkling wine
This Champagne is suitable for parties, weddings, or meals; its light fruity flavor leads to second or third glasses with no cloying aftertaste.
Brilliant pale straw color and a fruity, lively flavor with medium body. A wine that is great as a cocktail. **price range:** A

producer: Barengo Vineyards, Inc.
classification: Aromatized white table wine
This is a "May Wine" flavored with imported woodruff herbs. To make a "May Bowl," float bits of fresh fruit such as strawberries or peaches over a block of ice in a bowl of chilled May Wine. Add a few fresh-cut flowers to capture the essence of spring. Serve it "on the rocks" with a twist of lemon or in a highball glass with sparkling soda water.
A delicately scented bouquet and a light, fruity sweet flavor. The wine is suitable for all occasions and can be enjoyed before meals or with main dishes such as baked ham and barbecued meats. Serve ice cold. **price range:** A

producer: Barengo Vineyards, Inc.
classification: Red varietal table wine
grape variety: Petite Sirah
district: Lodi
city or village: Lodi

This wine is aged in oak casks in cellars built in the nineteenth century. It is similar to the fine wines of the Rhône Valley.

This full-bodied, unique dry wine is an excellent companion to meats, game, and seasoned dishes. Allow it to breathe for a half hour before serving. **price range:** A

producer: Barengo Vineyards, Inc.
classification: White table wine
district: Lodi

Called "Chablis," this wine is similar to the fine white wines of the French Chablis district.

Pale color and a clean, fresh taste with slight fruitiness. The wine is excellent with all foods, especially fish, fowl, light meats, and cold dishes. Chill thoroughly before serving. **price range:** A

producer: Barengo Vineyards, Inc.
classification: White varietal table wine
grape variety: Semillon
district: Lodi

Light, golden color, and a flowery bouquet. The wine is medium-bodied, with a rich flavor, and is dry. Well-suited to fish and poultry dishes, and light entrées with cream sauces. The wine should be served chilled. **price range:** A

producer: Bargetto Winery (Vine Hill Vineyard)
classification: White varietal table wine
grape variety: Chardonnay (100%)
district: Santa Cruz County

The vines at Vine Hill were planted in the late 1930s. The history of the vineyard dates back to the 1880s, when White Riesling grapes were planted there from cuttings taken from Schloss Johannisberg in the Rheingau. The vineyard now belongs to Dick Smothers of the Smothers Brothers comedy team. The vineyard totals 17 acres and is planted in Chardonnay, White Riesling, Sylvaner, and Pinot Blanc. This wine was aged in Yugoslavian and French Nevers 50-gallon oak barrels.

Light to medium straw-yellow color and a varietal Chardonnay bouquet with a touch of oak. The wine is very well-balanced and has great depth of flavor.
price range: C

producer: Barengo Vineyards, Inc.
classification: Red varietal table wine
grape variety: Gamay Beaujolais
district: Lodi
city or village: Lodi

This fresh, fruity red wine is similar to its French counterpart from the Beaujolais district.

Being light-bodied, this wine can be enjoyed quite young. It may be served at room temperature or slightly chilled, as the ideal accompaniment for a luncheon, picnic, or other light dishes. **price range:** A

producer: Barengo Vineyards, Inc.
classification: Red varietal table wine
grape variety: Ruby Cabernet
district: Lodi

Similar to the fine Clarets of Bordeaux, this wine is aged in small oak casks.

Rich bouquet and full-bodied on the palate. An excellent companion to meats, game, and cheeses; allow to breathe for a half hour before serving. **price range:** A

producer: Bargetto Winery
classification: Red varietal table wine
grape variety: Zinfandel (100%)
district: Amador County

This wine was aged in 50-gallon American white oak barrels.

Brilliant dark red color and a fruity varietal bouquet with a hint of oak. The wine has balance between fruit and acidity with good tannin and fruit to assure it of long life. **price range:** A

producer: Beaulieu Vineyards
classification: Rosé varietal table wine
grape variety: Grenache
district: Napa Valley
city or village: Rutherford

A *vin d'une nuit* ("wine of one night"), left on the skins only a few hours after the crushing, thus acquiring no more than a touch of color.

Pink color and a full Grenache fragrance. The wine is very fruity and is best served chilled. **price range:** A

producer: Barengo Vineyards, Inc.
classification: Red varietal table wine
grape variety: Cabernet Sauvignon
district: Lodi
city or village: Lodi

This full-bodied and distinctive red wine is similar to the Clarets of Bordeaux. It is aged in oak casks in cellars built in the nineteenth century.

An excellent companion to gourmet cuisine. Allow the wine to breathe by opening at least a half hour before serving.
price range: A

producer: Barengo Vineyards, Inc.
classification: White varietal table wine
grape variety: Pinot Chardonnay
district: Lodi

Similar to the great white Burgundies of France.

Full bouquet and a dry, full flavor. When served chilled, the wine is a fine companion to fish, shellfish, poultry, and veal.
price range: A

producer: Bargetto Winery (Eldorado Vineyard)
classification: White varietal table wine
grape variety: Chenin Blanc (100%)
district: Monterey County

This is one of the few late-harvest Chenin Blanc wines produced in California. The grapes were picked at the Eldorado Vineyard late in the season (November 21) in order to produce a sweet wine with high alcohol (14%) and good acid balance. It will be interesting to see how well and for how long this wine develops. It contains 1% residual sugar.

Brilliant straw-yellow color and a rich varietal bouquet. The wine is full-bodied, with a great depth of flavor.
price range: B

"You, invincible Paladins, celebrated talkative minstrels, after having cleft giants in twain, set free fair ladies, or exterminated armies, no black-eyed captive ever did offer you sparkling Champagne, Malmsey, or Madeira, or liqueurs the creation of Louis XIV. You had to be satisfied with beer or with some herb-flavored sour wine. How I pity you!"

producer: Beaulieu Vineyard
classification: Estate-bottled red varietal table wine
grape variety: Cabernet Sauvignon
district: Napa Valley

This wine is made only from Napa Valley grapes and is aged in 50-gallon American oak barrels for from one to two years. After bottling, it is ready to drink.

A deep red color and an oaklike bouquet characteristic of the varietal. The wine is fresh, full-bodied, and shows the effect of wood aging. Serve at room temperature with roasts, game, ham, meat sauce dishes, fowl, lamb, cheese, and all red meats.
price range: B

producer: Beaulieu Vineyard
classification: Red varietal table wine
grape variety: Cabernet Sauvignon (80%) and Merlot (20%)
district: Napa Valley
city or village: Rutherford

"Beau Tour." Beaulieu Vineyard's third Cabernet Sauvignon is distinguished by a slight admixture of Merlot, as opposed to the 100% Cabernets the winery also offers. Beau Tour is intentionally made in this manner to approximate the Clarets of Bordeaux, which contain this admixture. The wines are estate-bottled.

A dry, distinct Claret-type wine. It has a slight oak flavor from the brief period of aging in oak casks.
price range: B

producer: Beaulieu Vineyard
classification: Red varietal table wine
grape variety: Pinot Noir (100%)
district: Napa Valley
city or village: Rutherford

"Beau Velours." This rich and fruity wine is made in a younger style, emphasizing the intensely fruity varietal character of Pinot Noir. It was matured in large casks, ensuring that a minimum amount of wine would touch the wood and achieving the double benefit of maturing in wood while maintaining the wine's distinct style and bouquet.

Light red color; a dry, fruity, and full-bodied wine.
price range: B

producer: Beaulieu Vineyard
classification: White sparkling wine
district: Napa Valley
city or village: Rutherford

"Private Reserve Brut."

Pale color; the wine has an elegant bouquet and is completely dry.
price range: C

producer: Beaulieu Vineyard
classification: White varietal table wine
grape variety: Sylvaner (Riesling)
district: Napa Valley
city or village: Rutherford

When grown on the Beaulieu property in the Napa Valley, the Sylvaner yields a clean, fresh, and delightful white wine. The Sylvaner is responsible for many appealing wines in Alsace and Germany. Beaulieu's Sylvaner wines are estate-bottled.

Clear pale gold color and a fragrant bouquet. The wine is pleasantly dry and has the youth and freshness characteristic of the variety. Serve chilled with fish, seafoods, cream sauce dishes, and other light meats.
price range: B

producer: Beaulieu Vineyard
classification: Red varietal table wine
grape variety: Pinot Noir
district: Napa Valley
city or village: Rutherford

Pinot Noir is the grape responsible for the noble red wines of the Côte d'Or, Burgundy. As the grape is responsive to weather conditions during the growing season, its wines can vary from light to full-bodied, according to vintage. Called "Beau Mont," this Pinot Noir is estate-bottled from the Beaulieu property in the Napa Valley.

A dry, full-bodied red wine with the fruity, delicate flavor of the variety. Serve at room temperature with roasts, game, meat sauce dishes, lamb, and other red meats.
price range: B

producer: Beaulieu Vineyard
classification: White varietal table wine
grape variety: Pinot Chardonnay (100%)
district: Napa Valley
city or village: Rutherford

"Beau Fort." This wine is produced entirely from Pinot Chardonnay grapes grown on the property in the Napa Valley. The wines are estate-bottled. This grape is celebrated for producing the white Burgundies of France.

A dry, delightful white wine that retains the pleasant aroma and distinctive character of the variety.
price range: B

producer: Beaulieu Vineyard
classification: White varietal table wine
grape variety: Johannisberg Riesling (100%)

district: Napa Valley
city or village: Rutherford

"Beau Clair." This wine is made entirely from Johannisberg Riesling grapes grown on the Beaulieu property in the Napa Valley and is entitled to the "estate-bottled" designation. The grape is responsible for the finest Rhine and Mosel wines of Germany; the berries are small and intensely fragrant, and the yield is sparse.

Pale greenish color; the wine is light and delicate, with the distinctive fruitiness and flavor of the variety. Serve chilled with fish, seafood, cream sauce dishes, chicken, and light meats.
price range: B

producer: Beaulieu Vineyard
classification: White table wine
grape variety: Sauvignon Blanc and Muscadelle du Bordelais
district: Napa Valley
city or village: Rutherford

"Chateau Beaulieu." This white wine is made from grapes grown on the Beaulieu property in the Napa Valley. The blend is the same as that used in the Bordeaux district of France, and the wines are estate-bottled.

Delicate bouquet; the wine is deliciously fruity and moderately sweet.
price range: B

producer: Beaulieu Vineyard
classification: Red varietal table wine
grape variety: Cabernet Sauvignon (96%)
district: Napa Valley
city or village: Rutherford

1972 vintage. Lighter and less fruity than some of our other Cabernet Sauvignons, this wine requires less bottle age prior to drinking. In this vintage, a 96% proportion of Cabernet was selected for greater complexity. Cabernet Sauvignon is the grape responsible for the renowned château-bottled wines of the Médoc district in Bordeaux; Beaulieu's Cabernet Sauvignon is estate-bottled.

The wine is enjoyable immediately after opening. Serve at room temperature with roasts, game, ham, meat sauce dishes, fowl, lamb, and cheese.
price range: C

producer: Beaulieu Vineyard
classification: White table wine
grape variety: Pinot Blanc, Chenin Blanc, Melon, and French Colombard
district: Napa Valley
city or village: Rutherford

"Chablis." The composition of this blend was developed over many years and was devised to preserve the individual aroma of the grapes. An estate-bottled wine.

A round, mellow, and dry white wine with a characteristically fine aftertaste.
price range: B

producer: Boeger Winery
classification: White varietal table wine
grape variety: Johannisberg Riesling
district: El Dorado County

El Dorado County was planted extensively with grapes during the late 1800s and early 1900s to provide wines and spirits for the post-Gold Rush settlers of the area. Homesteaded in 1857, the winery occupies the site of a distillery and winery that was established in the 1870s.

A light, clear, and brilliant color and a bouquet that is fruity and shows varietal character; the wine has good acid and a smooth finish. It is a dry Johannisberg Riesling.
price range: A

producer: Boeger Winery
classification: White varietal table wine
grape variety: Chenin Blanc
district: El Dorado County

The grapes for this wine were grown in the Gold Hill district of El Dorado County. The ideal climate of warm days and cool nights prevalent in this district brought these grapes to maturity in mid-September. They were quickly picked, pressed gently in a Willmes pneumatic press, then slowly fermented under temperature-controlled conditions.

A clear, light color and fresh bouquet; the wine has high acid and a smooth finish. It is a dry Chenin Blanc.
price range: A

producer: Boeger Winery
classification: Red varietal table wine
grape variety: Cabernet Sauvignon
district: El Dorado County

The wine is aged in small oak casks.

A deep, intense ruby-red color. The wine appears to be clear and has a fruity oak bouquet. On the palate it is robust, with distinctive varietal flavor and high tannin. Although it has a delightful flavor now, the wine will reach full maturity with continued bottle aging.
price range: B

producer: Boeger Winery
classification: Red varietal table wine
grape variety: Zinfandel
district: El Dorado County

This wine is produced from Zinfandel grapes harvested from select vineyards in the Sierra Nevada foothills. Most of the grapes were grown in the well-known Shenandoah Valley of Amador County and were crushed and fermented with some Zinfandels from Placer and El Dorado counties.

A clear, bright red color coupled with a fruity bouquet. It is a characteristic Zinfandel without the harshness so often found in Zinfandels. The wine should be served at cellar temperature, about 60 degrees F.
price range: A

produrer: Bonesio Winery
classification: Red table wine
grape variety: Predominantly Carignane, Zinfandel
district: Santla Clara Valley

This is a reasonably priced, medium-bodied Burgundy-style wine.
price range: A

producer: Bonesio Winery
classification: White varietal table wine
grape variety: Malvasia Bianca
district: Santa Clara Valley

This is a medium-dry, extremely fruity white wine with a grapey bouquet. It is well balanced and flavorful and of almost clear white color.
price range: A

producer: Bonesio Winery
classification: White table wine
grape variety: Predominantly French Colombard

This Chablis-type wine is pleasant, dry, and well balanced.
price range: A

producer: Bonesio Winery
classification: Red varietal table wine
grape variety: Cabernet Sauvignon
district: Santa Clara Valley

This medium-red Cabernet Sauvignon is light-bodied and reasonably priced.
price range: A

producer: Borra's Cellar
classification: Red varietal table wine
grape variety: Barbera
district: Lodi
city or village: Lodi

This wine is produced from grapes grown solely on Borra's property. The winery had its first crush in 1975, and this first vintage is currently still aging; it should be available in late 1977 or early 1978. The picture on the label shows a three-story tank house on the winery property, which many years ago was used to store water. The grape vine in the foreground is a huge vine of unknown origin, which entirely covers an arbor fourteen feet square.

Deep red color and a fruity bouquet. The wine is robust and hearty.
price range: A

producer: Brookside Vineyard Co.
classification: White varietal table wine
grape variety: Pinot Chardonnay
district: San Joaquin Valley
city or village: Sacramento
price range: B

producer: Brookside Vineyard Co.
classification: Red varietal table wine
grape variety: Zinfandel
district: San Joaquin Valley
city or village: Sacramento
price range: B

producer: Brookside Vineyard Co.
classification: Red varietal table wine
grape variety: Cabernet Sauvignon
district: San Joaquin Valley
city or village: Sacramento
price range: B

producer: David Bruce Winery, Inc.
classification: Red varietal table wine
grape variety: Grenache
district: North Coast—Santa Cruz
city or village: Los Gatos

A Grenache from the 1971 vintage, this is one of the few red wines made wholly from this varietal.

A deep red color and a strong, berrylike bouquet. This big, rich, and full-blooded red wine is made in the late-harvest style.
price range: C

producer: David Bruce Winery, Inc.
classification: White varietal table wine
grape variety: Chardonnay
district: North Coast—Santa Cruz
city or village: Los Gatos

This Chardonnay is from the 1974 vintage and is sold in two lots. Lot 1, which must be carefully decanted, is bigger than lot 2. Lot 2 at this time need not be decanted.

A golden color and an aromatic, orangey bouquet. It is a big, mouth-filling, and somewhat woody Chardonnay.
price range: D

producer: David Bruce Winery, Inc.
classification: Red varietal table wine
grape variety: Cabernet Sauvignon
district: North Coast—Santa Cruz
city or village: Los Gatos

1973 vintage.

A purple-black color and a strong Cabernet-raspberry bouquet. This big, mouth-filling wine is eminently drinkable, but will be long-lived. **price range:** D

producer: David Bruce Winery, Inc.
classification: Red varietal table wine
grape variety: Zinfandel
district: North Coast—Santa Cruz
city or village: Los Gatos

This is a late-harvest Zinfandel from the 1971 vintage.

A purple-black color and a "chocolaty" bouquet. The wine is big and intense; it is sold in two grades, dry or sweet. It will be long-lived. **price range:** C

producer: David Bruce Winery, Inc.
classification: Red varietal table wine
grape variety: Pinot Noir
district: North Coast—Santa Cruz
city or village: Los Gatos

This big wine is from the 1970 vintage and has much potential.

A red-black color and a bouquet that does not immediately display its fruit. This big, tannic wine needs one or two hours' aeration. **price range:** C

producer: David Bruce Winery, Inc.
classification: Red varietal table wine
grape variety: Zinfandel
district: North Coast—Santa Cruz
city or village: Los Gatos

"Essence." It is from the 1971 vintage.
"Black" color and a chocolaty bouquet. The wine is big, intense, and sweet; it needs decanting prior to drinking.
price range: D

producer: Buena Vista Winery
classification: White varietal table wine
grape variety: Green Hungarian (100%)
district: Napa and Sonoma counties
city or village: Sonoma

Straw color and a full, smooth bouquet. The wine is round and full.
price range: A

producer: Buena Vista Winery
classification: White varietal table wine
grape variety: Gewürztraminer (100%)
district: Sonoma and Mendocino counties
city or village: Sonoma

Clear straw color and a spicy bouquet. The wine has an herby essence of the grape.
price range: B

producer: Buena Vista Winery
classification: Red varietal table wine
grape variety: Zinfandel (100%)
district: Sonoma County
city or village: Sonoma

Table wine from Zinfandel grapes was first produced at the Buena Vista winery.

Very clear, brilliant red color, and a full varietal bouquet. The wine is very fruity, with the pronounced raspberry flavor characteristic of Zinfandel.
price range: A

producer: Buena Vista Winery
classification: White varietal table wine
grape variety: Pinot Chardonnay (100%)
district: Sonoma and Mendocino counties
city or village: Sonoma

Very light straw color and a fresh, slightly fruity bouquet. The wine is very dry.
price range: B

producer: Burgess Cellars
classification: White varietal table wine
grape variety: Green Hungarian
district: Napa Valley
city or village: St. Helena

The grapes for this wine came from a mountain vineyard on the western side of the Napa Valley; hence its unique character.

A light gold color and a flowery, fruity bouquet. Fruity and off dry, it is a great sipping wine, very Germanic in character.
price range: B

producer: Burgess Cellars
classification: Estate-bottled rosé varietal table wine
grape variety: Grenache
district: Napa Valley
city or village: St. Helena

A bright pink color and a rich, flowery bouquet. On the palate the wine is medium dry and fruity; it is complex and a serious wine for the consumer. **price range:** A

producer: Burgess Cellars
classification: Red varietal table wine
grape variety: Zinfandel
district: Napa and Sonoma counties
city or village: St. Helena and Glen Ellen

This wine is made entirely from grapes grown in steep mountain vineyards, and that character shows in the bottle.

A ruby-red color and a complex bouquet with Zinfandel and oak. The wine is dry, long-lasting, and fruity; it is a big Zinfandel with character. **price range:** C

producer: Burgess Cellars
classification: Red varietal table wine
grape variety: Cabernet Sauvignon and Merlot
district: Napa Valley
city or village: St. Helena

This Cabernet Sauvignon contains about 12% Merlot.

A deep purple color with a bouquet rich in Cabernet Sauvignon character and oak. The wine is full-flavored, with plenty of fruit, oak, and tannin. It is complex, big, and unique in varietal character.
price range: D

producer: Burgess Cellars
classification: Red varietal table wine
grape variety: Petite Sirah
district: Napa Valley
city or village: St. Helena

The overall character of this wine relates to the fact that a majority of the grapes were grown in a mountain vineyard.

A "black" color and a spicy, fruit-oak bouquet. The wine has plenty of tannin and is a prime example of a big wine with complexities not normally encountered in this variety.
price range: C

producer: Burgess Cellars
classification: White varietal table wine
grape variety: Johannisberg Riesling
district: Napa Valley
city or village: St. Helena

The grapes for this wine came from the Winery Lake vineyards in the Carneros region of the Napa Valley. This region is very similar to the temperatures and climate of the Mosel region of Germany.

A light golden color and a bouquet that is rich in fruit and suggests apricots. On the palate the wine is medium dry, with a long finish. It is a wonderfully fruity, long-lasting wine—very delicious with light cheeses or fruits.
price range: C

producer: Burgess Cellars
classification: White varietal table wine
grape variety: Chenin Blanc
district: Napa Valley
city or village: St. Helena

The grapes for this wine came from the Steltzner vineyards, close to Yountville in the Napa Valley. The wine shows vineyard character as well as varietal character.

A light straw color and a full bouquet with oak and varietal characteristics. On the palate the wine is dry, full-bodied, and has a long finish. Unusual for a wine from this grape variety, it is completely dry and has great character.
price range: B

producer: Burgess Cellars
classification: White varietal table wine
grape variety: Chardonnay
district: Napa Valley
city or village: St. Helena

The grapes for this wine came from the Winery Lake vineyards in the Carneros region of the Napa Valley.

A straw color and a tremendous bouquet with fruit and oak predominant. The wine is full, dry, and has a long finish. It is a Chardonnay with sufficient character to be classified as a great wine. **price range:** D

producer: Burgess Cellars
classification: Red varietal table wine
grape variety: Cabernet Sauvignon
district: Napa Valley
city or village: St. Helena

This is a special selection of Cabernet Sauvignon that has outstanding traits in every respect. In the producer's judgment, it is one of the most complex and interesting Cabernet Sauvignons produced in California.

A black-red color and a huge, oaky bouquet. The wine is big, dry, and complex, with a long finish. **price range:** E

producer: California Growers Winery, Inc.
classification: Red varietal table wine
grape variety: Cabernet Sauvignon
district: San Joaquin Valley

This is a robust, flavorful Cabernet Sauvignon, well-balanced, with a mature, distinctive bouquet. It is of clear dark red color with a purple tint. This is a wine of superior quality and maturity.
price range: below A

producer: California Growers Winery, Inc.
classification: White varietal table wine
grape variety: French Colombard
district: San Joaquin Valley

This is a delightful varietal wine, well-balanced and medium-bodied, of unique fruity and perfumey character. The bouquet is delicate and fruity, the color a clear light gold. **price range:** below A

producer: California Growers Winery, Inc.
classification: White varietal table wine
grape variety: Johannisberg Riesling
district: San Joaquin Valley

This dry, medium-bodied Johannisberg Riesling has a delicate, fruity bouquet and slight green tint to its light straw color. It is a fine premium varietal wine with all the delicate and fruity characteristics of the varietal. It is at its best when very young.
price range: below A

producer: California Growers Winery, Inc.
classification: Red generic table wine
grape variety: Ruby Cabernet and Barbera
district: San Joaquin Valley

This brilliant, clear ruby-colored Chianti-style wine with fresh, fruity bouquet is light and full-flavored. It is properly aged at the winery and ready to be enjoyed right away.

This wine won a bronze medal at the 1976 California wine judging at the Los Angeles County Fair in its first participation in this prestigious U.S. wine competition.
price range: below A

producer: California Growers Winery
classification: Tokay wine
grape variety: Muscat, Carignane, and Palomino
district: San Joaquin Valley

This reddish-amber wine with light, fruity bouquet has a slightly nutty Sherry taste. It is mellow and well-balanced, showing its proper aging.

This prize-winning Tokay took a first award at the 1976 California wine judging at Los Angeles. **price range:** below A

producer: California Growers Winery, Inc.
classification: Rosé sparkling wine
grape variety: Predominantly Grenache
district: San Joaquin Valley

This is a fresh, faintly sweet, and fruity, clear pink Champagne. It is light-bodied, tart, and well-balanced, with a fruity, fresh bouquet.

This pink Champagne took a second award at the 1976 Los Angeles County Fair.
price range: A

producer: Callaway Vineyards and Winery
classification: White varietal table wine
grape variety: Sauvignon Blanc
district: South Coastal Mountains
city or village: Temecula

This Sauvignon Blanc was matured in Spessart white oak casks imported from Germany. Callaway is the only premium winery in southern California; the wine was bottled with less than 1.5 ppm dissolved oxygen and shows slightly sweeter than its measurement of 0.20 residual sugar.

Pale straw-gold color and a big, full bouquet with varietal fruit. The wine is clean, full in the mouth, and very fruity, with a long finish. **price range:** C

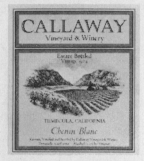

producer: Callaway Vineyard & Winery
classification: White varietal table wine
grape variety: Chenin Blanc
district: South Coastal Mountains
city or village: Temecula

Callaway is the only premium winery in southern California. This Chenin Blanc was matured in white oak from the Spessart Mountains in Germany and was bottled with less than 1.5 ppm dissolved oxygen.

Pale straw color and a medium varietal bouquet with fine depth. The wine is very clean and crisp, with fine balance, rich flavors, and a very long finish.
price range: B

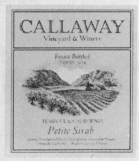

producer: Callaway Vineyard & Winery
classification: Red varietal table wine
grape variety: Petite Sirah
district: South Coastal Mountains
city or village: Temecula

One of the finest Petite Sirahs ever made in California. The wine was aged in 60-gallon German white oak barrels and will continue to improve for the next decade.

"Black" ruby-red color and a full

bouquet amply demonstrating the fruit inherent in this grape. The wine is huge—fruity, soft, with good tannin and a fine finish. You won't believe how good it is until you try it. **price range:** C

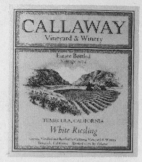

producer: Callaway Vineyard & Winery
classification: White varietal table wine
grape variety: Johannisberg (White) Riesling
district: South Coastal Mountains
city or village: Temecula

Callaway White Riesling was chosen to be served to Queen Elizabeth II of England at the time of her visit to New York in July 1976.

Medium yellow color and a slightly perfumed, varietal aroma. The wine is very fruity, with good balance in body, acid, and fruit, and has a long finish. **price range:** C

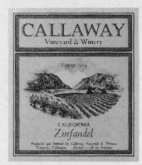

producer: Callaway Vineyard & Winery
classification: Red varietal table wine
grape variety: Zinfandel
district: South Coastal Mountains
city or village: Temecula

This is probably the first red wine in California that matured in white oak from the Spessart Mountains in Germany. It was fermented at 65 degrees F. and will improve over the next eight years or so.

Deep ruby-red color and a full, fruity bouquet. The wine is dry, with varietal "berry" fruit, and has good tannin balance; it is a unique Zinfandel, with a faint blackberry flavor. **price range:** C

producer: Callaway Vineyard & Winery
classification: Red varietal table wine
grape variety: Cabernet Sauvignon
district: South Coastal Mountains
city or village: Temecula

The first California Cabernet Sauvignon ever to be matured in white oak from the

Spessart Mountains in Germany. It is a very big wine that will live for many years.

Deep ruby-red color and a big, varietal bouquet. The wine shows good balance and has ample tannin but not the "bite" that excessive tannin gives. It has a fine, fruity finish. **price range:** C

producer: Callaway Vineyard and Winery
classification: White varietal table wine
grape variety: Chenin Blanc
district: South Central Mountains
city or village: Temecula

"Sweet Nancy," named for Ely Callaway's wife. This is the first late-harvested Chenin Blanc produced in California. The grapes were grown in northern California and picked in a state of overripeness as a result of Botrytis mold; they were rushed to the winery by refrigerated truck.

Full golden color, and a strong Botrytis nose showing extraordinary balance. The wine is rich and round, with full body, good acid, and luscious sweetness—though it is not at all cloying. It is similar to a Côteaux de Layon, and like that wine, it will improve with bottle age. **price range:** E

producer: Cambiaso Winery & Vineyards
classification: Red varietal table wine
grape variety: Ruby Cabernet
district: Sonoma County
city or village: Healdsburg

This wine is made from a new hybrid developed by the University of California at Davis, a cross between Cabernet and Carignane.

A deep purplish-red color and an excellent, full bouquet. The wine is very dry with low acid, yet tastes very full. It goes well with hearty meals. **price range:** B

producer: Cambiaso Winery & Vineyards
classification: Red varietal table wine

grape variety: Cabernet Sauvignon
district: Sonoma County
city or village: Healdsburg

This excellent Cabernet Sauvignon should be allowed to mature in the bottle after purchase.

A dark red color and an excellent bouquet. The wine tastes exceptionally rich and full-bodied, and it is dry.
price range: B

producer: Cambiaso Winery & Vineyards
classification: Red varietal table wine
grape variety: Petite Sirah
district: Sonoma County
city or village: Healdsburg

A deep red color and an excellent bouquet. On the palate the wine is very dry, with strong characteristics of Petite Sirah. The wine is great with cheese, spaghetti, stews, and casseroles. **price range:** B

producer: Cambiaso Winery & Vineyards
classification: White varietal table wine
grape variety: French Colombard
district: Sonoma County
city or village: Healdsburg

A clear straw color and a good bouquet. The wine is exceptionally dry with low acidity, and has the very distinct aroma and flavor of good French Colombard grapes.
price range: B

producer: Cambiaso Winery & Vineyards
classification: Red table wine
grape variety: Petite Sirah and Zinfandel
district: Sonoma County
city or village: Healdsburg

An excellent blend of Zinfandel and Petite Sirah, this is Giovanni Cambiaso's favorite wine, still produced today with the same traditional patience.

Dark red color and an excellent bouquet. The wine has exceptionally full body; it is very dry and mellow, with low acidity.
price range: A

producer: Caymus Vineyards
classification: Rosé varietal table wine
grape variety: Pinot Noir
district: Napa Valley
city or village: Rutherford

This true varietal rosé is made entirely from Pinot Noir, one of the few of its kind produced in California. Its counterparts may be found in Burgundy and Switzerland, also made from Pinot Noir and vinified in the same manner.

Salmon-pink to light orange color and a bouquet with good Pinot Noir character. The wine is clean and refreshing; it goes well with pork and veal dishes, especially ham, and is also very good with seafood and poultry. **price range:** B

producer: Caymus Vineyards
classification: Red varietal table wine
grape variety: Cabernet Sauvignon (100%)
district: Napa Valley
city or village: Rutherford

This wine was made entirely from Cabernet Sauvignon and was not blended with any other varieties. The grapes came from a small parcel of land, and the wine is vinified the same way each year, in a like manner as the famous Bordeaux château wines.

Deep ruby color and an herbaceous bouquet. The wine is clean, extremely fruity, and has a long, lingering aftertaste; it should be a winner, as was the 1973 vintage. **price range:** C

producer: Caymus Vineyards
classification: Red varietal table wine
grape variety: Zinfandel

This wine is made from a blend of Zinfandel grapes grown in three separate areas in California, two of them in Amador and Lake counties and the other in the Napa Valley. Each area gives its own character to the wine.

Medium red color and a typical "raspberry" bouquet. The wine combines good body with refreshing raspberrylike flavor; and the clean aftertaste lingers. A "drinking" wine: several glasses seem to require more. **price range:** B

producer: Chalone Vineyard
classification: Estate-bottled white varietal table wine
grape variety: Pinot Blanc
district: Monterey County
city or village: Pinnacles
1974 vintage.

A medium straw-yellow color. Some bottles may be slightly cloudy because the wine is shipped unfiltered. The bouquet resembles a Chardonnay, with good character and some oak. The wine is well-balanced and clean, with good body and a medium finish. **price range:** C

producer: Chalone Vineyard
classification: Estate-bottled white varietal table wine
grape variety: Chenin Blanc
district: Monterey County
city or village: Pinnacles

1974 vintage. The soil on the vineyard was discovered by a Frenchman seeking land comparable to that of France. It is sparse and reddish with underlying limestone, as is the Côte d'Or in Burgundy. Each acre of land yields only 600 bottles of wine. This wine is available only in California.

A light straw-yellow color and a big, fruity bouquet showing some oak. The wine is dry, rich, and has ripe fruit; it is well-balanced, with a medium finish.
price range: B

producer: Chalone Vineyard
classification: White varietal table wine
grape variety: French Colombard
district: Napa Valley
city or village: Calistoga
1975 vintage.

A light straw-yellow color and a vinous, clean, and fruity bouquet with light oak. On the palate it is dry, crisp, and fruity, with a medium body and a long finish. It is a good California "Chablis-type" wine.
price range: A

producer: Chateau Chevalier Winery
classification: Red varietal table wine
grape variety: Cabernet Sauvignon and Merlot
district: Napa Valley
city or village: St. Helena (Spring Mountain)

This is the first release of the chateau since a replanting program was started in 1970. The Chateau Chevalier winery was established in 1891, and the original vineyards were planted by Benger Bros. in 1876. A 7½% admixture of Merlot helps soften the tannin of this big wine, which will live for a great many years.

Deep, dark red color and an intense Cabernet nose that develops after five or six hours of breathing. The wine is a huge, well-balanced Cabernet, with immense fruit. **price range:** C

producer: Chateau St. Jean
classification: White varietal table wine
grape variety: Chardonnay
district: North Coast Counties

A 100% Chardonnay released in November/December 1976. While most of the chateau's Chardonnays bear a vineyard/estate designation, this one is a blend from several vineyards.

A wine that is medium in body and texture, fruity in style, and richly balanced in finish, with definite oak undertones. While drinkable now, it will continue to develop for some years to come. **price range:** C

producer: Chateau St. Jean (Robert Young Vineyards)
classification: White varietal table wine
grape variety: Johannisberg Riesling
district: Sonoma County—Alexander Valley

A bouquet with a complex array of fruit and earthiness and a fine, delicate flavor—almost dry, fruity, and earthy. The wine is true to its European ancestry—it is a perfect accompaniment to a meal.
price range: C

producer: Chateau Montelena Winery
classification: White varietal table wine
grape variety: Johannisberg Riesling
district: Napa and Alexander valleys

This wine was produced from late-harvested grapes that were affected by Botrytis mold. It has 1.2% residual sugar and 0.75% total acidity. 1974 vintage.

A light straw color and a perfumed, flowery bouquet. The wine is medium dry and has a crisp, clean finish. **price range:** C

producer: Chateau Montelena Winery
classification: Red varietal table wine
grape variety: Zinfandel
district: Napa Valley

This Zinfandel was made in a new, complex style combining the spice and fruit of the grape with the vanillalike flavor from

Nevers oak barrels. While in the barrel, the wine was kept from undergoing malolactic fermentation in order to preserve the varietal fruitiness. 1973 vintage.

A brilliant color true to the variety. The bouquet shows strong varietal characteristics of fruit and spice. There is rich fruit followed by a vanillalike finish.
price range: C

producer: Chateau Montelena Winery
classification: White varietal table wine
grape variety: Chardonnay
district: Napa and Alexander valleys

This big, powerful white wine was allowed to age in new Limousin oak barrels for eight months and has great aging potential.

A brilliant, characteristic color and a woody bouquet with strong varietal character. The wine has a full, rich body with nuances of wood; it was produced from fully mature grapes. **price range:** C

producer: The Christian Brothers
classification: White varietal table wine
grape variety: Chardonnay

The rare Chardonnay grape is considered to make the finest white Burgundies. It is one of the world's truly great white dinner wines.

A clear color and a full bouquet that is exquisitely subtle. It is indeed a wine of immense charm and finesse, with a superbly soft, mellow flavor. **price range:** B

producer: The Christian Brothers
classification: White varietal table wine
grape variety: Johannisberg (White) Riesling
district: Napa Valley

This wine is made from the most famed grape of the Rhineland—the peerless White Riesling.

A pale gold color and a fragrant, flowery bouquet. It is a delectably dry Riesling.
price range: B

producer: The Christian Brothers
classification: Red varietal table wine
grape variety: Pinot Noir
district: Napa Valley

This elegant wine is the finest of red Burgundies, pressed from the sparse crops of the true Pinot Noir grape grown in Napa Valley vineyards.

A clear color and a full bouquet. On the palate it is perfectly dry, with elegant flavor. **price range:** B

producer: The Christian Brothers
classification: Red varietal table wine
grape variety: Cabernet Sauvignon
district: Napa Valley

This truly superb dry red table wine is made from the most famous grape used for clarets: the noble and sparse-bearing Cabernet Sauvignon. It is grown in Napa Valley hillside vineyards and matured to its full flavor and bouquet.

A brilliant deep red color and a robust bouquet. The wine is dry and will stay in its prime for years. **price range:** B

producer: The Christian Brothers
classification: White varietal table wine
grape variety: Sauvignon Blanc
district: Napa Valley

This wine is made from the rare Sauvignon Blanc grape used for the fine white wines of Bordeaux.

A pale gold color and a spicy bouquet. The wine has an enticingly delicious taste, and a natural sweetness adds to its character. **price range:** B

producer: The Christian Brothers
classification: Estate-bottled white varietal table wine
grape variety: Sauvignon Blanc (Blanc Fumé)
district: Napa Valley

A special fermentation helps give Napa Fumé its character and taste. Juice is quickly extracted from the grapes and given a long, slow cold fermentation in specially designed, temperature-controlled stainless-steel tanks. The fermenting juice is kept at approximately 50 degrees for two months. The manner in which this is done helps retain more fruitiness and fragrance in the wine. It also helps retain a trace of the natural carbon dioxide gas produced by fermentation. This is the "fuming" implied in the name.

A clear color and a fragrant bouquet. The wine is dry, with a hint of fruitiness.
price range: B

producer: The Christian Brothers
classification: Red varietal table wine
grape variety: Zinfandel
district: Napa Valley

This refreshingly light, fruity dry dinner wine possesses a truly rare character. It has exceptional softness accompanied by a fragrant bouquet and a rich and satisfying aftertaste. **price range:** B

producer: The Christian Brothers
classification: Estate-bottled red varietal table wine
grape variety: Pinot St. George
district: Napa Valley

The grapes for this wine are picked at the moment of balanced ripeness, then the wine is aged in oak casks and later in bottle until it reaches a zestful flavor and mellow bouquet.

A red dinner wine with a full, mellow bouquet and a smoothly dry, uniquely satisfying flavor. **price range:** B

producer: The Christian Brothers
classification: White sparkling wine "Extra Dry Champagne."

This elegant premium "white" Champagne is a shade more generous in sweetness and fuller in flavor than Brut Champagne. It has a full bouquet.
price range: C

producer: Clos du Val Wine Co., Ltd.
classification: Red varietal table wine
grape variety: Cabernet Sauvignon and Merlot
district: Napa Valley

This wine is made from a blend of 87% Cabernet and 13% Merlot aged in small French oak cooperage. It is typical of the lower part of the Napa Valley, where Merlot plays a major part.

A brilliant medium-red color. The bouquet shows strong varietal character; on the palate the wine is soft, mellow, delicate, and not too deep, with a definite *gout de terroir.* Although not a huge wine, it has elegance, a nice aroma, and is ready to be enjoyed now. **price range:** C

producer: Clos du Val Wine Co., Ltd.
classification: Red varietal table wine
grape variety: Zinfandel
district: Napa Valley

The 1973 Clos du Val Zinfandel was made from a blend of grapes from two different ranches, one in the hills and the other on the valley floor. It was aged in small French oak cooperage.

A deep red color and a powerful "berry" bouquet characteristic of Zinfandel—very strong and long-lasting. The taste is powerful, tannic, and long-lasting. This is a powerful Zinfandel with a softness that lingers on the palate. It will age very nicely.
price range: B

producer: Coloma Winery
classification: White varietal table wine
grape variety: Chenin Blanc

One of five white varietal wines produced at this winery.

Light golden color and a clean bouquet with the crisp fruitiness of the grape variety. The wine is off-dry, soft, and delightfully fresh and fruity; it should be consumed when young. **price range:** A

producer: Concannon Vineyard
classification: White varietal table wine
grape variety: Johannisberg Riesling (100%)
district: Livermore Valley
city or village: Livermore

A pale gold color with greenish tints and a distinct flowery bouquet of Johannisberg Riesling. The wine is mildly tart with subtle sweet overtones, and finishes cleanly. It is one of California's dry Rieslings and is well-suited as a dinner beverage with lighter foods. **price range:** B

producer: Concannon Vineyard
classification: Estate-bottled white varietal table wine
grape variety: Rkatsiteli (100%)
district: Livermore Valley
city or village: Livermore

This is the only varietal wine produced in the United States at this time from grapes native to Russia.

A very pale straw color with green tints, and a tart, crisp bouquet. The wine is very dry, with slight spritz; it is clean, light-bodied, and very pleasant. It is ideal before dinner or as a companion to lighter foods. **price range:** B

producer: Concannon Vineyard
classification: Red varietal table wine
grape variety: Petite Sirah (100%)
district: Livermore Valley
city or village: Livermore

Concannon Vineyard was the first winery in America to bottle a varietal Petite Sirah.

A deep ruby color and a rich bouquet. The wine is dry, full-flavored, and has a lingering aftertaste. Serve at cool room temperature; it will harmonize well with rich stews, roasts, steaks, and pasta. **price range:** B

producer: Coloma Champagne Cellars
classification: White sparkling wine
grape variety: French Colombard and Chardonnay
district: Alameda County
city or village: Fremont

Made by the Charmat (bulk) process, this is an outstanding sparkling wine for the price.

Light gold color with greenish overtones and a fruity bouquet with a hint of apples. On the palate the wine is off-dry.
price range: A

producer: Concannon Vineyard
classification: White table wine
grape variety: Chenin Blanc and Riesling
district: Livermore Valley
city or village: Livermore

"Moselle." This wine is made by an old family secret formula. It is one of the few Moselles with a California appellation.

A pale straw color and a mildly sweet bouquet. The wine is medium dry, soft, and fruity; it is an ideal beverage wine and also would go well with light meats and fish. It is mildly sweet and finishes cleanly.
price range: A

producer: Concannon Vineyard
classification: Fortified wine
grape variety: Palomino
district: Livermore Valley
city or village: Livermore

"Prelude Dry Sherry." This wine is produced by the authentic Spanish flor technique.

An amber-gold color and a nutty bouquet. The wine is light, dry, and smooth; it is a good prelude to an evening meal. **price range:** A

producer: Concannon Vineyard
classification: White varietal table wine
grape variety: Semillon (100%)
district: Livermore Valley
city or village: Livermore

A golden straw color and a floral bouquet. The wine is full-bodied and rich, with a mildly tart flavor and a clean finish. It would be nice with any food.
price range: A

producer: Concannon Vineyard
classification: White varietal table wine
grape variety: Semillon (100%)
district: Livermore Valley
city or village: Livermore

This wine definitely improves with several years' bottle age.

A full straw color and a subtle fruity bouquet. The wine is medium-bodied, sweet, and slightly fruity. It would be best suited to a fresh fruit dessert and is also appropriate for those preferring a sweet aperitif. **price range:** A

producer: Concannon Vineyard
classification: White varietal table wine
grape variety: Chenin Blanc (100%)
district: Livermore Valley
city or village: Livermore

A straw color and a sweet, fruity bouquet. The wine is mildly sweet with the fresh fruit flavor of Chenin Blanc. It would be best suited to light meats or cream foods, or as an afternoon or evening beverage to be enjoyed with or without food.
price range: A

producer: Concannon Vineyard
classification: Red varietal table wine
grape variety: Zinfandel (100%)
district: Livermore Valley
city or village: Livermore

Enjoyable in its youth, this Zinfandel matures gracefully in the bottle.

A medium ruby color and a fruity bouquet. The wine has a rich, berrylike flavor. **price range:** A

producer: Concannon Vineyard
classification: Red varietal table wine
grape variety: Cabernet Sauvignon (100%)
district: Livermore Valley
city or village: Livermore

This Cabernet Sauvignon is aged four years in wood and one year in bottle before being shipped to the consumer.

A medium ruby color and a current-raspberry bouquet. The wine is rich, tart, and mildly tannic on the palate. It has a fruity character with a lingering aftertaste and is a red wine with considerable depth; it will probably be at its best between eight and twelve years of age. **price range:** D

producer: Concannon Vineyard
classification: White varietal table wine
grape variety: Sauvignon Blanc
district: Livermore Valley
city or village: Livermore

A pale straw color and a spicy bouquet. The wine has medium body with sweet overtones and a lingering aftertaste. It is a well-balanced, high-quality white wine, which typifies a true Livermore Sauvignon Blanc. **price range:** B

producer: Cresta Blanca Winery
classification: White varietal table wine
grape variety: Moscato di Canelli
district: Northern California

The Moscato di Canelli is well known in the Piedmont region in Italy. It produces a heavy, almost viscous wine suitable for aperitif use over fresh fruits, as well as a "hospitality" wine. Fewer than 750 acres have been planted in California. Perhaps as a result of increasing interest in wines, this wine is finding a large market. It bears a vintage date.

A medium yellow to light gold color with a very pungent Muscat bouquet. The wine is rich, very full, and fruity. It is best consumed when young. **price range:** B

producer: Cresta Blanca Winery
classification: Fortified wine
grape variety: Palomino and Pedro Ximenez
district: Northern California

"Cresta Blanca Triple Cream Sherry." It is the only California wine to be awarded the grand prize at the California state fair, among numerous other gold medals. The same formula has been used for more than thirty-five years: barrel aging.

A medium amber color and a very aged, full rich bouquet with cream Sherry character. The wine is very complex, with considerable character; it is a delightful aperitif or a fine dessert wine. **price range:** A

producer: Cresta Blanca Winery
classification: White sparkling wine

Cresta Blanca Champagnes have long been gold-medal winners in national and international competition.

A pale straw-yellow color and a true Champagne bouquet. The wine is very crisp and quite dry, the result of long bottle aging as is traditional in France. **price range:** C

producer: Cresta Blanca Winery
classification: Fortified wine
grape variety: Palomino

This dry Sherry is reminiscent of a Spanish Fino. The special formula for making it was developed a quarter of a century ago. Ample oak aging is evident in the smoothness and complexity of the wine. It has won many prizes.

Very pale straw color with a bouquet showing aged and subdued oak character. The wine tastes very smooth, is somewhat dry, and has an excellent finish. **price range:** A

producer: Cresta Blanca Winery
classification: White varietal table wine
grape variety: Chenin Blanc
district: Northern California

Chenin Blanc is a popular varietal made by many California wineries that is enjoying unprecedented demand with the trend towards light California wines. It is sold with a vintage date.

A light straw-yellow color and a distinct varietal bouquet. The wine is very fresh and well-balanced and is best consumed young. **price range:** A

producer: Cresta Blanca Winery
classification: Red varietal table wine
grape variety: Ruby Cabernet

This wine is made from a hybrid grape developed by the University of California at Davis. It is a crossbreed of Cabernet Sauvignon and California's prolific Carignane.

A medium to dark red color and a bouquet that shows strong varietal character. On the palate the wine is full and grapey; it is an excellent example of this grape variety. **price range:** A

producer: Cresta Blanca Winery
classification: Red varietal table wine
grape variety: Zinfandel
district: Mendocino County

The Cresta Blanca Zinfandel won numerous awards, most recently the San Francisco Vintners' Club award.

A medium red color and a faint raspberry bouquet with pronounced oak characteristics. The wine is very smooth and full and easy to drink. It is an excellent example of how good this variety can be when properly grown and vinified. **price range:** A

producer: Cresta Blanca Winery
classification: White varietal table wine
grape variety: Pinot Chardonnay
district: North Coast Counties

Cresta Blanca Pinot Chardonnay is vintage-dated. Unlike most other whites, it will improve with aging.

A faint straw color, which deepens with age, and a full, fruity bouquet showing varietal character. On the palate the wine is full and rich; it is dry yet smooth and well-balanced. It is an excellent example of a Chardonnay. **price range:** B

producer: Cresta Blanca Winery
classification: White varietal table wine
grape variety: Johannisberg Riesling
district: North Coast Counties

This wine is another excellent example of the growing trend for light and highly drinkable white wines. It is best served young and carries a vintage date.

A light straw-yellow color and a bouquet that shows distinct varietal character. The wine is well balanced between sugar and acid, and is full and grapey. **price range:** B

producer: Cresta Blanca Winery
classification: White varietal table wine
grape variety: Green Hungarian
district: Mendocino County

Green Hungarian is among California's rarest grape varieties. Fewer than 400 acres are planted in the state. This wine is styled for consumers with a taste for bone-dry white wine and bears a vintage date.

A light straw-yellow color and a very fresh and fruity bouquet. It is dry, but not astringent, and is best consumed young. **price range:** A

 *(upper)*

producer: Cresta Blanca Winery
classification: White varietal table wine
grape variety: Gewürztraminer
district: Northern California

Cresta Blanca Gewürztraminer was first offered in 1974. Since then, the wine has been highly acclaimed by press and critics. This variety is another relative newcomer to California; fewer than 3,000 acres have been planted. The wine bears a vintage date and is best consumed young.

A light straw-yellow color and the distinct spicy bouquet typical of this grape variety. Sugar and acidity are balanced, and the wine tends toward the sweet side. It is an excellent example of this grape variety. **price range:** A

 *(lower)*

producer: Cuvaison Winery
classification: White varietal table wine
grape variety: Chardonnay
district: Sonoma Valley
city or village: Calistoga

A medium straw-gold color. The bouquet shows good varietal character with some wood. There are rich Chardonnay and French oak flavors, and good acidity in the finish. This is a big-styled Chardonnay that will benefit from several years in the bottle. **price range:** B

producer: Cuvaison Winery
classification: Red varietal table wine
grape variety: Zinfandel
district: Napa Valley
city or village: Calistoga

A dark ruby color and a bouquet with intense fruit and wood. The wine is full-bodied, with good tannin and a long finish; it is a big, powerful Zinfandel with aging potential. **price range:** B

producer: Cuvaison Winery
classification: White varietal table wine
grape variety: Chardonnay
district: Napa Valley
city or village: Calistoga

A medium straw-gold color and a rich bouquet showing varietal character and spicy overtones. The wine has good acidity and oak, with a long finish. This is a full-bodied Chardonnay with lots of oak; it will benefit from bottle aging. **price range:** B

producer: Del Rey Coop
classification: Red table wine
grape variety: Grenache and Carignane
district: San Joaquin Valley
city or village: Fresno

This is a mellow, smooth Burgundy-style wine of dark red color. It has a rich, heady bouquet. **price range:** A

"How is Champagne made? By sheer genius, sir, sheer genius!"
—Conversation at Whites Club, London

producer: Del Rey Coop
classification: White table wine
grape variety: French Colombard and Thompson
district: San Joaquin Valley
city or village: Fresno

This is a crisp, clean Chablis-type wine with fruity bouquet. **price range:** A

producer: Delicato Vineyards
classification: Red varietal table wine
grape variety: Cabernet Sauvignon
district: San Joaquin Valley
city or village: Manteca

Deep red color and a fruity bouquet. The wine is dry. **price range:** B

producer: Delicato Vineyards
classification: Red varietal table wine
grape variety: Gamay Beaujolais
district: San Joaquin Valley
city or village: Manteca

Deep red color and a fruity bouquet. The wine is dry. **price range:** B

producer: Delicato Vineyards
classification: White varietal table wine
grape variety: Chenin Blanc

district: San Joaquin Valley
city or village: Manteca

Light golden color and a fruity, light bouquet. The wine is mellow to the taste. **price range:** A

producer: Delicato Vineyards
classification: Red varietal table wine
grape variety: Zinfandel
district: San Joaquin Valley
city or village: Manteca

Brilliant red color and a pleasant bouquet. The wine is dry and full-bodied. **price range:** A

producer: Delicato Vineyards
classification: White varietal table wine
grape variety: Johannisberg Riesling
district: San Joaquin Valley
city or village: Manteca

Light clear color with greenish tints and a dry, tart bouquet and flavor. **price range:** B

producer: Domaine Chandon
classification: White sparkling wine
grape variety: Pinot Noir
district: Napa Valley

Domaine Chandon is a wholly owned subsidiary of Moët-Hennessy, a French corporation that owns several Champagne firms, Hennessy Cognac, and Dior perfumes and cosmetics. Moët-Hennessy provides financial and technical assistance to the Domaine's efforts to providing the United States with a fine Napa Valley sparkling wine. California grapes lend a refreshing vigor to the typical Champagne yeastiness the wine develops while aging in bottle.

Oeil de perdrix color (pale apricot-salmon) and a yeasty bouquet showing

varietal fruit. The wine is very clean, with varietal character, and is light and dry: it shows the influence of the Moët & Chandon oenologist who blended the cuvée and directed the vinification. **price range:** D

producer: Domaine Chandon
classification: White sparkling wine
grape variety: Pinot Noir and Chardonnay
district: Napa Valley

California grapes lend a refreshing vigor to the typical Champagne yeastiness the wine develops while aging in bottle.

Brilliant pale straw-yellow color and a fruity, fresh Champagne bouquet. The wine is clean, with subtlety and definite Champagne style. **price range:** D

producer: Dry Creek Vineyard, Inc.
classification: Red varietal table wine
grape variety: Petite Sirah (60%) and Zinfandel (40%)
district: Sonoma County

This wine has consistently been considered one of California's finest Petite Sirahs.

An inky, deep garnet color and a powerful bouquet with oak overtones. The wine has a slight haze and has some sediment as it was not filtered. It has a strong varietal flavor and a long finish. **price range:** B

producer: Dry Creek Vineyard, Inc.
classification: Red varietal table wine
grape variety: Merlot (100%)
district: Sonoma County

This Merlot is made from an interesting varietal that is beginning to be recognized for its full-flavored red wines.

A medium red color and a bouquet with the essence of Merlot. The wine has varietal character typical of California Merlot, with a slight woody flavor and good finish. **price range:** B

producer: Dry Creek Vineyard, Inc.
classification: White varietal table wine
grape variety: Sauvignon Blanc (100%)
district: Sonoma County

This Sauvignon Blanc was grown in the cooler regions of Sonoma County. It was a gold-medal winner at the 1975 Los Angeles county fair, and top prize winner at the first Sonoma County wine judging in the fall of 1975. It was fermented in stainless steel and aged four months in small Limousin and American oak barrels.

A pale gold color and an essence of bell peppers, green olives, and fresh asparagus in the bouquet. The wine has intense varietal flavor enhanced by oak aging and is a classic example of a dry Sauvignon Blanc. **price range:** B

producer: Dry Creek Vineyard, Inc.
classification: Red varietal table wine
grape variety: Cabernet Sauvignon (70%) and Zinfandel (30%)
district: Sonoma County

This interesting red wine is Dry Creek's first release of Cabernet. A blend of approximately one-third Zinfandel gives it a unique richness. The wine was ranked first by the Vintners' Club at a January 1976 Cabernet Sauvignon tasting.

A deep garnet color and a full, rich bouquet with a hint of black currants and oak. The wine is full-bodied on the palate and shows good varietal character with a long finish. **price range:** C

producer: Dry Creek Vineyard, Inc.
classification: Red varietal table wine
grape variety: Zinfandel (100%)
district: Dry Creek Valley—Sonoma County

This Zinfandel is made from grapes grown on the world-famous benchland on the east side of Dry Creek Valley in Sonoma County. In this area many of California's greatest Zinfandels are grown.

A medium garnet color and a classic raspberry Zinfandel bouquet with complexities of oak. It is a well-balanced, medium-bodied Zinfandel with good varietal characteristics. **price range:** B

producer: Dry Creek Vineyard, Inc.
classification: White varietal table wine
grape variety: Gewürztraminer (100%)
district: Alexander Valley

This Gewürztraminer is Dry Creek's first release of this varietal. They plan to make larger quantities in future years.

A medium yellow color and a fruity, spicy bouquet. The wine has good varietal flavor, spiciness, and a pleasing finish. It finishes slightly sweet. **price range:** B

producer: Dry Creek Vineyard, Inc.
classification: Red varietal table wine
grape variety: Gamay Beaujolais (100%)
district: North Coast Counties

This Gamay Beaujolais is made from the Pinot Noir-related variety of Gamay, not from the more common Napa Gamay, which produces a more ordinary wine.

A ruby-red color and a heady, fruity bouquet. The wine is made in a youthful, fruity style of California Beaujolais and would be ideal for luncheon and light dinner entrees. **price range:** A

producer: Dry Creek Vineyard, Inc.
classification: White varietal table wine
grape variety: Chenin Blanc (100%)
district: Sonoma County

This Chenin Blanc won a medal at the 1975 Los Angeles county fair. It is cold-fermented in stainless steel and receives no oak aging.

A very pale gold color and a rich, flowery, and fruity bouquet. The wine is well-balanced with a tart, spicy, and lingering finish and is quite dry. **price range:** B

producer: Fetzer Vineyards
classification: Red table wine
district: Mendocino County

This wine won a silver medal at the Los Angeles county fair in 1975. Thousands of cases of it are sold each month in the San Francisco Bay area, and the wine has been praised by many critics. Always a nonvintaged blend.

A medium red color; very clean, fruity, and full-bodied. The wine has a direct, forthright taste with a touch of wood. It is a great wine for the price. Decant one hour before serving. **price range:** A

producer: Fetzer Vineyards
classification: Red varietal table wine
grape variety: Petite Sirah
district: Mendocino County

This robust "Petite Syrah" was judged superior (by many) to the 1973, which won a gold medal at the Los Angeles county fair. 1974 vintage.

A clean, deep purple color with a very good, fruity bouquet. On the palate the wine is full-bodied, woody, and very fruity. This rich and round wine is ready now, but is also worthy of laying down for further aging. Decant four hours before serving. **price range:** B

producer: Fetzer Vineyards
classification: Red varietal table wine
grape variety: Carignane
district: Mendocino County

1974 vintage.

A deep red color with clear brilliance. The bouquet is fruity, and on the palate the wine is full-bodied, with a complex aroma and a delicate, delightful flavor. It is a remarkable dry red wine that is charming and delightful when young, though it will improve with age. Decant a few hours before serving. **price range:** A

producer: Fetzer Vineyards
classification: Red varietal table wine
grape variety: Zinfandel
district: Mendocino County
city or village: Ricetti

1973 vintage. This Zinfandel earned a gold medal in a tasting of thirty-five California Zinfandels at the 1975 Los Angeles county fair. An outstanding Mendocino Zinfandel, it comes from the Ricetti Vineyards, located high in the eastern hills above Redwood Valley in Mendocino County, which enjoy a special, unique microclimate on red clay soil.

A deep red color, and clear. The bouquet is fruity, with heavy varietal aroma. On the palate the wine is well-balanced, with medium tannin and a lingering finish. Decant four hours before serving. **price range:** B

producer: Fetzer Vineyards
classification: Red varietal table wine
grape variety: Pinot Noir
district: Mendocino County

A medium red, clear color with an excellent fruity bouquet. On the palate the wine is full-bodied and fruity; soft, but very rich. This is a great wine to drink now, but it will improve with bottle age. Decant a few hours before serving. **price range:** B

producer: Fetzer Vineyards
classification: Red varietal table wine
grape variety: Cabernet Sauvignon
district: Mendocino County

This wine has won many competitive tastings; it sells for about half the price of many premium California Cabernet Sauvignons.

A dark purple color, with reddish robe. The wine has a perfumed, rich, and spicy varietal bouquet. On the palate it is clean, full-flavored and characteristic of the varietal. It is a great wine to drink now or lay away in your cellar. Decant four hours before serving. **price range: B**

producer: Fetzer Vineyards
classification: Red varietal table wine
grape variety: Zinfandel
district: Mendocino County

This wine has placed first in many Zinfandel tastings and was rated the Double Wine Glass award by an independent Buyer's Guide.

A deep red-purple color and a rich and fruity bouquet. On the palate it is well balanced, with medium tannin. You will find that this wine possesses all the exciting characteristics of the noble North Coast Zinfandels. Decant a few hours before serving. **price range: A**

producer: Ficklin Vineyards
classification: Fortified wine
grape variety: Tinta Madeira, Tinta Cao, Alvarelhao, Touriga, and Souzao
district: Madera County—Central Valley
city or village: Madera

Ficklin Vineyards is dedicated to making only one type of fortified wine: Port. Every step in its production is carefully executed to produce the best possible wine, with the result that it has often been proclaimed the finest Port wine made in America.

Deep blackish-red color and a full, berrylike bouquet. The wine is rich and full, with the depth and complex character of a true Port. **price range: B**

producer: J. Filippi Vintage Co.
classification: Red varietal table wine
grape variety: Zinfandel
district: Southern California—Cucamonga
city or village: Mira Loma

Clear ruby-red color and a fresh bouquet

with varietal character. The wine combines medium body with good complexity.
price range: A

producer: J. Filippi Vintage Co.
classification: White table wine
grape variety: French Colombard and Burger
district: Southern California—Cucamonga
city or village: Mira Loma

Pale straw color and a fruity, spicy bouquet. The wine is dry, clean, and fruity.
price range: A

producer: J. Filippi Vintage Co.
classification: White table wine
grape variety: Burger and Golden Chasselas
district: Southern California—Cucamonga
city or village: Mira Loma

Light yellow color and a fruity, vinous bouquet. The wine is medium sweet and full-bodied, with good acidity.
price range: A

producer: The Firestone Vineyard
classification: White varietal table wine
grape variety: White (Johannisberg) Riesling
district: Santa Barbara County—Santa Ynez Valley
city or village: Los Olivos

This Johannisberg Riesling represents the third release from the winery. They plan to change the drawing on the label with each subsequent release.

Light to medium yellow color and a full varietal bouquet that develops with airing. The wine is balanced between good acidity and medium residual sugar and body; it has a lingering finish. **price range:** B

producer: The Firestone Vineyard
classification: Rosé table wine
grape variety: Pinot Noir and Chardonnay
district: Santa Barbara County—Santa Ynez Valley
city or village: Los Olivos

On September 23, 1975, some three hundred friends, neighbors, and wine-industry people joined forces to help harvest the first grapes from the Firestone Vineyard. The Pinot Noir had excellent flavor, and it was decided that a rosé should be produced. With an addition of Chardonnay (34%), the result was a rich, full-flavored rosé with a generous alcoholic content of 12.7% by volume.

Rosé color, tending toward a darker pink, and a complex, fruity nose. The wine has good acid and fruit and a rounded character with extraordinary body and fullness. The Chardonnay adds to the complexity of the wine, making it a singular rosé with a smooth, lingering finish.
price range: B

producer: The Firestone Vineyard
classification: Rosé varietal table wine
grape variety: Cabernet Sauvignon (100%)
district: Santa Barbara County—Santa Ynez Valley
city or village: Los Olivos

In this rosé, only the free-run juice was used. Rather high in alcohol (13.1%), it represents the first release of the winery.

Brilliant clear rosé color and a fruity varietal bouquet. The fruity nose is carried onto the palate, where the grape identifies itself pleasantly; the wine is balanced, with low sugar, and its dryness makes it an excellent wine to be consumed either on its own or with food. **price range:** B

producer: Fortino Winery
classification: Red table wine

grape variety: Zinfandel, Carignane, and Grenache
district: Santa Clara Valley
city or village: Gilroy

"Burgundy Reserve."

Full, robust red color and a fruity bouquet. The wine is light, smooth, and dry. **price range:** A

producer: Fortino Winery
classification: Red varietal table wine
grape variety: Carignane (100%)
district: Santa Clara Valley
city or village: Gilroy

Vivid red color and a fruity bouquet. The wine is savory, dry, and medium-bodied—a delightful red wine.
price range: A

producer: Fortino Winery
classification: Red varietal table wine
grape variety: Petite Sirah (100%)
district: Santa Clara Valley
city or village: Gilroy

Robust, deep red color, and a fruity bouquet. The wine is rich, full-bodied, and very pleasing—the vintner's pride.
price range: B

producer: Fortino Winery
classification: White varietal table wine
grape variety: Sylvaner
district: Santa Clara Valley
city or village: Gilroy

A Rhine-type wine.

Clear color and a fruity bouquet. The wine is dry, crisp, and mellow.
price range: A

producer: Fortino Winery
classification: Red varietal table wine
grape variety: Cabernet Sauvignon (100%)
district: Santa Clara Valley
city or village: Gilroy
Vivid red color and a grapey bouquet. The wine is rich, robust, and distinctive, with a savory flavor. **price range:** C

producer: Freemark Abbey Winery
classification: White varietal table wine
grape variety: Johannisberg Riesling
district: Napa Valley
This is the famous 1973 "Edelwein," the first Johannisberg Riesling produced in California comparable to a great German Beerenauslese. In 1973, heavy botrytis mold concentrated sugar and flavor of the grapes to the point where they were harvested at an incredible 30 degrees Brix. The grapes were pressed and fermented at 45 degrees for nearly three months and bottle-aged for one year. The climatic conditions that permitted the making of this wine are rare and uncertain; Freemark may not be able to duplicate it, but offers it as a noble experiment in California wine making.
A bouquet of raisins, apricots, peaches, honeysuckle, and almonds. The lively fruit acids in the wine bring fruit into perfect harmony, and there is no cloying sweetness. The substance of flavor in the wine is equal to its tantalizing fragrance.
price range: E

---

*"Did you ever taste
Madeira?"
"I never before tasted
Madeira."
"Then you ask for a wine
without knowing what it is?"
"I ask for it, sir, that I may
know what it is."*
—George Borrow, *Lavengro*

producer: Freemark Abbey Winery
classification: Red varietal table wine
grape variety: Petite Sirah
district: Napa Valley (York Creek—Spring Mountain)
city or village: St. Helena
This wine comes from the York Creek vineyard. Although the vines are fully mature, their yield is exceedingly low due to the rugged growing conditions. The result is an uncommon concentration of varietal character, flavor, and fruit.
A deep red color and a rich, complex, and spicy bouquet. Although the wine's quality depends on the vintage, the 1971 is the most beautifully balanced if not the most tannic and dramatic Petite Sirah Freemark has produced. The wine is a delicious, heavy Rhone-style experience.
price range: C

producer: Freemark Abbey Winery
classification: White varietal table wine
grape variety: Johannisberg Riesling
district: Napa Valley
1972 vintage. The rains of that year, combined with an early-morning fog, encouraged a moderately heavy Botrytis condition ("noble mold"), which results in the honeylike complexity of this wine.
A full-bodied, rich, and dry Johannisberg Riesling with a hint of honey—it is a substantial compliment to well-seasoned white meat entrées, although not a light, delicate sipping wine. **price range:** B

producer: Freemark Abbey Winery
classification: Red varietal table wine
grape variety: Cabernet Sauvignon (100%)
district: Napa Valley—Bosché Vineyard
city or village: St. Helena

1972 vintage. The grapes for this wine come from the small John Bosché vineyard, and the wine is slightly more intense and complex than Freemark's regular Cabernet Sauvignon.
A light red color. The wine is soft and has considerable Cabernet fruit, with distinctive character. It has moderate aging potential. **price range:** C

producer: Freemark Abbey Winery
classification: Red varietal table wine
grape variety: Pinot Noir
district: Napa Valley
This wine was aged in 60-gallon French Nevers oak barrels.
The wine has abundant strawberrylike fruit balanced with a hint of Nevers oak and well-defined acidity. This wine will gratify the drinker who can appreciate subtlety of flavor as opposed to power, and who can understand the typically delicate character of California Pinot Noir. Three years' additional bottle age is recommended.
price range: C

producer: Freemark Abbey Winery
classification: White varietal table wine
grape variety: Chardonnay
district: Napa Valley
This celebrated Chardonnay benefits from a full year of bottle age prior to release, thus transforming simple fruitiness into a rich, complex bouquet. The wine is aged in 60-gallon Nevers oak barrels.
Rich, complex bouquet. The wine is full-bodied and classically balanced, with high acid. It is a wine of great finesse, drinkable now though it will improve with additional bottle age. **price range:** C

producer: Freemark Abbey Winery
classification: Red varietal table wine
grape variety: Cabernet Sauvignon

district: Napa Valley
1971 vintage. The growing season that year was long and cool, accounting for the elegant proportions of this wine. A small admixture of 7½% Merlot adds complexity.
A dark red color and a generous bouquet with complex herbaceous varietal character. This wine has more tannin than other vintages, and is agreeably balanced. Its 11% alcoholic content enhances its drinkability; two or three additional years of bottle age is recommended. **price range:** C

producer: Franciscan Vineyards
classification: White varietal table wine
grape variety: Johannisberg (White) Riesling
district: Napa Valley
city or village: Rutherford
1974 vintage.
Light straw color and a varietal bouquet. The wine is slightly sweet, with a tart flavor.
price range: A

producer: Franciscan Vineyards
classification: Red table wine
grape variety: Charbono and Petite Sirah
district: Napa Valley
city or village: Rutherford
"Burgundy." 1973 vintage.
Very deep red color and an aged bouquet with good oak aroma. The wine is balanced with medium tannin, and has an oaky flavor. **price range:** A

producer: Franciscan Vineyards
classification: Red varietal table wine
grape variety: Pinot Noir
district: Napa Valley

city or village: Rutherford
1974 vintage.
Brilliant medium red color and a fruity bouquet. The wine is dry and clean, with low tannin and a slight oak flavor.
price range: A

producer: Franciscan Vineyards
classification: Red varietal table wine
grape variety: Zinfandel
district: Napa Valley
city or village: Rutherford
1974 vintage.
Brilliant medium red color and a fruity varietal bouquet. The wine is dry, well-balanced, and light in tannin.
price range: A

producer: Franciscan Vineyards
classification: Red varietal table wine
grape variety: Cabernet Sauvignon
district: Napa Valley
city or village: Rutherford and Oakville
1973 vintage.
Brilliant dark red color and a slightly "peppery" bouquet characteristic of the varietal. The wine has medium tannin and is dry, with a slight oak flavor.
price range: B

producer: Gallo Winery
classification: Red table wine
This easy-drinking, mellow red wine is a favorite at cookouts or with everyday meals because it can be enjoyed in quantity as a result of its softness. It is made in the true Italian tradition.
Brilliant light red color and a clean, grapey bouquet. The wine is light-bodied and smooth. **price range:** A

producer: Gallo Winery
classification: White table wine
grape variety: French Colombard and other white varieties
Brilliant pale straw color and a strong bouquet characteristic of Colombard and mellowed with bottle aging. On the palate the wine has natural sharpness balanced by fruit; it is a hearty white wine that would be excellent with barbecued or roast game birds. **price range:** A

producer: Gallo Winery
classification: White varietal table wine
grape variety: Chenin Blanc and other white varieties
district: Modesto
Brilliant pale yellow-green color and a clean varietal bouquet that shows bottle aging. The wine is full-bodied, true to the variety, and has a crisp finish. It is a deliciously mellow yet distinct Chenin Blanc that is great with seafood or fresh fruit.
price range: A

producer: Gallo Winery
classification: White varietal table wine
grape variety: Sauvignon Blanc and other white varieties
district: Modesto
A "snappy" white wine made in the Bordeaux style.
Brilliant pale straw color and a clean, subtle bouquet. On the palate the wine is crisp, dry, "flinty," and has a tantalizingly true Sauvignon flavor. It is a perfect complement to many fish and poultry dishes; also, a fine appetizer. **price range:** A

producer: Gallo Winery
classification: Red varietal table wine
grape variety: Zinfandel and other red varieties
district: Modesto
Brilliant sharp red color and a penetrating berrylike aroma characteristic of Zinfandel. The wine is true to its type—dry, clean, and very attractive, with a slight tannic finish that compels one to take a second glass. This charming Zinfandel is what many other wineries are attempting to duplicate; drink it with your favorite beef dishes. **price range:** A

producer: Gallo Winery
classification: Red varietal table wine
grape variety: Ruby Cabernet and other red varieties
district: Modesto
Brilliant deep ruby color and a spicy, Cabernet-like nose with roundness from bottle aging. The wine is dry, has good fruit, and is clean and full-bodied. It is excellent with game or roasts.
price range: A

producer: Gallo Winery
classification: Red table wine

A light red wine much favored with steaks and roasts.
Brilliant medium red color and a clean, grapey bouquet. The wine is fruity, slightly tannic, and has good balance; it finishes cleanly, with no musty "tank" flavor.
price range: A

producer: Gallo Winery
classification: White table wine
A favorite white wine with seafood or light desserts; a thirst quencher as well as a fine dinner wine.
Brilliant pale gold color and a clean, zesty, and grapey bouquet. The wine is smooth drinking, with a crisp finish.
price range: A

producer: Gallo Winery
classification: Rosé table wine
A pleasant light rosé, good with light meals or desserts. It is made as a fine white table wine, then "blushed" pink.
"Blushing" pink color and a crisp, fruity bouquet. The wine has a pronounced, mouth-tingling flavor. **price range:** A

producer: Gallo Winery
classification: White table wine
A premium white table wine made from a blend of five different grape varieties.
Brilliant pale straw color and a bouquet with good fruitiness and clean character. The wine is a fresh, snappy mouthful; well-balanced, clean, straightforward, and well-made. It is very good with seafood or fowl. **price range:** A

producer: Gallo Winery
classification: White table wine
Brilliant pale gold color and a bouquet with grapey overtones—complex, yet clean. The wine is a zesty mouthful: full-bodied, mellow, with a crisp finish. It is good with seafood or dessert.
price range: A

producer: Gallo Winery
classification: Red table wine
Flavorful "Burgundy," very complementary with all types of red meats and roasts.
Brilliant dark red color and an exuberant, vinous, and berrylike nose. The wine is medium-bodied, with good tannin and body. **price range:** A

producer: Gallo Champagne Cellars
classification: White sparkling wine
grape variety: Chenin Blanc, French Colombard, and other white varieties
An excellent Champagne that compares favorably with many imports.
Brilliant pale straw color and a crisp, clean flavor that fills the mouth. It is especially good either as an aperitif or with dessert. **price range:** A

producer: Geyser Peak Winery
classification: Red varietal table wine
grape variety: Cabernet Sauvignon and Merlot

district: Sonoma County
Deep red color browning at the edges and a berrylike varietal bouquet. The wine is clean, with a complex, lingering flavor.
price range: A

producer: Geyser Peak Winery
classification: Red table wine
grape variety: Carignane and Petite Sirah
district: Sonoma County
"Burgundy."
Brilliant purple color and a grapey bouquet. The wine is low in acid and has good balance between body and flavor.
price range: A

producer: Geyser Peak Winery
classification: White varietal table wine
grape variety: Johannisberg Riesling
district: Sonoma County
This is a clean, mildly acidic, slightly oaky Johannisberg Riesling, with the characteristic Riesling nose. It is of brilliant medium straw color. **price range:** B

producer: Geyser Peak Winery
classification: Pink varietal table wine
grape variety: Cabernet Sauvignon
district: Sonoma County
city or village: Geyserville
This is a piquant, sprightly rosé wine with slight carbonation. It has a very fruity nose and is of sparkling strawberry-pink appearance. **price range:** B

producer: Geyser Peak Winery
classification: White table wine
grape variety: Golden Chasselas and French Colombard
district: Sonoma County
This is a mellow, light-bodied Chablis-style wine. Its color is brilliant light straw, and its aroma is clean. **price range:** A

producer: Geyser Peak Winery
classification: White varietal table wine
grape variety: Pinot Chardonnay
district: Sonoma County
The pronounced bouquet of this wine reflects a smooth, rich taste. The bouquet is fruity with a touch of oak. **price range:** B

producer: Geyser Peak Winery
classification: Red varietal table wine
grape variety: Cabernet Sauvignon and Merlot
district: Sonoma County
This deep red wine has a brownish rim. It is clean to the palate, complex, and lingering, with the berrylike varietal nose.
price range: B

producer: Geyser Peak Winery
classification: Red varietal table wine
grape variety: Zinfandel

district: Sonoma County
This clear dark purple wine has all the characteristics of a Zinfandel. It has an earthy, berrylike bouquet and pronounced Zinfandel palate, with a soft finish.
price range: B

producer: Grand Cru Vineyards, Inc.
classification: White varietal table wine
grape variety: Zinfandel
district: Sonoma Valley
city or village: Glen Ellen
This is a white wine produced from red grapes. Only the free-run juice is used. The wine is fermented in stainless-steel tanks and aged in white oak barrels.
A light gold color and a bouquet combining fruit and oak. The wine is clean and full-bodied, in the white Burgundy style.
price range: C

producer: Grand Cru Vineyards, Inc.
classification: White varietal table wine
grape variety: Gewürztraminer
Gewürztraminer is an artificially infected wine, produced by infecting the grapes with *Botrytis cinerea* spores after harvesting. It is a very expensive technique, but it produces outstanding wine.
A light gold color and an intense bouquet combining Gewürztraminer and Botrytis aromas. The wine is clean and very rich; "oily," with heavy Botrytis character. It should age well. **price range:** E

producer: Grand Cru Vineyards, Inc.
classification: White varietal table wine
grape variety: Gewürztraminer
district: Alexander Valley

This is the second crop from new vineyards in the Alexander Valley. The vineyard is primed to low production, and the grapes are field harvested.

A yellow color with green tinges. The bouquet shows intense varietal character, and the wine tastes clean, rich, and very spicy.
price range: B

producer: Grand Cru Vineyards, Inc.
classification: Red varietal table wine
grape variety: Zinfandel
district: Sonoma Valley

This is a late-harvest wine made from very ripe grapes. The vineyard is eighty-five years old.

A dark red, almost "black" color. The bouquet has rich oak and complex Zinfandel character. The wine is clean, full-bodied, with high alcohol. **price range: C**

producer: Griffin Vineyard (Hop Kiln Winery)
classification: White varietal table wine
grape variety: Gewürztraminer
district: Sonoma County
city or village: Healdsburg

The grapes for this wine were picked at 24 degrees Brix and then placed in #50 boxes to prevent premature fermentation. The wine was then fermented dry, in barrels.

Straw-yellow color and an extremely pungent, flowery bouquet. The wine is spicy and tart, yet tastes sweet.
price range: B

producer: Griffin Vineyard (Hop Kiln Winery)
classification: Red varietal table wine
grape variety: Gamay
district: Sonoma County
city or village: Healdsburg

Grown in a four-acre hill vineyard located above the Russian River, these Gamay grapes can produce either a delightful Beaujolais-type wine (pressed at about 12 degrees Brix when still fermenting), or a heavier, deep, dark, and full-bodied Burgundy-type wine. The wine is unfiltered and unfined; it is in limited production so it sells quickly.

Clear ruby color and a fresh, fruity flavor with a touch of French oak. The wine tastes youthful and fruity, without the acidity of many Beaujolais wines. **price range: B**

producer: Griffin Vineyard (Hop Kiln Winery)
classification: White varietal table wine
grape variety: Johannisberg Riesling
district: Sonoma County
city or village: Healdsburg

The grapes for this wine were picked in #50 boxes and immediately crushed, then left to ferment in barrel. The result was a dry Riesling in the Alsatian style, estate-grown and bottled. All Griffin wines spend the winter and spring without being moved, if possible.

Brilliant pale color and a classic, flowery Riesling bouquet. The wine is dry and slightly sweet-tart in flavor; it is a rare Johannisberg Riesling in the sense that its inherent grape flavors are not obscured by residual sugar. **price range: B**

producer: Griffin Vineyard (Hop Kiln Winery)
classification: Red varietal table wine
grape variety: Zinfandel
district: Sonoma County
city or village: Healdsburg

The Hop Kiln Winery was originally built in 1905. It was a hop-processing plant until 1952; the processing equipment has been left intact, and the tasting room was built around the two-story press. The hop kiln was designated a county and state landmark within the Sweetwater Springs Historic District, where very old Zinfandel vines are planted. In cool districts such as this, the grape produces a wine that can age as long as Cabernet, increasing in complexity and richness over a ten- to 15-year period. The wine is unfined and unfiltered; it is suggested that it be given five years' aging prior to drinking.

Very dark "carnelian" color and a pronounced "briar" nose typical of Zinfandel. The wine is rich, robust, and mouth-filling.
price range: B

producer: Griffin Vineyard (Hop Kiln Winery)
classification: White varietal table wine
grape variety: French Colombard
district: Sonoma County
city or village: Healdsburg

This grape in the past was primarily sold for Champagne production and for blending purposes. It is now in demand as a varietal, and in cool climatic regions develops great subtleties. Griffin Vineyard was one of the first wineries to recognize its qualities some ten years ago.

Straw-yellow color and a fruity bouquet. The wine is dry and slightly tart, but has a characteristic, sweet aftertaste.
price range: B

producer: Emilio Guglielmo Winery (Mount Madonna)
classification: Red varietal table wine
grape variety: Gamay Beaujolais (100%)
district: Santa Clara Valley
city or village: Morgan Hill
Aged in oak casks. **price range: A**

producer: Emilio Guglielmo Winery (Mount Madonna)
classification: White varietal table wine
grape variety: White Riesling (100%)
district: Santa Clara Valley
city or village: Morgan Hill
Aged in oak casks. **price range: A**

producer: Emilio Guglielmo Winery (Mount Madonna)
classification: Red varietal table wine
grape variety: Ruby Cabernet (100%)
district: Santa Clara Valley
city or village: Morgan Hill
Aged in oak casks. **price range: A**

producer: Emilio Guglielmo Winery (Mount Madonna)
classification: Red varietal table wine
grape variety: Petite Sirah (100%)
district: Santa Clara Valley
city or village: Morgan Hill
Aged in oak casks. **price range: B**

producer: Emilio Guglielmo Winery (Mount Madonna)
classification: White varietal table wine
grape variety: Semillon (100%)
district: Santa Clara Valley
city or village: Morgan Hill
Aged in oak casks. **price range: A**

producer: Emilio Guglielmo Winery (Mount Madonna)
classification: White table wine
grape variety: Riesling and Semillon
district: Santa Clara Valley
city or village: Morgan Hill
Aged three to four years in redwood.
price range: A

producer: Gundlach-Bundschu Winery
classification: Red varietal table wine
grape variety: Zinfandel (100%)
district: Sonoma Valley
city or village: Vineburg

From the Rhine Farm Vineyards.
Dark red color and a varietal "berry" bouquet. The wine is very smooth-tasting.
price range: B

producer: Gundlach-Bundschu Winery
classification: White varietal table wine
grape variety: Kleinburger
district: Sonoma Valley
city or village: Vineburg

This is the only Kleinburger varietal wine produced in the United States. Grown at the Rhine Farm Vineyards in Vineburg.

Light and fruity bouquet; the wine has a fresh-tasting flavor reminiscent of apricots.
price range: A

producer: Gundlach-Bundschu Winery
classification: White table wine
grape variety: Sonoma Riesling (Sylvaner)
district: Sonoma Valley
city or village: Vineburg

From the Rhine Farm Vineyards. Under California law, a wine made from Sylvaner may legally be called Riesling; this is not to be confused with the White (Johannisberg) Riesling that is native to Germany.

Brilliant clear color and a soft, clean bouquet. The wine is rich, with a hint of sweetness. **price range:** A

producer: Hacienda Wine Cellars
classification: White varietal table wine
grape variety: Gewürztraminer
district: Sonoma County
city or village: Sonoma

1975 vintage.
Brilliant straw color; the bouquet hints of citrus in youth but develops varietal spiciness later. The wine is slightly sweet but has balanced acidity, and the finish is long and flavorful. **price range:** B

producer: Hacienda Wine Cellars
classification: Red varietal table wine
grape variety: Cabernet Sauvignon
district: Sonoma County
city or village: Sonoma

1974 vintage. Aged in Nevers oak.
Medium red color and a mildly herbaceous Cabernet bouquet showing Nevers oak aroma. The wine is light-bodied and low in tannin. **price range:** B

producer: Hacienda Wine Cellars
classification: Red varietal table wine
grape variety: Pinot Noir
district: Napa/Sonoma/Mendocino counties
city or village: Sonoma

A nonvintage blend of wines from three counties, in two vintages (1973–74).
Medium red color and a hint of American oak in the bouquet combined with moderate varietal aromas. The wine is tart, full-bodied, and slightly astringent.
price range: B

producer: Hanzell Vineyards
classification: Red varietal table wine
grape variety: Pinot Noir
district: Sonoma County
city or village: Sonoma

Hanzell Vineyards was formerly the property of the late James D. Zellerbach, who built the winery in an attempt to duplicate the great French Burgundy wines. Because of Zellerbach's experiments with imported French oak barrels, the wines were among the first seriously to challenge great French Pinot Noirs and Chardonnay. The winery was constructed with a deliberate resemblance to the famous Clos de Vougeot monastery in the Côte de Nuits, Burgundy.

A well-constructed, excellent example of a California Pinot Noir.
price range: E

producer: Hoffman Mountain Ranch Vineyards
classification: White varietal table wine
grape variety: Chenin Blanc
district: San Luis Obispo County—Santa Lucia Mountains
city or village: Paso Robles

This is a fresh, clean Chenin Blanc with full, well-balanced flavor. The bouquet is clean, fresh, and fruity, with lots of varietal character. It is a brilliant pale gold color.
price range: B

producer: Hoffman Mountain Ranch Vineyards
classification: Red varietal table wine
grape variety: Zinfandel
district: San Luis Obispo County—Santa Lucia Mountains
city or village: Paso Robles

This wine is smooth, with light tannin and nice fruitiness of the Zinfandel grape. The bouquet is fruity, reminiscent of raspberries with a hint of American oak. It is a brilliant, medium ruby-red color.

The grapes are from eighty-year-old vines grown on chalky hillsides.
price range: B

producer: Hoffman Mountain Ranch Vineyards
classification: Red varietal table wine
grape variety: Pinot Noir
district: San Luis Obispo County—Santa Lucia Mountains
city or village: Paso Robles

This is a rich, full Pinot Noir with medium tannin and hints of French oak in the bouquet. It is a full, dark ruby color.
price range: B

producer: Hoffman Mountain Ranch Vineyards
classification: White varietal table wine
grape variety: Franken Riesling
district: San Luis Obispo County—Santa Lucia Mountains
city or village: Paso Robles

This is a fresh, fruity wine with Botrytis richness, well-balanced acid, and fresh, fruity bouquet. It is full-bodied and of brilliant light gold color.

The grapes are picked at high sugar with Botrytis injection, fermented cold, until fermentation is stopped to maintain natural sugar of 2%. **price range:** B

producer: Hoffman Mountain Ranch Vineyards
classification: Red varietal table wine
grape variety: Cabernet Sauvignon
district: San Luis Obispo County—Santa Lucia Mountains
city or village: Paso Robles

This elegant Cabernet could use some bottle aging before consumption. It is of medium body and tannin and has a spicy Cabernet nose and brilliant ruby-red appearance. **price range:** B

producer: Hoffman Mountain Ranch Vineyards
classification: White varietal table wine
grape variety: Chardonnay
district: San Luis Obispo County—Santa Lucia Mountains
city or village: Paso Robles

This is a rich, full-bodied Chardonnay with full flavor and good balance. The bouquet has a touch of French oak, as the wine was fermented in 60-gallon French Limousin oak barrels. **price range:** B

producer: Husch Vineyards
classification: Estate-bottled white varietal table wine
grape variety: Pinot Chardonnay (100%)
district: North Coast—Anderson Valley
city or village: Philo

This Pinot Chardonnay is one of California's great white wines. The emphasis at Husch Vineyards is on producing limited quantities of pure varietal wines, all aged in small oak barrels with much hand labor required. By specializing in three wines, Husch is able to control every step of the operation.

A straw-yellow color and a bouquet with tremendous Chardonnay character—just enough oak. It is a truly big wine with a long, lusty finish. **price range:** C

producer: Husch Vineyards
classification: Estate-bottled white varietal table wine
grape variety: Gewürztraminer
district: North Coast—Anderson Valley
city or village: Philo

This Gewürztraminer is unblended and carries a vintage date.

A white-gold color and a spicy, fruity bouquet. The wine is clean and crisp on the palate—a delightful Gewürztraminer.
price range: B

producer: Inglenook Vineyards
classification: Estate-bottled varietal table wine
grape variety: Cabernet Sauvignon
district: Napa Valley
city or village: Rutherford

This is a good drinking Cabernet with good aging capacity. It is of brilliant deep red appearance and smooth palate.
price range: B

producer: Husch Vineyards
classification: Estate-bottled red varietal table wine
grape variety: Pinot Noir (100%)
district: North Coast—Anderson Valley
city or village: Philo

This Pinot Noir is a big, complex Burgundy-style wine. The Husch vineyard was started in 1968 when Tony and Gretchen Husch moved to Philo from the San Francisco Bay area. They left behind short-lived careers as city planners and set out to find a more fulfilling life as wine makers. They settled on an old sheep ranch and planted vineyards in Gewürztraminer, Pinot Chardonnay, and Pinot Noir. Husch Vineyards was bonded in 1971, and grapes from the first harvest were crushed on the patio of the house.

A deep purple-red color and a very fruity bouquet with a hint of black cherries. The wine is velvety on the palate and will live long. **price range:** C

producer: Inglenook Vineyards
classification: Estate-bottled white varietal table wine
grape variety: Chenin Blanc
district: Napa Valley
city or village: Rutherford

This brilliant straw-gold wine is excellent for cocktails or dinner. It is slightly sweet, with a fresh and fruity bouquet.
price range: A

producer: Inglenook Vineyards
classification: Estate-bottled white varietal table wine
grape variety: Grey Riesling
district: Napa Valley
city or village: Rutherford

This is a clean, crisp white wine with a vinous bouquet. **price range:** B

producer: Inglenook Vineyards
classification: Red varietal table wine
grape variety: Ruby Cabernet

This is a smooth and clean red wine with a soft, fruity bouquet. It is of brilliant, deep, fiery red color. **price range:** A

producer: Windsor Vineyards
classification: White varietal table wine
grape variety: Johannisberg Riesling
district: Sonoma County

This is a rich, slightly sweet, brilliant golden Riesling with a fruity, mature bouquet. A very Germanic wine.
price range: B

producer: Inglenook Vineyards
classification: White varietal table wine
grape variety: Chenin Blanc

This is a crisp, clean, medium-dry white wine with a fresh, fruity bouquet and a clean, clear appearance. **price range:** A

producer: Kenwood Vineyards
classification: Red varietal table wine
grape variety: Pinot Noir
district: Sonoma Valley

This wine was aged in 50-gallon barrels and bottled in June 1975.

A deep garnet color and a full, spicy

bouquet. The wine is mouth-filling, long-lasting, and enhanced by oak background. It is big and Burgundian; already complex, it should improve with further bottle age.
price range: B

producer: Kenwood Vineyards
classification: Red varietal table wine
grape variety: Cabernet Sauvignon

This wine was extensively aged in 50-gallon oak barrels, and was bottled in August 1975. It is blended with 6% Merlot for added complexity. It won second place at the 1975 Sonoma fair.

A deep red color and an intense, complex bouquet. The wine has the rich taste of ripe grapes with distinct oak overtones; it has sufficient tannin to give it excellent aging potential. **price range:** B

producer: Kenwood Vineyards
classification: Red varietal table wine
grape variety: Zinfandel
district: Sonoma County

This wine was aged in 50-gallon oak barrels before being bottled in September 1975.

A deep red color and a berrylike bouquet that is minty and herbaceous. It is a complex but distinctive Zinfandel, being smooth and youthful. The wine is zesty, with a pleasant touch of oak; it is smooth enough to enjoy now, but has medium tannin levels and could benefit from further bottle age. **price range:** B

producer: F. Korbel & Bros.
classification: White table wine
grape variety: Pinot Blanc and French Colombard
district: Western Sonoma County
city or village: Guerneville

A clear color and a fruity bouquet. The wine is dry, light, harmoniously balanced, and should be served well chilled.
price range: B

producer: F. Korbel & Bros.
classification: Red table wine
grape variety: Zinfandel and Petite Sirah
district: Western Sonoma County
city or village: Guerneville

"Korbel Mountain Burgundy." The wine is carefully aged in oak and is ready to be enjoyed immediately on release.

Clear color. The wine exhibits the unique characteristics of the grape varieties from which it was produced. It should be served at cool room temperature. **price range:** B

producer: F. Korbel & Bros.
classification: White varietal table wine
grape variety: Chenin Blanc
district: Western Sonoma County
city or village: Guerneville

This grape variety is grown almost exclusively in the French provinces of Touraine and Anjou. In Sonoma, Napa, and other northern California counties, it is successful and produces an early-maturing wine of excellent quality.

Clear color. The wine is light, mellow, and fruity with a hint of sweetness.
price range: A

producer: F. Korbel & Bros.
classification: Red varietal table wine
grape variety: Cabernet Sauvignon
district: Western Sonoma County
city or village: Guerneville

Korbel has the distinction of growing Cabernet grapes in the coolest portions of Sonoma County. The variety is planted on the steep hillside vineyards adjacent to the winery, and the grapes are harvested in late October. The combination of moderate exposure to afternoon sunshine and purposefully restrictive growing practices yields a small crop of 2 to 3 tons per acre, with outstanding quality.

An aromatic, herbaceous bouquet with bottle aging. The wine tastes well-balanced and is ready to drink when shipped for the discriminating wine lover, but will respond favorably to further aging.
price range: B

producer: F. Korbel & Bros.
classification: Red varietal table wine
grape variety: Zinfandel
district: Western Sonoma County
city or village: Guerneville

Korbel vintage Zinfandel is produced from grapes grown near the winery on old, long-producing hillside vineyards. It is aged only long enough to soften the wine, producing an obvious youth and pronounced Zinfandel flavor.

Clear color and a unique bouquet. The wine is distinctly fruity, zesty, and has a berrylike character. It is not comparable to the Claret-type Zinfandels, which receive many years of oak aging to obtain their character. **price range:** A

producer: F. Korbel & Bros.
classification: White table wine
grape variety: Sauvignon Blanc, Semillon, and French Colombard
district: Western Sonoma County
city or village: Guerneville

"Korbel Sonoma Blanc" bears a vintage date. It is a distinctive, one-of-a-kind wine, produced only by Korbel from grapes grown on the hillside vineyards adjacent to the winery on the lower Russian River. Specially blended by Korbel's winemaster, it is predominantly a Sauvignon Blanc with a touch of Semillon and French Colombard.

Clear color and a fruity bouquet. The wine tastes fresh and well-balanced, with a dry finish. It has a loyal group of enthusiastic wine lovers who appreciate its uniqueness. **price range:** A

producer: F. Korbel & Bros.
classification: White varietal table wine
grape variety: Grey Riesling

district: Western Sonoma County
city or village: Guerneville

The Grey Riesling grape is particularly suited to the cool North Coast region of California. At Korbel, Grey Riesling vines are planted in the lower-river-bottom vineyards near the winery. Following fermentation, the wine is clarified at an early date and is usually bottled within nine months.

Clear color with a fragrant, delicate bouquet. The wine is fresh with distinctive varietal character and is best enjoyed when under two years old. **price range:** A

producer: F. Korbel & Bros.
classification: White varietal table wine
grape variety: Gewürztraminer
district: Western Sonoma County
city or village: Guerneville

In order to guarantee an abundance of varietal character and proper acidity, this variety can be grown only in the coolest region of California's North Coast region. After a long fermentation period and relatively short aging, the wine is bottled young, usually in its first year. The result is a wine with a flowery, distinctive aroma that is easily identified by the knowledgeable wine drinker.

A flowery, distinctive bouquet. The wine tastes spicy, with proper acidity and good varietal character. It is a delightful sipping wine or a substitute for cocktails.
price range: B

producer: F. Korbel & Bros.
classification: White varietal table wine
grape variety: Johannisberg Riesling
district: Western Sonoma County
city or village: Guerneville

At Korbel, Johannisberg Riesling has been planted on the steep slopes overlooking the Russian River. These precipitous, rocky vineyards bear a striking resemblance to the Rhine River of Germany, home of the White Riesling grapes for over two thousand years. Although viticultural problems in these vineyards border on the insurmountable, the resulting wines represent a very special and gratifying reward for the effort.

A delicate, varietal bouquet. The wine is drier than average, yet possesses optimum balance. Its dryness allows the delicate flavor of the grape to be appreciated without excessive sweetness. **price range:** B

producer: F. Korbel & Bros.
classification: White varietal table wine
grape variety: Chardonnay
district: Western Sonoma County
city or village: Guerneville

Chardonnay is the most difficult white grape to grow, and its yield of one to two tons per acre is very modest. Because of its finicky nature, only the coolest vineyards at Korbel, with well-drained gravelly soils, have been selected for growing Chardonnay. Precise balance in the wine is enhanced by the cool ocean fog that rolls nightly up the Russian River. The wine is offered only in limited quantities.

A truly great wine. Unlike many white wines, it may be laid away to develop additional complexity and character.
price range: B

producer: F. Korbel & Bros.
classification: Red varietal table wine
grape variety: Pinot Noir
district: Western Sonoma County
city or village: Guerneville

Korbel Pinot Noir is grown in the Armstrong Valley vineyard, one of the coolest growing areas on the Korbel ranch. Due to the prevailing ocean breezes, this low vineyard averages 10 degrees cooler during the day than other areas on the ranch. The cool climatic condition provides the proper environment for the delicate, early-ripening Pinot Noir grape.

A full-bodied red wine. Serve at approximately 60 degrees F. **price range:** B

producer: F. Korbel & Bros.
classification: Rosé varietal table wine
grape variety: Gamay and Zinfandel
district: Western Sonoma County
city or village: Guerneville

"Chateau Vin Rosé" is a varietal rosé comprised of approximately 80% Gamay, the balance being Zinfandel. The Gamay grapes were harvested from cool vineyards adjacent to the Russian River near the Korbel Winery. They were purposely picked at a somewhat low sugar level of 21 degrees Brix and 0.65% acidity to retain the natural acidity and thus provide the zesty freshness and aromatic bouquet evident in the wine.

A pink color and a fresh varietal aroma. The wine is balanced, light, youthful, and vigorous. **price range:** A

producer: F. Korbel & Bros.
classification: White sparkling wine
grape variety: Chardonnay, Sylvaner, French Colombard, Chenin Blanc, and Pinot Blanc
district: Western Sonoma County
city or village: Guerneville
Natural ("nature") Champagne.
price range: C

producer: Hanns Kornell Champagne Cellars
classification: White sparkling wine
district: Napa Valley
city or village: St. Helena
This Champagne is authentically fermented in the original bottle.
Pale gold color and an excellent bouquet. A delightful sparkling wine.
price range: C

producer: Hanns Kornell Champagne Cellars
classification: Red sparkling wine
district: Napa Valley
city or village: St. Helena
This Champagne is authentically fermented in the original bottle.
Beautiful deep red color and an excellent bouquet. A delightful sparkling wine.
price range: C

producer: Hanns Kornell Champagne Cellars
classification: White sparkling wine
district: Napa Valley
city or village: St. Helena
"Sehr Trocken" (very dry). This Champagne is authentically fermented in the original bottle.
Deep golden color and an excellent bouquet. A delightful sparkling wine.
price range: D

producer: Charles Krug Winery
classification: Rosé table wine
district: Napa Valley
city or village: St. Helena
This wine is produced in the traditional way, the juice being drained off the skins at precisely the right time for optimum rosé color and flavor. The wine is then fermented very cold to preserve the fragrant fruitiness of the grapes.
Very light red to pink color and a fruity, grapey bouquet. The wine has light to medium body, is nearly dry, and is delicate and well-balanced. It should be served very young to take advantage of its freshness. **price range:** A

producer: Charles Krug Winery
classification: Red varietal table wine
grape variety: Cabernet Sauvignon (100%)
district: Napa Valley
city or village: St. Helena
"Vintage Select" Cabernet Sauvignon, a superb Cabernet from carefully selected vineyards for which the Charles Krug Winery has a fine reputation.
A deep red color and a strong varietal bouquet brought out by bottle aging. The wine has rich varietal flavor; it is dry and well-balanced, a wine of great bearing that will generally age well to ten years and sometimes more. It is one of California's finest red wines. **price range:** C

producer: Charles Krug Winery
classification: Red varietal table wine
grape variety: Pinot Noir (100%)
district: Napa Valley
city or village: St. Helena
Medium red color and a varietal aroma in the aged bouquet, which shows "grapey" character. The wine is dry, medium-bodied, and well-balanced with varietal flavor. It is an exciting wine whose softness permits it to be drunk young, but it has sufficient character to age nicely for a few years. **price range:** B

producer: Charles Krug Winery
classification: Red varietal table wine
grape variety: Cabernet Sauvignon
district: Napa Valley
city or village: St. Helena
Nearly 100% of the variety is in this wine, which will age well for a few years or can be consumed soon after purchase. It is another Krug best-seller.
Medium red color and an aged bouquet with varietal aromas. The wine is dry, with characteristic varietal flavor and good bal ance. **price range:** B

producer: Charles Krug Winery
classification: White varietal table wine
grape variety: Grey Riesling (100%)
district: Napa Valley
city or village: St. Helena
This is one of Krug's largest-selling wines. The Charles Krug winery is still family-owned and operated, and no preservatives are ever added to the wine.
Light yellow co-or and a strong varietal bouquet; the wine is very fruity, fresh, and dry, with good body. This is an excitingly delicate varietal of superb balance: it should be drunk young while at peak fruitiness. **price range:** A

producer: Charles Krug Winery
classification: White varietal table wine
grape variety: Sauvignon Blanc (Blanc Fumé) (100%)
district: Napa Valley
city or village: St. Helena
This wine is one of two Krug whites that receive French oak barrel aging; it is very well-received when sampled. No preservatives are added.
A light to medium yellow bouquet and a strong, varietal bouquet. The wine is medium-bodied, dry, and well-balanced. It will improve with a year or so in the bottle and is an outstanding example of a dry California Sauvignon Blanc. **price range:** B

producer: Charles Krug Winery
classification: White varietal table wine
grape variety: Pinot Chardonnay (100%)
district: Napa Valley
city or village: St. Helena
This Pinot Chardonnay has perhaps the greatest longevity of all Krug white wines. It was aged in French Nevers oak barrels, and no preservatives were added.
Medium yellow color and a bouquet with strong varietal character. The wine is dry, medium-bodied, and slightly tart with good varietal flavor. This excellent Chardonnay should be bottle-aged for a minimum of one year to bring out its full potential. **price range:** B

producer: Charles Krug Winery
classification: White varietal table wine
grape variety: Gewürztraminer (100%)
district: Napa Valley
city or village: St. Helena
No preservatives added.
Medium yellow color and a strong, very spicy varietal nose. The wine is dry, medium-bodied, and flavorful with smooth balance. It is a delicate wine to be drunk young or aged a year or two in order to increase its complexity and overall character. **price range:** B

producer: Charles Krug Winery
classification: White varietal table wine
grape variety: Johannisberg Riesling (100%)
district: Napa Valley
city or village: St. Helena

This cross between a Moselle and a Rhine-type wine is one of Krug's best-selling wines. No preservatives are added.

Medium yellow color and a strong varietal nose with delicate fruitiness. The wine is dry, has medium body with a nice varietal flavor. It is a beautifully balanced wine ready to drink when released, but it will also age with an additional year or so of bottle aging. **price range:** B

producer: L. Le Blanc Vineyards
classification: Red varietal table wine
grape variety: Cabernet Sauvignon
district: San Joaquin Valley

This is a superb, robust red varietal wine that has been given ample time for its true character to develop. It has a pleasant and complex aroma and a purple tint to its clear dark red color. **price range:** below A

producer: L. Le Blanc Vineyards
classification: White varietal table wine
grape variety: Johannisberg Riesling
district: San Joaquin Valley

This slightly greenish-colored wine is crisp, refreshing, and fruity, with medium body. It is superbly dry and has a delicate, fruity bouquet. **price range:** below A

producer: L. Le Blanc Vineyards
classification: White sparkling wine
grape variety: French Colombard and Chenin Blanc
district: San Joaquin Valley

This well-balanced Champagne has a faint degree of sweetness combined with delightful freshness and fruity character. **price range:** A

producer: Llords & Elwood Winery
classification: White sparkling wine

"Extra Dry Champagne" is the only sparkling wine made by the Llords & Elwood Winery.

Pale gold color and a vinous, distinct bouquet. The wine is crisp, smooth, and light; it is quite dry, with a fruity flavor. Elegantly dry, refreshing, and sophisticated, it is ideal as an aperitif. **price range:** C

producer: Llords & Elwood Winery
classification: Red varietal table wine
grape variety: Cabernet Sauvignon

Matured in small oak cooperage.

Brilliant aged garnet color and a delicate, oaky bouquet typical of the variety. The wine is dry, medium-bodied, and has soft varietal flavor; it is a superb wine with the classic balance of a traditional Claret. **price range:** B

producer: Llords & Elwood Winery
classification: Fortified wine
grape variety: Palomino

This dry Sherry is aged naturally in small oak casks out-of-doors and is not "baked." Its uniform quality results from fractional blending from each cask via the Solera method.

Brilliant medium amber color and a "nutty" oak bouquet. The wine is dry, tantalizingly mellow and mature, with a nutty flavor that easily equals the qualities of many of its Spanish counterparts. **price range:** B

producer: Llords & Elwood Winery
classification: Fortified wine
grape variety: Tinta Madeira

This California Port is aged for years in small oak casks in order to retain its fruitiness and develop superior flavor and aroma. It is one of the very finest Ports made in America.

Deep ruby color and a vinous oak bouquet. The wine is drier than most ordinary Ports; it has a soft, zestful flavor, is fruity and complex, and is the equal of many fine Portuguese Ports. **price range:** B

producer: Llords & Elwood Winery
classification: Rosé varietal table wine
grape variety: Cabernet Sauvignon

Llords & Elwood was the first California winery to make a rosé wine from Cabernet Sauvignon and label it as a varietal. It is not to be confused with lesser rosé wines, which tend to lack breed.

Deep pink color and a fruity varietal bouquet. The wine is medium dry, full-bodied, and has a delicious fruity flavor. **price range:** B

producer: Llords & Elwood Winery
classification: White varietal table wine
grape variety: Johannisberg Riesling

Llords & Elwood was the first California winery to make and sell commercially a Spätlese (late harvest) type of Johannis-berg Riesling. All their Johannisberg Rieslings have the extracts of many German Spätleses but the dryness of those from the Mosel.

Pale straw color and a fruity varietal bouquet. The wine is medium dry, with the captivatingly fruity flavor of the variety; it has many characteristics of a fine Spätlese from the Mosel. **price range:** B

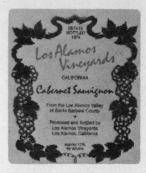

producer: Los Alamos Vineyards
classification: Red varietal table wine
grape variety: Cabernet Sauvignon
district: Central Coast—Santa Barbara County

This wine has a slightly herbaceous palate and scent and a clear, deep red color. On the whole, it has excellent varietal character and should age very well. **price range:** B

producer: Los Alamos Vineyards
classification: Red varietal table wine
grape variety: Gamay Beaujolais
district: Central Coast

This Gamay Beaujolais is smooth and ready to drink now, with a nice, smooth bouquet and a clear, unusually dark red appearance. **price range:** B

producer: Los Alamos Vineyards
classification: White varietal table wine
grape variety: Pinot Chardonnay
district: Central Coast

This light gold-colored wine is fruity and slightly dry, with quite a fruity bouquet. It is an excellent wine, and won the bronze medal at the 1976 Los Angeles county fair. **price range:** B

producer: Los Alamos Vineyards
classification: White varietal table wine
grape variety: Pinot Chardonnay
district: Central Coast

The nose on this clear straw-colored wine is fruity, with a trace of oak. To the palate, the wine is slightly tannic from being aged in oak barrels, and fruity, with a good Chardonnay character.
price range: B

producer: Louis M. Martini, Inc.
classification: White varietal table wine
grape variety: Johannisberg Riesling
district: Napa/Sonoma counties
city or village: St. Helena

This pale straw Johannisberg Riesling has a strong, fruity, varietal bouquet. It is a dry wine with medium acid and strong fruit; medium body.

This wine is also available as a private reserve, vintage 1972. **price range:** B

producer: Louis M. Martini, Inc.
classification: White table wine
grape variety: Predominantly French Colombard
district: Napa/Sonoma counties
city or village: St. Helena

This is a dry, light, slightly tart, fresh Chablis-type wine with a fresh, fruity bouquet. It is a brilliant pale straw color.
price range: A

producer: Louis M. Martini, Inc.
classification: Red varietal table wine
grape variety: Barbera
district: Napa/Sonoma counties
city or village: St. Helena

This is a heavy, acidic, robust wine with noticeable tannin and a strong, vinous bouquet. It is clear dark red.

This wine is also available as a private reserve, vintage 1969, at the winery.
price range: A

producer: Los Alamos Vineyards
classification: Red varietal table wine
grape variety: Zinfandel
district: Santa Barbara County

This is a somewhat tannic, sound wine with good character of the Zinfandel grape. It is bright red in color, with a deep varietal bouquet. **price range:** B

producer: Louis M. Martini, Inc.
classification: White varietal table wine
grape variety: Gewürztraminer
district: Napa/Sonoma counties
city or village: St. Helena

This is a strong, spicy, heavy-bodied wine, dry with low acid. Its bouquet is spicy and fruity and its appearance a brilliant straw color.

This wine is also available as a private reserve, vintage 1972. **price range:** B

producer: Louis M. Martini, Inc.
classification: Red varietal table wine
grape variety: Cabernet Sauvignon
district: Napa/Sonoma counties
city or village: St. Helena

This smooth Cabernet Sauvignon has a good, aged character and some tannin. It is clear medium red and has the typical Cabernet Sauvignon bouquet.

This wine is also available as a special selection, vintage 1969. **price range:** B

producer: Paul Masson Vineyards
classification: White sparkling table wine
grape variety: Pinot Chardonnay, Johannisberg Riesling, Chenin Blanc, French Colombard, and Emerald Riesling

This straw-colored Champagne, dry, crisp and noble, is called the "King of California Champagnes." **price range:** C

producer: Paul Masson Vineyards
classification: White table wine
grape variety: Franken Riesling (Sylvaner), French Colombard, and Emerald Riesling

This Rhine-style wine is graceful and delicate, with a soft, pleasing taste. The fragrance has a mysterious taste of sweetness. **price range:** A

producer: Louis M. Martini, Inc.
classification: Red varietal table wine
grape variety: Zinfandel
district: Napa/Sonoma counties
city or village: St. Helena

This clear medium-red Zinfandel has a spicy, berrylike bouquet. To the palate, it is smooth, with good tannin and strong grape flavor.

This wine is also available as a private reserve, vintage 1970. It is a heavier, more robust wine than the 1972 and will age well for ten years. **price range:** A

producer: Louis M. Martini, Inc.
classification: White varietal table wine
grape variety: Pinot Chardonnay
district: Napa/Sonoma counties
city or village: St. Helena

This is a dry, heavy-flavored Pinot Chardonnay with good acid and body and a slightly woody bouquet.

This wine is also available as a private reserve, vintage 1972. **price range:** B

producer: Louis M. Martini, Inc.
classification: Red varietal table wine
grape variety: Pinot Noir
district: Napa/Sonoma counties
city or village: St. Helena

This is a smooth, full-bodied, grapey Pinot Noir with good varietal character and a fruity, woody bouquet. It is clear light red in color.

This wine is also available as private reserve, vintage 1968; special selection, vintage 1968; and special selection, vintage 1969. **price range:** B

In the eighteenth century it was the custom for a Hungarian bridegroom to drink wine from his bride's slipper at the wedding feast. He was supposed to drink one slipperful with each course.

producer: J. Mathews Napa Valley Winery
classification: Red table wine
grape variety: Predominantly Petite Sirah
district: Napa Valley

This deep red Burgundy-style wine has a powerful bouquet and fresh taste. At present, it has some tannin, but it will soften with age. **price range: A**

producer: J. Mathews Napa Valley Winery
classification: Red varietal table wine
grape variety: Berbera
district: Napa Valley

This deep red Berbera has a powerful bouquet and a soft, smooth palate. It shows a complexity that comes with age.
price range: B

producer: J. Mathews Napa Valley Winery
classification: Red varietal table wine
grape variety: Cabernet Sauvignon
district: Napa Valley

This is a soft, smooth, complex wine with the pronounced Cabernet Sauvignon nose. It is of a brilliant medium red color.
price range: B

producer: J. Mathews Napa Valley Winery
classification: Red varietal table wine
grape variety: Pinot Chardonnay (100%)
district: Napa Valley

This wine is of brilliant pale straw appearance and has the typical Pinot Chardonnay bouquet. **price range: B**

producer: J. Mathews Napa Valley Winery
classification: Red varietal table wine
grape variety: Zinfandel
district: Napa Valley

This is a complex Zinfandel that shows some oak. Its bouquet is delightful, and its color is a brilliant medium red.
price range: A

producer: Mirassou Vineyards
classification: Rosé table wine
grape variety: Mainly Petite Sirah
district: North Coast Counties
city or village: Soledad/San Jose

"Petite Rosé." Fermented off the skins, it is a rosé in color only; the 1974 vintage won a gold medal at the international competition in Bratislava, Czechoslovakia. Mirassou is North America's oldest family wine-growing enterprise and is presently managed by the fifth generation. The Mirassous have grown wine grapes continuously since 1854.

Deep strawberry-pink color and a fresh, fruity bouquet. On the palate the wine is light, dry, and delicate, with a lingering aftertaste. "Petite Rosé" is a dry wine with unusually pronounced character.
price range: A

producer: Mirassou Vineyards
classification: Red table wine
grape variety: Petite Sirah, Zinfandel, and Gamay Beaujolais
district: North Coast Counties
city or village: Soledad/San Jose

"Burgundy."
Bright garnet color and a bouquet showing good balance of fruit and wood. This wine is a well-balanced blend that, unlike many generics, will develop into a lovely wine of surprising complexity with bottle age; it is very good dollar value.
price range: A

producer: Mirassou Vineyards
classification: White table wine
grape variety: Pinot Blanc and French Colombard
district: North Coast Counties
city or village: Soledad/San Jose

"Chablis."
Pale straw color and a vinous, clean bouquet with some fruit. On the palate the wine is crisp, light, and dry with a gentle roundness. It is an enjoyable dry white wine to complement any meal, and an excellent buy. **price range: A**

producer: Mirassou Vineyards
classification: White sparkling wine
district: North Coast Counties
city or village: Soledad/San Jose

"LD" Champagne. This wine was made via the *methode champenoise* and spent fifty months *en tirage*. Its dryness is between our Natural Champagne and Brut Champagne. It is made predominantly from Pinot Blanc with some Chenin Blanc.

A light gold color and bouquet suggesting yeastiness. The taste combines yeastiness, fruitiness, and richness; enjoy it leisurely with a favorite companion, a fireplace, soft music, and the fanciest of hors d'oeuvres. **price range: D**

producer: Mirassou Vineyards
classification: Red varietal table wine
grape variety: Zinfandel
district: North Coast Counties
city or village: Soledad/San Jose

The 1973 Zinfandel is one of the best of recent years. This young wine can be enjoyed now, but some should be cellared for future enjoyment.

A medium ruby color and a luscious, zesty, berrylike bouquet. The wine has excellent fruity flavor in good harmony with oak; zesty and enticing while young, this wine will achieve a great deal of elegance and enriched complexity with age. It is great now with pasta; when aged, with Beef Wellington. **price range: B**

producer: Mirassou Vineyards
classification: White sparkling wine
grape variety: Pinot Blanc
district: North Coast Counties
city or village: Soledad

"Brut Champagne." This was a gold-medal winner at the 1975 Los Angeles county fair. It is fermented in the traditional *methode champenoise*. A small amount of dosage is added to make it just "off dry."

A honey color and a delicate, yeasty bouquet. The yeastiness carries through in the taste. It is excellent as an aperitif or with an omelette, ham, and strawberries on a warm Sunday morning. **price range: C**

producer: Mirassou Vineyards
classification: White varietal table wine
grape variety: Pinot Chardonnay
district: North Coast Counties
city or village: Soledad

1974 was the best vintage for this Pinot Chardonnay since the 1969. Balanced acidity is typical of the wines made in 1974, one of the warmest years since the Monterey vineyards were planted. It was also one of the longest growing seasons—ideal for Pinot Chardonnay.

Medium gold color and a full varietal aroma with overtones of fresh fruit. The wine is well-balanced, full-bodied, and has a lingering finish. It is expected to reach its peak in 2½–3½ years.
price range: C

producer: Mirassou Vineyards
classification: Red varietal table wine
grape variety: Pinot Noir
district: North Coast Counties
city or village: Soledad

1973 vintage.
A brick-red color and a full varietal bouquet. The wine is rich, with balanced body; it is developing nicely at this young age and will continue to improve for the next six or seven years. Its flavor presents a developing complexity of wine and wood.
price range: B

producer: Mirassou Vineyards
classification: Red varietal table wine
grape variety: Petite Sirah
district: North Coast Counties
city or village: Soledad/San Jose

A deep, dark red color and a "peppery" bouquet characteristic of the variety; earthy. On the palate the wine is light yet rich, with a nice amount of tannin. This Petite Sirah is very enjoyable now and will continue to develop for from five to seven years. It is full, rich, and vigorous, yet possesses a soft, gentle character with a heady bouquet. It would be fantastic with stews. **price range:** B

producer: Mirassou Vineyards
classification: White varietal table wine
grape variety: Johannisberg Riesling
district: North Coast Counties
city or village: Soledad

1974 vintage. This wine was an award winner in Bratislava, Czechoslovakia, in international competition.

Light gold color and a flowery, varietal bouquet. The wine is well-balanced, full-bodied, and has a lingering finish. With just enough sweetness for balance and accenting its fruit, this wine should continue to develop nicely. **price range:** B

producer: Mirassou Vineyards
classification: White varietal table wine
grape variety: Chenin Blanc
district: North Coast Counties
city or village: Soledad

1973 vintage. This was an award winner in an international competition in Surrey, England. Steve Mirassou considers this Chenin Blanc to be the best he's ever produced.

A light to medium straw color and a strong varietal bouquet with intense fruitiness. Semisweet, the wine is well-balanced, with a rich lingering aftertaste. A classic Chenin Blanc—drinkable now for its freshness. At any stage of its development (one to two years), it is a perfect complement for fresh cracked crab, artichokes, and French bread. **price range:** B

producer: Mirassou Vineyards
classification: White varietal table wine
grape variety: Gewürztraminer
district: North Coast Counties
city or village: Soledad

A medium gold color and an intense varietal bouquet with much spiciness. "Harvest" Gewürztraminer is more concentrated than Mirassou's regular bottling. It is well-balanced with substantial character but has exceptional fruit and spice. Served with fruit or cheese, it is an excellent wine to linger over and will enhance many savory dishes—a favorite is mild curry. **price range:** B

producer: Mirassou Vineyards
classification: Red varietal table wine
grape variety: Cabernet Sauvignon
district: North Coast Counties
city or village: Soledad

A ruby color and a full, enticing varietal bouquet. The wine is emphatic—it has good tannin and a lingering finish. At this youthful stage it shows great promise for cellar aging, though it is not too powerful to preclude enjoyment now. It is one of the best Mirassou Cabernet Sauvignons to date, with intense varietal characteristics and outstanding fruit. Try some with your next roast leg or rack of lamb or with steak tartare. **price range:** B

producer: Mirassou Vineyards
classification: Red varietal table wine
grape variety: Gamay Beaujolais
district: North Coast Counties
city or village: Soledad

An extended period of fermentation marks this wine. It was fermented down to 10 degrees balling on the skins, lightly centrifuged, and then continued fermenting for nine months longer. Malolactic fermentation took place for forty to fifty days.

A bright ruby-red color and a fresh, fruity bouquet suggesting berries. The wine finishes rich and is very fresh, with slight tartness. The ideal time for consuming this wine is from one to two years following its release. Since it is light-bodied, it is excellent with a wide variety of foods. **price range:** B

producer: Mirassou Vineyards
classification: White varietal table wine
grape variety: Pinot Chardonnay
district: North Coast Counties
city or village: Soledad

A "Harvest" Pinot Chardonnay, that will develop complexity with bottle age.

A golden color and a bouquet with emphatic varietal aroma. The wine is well-balanced, with fine fruit and overtones of oak. It is a wine that will enhance a meal now and will also continue to improve for up to four years. It would be light and pleasant with a wide variety of seafood dishes. **price range:** B

producer: Mirassou Vineyards
classification: Red varietal table wine
grape variety: Pinot Noir
district: North Coast Counties
city or village: Soledad

A "Harvest" Pinot Noir bottled in April 1976.

A deep garnet color and an elegant, rich bouquet with somewhat spicy fruit. The wine has rich fruit and body, with soft tannin. It is a very young Pinot Noir that will age well for at least ten years. Both taste and bouquet promise a wine of elegance and finesse with time. **price range:** C

producer: Mirassou Vineyards
classification: Red varietal table wine
grape variety: Zinfandel
district: North Coast Counties
city or village: Soledad

1973 vintage. A "Harvest" Zinfandel produced in one of the finest vintages for this variety. It has an aging potential of eight to ten years.

A deep ruby-red color and a strong varietal bouquet. The wine is full-bodied, with well-balanced fruitiness. A very young wine at this time, it shows definite promise and is well worth cellaring. **price range:** B

producer: Mirassou Vineyards
classification: Red varietal table wine
grape variety: Cabernet Sauvignon

district: North Coast Counties
city or village: Soledad

A "Harvest" Cabernet Sauvignon to be released in September 1978. The wine rested in 58-gallon Limousin oak barrels until it was bottled in July 1975. A small amount was prereleased in June 1976.

A deep garnet color and a rich, fruity bouquet with a touch of oak. The wine is full-bodied, well-balanced, and has a long finish. This Cabernet has intense varietal characteristics and outstanding balance: it is definitely one to lay away for future enjoyment; a wine of distinction. **price range:** C

producer: C. K. Mondavi & Sons
classification: Red table wine
grape variety: Blend of selected red varieties
"Burgundy."

Medium red color and a bouquet rich with grapiness, though it shows some aging. The wine is dry, medium-bodied, well-balanced, flavorful, and savory. It is an abundantly pleasant wine that is a pleasurable companion to many foods.
price range: A (fifth), B (half gallon), C (gallon)

producer: C. K. Mondavi & Sons
classification: Red table wine
grape variety: Blend of selected red varieties
"Chianti."

Medium red color and a grapey, vinous bouquet with some aged character. The wine is medium-bodied, dry, well-balanced, and full-flavored.
price range: A (fifth), B (half gallon), C (gallon)

producer: C. K. Mondavi & Sons
classification: Red table wine
grape variety: Zinfandel

The Mondavi Winery is family owned and operated. No preservatives are added to the wine; their "C. K." line includes jug wines in fifths, half gallon, and gallon sizes. This one is called "Zinfandel."

Medium red color with a touch of purple; the bouquet is well-balanced, rich, and full. The wine tastes dry and well-balanced and is medium-bodied, with varietal flavor. It is an exciting rendition of this California classic and an unbeatable bargain.
price range: A (fifth), B (half gallon), C (gallon)

producer: Robert Mondavi Winery
classification: Red varietal table wine
grape variety: Petite Sirah
district: Napa Valley
city or village: Oakville
Dark red color and a big, full bouquet with varietal richness. The wine is full-bodied and quite tannic.   **price range:** B

producer: Robert Mondavi Winery
classification: White varietal table wine
grape variety: Johannisberg Riesling
district: Napa Valley
city or village: Oakville
Clean, clear color and a light, fragrant, and flowery bouquet. The wine is soft, round, and slightly sweet.   **price range:** B

producer: Robert Mondavi Winery
classification: White varietal table wine
grape variety: Chenin Blanc
district: Napa Valley
city or village: Oakville
Clean, clear color and a fresh, fruity and aromatic bouquet. The wine is slightly sweet with a delicate flavor. **price range:** B

producer: Robert Mondavi Winery
classification: Red varietal table wine
grape variety: Gamay

district: Napa Valley
city or village: Oakville
Red-purple color and a clean bouquet showing Gamay character. The wine is clean, dry, and medium-bodied, with characteristic Gamay flavor. **price range:** B

prodûcer: Robert Mondavi Winery
classification: Red varietal table wine
grape variety: Pinot Noir
district: Napa Valley
city or village: Oakville
Clean, full red color and a distinctive varietal bouquet. The wine is full-bodied but delicate, with a rich fruity flavor.
price range: C

producer: Robert Mondavi Winery
classification: Red varietal table wine
grape variety: Zinfandel
district: Napa Valley
city or village: Oakville
Rich, dark red color and a clean, deep varietal bouquet. The wine is dry and full-bodied, with clean varietal flavor.
price range: B

producer: Mount Eden Vineyards
classification: White varietal table wine
grape variety: Chardonnay
district: Santa Clara Valley
city or village: Saratoga
The 1972 Mount Eden Chardonnay was the first highly lauded Chardonnay to be released by the winery. It won a gold medal at the Los Angeles county fair in 1974. It has been sold out for some time. The wine was served at the State dinner given by Henry Kissinger for the French Premier upon the occasion of his visit to the United States in 1976.
Deep gold color and intense Chardonnay character in the well-developed bottle bouquet. The wine is rich, luscious, and almost syrupy, with medium acidity and a long finish. It should increase in complexity for several years at least. **price range:** E

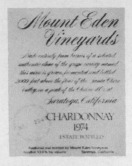

producer: Mount Eden Vineyards
classification: White varietal table wine
grape variety: Chardonnay
district: Santa Clara Valley
city or village: Saratoga
At Mount Eden Vineyards, four acres of Chardonnay vines produce a scant yield of one ton per acre from fifteen-year-old vines. Late in September of 1974, four tons of Chardonnay were harvested at 24.3 degrees Brix and 0.78% total acidity. The grapes were pressed when still cool, and the juice flowed directly into new 60-gallon Limousin oak barrels. The wine was fermented for about five weeks at a cellar temperature of about 55-60 degrees F. After several rackings and a light bentonite fining, the wine was given simple filtration and was bottled in May 1975.
Golden color; an aroma of ripe grapes, with lingering perfume. The wine tastes luscious, yet is well balanced, with a suggestion of ripe fruit. A delightful future is promised. **price range:** E

producer: Mount Eden Vineyards
classification: Red varietal table wine
grape variety: Pinot Noir
district: Santa Clara Valley
city or village: Saratoga
1972 vintage. This outstanding Pinot Noir was awarded the 1975 Wine of the Year award by *San Francisco* magazine. Magnums are available.
Aromatic complexity; velvety, rich, and well-balanced taste. Watch this wine grow! **price range:** E

producer: Mount Eden Vineyards
classification: Red varietal table wine
grape variety: Pinot Noir

district: Santa Clara Valley
city or village: Saratoga
The grapes for this wine were fermented on the stems for ten days, then pressed off into new 60-gallon Limousin oak barrels. By spring the wine had been softened and its complexity increased by the completion of malolactic fermentation. The wine spent sixteen months in barrel before being bottled in June 1975. It was neither fined nor filtered; racking allowed it to clarify itself naturally.
Medium body, quite delicate style. The wine is fruity, mellow, and well-balanced, with a soft silky finish. **price range:** D

producer: Mount Eden Vineyards
classification: Red varietal table wine
grape variety: Cabernet Sauvignon
district: Santa Clara Valley
city or village: Saratoga
The grapes for this wine were harvested at 25 degrees Brix during the second week of October 1973. The wine was fermented for two weeks at a relatively cool temperature before pressing, and after pressing was transferred to 60-gallon Nevers oak barrels. The malolactic fermentation was completed by the following spring. The wine was then given a fresh egg-white fining in the spring of 1975 and was bottled that summer. Magnums are available.
Ruby color and a rich, fruity, and intensely varietal bouquet with peppery undertones. On the palate the wine is mouth-filling, a fine balance of ripe fruit and oak. Its future is assured by generous amounts of acid and tannin. **price range:** E

producer: Mount Eden Vineyards
classification: Red varietal table wine
grape variety: Cabernet Sauvignon
district: Santa Clara Valley
city or village: Saratoga
This wine spent almost two and one-half years in small cooperage made of Nevers oak.
Woody bouquet and a mellow, complex flavor. It should have a long life.
price range: E

producer: The Monterey Vineyard
classification: White varietal table wine
grape variety: Chenin Blanc (100%)
district: Monterey County
city or village: Gonzales

This Chenin Blanc was made from grapes attacked by Botrytis mold, noticeably increasing the body of the wine.

A light straw color and an intense varietal bouquet. The wine is slightly sweet but well-balanced, with true varietal character. **price range:** A

producer: The Monterey Vineyard
classification: Red varietal table wine
grape variety: Zinfandel
district: Monterey County
city or village: Gonzales

Zinfandel, in the cool upper Monterey County region, is one of the latest-ripening wine grapes. "Normal" picking date is mid- to late November. The long, cool season is thought to be a major factor in the exceptional "raspberry" character of this wine.

A light-medium red color and a raspberrylike bouquet with some oak character. The wine is soft, very fruity, and has a strong Zinfandel taste. It is comparatively light in body but has good balance and is very easy to drink. It would go well with delicately flavored foods. **price range:** B

producer: The Monterey Vineyard
classification: Red varietal table wine
grape variety: Zinfandel
district: Monterey County
city or village: Gonzales

This is a "late harvest" Zinfandel made from the last grapes to be picked by the Monterey Vineyard each year. Considerable drying of the grapes on the vine concentrates the flavor and extracts, giving the wine good viscosity ("legs"), body, and long life.

A medium ruby-red color and a spicy, intense raspberry bouquet that is very complex. The wine is a soft mouthful; it is dry, fruity, and full-bodied, a big Zinfandel without the "alcoholic" character usually found in late-harvest California Zinfandels. The influence of oak barrel aging is noticeable. **price range:** B

producer: The Monterey Vineyard
classification: Red varietal table wine
grape variety: Gamay Beaujolais (100%)
district: Monterey County
city or village: Gonzales

This wine was made from Gamay Beaujolais, the Beaujolais clone of Pinot Noir. No Napa Gamay was used, and the wine was aged in oak.

Medium red color and a fruity, fresh, and complex bouquet. The wine tastes soft and fruity; it is dry and not harsh. Though fruity, it is not in the nouveau style and is definitely an "aging" Beaujolais-type wine that has more body than most California "Beaujolais." **price range:** B

producer: The Monterey Vineyard
classification: Rosé varietal table wine
grape variety: Cabernet Sauvignon
district: Monterey County
city or village: Gonzales

This wine was produced from Cabernet Sauvignon grapes harvested in December. The very long, cool season develops a unique style of wine with distinctive flavor.

A rosé with crystal-clear color and a very fresh, light fruity bouquet. On the palate the wine is light, dry, and unusually delicate considering it was made from Cabernet Sauvignon. **price range:** B

producer: The Monterey Vineyard
classification: White varietal table wine
grape variety: Gewürztraminer
district: Monterey County
city or village: Gonzales

This wine was made from grapes grown in the cool region around Gonzales, where heat summation totals less than two thousand degree days annually—similar to the coolest regions of northeastern France. Vineyards are irrigated, however, for there are very low levels of rainfall in Gonzales.

A straw-gold color and a spicy, intense bouquet typical of Traminer. The wine is not quite dry, but gives a dry impression; it is exceptionally clean, with distinct Gewürztraminer flavor, and finishes dry so that the intense varietal character is not overwhelming. **price range:** B

producer: The Monterey Vineyard
classification: Red varietal table wine
grape variety: Pinot Noir (100%)
district: Monterey County
city or village: Gonzales

This Pinot Noir was produced in the coolest grape-growing region in California. The grapes were not harvested until November.

A medium red color and a woody, vinous, and complex bouquet. The wine combines medium body with softness. **price range:** B

producer: The Monterey Vineyard
classification: White varietal table wine
grape variety: Sylvaner
district: Monterey County
city or village: Gonzales

"Grüner Sylvaner." This wine is made from grapes attacked by considerable Botrytis mold, though not to the degree of Monterey's Johannisberg Riesling.

A light greenish-gold color and an almost spicy, intensely fruity bouquet. The wine finishes dry, although it contains a bit of residual sugar. This coolest-climate Sylvaner is amazingly intense in varietal character, yet will develop subtlety with additional bottle aging. **price range:** A

producer: The Monterey Vineyard
classification: White varietal table wine
grape variety: Chardonnay (100%)
district: Monterey County
city or village: Gonzales

This Chardonnay was produced from grapes grown in the northernmost section of Monterey County. This is the coolest major wine region in the United States in terms of total heat summation, and several vineyard blocks receive less than two thousand degree days per year. Intense Chardonnay character results from the exceptionally cool climate and the well-drained, decomposed granite soil. This wine received no wood aging and hence has none of the common oak character of Monterey's other Chardonnay.

A light straw color with greenish tints; the bouquet is intense and distinctly Chardonnay. The wine tastes crisp, clean, and dry. **price range:** B

producer: The Monterey Vineyard
classification: Red varietal table wine
grape variety: Cabernet Sauvignon and Merlot
district: Monterey County
city or village: Gonzales

This Cabernet Sauvignon contains 10% Merlot for added complexity.

A heavy red color and a distinctive Cabernet bouquet—heavy and full. The wine has soft body and velvet smoothness, and is dry. This wine is unusual in that it combines body with softness; it is drinkable now with its fruity and definite character, but will improve with age for several years. **price range:** B

producer: The Monterey Vineyard
classification: White table wine
grape variety: Pinot Blanc, Chenin Blanc, and Sylvaner
district: Monterey County
city or village: Gonzales

"Del Mar Ranch." This wine is a unique blend of three varietals that come from a specific vineyard block of the same name.

A light straw color and a pleasantly fruity, complex bouquet. The wine tastes totally dry but distinctly fruity; its dryness and unique fruity character would make it an excellent wine to serve with hors d'oeuvres. **price range:** A

producer: The Monterey Vineyard
classification: White varietal table wine
grape variety: Johannisberg Riesling
district: Monterey County
city or village: Gonzales

This wine was made from grapes grown in the coolest vineyards of Monterey County. *Botrytis cinerea* mold was widespread, and the wine shows good body with relatively high glycerin content as a result of the mold.

A light straw-gold color and an intense bouquet typical of White Riesling. On the palate the wine is slightly sweet but retains a basically dry finish. This is a very "big" Johannisberg Riesling, Botrytis contributing to the honeylike flavor and good "legs." **price range:** B

producer: The Monterey Vineyard
classification: White varietal table wine
grape variety: Chardonnay (100%)
district: Monterey County
city or village: Gonzales

This Chardonnay was produced from grapes grown in the northernmost section of Monterey County. This is the coolest major wine region in the United States in terms of total heat summation, and several vineyard blocks receive less than two thousand degree days per year. One of the finest Chardonnays made in California, it has a distinctive Montrachet-like character, yet has a characteristic Monterey flavor. It is aged in oak, giving a notable constituent to its flavor.

A light golden-straw color and a complex bouquet of Chardonnay with Limousin oak overtones. The wine tastes smooth, crisp, and dry, with a noticeable oak flavor.
price range: B

producer: The Monterey Vineyard
classification: White varietal table wine
grape variety: Sylvaner
district: Monterey County
city or village: Gonzales

The grapes for this wine had considerable Botrytis mold. This cool-climate Sylvaner is produced from 100% Monterey County grapes.

A light greenish-gold color and an almost spicy, intensely fruity bouquet. The wine is remarkably fruity and very easy to drink; it finishes dry, although it contains some residual sugar. It is amazingly intense in varietal character, yet has subtle overtones, especially after bottle aging.
price range: B

producer: The Monterey Vineyard
classification: White varietal table wine
grape variety: Chardonnay
district: Monterey County
city or village: Gonzales

This wine is a blend of the 1974 and 1975 vintages and is aged in barrel. It is owned by Ernie's Wine & Liquor Corp. in San Francisco.

A light straw-gold color and a complex Chardonnay bouquet with oak overtones from Limousin oak. The wine is smooth, crisp, and dry; light in body; and has a distinctive north coast California Chardonnay character.
price range: A

producer: The Monterey Vineyard (Los Alamos Vineyards)
classification: White varietal table wine
grape variety: Johannisberg Riesling
district: Santa Barbara County
city or village: Los Alamos

This particular wine was produced by the Monterey Vineyard from grapes grown by Los Alamos. Botrytis mold significantly contributes to its character.

A light golden color and a distinctive varietal bouquet. The wine is crisp and dry, with clean varietal character, and it is fuller-bodied than most other dry Rieslings from California.
price range: B

producer: Monteviña
classification: White varietal table wine
grape variety: Zinfandel
district: Shenandoah Valley

This is a soft, full wine, faintly sweet, with a fine, light Zinfandel nose. It is brilliant in appearance, with a faint "Partridge Eye."
price range: A

producer: Monteviña
classification: Red varietal table wine
grape variety: Barbera
district: Shenandoah Valley

This is a brilliant, very dark wine, with big, beautiful, Italian-style bouquet. To the palate it is full and long.

This wine has lots of aging potential.
price range: A

producer: Monteviña
classification: Red varietal table wine
grape variety: Ruby Cabernet
district: Shenandoah Valley

This is a very big, rich, full wine with thick flavors, which can benefit from many years' aging. Its bouquet is intense, of Ruby Cabernet and oak. It is brilliant black-red to the eye.
price range: A

producer: Monteviña
classification: White varietal table wine
grape variety: Sauvignon Blanc
district: Shenandoah Valley

This is a clean, full Sauvignon Blanc with a long finish. Its bouquet is luscious and full and its color a brilliant, rich gold.
price range: B

producer: A. Nonini Winery
classification: Red varietal table wine
grape variety: Barbera
district: San Joaquin Valley
city or village: Fresno
Estate-bottled.

Dark red color and a full, dry, and mild bouquet. The wine is soft, full-bodied, and excellent—a good dinner wine.
price range: A

producer: A. Nonini Winery
classification: Red varietal table wine
grape variety: Zinfandel
district: San Joaquin Valley
city or village: Fresno
Estate-bottled.

Medium red color and an excellent bouquet. The wine is light-bodied, medium dry, and soft—a good dinner wine.
price range: A

producer: Notivitate of Los Gatos
classification: White varietal table wine
grape variety: Johannisberg Riesling
district: Santa Clara
city or village: Los Gatos

Light golden color and a sweet bouquet with light fruit. The wine combines good acid/sugar balance with ample fruit and has a good, clean finish.
price range: B

producer: Novitiate of Los Gatos
classification: Fortified wine
grape variety: Tinta Madeira
district: Central Valley
city or village: Los Gatos

An estate-bottled California Port made from original Port grape varieties.

Dark red color and a sweet, fruity bouquet. The wine is light, sweet, and has a brandy "snap"; it has good body and will improve in bottle.
price range: A

"It warms the blood, adds luster to the eyes, And wine and love have ever been allies."
—Ovid

producer: Novitiate of Los Gatos
classification: Fortified wine
grape variety: Palomino
district: Central Valley
city or village: Los Gatos
This estate-bottled flor Sherry spends three to five years in oak, then eighteen months under flor yeast.
Medium gold color and a "thick" bouquet with caramel undertones. The wine is light, dry, and clean, with a subtle hint of flor yeast. **price range:** B

producer: Novitiate of Los Gatos
classification: White varietal table wine
grape variety: Pinot Blanc
district: Santa Clara
city or village: Los Gatos
Estate-bottled.
Clear light straw color and a subtle floral bouquet. The wine is dry and crisp, lightly fruity, and finishes cleanly. **price range:** A

producer: Oakville Vineyards
classification: Red varietal table wine
grape variety: Cabernet Sauvignon and Gamay
district: Napa Valley
city or village: Rutherford
An addition of 15% Gamay to this Cabernet produces an early-maturing, delightfully soft wine of good breeding.
Medium garnet color and a bouquet with Cabernet earthiness and a touch of oak. The wine is dry and soft; even with two years of bottle age the wine has not yet reached its peak; it will improve until 1979. **price range:** B

producer: Oakville Vineyards
classification: Red varietal table wine
grape variety: Zinfandel
district: Napa Valley
city or village: Rutherford
A blend of 60% Mother Lode Zinfandel 1974 and 40% Napa Valley 1973.
Deep ruby color and a typical berrylike Zinfandel bouquet. The wine is dry, with a touch of oak. The excellent marriage of Mother Lode/Napa Valley grapes produced this early-drinking, flavorful wine. **price range:** A

producer: Papagni Vineyards
classification: Red varietal table wine
grape variety: Alicante-Bouschet
district: Madera County—San Joaquin Valley
city or village: Madera
The Alicante-Bouschet is a red hybrid grape variety developed by the brothers Bouschet during the nineteenth century. This is the only commercially available varietal wine made from this grape. The 1973 vintage was produced from eighty-year-old vines in the Madera district.
Deep red—almost black—color and a bouquet with definite varietal character balanced by oak, with a hint of chocolate. The wine is very big, full-bodied, and dry, with good acid and tannin and strong, robust flavor. It is ready to drink now but has definite aging potential. **price range:** A

producer: Papagni Vineyards
classification: Red varietal table wine
grape variety: Barbera
district: Madera County—San Joaquin Valley
city or village: Madera

Brilliant rich red color and a varietal bouquet showing oak balance. The wine is dry, soft, and full-bodied; although ready to drink now, it will develop further and mellow with bottle aging. **price range:** A

producer: Papagni Vineyards
classification: Red varietal table wine
grape variety: Carignane
district: Madera County—San Joaquin Valley
city or village: Madera
Brilliant clear red color and a varietal bouquet with a hint of oak. The wine is dry, medium-bodied, and very smooth; it is a very good complement to a wide variety of foods. **price range:** A

producer: Papagni Vineyards
classification: Red varietal table wine
grape variety: Zinfandel
district: Madera County—San Joaquin Valley
city or village: Madera
Brilliant ruby-red color and a zesty, berrylike bouquet with varietal character balanced by oak. The wine is well-balanced, smooth, and dry, with medium to full body; it is fruity, soft, and ready to serve now, but will develop further in the bottle. **price range:** A

producer: Papagni Vineyards
classification: White varietal table wine
grape variety: Muscat of Alexandria
district: Madera County—San Joaquin Valley
city or village: Madera
This is one of the very few commercially available varietal wines made from the Muscat of Alexandria.

Brilliant clear-white color and a fresh, spicy, and distinctive varietal fragrance. The wine is medium-bodied, generously crisp and fruity, and is off-dry; it is an excitingly flavorsome white wine suitable before or after meals and is delightfully different. **price range:** A

producer: Papagni Vineyards
classification: White sparkling wine
district: Madera County—San Joaquin Valley
city or village: Madera
"Brut Champagne."
Brilliant clear color and a fruity, crisp, and yeasty bouquet. The wine is dry and elegant, unique in its display of freshness and yeasty fragrance. **price range:** A

producer: Papagni Vineyards
classification: White sparkling wine
grape variety: Muscat
district: Madera County—San Joaquin Valley
city or village: Madera
A Moscato *spumanto*.
Clear sparkling color and a crisp, lusciously sweet, and fresh perfumey bouquet. The wine is full, complex, and sweet, with rich effervescence—a great achievement in a sparkling Muscat wine. **price range:** B

producer: Parducci Wine Cellars
classification: White varietal table wine
grape variety: Pinot Chardonnay
district: Mendocino County
city or village: Ukiah
Like other Parducci white wines, this wine is made totally from free-run juice; no press wine is blended. It is bottled when young, without prolonged aging in oak, in order to preserve the delicate light character of Chardonnay grown in Mendocino. The 1974 vintage Parducci Chardonnay won a gold medal at the 1975 Los Angeles county fair.
A ripe fruity bouquet and a light flavor with lingering finish. This unique wine is crisp, fruity, and dry and is a great companion for meals. **price range:** B

producer: Parducci Wine Cellars
classification: White varietal table wine
grape variety: Chenin Blanc (100%)
district: Mendocino County
city or village: Ukiah

Like other Parducci white wines, this wine is made totally from free-run juice; no press wine is blended. Parducci Chenin Blancs gained recognition as among the best Chenin Blancs featured at the Los Angeles county fair in 1975, and the 1974 vintage won a gold medal.

A clean, intensive varietal bouquet suggesting honey and ripe melons; on the palate the wine is well-balanced, harmonious and refreshing, and off-dry.
price range: B

producer: Parducci Wine Cellars
classification: Red varietal table wine
grape variety: Cabernet Sauvignon
district: Mendocino County
city or village: Ukiah

Aged in American oak.

Intensive varietal bouquet with pepper and spice overtones. The wine is robust and well-balanced, with full body, rich flavor, and an excellent finish.
price range: B

producer: Parducci Wine Cellars
classification: Red varietal table wine
grape variety: Petite Sirah
district: Mendocino County
city or village: Ukiah

A big wine, aged in oak and with a good future.

A complex bouquet with a sweet, spicy background; the wine is medium-bodied, harmoniously round, and has good tannin.
price range: B

producer: Parducci Wine Cellars
classification: Red table wine
grape variety: Pinot Noir and various other Mendocino County grapes
district: Mendocino County

The quality of Parducci "Burgundy" is comparable to the winery's premium varietal wines.

A complex bouquet with a pleasant oaky background; on the palate the wine is soft with satisfying tannin and pleasantly mellow fruit. It finishes dry and goes well with meals.
price range: A

producer: Parducci Wine Cellars
classification: Red varietal table wine
grape variety: Zinfandel
district: Mendocino County
city or village: Ukiah

The delightful character of this wine is a result of nonirrigated vines grown on hillside vineyards.

Light wood bouquet showing intense varietal characteristics; the wine has a velvety touch, with good acidity and balance. It is an excellent wine that finishes well.
price range: B

producer: Parducci Wine Cellars
classification: White varietal table wine
grape variety: French Colombard
district: Mendocino County
city or village: Ukiah

Parducci was the first California winery to introduce a varietal made from French Colombard. Wine critics agree that Parducci's Mendocino County French Colombards, harvested from the Home Ranch Hills, have an outstanding quality year after year.

A fruity, varietal bouquet with floral fragrance; on the palate the wine is delicate, lively, and fresh, with a honey-and-spice flavor.
price range: B

producer: Pedrizzetti Winery
classification: Red varietal table wine
grape variety: Zinfandel
district: Santa Clara Valley
city or village: Morgan Hill

The warm days, foggy nights, and gravelly soil of the south Santa Clara Valley produces some of the finest red wines in the world.

The color is medium red, and the wine is clear and clean. It has a very grapey but not woody bouquet. The taste has the typical berryish character of Zinfandel, with low acid. The wine is ready to enjoy when shipped and is good with all kinds of meat or wild game.
price range: A

producer: Pedrizzetti Winery
classification: Red varietal table wine
grape variety: Barbera
district: Santa Clara Valley
city or village: Morgan Hill

The name Pedrizzetti is synonymous with Barbera in California. This lovely wine is made from vines brought from Italy and continuously producing since 1923. The vines are very old and grow adjacent to the winery.

The color is medium red, and the wine is clear and clean. It has a very vinous, grapey, and woody bouquet. The taste is slightly astringent and is typical of Italian wines. A true estate-bottled wine.
price range: A

producer: Pedrizzetti Winery
classification: Red varietal table wine
grape variety: Cabernet Sauvignon

This Cabernet is one of the finest in its price range.

The color is medium red, and the wine is clear and clean. It has a vinous bouquet, moderate acidity, and good varietal character. This is a departure from the heavy oak taste common to most California Cabernets. The predominant taste is wine, not wood.
price range: B

producer: Pedrizzetti Winery
classification: Red varietal table wine
grape variety: Petite Sirah
district: Santa Clara Valley
city or village: Morgan Hill

This true estate-bottled wine is made entirely from grapes grown adjacent to the winery.

The color is deep purple-red, and the wine is clear though deeply colored. It has a very grapey, vinous bouquet; in character it is huge and robust, yet the finish is soft and lingering. Although ready to drink now, this wine has a potential layaway life of seven to ten years.
price range: B

producer: Pedrizzetti Winery
classification: White varietal table wine
grape variety: Chenin Blanc
district: Monterey and Santa Barbara counties

The coastal counties of Monterey and Santa Barbara are the future premium wine-growing areas for California.

A pale straw color. Clear and clean in appearance, the wine has a very fragrant nose—like ripe grapes. This grape has the "Monterey nose," that is, characteristics of the Monterey County region. It is different from any other Chenin Blanc grown in California.
price range: A

producer: Pedrizzetti Winery
classification: White varietal table wine
grape variety: Chardonnay

These grapes are from a new California growing area, Santa Maria, in Santa Barbara County. Big things are expected from this area. Watch for it on labels.

A pale gold color. Clear and clean in appearance, the wine has definite varietal characteristics. It is crisp, clean, and true to white Burgundy. This rare white wine has tremendous potential: it may be consumed now or left to improve for two to five years.
price range: B

producer: Pedrizzetti Winery
classification: Rosé varietal table wine
grape variety: Zinfandel
district: Santa Clara Valley
city or village: Morgan Hill
This true estate-bottled wine is made from grapes grown immediately adjacent to the winery in Morgan Hill, California.
A pale pink, clear, and definite rosé color. The bouquet is very faint and elusive; the wine is soft, clean, and has a light varietal taste. This rosé is made entirely from the juice of the Zinfandel grape, left on the skins long enough to attain the desired color and taste. **price range:** A

producer: Pedrizzetti Winery
classification: White varietal table wine
grape variety: Johannisberg Riesling
This wine was crushed in late November 1975, finished and bottled in March 1976. The grapes are from the Gonzales area in Monterey County, a new grape-growing area in California. As the vineyards lie very near the Pacific Ocean, the taste of the sea breezes is very evident in the grapes.
A pale gold, brilliant straw color. The bouquet shows strong varietal characteristics; the taste is very assertive, slightly sweet, and lingering. This Johannisberg Riesling is typical of the grapes from Monterey County and must not be compared to the same varietal grown elsewhere in the state. **price range:** A

producer: J. Pedroncelli Winery
classification: White varietal table wine
grape variety: Pinot Chardonnay
district: Sonoma County
city or village: Geyserville
Barrel-aged.
Brilliant light gold color and a bouquet acknowledging barrel age. The wine is dry.
price range: B

producer: J. Pedroncelli Winery
classification: White varietal table wine
grape variety: Johannisberg (White) Riesling
district: Sonoma County
village: Geyserville
Brilliant straw color and a characteristic varietal bouquet. The wine is medium dry.
price range: B

producer: J. Pedroncelli Winery
classification: Red varietal table wine
grape variety: Gamay
district: Sonoma County
city or village: Geyserville
Brilliant light red color and a varietal bouquet. The wine is dry. **price range:** A

producer: J. Pedroncelli Winery
classification: Red varietal table wine
grape variety: Pinot Noir
district: Sonoma County
city or village: Geyserville
Barrel-aged.
Clear medium red color and a bouquet acknowledging barrel aging. The wine is dry. **price range:** B

producer: J. Pedroncelli Winery
classification: Red varietal table wine
grape variety: Cabernet Sauvignon
district: Sonoma County
village: Geyserville
Barrel-aged.
Clear dark red color and a varietal bouquet acknowledging barrel aging. The wine is dry. **price range:** B

producer: J. Pedroncelli Winery
classification: Red varietal table wine
grape variety: Zinfandel
district: Sonoma County
city or village: Geyserville
Medium red color and a varietal bouquet. The wine is dry. **price range:** A

producer: J. Pedroncelli Winery
classification: White varietal table wine
grape variety: Chenin Blanc
district: Sonoma County
city or village: Geyserville
Brilliant light yellow color and a varietal bouquet. The wine is low in sugar and fresh-tasting. **price range:** A

producer: Joseph Phelps Vineyards
classification: White varietal table wine
grape variety: Johannisberg Riesling
district: Napa Valley
Wine-maker Walter Schug is a native of Germany's Rheingau district.
A straw-gold color and an intensely fruity bouquet. The wine is crisp and refreshing, with a trace of residual sugar.
price range: B

producer: Joseph Phelps Vineyards
classification: White varietal table wine
grape variety: Gewürztraminer
district: Napa Valley
A pale straw-gold color and a spicy, fruity bouquet. The wine is medium-bodied with a trace of residual sweetness and has a lingering finish. **price range:** B

producer: Joseph Phelps Vineyards
classification: White varietal table wine
grape variety: Chardonnay
district: Napa Valley
Medium golden-hued color and a strong aroma of the varietal enhanced by French oak. The wine is rich, creamy, and full-bodied. **price range:** C

producer: Joseph Phelps Vineyards
classification: White varietal table wine
grape variety: Sauvignon Blanc (100%)
district: Napa Valley
This wine is aged in new Limousin oak and German oak.
Pale yellow color and a grassy bouquet with medium fruit. The wine is medium-bodied, crisp, and austere. **price range:** B

producer: Joseph Phelps Vineyards
classification: Red varietal table wine
grape variety: Cabernet Sauvignon and Merlot
district: Napa Valley
This Cabernet Sauvignon is blended with 10% Merlot for added complexity and is aged in French oak.
Garnet-red color and a strong varietal Cabernet bouquet. The wine is rich and tannic and requires several years of bottle aging. **price range:** C

producer: Joseph Phelps Vineyards
classification: Red varietal table wine
grape variety: Zinfandel
district: Sonoma County
city or village: Dry Creek Benchlands

This wine is made from grapes of an old, nonirrigated vineyard in the red volcanic soil of Sonoma's Dry Creek Valley.

Opaque ruby color with purple edges and an intensely fruity, raspberrylike bouquet with underlying hints of French oak. The wine is full-bodied and quite tannic. **price range:** C

producer: Joseph Phelps Vineyards
classification: Red varietal table wine
grape variety: Zinfandel
district: Napa and Sonoma counties

Unlike Phelps' other Zinfandel, this wine is approximately a fifty/fifty blend of grapes from Napa and Sonoma counties.

Deep ruby color and a raspberry bouquet suggestive of a young Beaujolais. The wine is deep and full-bodied with developing complexity; it is soft, however, with little tannin. **price range:** B

producer: Joseph Phelps Vineyards
classification: Red varietal table wine
grape variety: Pinot Noir
district: Napa Valley

This Pinot Noir was produced from grapes grown in the Yountville benchland vineyard of John Stanton.

Medium tawny color with developing brick edges. The bouquet is fruity, with the slight vanilla component from the new wood. On the palate the wine is medium-bodied and has the typical flavors of Pinot Noir and a satisfying aftertaste.

price range: B

producer: Joseph Phelps Vineyards (Heinemann Mountain Vineyard)
classification: Red varietal table wine
grape variety: Pinot Noir
district: Napa Valley

This wine is the first produce from a dramatic hillside vineyard in the volcanic ash soil of the Mayacamas Range; it is fuller-bodied than Phelps' other Pinot Noir.

A deep garnet color and a big "Pinot Noir" bouquet with rich Limousin oak components. The wine is full-bodied with strong, rich berrylike fruitiness and has good tannin. **price range:** C

producer: Pope Valley Winery (Eagen Vineyards)
classification: Rosé varietal table wine
grape variety: Zinfandel
district: Napa Valley

This Zinfandel rosé was fermented on the skins for ten days without pumping the juice over the cap, a unique method that produces a superior wine. It contains 12% alcohol by volume, 0.68% total acidity, and 5% residual sugar.

Deep pink color and a slight berry bouquet with some spice. The wine is well-balanced in fruit acidity; it is a very pleasant rosé. **price range:** A

producer: Pope Valley Winery
classification: Red table wine
grape variety: Gamay Beaujolais, Pinot Noir, and Petite Sirah
district: Napa Valley
city or village: Yountville

"House Burgundy." Almost French Burgundy in style, this wine contains 0.6% total acidity, 12% alcohol by volume, and good acid-fruit combination.

Light brick-red color and a fruity, Pinot Noir bouquet with some oak. A nice red table wine for everyday use; easy to drink and very dry. **price range:** A

producer: Pope Valley Winery (D'Anneo Vineyard)
classification: White table wine
grape variety: Sauvignon Vert and French Colombard
district: Napa Valley

Medium golden color and a nice apricot bouquet. The wine is slightly sweet but well-balanced and easy to drink. Serve well chilled. **price range:** A

producer: Pope Valley Winery
classification: Red varietal table wine
grape variety: Gamay Beaujolais
district: Napa Valley
city or village: St. Helena

1972 vintage.

A medium-light brick-red color, and a bouquet showing nice Pinot Noir character. This nice, light red wine is comparable to other California Gamays. **price range:** A

producer: Pope Valley Winery
classification: White varietal table wine
grape variety: Semillon and other varieties
district: Napa Valley
city or village: Pope Valley

This is the first wine with this label that has been marketed. Only 600 gallons were produced; the wine has 12.4% alcohol by volume, 1.5% residual sugar, and 0.68% total acid. It is a blend of Semillon, Grey Riesling, Muscat, and French Colombard.

A light green-gold color and a nice fruity bouquet with suggestions of Semillon and Muscat. The wine is slightly sweet, well-balanced, and clean. A very pleasant picnic-type wine; serve very cold.
price range: A

producer: Pope Valley Winery
classification: Red varietal table wine
grape variety: Cabernet Sauvignon and Ruby Cabernet
district: North Coast Counties
city or village: Dry Creek Valley

This is a blend of 80% Sonoma Cabernet Sauvignon and 20% Napa Valley Ruby Cabernet, both from the 1974 vintage. The wine contains 0.62% total acidity and 13.4% alcohol by volume; it is the best currently available from this winery.

Deep red color and an herbaceous bouquet with good fruit and slight wood. The wine is mouth-filling, well-balanced, and smooth, with slight tannin and good fruit. **price range:** A

producer: Rapazzini Winery
classification: White varietal table wine
grape variety: Green Hungarian
district: Santa Clara County

Off-white color and a fruity bouquet. The wine has a touch of sweetness.
price range: A

producer: Rapazzini Winery
classification: White varietal table wine
grape variety: Chenin Blanc

The best semi-dry white wine this winery produces.

Good clear color and a fruity bouquet. The wine is crisp, soft, and excellent.
price range: A

producer: Rapazzini Winery
classification: Red varietal table wine
grape variety: Barbera
district: Santa Clara County
Deep red color and a full bouquet. A soft, excellent red wine. **price range:** A

producer: Rapazzini Winery
classification: Red varietal table wine
grape variety: Zinfandel
district: Santa Clara County
A well-aged, dry red wine.
Clear medium red color and a full bouquet. The wine is well-aged, dry, and full-bodied. **price range:** A

producer: Martin Ray
classification: Red varietal table wine
grape variety: Cabernet Sauvignon
district: Santa Clara County
city or village: Saratoga
This deep, dark bluish-red Cabernet Sauvignon has a very full, herbaceous, eucalyptus bouquet and excellent aging capacity, up to forty years.
price range: E

producer: Martin Ray
classification: Red varietal table wine
grape variety: Pinot Noir

district: Santa Clara County
city or village: Saratoga
This is a full, rich wine with distinct Pinot character. It is brilliant brick red.
price range: E

producer: Martin Ray
classification: White varietal table wine
grape variety: Chardonnay
district: Santa Clara County
city or village: Saratoga
This is a brilliant deep gold Chardonnay, fruity and full of the special characteristics of the grape. **price range:** E

producer: Richert & Sons Winery
classification: Fortified wine
grape variety: Blend
district: Santa Clara
city or village: Morgan Hill
This Cream Sherry is Richert's best-selling wine, and they believe it to be comparable to the finest produced anywhere.
Golden-brown color and a full-bodied, smooth bouquet. The wine is mild, but rich, and creamy smooth. **price range:** B

producer: Ridge Vineyards
classification: Red varietal table wine
grape variety: Cabernet Sauvignon
district: Santa Cruz Mountains—Monte Bello Ridge
city or village: Cupertino
This estate-grown Cabernet Sauvignon is made by traditional Claret techniques to be as full and rich as the vintage will allow. It comes from nonirrigated mountain vineyards and is one of the very best of the 1972 vintage.
A deep red color and a rich Cabernet bouquet complemented by oak aromas. It is a full, rich wine that is complex and long-lingering on the palate.
price range: E

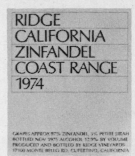

producer: Ridge Vineyards
classification: Red varietal table wine
grape variety: Zinfandel
district: Amador County—Sierra Foothills
city or village: Plymouth—Shenandoah Valley
"Shenandoah." This wine was made from grapes grown from old vines planted in two nonirrigated, neighboring hill vineyards.
A medium red color and a bouquet rich in oak and Zinfandel fruity. The wine is warm, full, and medium-bodied; it needs several years of bottle aging to develop fully. **price range:** C

producer: Ridge Vineyards
classification: Red varietal table wine
grape variety: Petite Sirah
district: Napa Valley—Spring Mountain
city or village: St. Helena—York Creek Vineyard
"York Creek." This wine was made from grapes grown from very old vines planted in a nonirrigated hillside vineyard.
A very deep red color and a peppery varietal bouquet with characteristic spice. The wine is full, heavy, and tannic. It needs aeration; open early or decant before drinking. It is made in the traditional style.
price range: C

producer: Ridge Vineyards
classification: Red varietal table wine
grape variety: Zinfandel
district: Sonoma County
city or village: Geyserville
This wine comes from nonirrigated hill vineyards in Sonoma County planted in old vines and is one of the finest Zinfandels from the 1973 vintage.
A deep red color and a bouquet displaying rich varietal character complemented by oak aging. The wine tastes full and

heavy, but it is smooth with good tannin. It will age very well and needs at least three years' aging after purchase.
price range: C

producer: Ridge Vineyards
classification: Red varietal table wine
grape variety: Zinfandel and Petite Sirah
district: North Coast Counties
"Coast Range." This is Ridge's one Zinfandel blended from grapes grown in different vineyards. The grapes come from a number of nonirrigated hill vineyards in the North Coast Counties. The wine is a blend of 97% Zinfandel and 3% Petite Sirah.
A medium red color and a bouquet characteristic of Zinfandel fruit with oak overtones. The wine tastes round, full, and well-balanced. It can be enjoyed young but will profit from a year or two of bottle age. **price range:** B

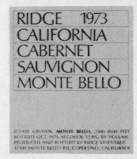

producer: Ridge Vineyards
classification: Red varietal table wine
grape variety: Zinfandel and Petite Sirah
district: Sonoma County
city or village: Lytton
"Lytton Springs." This Zinfandel comes from an old hill vineyard that has two grape varieties interplanted. The few Petite Sirah vines add complexity and tannin to the Zinfandel, and the final percentage is 96% Zinfandel to 4% Petite Sirah. 1973 vintage.
A deep red color and a peppery bouquet with Zinfandel fruit. The wine is rich, full, and complex. **price range:** C

producer: Ridge Vineyards
classification: Red varietal table wine
grape variety: Cabernet Sauvignon (100%)
district: Santa Cruz Mountains
city or village: Monte Bello Ridge

These estate-grown grapes are planted in light, nonirrigated soils that limit production to about two tons per acre. The wine is fermented approximately eighteen days on the skins, then a complete malolactic fermentation follows. The wine is subsequently aged for two years in small cooperage.

Medium dark red color and a fine bouquet with Cabernet fruit and oak overtones. The wine has good fruit, medium tannin, and a good finish; it is an excellent example of a full, complex, and medium-bodied Cabernet that will need at least five years of bottle aging to show its potential.
price range: D

producer: Carlo Rossi Vineyards (Gallo Winery)
classification: Rosé table wine
A durable rosé wine that many enjoy with light meats, poultry, and fish.
Brilliant pink color and a clean, fruity bouquet. The wine has a berrylike flavor, is crisp, and has a pleasant finish.
price range: A

producer: Carlo Rossi Vineyards
classification: White table wine
A crisp, bracing white wine that may be enjoyed before, during, or after a light meal.
Brilliant pale gold color and a refreshing, grapey bouquet. The wine is a well-rounded combination of mellowness and tartness.
price range: A

producer: Roudon-Smith Vineyards
classification: White varietal table wine
grape variety: Sauvignon Blanc
district: San Benito County
city or village: Hollister

This vintage-dated Sauvignon Blanc was aged half in French Limousin oak and half in Canadian oak, each providing a distinctive character.

Straw to light gold color and a bouquet with a full aroma of gardenias. On the palate the wine is big, full, and oaky, characteristic of the varietal; it is suggested that it be opened sometime before serving in order to "breathe."
price range: B

producer: Roudon-Smith Vineyards
classification: White varietal table wine
grape variety: Chardonnay
district: North Coast Counties
city or village: San Luis Obispo

Medium gold color and a flowery bouquet with hints of oak. On the palate the wine is full, round, and sturdy; it is a big Chardonnay, with initial fruit that gives way to huge body and distinctive varietal character.
price range: C

producer: Roudon-Smith Vineyards
classification: Red varietal table wine
grape variety: Pinot Noir
district: Santa Cruz County
city or village: Vinehill

Additional bottle aging is suggested. Deep russet-red color and a bouquet with considerable fruit. Oak underlies the fruit flavor.
price range: C

producer: Russian River Vineyards
classification: Red varietal table wine
grape variety: Zinfandel, Cabernet, and Merlot
district: Sonoma County
city or village: Forestville (Russian River)

This wine is a blend of Zinfandels of the 1967 and 1968 vintages, with a 20% blend of Cabernet and Merlot for added freshness, interest, and complexity.

Magenta color and a fresh, fruity bouquet. It is a full-bodied Zinfandel.
price range: B

producer: Russian River Vineyards
classification: White varietal table wine
grape variety: Chardonnay (100%)
district: Sonoma County
city or village: Forestville (Russian River)

This Chardonnay is from a tributary-nestled vineyard.

Golden straw color and an intense varietal bouquet. The wine is full-bodied and shows river-country character.
price range: B

producer: Russian River Vineyards
classification: Red varietal table wine
grape variety: Cabernet Sauvignon
district: Sonoma County
city or village: Forestville (Russian River)

This wine comes from the rich bottom-land of the wine country's most famous river.

A deep garnet color and a forceful bouquet. The wine is light, with a European character reminiscent of St. Julien.
price range: B

producer: Santa Barbara Winery
classification: White varietal table wine
grape variety: Pinot Chardonnay
district: Central Coast

The grapes are crushed in the field, then cold fermented at 45 degrees F. The wine is then aged eight months in Yugoslavian oak.

This is a smooth, well-balanced Pinot Chardonnay with a fresh varietal scent and brilliant light gold appearance. It is a nice, fresh wine.
price range: A

producer: Santa Barbara Winery
classification: Rosé table wine
grape variety: Pinot Noir and Chardonnay
district: Santa Barbara County—Santa Ynez Valley
city or village: Solvang

This wine is a blend of 80% Pinot Noir and 20% Chardonnay.

This clear, light rosé is smooth to the palate, with the Chardonnay flavor quite distinct. Its bouquet is soft and fruity. This is a very pleasant wine.
price range: A

producer: V. Sattui Winery
classification: Red varietal table wine
grape variety: Zinfandel (100%)
district: Napa Valley
city or village: St. Helena

1973 vintage. This wine is unfined and unfiltered. The grapes come from forty-year-old vines, and the wine is aged in American oak for twenty-five months before bottling. The wines are sold only at the winery; there is no distributing agent.

Red color with brownish tinges; a fruity bouquet suggesting peppermint. The wine is medium-bodied, fruity, and has many complex flavors; it is typical of a good Napa Valley Zinfandel.
price range: B

producer: V. Sattui Winery
classification: Red varietal table wine
grape variety: Cabernet Sauvignon (100%)
district: Napa Valley
city or village: St. Helena

1973 vintage. This wine is unfined and is aged in French Nevers oak for twenty-five months before bottling. The wines are sold only at the winery; there is no distributing agent.

Medium dark red color with brownish tinges and a typical Napa Valley Cabernet Sauvignon nose. The wine is fruity, has many complex flavors, and is true to its type.
price range: B

producer: Ste. Claire Vintners
classification: Red sparkling wine
district: Central Valley
city or village: Acampo
"Sparkling Burgundy" fermented by the Charmet (bulk) process.
Brilliant dark red color and a fruity bouquet and flavor. **price range:** A

producer: Ste. Claire Vintners
classification: Red table wine
district: Central Valley
city or village: Acampo
"Burgundy."
Medium red color; an astringent, full-bodied wine. **price range:** A

producer: Ste. Claire Vintners
classification: White table wine
grape variety: Blend
district: San Joaquin Valley
city or village: Acampo
Straw color and a vinous, fruity bouquet. The wine is fruity and slightly sweet.
price range: A

producer: San Martin Vineyards
classification: White varietal table wine
grape variety: Chenin Blanc
district: Monterey County

This wine comes from 117 acres planted in Chenin Blanc grapes in the foothills of the Santa Lucia Mountains in Monterey County. It is produced by the cold fermentation process, filtered for brilliance, then allowed to settle. It should be enjoyed when it is very young.
Brilliant pale gold color with slight spritz and a big, fruity varietal bouquet. The wine is clean, crisp, and medium sweet, with good acid balance. It is a perfect wine with meals. **price range:** A

producer: San Martin Vineyards
classification: White varietal table wine
grape variety: Johannisberg Riesling
district: Santa Barbara County—Santa Clara Valley

This distinguished wine is cold-fermented in order to preserve its fruitiness. After filtering for brilliance, it is aged in German white-oak casks in order to develop a rich quality prized by many wine connoisseurs. It should be considered the standard of excellence for this grape variety.
Clear pale straw color and a very fruity bouquet characteristic of the variety with a suggestion of Botrytis mold. The wine is fresh, dry, crisp, and fruity; it is extremely well-made. **price range:** B

producer: San Martin Vineyards
classification: Fortified wine
grape variety: Montonico
district: Santa Clara Valley

The small (8.4 acres) planting of Montonico in Santa Clara is believed to be the only planting of this grape on the continent. Cuttings were first brought from Calabria, Italy, in the province of Cosenza in 1938, and the present vineyard was planted in 1949. This wine has been aged since 1967 in 11,000-gallon American white oak; it has not been heated or "baked" as are most inexpensive Sherries. It was used in Sherry blending until 1973 when it was found to be an unusual and well-balanced wine unblended. This wine is often called "Wine of the Saints" because of its long aging process.
Light amber color with tints of orange; a light bouquet blending honey, mint, and oranges. The wine is sweet, light-bodied, and very fruity; although a dessert wine, it is not similar to Sherries and stands alone, unique. **price range:** C

producer: San Martin Vineyards
classification: Red varietal table wine
grape variety: Grignolino
district: Santa Clara Valley

This wine is made in the classic Italian tradition and is aged in small oak barrels before bottling.
Light red color browning at the edges and a fruity nose with subdued oak. The wine is slightly tart and has tannin; it is ready to enjoy immediately with pasta.
price range: A

producer: San Martin Vineyards
classification: Red varietal table wine
grape variety: Pinot Noir
district: Santa Clara Valley

This wine was produced from grapes grown in the ideal climate and soil of the Santa Clara Valley. It was matured in small oak barrels before bottling, and is ready to drink now.
Deep ruby color and a full varietal aroma that develops complexities. The wine is full in the mouth, with good acid balance, and is smooth and soft. It is a very well made example of this variety. **price range:** B

producer: San Martin Vineyards
classification: Red varietal table wine
grape variety: Cabernet Sauvignon
district: Santa Clara Valley

Probably no locale in the North Coast region is more favored than the San Ysidro Vineyards, the source of this great wine. The warmth of the Santa Clara Valley is tempered by cool breezes off Monterey Bay and favors the growing of classic varietal grapes. This wine was a bright spot among generally poor 1972 vintage Cabernet Sauvignons.
Medium to dark ruby color with brown edges; a strong varietal bouquet with a balance of wood and spice. The wine is soft in the mouth, with medium tannin and good varietal flavor. **price range:** B

"Wine is light, held together by water." —Galileo

producer: San Martin Vineyards
classification: Red varietal table wine
grape variety: Ruby Cabernet
district: Santa Clara Valley

This wine comes from a fairly new hybrid grape variety developed in California, though its proud heritage is very evident. The wine is matured in small oak barrels before bottling.
Brilliant, "thick" deep red color and a big bouquet with a characteristic "spicy" quality. The wine is big in the mouth, with a spicy, complex flavor and lots of tannin to assure good aging potential.
price range: A

---

*"I tasted—careless—then.
I did not know the wine.
Came once a world—did
you?
Oh, had you told me so,
This thirst would blister
easier now!"*

—Emily Dickinson

producer: San Martin Vineyards
classification: White varietal table wine
grape variety: Emerald Riesling
district: Santa Clara Valley

The Emerald Riesling is a unique grape variety developed in California from a cross between the Johannisberg Riesling and the Muscadelle. A light, fragrant wine, it is cold-fermented to preserve its youthful qualities.

Pale straw color with hints of gold and a clean, fruity bouquet with vinous character. The wine is tart, slightly sweet, and well-balanced, characteristic of the varietal; it is a pleasant "picnic" wine. **price range:** A

producer: San Martin Vineyards
classification: White varietal table wine
grape variety: Pinot Chardonnay
district: Monterey County—Santa Clara Valley

This limited vintage is produced from selected Pinot Chardonnay grapes grown in the Santa Clara Valley and Monterey County vineyards. There the grape matures with an unusual "earthy" quality and is blessed by an ideal combination of sun, soil, and sea breezes. Although completely dry, it gives an impression of sweetness from a high level of glycerin.

Brilliant medium straw color and a bouquet with good balance of wood and fruit. The wine has good acid, is dry and fairly big; although still in its youth, it should still develop. **price range:** B

producer: Schramsberg Vineyards
classification: White varietal table wine
grape variety: Pinot Noir (blanc) and Chardonnay
district: Napa Valley

This is a still white wine made from a Champagne base in a most unusual style. Not really directly comparable with other wines, it is a specialty.

A pale gold, limpid color and a complex bouquet dominated by Pinot Noir. The wine is very dry and has high acidity; it is really a wine to be enjoyed with food, not sipped. **price range:** C

producer: Schramsberg Vineyards
classification: White sparkling wine
grape variety: Pinot Noir and Chardonnay
district: Napa Valley

This wine is sold as a "Blanc de Noirs," a white wine made from black grapes. It is marketed three to four years after the vintage and is bottle-fermented.

A gold color with a very complex bouquet of fruit and yeast. Quite dry, it is medium in body and has good fruit and acidity. **price range:** E

producer: Schramsberg Vineyards
classification: Pink sparkling wine
grape variety: Napa Gamay and Pinot Noir
district: Napa Valley

"Cuvée de Gamay." This wine is colored by a very brief contact with the skins while fermenting. Bottle-fermented, it is sold eight months after the vintage.

Light salmon or peach color, clear and limpid. The bouquet is spicy, with good fruit; on the palate it is dry, with spice and fruit. **price range:** C

producer: Schramsberg Vineyards
classification: White sparkling wine
grape variety: Chardonnay and Pinot Blanc
district: Napa Valley

A "Blanc de Blancs," this wine is made exclusively from white grapes. Bottle-fermented, it is sold two to three years after the vintage.

A light gold color with green tints. The complex bouquet blends Chardonnay, Pinot Blanc, and yeast; on the palate the wine is dry, with medium to high acidity. **price range:** D

producer: Sebastiani Vineyards
classification: Red table wine
grape variety: Blend of mostly Zinfandel, Carignane, and Petite Sirah
district: North Coast Counties

"Sebastiani Burgundy." The Sebastianis have made this name into almost a proprietary brand by producing very big, full-flavored "Burgundies" consistently over a number of years. They believe that it is a combination of outstanding grapes and proper aging that are responsible. This is one of several wines selected for aging in the Sebastiani cellars, which house a collection of 5,000 American white oak barrels with a capacity of 50 gallons each.

Deep garnet-red color with slight tawny tinges and a full, round, smooth, and complex bouquet. The wine is very full-flavored, complex, and smooth; it is full-bodied not only in color but also in taste, and has a very smooth, flavorful finish. The

spiciness of the grapes is rounded out by aging in casks. **price range:** A

producer: Sebastiani Vineyards
classification: Red varietal table wine
grape variety: Cabernet Sauvignon
district: North Coast Counties

Prior to its release in 1974, the Sebastiani Cabernet Sauvignon 1968 spent three years in redwood casks, one year in oak, and one in bottle. Total acidity at the time of bottling, 0.609; volatile acidity at bottling, 0.071; residual sugar at bottling, 0.19.

Garnet-red color with tawny tinges and a smooth, complex Cabernet bouquet with a light touch of smoothness given by oak. The wine is smooth and soft on the palate, a perfectly balanced Cabernet Sauvignon with proper aging and just enough oak to blend perfectly with the Cabernet varietal flavor. **price range:** C

producer: Sebastiani Vineyards
classification: Rosé varietal table wine
grape variety: Pinot Noir
district: North Coast Counties

"White of Reds" is a "partridge eye" wine; the slight pink color is extracted from the grape skins during fermentation, the result of a short time when the juice was left on the skins and seeds of the grapes. The color is quite unusual. The grapes were hand-picked at 24.9% Brix; the wine at the time of bottling had 0.65 total acidity 0.15 residual sugar, and 13.8% alcohol by volume.

Partridge eye, suggesting opalescent pale copper color, and aroma evident of the grape—spicy. The wine tastes young and zesty, with good Pinot Noir flavor and a great deal of fruitiness—very zesty for a Pinot Noir. It is a uniquely young and spry wine with an interesting combination of red and white wine characteristics. **price range:** B

producer: Sebastiani Vineyards
classification: Red varietal table wine
grape variety: Gamay Beaujolais
district: North Coast Counties

Sebastiani Gamay Beaujolais Nouveau was the first wine of this type produced in California. In 1972, Sebastiani Vineyards brought a tradition from France to the United States, and an annual festival in Sonoma has announced its release ever since. The young, piquant flavor of this wine is vastly different from the flavor of most older wines, and it is meant to be consumed within a few months after its release.

Deep purplish-red color and a light, almost indescribable bouquet. On the palate the wine is sprightly, lively, and young, with a flavor strongly reminiscent of the grape—clean and berrylike. **price range:** B

producer: Sebastiani Vineyards
classification: Red varietal table wine
grape variety: Barbera
district: North Coast Counties

For years, the Sebastiani Vineyards in Sonoma have made a varietal Barbera their specialty. As with the Sebastiani family, the Barbera grape originally came from Italy, and for years the Sebastianis have offered outstanding Barberas. In every single year between 1953 and 1975 the Sebastianis have won an award for their Barbera, including seventeen gold medals at the Los Angeles county fair.

Deep red color and a typical, attractive bouquet showing Barbera spiciness. On the palate the wine is very smooth and soft, with a pleasant woody character. An outstanding Barbera, it is enjoyable either when released or after further bottle aging. **price range:** B

producer: Sebastiani Vineyards
classification: Fortified wine
grape variety: Palomino
district: Northern California

Amore Cream Sherry is aged in the Sebastiani Solera Terrace, where dessert wines are placed in 50-gallon oak barrels. The sun evaporates moisture out of the wines, making them creamier and richer while caramelizing their natural sugars to a golden-brown color.

Deep, caramel-gold color and a smooth, sweet bouquet. On the palate the wine is creamy, smooth, and sweet, with a perfectly rounded texture from bouquet to taste and then to finish. It is an excellent dessert complement to nuts, cheeses, and fresh fruit. **price range:** B

producer: Sebastiani Vineyards
classification: White varietal table wine
grape variety: Green Hungarian
district: North Coast Counties

For several years, Green Hungarian has been the Sebastianis' best-selling wine. It is now fermented in stainless-steel tanks installed in the winery's new cold-fermentation cellar, allowing the light aromas of the grape to be preserved in the wine.

Pale clear straw color and a very fragrant, flowery bouquet. On the palate the wine is light and delicate, semi-dry with a slight touch of sweetness. It would be of interest to white-wine drinkers who draw fine lines between degrees of sweetness in wines.　　**price range:** A

producer: Sebastiani Vineyards
classification: Fortified wine
district: Northern California

Arenas,Dry Sherry is aged in the Sebastiani Solera Terrace, where dessert wines are placed in 50-gallon oak barrels. The sun evaporates moisture out of the wines, making them creamier and richer while caramelizing their natural sugars to a golden-brown color.

Pale golden color and a slightly nutty bouquet that retains good fruit. On the palate the wine is clean and nutty; it is not completely bone dry, but tart with the slightest touch of sweetness. It is excellent when served chilled, allowing its clean finish and balanced fruitiness to show through.　　**price range:** B

producer: Sebastiani Vineyards
classification: Red varietal table wine
grape variety: Pinot Noir
district: North Coast Counties

The grapes for Sebastiani Pinot Noir come from the Sonoma Valley with cool (region 1) temperatures. Aged for three years in redwood casks, six months in American white oak casks, and three months in bottle prior to release, the wine should become even more interesting after further bottle aging and should be quite long-lived.

Deep, tawny-red color and a pungent varietal bouquet showing the smoothness of prolonged aging. The wine is very round, full, and soft on the palate, with the slight characteristic spiciness of Pinot Noir. A Pinot Noir made in the California style rather than the French style, it makes an excellent impression on the palate, with a long taste and good tannin.
price range: C

producer: Sebastiani Vineyards
classification: White varietal table wine
grape variety: Chenin Blanc
district: North Coast Counties

The 1975 vintage Chenin Blanc was the first that Sebastiani produced in their new cold-fermentation cellar for white wines. Its light, fresh, and clean taste and intense character are a result of cold fermentation in stainless steel tanks. It has 3.0 reducing sugar and considerable fruitiness.

Pale, clear color with faint pink tinges and a sweet, pronounced fruity bouquet. On the palate the wine shows smooth sweetness and a clean, lingering varietal character. Its fresh, clean taste makes it highly recommended, and it is suggested that it be chilled even colder than normal in order that it display all its qualities.
price range: A

producer: Sebastiani Vineyards
classification: White varietal table wine
grape variety: Gewürztraminer
district: Sonoma County

Sebastiani's copper-hued Traminer grapes come largely from a hillside vineyard set deep in the Sonoma foothills overlooking the Sonoma Valley vineyards. *Gewürz* means "spicy" in German, and the clean, spicy fruit taste of this wine is characteristic of the varietal, which is native to Alsace. The wine is well complemented by 2.5 reducing sugar.

Pale straw color and a very spicy bouquet carrying into the flavor, blended with some residual sweetness. The clean, spicy taste is uniquely Gewürztraminer; it is an outstanding sipping wine when served chilled, as well as being an ideal complement to virtually any seafood or fowl dish.　　**price range:** B

producer: Robert Setrakian Vineyards
classification: Fortified wine
grape variety: Predominantly Palomino
city or village: Yettem

This is a well-aged and masterfully finished dry Solera Sherry of the same premium class as the award-winning Solera Cream Sherry from Robert Setrakian Vineyards. It is of clear, medium golden-amber color and has a nutty, well-aged, and well-developed Sherry character.

This fine dry Sherry is made after the famous three-tier Solera process, as are all the premium Setrakian Ports and Sherries.
price range: B

producer: Robert Setrakian Vineyards
classification: Rosé varietal table wine
grape variety: Grenache
city or village: Yettem

This clear pink, orange-tinted wine is extremely light in body, clean, fresh and crisp with delicately fruity undertones.

The wine won a gold medal at the 1976 California wine judging at Los Angeles.
price range: below A

producer: Robert Setrakian Vineyards
classification: Red varietal table wine
grape variety: Cabernet Sauvignon
city or village: Yettem

This classic Claret has a brilliant and clear appearance. Its very pleasant and complex aroma reflects superior quality and maturity; it is robust, flavorful, and well-balanced. Always properly aged at the winery, it is ready to be enjoyed immediately.　　**price range:** below A

producer: Robert Setrakian Vineyards
classification: White sparkling wine
grape variety: French Colombard and Chenin Blanc
city or village: Yettem

This premium Champagne is a truly dry sparkling wine and a perfect blend of crisp, clean, and fruity characteristics that makes it enjoyable for any occasion and with any food. The wine has good acidity and body and is well-balanced; it has a fresh, fruity bouquet.

This Champagne received the distinction of an honorable mention at the 1976 California wine judging at Los Angeles. The wine has cork-finish and a very distinguishable private mold bottle.
price range: B

producer: Robert Setrakian Vineyards
classification: White varietal table wine
grape variety: Johannisberg Riesling
city or village: Yettem

This is a true white Riesling with all the piquantly fresh fruity characteristics of this premium varietal. The wine is dry and medium-bodied and should be drunk young.　　**price range:** below A

producer: Robert Setrakian Vineyards
classification: Red varietal table wine
grape variety: Ruby Cabernet
city or village: Yettem

The brilliant and clear appearance of this wine anticipates the clean, fresh bouquet and smooth, well-balanced taste. The bouquet is grapey and complex; to the palate the wine is full-bodied and mature.

This wine received honorable mention at the 1976 California wine judging in Los Angeles, for excellence in its classification.　　**price range:** below A

producer: Robert Setrakian Vineyards
classification: Fortified wine
grape variety: Predominantly Mission
city or village: Yettem

This is an outstanding, rich, full-bodied, and flavorful Solera-processed Cream Sherry. The bouquet is rich and well aged, with the distinct character of sherry.

This was a silver-medal winner in its first participation in the 1976 California wine judging at Los Angeles. The distinctive private-mold bottle contains premium three-tier Solera blended Cream Sherry comparable to the finest.　　**price range:** B

producer: Robert Setrakian Vineyards
classification: Fortified wine
grape variety: Predominantly Carignane
city or village: Yettem
  This is a true Port wine, full-bodied and rich, with a mature, well-aged bouquet. Its tawny color has a reddish tint. A three-tier Solera-blended wine. **price range:** B

producer: Silveroak Cellars
classification: Red varietal table wine
grape variety: Cabernet Sauvignon
district: Napa Valley
city or village: Oakville
  1972 vintage.
  Brilliant medium red color and an herbaceous varietal bouquet with some oak. The wine is smooth and light, typical of the variety in the vintage. **price range:** C

producer: Simi Winery
classification: **Red varietal table wine**
grape variety: **Gamay Beaujolais**
district: **Sonoma County—Alexander Valley**
city or village: **Healdsburg**
  Ruby-red color and a fruity, elegant bouquet. The wine's complex flavors show the superb influence of soil and climate, and the finish is long. **price range:** A

producer: Simi Winery
classification: Red varietal table wine
grape variety: Pinot Noir

---

district: Sonoma County—Alexander Valley
city or village: Healdsburg
  Medium red color and a "gentle" bouquet. The wine is a delicate composition of clean, nonaggressive flavors and is easy to drink. **price range:** B

producer: Simi Winery
classification: Red varietal table wine
grape variety: Zinfandel
district: Sonoma County
city or village: Healdsburg
  Deep red color and a delightful, full "raspberry" bouquet. The wine has strong Zinfandel character and is fruity.
price range: B

producer: Simi Winery
classification: Rosé varietal table wine
grape variety: Cabernet Sauvignon
district: Sonoma County—Alexander Valley
city or village: Healdsburg
  Dark pink color and a very fruity varietal bouquet. The wine has full varietal flavor and is fresh-tasting. **price range:** B

producer: Simi Winery
classification: White varietal table wine
grape variety: Gewürztraminer
district: Sonoma County—Alexander Valley
city or village: Healdsburg
  Pale straw color with slight green tinges and a fruity, spicy bouquet. The wine has an excellent balance of sweetness and acidity and shows potential for long life.
price range: B

producer: Simi Winery
classification: White varietal table wine
grape variety: Johannisberg Riesling
district: Sonoma County—Alexander Valley
city or village: Healdsburg
  Pale straw color and a bouquet reminiscent of green apples (malic acid). The wine is smooth and soft, with a mellow flavor and an excellent finish; it is reminiscent of a Rhine wine. **price range:** B

producer: Simi Winery
classification: White varietal table wine
grape variety: Chardonnay
district: Sonoma County—Alexander Valley
city or village: Healdsburg
  Fermented and aged in Limousin oak.
  Clean pale gold color and a delicate varietal bouquet. The wine is fresh and round, with a slight fruity flavor.
price range: B

producer: Sonoma Vineyards
classification: Red varietal table wine
grape variety: Petite Sirah
  Ruby-red color and a woody, varietal bouquet. The wine is rich and velvety, very characteristic of the varietal and typically "hearty drinking" in style. It is well-aged and ready to drink when shipped.
price range: A

producer: Sonoma Vineyards
classification: White varietal table wine
grape variety: Johannisberg Riesling
  Light straw-yellow color and a fruity, rich bouquet that is true to type. The wine is

---

light, elegant, and slightly sweet; it retains a natural sweetness characteristic of Rieslings. Although enjoyable and drinkable now, it will mature even further.
price range: B

producer: Sonoma Vineyards
classification: White varietal table wine
grape variety: French Colombard
  Medium yellow color and a light, fresh French Colombard nose. On the palate the wine is semi-dry and rather rich for its type. It is an excellent Chablis-type wine.
price range: A

producer: Sonoma Vineyards
classification: Red varietal table wine
grape variety: Ruby Cabernet
district: North Coast Counties
  Dark ruby color and a very woody, varietal bouquet. The wine is rich, smooth, and woody, excellent for drinking now.
price range: A

producer: Sonoma Vineyards
classification: Red varietal table wine
grape variety: Zinfandel
  Medium red color and a fruity, well-aged bouquet characteristic of Zinfandel. On the palate the wine is rich, well-aged in wood; it is not overly tannic but has great aging ability. **price range:** A

producer: Sonoma Vineyards
classification: Red varietal table wine
grape variety: Cabernet Sauvignon
district: Sonoma County
  A well-aged, Claret-type wine.
  Brick-red color and a very smooth, woody flavor. It is a wine to drink now, at the peak of its development. **price range:** B

producer: Sonoma Vineyards
classification: White varietal table wine
grape variety: Pinot Chardonnay

The dark color of this wine comes from contact with the skins during fermentation to give it added varietal character.

Straw color and a rich varietal bouquet blended with ample wood. On the palate it is a rich, chewy wine with ample body; it is well-aged and characteristic of the varietal. **price range:** B

producer: Sonoma Vineyards
classification: Rosé varietal table wine
grape variety: Grenache
A naturally sweet Grenache, ready to drink when shipped.

Medium pink color and a characteristic Grenache bouquet—light and fruity. The wine is light, fruity, and slightly sweet.
price range: A

producer: Sonoma Vineyards
classification: Red varietal table wine
grape variety: Zinfandel
district: Sonoma County
Brick-red color and a well-aged bouquet typical of the varietal. The wine is mature and sophisticated; ready to drink, it shows all the characteristics of a well-aged Zinfandel. **price range:** B

producer: Sonoma Vineyards
classification: Red varietal table wine
grape variety: Pinot Noir
district: Sonoma County
A rich, deep wine made in the classical Pinot Noir style.

Medium red color and a woody, sophisticated bouquet that is true to type. The wine is rich, woody, and smooth—typical of the varietal; it has substantial tannin and wood for further aging but is excellent to drink now. **price range:** B

producer: Sotoyome Winery
classification: Red table wine
grape variety: Gamay and Cabernet Sauvignon

district: Sonoma County
city or village: Healdsburg
An unfiltered wine containing about 20% Cabernet Sauvignon.

Medium red color; a light-bodied, flavorful red wine. **price range:** A

producer: Sotoyome Winery
classification: Red varietal table wine
grape variety: Cabernet Sauvignon (100%)
district: Sonoma County
city or village: Healdsburg
Produced from grapes grown in the Dry Creek area in Sonoma County.

Medium red color and a fruity bouquet.
price range: B

producer: Sotoyome Winery
classification: Red varietal table wine
grape variety: Zinfandel and Petite Sirah
district: Sonoma County
city or village: Healdsburg
A nonvintage blend of 1974 and 1975 Zinfandels. The grapes came from fully mature vines, many over forty years old. About 10% Petite Sirah was used in the blend, which was unfiltered.

Dark red color; the wine is medium-bodied and full-flavored.
price range: A

producer: Souverain of Alexander Valley
classification: Red varietal table wine
grape variety: Gamay Beaujolais (100%)
district: Sonoma County
city or village: Geyserville

This wine was made from both Sonoma and Mendocino county grapes, hence its "North Coast" designation. In some vintages the method of carbonic maceration is used, by which the grapes ferment slightly before crushing; this can be discerned in the aromatic, rather ethereal bouquet.

Medium ruby-red color and a fresh, typically varietal bouquet often similar to wild cherries. The wine is fruity and has a medium-light body with some tannin; it is meant to be drunk while it is still young and fresh. **price range:** A

producer: Souverain of Alexander Valley
classification: Red varietal table wine
grape variety: Pinot Noir (100%)
district: Sonoma County
city or village: Geyserville
This is an outstanding example of a Pinot Noir made from carefully selected grapes grown in superior micro-climates for Pinot Noir in the Sonoma-Mendocino area. The grapes came from certified virus-free vines, and the wine was matured in French and Yugoslavian oak barrels. Pinot Noir is normally a difficult variety to grow in California.

Brilliant deep garnet color and a distinctive Pinot Noir bouquet with attractive fruit. The wine is soft and elegant to the taste, with considerable finesse. **price range:** B

producer: Souverain of Alexander Valley
clasification: White varietal table wine
grape variety: Chardonnay (100%)
district: Sonoma County
city or village: Geyserville
Like all Souverain wines, this Chardonnay was cold-fermented for about six weeks at about 50–55 degrees F. and was aged in French Nevers oak barrels. Because the grapes were fully ripe at the time of picking, it is high in alcohol and rich in grape extracts.

Rich yellow-green color and a characteristic "white sage" aroma typical of Chardonnay, with a hint of oak from the casks. The wine is dry, rounded, and full-bodied—a superb example of a "big style" Chardonnay. If properly stored, it should age very well. **price range:** B

producer: Souverain of Alexander Valley
classification: Red table wine
grape variety: Blend
district: Sonoma County
city or village: Geyserville
This versatile generic red "Burgundy" was made from grapes grown in Sonoma and Mendocino counties, hence its "North Coast" classification. Various premium red grape varieties were used in making it, and the wine was aged in oak; it is now ready to drink.

Medium dark red color with brick overtones and a bouquet showing good aging and distinction. The wine is well-balanced and well-aged, with good tannin.
price range: A

producer: Souverain of Alexander Valley
classification: Red varietal table wine
grape variety: Cabernet Sauvignon (100%)
district: Sonoma County
city or village: Geyserville
This classic Claret-type wine was made from grapes grown in the Alexander Valley, Sonoma County, with some grapes from Mendocino County as well. It was matured in small Yugoslavian oak barrels until bottling, and though drinkable, will continue to improve for several years.

Deep garnet color with brick-red overtones and a typical bouquet of Cabernet suggestive of green peppers. The wine combines full body with good tannin and has a long finish. **price range:** B

producer: Souverain of Alexander Valley
classification: Red varietal table wine
grape variety: Petite Sirah

district: Sonoma County
city or village: Geyserville

This full-bodied red wine was matured in small oak casks, mostly American white oak. Though drinkable when released, it should age well.

Deep red color with purple overtones and an intense bouquet suggestive of berries, with distinct oak aromas. The wine is full-bodied, with good acid and tannin; it is good with hearty meals such as steak or venison or with game dishes.

price range: A

producer: Souverain of Alexander Valley
classification: White varietal table wine
grape variety: Johannisberg Riesling (100%)
district: Sonoma County
village: Geyserville

This Johannisberg Riesling was made from fully mature vines, partly in the Alexander Valley district of Sonoma County and partly in Mendocino. Slow, cold fermentation resulted in a small amount of residual sugar in the wine; it will continue to develop and age well in the bottle.

Brilliant light yellow-green color and a classic Riesling bouquet with much fruit. The wine is well-balanced with good acidity and a hint of sweetness. **price range:** B

producer: Souverain of Alexander Valley
classification: White varietal table wine
grape variety: Grey Riesling
district: Mendocino County
city or village: Geyserville

This grape variety is known as *Chauche Gris* in France, but because of the attractive gray- to greenish-pink color that the grapes develop at harvest time, it is now known in California as Grey Riesling. This attractive, light white wine was made from choice grapes grown in Mendocino County. It needs no further aging after release for sale.

Brilliant light straw color and a fresh, fruity bouquet. The wine is dry but not austerely so; it is well-balanced, with a nice finish. **price range:** A

producer: Souverain of Alexander Valley
classification: White varietal table wine
grape variety: Green Hungarian
district: Sonoma County
city or village: Geyserville

Lee Stewart, who first founded Souverain Cellars in 1943, was the first wine maker in California to market Green Hungarian wines as a varietal. This wine was matured in 3,000-gallon Yugoslavian oak tanks and is best drunk within three years of the vintage date.

Pale yellow-green color and a fresh bouquet that develops with bottle age. The wine is light, dry, and crisp, ideal with fish or shellfish. **price range:** A

producer: Souverain of Alexander Valley
classification: White varietal table wine
grape variety: French Colombard (Colombard Blanc)
district: Sonoma County
city or village: Geyserville

Cold-fermentation techniques as well as judicious blending of premium Sonoma and Mendocino county grapes give this wine its distinctive characteristics.

Pale straw color and a flowery, fragrant bouquet. The wine has a slight spritz or "petillant" quality; it combines pleasant natural tartness with a slight residual sweetness. It is lively and youthful, uniquely Souverain in style. **price range:** A

producer: Souverain of Alexander Valley
classification: White varietal table wine
grape variety: Chenin Blanc (100%)
district: Sonoma County
city or village: Geyserville

Made from a blend of Sonoma and Mendocino county grapes—hence its "North Coast" designation—this wine was cold-fermented and later matured in 3,000-gallon oak tanks. It is best drunk within three years of the vintage date.

Brilliant light straw-yellow color and a bouquet with a ripe peach fragrance. The wine is dry, soft, and well-balanced, a classic example of a drier Chenin Blanc.

price range: A

producer: Souverain of Alexander Valley
classification: Red varietal table wine
grape variety: Zinfandel
district: Sonoma County
city or village: Geyserville

This is a traditional Sonoma County Zinfandel made in a "big" style entirely from grapes grown in Sonoma and Mendocino counties. The wine was aged in small 60-gallon oak barrels and should age well.

Brilliant dark garnet-red color and a "briar" or "berry" aroma, with good fruit. The wine is robust and full-bodied, with good tannin. **price range:** A

producer: Souverain of Rutherford
classification: White varietal table wine
grape variety: Chardonnay (100%) **district:** Napa Valley
city or village: Rutherford

This elegant Napa Valley Chardonnay was made in the classic way. Only free-run juice was used for the wine, and maturity took place in 60-gallon French Limousin oak barrels prior to bottling.

Brilliant yellow-green color and a classic Chardonnay bouquet with a trace of oak. The wine is dry and full-bodied, with good fruit. While drinkable, it will continue to improve for three to four years if properly stored. **price range:** B

producer: Souverain of Rutherford
classification: Red varietal table wine
grape variety: Cabernet Sauvignon (100%)

district: Napa Valley
city or village: Rutherford

Made entirely from Napa Valley Cabernet Sauvignon grapes, this wine was made only from free-run juice and was matured in 60-gallon French Nevers oak before bottling. It has the body and tannin to age well and will continue to improve in bottle for several years.

Brilliant deep garnet color and a typical Cabernet bouquet. The wine is rich and full-bodied, with good tannin.

price range: B

producer: Souverain of Rutherford
classification: White varietal table wine
grape variety: Johannisberg Riesling (100%)
district: Napa Valley
city or village: Rutherford

Made entirely from free-run juice, this Johannisberg Riesling spent a short time in wood to give its unique Souverain of Rutherford personality. It is fuller-bodied than most German Rieslings but has true varietal character and style.

Light yellow-green color and a true Riesling bouquet with good fruit. The wine is dry, with good acid balance and a hint of spiciness. It should age well for several years if properly stored. **price range:** B

producer: Spring Mountain Vineyards
classification: Red table wine
grape variety: Cabernet Sauvignon, Cabernet Franc, and Merlot
district: Napa Valley
city or village: St. Helena

This big Cabernet has some Pauillac characteristics. The final blend, which may include Petit-Verdot, has not been settled upon but will evolve after a few more vintages.

Brilliant deep red color and a bouquet showing Cabernet character with overtones of raspberries. The wine is full-bodied, with excellent tannin and a suggestion of violets. **price range:** C

bouquet with fruit and a "gunflint" quality typical of this grape. The wine is dry, crisp, and full-bodied—great with fish.

price range: B

producer: Spring Mountain Vineyards
classification: Red varietal table wine
grape variety: Cabernet Franc (100%)
district: Napa Valley
city or village: St. Helena

1973 was the only vintage of this wine, a late-harvest wine with 16.9% alcohol and 0.7% sugar.

Brilliant deep red color and an intense and powerful bouquet. The wine is huge, with plenty of tannin; it could be served with the cheese course, in place of Port.

price range: E

producer: Stag's Leap Winery, Inc.
classification: Red varietal table wine
grape variety: Petite Syrah
district: Napa Valley
city or village: Napa

price range: C

producer: Sterling Vineyards
classification: Rosé varietal table wine
grape variety: Cabernet Sauvignon
district: Napa Valley
city or village: Calistoga

An unusual rosé wine made from a premium red-wine grape variety.

Flame or salmon-pink color and a fruity bouquet in youth that by six months' time shows some Cabernet intensity. The wine is fresh, tart, dry, and flavorful; it is a surprisingly austere and assertive rosé.

price range: B

producer: Sterling Vineyards
classification: Red varietal table wine
grape variety: Merlot
district: Napa Valley
city or village: Calistoga

This wine is made from a variety grown in Bordeaux and is suggestive of a Pomerol. It is somewhat quicker to mature than a Cabernet Sauvignon but tenacious in holding its lovely peak.

Intense ruby-garnet color and a full, flowery and fruity bouquet with good oak. The wine is round, full-flavored, and softly tannic. **price range:** C

producer: Spring Mountain Vineyards
classification: White varietal table wine
grape variety: Chardonnay (100%)
district: Napa Valley
city or village: St. Helena

Beginning in 1976, the vineyard converted to in-field crushing of the grapes, resulting in a wine with greater fragrance and freshness.

Brilliant golden color and an intense varietal bouquet. The wine is full-bodied, huge, and luscious, with ideal balance.

price range: C

producer: Stag's Leap Winery, Inc.
classification: White varietal table wine
grape variety: Chenin Blanc
district: Napa Valley
city or village: Napa

price range: A

producer: Sterling Vineyards
classification: White varietal table wine
grape variety: Sauvignon Blanc
district: Napa Valley
city or village: Calistoga

A dry white wine reminiscent of a Graves, it profits from bottle aging.

Pale gold color and a bouquet rich in pear and grass aromas combined with wood from Nevers oak. The wine is full-bodied and develops full flavors with bottle age. **price range:** B

producer: Sterling Vineyards
classification: White varietal table wine
grape variety: Pinot Chardonnay
district: Napa Valley
city or village: Calistoga

A very complex white wine requiring some bottle aging.

Light gold-green color and a rich bouquet combining apples and "butterscotch" with the aromas of the Limousin oak in which the wine is aged. On the palate the wine is full-bodied, soft, and full-flavored. **price range:** C

producer: Spring Mountain Vineyards
classification: White varietal table wine
grape variety: Sauvignon Blanc with a touch of Chardonnay
district: Napa Valley
city or village: St. Helena

Produced entirely from Spring Mountain's Wildwood vineyards.

Brilliant straw color and a "steely"

producer: Sterling Vineyards
classification: Red varietal table wine
grape variety: Cabernet Sauvignon
district: Napa Valley
city or village: Calistoga

A well-balanced Cabernet Sauvignon in every respect that will age very well to a refined maturity.

Deep garnet-red color and an herbaceous nose showing Cabernet fruit and clean Nevers oak from cask aging. On the palate the wine is balanced with many complex flavors; it is full-bodied and rather tannic. **price range:** C

producer: Sterling Vineyards
classification: Red varietal table wine
grape variety: Pinot Noir
district: Napa Valley
city or village: Calistoga

More than most California Pinot Noirs, this wine requires extensive bottle aging.

Medium to dark ruby color and an intense violet fragrance from both the grapes and the pungent Limousin oak in which the wine is aged. The wine is full-bodied on the palate, moderately tannic, and has many berrylike flavors. **price range:** C

producer: Sterling Vineyards
classification: White varietal table wine
grape variety: Gewürztraminer
district: Napa Valley
city or village: Calistoga

A big, graceful, and assertive wine displaying the uniquely aromatic qualities of this grape variety.

Pale gold color and a bouquet showing the tempered but unmistakable spice of Gewürztraminer. The wine is full, dry, and freshly spicy without being cloying.

price range: B

producer: Sutter Home Winery, Inc.
classification: White varietal table wine
grape variety: Zinfandel
district: Shenandoah Valley, Amador County
city or village: Plymouth

This is one of the few white wines made from the red Zinfandel grape. An "Oeil de Perdrix," or "partridge eye"—a white Zinfandel wine. The Trinchero family has owned Sutter Home Winery since 1946.

A brilliant, very light pink-salmon color with a light, fruity bouquet. Being slightly sweet, the wine is delightful when consumed young, as a light aperitif or as a light dessert wine. **price range:** B

producer: Sutter Home Winery, Inc.
classification: White varietal table wine
grape variety: Muscat of Alexandria
district: San Joaquin Valley

A pale gold color, followed by a rich Muscat varietal nose. The wine is full and sweet on the palate and is perfect as a light dessert wine. **price range:** A

producer: Sutter Home Winery, Inc.
classification: Red varietal table wine
grape variety: Zinfandel
district: Shenandoah Valley, Amador County
city or village: Plymouth

Zinfandel represents 80% of Sutter Home's total production; it is their specialty. This wine is typical of the best Zinfandels produced in this area.

A clear, deep red color; the bouquet is rich, with strong varietal character. It is a full, tannic, and fat Zinfandel. **price range:** B

producer: Tiburon Vintners
classification: White sparkling wine
grape variety: Blend

This is a straw-colored sparkling wine produced by the Charmat (bulk) process. Its bouquet and palate are true to type. It is extra dry. **price range:** B

producer: Trefethen Vineyards
classification: White varietal table wine
grape variety: Chardonnay (100%)
district: Napa Valley
city or village: Oak Knoll

This wine is made from Chardonnay grapes grown in vineyards owned by the Trefethen family. The grapes were picked at 23.5% Balling on September 30 and October 1, 1974; of 31.44 tons, approximately 75% was picked by hand. The remainder was picked by machine and field-crushed. 3,250 gallons of Chardonnay were bottled and were released in October 1976.

Pale straw-gold color tinged with green and a very distinct, pure Chardonnay bouquet without intrusive oakiness. The wine is distinctive and full of varietal character; it has good sugar-acid balance, full body, and characteristic varietal flavor.
price range: C

producer: Trentadue Winery
classification: Red varietal table wine
grape variety: Petite Sirah
district: Sonoma County
city or village: Geyserville

A 100% Sonoma County wine made from Leo Trentadue's own vineyards in the Alexander Valley. No filtering or fining. The wine is stored in 50-gallon barrels for two years.

A deep purple color. The 1973 vintage is heavy-bodied and could use more bottle age. **price range:** A

producer: Trentadue Winery
classification: White varietal table wine
grape variety: Chardonnay
district: Sonoma County
city or village: Geyserville

A 100% Sonoma County wine made from Leo Trentadue's own vineyards in the Alexander Valley. Practically no filtering or fining. Vintaged and stored in 50-gallon oak barrels for nine months. **price range:** B

producer: Trentadue Winery
classification: Red varietal table wine
grape variety: Carignane
district: Sonoma County
city or village: Geyserville

A 100% Sonoma County wine made from Leo Trentadue's own vineyards in the Alexander Valley. No filtering or fining. The wine is stored in 50-gallon oak barrels for two years.
1972 vintage. **price range:** A

producer: Trentadue Winery
classification: Red varietal table wine
grape variety: Cabernet Sauvignon
district: Sonoma County
city or village: Geyserville

A 100% Sonoma County wine made from Leo Trentadue's own vineyards in the Alexander Valley. No filtering or fining. The wine is stored in 50-gallon oak barrels for three years.

Very heavy; 14% alcohol. Could use more bottle age. 1971 vintage.
price range: B

producer: Trentadue Winery
classification: White varietal table wine
grape variety: Sauvignon Vert
district: Sonoma County
city or village: Geyserville

A 100% Sonoma County wine made from Leo Trentadue's own vineyards in the Alexander Valley. Very little filtering or fining.

1973 vintage. Ready to drink when shipped. **price range:** A

producer: Trentadue Winery
classification: Red varietal table wine
grape variety: Gamay
district: Sonoma County
city or village: Geyserville

A 100% Sonoma County wine made from Leo Trentadue's own vineyards in the Alexander Valley. No filtering or fining.

1973 vintage. Ready to drink when shipped. **price range:** A

producer: Trentadue Winery
classification: White varietal table wine
grape variety: Semillon
district: Sonoma County
city or village: Geyserville

A 100% Sonoma County wine made from Leo Trentadue's own vineyards in the Alexander Valley. Very little filtering or fining.

Dry. 1973 vintage. Ready to drink when shipped. **price range:** A

producer: Trentadue Winery
classification: Red varietal table wine
grape variety: Zinfandel
district: Sonoma County
city or village: Geyserville
A 100% Sonoma County wine made from Leo Trentadue's own vineyards in the Alexander Valley. No filtering or fining.
1972 vintage. Ready to drink when shipped. **price range:** A

producer: Trentadue Winery
classification: White varietal table wine
grape variety: Chenin Blanc
district: Sonoma County
city or village: Geyserville
A 100% Sonoma County wine made from Leo Trentadue's own vineyards in the Alexander Valley. Very little filtering or fining.
1971 vintage. Ready to drink when shipped. **price range:** A

producer: Trentadue Winery
classification: White varietal table wine
grape variety: French Colombard
district: Sonoma County
city or village: Geyserville
A 100% Sonoma County wine made from Leo Trentadue's own vineyards in the Alexander Valley. Almost no filtering or fining.
1973 vintage. Ready to drink when shipped. **price range:** A

producer: Turgeon & Lohr Winery
classification: White table wine
grape variety: White Riesling (80%), Sylvaner (17%), and Gewürztraminer (3%)
district: Monterey
This wine was made entirely from Monterey grapes and is their first crop of white Riesling.
Light straw color and a subtle honey-and-apricots bouquet. On the palate the wine is medium dry, *petillant*, well-balanced, and has a refreshing and pleasant aftertaste. The classic Riesling nose is present, and the wine is light and similar in style to Mosel. It is made to be consumed with light foods, fish, and cheese.
price range: B

producer: Turgeon & Lohr Winery
classification: Red table wine
grape variety: Pinot Noir (22%), Gamay (20%), Cabernet Sauvignon (16%), and Zinfandel (43%)
district: Northern California
The first three grape varieties came from the Monterey area and were aged in small European oak barrels; the Zinfandel came from Sonoma and was aged in American oak.
A ruby-red color and a bouquet suggesting violets, cassis, straw, and oak. The wine is soft, aromatic, light, and drinkable. It is a well-made "Burgundy" from premium grapes and will improve with age; it is very good value. **price range:** A

producer: Turgeon & Lohr Winery
classification: Red varietal table wine
grape variety: Petite Sirah
district: Northern California

This was the first wine made at this winery. The grapes were in perfect condition and measured 24.5 degrees Brix and 0.80% acidity. The wine underwent a complete malolactic fermentation and spent nine months in Yugoslavian oak barrels.
Deep red color and a raspberry, black-pepper bouquet showing subtle oak. The wine has an intense, full-bodied berry flavor with a lingering aftertaste; there is still some tannin. It is a classic wine from this variety: deep color, intense bouquet, and full-bodied. **price range:** B

producer: Turgeon & Lohr Winery
classification: White varietal table wine
grape variety: Chenin Blanc
district: Northern California
A deep straw-yellow color and a bouquet showing some oak; it has a subtle Chenin Blanc aroma. The wine is very light with a dry oak finish; unlike most California Chenin Blancs, it is very dry and light, palatable, and with a style like Vouvray.
price range: A

producer: Valley of the Moon Winery
classification: White varietal table wine
grape variety: French Colombard
district: Sonoma Valley
city or village: Glen Ellen
This light white French Colombard is semi-sweet. **price range:** A

producer: Valley of the Moon Winery
classification: Red varietal table wine
grape variety: Zinfandel (100%)
district: Sonoma Valley
city or village: Glen Ellen
This amber-red Zinfandel is dry to the palate. **price range:** A

producer: Valley of the Moon Winery
classification: White varietal table wine
grape variety: Semillon (100%)
district: Sonoma Valley
city or village: Glen Ellen
This clear white Semillon is dry to the palate. **price range:** A

producer: Valley of the Moon Winery
classification: Red varietal table wine
grape variety: Zinfandel, with others added
This light red Zinfandel is dry.
price range: A

producer: Veedercrest-Ringsbridge Cellars
classification: White varietal table wine
grape variety: Johannisberg (White) Riesling
district: Napa Valley
city or village: Yountville
From the Richard Steltzner vineyard, a late-harvest (formerly called "spätlese") Johannisberg Riesling from the 1975 vintage. **price range:** C

producer: Veedercrest-Ringsbridge Cellars
classification: White varietal table wine
grape variety: Johannisberg (White) Riesling and Gewürztraminer
district: Napa Valley—Carneros District

From the Winery Lake Vineyard in Carneros, blended with 11% Gewürztraminer. An "auslese" (selected late-picking) from the 1975 vintage. **price range:** C

producer: Veedercrest-Ringsbridge Cellars
classification: White varietal table wine
grape variety: Johannisberg (White) Riesling and Gewürztraminer
district: Napa Valley—Carneros District
1973 and 1974 vintages. A "beerenauslese" (individually selected berries, late harvest) believed to be the first commercially produced wine in California to be made of individually selected grapes affected by Botrytis (noble mold). Blended with 26% Gewürztraminer for complexity.
Brilliant pale yellow color; luscious sweet, fruity flavor. **price range:** E

producer: Veedercrest-Ringsbridge Cellars
classification: White varietal table wine
grape variety: Gewürztraminer (76%), White Riesling (9%) and Muscat di Canelli (15%)
district: Napa Valley—Carneros District
1975 vintage, a late harvest ("spätlese"). From the Winery Lake Vineyards in the Carneros District. **price range:** C

producer: Veedercrest Vineyards
classification: Red varietal table wine
grape variety: Merlot (predominantly) blended with Cabernet Sauvignon, Malbec, Petit-Verdot, and Cabernet Franc
district: Napa Valley
city or village: St. Helena
1974 vintage. Believed to be the only American Claret-type wine containing all five of the major grape varieties grown for Bordeaux wines. **price range:** E

producer: Nicholas G. Verry, Inc.
classification: Retsina wine (light wine with resin flavor)
grape variety: Blend
district: San Joaquin Valley
city or village: Parlier
This light amber wine is produced in the traditional Greek fashion, its resin imported from Greek pine trees. It has a bitter flavor.
Pine resin is a mark of Greek wine because the Greeks aged and stored their wines in pine barrels instead of the European oak. **price range:** A

producer: Villa Bianchi Winery
classification: Rosé varietal table wine
grape variety: Grenache
district: San Joaquin Valley
city or village: Kerman
Rose-pink color and a varietal bouquet. A soft, tantalizing rosé. **price range:** A

May our wine brighten the mind and strengthen the resolution.

producer: Villa Bianchi Winery
classification: Red varietal table wine
grape variety: Zinfandel
district: San Joaquin Valley
city or village: Kerman
Brilliant light red color and a vinous, raspberry bouquet. The wine is fruity.
price range: A

producer: Villa Mt. Eden Winery
classification: White varietal table wine
grape variety: Gewürztraminer (100%)
district: Napa Valley
city or village: Oakville
The wine is grown, produced, and bottled at the estate.
A clear straw color. The bouquet is fruity, with good varietal aroma. On the palate it is dry; there is a hint of oak and a long finish. The wine is balanced, in the light dry style of a fine Gewürztraminer.
price range: B

producer: Villa Mt. Eden Winery
classification: Red varietal table wine
grape variety: Napa Gamay (100%)
district: Napa Valley
city or village: Oakville
The wine is grown, produced, and bottled at the estate.
A ruby-red color. The bouquet is fruity, a high varietal nose with lots of American oak: On the palate the wine is fruity, oaky, with good flavor and finish. It has a dry Beaujolais style with outstanding varietal character. **price range:** B

producer: Villa Mt. Eden Winery
classification: White varietal table wine
grape variety: Chenin Blanc (100%)
district: Napa Valley
city or village: Oakville
The wine is grown, produced, and bottled at the estate.
A clear light straw color. The bouquet is rich, fruity, and shows varietal character. On the palate it is dry, fruity, and has good acid with light oak. The wine shows exceptional balance and powerful fruit, yet is bone-dry. **price range:** B

producer: Weibel Champagne Vineyards
classification: Flavored wine
grape variety: Blend flavored with Woodruff herbs
district: Napa and Santa Clara valleys
city or village: Mission San Jose
"May Wine." This is an enjoyable light wine that is wonderful when served in summer with just about anything.
Light gold color and a delicate bouquet. The wine is light and slightly sweet.
price range: A

"In wine there is truth."
—Pliny

producer: Weibel Champagne Vineyards
classification: White varietal table wine
grape variety: Johannisberg Riesling
district: Alameda County
city or village: Mission San Jose
This distinctive and fresh white wine is made from the celebrated Johannisberg Riesling grape.
Very light color and a fruity, fragrant bouquet. The wine is medium dry, with medium body. **price range:** B

producer: Weibel Champagne Vineyards
classification: White sparkling wine
grape variety: White Pinot
district: Santa Clara and Napa valleys
city or village: Mission San Jose
Weibel's finest-quality Champagne, naturally fermented in the bottle by the traditional method.
Light gold color with aristocratic sparkles and a delicate bouquet. The wine is dry and crisp. **price range:** C

producer: Weibel Champagne Vineyards
classification: Red varietal table wine
grape variety: Pinot Noir
district: Santa Clara and Napa valleys
city or village: Mission San Jose

A "gentleman's wine," to be shared with the ladies while dining with steaks, roasts, or game.

Clean ruby color and a full, slightly woody bouquet. On the palate the wine is robust and full-bodied. **price range:** B

producer: Weibel Champagne Vineyards
classification: White varietal table wine
grape variety: Pinot Chardonnay
district: Napa Valley
city or village: Mission San Jose

Grapes grown in the Napa Valley, but the wine is produced at Mission San Jose in Alameda County.

Medium clear gold color and a full, fragrant bouquet. On the palate the wine is dry, with authoritative Chardonnay character. **price range:** B

producer: Wente Bros.
classification: White varietal table wine
grape variety: Johannisberg (White) Riesling
district: Monterey
city or village: Arroyo Seco (Greenfield)

This wine is made from special handpicked Johannisberg Riesling grapes that have been saturated with the *Botrytis cinerea* mold. The grapes are dependent on the weather in Monterey County; hence, this wine is made only once every two or three years. It is an extremely popular wine for which demand is greater than supply.

A clear golden color and a very fruity bouquet. On the palate the wine is sweet and fruity, with a very smooth texture and

good aftertaste. It is sweet but not overly so—an ideal dessert wine or a very good dessert in itself, being quite enjoyable sipped on its own. **price range:** C

producer: Wente Bros.
classification: White table wine
grape variety: Chenin Blanc and Ugni Blanc
district: Livermore and Monterey

"Le Blanc de Blancs." This is Wente Bros. second most popular wine, with popularity continuing at a rapid pace.

A clear gold color coupled with a fruity bouquet. On the palate the wine is semisweet, with the flavor of fresh grapes. Being off-sweet, it is delicious alone or with light entrées. **price range:** A

producer: Wente Bros.
classification: White varietal table wine
grape variety: Johannisberg (White) Riesling
district: Monterey

A Rhine-type wine first produced in 1974 and fast becoming one of Wente Bros. most popular wines.

A slight golden color. The bouquet is distinctive and fruity; on the palate the wine is dry but fruity. This wine has the fruit acidity and flowery aroma of the finest Rhine types. It is delicious alone or with a light lunch or supper. **price range:** A

producer: Wente Bros.
classification: White varietal table wine
grape variety: Pinot Blanc.
district: Livermore and Monterey

A white Burgundy-type wine made from a variety that is close cousin of the Chardonnay.

A clear, light gold-straw color and a slightly fruity and woody bouquet. On the palate it is dry and crisp; being mediumbodied, it enhances many dishes, including chicken, fish, and shellfish.
price range: A

producer: Wente Bros.
classification: Red varietal table wine
grape variety: Petite Sirah
district: Livermore and Monterey

A red Burgundy-type wine born of the legendary grape of the Rhone Valley. It is matured in small casks to develop fully its hearty aroma and intriguing flavor.

A very dark red-ruby color and a nutty aroma. On the palate it is somewhat tannic, but quite smooth. It is a dry and full-bodied red wine that would be excellent with red meats and other full-flavored dishes.
price range: A

producer: Wente Bros.
classification: White varietal table wine
grape variety: Chardonnay
district: Livermore and Monterey

A white Burgundy-type wine that is one of the most sought-after Chardonnays on the market. In recent years, the winery has not been able to make enough to meet the increased demand for this wine.

A clear straw-yellow color and a slightly spicy bouquet with a hint of wood. The wine is dry and has a good strong flavor with a clean aftertaste. It is full-bodied but very elegant; it would be a sophisticated accompaniment to crab, lobster, veal, and wild fowl. **price range:** B

producer: Wente Bros.
classification: White varietal table wine
grape variety: Sauvignon Blanc
district: Livermore

A very distinctive dry Sauterne-type wine made from grapes that are well suited to the climate and soil of the Livermore Valley.

The color is straw to deep gold, with a spicy-earthy bouquet. On the palate the wine is dry, with a clean, crisp taste. Being dry, it is outstanding with lightly seasoned foods and fowl. **price range:** A

producer: Wente Bros.
classification: White varietal table wine
grape variety: Grey Riesling
district: Livermore and Monterey

A Rhine-wine type that is the most popular of all Wente Bros. wines.

A clear, slightly golden color and a soft, slightly fruity bouquet. The wine is dry, with a slight fruitiness and medium body. It is a delicate wine to accompany lightly seasoned dishes. **price range:** A

producer: Windsor Vineyards
classification: White varietal table wine
grape variety: Johannisberg Riesling

This is a very Germanic wine, slightly sweet, rich, and complex. The bouquet is light, fruity, and clean. It is not grown at one particular vineyard, unlike their other Johannisberg Riesling. **price range:** B

producer: Windsor Vineyards
classification: White varietal table wine
grape variety: Grey Riesling

This slightly sweet, brilliant strawcolored wine is true to type in bouquet and palate. **price range:** A

producer: Windsor Vineyards
classification: White varietal table wine
grape variety: French Colombard

This is an excellent Chablis-type wine. It is rather rich for its type, semi-dry, with a light, fresh, Colombard nose.
price range: A

producer: Windsor Vineyards
classification: Red varietal table wine
grape variety: Pinot Noir
This is a light, fresh, slightly tannic Pinot Noir, true to its type. The bouquet is slightly woody, the color a brilliant dark ruby.
price range: A

producer: Windsor Vineyards
classification: White varietal table wine
grape variety: Chardonnay
district: Sonoma County
This is a truly excellent Chardonnay, with fine aging potential. It is very rich and silky with ample wood and acid, a rich bouquet, and a brilliant golden color.
Windsor will be one of the great California vineyards. **price range:** B

producer: Windsor Vineyards
classification: Red varietal table wine
grape variety: Cabernet Sauvignon
This is a deep, flavorful wine with a rich, Cabernet-like, quite woody bouquet. It is ready to drink now but will respond well to bottle aging. **price range:** A

producer: Windsor Vineyards
classification: Red varietal table wine
grape variety: Zinfandel
This is a woody, well-aged Zinfandel with a fruity bouquet characteristic of the variety. It is a brilliant medium red.
price range: A

producer: Windsor Vineyards
classification: Red varietal table wine
grape variety: Grenache
district: Mendocino County
This is a light Chateauneuf-du-Pape-type wine, fruity but mature. It is darker than most Grenache wines, with a slightly richer bouquet as well. It is brilliant medium red.
price range: A

producer: Windsor Vineyards
classification: White varietal table wine
grape variety: Pinot Chardonnay
This is a pleasant-quaffing Chardonnay wine with a grassy palate and fresh, clean bouquet. **price range:** B

producer: Woodbridge Vintners
classification: Red varietal table wine
grape variety: Ruby Cabernet
district: San Joaquin Valley
city or village: Lodi
Medium red color and a distinctive varietal bouquet and flavor. **price range:** A

producer: Woodbridge Vintners
classification: Rosé sparkling wine
district: San Joaquin Valley
city or village: Acampo

Pink Champagne, bulk-fermented via the Charmat process.
Light pink color with slight orange tints; fruity bouquet and flavor. **price range:** A

producer: Woodbridge Vintners
classification: White table wine
grape variety: Blend
district: San Joaquin Valley
city or village: Lodi
"Chablis."
Brilliant light straw color and a fruity bouquet. The wine is light and dry.
price range: A

producer: Woodbridge Vintners
classification: Red varietal table wine
grape variety: Zinfandel
district: San Joaquin Valley
city or village: Lodi
Deep red color and a fruity bouquet. The wine has the characteristic flavor of Zinfandel. **price range:** A

producer: Woodland Vineyards
classification: Red varietal table wine
grape variety: Zinfandel
district: San Joaquin Valley
A well-balanced and sensibly priced Central Valley Zinfandel.
Clear purple-red color and a berrylike bouquet. The wine is fresh, with berry spiciness, and is ready to drink when shipped.
price range: A

producer: Yankee Hill Winery
classification: Red varietal table wine
grape variety: Zinfandel
district: Central Valley
city or village: Columbia
Dark red color and a varietal bouquet showing lots of wood. The wine is dry, with a pleasing aftertaste. **price range:** A

producer: Yankee Hill Winery
classification: Red varietal table wine
grape variety: Zinfandel
district: Central Valley
city or village: Columbia
Medium red color and a bouquet characteristic of the varietal. The wine is dry and still young; it should improve with additional bottle age. **price range:** A

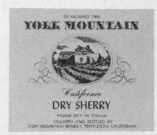

producer: York Mountain Winery
classification: Fortified wine
grape variety: Palomino
district: Central Coast
city or village: Templeton
This wine is basically comprised of an eight-year old Sherry with some four-year-old. To complete the blend, small amounts of flor and Cream Sherry were added to intensify the character.
A dark straw color and a nutty, woody bouquet. The wine is full-bodied with a slightly creamy, lingering aftertaste.
price range: A

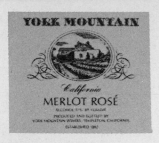

producer: York Mountain Winery
classification: Rosé varietal table wine
grape variety: Merlot
district: Santa Lucia Mountains
city or village: Templeton

This is the first rosé wine made principally from Merlot in California.

Ruby-pink color with orange tinges; fruity bouquet. The wine is dry, fruity, and has a slight spritz with hints of oak. It is a very versatile rosé—light and fruity, yet dry. **price range:** A

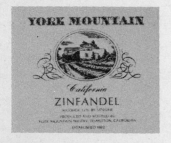

producer: York Mountain Winery
classification: Red varietal table wine
grape variety: Zinfandel
district: Santa Lucia Mountains
city or village: Templeton

Unfiltered and unfined; hence, a high tannic wine with good aging qualities. It has more Cabernet characteristics than most young Zinfandels.

Deep red color and a fruity bouquet showing slight wood. The wine is dry, balanced, and has high acidity and alcohol.
price range: B

producer: ZD Wines
classification: Red varietal table wine
grape variety: Zinfandel
district: Amador County—San Joaquin County
city or village: Sonoma

This wine is a blend of two Zinfandels, one from an old hillside vineyard in the Shenandoah Valley, Amador County, owned by Cary Gott, and the other from the Clements Vineyard in the northeastern part of San Joaquin Valley. Blending resulted in a wine that many tasters consistently preferred to either of the individual wines. The blend was stored in oak cooperage until it was bottled in July 1975.

Brilliant medium color and a "tapestry of varietal aromas" in the bouquet—raspberry, with an earthy undertone. The wine is medium-bodied, varietal flavors blending with wood undertones from the cask aging. **price range:** B

producer: ZD Wines
classification: Red varietal table wine
grape variety: Pinot Noir
district: Napa Valley—Carneros district
city or village: Sonoma

This Pinot Noir was made entirely from grapes grown at the Winery Lake Vineyards in the cool Carneros district of Napa County. The 1973 vintage was an extraordinarily good one for Pinot Noir; the grapes were picked on September 27–28 at an average sugar content of 24.2 degrees Brix. The must was fermented for four days in redwood tanks and then fermented dry in 50-gallon oak barrels. It underwent a malolactic fermentation during aging in American and French Limousin oak barrels and was bottled on August 3, 1975.

Brilliant dark red color and a very mature varietal bouquet coupled with oak aromas. The wine is very full on the palate, with many varietal flavors, and has a long, tannic finish. **price range:** C

producer: ZD Wines
classification: Red varietal table wine
grape variety: Pinot Noir (100%)
district: Napa Valley—Carneros district
city or village: Sonoma

The grapes for this wine came from the cool Carneros district in the Napa Valley and were grown at the Winery Lake Vineyards. The wine was fermented in oak barrels and left to age in 50-gallon oak casks.

Brilliant medium red color and a light, fruity bouquet with noticeable oak aromas from cask aging. The wine is medium-bodied, with good balance, and has a lingering finish. **price range:** B

producer: ZD Wines
classification: White varietal table wine
grape variety: Chardonnay
district: Sonoma County—Valley of the Moon
city or village: Sonoma

This was the second harvest from the small La Casa Zepponi Vineyard in the Valley of the Moon, just south of Sonoma city. The grapes were picked at a sugar content of 22.6 degrees Brix on September 17, 1974, and the wine was fermented to complete dryness in 50-gallon oak barrels and left to age in American and French oak. It was bottled on August 17, 1975 and should improve with further bottle age.

Brilliant light straw color and a delicate varietal aroma with a hint of oak. The wine is medium-bodied, with good fruit and noticable vanilla from the oak, and has a lingering finish. **price range:** C

producer: ZD Wines
classification: White varietal table wine
grape variety: Chardonnay
district: Napa Valley—Carneros district
city or village: Sonoma

This wine was produced entirely from grapes grown at the Winery Lake Vineyards in the cool Carneros region of Napa County. The 1974 vintage produced a bountiful crop of Chardonnay grapes, which were picked on September 28 at 23.3 degrees Brix. The wine was fermented in 50-gallon American and Limousin oak barrels and then aged in the same barrels until bottling on August 16, 1975. It was neither filtered nor fined and should improve with bottle age.

Brilliant light straw color and an intense varietal aroma with complexity from oak. The wine is full-bodied, with rich Chardonnay character and a hint of vanilla from the Limousin oak, and is well-balanced.
price range: C

producer: ZD Wines
classification: White varietal table wine
grape variety: Gewürztraminer (100%)
district: Napa Valley—Carneros district
city or village: Sonoma

This wine was produced from grapes grown at the Winery Lake Vineyards in the cool Carneros district of the Napa Valley. The 1974 vintage produced a bountiful crop, and the grapes were harvested late on October 9 with a sugar content of 22.1 degrees Brix. The wine was fermented to dryness (less than 0.2% sugar) in 50-gallon oak barrels and was aged in the same barrels until it was bottled on April 6, 1975.

Brilliant medium straw color and a varietal bouquet with fine spiciness. The wine is balanced with fruity acidity, is medium-bodied, and has a lingering finish.
price range B

Any wine produced in the United States can be correctly referred to as an American wine. However, the term "Native American" is applied only to wines produced from grapes grown east of the Rocky Mountains because these grapes are native to our country. They are of the Labrusca type, and hybrids of the same, but all are predominantly American. Native American grapes differ greatly in taste and aroma from the vinifera varieties grown in California and Europe.

Certain parts of New York State are very favorably adapted to the growing of these quality native wine grapes. As a result, New York State vineyards yield a high volume of wine.

Although history records the presence of wild grapes during the days when Viking adventurers set foot on America's shores, it was not until the late 1700s that wild vines were domesticated in Kentucky. Cross-breeding and domestication of a variety of grapes continued. A former officer of the American Revolution, Major John Adlum, is credited with early missionary work for the native American grapes. In the 1800s he generously shared information and grapevine cuttings with interested growers. Another leading advocate for the native American grape was the Reverend William Warner Bostwick, rector of St. James Episcopal Church of Hammondsport in the Finger Lakes district of west-central New York. Obtaining young shoots, such as the Isabella, from Hudson Valley vineyards, the minister planted them in 1829 in his rectory garden. He had no idea that he was actually launching a multimillion-dollar wine industry. His native vines took hold. They grew, and the grapes were so plentiful and wholesome that the wines produced from them caused other residents of the Hammondsport area to emulate the minister's efforts. Vineyards and wine cellars dotted the steep hillsides and shores of the deep, narrow waters of Lake Keuka; and still wines were shipped in barrels by canal boat to the important wine market of New York City.

Shortly before the Civil War, the first American Champagne was produced. It received such acclaim in New York, Boston, and Philadelphia that the Lake Keuka area, from Hammondsport on the south to Penn Yan on the north, was popularly known as the "Champagne region of America."

The quality of Finger Lakes grapes and the wines produced from them is credited to the geographical contours of the region. It is a stony land, similar to the Rhine or Mosel districts in Europe. Lake Keuka itself is an important factor. Its clear waters act as a moderator of the extremes of heat and cold. In spring, the lake's frigid temperature helps keep the buds dormant on their vines until danger from spring frosts have passed. In the fall, the lake's warmth acts as a barrier to early frosts until final harvesting.

Although native American grapes (*Vitis labrusca*) such as Concord, Delaware, Catawba, Dutchess, Elvira, Niagara, and Ives account for most of the wine, a dedicated group of winegrowers is beginning to use Rieslings, Chardonnays, Cabernet, and Pinot Noir in the hope that these grapes, which are so successful in other parts of the world, will be able to survive the short summer of the Finger Lakes and bring additional flavor and aroma to the already carefully produced New York State wines.

HOW TO READ A NEW YORK STATE WINE LABEL

GENERIC OR DESCRIPTIVE

NEW YORK STATE This indicates that 75% of the wine has been made from grapes grown in New York State.

DESCRIPTION This is the producer's optional description of the wine.

ALCOHOL 12% BY VOLUME This simply states that the wine contains 12% alcohol by volume. Federal regulations allow up to 1.5% variation.

NAME OF WINE This is producer's name for the wine.

NAME OF PRODUCER This is the company that has produced and bottled the wine.

VARIETAL

NAME OF GRAPE At least 51% of the wine in the bottle must be made from the named grape.

REGION NAME This means that the grapes and thus the wine must be 100% from that region (Finger Lakes, Seneca Lake, .etc.).

ESTATE-BOTTLED The grapes from which the wine in the bottle was made must have been grown on the property of the winery.

YEAR OF VINTAGE This is optional and is usually placed on bottle to indicate year bottled. Does not necessarily indicate that it was an outstanding year.

NAME OF PRODUCER Same as required on generic or descriptive lable.

ALCOHOL Same as required on generic or descriptive label.

NEW YORK STATE Same as required on generic or descriptive label.

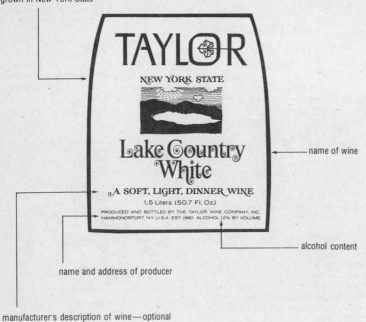

at least 75% of this wine is made from grapes grown in New York State

name of wine

alcohol content

name and address of producer

manufacturer's description of wine—optional

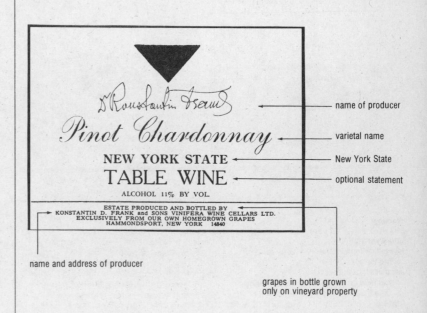

name of producer

varietal name

New York State

optional statement

name and address of producer

grapes in bottle grown only on vineyard property

producer: Benmarl Wine Company
classification: White varietal table wine
grape variety: Seyval Blanc
district: Hudson River Valley
city or village: Marlboro, Ulster County

This fine white wine is estate grown and bottled, demonstrating the regional character of Hudson region slate soils. It is made from Seyval Blanc (Seyve Villard 5276), one of the best white hybrid grape varieties grown in the eastern United States.

Brilliant clear color with shades of green and straw, depending on the vintage; the bouquet is fruity and Loire-like, softening to Chardonnay-like characteristics with bottle age. The wine is dry, terse, and has fresh fruit flavor and acidity; it is clean, delicious, and so easy to drink in its youth that we rarely think of it as an older wine. The regional characteristics show in the finish and flavor. **price range:** B

producer: Benmarl Wine Company
classification: Red table wine
grape variety: Baco Noir, Chelois, Chancellor Noir, De Chaunac, and Maréchal Foch
district: Hudson River Valley
city or village: Marlboro, Ulster County

This fine estate-bottled red wine was handmade and aged in new American Ozark oak and French Nevers oak barrels. Only a limited bottling takes place each year, and the 1975 vintage produced only 150 cases. It has good potential and tremendous aging possibilities.

Young red color and a full and heady bouquet with deep fruit and wood. The wine is somewhat astringent in youth, but keeps the deep fruit flavor; it is powerful, rich, and quite dry. **price range:** B

producer: Benmarl Wine Company
classification: Red varietal table wine
grape variety: Baco Noir
district: Hudson River Valley
city or village: Marlboro, Ulster County

The Baco Noir grape produces quite a different character of wine outside the Hudson River region; outside this area, it is highly productive but generally gives less

fine wines than in the Hudson region. This wine is estate-bottled.

Brilliant red color with slight purple hues and a fresh, fruity Beaujolais-like aroma. The wine is light, fruity, and pleasant; it can be enjoyed now and over the next five years. It has good acidity and complexity and is reminiscent of the bigger Beaujolais wines, such as Brouilly, yet preserves its regional character. **price range:** B

producer: Benmarl Wine Company
classification: Rosé varietal table wine
grape variety: Baco Noir
district: Hudson River Valley
city or village: Marlboro, Ulster County

This light red wine was produced by allowing only a short fermentation on the skins. It is produced annually for early consumption—within 24 months; 180 cases are produced each year, all estate-bottled.

Light red color and a light, spicy bouquet. The wine is soft but fresh on the palate and has a spicy character; it is an unusually light dry wine from the Baco Noir grape. **price range:** B

producer: Benmarl Wine Company
classification: White table wine
grape variety: Verdelet, Burdin, Vignole, Seyval Blanc, and Chardonnay
district: Hudson River Valley
city or village: Marlboro, Ulster County

A blend of several white varieties to improve a single offering, using blends in the 1973 Chardonnay or Riesling. Such wines are always popular, although offerings are limited: only seventy-five cases were produced in 1973.

Green to straw-shaded color and a fresh, nutty bouquet with fruity undertones. The wine is alive and fresh, with a clean, long finish; it is quite dry and can be enjoyed in its youth as it is "dangerously drinkable." **price range:** B

producer: Boordy Vineyards
classification: Red table wine
grape variety: Blend of French hybrids

district: Chautauqua
city or village: Penn Yan
Made to be drunk young.

Ruby-red color and a fruity bouquet reminiscent of Beaujolais. The wine is fairly full-bodied, has fruit, freshness, and a soft finish. **price range:** A

producer: Boordy Vineyards
classification: White table wine
grape variety: Blend of French hybrids
district: Chautauqua
city or village: Penn Yan

Although this wine is produced in the heart of the Finger Lakes, the grapes come from Chautauqua, a world-famous vineyard area. The wine is meant to be drunk young.

Fair color and a very distinctive bouquet similar to Loire Valley white wines. The wine has fruit and freshness and a long finish. **price range:** A

producer: Boordy Vineyards
classification: White varietal table wine
grape variety: Seyval Blanc (Seyve-Villard 5276)
district: Finger Lakes
city or village: Penn Yan

The Seyve-Villard 5276 (Seyval Blanc) yields a wine of exceptional character. The 1973 vintage won the Diplome d'Honneur at the international wine competition at Bratislava, Czechoslovakia, in the fall of 1975.

Pale yellow color and a very discreet bouquet. The wine is light, with crisp dryness. **price range:** A

producer: Boordy Vineyards
classification: White varietal table wine
grape variety: Dutchess
district: Chautauqua
city or village: Penn Yan

The Dutchess grape originated in the vineyards of A. J. Cywood on the banks of

the Hudson River in Dutchess County, New York, in the mid-nineteenth century. It yields an extraordinarily aromatic wine and is one of the best American grapes despite the great care it demands.

Light pale color and a subtle, delicately aromatic bouquet with deep fruit. The wine is dry and finishes smoothly. **price range:** A

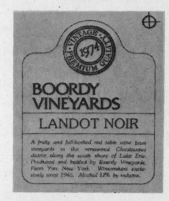

producer: Boordy Vineyards
classification: Red varietal table wine
grape variety: Landot 4511
district: Chautauqua
city or village: Penn Yan

This unique wine is produced exclusively from the Landot grape variety, a new hybrid grape grown nowhere else in the United States and perhaps nowhere else in the world. The 1972 vintage won the Grand Diplome d'Honneur and silver medal at an international competition in Bratislava, Czechoslovakia, in the fall of 1975.

Beautiful red color, similar to a Beaujolais, and a dominantly fruity, fresh bouquet. **price range:** A

producer: Boordy Vineyards
classification: Red varietal table wine
grape variety: Baco Noir
district: Chautauqua
city or village: Penn Yan

The first twenty-five Baco Noir vines were brought from France to the United States in 1938 by Boordy Vineyards. All Baco vineyards now yielding in America are descended from these original vines.

Very pronounced red color and an extremely fruity bouquet. The wine is dry, fruity in its youth, and medium-bodied; no other wine resembles it closely. Outstanding with spaghetti. **price range:** A

"If I had a thousand sons, the first humane principle I would teach them should be . . . to addict themselves to sack."
—Shakespeare, *Henry IV, Part II*

producer: Brotherhood Corporation
classification: Fortified wine
grape variety: Concord
  Brotherhood Corporation is America's oldest winery.
  This Sherry is richly mellowed to velvety smoothness. It is amber in color.
price range: A

producer: Brotherhood Corporation
classification: White table wine
grape variety: Delaware and Catawba
  This softly sweet wine has a fruity after-taste and a rich bouquet.
price range: A

producer: Brotherhood Corporation
classification: White table wine
grape variety: Aurora, Keuka White, and Seyval Blanc
  This delicate Chablis-type wine has a fresh bouquet and surprisingly full body.
price range: A

producer: Brotherhood Corporation
classification: Flavored wine
  This is a special natural wine with herbs and spices added, which give it a festive aroma and flavor. Serve it piping hot, over ice, or with soda on a hot day.
price range: A

producer: Brotherhood Corporation
classification: Fortified wine
grape variety: Delaware
  This wine is fine and dry, with the traditional flor taste. It is pale amber. The flor flavor is most distinctive.
price range: A

producer: Brotherhood Corporation
classification: White table wine
grape variety: Aurora, Keuka White, and Seyval Blanc
  This is a well-balanced medium-dry white wine with a mild and fragrant bouquet.
price range: A

producer: Brotherhood Corporation
classification: Rosé table wine
grape variety: Chancellor, Cascade, and Pink Catawba
  This fragrant, fruity wine is moderately dry.
price range: A

producer: Brotherhood Corporation
classification: White table wine
grape variety: Aurora hybrid
  This is a dry yet lilting white wine with the taste of the Aurora Blanc. Its bouquet is light and delicate.
price range: A

producer: Brotherhood Corporation
classification: Rosé sparkling wine
grape variety: Catawba, Cascade, and Concord
region: New York State
  This sweet pink sparkling wine is fermented in the bottle.
price range: B

producer: Brotherhood Corporation
classification: Fortified wine
grape variety: Concord, Chancellor, De Chaunac, and Chelois
  This is a velvety smooth wine. A delight to sip with dessert or after dinner.
price range: A

producer: Brotherhood Corporation
classification: Red table wine
grape variety: Chancellor, Cascade, De Chaunac, and Chelois
  This is a dry Burgundy-type wine with a full bouquet and rich ruby-red color.
price range: A

producer: Brotherhood Corporation
classification: White table wine
grape variety: Delaware, Catawba, and White Concord
  This is a light white wine with woodruff herbs, strawberry, and other natural flavors added. The herbs add a flowery fragrance, the strawberries a sweet taste.
price range: A

producer: Brotherhood Corporation
classification: White sparkling wine
grape variety: Delaware, Catawba, and Aurora
  This bottle-fermented dry sparkling wine is perfect for festive occasions.
price range: B

producer: Bully Hill Vineyards, Inc.
classification: Red table wine
grape variety: Blend of French hybrids
district: Finger Lakes
city or village: Hammondsport
  Alcoholic content below 14%; made for early consumption; a hint of residual sugar. Estate-bottled.
  Bright red color and a light, "friendly" bouquet. The wine is soft and smooth.
price range: B

producer: Bully Hill Vineyards, Inc.
classification: Red table wine
grape variety: Chelois S-10878 (55%), Cascade Noir S-13503 (35%), Colobel Noir (5%), and Rougeon Noir (5%)
district: Finger Lakes
city or village: Hammondsport
  Bright red color and a light, vinous bouquet. The wine is dry and sturdy and has a fresh, clean taste.
price range: B

Bully Hill Champagne is made according to the time-honored bottle-fermented *methode champenoise*; it is hand-riddled, hand-disgorged, corked, and wire-hooded. In order to acknowledge official sanctity of the French Champagne district, it is carefully labeled "sparkling wine."
  Pale yellow color and a bouquet characteristic of Seyval Blanc. The wine is clean, light, and has small but long-lasting bubbles.
price range: C

producer: Bully Hill Vineyards, Inc.
classification: Red varietal table wine
grape variety: Baco Noir
district: Finger Lakes
city or village: Hammondsport
  Estate-bottled.
  Brilliant red color and a bouquet combining fruit and pleasing pepperspice. The wine is medium-bodied, dry, and crisp.
price range: B

producer: Bully Hill Vineyards, Inc.
classification: White varietal table wine
grape variety: Aurora (Seibel 5279)
district: Finger Lakes
city or village: Hammondsport
  Estate-bottled.
  Pale straw color; sometimes the wine may throw some tartrate crystals, otherwise it is crystal clear. The wine is semi-dry.
price range: B

producer: Bully Hill Vineyards, Inc.
classification: White table wine
grape variety: Seyval Blanc and Aurora
district: Finger Lakes
city or village: Hammondsport
  Estate-bottled.
  Pale straw color with greenish highlights and a light bouquet showing delicate fruitiness. The wine is semi-dry, is clean, and has good balance.
price range: B

producer: Bully Hill Vineyards, Inc.
classification: White varietal table wine
grape variety: Seyval Blanc (Seyve-Villard 5276)
district: Finger Lakes
city or village: Hammondsport
  Bully Hill considers this fine white wine its best.
  Pale color with greenish tints and a bouquet showing Riesling-like fruitiness. The wine is delicately smooth and dry, with a tart finish.
price range: B

producer: Gold Seal Vineyards
classification: White varietal table wine
grape variety: Pinot Chardonnay (100%)
district: Finger Lakes
city or village: Hammondsport
  This rare vinifera varietal was made from grapes grown on the hillsides of Lake Keuka and Lake Seneca in the Finger Lakes district. It derives its powerful and delightful character from the superior Finger Lakes soil and climate.
  Clear straw color and a characteristic Chardonnay bouquet. It is a powerful wine.
price range: B

producer: Bully Hill Vineyards, Inc.
classification: Red table wine
grape variety: Blend of French hybrids
district: Finger Lakes
city or village: Hammondsport
  Medium red color; a balanced, natural wine that will continue to develop in the bottle.
price range: B

producer: Bully Hill Vineyards, Inc.
classification: White sparkling wine
grape variety: Seyval Blanc (100%)
district: Finger Lakes
city or village: Hammondsport

producer: Bully Hill Vineyards, Inc.
classification: Red varietal table wine
grape variety: Chancellor Noir (80%), Baco Noir (7%), Chelois Noir (4%), Colobel Noir (3%), Rougeon Noir (3%), Cascade Noir (2%), and Foch (1%)
district: Finger Lakes
city or village: Hammondsport
  Bully Hill's best red varietal, made from a grape variety largely discarded by high-volume New York State wineries because of its susceptibility to mildew. With timely spraying and careful pruning, Bully Hill has demonstrated the Chancellor's viability and produces an excellent red wine.
  Deep red color and a rich, heavy bouquet with hints of oak. It is a big, dry wine with great body.
price range: B

producer: Gold Seal Vineyards, Inc.
classification: Rosé varietal table wine
grape variety: Catawba
district: Finger Lakes
city or village: Hammondsport
  This light, semi-sweet rosé wine comes from the native American Catawba grape. Its special flavor and color derive from skillfuly controlled fermentation.
  Attractive pink color and a fruity bouquet. The wine is semi-dry, delicious, and versatile. It has a fine, fruity flavor.
price range: A

producer: Gold Seal Vineyards, Inc.
classification: White table wine
grape variety: White Riesling, Delaware, and hybrids
district: Finger Lakes
city or village: Hammondsport

This unique wine is a blend of native American Labrusca varieties, European vinifera varieties, and hybrids grown on the hillsides of the Finger Lakes region.

Brilliant clear white color and a soft, flowery bouquet. It has great delicacy and softness arising from the famous German White Riesling grapes. **price range:** A

producer: Gold Seal Vineyards, Inc.
classification: White varietal table wine
grape variety: Chardonnay and white hybrids
district: Finger Lakes
city or village: Hammondsport

The "nature" wines are some of the most interesting white wines made and are especially sought after by sophisticated wine lovers in France. They are bottled without being made into sparkling wines in the Champagne district, and this especially elegant wine is quite scarce. The informing grape variety is the Chardonnay, which also produces the famous wines of Chablis to the south of the Champagne district. Gold Seal Chablis Nature is a blend of the best Champagne grapes, including Pinot Chardonnay.

Clear, brilliant color and a Chablis nose. The wine combines the elegance of a "nature" wine and the body of a Chablis with a vinous flavor. The French prefer to serve this dry wine well-chilled. **price range:** A

producer: Frederick S. Johnson Vineyards
classification: White varietal table wine
grape variety: Seyval Blanc (S.V. 5276)
district: Chautauqua County
city or village: Westfield

Seyval Blanc is a French hybrid that is considered to be among the best white grapes for making an outstanding white table wine.

Brilliant clear color and a clean, fruity bouquet. The wine is delicate, very dry, and has a fresh, clean after-taste.
price range: A

producer: Frederick S. Johnson Vineyards
classification: Red table wine
grape variety: Chancellor Noir
district: Chautauqua County
city or village: Westfield

Chancellor Noir (Seibel 7053) is a French-American hybrid that gives a red Burgundy-type wine with a very distinct character.

Very dark red color and a mature bouquet with the character of the grape. The wine is very dry, with a full rich flavor and a pleasant, lingering aftertaste.
price range: A

producer: Monarch Wine Co., Inc.
classification: Rosé table wine
grape variety: Concord

Deep pink color and a fruity bouquet. A well-balanced, smooth-tasting pink wine.
price range: A

producer: Monarch Wine Co., Inc.
classification: White table wine
grape variety: Niagara

Fruity bouquet; the wine is light and bright. **price range:** A

producer: Pleasant Valley Wine Co.
classification: Rosé table wine
grape variety: Niagara and Isabella

district: Finger Lakes
city or village: Hammondsport

Clear, clean rosé color and a fruity bouquet. The wine is semi-dry and well-balanced; it is marked by the presence of tiny bubbles. **price range:** A

producer: Pleasant Valley Wine Co.
classification: Red sparkling wine
grape variety: Concord, Baco Noir, and De Chaunac
district: Finger Lakes
city or village: Hammondsport

This "Sparkling Burgundy" is fermented in the bottle and contains 12% alcohol. It is sold under the Great Western label.

Ruby-red color and a very fruity bouquet. The wine is semi-sweet and well-balanced. **price range:** C

producer: Pleasant Valley Wine Co.
classification: White sparkling wine
grape variety: Delaware, Dutchess, Catawba, and Muscat
district: Finger Lakes
city or village: Hammondsport

"Spumante Champagne" is fermented in the bottle and contains 12% alcohol. It is sold under the Great Western label.

Pale straw-yellow color and a fruity bouquet with a slight hint of Muscat. The wine is sweet and well-balanced.
price range: C

producer: Pleasant Valley Wine Co.
classification: White sparkling wine
grape variety: Delaware, Dutchess, and Catawba
district: Finger Lakes
village: Hammondsport

"Extra Dry Champagne" is fermented in the bottle and contains 12% alcohol. It is sold under the Great Western label.

Pale straw-yellow color and a slightly fruity bouquet. The wine is semi-dry and well-balanced. **price range:** C

producer: Pleasant Valley Wine Co.
classification: White sparkling wine
grape variety: Delaware, Dutchess, and Catawba
district: Finger Lakes
city or village: Hammondsport

"Champagne Naturel" is an excellent Champagne produced by fermentation in the bottle. The wine is disgorged by the transfer process, and no shipping dosage is added that would make the wine sweet. It contains approximately 12% alcohol and is sold under the Great Western label.

Pale straw-yellow color and a slightly fruity bouquet. The wine is very dry and well-balanced. **price range:** C

producer: Pleasant Valley Wine Co.
classification: White table wine
grape variety: Aurora
district: Finger Lakes
city or village: Hammondsport

"Aurora Sauterne" is named for the Aurora grape, a hybrid developed many years ago by Louis Seibel, who succeeded in crossing the best of the French and American vine types. The wine is sold under the Great Western label.

Pale yellow color and a bouquet that displays vinifera characteristics. The wine is semi-dry and well-balanced.
price range: A

producer: Pleasant Valley Wine Co.
classification: Rosé varietal table wine
grape variety: Isabella (100%)
district: Finger Lakes
city or village: Hammondsport

The Isabella grape is a native American variety that was the first commercially planted grape in the famous New York Finger Lakes district in the 1800s.

Rosé color and a fruity bouquet. The wine is semi-sweet and well-balanced.
price range: B

producer: Pleasant Valley Wine Co.
classification: Fortified wine
grape variety: Concord
district: Finger Lakes
city or village: Hammondsport

Great Western "Solera Cocktail Sherry" is produced in four stages via the Solera system used in the Spanish Sherry country. The wine remains in each stage for one full year; at the end of the year, half the wine is advanced, leaving each cask half full. This blending of younger wines with older ones increases the average age in each cask, allowing Great Western Ports and Sherries to be smooth and mellow.

Pale yellow color and a Sherry bouquet. The wine is dry, with a crisp nutty flavor.

price range: A

producer: Pleasant Valley Wine Co.
classification: Red table wine
grape variety: Baco Noir and De Chaunac
district: Finger Lakes
city or village: Hammondsport

Baco Noir was developed by Maurice Baco in the Burgundy district of France by crossing French and American vine types. As Great Western "Baco Noir Burgundy" is sealed with a cork closure, the wine should be stored on its side, like any other fine wine.

Ruby-red color and a robust bouquet. The wine is robust, dry, and full-bodied.

price range: A

producer: Pleasant Valley Wine Co.
classification: White table wine
grape variety: Moore's Diamond (100%)
district: Finger Lakes
city or village: Hammondsport

The Moore's Diamond is a native American grape variety first developed by Jacob More, a grape hybridizer, in the 1870s. It

produces a very dry white wine that preserves a briskness and spicy fragrance. Great Western "Diamond Chablis" is sealed via a cork closure; it should be stored on its side, like all fine wines.

Pale yellow color and an austere bouquet. The wine is dry and well-balanced. **price range:** A

producer: Pleasant Valley Wine Co.
classification: White table wine
grape variety: Dutchess
district: Finger Lakes
city or village: Hammondsport

The Dutchess grape is a native American variety developed by A. J. Caywood of Marlboro, New York, in 1868. Great Western "Dutchess Rhine Wine" is sealed via a cork closure, and hence should be stored on its side, like any other fine wine.

Pale yellow color and a slightly fruity bouquet. The wine is well-rounded and semi-dry. **price range:** A

producer: Taylor Wine Co., Inc.
classification: Fortified wine
grape variety: Predominantly Concord and Ives
district: Finger Lakes

This is a sweet, full-bodied wine of a brilliant deep ruby color. The bouquet is sweet and fruity. **price range:** A

producer: Taylor Wine Co., Inc.
classification: White table wine
grape variety: Predominantly White Concord
district: Finger Lakes

This is a well-balanced, fresh, and fruity wine of good body. The aroma is of White Concord grapes. The wine is clear gold.

price range: A

producer: Taylor Wine Co., Inc.
classification: White table wine
grape variety: Niagara
district: Finger Lakes

This soft, light dinner wine is slightly sweet, slightly tart, because of the Niagara grapes. It is of a brilliant straw appearance with a strong Niagara nose.

price range: A

producer: Taylor Wine Co., Inc.
classification: Red table wine
grape variety: De Chaunac
district: Finger Lakes

This is a dry, well-balanced, light-bodied wine with the distinctive Seibel nose. It is deep red in color.

price range: A

producer: Taylor Wine Co., Inc.
classification: Red table wine
grape variety: Baco Noir and Concord
district: Finger Lakes

This wine has good body and a strong Labrusca nose. It is brilliant medium red.
price range: A

producer: Taylor Wine Co., Inc.
classification: Red table wine
grape variety: Predominantly Red Seibels with native varieties
district: Finger Lakes

This wine is full-bodied with a robust,

fresh bouquet. It is of brilliant medium red.
price range: A

producer: Taylor Wine Co., Inc.
classification: White varietal table wine
grape variety: Emerald Riesling

This is a fruity wine of brilliant medium yellow appearance. **price range:** A

producer: Taylor Wine Co., Inc.
classification: White table wine
grape variety: Predominantly Aurore with native varieties
district: Finger Lakes

This is a light, crisp wine with a light, fruity nose. It is brilliant pale yellow.
price range: A

producer: Taylor Wine Co., Inc.
classification: White table wine
grape variety: French Colombard and hybrids
district: Finger Lakes

The wine is tart, yet slightly sweet, with a fruity bouquet.

This is different from other "Chablis" wines due to the addition of both native and French hybrid grapes to the French Colombard. **price range:** A

producer: Taylor Wine Co., Inc.
classification: Fortified wine
grape variety: Predominantly Concord and Elvira
district: Finger Lakes

This is a dry, tart, fine Sherry of clear, light amber appearance and a light, nutty nose. **price range:** A

Three states account for almost all the wine produced in America. Over 75 percent comes from California. The Finger Lakes district of New York follows that lead, and the Sandusky Lake Region of Ohio is the last area in this important triumvirate.

A small proportion of the American wine output, however, comes from a few other districts worthy of mention: Yakima Valley in Washington; Willamette Valley in Oregon; the Council Bluffs area of Iowa; southwestern Michigan; the area around Cincinnati, Ohio; the Hudson River Valley in New York; the Egg Harbour district in northern and north-central New Jersey; the area around Charlottesville, Virginia; sections in the Ozark Mountains of Arkansas; and the eastern part of Pennsylvania.

In most cases eastern and midwestern wine productions are comprised of sparkling and table wines made from native American grapes. Growers in the southeastern and northwestern states concentrate on fruit and berry wines.

A recent movement, championed several years ago by Konstantin Frank of New York State, seems to indicate that Rieslings, Chardonnays, Cabernet, Pinot Noir, and other European grapes can survive the hard winters and short summers of that territory. Dr. Frank has had reasonable success in his own winery, Vinifera Wines, and other winegrowers are beginning to follow his lead. No doubt, in the years to come, we shall be drinking more and more European-type wines that will have been produced in other areas of the United States. At the present time, however, the range of fruits used to make American wines in states other than California, New York, and Ohio stacks up something like this:

Arkansas The Concord, Niagara, Catawba, Scuppernong, Delaware, and Campbell's Early are widely used.

Florida Citrus fruits produce interesting fruit wines in this state.

Indiana Such varietals as Seyval Blanc, Baco Noir, Maréchal Foch, and Cabernet Sauvignon are grown.

Massachusetts The first bonded winery in the state, located on Martha's Vineyard, has recently produced its first wine from Johannisberg Riesling.

Michigan They grow the Ives, Concord, Niagara, and Aurora Blanc predominantly. Some vineyards also grow Johannisberg Riesling and Chardonnay.

Missouri The Seyval Blanc, Concord, and French hybrids are grown here.

New Jersey The Concord, Niagara, Catawba, Baco Noir, and Chelois are popular grape types.

Oregon Growers prefer the Pinot Noir, Chardonnay, Pinot Meunier, Pinot Blanc, Gewürztraminer, and Johannisberg Riesling.

Pennsylvania The Delaware, Dutchess, and Niagara are used, and there is a small production of Maréchal Foch, Seyval Blanc, Pinot Chardonnay, and Baco Noir.

Texas Two unusual varieties of grape flourish here, the Lenoir and the Herbemont.

Washington They grow the Pinot Noir, Chardonnay, Gewürztraminer, Semillon, and Grenache.

Wisconsin The Baco Noir, Seyval Blanc, Chelois, and Aurora Blanc are the backbone of this state's viticulture.

The variety of grapes used in these and other states has changed in the concourse of cultivation, and it goes on changing. I mention only a few varieties here. Even from this short list, however, you can get an indication of characteristics that predominate in America's "local wines."

ARKANSAS

producer: Robert G. Cowie
classification: Red table wine
grape variety: Cynthiana
The wine is of a very deep red color; its taste and bouquet are not foxy.
price range: A

producer: Robert G. Cowie
classification: Red table wine
grape variety: Campbell's Early
price range: A

producer: Robert G. Cowie
classification: Red table wine
grape variety: Ives
This wine has a foxy bouquet.
price range: A

producer: Post Winery, Inc.
classification: Red table wine
grape vareity: Concord
district: Ozark Mountains
village: Altus
A good source of iron.
Deep red color and a fruity bouquet. A fruity, medium-sweet red wine.
price range: A

producer: Post Winery, Inc.
classification: Red table wine
grape variety: Campbell's Early
district: Ozark Mountains
village: Altus
One of their best-selling wines.
A medium-sweet red wine.
price range: A

producer: Post Winery, Inc.
classification: White table wine
grape variety: Blend of French hybrids
district: Ozark Mountains
city or village: Altus
A semi-sweet white wine.
price range: A

producer: Post Winery, Inc.
classification: White table wine
grape variety: Niagara
district: Ozark Mountains
city or village: Altus
Clear color and a fruity bouquet. The wine is sweet.
price range: A

producer: Post Winery, Inc.
classification: Fortified wine
district: Ozark Mountains
city or village: Altus
Cream Sherry made by the Spanish Solera system; the base wine is fifteen years old.
Light golden color and smooth, mellow flavor: a premium Sherry.
price range: A

producer: Post Winery, Inc.
classification: Rosé table wine
grape variety: Blend
district: Ozark Mountains
city or village: Altus
Light pink color and a fruity bouquet. The wine is medium sweet.
price range: A

producer: Post Winery, Inc.
classification: Red/white table wine
grape variety: Scuppernong (Muscadine)
district: Ozark Mountains
city or village: Altus

Post's is very proud of this wine, which they consider a specialty.

Fruity bouquet; a medium-sweet table wine. **price range: A**

producer: Post Winery, Inc.
classification: White table wine
grape variety: Blend of French hybrids
district: Ozark Mountains
city or village: Altus

The winery specializes in varietal wines, but their table wines are the best in the area.

Mild, pleasing bouquet; the wine is dry and crisp. **price range: A**

producer: Sax Winery
classification: White varietal table wine
grape variety: Delaware
district: Ozark Mountains
city or village: Altus
price range: A

producer: Sax Winery
classification: Red table wine
grape variety: Campbell's Early
district: Ozark Mountains
city or village: Altus

Light red color and medium body.
price range: A

producer: Sax Winery
classification: Red varietal table wine
grape variety: Cynthiana
district: Ozark Mountains
city or village: Altus

An excellent medicinal wine, owing to its high iron content.

Deep red color and a foxy bouquet. A dry, full-bodied wine with excellent flavor. **price range:** A

producer: Sax Winery
classification: White varietal table wine
grape variety: Niagara
district: Ozark Mountains
city or village: Altus

White to pale yellow color and a grapey bouquet. The wine has a full grape flavor and is an excellent dinner wine.
price range: A

FLORIDA

producer: Fruit Wines of Florida, Inc.
classification: Fruit wine
variety: Orange

This is a naturally fermented wine made from pure Florida orange juice. The brand is being sold in Florida, Georgia, Louisiana, Texas, Arizona, California, Minnesota, Wisconsin, Illinois, Tennessee, and Pennsylvania, and requests have been received from Canada, Italy, Germany, and Africa.

Light amber-gold color and a pronounced orange aroma. The wine is slightly sweet. **price range:** A

producer: Fruit Wines of Florida, Inc.
classification: Fruit wine
variety: Grapefruit

This wine is naturally fermented from pure grapefruit juice.

Light yellow color and an aroma of grapefruit. The wine is slightly sweet.
price range: A

producer: Fruit Wines of Florida, Inc.
classification: Fruit wine
variety: Tangerine

This is the first tangerine wine ever made commercially; its unique flavor is a new dimension in wine making.

Golden-bright clear color and a tangerine bouquet. The wine is very flavorful. **price range:** A

ILLINOIS

producer: Thompson Winery
classification: White sparkling wine
grape variety: Blend of American and European hybrids
district: Northeast
city or village: Monee

This wine is made in strict adherence to the Champagne tradition. The grapes are selected by hand (*epluchage*), and the juice is expressed from red grapes (*blanc de noirs*). Fermentation is carried out in bottle according to the traditional *methode champenoise*.

Pale bright-yellow color and a fruity bouquet. The wine is complex and has a slight oak flavor. **price range:** C

producer: Thompson Winery
classification: Pink sparkling wine
grape variety: Blend of American and European hybrids
district: Northeast
city or village: Monee

This wine is made in strict adherence to the Champagne tradition. The grapes are selected by hand (*epluchage*), and the juice is expressed from red grapes (*blanc de noirs*). Fermentation is carried out in bottle according to the traditional *methode champenoise*.

Bright pink color; a fruity bouquet; and a fresh, fruity flavor. **price range:** C

INDIANA

producer: Banholzer Winecellars Ltd.
classification: Red table wine
grape variety: Foch and Cabernet Sauvignon
district: Northwest Indiana
city or village: New Carlisle

The deep-colored red hybrid Foch was made via the carbonic-maceration method, producing a very fruity, light-bodied Beaujolais-type wine. Long-vatted Cabernet was added to increase body, alcohol, and bouquet, then the blend was aged in French oak for one year.

Deep inky color, very intense, a fruity bouquet, but the oak shows through. The wine is rich, not too heavy-bodied or tannic; it is a fine dry red dinner wine, with Cabernet dominant in the blend. The wine is lighter and lower in alcohol than its bouquet and color suggest.
price range: B

producer: Banholzer Winecellars Ltd.
classification: White table wine
grape variety: Chardonnay, Ravat Blanc, and Seyval Blanc
district: Northwest Indiana
city or village: New Carlisle

Much like an authentic Chablis, this wine was aged one year in French Limousin oak. It developed very slowly and was not ready to drink until it was eighteen months old. It should be quite long-lived.

Almost white color with green and gold at the edges; a steely, strong bouquet with wood stands out. The wine is crisp, assertive, and powerful; it is dry, with good body and high acidity and alcohol. A first-class white dinner wine. **price range:** A

producer: Banholzer Winecellars Ltd.
classification: White table wine (flavored)
grape variety: Seyval Blanc and Aurora
district: Northwest Indiana
city or village: New Carlisle

This is perhaps the first American "May Wine" made entirely from French hybrid grapes.

Bronze-white color with some green around the edges and a light bouquet with faint woodruff overtones. The wine is light, delicate, and sweet, a typical May Wine in the German style; it is clean-flavored, with modest alcohol and good acidity.
price range: A

producer: Banholzer Winecellars Ltd.
classification: Red varietal table wine
grape variety: Cabernet Sauvignon (100%)
district: Northwest Indiana
city or village: New Carlisle

This is the Midwest's first Cabernet. A scant 300 gallons were produced after being described in the *New York Times, Le Monde,* the *Chicago Tribune,* and others; the harvest was covered by ABC-TV, and the wine sold on the futures market for $21 the bottle. Delivery is scheduled for 1978. The grapes showed 23 degrees Brix and 0.77 acid at harvest in an extraordinarily long, warm growing season.

Medium-red color; good legs, medium-hued, young appearance; a bouquet very rich in fruit, with a distinct varietal aroma. The wine is very rich but not overly heavy or tannic; it is dry, with a very rich aftertaste, more like a Margaux than any other Médoc.
price range: E

producer: Banholzer Winecellars Ltd.
classification: White table wine
grape variety: Pinot Noir and Chardonnay in equal proportions

district: Northwest Indiana
city or village: New Carlisle

This is probably the first wine of its type produced in this country. The Pinot Noir was cold-pressed and later blended with Chardonnay, then the wine was aged in French oak casks.

Amber-gold color and a rich Pinot Noir nose with some French oak evident. The wine is heavy, with a very complex flavor; it is dry, with great body. Although blended in a traditional Champagne cuvée, the wine is modest in acid and is much like a white Burgundy, yet the Pinot Noir dominates.
price range: C

producer: Banholzer Winecellars Ltd.
classification: White varietal table wine
grape variety: Vidal Blanc
district: Northwest Indiana
city or village: New Carlisle

The grapes for this wine were heavily Botrytised and weighed in at 29 degrees Brix at the time of harvest. They were picked and the wine was fermented for nearly four months at 36 degrees F., then racked twice and bottled early so as to preserve its lovely fruitiness. It is much like a German Beerenauslese or a French Sauternes, and was produced in a like manner.

Light gold color and heavy viscosity; the bouquet is very rich and fruity and suggests figs and raisins. The wine is lovely with summer fruit and heavy with 5% residual sugar; it is truly a dessert wine.
price range: B

producer: Banholzer Winecellars Ltd.
classification: Red table wine
grape variety: Maréchal Foch and Baco Noir
district: Northwest Indiana
village: New Carlisle

One of the winery's three "picnic" wines, this red wine bridges the gap between popular, unsophisticated wines and the higher-priced dry red varietals.

Medium-red color with gold around the edges and a light, fruity bouquet. The wine is delicate, with a slight sweet flavor and some wood. It is low in tannin and acidity, with good body, and would go well with cold cuts.
price range: A

producer: Banholzer Winecellars Ltd.
classification: Rosé varietal table wine
grape variety: Baco Noir
district: Northwest Indiana
city or village: New Carlisle

Until tasted, this wine might be mistaken for a rosé fermented totally off the skins; the wine's tannin derives largely from aging in American white oak casks. It was cold-pressed to produce a medium-bodied red wine of considerable character.

Deep rosé color—not quite red, with some gold at the edges—and a woody bouquet with hints of raspberries. The wine is fuller and more assertive than its appearance suggests; it is dry and would stand up well with pasta dishes.
price range: B

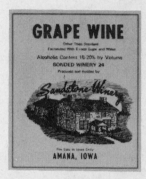

producer: Villa Medeo Vineyards
classification: Red varietal table wine
grape variety: Baco Noir
district: Southeastern Indiana
city or village: Madison

This wine, made from a popular red hybrid, is fermented in the Old World Italian style.

Garnet-red color and a fruity bouquet. The wine is medium-bodied, with a berry flavor and good varietal character, it is crisp, dry, and has a touch of oak in the finish.
price range: B

producer: Villa Medeo Vineyards
classification: Red table wine
grape variety: Hybrid blend
district: Southeastern Indiana
city or village: Madison

Deep, rich red color and a sweet, fruity bouquet. The wine has good fruit flavor and body; it is slightly sweet, and a good wine experience.
price range: B

producer: Villa Medeo Vineyards
classification: White varietal table wine
grape variety: Vidal 256
district: Southeastern Indiana
city or village: Madison

Gold-yellow color and a dry, complex bouquet. The wine is quite refreshing; it is spicy, with slight acidity making it clean and crisp, and has a good finish.
price range: B

IOWA

producer: Sandstone Winery, Inc.
classification: Red and white table wines
grape variety: Concord and Niagara
district: Eastern Iowa
city or village: Amana

This is a homemade wine with sugar and water added; alcoholic content ranges from 10% to 19%.

Clear color and a definite bouquet.
price range: A

MARYLAND

producer: Provenza Vineyards
classification: Red, white, and rosé table wines
grape variety: French hybrids
district: Washington, D.C., suburbs
city or village: Brookeville

The first winery in the Washington, D.C., metropolitan area.
price range: A

MASSACHUSETTS

producer: Chicama Vineyards
classification: White varietal table wine
grape variety: Chardonnay
district: Martha's Vineyard
city or village: West Tisbury
This is the first commercial bottling from Chicama Vineyards, the first bonded winery in Massachusetts. The wine was made from four-year-old vines and is estate-bottled.
Very pale straw color and a light bouquet. The wine is assertive, very dry, flinty, and austere. **price range:** C

producer: Chicama Vineyards
classification: White varietal table wine
grape variety: White (Johannisberg) Riesling
district: Martha's Vineyard
city or village: West Tisbury
This is the first commercial bottling of Riesling from Chicama Vineyards, the first bonded winery in Massachusetts. The wine came from four-year-old vines and is estate-bottled.
Clear pale color and a light bouquet that develops with bottle age. The wine is extremely dry. **price range:** C

MICHIGAN

producer: Fenn Valley Vineyards
classification: White table wine
grape variety: Blend of French hybrids, predominantly Seyval Blanc
district: Kalamazoo River Valley
city or village: Fennville
A blend of well-ripened grapes was used to produce this wine. Fenn Valley combines the art of Old World techniques with modern vinification to produce this superior dry white wine.
Brilliant clear color and a delicate fruity bouquet. The wine is lightly dry with a soft fruity taste and a tangy finish.
price range: A

producer: Fenn Valley Vineyards
classification: White table wine
grape variety: Blend of Seyval and Vidal
district: Kalamazoo River Valley
city or village: Fennville
Crystal-clear color and a fruity bouquet with strong Vidal aroma. The wine is smooth, semi-dry, and well-balanced; it is a fine accompaniment to fowl, seafood, and delicate foods. It is made in the German style. **price range:** B

producer: Fenn Valley Vineyards
classification: White varietal table wine
grape variety: White (Johannisberg) Riesling (100%)
district: Kalamazoo River Valley
city or village: Fennville
This premium varietal wine is made via the traditional German method.
Brilliant crystal-clear color and a strong, fruity bouquet typical of Riesling. The wine is dry, full-bodied, and has a delicate fruity taste; it is characteristic of German wines. It may be drunk alone or with cheese, fowl, fish, or white meats. **price range:** B

producer: Fenn Valley Vineyards
classification: White varietal table wine
grape variety: Vidal Blanc
district: Kalamazoo River Valley
city or village: Fennville
This premium white varietal wine is made from Vidal Blanc, a French-American hybrid, in the German style.
Brilliant crystal-clear color and a very fruity bouquet. The wine is typical of the German style—it is semi-dry, with slight residual natural sugar.

producer: Fenn Valley Vineyards
classification: Rosé table wine
grape variety: Blend of French hybrids
district: Kalamazoo River Valley
city or village: Fennville
An all-around table rosé that compliments any meal.
Clear pink color; the wine is semi-dry, balanced, and has a pleasant fruity flavor.
price range: A

producer: St. Julian Wine Co., Inc.
classification: Fortified wine
grape variety: Concord blend
district: Van Buren County
city or village: Paw Paw
This light Port is a sweet, rich-flavored, ruby-red wine. Excellent after dinner, with dessert, or as a nightcap.
price range: A

producer: St. Julian Wine Co., Inc.
classification: Fortified wine
grape variety: Niagara
district: Van Buren County
city or village: Paw Paw
This is a semi-sweet, nutty, amber-colored Sherry with a distinct flor nose and clean finish. **price range:** A

producer: St. Julian Wine Co., Inc.
classification: Red table wine
grape variety: Concord

district: Van Buren County
city or village: Paw Paw
This is a sweetened Concord wine with a fruity Concord bouquet and clean finish.
price range: A

producer: St. Julian Wine Co., Inc.
classification: White table wine
grape variety: Niagara blend
district: Van Buren County
city or village: Paw Paw
This is a dry white wine with a fruity nose and clear white appearance. It was rated extremely high in Peter Sichel's book *Which Wine*. **price range:** A

producer: St. Julian Wine Co., Inc.
classification: Red table wine
grape variety: Concord blend
district: Van Buren County
city or village: Paw Paw
This is a dry, hearty Burgundy-type wine with a clean red appearance.
price range: A

producer: St. Julian Wine Co., Inc.
classification: White table wine
grape variety: Niagara blend
district: Van Buren County
city or village: Paw Paw
This straw-colored white wine is sweet to semi-sweet and has a very fruity bouquet.
price range: A

producer: St. Julian Wine Co., Inc.
classification: Rosé table wine
grape variety: Niagara-Concord blend
district: Van Buren County
city or village: Paw Paw
This brilliant pink table wine has a fruity bouquet and a semi-dry taste.
price range: A

producer: St. Julian Wine Co., Inc.
classification: Rosé table wine
grape variety: Delaware and Riesling
district: Van Buren County
city or village: Paw Paw
St. Julian "Chateau Rosé" is a semi-dry all-purpose rosé table wine carbonated to the legal limit. **price range:** A

producer: St. Julian Wine Co., Inc.
classification: Varietal white table wine
grape variety: Vidal Blanc
district: Van Buren County
city or village: Paw Paw
This is the first French-hybrid grape ever crushed by the St. Julian Wine Co.
Vidal Blanc is a bone-dry white wine with strong varietal aroma and palate. It is of brilliant straw color.
price range: B

producer: St. Julian Wine Co., Inc.
classification: Fortified flavored wine
grape variety: Niagara blend with natural flavor added
district: Van Buren County
city or village: Paw Paw
This is St. Julian's best-selling wine. It is of dark amber color with a strong almond nose and almond flavor and a very clean finish. **price range:** A

producer: St. Julian Wine Co., Inc.
classification: Pink table wine
grape variety: Niagara-Concord blend and Delaware

district: Van Buren County
city or village: Paw Paw
This is the most popular of St. Julian's generic table wines. It is semi-dry and fruity, with a fruity bouquet and clean finish. **price range:** A

producer: St. Julian Wine Co., Inc.
classification: White table wine
grape variety: Niagara blend
district: Van Buren County
city or village: Paw Paw
This dry Rhine-style wine has the varietal Niagara bouquet and is of pale straw color.
price range: A

producer: St. Julian Wine Co., Inc.
classification: White varietal sparkling wine
grape variety: Vidal Blanc with some Seyval Blanc
district: Van Buren County
city or village: Paw Paw
St. Julian "Vidal Champagne" is the first varietal (hybrid) Champagne to be produced in Michigan.
This naturally fermented Champagne is dry to the palate and fruity to the nose. It is very clear white in color.
price range: B

producer: St. Julian Wine Co., Inc.
classification: White sparkling wine
grape variety: Niagara, Seyval Blanc, and Delaware
district: Van Buren County
city or village: Paw Paw
This sparkling wine is produced via natural-fermentation bulk process (Charmat).
St. Julian's "Brut Champagne" is dry. It is pale almost to the point of being clear.
price range: B

producer: Tabor Hill Vineyard & Winecellar, Inc.
classification: White varietal table wine
grape variety: Vidal Blanc
district: Berrien County
city or village: Buchanan
This wine was served at the White House by President Ford.
Brilliant pale straw color and a fruity Muscat nose. The wine is clean, crisp, and pleasant; being slightly sweet, it is reminiscent of a Rhine or Alsatian wine.
price range: B

producer: Tabor Will Vineyard & Winecellar, Inc.
classification: White varietal table wine
grape variety: Johannisberg Riesling
district: Southwestern Michigan
city or village: Buchanan
This was the first wine produced in the Midwest to show the character of late-harvested grapes affected by Botrytis mold. The best wine from the winery to date.
Light gold color and a fruity bouquet suggestive of apricots. The wine is clean, crisp, and sweet. **price range:** C

producer: Tabor Hill Vineyard & Winecellar, Inc.
classification: Red varietal table wine
grape variety: Baco Noir
district: Berrien County
city or village: Buchanan
This was Tabor Hill's first Baco Noir to be aged nine months in French oak.
Deep red color and a varietal bouquet with an underlying oak aroma from barrel aging. The wine is dry and full-bodied.
price range: B

producer: Tabor Hill Vineyard & Winecellar, Inc.
classification: White varietal table wine
grape variety: Chardonnay
district: Berrien County
city or village: Buchanan
Brilliant pale straw color and a true varietal bouquet with a suggestion of oak. The wine is light and dry, with some tannin.
price range: B

producer: Tabor Hill Vineyard & Winecellar, Inc.
classification: Rosé table wine
grape variety: Blend
district: Berrien County
city or village: Buchanan
A rosé for non-rosé drinkers.
Deep rosé color and a clean, fruity bouquet. The wine is crisp and full-bodied and is blended for those who enjoy big wines. **price range:** B

producer: Tabor Hill Vineyard & Winecellar, Inc.
classification: White table wine
grape variety: Blend
district: Berrien County
city or village: Buchanan
Named one of the best wines produced in 1976.
Golden to light gold color and a soft, fruity bouquet. The wine is clean, crisp, and pleasant, with a soft, full taste of sweetness. **price range:** B

producer: Tabor Hill Vineyard & Winecellar, Inc.
classification: White varietal table wine
grape variety: Johannisberg Riesling
district: Berrien County
city or village: Buchanan
Pale straw color and a typical varietal bouquet. The wine has full Riesling flavor and character.　**price range:** B

producer: Warner Vineyards, Inc.
classification: White sparkling wine
grape variety: Seyval Blanc and Delaware
district: Van Buren County
city or village: Paw Paw
A light white sparkling wine sold as "Imperial Brut Champagne."
Pale straw-gold color and a vinous, delicate bouquet. The wine effervesces nicely, is light bodied, and off dry.
price range: A

producer: Warner Vineyards, Inc.
classification: White varietal table wine
grape variety: Seyval Blanc
district: Van Buren County
city or village: Paw Paw
A light, dry Chablis-type wine.
Very pale straw-gold color and a vinous, complex bouquet. The wine has an unusual herbaceous flavor—slightly metallic and "sandy."　**price range:** B

producer: Warner Vineyards, Inc.
classification: White sparkling wine
grape variety: Delaware and Niagara

district: Van Buren County
city or village: Paw Paw
A medium-sweet white sparkling Champagne.
Light straw-gold color, and a slightly fruity bouquet. The wine is effervescent, slightly fruity and has residual sugar.
price range: A

producer: Warner Vineyards, Inc.
classification: White table wine
grape variety: Aurora Blanc
district: Van Buren County
city or village: Paw Paw
A Barsac-type wine; slightly sweet.
Light straw-gold color and a slightly fruity, complex bouquet. The wine is fruity, medium-bodied, and has residual sugar.
price range: B

producer: Warner Vineyards, Inc.
classification: Fortified wine
grape variety: Niagara and Concord
district: Van Buren County
city or village: Paw Paw
A light Oloroso-type of Cream Sherry.
Medium-dark amber-brown color and a heavy aldehyde bouquet. The wine is maderized, with heavy aldehydes, and tastes sweet.　**price range:** A

producer: Warner Vineyards, Inc.
classification: Rosé varietal table wine
grape variety: De Chaunac
district: Van Buren County
city or village: Paw Paw
Similar to a Tavel.
Pink to orange color and a vinous, complex bouquet. The wine is dry, full-bodied, and complex, like a Tavel.
price range: B

producer: Warner Vineyards, Inc.
classification: White sparkling wine
grape variety: Seyval Blanc, Chardonnay, and Aurora Blanc
district: Van Buren County
city or village: Paw Paw
Warner Vineyards "Brut Champagne" is truly a legendary American Champagne, bottle-fermented by the traditional *methode champenoise*.
Pale straw-gold color and a light, complex, and yeasty bouquet. The wine effervesces nicely, has a slight yeasty flavor, and is very dry.　**price range:** C

producer: Warner Vineyards, Inc.
classification: White table wine
grape variety: Delaware and Liebestrauben
district: Van Buren County
city or village: Paw Paw
Made from late-harvested grapes, like a Mosel Spätlese.
Light straw-gold color and a full, complex, and flowery bouquet. The wine is slightly fruity and residually sweet, like a Mosel.　**price range:** B

producer: Warner Vineyards, Inc.
classification: Red table wine
grape variety: Baco Noir and Maréchal Foch
district: Van Buren County
city or village: Paw Paw
A light red Burgundy-type wine.
Slightly tawny, ruby-red color, and a vinous, complex bouquet. The wine is medium-bodied and quite dry.
price range: A

producer: Warner Vineyards, Inc.
classification: White table wine
grape variety: Seyval Blanc and Delaware
district: Van Buren County
city or village: Paw Paw
"Chablis."
Pale straw-gold color and a vinous, delicate bouquet. The wine is dry, vinous, and light bodied, like a light Chablis.
price range: A

MISSOURI

producer: Ashby Vineyards, Inc. (Rosati Winery)
classification: White table wine
grape variety: Concord
district: Central Missouri—Phelps County
city or village: St. James
This sweet white dessert wine is made from red Concord grapes picked pink and quickly cold-pressed, with no white varieties blended in. The wine is not fortified and is less than 14% alcohol by volume.
Deep golden color and a mellow bouquet. The wine is smooth, full-bodied, and sweet—a fine dessert wine.
price range: A

producer: Ashby Vineyards, Inc. (Rosati Winery)
classification: Red table wine
grape variety: Concord
district: Central Missouri—Phelps County
city or village: St. James
A sweet, mellow red wine made from Concord grapes. It is similar to the homemade wines German farmers in the St. James area produce for themselves.

Tawny-red color and a pungent bouquet with evident sweetness and oak overtones. The wine is very sweet and mellow and is full-bodied. **price range: A**

producer: Ashby Vineyards, Inc. (Rosati Winery)
classification: White table wine
grape variety: Blend of Labrusca varieties
district: Central Missouri—Phelps County
city or village: St. James

A very popular wine, slightly different from the usual Chablis.

Sparkling clear straw color and a slightly heady bouquet characteristic of Labrusca. The wine is slightly sweet, with less tannin than some California wines. **price range: A**

producer: Ashby Vineyards, Inc. (Rosati Winery)
classification: Red table wine
grape variety: Blend of Concord, Foch, and Baco Noir
district: Central Missouri—Phelps County
city or village: St. James

This small winery has developed a method of handling Concords so as to reduce the foxy taste and aroma inherent in the variety. This shows up best in their "Burgundy," which is patterned on the "home" wines of local Italian-Americans.

Deep red color typical of a Burgundy and a slightly musky, "peppery" bouquet. The wine has less astringency than most Burgundies and is mellow and dry. **price range: A**

producer: Ashby Vineyards, Inc. (Rosati Winery)
classification: White table wine

grape variety: Missouri Riesling
district: Central Missouri—Phelps County
city or village: St. James

A fine native white variety, Missouri Riesling gives wines that do not resemble vinifera Rieslings. It gives extremely flavorful wines, perhaps too fruity for some palates, that have made it a popular grape in Missouri since it was developed in Hermann, Missouri in the mid-1800s.

Golden-straw color and an extremely fruity, pronounced bouquet. The wine is youthful and crisp, with some foxiness—a fine native varietal wine, dry and light. **price range: A**

producer: Green Valley Vineyards
classification: Red table wine
grape variety: French-American hybrids
district: North of the Missouri River

This brilliant red wine is of medium color, with an earthy, pleasant bouquet. It is soft to the palate, well-balanced, with light fruit. **price range: A**

producer: Green Valley Vineyards
classification: White table wine
grape variety: French-American hybrids, Missouri grown
district: North of the Missouri River

This white wine has a light greenish-yellow tint and a distinctive, clean bouquet. It is dry and well-balanced. **price range: A**

producer: Mount Pleasant Vineyards
classification: White varietal table wine
grape variety: Seyval Blanc (100%)
district: Missouri River
city or village: Augusta

This is a fresh, clean-tasting white wine, somewhat reminiscent of a Loire wine, made entirely from the Seyval Blanc grape.

The wine goes very well with seafood and never leaves the unpleasant aftertaste so typical of many poorly made whites. It should be blind-tasted against your favorite California white wine. **price range: A**

producer: Mount Pleasant Vineyards
classification: Red varietal table wine
grape variety: Münch
district: Missouri River
city or village: Augusta

Mount Pleasant Vineyards has the world's largest planting of Münch (1 acre), and the grape must surely be on someone's endangered species list. The Münch is a cross between Herbemont and Post-Oak; its developer, Texan Thomas V. Munson, received the French Legion of Honor in Agriculture for this (1888) and other wine developments. In his native country he was treated with scorn and relegated to gradual obscurity.

Brilliant red color and a Pinot-like bouquet. The wine is light-bodied; perfectly dry, like a Valpolicella. **price range: A**

producer: Mount Pleasant Vineyards
classification: Rosé table wine
grape variety: French hybrid
district: Missouri River
city or village: Augusta

This is a totally different type of wine made from the Emigré Rosé; it is made to be drunk before it is two years old. It has about the same keeping qualities as cottage cheese, so it should be aged only with regret. Mount Pleasant's most popular wine; the 1975 vintage is better than any other.

Bright pink color and a slight sweet flavor like a Rhine wine. It is fresh-tasting and clean, with a light, subtle bouquet. **price range: A**

producer: Mount Pleasant Vineyards
classification: Red varietal table wine
grape variety: Cynthianna

district: Missouri River
city or village: Augusta

If you think your forefathers were relegated prior to Prohibition to drinking foxy (Labrusca) wines, you should try Cynthianna. This grape was formerly the basis of a substantial dry red wine industry in Missouri. It is not of the species Labrusca, but rather Aestivalis, and the wine benefits from prolonged bottle aging.

Purple color and a spicy (nonfoxy) bouquet. The wine is completely dry, with a unique bouquet. The 1975 vintage is somewhat tart; those who are interested in the 1974 might still find some at the Restaurant Femme Osage in Washington, Missouri. **price range: A**

producer: Mount Pleasant Vineyards
classification: White varietal table wine
grape variety: Missouri Riesling
district: Missouri River
village: Augusta

As red Cynthianna represented the standard in Missouri red grapes before 1919, so Missouri Riesling represented the standards in whites. It was bred in 1860 in Hermann, Missouri, by Nicholas Grein, by crossing *Vitis riparia* with an unknown Labrusca variety. It does not impart a foxy flavor to the wines; as with many Rhinewine types, this wine has about 2% sugar. This vintage is the first time Mount Pleasant has made this wine, and it is sure to have a following.

Clear color and a fruity bouquet. The wine has no foxy flavor and is slightly sweet. **price range: A**

NEW JERSEY

producer: B & B Vineyards, Inc.
classification: Honey wine
variety: Honey
district: Delaware River Valley—Hunterdon County
city or village: Stockton

A traditional after-dinner wine. **price range: A**

producer: B & B Vineyards, Inc.
classification: Rosé table wine
grape variety: Niagara, Concord, and Catawba
district: Delaware River Valley—Hunterdon County
city or village: Stockton
A medium-dry rosé.
price range: A

producer: B & B Vineyards, Inc.
classification: Red table wine
grape variety: Baco Noir and Chelois
district: Delaware River Valley—Hunterdon County
city or village: Stockton
price range: A

producer: B & B Vineyards, Inc.
classification: White table wine
grape variety: Cascade and Gewürztraminer
district: Delaware River Valley—Hunterdon County
city or village: Stockton
A very dry white dinner wine.
price range: B

producer: Tomasello Winery
classification: White varietal table wine
grape variety: Villard Blanc

district: Atlantic and Camden counties
city or village: Hammonton
Pale gold color and a delicate bouquet. Though made from a hybrid, the wine has a subtle vinifera flavor. **price range:** A

producer: Tomasello Winery
classification: Red varietal table wine
grape variety: De Chaunac
district: Atlantic and Camden counties
city or village: Hammonton
Dark Burgundy-like color and a delicate aroma. Though made from a hybrid, the wine has the subtle taste of vinifera.
price range: A

OHIO

producer: Hafle Vineyards & Winery
classification: Red table wine
grape variety: Concord and French hybrids
district: Southwest Ohio
city or village: Springfield
This wine is a best-seller; to date, it has preference in the eastern United States and Ontario, but hybrids are rapidly changing wine tastes in the East.
A fruity bouquet and a semi-sweet, hearty Labrusca flavor. **price range:** A

producer: Hafle Vineyards & Winery
classification: Rosé table wine
grape variety: French hybrids
district: Southwest Ohio
city or village: Springfield
This semi-dry rosé wine is Hafle's #1 best-seller.
Brilliant rosé color and a slightly fruity bouquet. The wine is semi-dry, soft, and delicate; it is perfect for entertaining.
price range: A

producer: Cedar Hill Wine Co.
classification: Red table wine
grape variety: Leon Millot (60%) and Chelois (40%)
district: Lake Erie
city or village: Cleveland
This 200-gallon-capacity winery produces wine for sale only in its restaurant, Au Provençal. The restaurant seats 32 and specializes in creole and French foods, and the winery is located in the basement of the restaurant. This wine is made from a combination of two French-American hybrids.
Clear red color, and a vinous bouquet. The wine is dry, medium-bodied, and fresh. **price range:** B

producer: Cedar Hill Wine Co.
classification: Red varietal table wine
grape variety: Dhambourcin (J.S. 26-205)
district: Lake Erie
city or village: Cleveland
This French-American hybrid grape is capable of producing a superior "Burgundy" wine.
Clear purple color and a vinous bouquet. The wine is dry, full-bodied, and rather high in tannin. **price range:** B

producer: Cedar Hill Wine Co.
classification: White varietal table wine
grape variety: Seyval Blanc (S.V. 5276)
district: Lake Erie
city or village: Cleveland

This 200-gallon-capacity winery produces wine for sale only in its restaurant, Au Provençal, which specializes in Creole and French foods. The winery is located in the basement of the restaurant. This wine is made from a popular French-American hybrid.
Light yellow-green color and a vinous bouquet that is European in character. The wine is medium-bodied and dry.
price range: B

producer: Mantey Vineyards, Inc.
classification: Red table wine
grape variety: Baco Noir
district: Lake Erie
city or village: Sandusky
Rich red color and a heavily tart, robust flavor. **price range:** A

producer: Mantey Vineyards, Inc.
classification: Rosé table wine
grape variety: French-American hybrids
district: Lake Erie
city or village: Sandusky
Light pink color and a soft, slightly spicy bouquet. The wine is sweet and tart.
price range: A

producer: Dover Vineyards, Inc.
classification: Red table wine
grape variety: Concord and Niagara
district: Lake Erie
city or village: Westlake
Medium-sweet red wine.
price range: A

producer: Dover Vineyards, Inc.
classification: Rosé table wine
grape variety: Catawba
district: Lake Erie
city or village: Westlake
price range: A

producer: Dover Vineyards, Inc.
classification: Red table wine
grape variety: Concord
district: Lake Erie
city or village: Westlake
price range: A

producer: Moyer Vineyards
classification: Rosé table wine
grape variety: Blend of viniferas and
French hybrids
district: Ohio River Valley
city or village: Manchester
Deep pink color; the wine is dry and
fruity. **price range:** A

producer: Moyer Vineyards
classification: White table wine
grape variety: Blend of French hybrids and
vinifera

district: Ohio River Valley
city or village: Manchester
Pale straw color; the wine is dry and
crisp. **price range:** A

producer: Moyer Vineyards
classification: Red table wine
grape variety: Blend of French hybrids and
vinifera
district: Ohio River Valley
city or village: Manchester
"River Valley Red."
Medium red color; a moderately dry red
wine. **price range:** A

producer: Moyer Vineyards
classification: White table wine
grape variety: Blend of French hybrids and
vinifera
district: Ohio River Valley
city or village: Manchester
"River Valley White."
Pale yellow color; the wine is moderately
dry. **price range:** A

producer: Markko Vineyard
classification: White varietal table wine
grape variety: Johannisberg (White)
Riesling
district: Lake Erie
city or village: Conneaut
This White Riesling comes from grapes
grown on the heavier soil (silt-loam) in the
Lake Erie district of Ohio and has distinct
character. It is low in alcohol and semi-
sweet (1% residual sugar); it comes from a
blend of the latest clonal selections of
Riesling from Germany: #239, #356, and
#90.
Light straw color and a typical Riesling
bouquet. The wine is semi-sweet, smooth,
light, and fresh, with the characteristic balance of wines made from this noble grape
variety. **price range:** B

producer: Markko Vineyard
classification: White varietal table wine
grape variety: Pinot Chardonnay
district: Lake Erie
city or village: Conneaut
Chardonnay, when grown in the heavy
silt-loam soil of Lake Erie, has the distinct
characteristics of the region. This wine is
lighter than the 1973 vintage, but it will
develop full balance and character with
added bottle age.
Light straw color and a typical bouquet.
The wine is fresh and crisp.
price range: B

producer: Markko Vineyard
classification: White table wine
grape variety: White Riesling
district: Lake Erie
city or village: Conneaut
This semi-sweet white wine is a blend of
the latest clonal selections of Riesling imported from Germany: #239, #90, and
#356.
Light straw color and a distinct Riesling
bouquet. The wine is fresh, clean, and
crisp; it is semi-sweet and especially light
and delicate. **price range:** B

producer: Markko Vineyard
classification: Red table wine
grape variety: Cabernet Sauvignon and
Chambourcin
district: Lake Erie
city or village: Conneaut
The blend of grapes used for this wine
varies, and plantings are adjusted to improve the wine's characteristics. Markko is
increasing their proportions of Cabernet
Sauvignon.
Deep red-purple color and a medium
bouquet. The wine has medium to full body
and is ready to drink upon release.
price range: B

producer: Markko Vineyard
classification: White varietal table wine
grape variety: Chardonnay
district: Lake Erie
village: Conneaut
The grapes for this wine were grown in
Dunkirk, New York, on the deep gravelly
soil at the Woodbury Fruit Farm, and made
at the Markko winery in Conneaut. It was
aged in white oak casks.
Light yellow color and a full Chardonnay
bouquet. The wine is complex, with full
body and character developed from aging
in oak. **price range:** B

*"Bronze is the mirror of the
form; wine, of the heart."*
—Aeschylus

producer: Meier's Wine Cellars, Inc.
classification: White table wine
grape variety: Labrusca varieties
district: Lake Erie
Very light amber color and a fruity
bouquet. A clean, dry wine.
price range: A

producer: Meier's Wine Cellars, Inc.
classification: White table wine
grape variety: Labrusca varieties
district: Lake Erie
Clear light amber color and a fruity
bouquet. A clean, sweet white wine.
price range: A

producer: Meier's Wine Cellars, Inc.
classification: Rosé table wine
grape variety: Labrusca varieties/Catawba
district: Lake Erie
Pink rose-petal color and a fruity bouquet. The wine is clean-tasting.
price range: A

producer: Meier's Wine Cellars, Inc.
classification: Red table wine
grape variety: Labrusca varieties
district: Lake Erie
Deep ruby-red color and a fruity bouquet. The wine is clean and dry.
price range: A

producer: Meier's Wine Cellars, Inc.
classification: Red table wine
grape variety: Labrusca varieties
district: Lake Erie
Deep ruby-red color and a fruity bouquet. The wine is dry and clean-tasting.
price range: A

producer: Meier's Wine Cellars, Inc.
classification: Red sparkling wine
grape variety: Labrusca varieties
district: Lake Erie
Clear red color and a fruity bouquet. The wine is clean-tasting. **price range:** A

producer: Meier's Wine Cellars, Inc.
classification: Rosé sparkling wine
grape variety: Labrusca varieties
district: Lake Erie
Clear rosé-pink color and a fruity bouquet. The wine is clean-tasting.
price range: A

producer: Meier's Wine Cellars, Inc.
classification: White sparkling wine
grape variety: Labrusca varieties
district: Lake Erie
Clear color and a fruity bouquet. The wine is clean-tasting. **price range:** A

producer: Meier's Wine Cellars, Inc.
classification: Red sparkling wine
grape variety: Labrusca varieties
district: Lake Erie
Clear ruby-red color and a fruity bouquet. The wine is clean-tasting.
price range: B

producer: Meier's Wine Cellars, Inc.
classification: Rosé table wine
grape variety: Catawba
district: Lake Erie
Fresh pink color and a fruity bouquet. The wine is semi-dry and clean-tasting.
price range: A

producer: Meier's Wine Cellars, Inc.
classification: Red sparkling wine
grape variety: Labrusca varieties
district: Lake Erie
Clear red "Burgundy" color and a fruity bouquet. The wine is clean-tasting.
price range: B

producer: Meier's Wine Cellars, Inc.
classification: Rosé sparkling wine
grape variety: Labrusca varieties
district: Lake Erie
Clear pink color and a fruity bouquet. The wine is clean-tasting.
price range: B

producer: Meier's Wine Cellars, Inc.
classification: White sparkling wine
grape variety: Labrusca varieties
district: Lake Erie
Clear white color and a fruity bouquet. The wine is clean-tasting.
price range: C

producer: Meier's Wine Cellars, Inc.
classification: White sparkling wine
grape variety: Labrusca varieties
district: Lake Erie
Clear color and a fruity bouquet. The wine is clean and dry. **price range:** B

producer: Meier's Wine Cellars, Inc.
classification: Fortified wine
grape variety: Labrusca varieties
district: Lake Erie
Dark amber color and a fruity bouquet. The wine is sweet and clean-tasting.
price range: B

producer: Meier's Wine Cellars, Inc.
classification: Rosé sparkling wine
grape variety: Labrusca varieties
district: Lake Erie
Clear pink color and a fruity bouquet. The wine is clean-tasting. **price range:** C

producer: Meier's Wine Cellars, Inc.
classification: White sparkling wine
grape variety: Labrusca varieties
district: Lake Erie
Clear natural-white color and a fruity bouquet. The wine is clean-tasting.
price range: B

producer: Meier's Wine Cellars, Inc.
classification: Red sparkling wine
grape variety: Labrusca varieties

district: Lake Erie
Royal-red "Burgundy" color and a fruity bouquet. The wine is clean-tasting.
price range: C

producer: Valley Vineyards Farm Inc.
classification: Red varietal table wine
grape variety: Blue Eye
district: Southwestern Ohio
city or village: Morrow
Probably the only winery making wine from the Blue Eye grape, a new American hybrid that makes unique and delicious red wine. There is only limited production.
Light red color and a delicate bouquet and flavor. A truly delicious red wine.
price range: B

producer: Valley Vineyards Farm, Inc.
classification: Red varietal table wine
grape variety: Baco Noir (90%) and Foch (10%)
district: Southwestern Ohio
city or village: Morrow
This estate-bottled wine has the distinctive character of Baco Noir, the French hybrid grape, and as it improves considerably with age, is ideal to lay down in your cellar.
Medium body and a soft, delicate bouquet. The wine has distinctive varietal characteristics. **price range:** B

producer: Valley Vineyards Farm, Inc.
classification: White varietal table wine
grape variety: Seyve-Villard 5276 (Seyval Blanc)
district: Southwestern Ohio
city or village: Morrow
A dry white wine made entirely from select premium Seyval Blanc grapes, not blended with any other varieties.
Delicate golden color and a light bouquet. The wine is delicately dry and delicious. **price range:** A

producer: Valley Vineyards Farm, Inc.
classification: Red varietal table wine
grape variety: De Chaunac (Seibel 9549)
district: Southwestern Ohio
city or village: Morrow
This estate-bottled red wine is made from the De Chaunac grape, a French hybrid; at the 1975 American Wine Society Conference, this wine was voted "best in the nation" at a blind tasting by professional judges.
Deep red color and a full-bodied, distinctive bouquet. The wine has the full body and rich flavor of wines from this variety.
price range: B

producer: Valley Vineyards Farm, Inc.
classification: Rosé table wine
grape variety: Concord
district: Southwestern Ohio
city or village: Morrow
Made from the well-known Concord grape, this is the vineyard's most popular wine. It had its beginnings when they made the mistake of not letting it ferment on the skins for the proper length of time, the end result being a "pink" wine instead of a deep red the way most Concords are.
Soft red-pink color and a foxy bouquet. The wine is sweet and mellow; a pleasant, distinctive rosé produced by an unusual cellar treatment. **price range:** A

producer: Valley Vineyards Farm, Inc.
classification: Honey wine
variety: Honey
district: Southwestern Ohio
village: Morrow
This wine is a true mead, a rich, full-bodied sweet wine made from pure clover honey. First it is fermented dry, then sweetened with more clover honey before bottling to preserve its unique flavor.
Golden color and a slightly viscous appearance. The wine has a honey bouquet and flavor, like mead.
price range: B

producer: Valley Vineyards Farm, Inc.
classification: White table wine
grape variety: Seyve-Villard 12375 (Villard Blanc)
district: Southwestern Ohio
city or village: Morrow
"Mellow White" is a full-bodied white wine reflecting the mellowness and fragrance of a fine French hybrid grape.
Soft, clear color; the flavor is not too dry and very distinct. **price range:** A

OREGON

producer: Charles Coury Vineyards
classification: Red varietal table wine
grape variety: Pinot Noir (100%)
This is an elegant, aristocratic red wine made entirely from Pinot Noir grapes. All the varietal wines produced by Charles Coury Vineyards are 100% varietal wines.
price range: B

producer: Charles Coury Vineyards
classification: White varietal table wine
grape variety: Chardonnay (100%)
This is a nutty, dry white wine with a strong bouquet. **price range:** B

producer: Charles Coury Vineyards
classification: White varietal table wine
grape variety: Riesling (100%)

This is a superb, fragrant, semi-dry white wine made entirely from Washington State White Riesling grapes. It has a German/Alsatian tone and a fragrant bouquet.
price range: B

producer: The Eyrie Vineyards
classification: White varietal table wine
grape variety: Johannisberg (White) Riesling
district: Willamette Valley
city or village: Dundee
This is one of the very few totally dry Rieslings produced in the United States: it has only 0.2% reducing sugar.
Light color and a full, powerful varietal aroma. The wine is dry but very well-balanced. **price range:** B

producer: The Eyrie Vineyards
classification: Red varietal table wine
grape variety: Pinot Noir (100%)
district: Willamette Valley
village: Dundee
The 1973 vintage Pinot Noir was aged for two years in French Limousin oak barrels and was not filtered, fined, or centrifuged. The wine is quite drinkable now but will gain complexity with further bottle aging.
Color and bouquet typical of the variety—fruity, clean, full, and fresh. The wine shows good balance of tannin and acidity and is full-flavored.
price range: C

producer: The Eyrie Vineyards
classification: White varietal table wine
grape variety: Chardonnay (100%)
district: Willamette Valley
city or village: Dundee

The 1974 vintage was excellent in Oregon for Chardonnay. The wine was both fermented and aged in French Limousin oak barrels, as is the practice in the Burgundy district in France.

Straw color and a typical varietal bouquet. The wine shows good balance in wood, body, and acidity.
price range: C

producer: The Eyrie Vineyards
classification: Red varietal table wine
grape variety: Pinot Meunier (100%)
district: Willamette Valley
city or village: Dundee

The Pinot Meunier variety is native to the Champagne district in France, where it is one of the principal varieties used for Champagne and sometimes used to make a still red wine. The Eyrie Vineyard is the only producer in the United States to make a varietal wine from Pinot Meunier, and the wine is available only at the winery in limited quantities.

Medium-dark red color and a big, complex bouquet. The wine has unique character, good balance, and sufficient tannin to age gracefully; it is a very good and unique red wine. **price range:** C

"Taste cannot be controlled by law." —Thomas Jefferson

producer: The Eyrie Vineyards
classification: White varietal table wine
grape variety: Pinot Gris (100%)
district: Willamette Valley
city or village: Dundee

This unusual variety is native to the Baden region in Germany and the Alsace region in France, but it is not widely planted in the United States; at this time, a 100% Pinot Gris is produced only by the Eyrie Vineyards in this country, and the wine is available only at the winery.

Straw color with orange tints and a pronounced, full bouquet with applelike fruitiness that is characteristic of the variety. The wine is very full and flavorful, yet it is crisp and clean, with balanced acidity; it finishes beautifully and is a perfect accompaniment to salmon. **price range:** C

producer: Knudsen Erath Winery
classification: Red varietal table wine
grape variety: Pinot Noir
district: Willamette Valley
　This is a dry red Pinot Noir.
price range: B

producer: Knudsen Erath Winery
classification: Red varietal table wine
grape variety: Gamay
district: Willamette Valley
　This is a dry red Gamay wine.
price range: B

producer: Knudsen Erath Winery
classification: White varietal table wine
grape variety: White Riesling
district: Willamette Valley
　This medium yellow White Riesling is slightly sweet. **price range:** B

producer: Knudsen Erath Winery
classification: White varietal table wine
grape variety: Pinot Blanc
district: Willamette Valley
　This medium yellow Pinot Blanc is dry.
price range: B

producer: Knudsen Erath Winery
classification: White varietal table wine
grape variety: Gewürztraminer
district: Willamette Valley
　This is a slightly sweet, medium yellow Gewürztraminer. **price range:** B

producer: Knudsen Erath Winery
classification: White varietal table wine
grape variety: Sauvignon Blanc
district: Willamette Valley
　This is a dry Sauvignon Blanc
price range: B

producer: Ponzi Vineyards
classification: Red varietal table wine
grape variety: Pinot Noir
district: Willamette Valley
city or village: Beaverton

This was the first harvest of Pinot Noir, and it represents Ponzi Vineyards' first release. Only free-run juice was used, and the wine was aged in new French oak barrels. The vineyard and winery are limited in size to a family operation, as is traditional in Europe.

Deep ruby-red color and a fruity, full aroma. The wine is full-bodied, with a moderately long finish; it is best served with steak or an Italian feast.
price range: B

producer: Tualatin Vineyards, Inc.
classification: White varietal table wine
grape variety: Pinot Blanc (100%)
district: Willamette Valley
city or village: Beaverton

This was the first harvest of Pinot Blanc, and it represents the first release by the Ponzi Vineyard. It is ready to drink when shipped.

Straw-yellow color and a full, fruity bouquet with good varietal character. The wine shows good balance and has a pleasant varietal character reminiscent of an Alsatian Pinot Blanc; the finish is good.
price range: B

producer: Tualatin Vineyards
classification: White varietal table wine
grape variety: Gewürztraminer
district: Willamette Valley
city or village: Forest Grove

The grapes for this wine came from a vineyard set on a sloping bench above the Columbia River in central Washington State. They were harvested at optimum ripeness in mid-September 1975. After a cool, temperature-controlled fermentation, the wine was held in jacketed stainless-steel tanks to preserve its freshness and varietal character. It was bottled in late March 1976; only eight hundred cases were produced.

Clear color and a fruity bouquet typical of the varietal. The wine is spicy, dry, and pleasant, in the Alsatian style.
price range: B

producer: Tualatin Vineyards
classification: White varietal table wine
grape variety: Johannisberg (White) Riesling (100%)
district: Willamette Valley
city or village: Forest Grove

This wine is a happy marriage of two vintages of White Riesling, 1974 and 1975. The grace and complexity of the older wine beautifully complements the freshness of the younger wine. Both wines are 100% White Riesling from two vineyards in neighboring Washington State, one in the Yakima Valley and the other along the Columbia River. The wines were fermented slowly under refrigeration and held in stainless-steel tanks to preserve their full varietal character. Only 1850 cases were produced, and the wine was bottled in the spring of 1976.

Clear color and a fruity, varietal bouquet. The wine is soft, balanced, and medium dry. **price range:** B

producer: Tulatin Vineyards, Inc.
classification: White varietal table wine
grape variety: White Riesling
district: Willamette River valley
city or village: Forest Grove

Pale straw color and a fresh, fragrant, and fruity bouquet. The wine is medium-dry, soft, and round, with a characteristic varietal flavor. **price range:** B

PENNSYLVANIA

producer: Adams County Winery
classification: White varietal table wine
grape variety: Seyval Blanc (100%)
district: Southern Pennsylvania
city or village: Orrtanna

No water or sugar is added to the must. The juice is settled for many days before fermentation is started, resulting in a very pale color. Later bottles are demonstrating the result of white oak barrel aging. Very heavy rainfall prior to picking did not drop the grape sugar. No sorbate preservatives are added.

Pale green color and a very pronounced sweet Seyval aroma. The wine is crisp and clean and quite full-bodied; it has a long, fruity aftertaste. **price range:** B

producer: Adams County Winery
classification: White table wine
grape variety: Vidal Blanc (85%) and White Riesling (15%)
district: Southern Pennsylvania
city or village: Orrtanna

This wine was fermented at low temperature (45 degrees F.), and no sugar or water was added to the must, which was settled

for several days prior to fermentation. No sorbate preservatives were added.

Pale green-yellow color and an extremely sweet bouquet with traces of oak. The wine is more neutral than Adams' other whites, but it does have an extremely aromatic Vidal varietal aroma. The wine is full-bodied, and a pronounced oak/vanillin aftertaste results from lengthy aging in cask. **price range:** B

producer: Adams County Winery
classification: White varietal table wine
grape variety: Pinot Chardonnay (100%)
district: Southern Pennsylvania
city or village: Orrtanna

The vines were only five years old, yet they produced a wine rich in varietal characteristics. No sugar or water was added to the must; heavy rains before picking did not reduce the sugar content in the grapes. In this area, vinifera varieties seem to be even hardier than hybrids. After the juice was settled for many days, the wine was cold-fermented at 45 degrees F.; no sorbate preservatives were added.

Pale green color and a pronounced, varietal bouquet. The wine is crisp and clean, with a dry apple flavor; it is very dry. **price range:** B

producer: Adams County Winery
classification: Red table wine
grape variety: Chancellor Noir and De Chaunac
district: Southern Pennsylvania
city or village: Orrtanna

The grapes for this wine were fermented at lower than normal temperature (60 degrees F.); no sulphur dioxide was used after initial heavy sulphuring prior to the grape crush. The wine resembled a young Burgundy in taste by late 1975, but with age has tended toward a Bordeaux in character. No water was added to the must, though sugar was added to raise the Brix reading 2%; no sorbate preservatives were added.

Extremely deep red color when viewed against a bright light, and an extremely fruity bouquet. The wine is very full-bodied, fruity, and slightly tart; it was bottled early and shows neither a trace of residual sweetness nor a trace of wood tannin. **price range:** B

producer: Adams County Winery
classification: White table wine
grape variety: Chardonnay (50%) and Seyval Blanc (30%)
district: Southern Pennsylvania
city or village: Orrtanna

Neither water nor sugar was used in the making of this wine. Over 50% Chardonnay was used, but the wine has a slight aroma from an addition of approximately 2% Muscat de Frontignan. The wine was neither filtered nor stabilized with potassium sorbate. Because the wine has low acidity, it appears to have some residual sugar, though none is measurable.

Very pale green-yellow color and an extremely sweet aroma suggestive of Gewürztraminer. The wine is soft, round, and fruity; it has lower acidity than other Adams County wines and is close in style to those produced in cooler California climates. The finish reveals some wood as a result of aging in white oak barrels. **price range:** B

producer: Buckingham Valley Vineyards
classification: Red varietal table wine
grape variety: Maréchal Foch
district: Eastern Pennsylvania—Bucks County
city or village: Buckingham

At present, the only estate-bottled vintage wine produced in Bucks County.

Deep ruby-red color and a big, full bouquet. The wine is dry and clean, with excellent flavor. **price range:** A

producer: Buckingham Valley Vineyards
classification: White varietal table wine
grape variety: Seyval Blanc
district: Eastern Pennsylvania—Bucks County
city or village: Buckingham

An estate-bottled vintage wine.

Light color and a fruity bouquet. The wine is clean, with light body and a touch of sweetness—an excellent Seyval Blanc. **price range:** A

producer: Buckingham Valley Vineyards
classification: Rosé table wine
grape variety: Rosette, Seyval, Vidal, and Baco blend
district: Eastern Pennsylvania—Bucks County
city or village: Buckingham

An estate-bottled vintage wine.

Clear light rosé color and a fruity bouquet. The wine is clean, with excellent flavor and light body, and is slightly sweet. **price range:** A

producer: Bucks Country Vineyards
classification: Red table wine
grape variety: Chancellor, Foch, Baco Noir, and Chambourcin
district: Bucks County
city or village: New Hope

The current vintage of this young, fruity wine is blended with barrel-aged older vintages to yield a Burgundy-type wine.

Red color with medium purple tints and a distinctive, herbaceous, and fruity bouquet with some oak. The wine is soft, dry, and full-bodied, with a long, earthy finish; it is velvety, complex, and ready to drink now. **price range:** A

producer: Bucks Country Vineyards
classification: Rosé table wine
grape variety: Red and white hybrids and Catawba
district: Bucks County
city or village: New Hope

An interesting blend of hybrid and Labrusca grapes.

Medium pink color and a strong, spicy, and fruity bouquet. The wine is slightly sweet, soft, and fruity; serve chilled, with luncheon. **price range:** A

producer: Bucks Country Vineyards
classification: White varietal table wine
grape variety: Aurora Blanc
district: Bucks County
city or village: New Hope

This very attractive wine is made in the Loire Valley style, and though it is very attractive when young, it develops interesting complexity after two years' bottle age.

Brilliant light yellow color and a fresh, clean, and fruity varietal bouquet. The wine is dry, light-bodied, and has good acidity with a long fruity finish.
price range: A

producer: Bucks Country Vineyards
classification: Red varietal table wine
grape variety: Chelois
district: Bucks County
city or village: New Hope

Though fruity and smooth enough to drink young, in the Beaujolais style, this wine improves for several years to become soft, complex, and mature.

Medium red color with light purple tints and an intense varietal bouquet with some oak spice. The wine is dry, has medium body and acidity, and strong fruit.
price range: A

producer: Bucks Country Vineyards
classification: White table wine
grape variety: Villard, Seyval Blanc, Vidal Blanc, and Rayon d'Or
district: Bucks County
city or village: New Hope

Bottled after a very short period in the cellar, this wine is best enjoyed young, while its fruit is still at its peak.

Brilliant straw-yellow color and a strong, fruity, and pearlike bouquet. The wine is medium-bodied, semi-dry, and balanced with acid and fruit.   **price range:** A

producer: Bucks Country Vineyards
classification: Rosé varietal table wine
grape variety: Catawba
district: Bucks County
city or village: New Hope

This classic rosé wine is made from native eastern American grapes.

Brilliant light pink color and a strong varietal bouquet showing some wood. The wine combines sweetness with smooth fruit and is very good with fruits.
price range: A

producer: Conestoga Vineyards Inc.
classification: Red table wine
grape variety: Cascade blend

This is a fresh, fruity wine, whose rosé color has a slight orange-red tint to it.
price range: A

producer: Conestoga Vineyards, Inc.
classification: White table wine
grape variety: Seyval Blanc blend
city or village: Birchrunville

This brilliant light yellow wine has a subtle flavor and a fresh taste.
price range: A

producer: Conestoga Vineyards, Inc.
classification: Red table wine
grape variety: Blended French hybrids
city or village: Birchrunville

This light red wine has a slight oak taste; a mellow flavor; and a full, winey bouquet.
price range: A

producer: Penn-Shore Vineyards, Inc.
classification: White table wine
grape variety: Pinot Chardonnay
district: Lake Erie
city or village: North East

Estate-bottled, 1971 vintage.

Pale straw color and a varietal bouquet. The wine is crisp and dry.
price range: B

producer: Penn-Shore Vineyards, Inc.
classification: Red sparkling wine
grape variety: Blend
district: Lake Erie
city or village: North East

An estate-bottled sparkling wine made via the *methode champenoise* and disgorged by hand.

Deep red color and a complex bouquet. A distinctly different red sparkling wine.
price range: C

producer: Penn-Shore Vineyards, Inc.
classification: White sparkling wine
grape variety: Blend
district: Lake Erie
city or village: North East

An estate-bottled sparkling wine produced via the *methode champenoise* and disgorged by hand.

Brilliant pale straw color and a fruity bouquet. A crisp, aristocratic sparkling wine.   **price range:** C

producer: Penn-Shore Vineyards, Inc.
classification: White table wine
grape variety: Seyval Blanc

district: Lake Erie
city or village: North East

Estate-bottled.

Brilliant pale straw color and a varietal bouquet. A crisp, dry white wine.
price range: A

producer: Penn-Shore Vineyards, Inc.
classification: Red table wine
grape variety: Cascade
district: Lake Erie
city or village: North East

An estate-bottled red wine made from a French hybrid grape variety.

Brilliant deep red color and a fruity bouquet. A crisp, dry red wine.
price range: A

producer: Penn-Shore Vineyards, Inc.
classification: White table wine
grape variety: Dutchess
district: Lake Erie
city or village: North East

Made from an American Labrusca variety and estate-bottled.

Pale straw color and a bouquet characteristic of the varietal. The wine is crisp but smooth.   **price range:** A

producer: Penn-Shore Vineyards, Inc.
classification: White table wine
grape variety: Catawba
district: Lake Erie
city or village: North East

Estate-bottled.

Pale straw color and a fruity bouquet. A crisp, dry white wine.   **price range:** A

producer: Pequea Valley Vineyard & Winery
classification: White varietal table wine
grape variety: Seyval Blanc
district: Lancaster County
city or village: Willow Street

Under the Pennsylvania Limited Winery Act of 1972, the Pequea Valley Vineyard was established by the Monsey Corporation.

Typical clear color and a distinctive bouquet characteristic of Seyval Blanc. The wine is clean, light, and dry, with a pleasant aftertaste; it is an excellent example of a wine made from this variety.
price range: A

producer: Pequea Valley Vineyard & Winery
classification: Red table wine
grape variety: Blend of Cascade, Foch, and Chelois
district: Lancaster County
city or village: Willow Street

Clear red color and a pronounced, pleasant nose typical of hybrids. The wine is clean and dry; typical of its area, it has flavor characteristics of hybrid grapes grown in southeastern Pennsylvania. It is a smooth, medium-red dinner wine.
price range: A

producer: Chateau Piatt Winery, Inc.
classification: White varietal table wine
grape variety: Niagara (100%)
district: Eastern Pennsylvania
city or village: Allentown

Although the Niagara is a native American grape variety of the species Labrusca, it is our most popular wine, especially with beginning wine drinkers. Total production ranges from 5,000 to 8,000 gallons per year; this particular varietal wine is made from 100% Niagara grapes with no water added. The wine is available in Pennsylvania State Liquor Stores, in some stores in New Jersey, and at the winery.

Clear color and a distinctly fruity bouquet. The wine has a native American grape flavor and is medium sweet.
price range: A

producer: Chateau Piatt Winery, Inc.
classification: Red table wine
grape variety: De Chaunac
district: Eastern Pennsylvania
city or village: Allentown

French hybrid grapes produce wines similar to those of Europe, yet the wines, like all varietals, retain their own character, producing more vinous wines than the fruity native American varieties. This is a good dinner wine, closer in style to a Burgundy rahter than a Bordeaux; serve with red meats. Although it was aged in 50-gallon white oak barrels, further bottle aging is recommended.

Deep red color and a complex, weedy bouquet. The wine is hearty, light-bodied, and fresh, with some oak flavor from the cask aging. **price range:** A

producer: Presque Isle Wine Cellars
classification: Red table wine
district: Lake Erie
city or village: North East **price range:** A

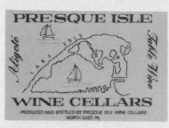

producer: Presque Isle Wine Cellars
classification: White varietal table wine
grape variety: Aligoté
district: Lake Erie
city or village: North East **price range:** A

producer: Presque Isle Wine Cellars
classification: Red varietal table wine
grape variety: Cabernet Sauvignon
district: Lake Erie
city or village: North East **price range:** B

producer: Presque Isle Wine Cellars
classification: White table wine
grape variety: Riesling
district: Lake Erie
city or village: North East **price range:** A

TEXAS

producer: Val Verde Winery
classification: White table wine
grape variety: Herbemont
district: Val Verde County
city or village: Del Rio

Val Verde is Texas' oldest winery: founded 1883. The wine is sold only at the winery, and the wine maker is a third-generation craftsman.

Brilliant amber color and a varietal bouquet. The wine shows a pleasing dryness. **price range:** A

producer: Val Verde Winery
classification: Red table wine
grape variety: Lenoir

district: Val Verde County
city or village: Del Rio

Medium red color and a varietal bouquet. The wine is extra dry.
price range: A

producer: Val Verde Winery
classification: Red table wine
grape variety: Lenoir
district: Val Verde County
city or village: Del Rio

Medium red color and a varietal bouquet. The wine is hearty and naturally sweet. **price range:** A

VERMONT

producer: Vermont Wineries, Inc.
classification: Honey wine
variety: Honey

A still wine, cork-finished.

Pale gold color and a floral, citrus bouquet. The wine is semi-dry.
price range: B

VIRGINIA

producer: Meredyth Vineyards
classification: White varietal table wine
gtape variety: Seyval Blanc (5276)
district: Fauquier County
city or village: Middleburg

This wine is from one of the first two vineyards in northern Virginia to produce wine.

Clear light golden color and a fruity bouquet still developing. The wine is clean and light, but it has body.
price range: B

producer: Meredyth Vineyards
classification: Rosé table wine
grape variety: Rougeon (Seibel 5898)
district: Fauquier County
city or village: Middleburg

This is the first wine produced from this grape variety in Virginia. Its initial popularity suggests that it will be promising. There are now two wineries in Virginia that produce estate-bottled wines; Meredyth is one of them. The winery has over a dozen different varieties planted over its 27 acres.

Clear rose-red color, deeper than most rosés, and a generous, outstanding bouquet. **price range:** B

producer: Meredyth Vineyards
classification: Red varietal table wine
grape variety: Maréchal Foch
district: Fauquier County
city or village: Middleburg

Clear red color with appropriate saturation and a full, developing bouquet suggesting a Burgundy—which carries into the flavor. **price range:** B

WASHINGTON

producer: Associated Vintners, Inc.
classification: Red varietal table wine
grape variety: Pinot Noir (100%)
district: Yakima Valley
city or village: Sunnyside

In Washington, Pinot Noir produces an excellent red wine if crop yields are kept low. The wine is more like a French Burgundy than a California Pinot Noir. The wine is aged for four years prior to sale.

Good red color, not as deep as a California Pinot Noir, and a rich Burgundy bouquet. Fine vintages show a marked similarity to French Burgundies; it is an excellent wine with red meats.
price range: B

producer: Associated Vintners, Inc.
classification: White varietal table wine
grape variety: Gewürztraminer (100%)
district: Yakima Valley
city or village: Sunnyside

Gewürztraminer is one of this vintner's specialties, and André Tchelistcheff said that theirs was one of the best Gewürztraminers made in the United States. This wine receives two years of bottle aging prior to sale.

Slight golden color and a characteristic spicy bouquet like an Alsatian Gewürztraminer. The wine has a full, spicy flavor; it is excellent with salmon, lobster, and crab, though its flavor might be too pronounced for more delicate seafood.
price range: B

producer: Associated Vintners, Inc.
classification: White varietal table wine
grape variety: Chardonnay
district: Yakima Valley
city or village: Sunnyside

To obtain the richness of a white "Burgundy," Chardonnay vines must be pruned back to two-thirds the expected crop from other varieties. This wine receives two years of aging prior to sale, one in the bottle.

Pale golden color and a well-made bouquet similar to a white Burgundy. It is an excellent white wine with stronger-flavored fish or turkey. **price range:** B

producer: Associated Vintners, Inc.
classification: White varietal table wine
grape variety: Johannisberg Riesling (100%)
district: Yakima Valley
city or village: Sunnyside

This is one of the few totally dry wines made from this varietal. It is aged one year in barrel and one year in bottle prior to sale.

Pale straw color and a characteristic Riesling bouquet. The wine is slightly tart, with fine Riesling flavor; it is an excellent dry white wine to accompany fish and chicken. **price range:** B

producer: Associated Vintners, Inc.
classification: White varietal table wine
grape variety: Semillon (10%)
district: Yakima Valley
city or village: Sunnyside

This variety is a very consistent producer of good-quality wine reminiscent of a fine white Graves. This Semillon receives two years of aging prior to sale, one in the bottle.

Golden color and a characteristic bouquet of Semillon or Graves. When aged, the wine develops rich flavor; it is an excellent wine with chicken and turkey.
price range: A

producer: Associated Vintners, Inc.
classification: Red varietal table wine
grape variety: Cabernet Sauvignon (100%)
district: Yakima Valley
city or village: Sunnyside

This is the most consistently excellent of six varietals grown in the cooler part of the Yakima Valley. It is aged four years prior to release, two in cask and then two in bottle.

Deep garnet-red color and a full bouquet characteristic of a good Bordeaux. The wine is slightly tannic and shows Bordeaux character; it will continue to improve for ten years. **price range:** C

producer: Boordy Vineyards
classification: Red varietal table wine
grape variety: Pinot Noir
district: Yakima Valley
city or village: Prosser

Boordy Vineyards Pinot Noir is produced in the Yakima Valley, Washington, along the same parallel as the Burgundy wine district of France.

Deep red color and the bouquet, deep color, and authority characteristic of Pinot Noir. The wine is full-bodied and dry; it is best with steak, roasts, game, or cheese but may be enjoyed on any occasion. Serve at room temperature.
price range: A

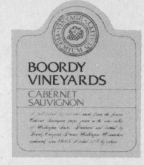

producer: Boordy Vineyards
classification: Red varietal table wine
grape variety: Cabernet Sauvignon
district: Yakima Valley
city or village: Prosser

Boordy Vineyards Cabernet Sauvignon is produced in the Yakima Valley, Washington, along the same parallel as the Burgundy wine district of France. When grown in Washington, this celebrated grape delivers all the authority for which it is famous.

A fine, full-bodied dry red wine. It is best with steak, roast, game, or cheese, but its full, delicate pleasure may be enjoyed on any occasion. Serve at room temperature.
price range: A

producer: Boordy Vineyards
classification: White varietal table wine
grape variety: Pinot Chardonnay
district: Yakima Valley
city or village: Prosser

Boordy Vineyards Pinot Chardonnay is produced in the Yakima Valley, Washington, along the same parallel as the Burgundy wine district of France.

A fine Washington State white "Burgundy" of exceptional integrity, harkening in taste to the full, rich character of the great French white Burgundies. For the neophyte wine drinker, its fullness may be surprising, since the wine is very dry and pale in color; serve well-chilled.
price range: A

producer: Ste. Michelle Vineyards
classification: White varietal table wine
grape variety: Gewürztraminer
district: Yakima Valley

Ste. Michelle's first bottling of Gewürztraminer is a well-balanced, outstanding example of this varietal; it is full and luscious, with the varietal spice, but not sweet. The true character of the grape has been allowed to come out. To the eye, it is a brilliant, viscous golden-yellow; its bouquet is fruity, spicy, and honeylike.
price range: B

producer: Ste. Michelle Vineyards
classification: White varietal table wine
grape variety: Semillon (100%)
district: Yakima Valley
city or village: Grandview
Earlier vintages of Semillon have been likened to the style of "Château Y," the dry wine of Château Yquem.
Pale straw-yellow color with green hints and a fine, citrusy, applelike bouquet. The wine is crisp and fruity, with a hint of flint—it is an excellent dry Semillon with a clean nose and full fruity flavor. It shows excellent varietal character.
price range: A

producer: Ste. Michelle Vineyards
classification: Rosé varietal table wine
grape variety: Grenache (100%)
district: Yakima Valley
city or village: Grandview
For the second consecutive year, this Grenache has been judged one of the best rosés produced in America by several tasting groups.
Medium-dark strawberry color and a bouquet suggesting both grapes and berries. The wine has a clean, lingering fruity flavor; varietal character is unmistakable, but a berrylike quality is present, with loads of fruit, excellent balance, and a touch of residual sugar. **price range:** A

producer: Ste. Michelle Vineyards
classification: Red varietal table wine
grape variety: Cabernet Sauvignon (100%)

district: Yakima Valley
city or village: Grandview
In 1974 this vineyard achieved a malolactic fermentation for the first time with their Cabernet, and the results are rewarding: the wine is softer and much more complex than previous vintages.
Deep purple-red color and a rich, fruity Cabernet bouquet showing some oak. The wine tastes young, grapey, and spicy; it is well-balanced, an outstanding Cabernet with great aging potential and fine varietal character. It should age well.
price range: B

producer: Ste. Michelle Vineyards
classification: White varietal table wine
grape variety: Johannisberg Riesling (100%)
district: Yakima Valley
city or village: Grandview
In 1974 this 1972 vintage Johannisberg Riesling beat twenty Rieslings from California, Australia, and Germany in a blind tasting sponsored by the *Los Angeles Times*. This vintage in many ways resembles that famous award-winner.
Pale straw color and a varietal bouquet with hints of flowery and citrus elements. The wine is opulent, rich, and fruity, with citrus-Riesling character. It shows outstanding varietal character in the bouquet and on the palate. **price range:** B

producer: Ste. Michelle Vineyards
classification: White varietal table wine
grape variety: Chenin Blanc (100%)
district: Yakima Valley
city or village: Grandview
This is one of the most luscious Chenin Blancs to date. The wine often ages well because of its inherently high acidity; even three or four years later it still shows excellent balance.
Clear, brilliant pale straw color with hints of gold and a very strong, fruity varietal bouquet. The wine is fruity and a touch sweet, but is balanced by high acid; it has very good Chenin Blanc character and finishes with a bit of nuttiness.
price range: A

And Noah he often said to his wife when he sat down to dine,
"I don't care where the water goes if it doesn't get into the wine."
—G. K. Chesterton,
"Wine and Water"

WISCONSIN

producer: Wollersheim Winery, Inc.
classification: Red varietal table wine
grape variety: Baco Noir
district: Wisconsin River Valley
city or village: Prairie du Sac
The Wollersheim Baco Noir won a gold medal in the international wine and spirits competition in Surrey, England, in April 1974. It received an *A* rating and was the sixth highest of all U.S. wines that won awards.
Very deep red color and a full, big bouquet showing very slight yeast. The wine is big, full-bodied and pleasant, like a Burgundy; it is tannic and still slightly young, but shows great potential.
price range: A

producer: Wollersheim Winery, Inc.
classification: Red table wine
grape variety: Blend of Seyval Blanc and Chelois
district: Wisconsin River Valley
city or village: Prairie du Sac
Light red color, like a Beaujolais, and a very fruity, slightly "citric" bouquet. The wine is light-bodied and very fruity, with a long, pleasant aftertaste. It is very much like a French Beaujolais.
price range: A

producer: Wollersheim Winery, Inc.
classification: White varietal table wine
grape variety: Seyval Blanc (S.V. 5276)
district: Wisconsin River Valley
city or village: Prairie du Sac
Pale gold color and a very fruity, Mosel-like bouquet. The wine is smooth, soft, and well-balanced; it is semi-dry, with big fruit and no foxy flavor, typical of Labrusca wines. **price range:** A

producer: Wollersheim Winery, Inc.
classification: Red varietal table wine
grape variety: Chelois
district: Wisconsin River Valley
city or village: Prairie du Sac
This wine also won a gold medal in the international wine and spirits competition in Surrey, England, in April 1974. The Chelois has been exclusively aged in French Nevers oak, giving it a true European style.
Medium-bright crimson-red color and a rich, slightly "smoky," and pleasant bouquet suggestive of a Bordeaux. The wine is round, medium-bodied, and full, with slight wood; it is still developing and hints at Cabernet Sauvignon.
price range: A

Wine has been known for many centuries in all the Mediterranean countries, but in France the growing of vines and the making and appreciation of wine have been considered an art for more than two thousand years. Wine making and wine drinking have become an integral part of French civilization.

Tradition, experience, and know-how contribute greatly to the quality of French wines, but other essential factors control the types and characters of the wines. Foremost among them are: the geographical location of the vineyard, the geology of the soil in which the grapes are grown, the climate of the region or district, and subtle influences of light and irrigation, all of which cause the vineyards to vary one from the other. Because the character of the wine is so dependent on these factors and on the exposure of each separate vineyard to sun and water, even in France the wine of one place cannot be duplicated in another. Each wine is unique.

Bordeaux growers have been producing wines for more than twenty centuries. No other region can boast of the tremendous variety of wines such as exist in Bordeaux; only the wines of Burgundy can match their greatness.

The Bordeaux region spreads along both banks of the Garonne River in the southwestern part of France and produces red wines and rosé wines that are dry, medium dry, sweet, and very sweet. The principal wines of Bordeaux are:

Bordeaux Rouge　This moderately priced wine is a blend of grapes gathered from the entire region. Its quality is equal to the reputation and name of the shipper.

Entre-Deux-Mers　This large district within Bordeaux produces dry white wines that are soft and round and have a pleasant fruitiness to their bouquet.

Médoc　Some of the famous parishes of the Médoc are St.-Estèphe, Pauillac, St.-Julien, Moulis, and Margaux, each of which is famous for its own special wines. The Médoc produces red wines that are light-bodied and unique for their delicate fragrance, their mellowness, and their light long-lasting taste.

St.-Émilion　The wines of this district are red, full-bodied, robust. They have a strong bouquet and a distinguished taste.

Pomerol　A very small district that produces red wines a little lighter than those of St.-Émilion, with which they share most of the characteristics of bouquet and taste.

Graves　Graves produces both red and white wines. The whites may be either dry or medium-dry. They are well-balanced, elegant wines with a delicate bouquet and fruity taste.

Sauternes-Barsac　Sauternes, which includes the township of Barsac, produces the greatest naturally sweet wines in the world. They have a beautiful deep golden color; are mellow and very fruity; and have a long-lasting, extremely rich flavor.

The greatest wines of Bordeaux are from these sections of the region, but other excellent wines, all worthy of your consideration, are produced elsewhere in Bordeaux. Such wines are Cérons, *Ste.-Croix-du-Mont, Loupiac, Côtes-de-Bordeaux-St.-Macaire*, Premières Côtes de Bordeaux, Ste.-Foy, Graves de Vayres, Canon (Fronsac), and Côtes de Fronsac.

Burgundy, too, has been famous for its wines for more than two thousand years. The red wines have warmth and a strong bouquet. They are full-bodied and mellow. The whites are very dry and exceedingly refreshing. Burgundy wines are sold under the name of the township or district from which they come. The districts of Burgundy are:

Chablis　The small town of Chablis in northern Burgundy produces a dry white wine so famous that it has been imitated in many other countries. The wine of Chablis is very dry, light, and heady. It has a characteristic flavor, usually described as a flinty taste. Its color is light yellow with a slight greenish overtone.

The Côte d'Or　The Côte d'Or, which produces the greatest of the great Burgundies, is divided into two parts: the Côte de Nuits to the north and the Côte de Beaune to the south. The wines of the Côte d'Or possess the strong qualities of Burgundies to the highest degree. They age well although they mature quicker than the corresponding Bordeaux.

　Côte de Nuits　The wines of the Côte de Nuits are very full-bodied and generous with a remarkable bouquet. The best-known wines come from the following townships: Fixin, Gevrey-Chambertin, Morey-St.-Denis, Chambolle-Musigny, Vougeot, Flagey-Echezeaux, Vosne-Romané, and Nuits-St.-Georges.

　Côte de Beaune　The wines of Côte de Beaune are somewhat lighter than those of Côte de Nuits. They are delicate and smooth with a very strong bouquet. The whites are dry and fruity and rank among the very best. The principal townships are: Aloxe-Corton, Pernand-Vergelesses, Beaune, Pommard, Volnay, Meursault, Chassagne, and Puligny-Montrachet.

Southern Burgundy　The wines of southern Burgundy are lighter than Côte d'Or wines. They are fruity with a delicate bouquet. They have a freshness and are excellent when young. Southern Burgundy includes the regions of Chalon, Mâcon, and Beaujolais. Chalon produces the well-known wines of Mercurey, Rully, Givray, and in Montagny, *Mâcon Blanc*. This wine, made from the superb Pinot Chardonnay grape, is dry and full-flavored, with much charm. Famous **Pouilly Fuissé** comes from this area, which also produces some red wines. Beaujolais wines are fresh, light, with an earthy flavor and bouquet. They are best when young. The principal wine areas of Beaujolais are St.-Amour, Juliénas, Fleurie, Chiroubles, Morgon, Brouilly, and Moulin-à-Vent.

Champagne　One of France's most famous wine areas and wines. Ever since the "creation" of this splendid drink by the monk Dom Perignon at the end of the seventeenth century, it has been associated everywhere with festivities and celebrations. It is also an excellent dinner wine that goes with everything— meat, fish and poultry. According to French law, wines may be called Champagne only when they are made from grapes grown in the Champagne region. All other sparkling wines are called *vins mousseaux*. Even the best sparkling wines do not approach the quality of Champagne because the unique combination of soil and climate needed for the best development of the vines can be found only within the designated area set aside for their cultivation. The result is a very special taste that can be found nowhere else.

Alsace　This is a region that spreads along the French bank of the Rhine and produces dry, fresh, fruity, white wine. The principal wines of Alsace are: *Riesling*, which is a dry, elegant, and classic wine; *Gewürtztraminer*, a very fruity wine that holds the distinction of having a magnificent bouquet; and *Sylvaner*, a fresh, light, fruity wine.

Côtes du Rhône　Red wines are full-bodied with vigor and warmth. They have a rich bouquet and a luscious taste. Within Côtes du Rhône, other grand wines come from Côte-Rôtie, Condrieu, Hermitage, Cornas, St. Péray, Lirac, and Châteauneuf-du-Pape. The pink wine of Tavel is noted as one of the world's best rosés.

The Loire　Wines are produced along the banks of that much-written-about river. The best known among them are the dry still white wines of Pouilly-Fumé and Sancerre; the still and crackling white wines of Vouvray, which range from dry to sweet; the red wines of Chinon and Bourgueil; the dry and sweet white wines of Saumur. Anjou produces about half of all the wines of the Loire— red, white, and rosé.

Côtes de Provence　These wines should be drunk when young. The reds are full-bodied and full-flavored; the rosés are light, fresh, and fruity; the whites are full-bodied, dry, and sometimes lightly sparkling.

HOW TO READ A FRENCH WINE LABEL

VINTAGE YEAR　"Vintage" refers to the year conspicuously displayed on the wine label. It is the year of the grape harvest from which a wine is made. A vintage year does not ensure exceptional qualities for every variety of French wine.

CHÂTEAU　The label may include the name of the Château or particular vineyard where the wine was produced; the name of the owner (*propriétaire*) of the vineyard; or that of the wine dealer (*négociant*), who may buy, bottle, and ship the wine, marketing it under his own name.

PROPRIÉTAIRE　The name of the owner and the town. By placing the name of the town on his label, the owner is being exceedingly specific about his production.

APPELLATION (name of town) **CONTRÔLÉE**　The character of a wine is bound up with the place where it is produced—the soil, the subsoil, climate, situation, and local vegetation all play a part in imparting special qualities to the wine. Should any one of these elements change, the wine would change also. But these natural factors, although they are essential, are not the only ones involved. Man, in the person of the *vigneron*, also plays a decisive role by choosing the varieties of vines, the methods of cultivation and wine making, and by deciding how to store the wine when it is finished. The combination of these human and natural factors give the wine its own originality, and this is expressed not only by the *Appellation Contrôlée*, which is a legal requirement, but also by adding the specific town (Pauillac, for example). The producer thus gives the consumer a double guarantee of the wine's origin and quality.

MISE EN BOUTEILLE AU CHÂTEAU: MISE DE LA PROPRIÉTÉ, MISE EN BOUTEILLE PAR LA PROPRIÉTAIRE, MISE Á LA PROPRIÉTÉ, MISE DU DOMAINE, MISE EN BOUTEILLE AU DOMAINE All these terms mean that the wine has been bottled by the proprietor on his property and indicates the purity and integrity of his product.

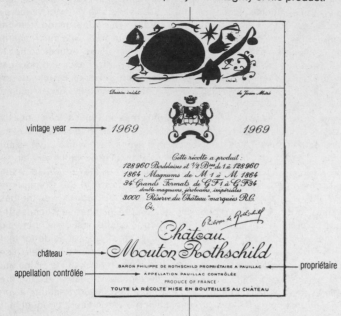

vintage year → 1969　1969

château → Château Mouton Rothschild

appellation contrôlée → ← propriétaire

FRANCE, ALSACE

producer: Léon Beyer
classification: White varietal table wine
grape variety: Gewürztraminer
district: Haut-Rhin
city or village: Equisheim
Clear color and a bouquet that shows the fruitiness of the grape. The wine has a rich body and a very long finish.
price range: B

producer: Domaine Weck
classification: White table wine
grape variety: Chasselas (20%), Muscat (14%), Sylvaner (28%), Riesling (10%), and Gewürztraminer (28%)
district: Haut-Rhin
city or village: Gueberschwihr
Gueberschwihr is an old and very pretty Alsatian village located in the middle of the vineyards, where some of the best and most exceptional wines are produced.
A delicate and subtle bouquet; the wine

is dry, *nerveux*, with perfumey characteristics. It is very fine and elegant.
price range: B

producer: Dopff & Irion
classification: White varietal table wine
grape variety: Gewürztraminer (100%)
Gewürztraminer wines often improve with age.
Slight pink color and an extremely appealing, flowery bouquet. The wine is spicy, soft, and finishes dry; it is particularly excellent with spicy foods and cold cuts, as well as cheeses.
price range: B

producer: Dopff & Irion
classification: White table wine
grape variety: Riesling (100%)
"Princesse d'Alsace" is an inexpensive Riesling sold in half-liter bottles.

Delicately fruity aroma; the wine is dry, well-balanced, and has good style and body; it is delicious with all seafood and also delightful as an aperitif instead of cocktails.
price range: A

producer: Dopff & Irion
classification: White table wine
grape variety: Riesling (100%)
"Ami des Crustacés" (crustacaeans' friend) is an elegant wine designed to be enjoyed with seafood, as its name indicates.
A delicate, fruity bouquet; the wine is very dry, with a crisp, clean, and "steely" quality.
price range: B

producer: Dopff
classification: White varietal table wine
grape variety: Riesling
district: Schoenenburg
city or village: Riquewihr
This prestigious wine comes from Dopff's own harvest in one of the best areas in Alsace for Riesling: the Schoenenburg Hill in Riquewihr.
Clear yellow color and a very fine, subtle bouquet. The wine is dry, very fruity, and elegantly delicate: its subtlety will enhance oysters and seafood; in fact, all fine food.
price range: C

producer: Dopff
classification: White varietal table wine
grape variety: Gewürztraminer
district: Eichberg
city or village: Turckheim
A very prestigious wine from a late harvest in Dopff's own vineyards.

Clear color and a very characteristic, fine, and delicate bouquet. The wine is velvety, powerful, and full-bodied; it is delicious with spicy meals, cheeses, and sweets.
price range: C

producer: Dopff
classification: White varietal table wine
grape variety: Riesling
district: Haut-Rhin
city or village: Riquewihr
Clear color and a fine, subtle bouquet. The wine is delicate and fruity—a typical wine from Alsace, suitable with hors d'oeuvres, fish, or seafood.
price range: B

producer: Antoine Gaschy
classification: White varietal table wine
grape variety: Gewürztraminer
district: Haut-Rhin
city or village: Wettolsheim
The Gaschy family have been wine growers at Wettolsheim and Equisheim since 1619.
Light yellow color and a very flavorful bouquet. The wine is rich, well-rounded, and full-bodied; it is dry, pleasantly tart, and has fine bouquet and flavor.
price range: B

"A ray of sun—and all the slope laughs with its lovely, lovely pink."
—William Bainbridge, *"April"*

producer: F. E. Hugel & Fils
classification: White varietal table wine
grape variety: Gewürztraminer
district: Haut-Rhin
city or village: Riquewihr

"Réserve Exceptionnelle." This Gewürztraminer is slightly fuller and higher in alcohol than Hugel's regular Gewürztraminer.

Clear yellow color and a flowery, perfumed bouquet. The wine is medium dry, well-balanced and full-bodied, with a characteristic spice.   **price range:** C

producer: F. E. Hugel & Fils
classification: White varietal table wine
grape variety: Riesling
district: Haut-Rhin
city or village: Riquewihr

A "Réserve Exceptionnelle," fuller in flavor and alcohol than Hugel's regular Riesling.

Clean straw color and a fragrant, distinguished bouquet. The wine is medium dry, with good body, and is nicely balanced.
price range: C

producer: F. E. Hugel & Fils
classification: White varietal table wine
grape variety: Sylvaner
district: Bas-Rhin

Made from grapes containing 17% minimum natural sugar.

Pale straw-gold color and a flinty, fresh bouquet. The wine tastes crisp, light, and fruity; it can be consumed any time of the day and is an excellent aperitif. Its freshness also makes it an ideal luncheon wine.
price range: B

producer: F. E. Hugel & Fils
classification: White table wine
grape variety: Pinot Blanc
district: Haut-Rhin
city or village: Riquewihr

"Cuvée Les Amours," a monopole of F. E. Hugel & Fils.

Clean pale gold color and a fruity bouquet; the wine is clean, dry, and medium-bodied.   **price range:** B

producer: F. E. Hugel & Fils
classification: White varietal table wine
grape variety: Pinot Blanc
district: Haut-Rhin

"Cuvée des Amours" is made from grapes containing 20% minimum natural sugar.

Pale straw-gold color and an attractive, delicately fruity bouquet. On the palate the wine is round, with a *gout de terroir*. It is a good general-purpose light dry wine, attractive as a luncheon wine and superb with shellfish.   **price range:** B

producer: F. E. Hugel & Fils
classification: White varietal table wine
grape variety: Riesling
district: Haut-Rhin

Made from grapes containing 18% minimum natural sugar.

A pale green-gold color and a typically discreet Riesling bouquet. The wine is dry on the palate; elegant but not too acid. It is ideal with shellfish and other fish cooked in butter, and with other simple fish dishes.
price range: B

producer: F. E. Hugel & Fils
classification: White varietal table wine
grape variety: Gewürztraminer
district: Haut-Rhin
city or village: Riquewihr

A "Réserve Exceptionelle", made from late-harvested grapes that have not been subject to "noble rot." The grapes contain 23% minimum natural sugar.

A pale golden-yellow color and a full, deep, spicy bouquet. The wine is extremely full, round, and fruity; it is a dessert wine par excellence, being distinctively rich and spicy. Serve with all spicy/smoked/pepper dishes and with cheese and dessert.   **price range:** C

producer: F. E. Hugel & Fils
classification: White varietal table wine
grape variety: Gewürztraminer
district: Haut-Rhin

Until 1972, this wine could also be called Traminer. The grapes contain 20.5% minimum natural sugar.

A pale straw-gold color and a distinctive, spicy, and delicate bouquet. On the palate it is dry and fruity; it is a typical traditional Gewürztraminer, delicate and not as perfumy as most that are overpressed. It would be nice with Thanksgiving turkey.   **price range:** B

producer: F.E. Hugel & Fils
classification: White varietal table wine
grape variety: Riesling

district: Haut-Rhin
city or village: Riquewihr

1973 vintage; "Beerenauslese." This is the greatest dry wine of the Rhine Valley and is extremely rare. Not a wine for the amateur, its qualities lie very deep, and it ages beautifully. The grapes were picked in late November in a stage of "noble rot," which occurs on an average of every three years. The maximum production never exceeds 900 cases and is selected personally by M. Jean Hugel. The grapes contain 24% minimum natural sugar.

A green-gold color and a delicate violet Botrytis fruit bouquet—spicy. The wine is full-bodied but delicate.
price range: E

producer: F. E. Hugel & Fils
classification: White varietal table wine
grape variety: Chasselas

This wine is sold under the brand name "Flambeau d'Alsace Hugel" and is sold mainly in Britain. Although not vintage-dated, it is in fact always the wine of one year.

A pale green-gold color and a light, fresh, and flowery bouquet. On the palate it is round, fresh, and agreeable; a simple, light luncheon wine.   **price range:** A

producer: F. E. Hugel & Fils
classification: White varietal table wine
grape variety: Gewürztraminer
district: Haut-Rhin
city or village: Riquewihr

"Beerenauslese." It is made from grapes picked late in November, in a state of "noble rot." It is produced on the average every three years and is very rare; production never exceeds 900 cases. The grapes contain 25.5% minimum natural sugar, and the wine is selected personally by Jean Hugel.

A golden-yellow color and an overwhelming bouquet with deep, rich spiciness. The wine is extremely round, fruity, and full—the supreme dessert wine.
price range: E

producer: F. E. Hugel & Fils
classification: White varietal table wine
grape variety: Riesling
district: Haut-Rhin
city or village: Riquewihr

"Réserve Exceptionnelle." Made from grapes containing 21.5% minimum natural sugar, harvested late in the season.

A green-gold color and an elegant, ripe Riesling bouquet suggesting violets. On the palate the wine is fruity, fine, dry, and long-lasting. It ages elegantly and is suited to fish dishes produced by great chefs.
price range: C

producer: F. E. Hugel & Fils
classification: White varietal table wine
grape variety: Pinot Gris (Tokay d'Alsace)
district: Haut-Rhin
city or village: Riquewihr

This grape should not be confused with Tokay from Hungary. There is only a small production in Alsace, with 3% of the total acreage. The grape ripens early and gives irregular yield. The grapes contain 24% minimum natural sugar.

A green-gold color and an earthy, discreet bouquet suggesting wood smoke when aged. On the palate the wine is round, with a characteristic "smoky" taste. It is full and rich when aged; it is ideal with foie gras and other pâtés, and with roast meats and game.
price range: C

producer: Josmeyer & Fils
classification: White varietal table wine
grape variety: Gewürztraminer (100%)
district: Haut-Rhin

---

city or village: Wintzenheim

Light yellow color and a spicy and fruity bouquet. It is a full-bodied Gewürztraminer, typical of wines made from this variety.
price range: B

producer: Josmeyer & Fils
classification: White varietal table wine
grape variety: Riesling (100%)
district: Haut-Rhin
city or village: Wintzenheim

Light yellow color and a fine and delicate bouquet. The wine is dry and suggests long life.
price range: B

producer: Charles Jux
classification: White varietal table wine
grape variety: Riesling (100%)
district: Bas-Rhin
city or village: Colmar

In accordance with the *Appellation Contrôlée* laws, this wine is a 100% Riesling—no other grapes are allowed to be blended. To be entitled to the appellation, the wine must attain a minimum of 11% alcohol.

Green-gold color and a fruity bouquet. The wine is very dry and elegant; a noble wine made from one of the greatest white wine grapes in the world. Very long-lived, it is a splendid wine to accompany all seafood, whether oily or dry. It is also an excellent accompaniment to many cheeses and shellfish. It should be served cool, around 50 degrees F.
price range: B

producer: Charles Jux
classification: White varietal table wine
grape variety: Gewürztraminer (100%)
district: Bas-Rhin
city or village: Colmar

Gewürztraminer is the most individual of Alsatian wines. Only very ripe grapes are used in the production of this wine in order to ensure the characteristic "spicy" characteristics of the variety. The laws of *Appellation Contrôlée* specify that the

---

wine must attain a minimum of 11% alcohol.

Straw to green-gold color and a flowery, pungent bouquet. The wine is quite spicy on the palate, with great character and, at times, a certain "spritz" or residual fermentation. The wine is quite long-lived.
price range: B

producer: Charles Jux
classification: White varietal table wine
grape variety: Sylvaner (100%)
district: Bas-Rhin
city or village: Colmar

This Sylvaner is made without any sugar added to the finished wine. The *Appellation Contrôlée* law specifies that it must attain 11% alcohol.

Pale gold color and a fruity bouquet. The wine is light, pleasant, and refreshing, with a crispness that makes it thoroughly enjoyable—at its best when drunk young. It can be served as an aperitif but also goes well with fish, mild shellfish, and white meats. It should be served cool, around 50 degrees F.
price range: A

producer: Kuentz-Bas
classification: White varietal table wine
grape variety: Gewürztraminer
district: Haut-Rhin
city or village: Colmar
(Husserenles-Châteaux)

Fruity bouquet; the wine is dry, clean, and spicy on the palate. It blends harmoniously with foie gras, shellfish, and dessert, and should be drunk chilled but not iced.
price range: B

producer: A & O Muré
classification: White varietal table wine
grape variety: Gewürztraminer
district: Haut-Rhin

---

city or village: Rouffach
vineyard: Clos St. Landelin

The Clos St. Landelin is a 17-hectare vineyard consisting of one undivided parcel—very scarce in Alsace. The vineyard faces southeast and has a calcareous (chalky), pebbly soil; it is planted in Gewürztraminer and Riesling, the *cépages nobles* of Alsace. 1975 vintage.

A gold color typical of Gewürztraminer and a fine bouquet characteristic of the variety. The wine is full-bodied, and the flavor lingers; a well-balanced and promising Gewürztraminer.
price range: B

"O thou invisible spirit of wine!"
—Shakespeare, *Othello*

producer: Quien & Co.
classification: White varietal table wine
grape variety: Riesling
district: Haut-Rhin
city or village: Guebwiller

The most popular Alsace wine.

Light yellow color and a very characteristic bouquet showing finesse. The wine is dry and fresh.
price range: B

producer: Salzmann/Thomann
classification: White varietal table wine
grape variety: Gewürztraminer
district: Haut-Rhin
city or village: Kayserberg—Colmar

This Gewürztraminer is entitled to the appellation "Schlossberg" and is produced from the Schlossberg vineyard, one of the best hillside vineyards in Alsace. Schlossberg Gewürztraminers are particularly famous for their great delicacy and finesse.

Pale green color and a very pronounced and characteristic bouquet. Less dry than a Riesling, the wine is fine-flavored, elegant, and full-bodied. Its heady bouquet invades the senses, and the flavor is a perfect companion with seasoned dishes and strong cheeses like Muenster.
price range: B

producer: Salzmann/Thomann
classification: White varietal table wine
grape variety: Riesling
district: Haut-Rhin
city or village: Kayserberg—Colmar

This Riesling is entitled to the appellation "Schlossberg" and is produced from the Schlossberg vineyard, one of the best hillside vineyards in Alsace. Rich soil and favorable exposure to the sun facilitates the production of a superior wine.

Pale green color and a delicate, fruity bouquet. The wine is lively and full of breeding; the "king of Alsatian *cepages*," Riesling harmonizes perfectly with all kinds of food and is unsurpassed with fish and seafood. **price range: B**

producer: Pierre Seltz
classification: White varietal table wine
grape variety: Gewürztraminer
district: Haut-Rhin
city or village: Mittelbergheim

Mittelbergheim produces some of Alsace's best wines; Pierre Seltz uses only clonal selections of superior grape varieties.

Green-yellow color and a bouquet of "roses." The wine is full, heavy yet elegant; it is one of the finest of its type.
price range: C

producer: Louis Sipp
classification: White table wine
grape variety: Chasselas
district: Haut-Rhin
city or village: Ribeauvillé

Alsatian wines, while made from similar gaprapes, differ markedly from their German counterparts.

Pale straw color and a fresh, grapey bouquet. The wine is light, clean, and very dry; it is a pleasant light wine, good as an aperitif or with a meal. **price range: A**

producer: Louis Sipp
classification: White varietal table wine
grape variety: Gewürztraminer
district: Haut-Rhin
city or village: Ribeauvillé

Few other regions produce such distinctive wines from Gewürztraminer as Alsace.

Bright golden color and a very flowery, "peppery" bouquet. The wine acknowledges a full grape flavor and is quite strong-flavored. **price range: B**

producer: Pierre Sparr & Ses Fils
classification: White varietal table wine
grape variety: Gewürztraminer
district: Haut-Rhin
city or village: Sigolsheim

Piorro Sparr offers a complete range of Alsatian wines, which have won many medals at fairs and exhibitions held throughout the world.

Light golden color and a pronounced varietal bouquet. The wine has an excellent finish and is a good representative of an Alsatian wine. **price range: B**

producer: Pierre Sparr & Ses Fils
classification: White varietal table wine
grape variety: Riesling
district: Haut-Rhin
city or village: Sigolsheim

A good and very representative Alsatian wine.

Light golden color and a pronounced varietal bouquet. The wine has an excellent finish. **price range:** B

producer: Domaines Viticoles Schlumberger
classification: White varietal table wine
grape variety: Riesling
district: Haut-Rhin
city or village: Guebwiller

Domaines Schlumberger is a family firm that owns a 140-hectare vineyard in Guebwiller, the southernmost part of the central and best vineyard section in Alsace. This vineyard has enjoyed a very special prestige for centuries.

Pretty yellow color and a delicate bouquet. The wine is very dry, with exquisite fruitiness; it is a "proud" wine; racy, and an Alsatian wine par excellence.
price range: B

producer: A. Willm
classification: White table wine
district: Haut-Rhin
city or village: Barr

An inexpensive yet delightfully typical Alsatian white wine. **price range: A**

producer: A. Willm
classification: White varietal table wine

grape variety: Gewürztraminer
district: Haut-Rhin
city or village: Barr
vineyard: Clos Gaesbronnel

Considered the finest Gewürztraminer vineyard in Alsace.

Deep, fragrant bouquet and a flavorful rich taste. A truly superior wine.
price range: C

producer: Zind Humbrecht
classification: White varietal table wine
grape variety: Sylvaner
district: Haut-Rhin
city or village: Wintzenheim—Colmar

Zind Humbrecht only sells wines from their vineyards, located in Wintzenheim, Turkheim, and Gueberschwihr.

Fresh green-tinged color; light and dry flavor, with the faintest hint of sparkle. This Sylvaner quenches the deepest thirst and goes well with cold meats.
price range: A

producer: Zind Humbrecht
classification: White varietal table wine
grape variety: Riesling
district: Haut-Rhin
city or village: Wintzenheim—Colmar

Dry and flavorsome bouquet; on the palate the wine shows outstanding finesse and breeding. It marries well with seafood and shellfish. **price range:** B

FRANCE, CHAMPAGNE

producer: Canard-Duchêne
classification: Champagne
grape variety: Pinot Chardonnay
district: Marne
city or village: Epernay

A "Blanc de Blancs" vintage Champagne fermented in the bottle.

Light, crisp color and a delicate, fruity bouquet. The wine is dry and elegant; it should go well as an aperitif or with all types of food (especially shellfish)—serve chilled. **price range:** E

producer: Cockburn & Campbell Ltd.
classification: Champagne
grape variety: Pinot Noir and Chardonnay

A very-good-quality nonvintage Champagne.

Good Champagne bouquet; the wine is crisp, dry, and has good froth.
price range: C

producer: de Venoge & Cie.
classification: Champagne
grape variety: Pinot Chardonnay and Pinot Noir
district: Côte des Blancs
city or village: Épernay

The best Champagne produced by the single-largest independent (single family) firm in Champagne, "Vin des Princes—Vintage."

Clear light straw color and a clean, fresh bouquet with a hint of fruit. The wine is very dry, its appearance marked by small bubbles. **price range:** E

producer: Findlater Mackie Todd & Co., Ltd.
classification: Champagne
grape variety: Pinot Noir, Chardonnay, and Pinot Meunier
district: Marne

"Duc de Marne" is a classic light Champagne.

Light sparkling color and a fresh, fruity bouquet. The wine is light, clean, and fruity, with good acid balance.
price range: C

producer: Charles Heidsieck
classification: Champagne
grape variety: Pinot Noir and Chardonnay
district: Montagne de Reims
city or village: Reims

Charles Heidsieck is one of the few Champagne firms still owned and operated by the family for whom it is named. Reasonably priced, the wines are often referred to as "Champagnes for the connoisseur."

Clear color and an elegant bouquet. The wine is light and dry. **price range:** C

"We cannot say this of any other wine, Port is deep-sea deep." —George Meredith

producer: Heidsieck Monopole
classification: Champagne
grape variety: Pinot Noir and Chardonnay
district: Montagne de Reims
city or village: Verzenay

"Heidsieck Monopole Dry" is a world-renowned wine, having enjoyed a long-standing tradition for quality since the firm was established in 1785. Their vineyards surround the famous windmill at Verzenay, famous as a lookout point in both world wars.

A delicate perfume of grapes; the wine is light, dry, and fresh. It is a great Champagne with finesse and character, ideal for all occasions. **price range:** E

producer: Joseph Henriot
classification: Champagne
grape variety: Pinot Noir and Chardonnay
district: Montagne de Reims
city or village: Reims

Great French Champagnes have a style that cannot be duplicated anywhere else in the world. Baron Philippe de Rothschild has long enjoyed this magnificent Champagne at Château Mouton-Rothschild in Bordeaux. His own special cuvée is now being imported to the United States and will soon be available on a nationwide basis.

Light golden color, with tiny bubbles; the bouquet is light and fragrant, with that delicate, classic Champagne aroma. The wine is full and rich, with a lingering finish; it should be chilled for two or three hours prior to serving. **price range:** E

producer: René Jardin
classification: Champagne
grape variety: Chardonnay
district: Côte des Blancs
city or village: Le Mesnil-sur-Oger

The little village of Le Mesnil lies on the Oger River in the Côte des Blancs, the southernmost portion of the Champagne district where primarily Chardonnay grapes are grown. The village's vineyards are officially rated 99% Premier Cru, one of the highest classifications allowed in the Champagne vineyards. Because this wine is a Blanc de Blancs, the exclusive use of

white grapes make it much lighter than most other nonvintage Champagnes.

Clear, pale color and a "gun-flint" bouquet. The wine is light and delicate, extremely refreshing, and ideal as an aperitif. **price range:** C

producer: Krug
classification: Champagne
grape variety: Chardonnay and Pinot Noir
district: Haut-Marne
city or village: Reims

The House of Krug still uses traditional methods of production, which most other firms have abandoned; hence it is essentially a handmade Champagne, one of the "Grand Marques."

Mature polished-gold color and a deep, full, and rich bouquet. On the palate the wine is mature, expansive, and full-bodied. **price range:** E

producer: Lanson Père & Fils, S.A.
classification: Champagne
grape variety: Pinot Blanc, Pinot Noir, and Pinot Meunier
district: Montagne de Reims—Vallée de la Marne
city or village: Reims

Lanson Père et Fils produces four different styles of Champagne: Brut vintage (Red Label), Brut nonvintage (Black Label), Extra-quality dry nonvintage, and extra-quality Brut rosé nonvintage. 450 acres of top-rated vineyards are family-owned and provide about 75% of the grapes used by Lanson, permitting an extraordinary degree of quality control.

Straw color and a delicate bouquet. The wine is quite dry. **price range:** D

producer: Lanson Père & Fils, S.A.
classification: Champagne
grape variety: Pinot Noir, Pinot Meunier, and Chardonnay
district: Montagne de Reims—Vallée de la Marne—Côte des Blancs
city or village: Reims

"Black Label Brut N/V" is a type of Champagne that is exported worldwide. It is a blend of wines from different properties

and from different vintages, permitting quality to be very consistent.

Very delicate bouquet; the wine is light and fruity and is excellent as an aperitif or anytime one desires a glass of Champagne. **price range:** E

producer: Launois Père & Fils
classification: Champagne
grape variety: Pinot Chardonnay
village: Le Mesnil-sur-Oger

An excellent wine from a small producer. This "Blanc de Blancs" is delicate, with breed and character. **price range:** E

producer: Laurent Perrier
classification: Champagne
grape variety: Pinor Noir and Chardonnay
district: Vallée de la Marne
city or village: Tours-sur-Marne

A well-balanced blend of various vintages and vineyards. Consistent quality and character. Sold as "Extra Dry."

Dry flavor, but less so than their "Brut." Serve chilled with all foods at any time.
price range: D

producer: Laurent Perrier
classification: Champagne
grape variety: Pinot Chardonnay
district: Côte des Blancs—Vallée de la Marne
city or village: Tours-sur-Marne

A "Blanc de Blancs," made from white grapes grown in selected, highly rated villages in the Champagne district.

Very dry, light, and delicate flavor.
price range: E

producer: Laurent Perrier
classification: Champagne
grape variety: Pinot Noir and Chardonnay

district: Vallée de la Marne
city or village: Tours-sur-Marne
A well-balanced, nonvintage Brut Champagne made from a blend of wines of various vintages and vineyards; consistent quality and character.
Very dry flavor, with fruit and body; serve chilled with all foods at any time.
price range: D

producer: Laurent Perrier
classification: Champagne
grape variety: Pinot Noir and Chardonnay
district: Vallée de la Marne
city or village: Tours-sur-Marne
"Cuvée Grand Siècle" is made from a blend of only the very best wines from the finest villages in the Champagne district. It is bottled in an authentic seventeenth-century bottle.
A dry Champagne of supreme quality, great breeding, and elegance.
price range: E

producer: Laurent Perrier
classification: Champagne
grape variety: Pinot Noir and Chardonnay
district: Côteaux Champenois
city or village: Tours-sur-Marne
A new appellation, Côteaux Champenois was created for the dry still white wines of the Champagne district formerly known as "Champagne Nature."
An elegant, dry, crisp, and fruity white wine. **price range:** B

producer: Abel Lepitre
classification: Champagne
grape variety: Chardonnay
city or village: Reims
A "Blanc de Blancs" Champagne that is said to have thwarted a mutiny that threatened the ocean liner *France*. The crew abandoned their plans to take over when they discovered they had run out of cuvée 134.
A fine Champagne perfume; the wine is supple, without a trace of acidity, and is light and elegant on the palate. A particularly superb Champagne.
price range: D

producer: Abel Lepitre
classification: Champagne
grape variety: Pinot
city or village: Reims
This nonvintage Champagne was classed as the best wine of its type in the Gault-Millau tasting of December 1973.
A complete bouquet; the wine is rich, full, and dry on the palate.
price range: C

producer: Moët & Chandon
classification: Champagne
grape variety: Pinot Noir, Chardonnay, and Pinot Meunier
district: Haut-Marne
city or village: Épernay
Founded in 1743, Moët & Chandon is by far the biggest of the Champagne firms.
Golden color, fruity bouquet, and a delicate flavor with a touch of sweetness in the finish. An ideal accompaniment for dessert. **price range:** D

producer: Moët & Chandon
classification: Champagne
grape variety: Pinot Noir, Chardonnay, and Pinot Meunier
district: Haut-Marne
city or village: Épernay
"Cuvée Bicentenaire" is a limited bottling commemorating the two hundred-year-old bond of friendship between France and America. The wine is made from Moët's most select grapes, reflecting the house's world-famous style of fruit and elegance.
Golden color, fruity bouquet, and very clean and soft on the palate.
price range: E

producer: Moët & Chandon
classification: Champagne
grape variety: Pinot Noir, Chardonnay, and Pinot Meunier
district: Haut-Marne
city or village: Épernay
Founded in 1743, Moët & Chandon is the largest of the Champagne houses.
Golden color; a fruity bouquet; and a clean, dry flavor.
price range: E

"From wine what sudden friendship springs."
—John Gay,
"The Squire and His Cur"

producer: Moët & Chandon
classification: Champagne
grape variety: Pinot Noir, Chardonnay, and Pinot Meunier
district: Haut-Marne
city or village: Épernay
This wine is called "Dom Pérignon," after the man who is said to have first prepared Champagne. It is the *ne plus ultra* of sparkling wines.
Golden color, a fruity bouquet, and a full flavor combined with incredible elegance. A peerless wine. **price range:** E

producer: Moët & Chandon
classification: Champagne
grape variety: Chardonnay
district: Côte des Blancs
city or village: Saran
Château: de Saran
This still white wine, entitled to the appellation Côteaux Champenois, is produced from a cuvée prepared by Moët & Chandon from grapes gathered from the vineyards surrounding the Château de Saran in the Côte des Blancs. Only Chardonnay grapes are used to prepare the cuvée, considered to be the *ne plus ultra* of the Côteaux Champenois.
Extremely pale color and a clean, flinty bouquet. The wine is extremely dry and finishes well. **price range:** E

producer: Oudinot
classification: Champagne
grape variety: Pinot Chardonnay
district: Côte des Blancs
village: Avize
Oudinot specializes in the making of a first-class Champagne from grapes grown on the famous Côte des Blancs in the southern part of Champagne. It is made from the first pressing.
A delightful and fresh wine. Dry, crisp, and well-rounded. Its special characteristics are body and vigor. **price range:** C

producer: Piper-Heidsieck
classification: Champagne
grape variety: Pinot Noir and Chardonnay
district: Montagne de Reims
city or village: Reims
Brut Champagne, vintage-dated.
price range: E

producer: Piper-Heidsieck
classification: Champagne
grape variety: Chardonnay
district: Côte des Blancs
city or village: Reims
Cuvée Florens-Louis Blanc de Blancs, vintage-dated. **price range:** E

producer: Pommery & Greno, S.A.
classification: Champagne
grape variety: Pinot Noir, Pinot Chardonnay, and Pinot Meunier
district: Montagne de Reims
city or village: Reims
Pommery & Greno S.A. is the second-largest vineyard owner in the Champagne district. They are the only Champagne house to have been awarded the coveted "Prestige de France" insignia.
Pale straw color and a good, fruity, and yeasty nose typical of classic Champagne. The wine is clean and fruity, with a long finish—it is one of the finest "Grand Marques." Fine when lightly chilled, as an ideal aperitif. **price range:** D

producer: Louis Roederer
classification: Champagne
grape variety: Pinot Noir and Chardonnay
district: Marne
city or village: Reims

An excellent example of a quality vintage Champagne.

A fruity bouquet; the wine is dry, with a grapey flavor. **price range:** E

producer: Louis Roederer
classification: Champagne
grape variety: Pinot Noir and Chardonnay
district: Marne
city or village: Reims

"Cristal" is a premium-quality Champagne sold in a special clear bottle, from which its name derives. It was originally produced for the tsar of Russia and is one of the very greatest Champagnes.

Fruity bouquet; the wine is full-bodied and grapey. **price range:** E

producer: Ruinart Père et Fils
classification: Champagne
grape variety: Chardonnay
district: Montagne de Reims
city or village: Reims

"Dom Ruinart" is an extremely pale, light, and delicate Champagne made exclusively from Chardonnay grapes grown in Ruinart's famed Sillery vineyards, which enjoy optimum soil and exposure to the sun. The wine is a Blanc de Blancs and is shipped in a classic-shape bottle. The house of Ruinart is the oldest of the existing Champagne firms; this wine is dedicated to Dom Thierry Ruinart, priest of Reims, monk at Saint-Germain-des-Prés, a well-known scholar and a friend and contemporary of Dom Pérignon. 1969 vintage.

Very light golden color and a delicate, fruity bouquet. The wine is very clean and dry. **price range:** E

producer: André Simon
classification: Champagne
grape variety: Pinot Noir, Pinot Meunier, and Chardonnay

Pale yellow color and good bubbles; the wine is light, dry, and has a clean, long finish. **price range:** C

producer: Taittinger
classification: Champagne
grape variety: Chardonnay
district: Montagne de Reims
city or village: Reims

"Comtes de Champagne Blanc de Blancs Brut" is named for the ancient and historical home of the Comtes de Champagne. Taittinger is the third-largest vineyard owner in the Champagne district, having holdings in thirty of the most famous hillside vineyards classified as the finest for producing Champagne. Their long, deep wine cellars reaching into the chalk earth are an historical monument and a showplace in Reims. Skilled workers perform every step of the complex process of developing and maturing the wine. This wine is made only from the first pressing of selected Chardonnay grapes. It has extraordinary delicacy and lightness in both bouquet and flavor. Produced in only the best vintages, it is presented in a striking eighteenth-century bottle.

Brilliant clear color and a delicately fragrant bouquet. The wine combines exquisite lightness and delicacy of flavor. **price range:** E

producer: Taittinger
classification: Champagne
grape variety: Chardonnay
district: Montagne de Reims
city or village: Reims

"Brut Réserve" is produced only in great years. It continues the Taittinger tradition for quality and is a Champagne of rare excellence. Champagne Taittinger is one of the rare firms controlled by a member of the family that first founded it.

Sparkling gold-tinted color and a delicately fragrant bouquet. The wine is light and delicate and has a special distinctive quality. **price range:** E

producer: Taittinger
classification: Champagne
grape variety: Chardonnay
district: Montagne de Reims
city or village: Reims

Taittinger Champagne has achieved worldwide reputation for excellence. The firm produces a lighter, superior-quality Champagne by using a preponderance of Chardonnay grapes, which are only pressed once. The firm has holdings in thirty of the most famous vineyards and now owns Château La Marquetterie, the place where the secret of making Champagne was first discovered. This wine is a Brut Champagne called "La Française" and is made from a preponderance of Chardonnay grapes that gives it special delicacy and finesse.

Very pale golden color and a delicate, fruity bouquet. The wine is light, dry, and exceptionally delicate. **price range:** E

producer: Taittinger
classification: Pink Champagne
grape variety: Pinot Noir
district: Montagne de Reims
city or village: Bouzy

Skilled workers perform every step in the complex process of developing and maturing the wine. This pink Champagne is made only from the first pressing of Pinot Noir grapes. Carefully controlled supervision of fermentation brings out its appealing rose color. It is produced only in the best vintages and is bottled in a striking eighteenth-century bottle.

A brilliant rosé color and a delicate fragrance. The wine tastes exquisitely light and delicate. **price range:** E

producer: Veuve Clicquot-Ponsardin
classification: Champagne
grape variety: Blend of Pinot Noir and Chardonnay
district: Haute-Marne
city or village: Reims

Founded in 1772, Veuve Clicquot-Ponsardin enjoys a worldwide reputation for quality. "The widow," Veuve Clicquot, managed the company from 1805 (when her husband died) until her death in 1866 and was the originator of the system of *remuage*, or riddling, by which sediment is removed from the Champagne bottle. 1970 vintage.

Clear color and a fully aromatic bouquet. The wine is elegant, fresh, and delicate, with a long-lasting flavor; it is one of the best Champagnes of its vintage. **price range:** E

producer: Veuve Clicquot-Ponsardin
classification: Champagne
grape variety: Blend of Pinot Noir and Chardonnay
district: Haute-Marne
city or village: Reims

"Yellow Label" is a non-vintage Brut Champagne. The label is synonymous with the annual tradition held by the top managers of Veuve Clicquot: tasting and blending their wines always to obtain the same flavor and taste, practiced since 1772.

Clear color and a pronounced bouquet. The wine is charming, versatile, and romantic; it is full of character and sure to delight all connoisseurs. **price range:** E

producer: Marcel Sautejeau
classification: White table wine
grape variety: Muscadet (Melon de Bourgogne)
district: Muscadet de Sèvre-et-Maine
city or village: Le Pallet

One of the better Muscadets, the Domaine de l'Hyvernière is bottled *sur lie*; that is, without a final racking.

Bright silver-gold color and a light, fine bouquet. The wine is dry, quite clean, and thirst-quenching. **price range:** B

producer: Château du Nozet (de Ladoucette)
classification: White table wine
grape variety: Sauvignon Blanc
district: Nièvre
city or village: Pouilly-sur-Loire

De Ladoucette was first introduced into the United States about twenty years ago. The wine has been produced and bottled at Château du Nozet since 1787; among its most famous customers were Marie-Antoinette, King Louis XVI, and Napoleon.

A wine as beautiful as the château from which it comes. **price range:** C

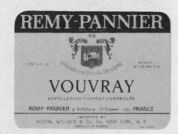

producer: Remy-Pannier
classification: White table wine
grape variety: Chenin Blanc
district: Touraine (Middle Loire)
city or village: Vouvray

The Vouvray vineyards date from the eighth century. The wines are usually semi-dry, but some are quite dry; some sparkling wines are made, but most are still. Sweet Vouvrays keep longer than their dry counterparts. **price range:** B

producer: Remy-Pannier
classification: White table wine
grape variety: Sauvignon Blanc
district: Nièvre
city or village: Sancerre

A fine alternative to the medium-priced wines of Burgundy.

Very pale color; well-scented, medium to full body. A more mellow wine than Pouilly-Fumé. **price range:** B

producer: Barré Frères
classification: White table wine
grape variety: Muscadet
district: Muscadet
city or village: Gorges

Clear color with tints of greens; the bouquet is fruity; and the wine is light, crisp, and fresh. This Muscadet is best served with seafood, particularly oysters, where its merits are most easily appreciated. **price range:** B

producer: Francis Cotat
classification: White table wine
grape variety: Sauvignon Blanc
district: Sancerre
city or village: Chavignol (Les Monts Damnés)

This estate-bottled, delicate white wine is renowned for its distinct bouquet and spicy flavor.

Pale straw color and a crisp, slightly smoky bouquet. The wine is clean and dry, with a hint of spice. It should be drunk very young. **price range:** C

producer: Comte de Malestroit
classification: White table wine

---

grape variety: Muscadet
district: Sèvre-et-Maine
city or village: Vallet

The only wine made by the Comte de Malestroit, this is one of the few estate-bottled Muscadets from the Sèvre-et-Maine. Unlike most Muscadets, this wine improves with a little bottle age.

Pale gold color and a full, slightly pungent bouquet. The wine is rich, very dry, soft, and crisp, with an excellent finish. **price range:** B

producer: Comte Lafond
classification: White table wine
grape variety: Sauvignon Blanc
district: Sancerre
city or village: Pouilly-sur-Loire

A fine dry wine with great character.
price range: C

producer: Chanson Père & Fils
classification: White table wine
grape variety: Sauvignon Blanc
district: Nièvre
city or village: Pouilly-Fumé

Pleasing bouquet; a delicate, medium-dry white wine, fruity and fresh.
price range: B

producer: Chanson Père & Fils
classification: White table wine
grape variety: Muscadet
district: Lower Loire—Muscadet de Sèvre-et-Maine

A pale yellow wine with a delicate, fruity taste. **price range:** B

producer: Les Celliers du Prieuré
classification: White table wine
grape variety: Melon
district: Muscadet
city or village: St. Georges-sur-Loire

Bright clear color and a light bouquet. The wine is very dry. **price range:** A

producer: Marnier-Lapostolle
classification: White table wine
grape variety: Sauvignon Blanc
district: Nièvre
city or village: Sancerre

This estate-bottled white wine is called "Château de Sancerre" and is one of the most famous châteaux in the Loire Valley. It is owned by the Marnier Lapostelle family; its previous owner was Louis de Sancerre (1342–1402), constable and marshal of France.

Clear color with slight greenish tinges and a mellow bouquet. The wine is fruity and very dry.

price range: B

producer: Jean-Claude Bougrier
classification: White table wine
grape variety: Chenin Blanc
district: Touraine
city or village: Vouvray

A fruity, semi-sweet white wine.
price range: A

"What can winemakers buy, one half so precious as they sell?"
—Omar Khayyám

producer: Alexis Lichine & Co.
classification: White table wine
grape variety: Blanc Fumé (Sauvignon Blanc)
district: Nièvre
city or village: Pouilly-Fumé
Clear; slight straw color; fruity bouquet. The wine is crisp, delicate, and refreshingly soft. **price range:** C

producer: Denis Marchais
classification: White table wine
grape variety: Muscadet
district: Muscadet de Sèvre-et-Maine
city or village: Vallet
The bouquet intensifies after some months spent in bottle.
Clear limpid color and a delicate, fruity bouquet. The wine is delicately dry; a wine to serve cold but not iced, accompanying fresh water fish or seafood (crustacés).
price range: B

producer: B. B. Mason & Co., Ltd.
classification: White table wine
Pale green color and a light, fruity bouquet. The wine is very dry and crisp, an inexpensive everyday wine similar to Muscadet. **price range:** B

producer: Chapin & Landais
classification: White table wine
grape variety: Muscadet

---

district: Muscadet de Sèvre-et-Maine
Light pale yellow color and a delicate and flinty bouquet. The wine is dry, fruity, and slightly "steely." **price range:** A

producer: André Simon
classification: White table wine
grape variety: Muscadet
district: Muscadet de Sèvre-et-Maine
Very pale yellow-white color and a crisp bouquet with fruity acidity. The wine is fresh, with good acidity: an excellent wine for seafood. **price range:** A

producer: M. Jean Segers
classification: White table wine
grape variety: Sauvignon Blanc
district: Nièvre
city or village: Pouilly-sur-Loire
Clear color with greenish tinges and a pronounced, delicately fruity bouquet. The wine is dry, full-bodied, elegant, and firm, with a "flinty" flavor characteristic of the region combined with the delicacy of Sauvignon. **price range:** B

producer: M. P. Millérioux
classification: White table wine
grape variety: Sauvignon Blanc
district: Nièvre
city or village: Sancerre—Champtin
vineyard: Clos du Roy
The grapes that go into Sancerre Clos du Roy are grown on limestone soil, giving the wine its long-lasting properties. It should be drunk young, however, to appreciate its fruity flavor.
Brilliant golden color and an aromatic, fruity bouquet. The wine is rich and full-bodied; it is quite dry, and in its first few months has a "flinty" taste characteristic of wines from this region. **price range:** B

producer: Ets. Marcel Martin
classification: White table wine
grape variety: Muscadet
district: Muscadet de Sèvre-et-Maine
city or village: Vallet
Slow fermentation produces this very delicate, fruity wine.
Pale yellow color and an aromatic bouquet. The wine tastes fruity and delicate, with a pronounced acidity that makes it suitable for serving with fish.
price range: B

producer: Ets. Marcel Martin
classification: White table wine
grape variety: Gros Plant
district: Gros Plant du Pays Nantais V.D.Q.S.
city or village: La Sablette de Mouzillon
This wine is bottled straight from the cask as soon as fermentation is completed. Though similar to a Muscadet, it is drier and, being less expensive, has become quite popular in recent years.
Clear, pure color and a very fruity bouquet. The wine is drier than a Muscadet and has more acidity; it is very crisp and refreshing and should be drunk with oysters and other seafood. **price range:** A

producer: E. Angenault
classification: White table wine
grape variety: Muscadet
district: Muscadet (Maine-et-Loire)
The fermentation of Muscadet is slow, and the wine is often kept *sur lie* (on the lees) without any racking. Too many Loire wine makers sulfur excessively so as to stabilize the wine, but of course this ruins its delicacy. Though the grape is, like the wine, called Muscadet, its original name was Melon, and it is native to Burgundy.
Pale yellow color and a pleasant—difficult to define—bouquet. The wine is fresh and dry, but not acidic; it is delicate and fruity, with many nuances in the taste and bouquet. Unlike many Loire white wines with a trace of sulfur, this wine has none; its color and bouquet benefit from the time spent *sur lie*. **price range:** B

producer: E. Angenault
classification: White table wine
grape variety: Sauvignon Blanc
district: Nièvre
city or village: Sancerre
Rounder than Pouilly-Fumé (which is produced nearby), Sancerre reaches maturity sooner and is best drunk within a year or so.
Pale color and a fine bouquet. The wine is mellow, dry, and fresh. **price range:** B

producer: E. Angenault
classification: White table wine
grape variety: Chasselas and Sauvignon Blanc
district: Nièvre
city or village: Pouilly-sur-Loire
Pouilly-sur-Loire is a refreshing wine with a distinct bouquet, best consumed the year after it is made. The confréries of Pouilly and Sancerre meet at a ceremony with a banner that means (freely translated): "Water divides us, but wine unites us."
Clear, fresh color and a musky, "smoky" bouquet. The wine is delightfully fresh. **price range:** A

producer: E. Angenault
classification: White table wine
grape variety: Sauvignon Blanc
district: Nièvre
city or village: Pouilly-sur-Loire
The soil in the Pouilly-Fumé region is argillaceous (limey); however, the most argillaceous plateaus overlooking the slopes are not appropriate for vineyards. Pouilly-Fumé is probably the one Loire white wine that benefits from a little bottle age, the bouquet and taste becoming more distinctive.
Pale, clear color and a full "musky" or "smoky" bouquet. The wine is very dry.
price range: C

producer: M. Redde
classification: White table wine
grape variety: Sauvignon Blanc
district: Nièvre
city or village: Pouilly-sur-Loire
vineyard: Les Berthiers

Pouilly-Fumé reaches its peak soon after it is made, and the wine can be sold just after bottling—usually in April.

Clear color with green tinges and a "spicy" bouquet. The wine is dry and supple, ideal with hors d'oeuvres, fish, and crustaceans. It should be served very cold.
price range: B

producer: Marquis de Goulaine
classification: White table wine
grape variety: Muscadet (Melon)
district: Lower Loire (Val de Loire)—Muscadet de Sèvre-et-Maine
city or village: Haute Goulaine

Muscadet is a wine that has become extremely popular since World War II. It is found in all good restaurants in France, particularly in Paris, and is now exported all over the world. Its price range, popularity, and number of bottles sold is comparable only to Beaujolais. The best Muscadet comes from the region of Sèvre-et-Maine, named for two rivers, and is bottled *sur lie*; i.e., not racked before bottling, which allows more flavor and purity in the wine.

Very pale color, with slight greenish-gold tinges, and a light aroma of "musk"—from which supposedly the name of the wine derived. The wine is light, dry, and pleasant, ideal with any sort of fish or seafood, as well as with white meats or hors d'oeuvres. It is also delightful on its own and makes an excellent *kir* aperitif when mixed with a dash of Cassis liqueur.
price range: B

producer: Confrérie des Vignerons de Oisly et Thésée
classification: White table wine
grape variety: Sauvignon Blanc
district: Touraine

Very pronounced bouquet and a clean, fresh flavor.
price range: B

producer: Comte de Malestroit
classification: White table wine
grape variety: Muscadet
district: Muscadet de Sèvre-et-Maine
city or village: Vallet

The Château la Noë is the largest single estate in the district. The Comte de Malestroit bottles the entire production in his own cellars.

Pale color and a scented bouquet. The wine is very dry and refreshing—an ideal wine to enjoy with fish.
price range: B

producer: Alphonse Mellot
classification: White table wine
grape variety: Sauvignon Blanc
district: Nièvre
city or village: Sancerre

Golden color with slight greenish tinge and a clean, fresh bouquet. The wine is quite dry and refreshing.
price range: B

producer: Marcel Dubois
classification: White table wine
grape variety: Various, mostly Chenin Blanc

A blend of seven vineyards in the Loire Valley.

Pale yellow color and a clean, flowery bouquet. The wine is fruity with balanced acidity—the complete, easy-to-drink, all-purpose wine.
price range: A

producer: Ets. Marcel Martin
classification: Red table wine
grape variety: Cabernet Franc

district: Touraine
city or village: Bourgueil—La Sablette de Mouzillon

This wine is generally at its best after three or four years in bottle, although it is very pleasant when drunk young.

Full red color and a beautiful bouquet of strawberries. The wine is fruity and delicate.
price range: A

producer: Ets. Marcel Martin
classification: Red table wine
grape variety: Cabernet Franc
district: Touraine
city or village: Chinon

This wine is particularly attractive when drunk young.

Full red color and a perfumed bouquet of violets. The wine is elegant and medium sweet; serve with meats and game.
price range: A

producer: Les Vins Touchais
classification: Red table wine
grape variety: Cabernet (Breton)
district: Touraine
city or village: Bourgueil

Light red color and a fresh, fruity bouquet. The wine is fruity and refreshing; a delicious luncheon wine in the summertime.
price range: A

producer: Bouvet-Ladubay
classification: White sparkling wine
grape variety: Chenin Blanc
district: Saumur
city or village: St. Hilaire–St. Florent

The firm of Bouvet-Ladubay is one of the oldest and most respected in the Loire Valley. They first produced their sparkling Saumur in 1851, and so fine is its quality that in many tastings Bouvet Brut has been judged better than some of the better-known French Champagnes. It is made by the *méthode champenoise*.

Light and dry bouquet, with a refreshing clean taste. The wine is light and dry, with the refreshing sparkle of delicate bubbles.
price range: C

producer: Duplessis Mornay
classification: White sparkling wine
grape variety: Chenin Blanc and Chasselas
district: Touraine
city or village: Vouvray

An excellent sparkling wine (*vin mousseux*) produced by the *méthode champenoise*. Entitled to the appellation Vouvray, it is called "Cuvée Florent."

Pale straw-gold color and a light, clean bouquet. The wine is dry, fruity, and effervescent.
price range: B

producer: Ackerman-Laurance
classification: White sparkling wine
grape variety: Pineau Blanc de la Loire
district: Touraine
city or village: Vouvray

A Brut sparkling Vouvray made by the Champagne method.

Very light gold color; a rich, fine bouquet. The wine is mellow and flinty, with good balance; goes well with fish, oysters, shellfish, and dessert. It flatters any meal.
price range: A

producer: Remy-Pannier
classification: White sparkling wine

"Remy Pannier Vin Mousseux" is naturally fermented in the bottle.

A well-scented challenge to the critical Champagne drinker.
price range: B

producer: J. R. Parkington & Co.
classification: White sparkling wine
grape variety: Chenin Blanc
district: Touraine
city or village: Vouvray

J. R. Parkington owns the label of this wine, referred to in the book *Wine* by Hugh Johnson.

Golden color and a fruity bouquet. With a slightly sweet taste, it is a lovely dessert wine. **price range:** B

producer: de Neuville
classification: White sparkling wine
grape variety: Chenin Blanc and Chardonnay
district: Saumur
city or village: St. Hilaire–St. Florent

This classic *vin mousseux* (sparkling wine) is produced by the classic *méthode champenoise* and is aged for many months at a constant temperature in limestone cellars. The entire aging process requires two years in the cellar after the final bottling. The blending of Chenin Blanc and Chardonnay grapes adds extra flavor; and the wine offers all the advantages, sparkle, and flavor of many more expensive Champagnes. The wine is quite long-lived.

Pale gold color and a fruity bouquet. The wine is quite dry and lively, with a faint honey taste; it can be served throughout the meal. **price range:** C

producer: Bouvet-Ladubay S.A.
classification: White sparkling wine
grape variety: Chenin Blanc
district: Saumur
city or village: Saumur

This wine, a Saumur *mousseux*, was awarded a gold medal and diploma for excellence in its class at the British Bottlers' Institute Brewers' Exhibition in London, 1972. It also won a gold seal in its class at the International Wine & Spirits Competition of the Club Oenologique, London, in 1975. It is a fine example of a good sparkling wine produced by the traditional Champagne method.

Pale gold color with a steady stream of small bubbles; a pleasant, fruity bouquet. The wine is clean, fresh, and slightly sweet; its medium-dry taste has made it very popular as a wine for all occasions.
price range: C

producer: Bouvet-Ladubay S.A.
classification: White sparkling wine
grape variety: Chenin Blanc
district: Saumur
city or village: Saumur

A Saumur *Brut mousseux* (dry sparkling wine), this wine was awarded a diploma for excellence in its class at the competition held by the British Bottlers' Institute at the Brewers' Exhibition in London, 1972. It later won a silver seal in its class at the International Wine & Spirit Competition held at the Club Oenologique in London, 1975.

Pale gold color with a steady stream of small bubbles; a bouquet similar to Champagne, though with more fruit. The wine is clean, fresh, and dry, with a good fruity taste; it is an excellent aperitif and is eminently suitable for all occasions by connoisseurs. **price range:** C

producer: J. R. Parkington & Co., Ltd.
classification: White sparkling wine
grape variety: Chenin Blanc
Either Brut or Demi-sec (semi-sweet), made by the *méthode champenoise*.
price range: C

producer: Ackerman-Laurance
classification: Rosé varietal table wine
grape variety: Cabernet Franc
district: Anjou
Entitled to the appellation "Cabernet d'Anjou."

Agreeable rose-hued color and a fresh, fruity bouquet. The wine is dry, well-balanced, and has finesse; it goes well with white meat and shellfish.
price range: B

producer: Domaine Laporte
classification: White table wine
grape variety: Sauvignon Blanc
district: Nièvre
city or village: Sancerre

The dry white wines of Sancerre owe their reputation to the chalk soil of the region, on which the Sauvignon Blanc grape thrives. The wines of the Domaine Laporte have won gold medals in Paris in 1967 and 1973 and bronze medals in 1969, 1970, and 1971.

Fruity bouquet; the wine is fresh, fruity, and excellent. **price range:** B

producer: Albert Besombes
classification: Rosé table wine
grape variety: Cabernet Franc
district: Anjou
city or village: St. Hilaire–St. Florent

Made exclusively from the Cabernet grape, Moc-Baril Rosé d'Anjou is produced by the Besombes family, wine makers for over one hundred years.

Clear pink color and a fresh, delicate bouquet. The wine is fruity, uniquely fresh, and delicate—just a touch sweet.
price range: A

ROYAL DE NEUVILLE

producer: de Neuville
classification: Rosé table wine
grape variety: Groslot and Cabernet
district: Saumur
city or village: St. Hilaire–St. Florent

This wine can be classified as a "crackling" or *petillant* rosé. Royal de Neuville is produced by the classic Champagne method and is aged for nine months in limestone cellars at a constant temperature of 54 degrees prior to bottling. It is one of the largest-selling wines in Canada.

Delightful pink color with orange highlights; a soft, fruity bouquet. The wine is soft, with a refreshing tingle, and has a slight touch of sweetness that is not offensive but pleasing to the palate. It is an elegant wine usually served on special occasions in a tulip or Champagne glass. **price range:** C

producer: Duplessis Mornay
classification: Rosé table wine
grape variety: Groslot
district: Anjou

Medium-full pink color and a fresh, fruity bouquet. The wine is medium dry, not sweet and cloying. **price range:** A

producer: Blanchard Wine Merchants
classification: Rosé table wine
grape variety: Groslot
district: Anjou
city or village: ▮mbert-du-Lattay

Bright pi▮ Go▮▮▮ and a light bouquet. The wine▮ table ▮ ▮weet flavor.
price rancadet ("▮
Vo▮

SAINT MICHEL

producer: François Neveu Saint-Michel
classification: Rosé table wine
grape variety: Cabernet
district: Anjou

Light color and a soft, flowery bouquet.
price range: A

producer: Caves Saint-Eutrope
classification: Rosé table wine
grape variety: Cabernet Franc (Cabernet d'Anjou)
district: Anjou
city or village: Chapelle-Heulin

A pleasant everyday wine.

Good bouquet; the wine is pleasant, fruity, and slightly sweet. **price range:** A

producer: Guenault-Cousin-La Chaise
classification: Rosé table wine
district: Anjou   **price range:** B

producer: Guenault-Cousin-La Chaise
classification: Red table wine
district: Touraine   **price range:** B

producer: Guenault-Cousin-La Chaise
classification: White table wine
grape variety: Sauvignon Blanc
district: Touraine   **price range:** B

producer: Guenault-Cousin-La Chaise
classification: White table wine
grape variety: Chenin Blanc
district: Vouvray
city or village: Montrichard   **price range:** B

producer: Vacheron
classification: White table wine
grape variety: Sauvignon Blanc
district: Cher
city or village: Sancerre   **price range:** B

producer: Henri Tytell & Fils
classification: White table wine
district: Sèvre-et-Maine
   This is a pale, dry white wine with a light bouquet.
   Mis en bouteilles sur lie.
price range: A

producer: Remy-Pannier
classification: Rosé table wine
grape variety: Groslot and Cabernet
district: Anjou
   Remy-Pannier is the largest *négociant* (shipper) in the Loire Valley.
   Light pink color and a light, fruity bouquet. The wine is medium sweet and has balanced acidity—a classic example of a Rosé d'Anjou.   **price range:** A

producer: Domaine Fontaine
classification: Rosé table wine
grape variety: Pinot Noir
district: Nièvre
city or village: Sancerre
   Sancerre rosés are among the most interesting rosé wines. The Pinot Noir is new to the Sancerre region, but the wines are rapidly gaining in popularity.
   Very pale rose color and a flowery bouquet. The wine is quite dry.
price range: B

producer: Cave des Viticulteurs de Vouvray
classification: White table wine
grape variety: Chenin Blanc
city or village: Château de Vaudenuits à Vouvray
   Greenish in color; fruity, with a rich finish. This demi-sec Vouvray is a delightful wine with a hint of mint, not too sweet, with the finish on the dry side.   **price range:** B

FRANCE, PROVENCE

producer: Baron de Basque de Laval
classification: Rosé table wine
grape variety: Grenache and Cinsault
district: Côtes de Provence
city or village: Les Arcs-sur-Argens
   A light, dry, and elegantly delicate rosé wine.   **price range:** B

producer: Jacques Louissier
classification: Rosé table wine
grape variety: Grenache and Mourvèdre
district: Côtes de Provence—Var
city or village: Correns
château: Miraval
   Bright pink color and a fruity bouquet. The wine is dry and full.   **price range:** A

producer: Marquis de Saporta
classification: Red, white, and/or rosé table wine
grape variety: Grenache, Cinsault, Cabernet Sauvignon (red); Ugni Blanc and Clairette (white)
district: Côteaux d'Aix en Provence
city or village: Le-Puy-Sainte-Réparade
château: Fonscolombe
   The Château de Fonscolombe is an historic château and vineyard in the Durance Valley, near Aix-en-Provence, which produces wine sold widely in Switzerland, Germany, and England. Visitors to the château are welcome. A high percentage of Cabernet Sauvignon lends style and depth to the red wines.
   Reds are medium red, rosés are tawny, and whites are clear in color; fresh bouquet. All the wines are fruity, dry, and finish well; they are meant to be drunk young while their fruitiness is still in evidence.
price range: B

producer: Pradel
classification: Rosé table wine
grape variety: Grenache, Cinsault, Mourvèdre, Carignane, and Clairette
district: Côtes de Provence V.D.Q.S.
city or village: Villeneuve-Loubet
   With modern equipment, Pradel is producing eight million bottles of wine a year; the wines are sold not only in France but also in ninety other countries. The United States and West Germany consume over one million bottles a year. Pradel rosés are the most popular.
   Fruity bouquet; the wine is full-bodied and fruity; an excellent dry rosé.
price range: A

producer: Maison Sichel
classification: Rosé table wine
grape variety: Various
district: Côtes de Provence V.D.Q.S.
   Bright red color and a fresh, delightful bouquet. The wine is dry and full-bodied and should be drunk young.
price range: B

> *"Wine that maketh glad the heart of man."*
> —Psalm 104:15

producer: Vincent Vial
classification: Rosé table wine
grape variety: Blend
district: Côtes de Provence V.D.Q.S.
   "Quai de Provence" is a blend of the finest rosé wines of Provence, produced by several growers and blended so that consistent quality is always available.
   Dry and fruity flavor.   **price range:** B

HAUTE-MÉDOC

producer: M. Aymar Achille-Fould
classification: Château-bottled red table
wine
grape variety: Cabernet Sauvignon (25%),
Cabernet Franc, and Merlot
city or village: St.-Julien-Beychevelle

Château Beychevelle is one of the best
known and most prized Médocs. Officially
rated *quatrième cru* (fourth growth) in the
1855 classification, it fetches prices today
that are higher than many second growths.
The château itself is one of the most beautiful in the Médoc; the name *Beychevelle*
stems from the French *basse voile*, or
"strike sail," and was a command given by
the Duc d'Épernon to ships passing by the
property on the River Gironde. This gesture
was a salute to the Grand Admiral of
France, who at one time owned the estate.

Deep, full, and distinguished color and a
highly fragrant and complex bouquet. On
the palate the wine is delicate and well-
structured, with an even texture.
price range: C

producer: M. Arnaud
classification: Château-bottled red table
wine
grape variety: Cabernet Sauvignon and
Merlot
city or village: St.-Estèphe
château: Pomys

Ruby-red color and a bouquet characteristic of St.-Estèphes. The wine is very dry
and tannic: it needs three to five years of
aging in the bottle to reach its full maturity.
price range: C

*"Five qualities there are
wine's praise advancing:
Strong, beautiful, fragrant,
cool, and dancing."*
—John Harrington, 1608

producer: Château Beauregard
classification: Château-bottled red table
wine
grape variety: Cabernet and Merlot
city or village: St.-Julien

The vineyards adjoin those of Château
Léoville-Las-Cases.

Brilliant red color and a fine, delicate
bouquet. The wine is very tasty—soft but
well-balanced. **price range:** C

producer: Borie-Manoux
classification: Château-bottled red table
wine
grape variety: Cabernet Sauvignon (33%),
Cabernet Franc (33%), and Merlot
(33%)
city or village: Pauillac
château: Batailley

Classified as a fifth growth (*cinquième
cru*) in 1855, Château Batailley presently
consists of 135 acres of vineyards that surround an eighteenth-century château. The
château is encircled by a magnificent
park, with many species of old trees.

Full bouquet and a round, elegant flavor
typical of a fine *grand cru classé*.
price range: B

producer: Calvet
classification: Red table wine
grape variety: Cabernet Sauvignon, Merlot,
and Carmenère

city or village: Pauillac

Calvet offers this wine as an introduction
to the wines of Pauillac, which are usually
more expensive. Planted in the soil of
Pauillac, the vines produce some of the
noblest wines in the world, yet the ground
suits no other crop.

A subtle bouquet and a smooth, even
taste. This totally satisfying wine has some
tannin and finishes well. **price range:** B

producer: Château de Camensac
classification: Château-bottled red table
wine
grape variety: Cabernet Sauvignon and
Merlot
city or village: St.-Laurent

Since it was bought by new owners in
1967, Château de Camensac has markedly
improved in quality. Officially it is classified as a *cinquième cru* (fifth growth), but
in a new classification it might rate higher.

Brilliant deep red color and an intense,
fruity bouquet. The wine is soft, graceful,
and has depth. **price range:** B

producer: Delbos-Bouteiller
classification: Château-bottled red table
wine
grape variety: Cabernet Franc, Cabernet
Sauvignon, and Merlot
city or village: Cussac–Fort Médoc
château: Lanessan

Château Lanessan is among the most
esteemed of the Haut-Médoc *cru
bourgeois* châteaux and for many years
has been producing wines equal to those
of the classified growths. The vineyard is
planted in *cépages nobles* (noble varieties), giving finesse and remarkable flavor to the wines. M. Delbos-Bouteiller was
awarded the gold medal of the Société Agricole for the best-kept vineyard in the de-
partment of the Gironde.

Fine bouquet; the wine is extremely
elegant, fine, and full-bodied. The 1973
Lanessan is superior to many classified
growths of that vintage. **price range:**

producer: Descas Père & Fils
classification: Red table wine
grape variety: Cabernet Sauvignon and
Merlot
city or village: St.-Estèphe

An excellent value in Bordeaux red.

Clear ruby-red color and a woody
bouquet with delicate Cabernet nuances.
The wine has some wood and spice with
rich fruit. **price range:** A

producer: Dourthe Frères
classification: Château-bottled red table
wine
grape variety: Cabernet Sauvignon and
Merlot
city or village: Moulis
château: Maucaillou

Château Maucaillou is officially classified as a *cru exceptionnel* (exceptional
growth) of the Médoc.

A "definite" bouquet and a mellow
flavor; the wine has finesse and character.
price range: C

producer: M. Duboscq
classification: Château-bottled red table
wine
grape variety: Merlot and Cabernet
Sauvignon
city or village: St.-Estèphe
château: Hostein-Marbuzet

Said the ancients: "Wines gathered at
Marbuzet are the gems of Médoc wines.
They have the body of Pauillacs and the
finesse of the St.-Juliens." The owners of
Château Haut-Marbuzet, Messrs. Duboscq
and Besse, give special attention to the
wine, which has earned much praise and

great success. There is another, unrelated château in close proximity also called Marbuzet; the two should not be confused.

A bouquet full of delicacy; the wine is full, fruity, and very elegant. In good vintages, this wine is easy to drink when young but will continue to improve for up to twenty-five years. **price range:** C

producer: Marc Faure
classification: Château-bottled red table wine
grape variety: Merlot (50%) and Cabernet Sauvignon (50%)
city or village: Soussans-Margaux
This wine won a gold medal at the general agricultural contest in Paris in 1962.

A complex, typical Margaux bouquet; the wine is harmonious, characteristic of its area of production, and very good quality. **price range:** B

producer: M. Fort
classification: Château-bottled red table wine
grape variety: Cabernet Sauvignon, Cabernet Franc, and Merlot
city or village: St.-Julien
A typical wine of its commune; the vines are excellently situated.

Rich red color and a fine, perfumed bouquet. The wine is smooth, elegant, and offers excellent value. **price range:** B

producer: Gilbey S.A.
classification: Red table wine
grape variety: Cabernet Sauvignon, Cabernet Franc, and Merlot
city or village: St.-Yzans-de-Médoc
LaCour Pavillon, the proprietary branded wine of Gilbey's S.A., is a blend of several wines produced only in the Haut-Médoc region. The wines are produced, vinified, and bottled in the Médoc, under the supervision of Martin Bamford, director of Gilbey's S.A. and a Master of Wine. The wines are aged in small wooden casks for up to two years before being bottled; although not a château-bottled wine, La Cour Pavillon has many of the same characteristics and quality and compares most favorably in blind tastings with the *cru bourgeois* châteaux of the Médoc. It is one of the best wine bargains around.

Deep, full ruby color, turning to garnet with age; a full, complex bouquet with unmistakable Cabernet aroma. The wine is dry, medium-full bodied, and smooth. **price range:** B

producer: F. Ginestet
classification: Château-bottled white table wine
grape variety: Semillon and Sauvignon Blanc
city or village: Margaux
château: Margaux
Pavillon Blanc du Château Margaux is the only white wine produced at the world-famous Château Margaux. In the middle of the gravelly soil where red grapes grow, there is a strip of Pliocenic chalk ideal for white grapes. This small area is planted in Semillon and Sauvignon Blanc, and the wine is given the same care from grape to bottle as Château Margaux.

Brilliant pale gold color and a distinguished, fragrant bouquet. The wine is dry, elegant, and flavorful and has a clean taste. **price range:** C

producer: F. Ginestet
classification: Château-bottled red table wine
grape variety: Cabernet Sauvignon, Cabernet Franc, Merlot, Malbec, and Petit-Verdot
city or village: Margaux
château: Margaux
Château Margaux was selected in 1855 as one of three *premier grand cru classé* (classified first great growth) wine estates in the Haut-Médoc. It is produced and bottled at the château under supervision of the Ginestet family. It is the only great growth to remove the stalks and imperfect grapes by hand. The wine is aged in new oak barrels longer than the average of other first great growths. The Ginestet family owns Château Margaux exclusively.

Deep rosy-red color and an unsurpassed, fruity, and subtle bouquet. The wine combines remarkable depth and balance with great finesse. It is produced only in great vintage years, then carefully selected, so only the best is awarded the title of Château Margaux. The wine has great elegance, depth and balance, and the longevity characteristic of Château Margaux. **price range:** E

producer: F. Ginestet
classification: Red table wine
grape variety: Cabernet Sauvignon and Merlot
city or village: Fort Médoc
The name Fort Médoc comes from the fort built by Louis XIV to guard the entrance of the Garonne River. In the heart of the Haut-Médoc, the estate produces rich, vigorous, and velvety red wines.

Warm ruby color and a beautiful fruity bouquet. The wine tastes clean and velvety and is very clean. **price range:** B

producer: F. Ginestet
classification: Red table wine
grape variety: Cabernet Sauvignon, Cabernet Franc, Merlot, Malbec, and Petit-Verdot
city or village: Margaux
F. Ginestet, owners of Château Margaux, are closely identified with the Margaux district. Elegant wines are the result of the rough, gravelly soil.

Ruby color and a delicate, well-balanced bouquet. The wine is supple, delicate, and possesses fine balance; a true Margaux with characteristic finesse. **price range:** C

producer: Holt Frères et Fils
classification: Château-bottled red table wine
grape variety: Cabernet and Merlot
city or village: Margaux
château: Rausan-Ségla
Rausan-Ségla was rated directly after Mouton-Rothschild in the 1855 classification of Bordeaux wines. In the commune of Margaux, it is considered second in quality only to Château Margaux.

Brick-red color and an exceptionally fragrant, fine "nose" typical of Margaux. The wine is full, soft, round, and finishes well; a great wine for meat and nut dishes. **price range:** C

producer: C. Jouvet, S.A.
classification: Red table wine
grape variety: Cabernet and Merlot
city or village: Margaux
Margaux is renowned for the bouquet and silky texture of its wines.

A high degree of aroma, characteristic of Margaux; the wine is light, dry, and has a soft finish. **price range:** B

producer: C. Jouvet S.A.
classification: Red table wine
grape variety: Cabernet and Merlot
city or village: St.-Julien
Light, dry bouquet; the wine has great finesse and delicacy of taste. **price range:** B

producer: B. Jugla
classification: Château-bottled red table wine
grape variety: Cabernet Sauvignon, Cabernet Franc, and Merlot
city or village: Pauillac
A lesser-known property offering excellent value.

Deep ruby-red color and a full, fruity bouquet that develops well with age. The wine is round and has interesting character. **price range:** B

producer: L. Lurton
classification: Château-bottled red table wine
grape variety: Cabernet and Merlot
city or village: Margaux
château: Durfort-Vivens

Château Durfort-Vivens was officially classified as a *deuxième cru classé* (classified second growth) in 1855.

Bright red color and a powerful bouquet. The wine is dry and full-bodied for a Margaux. **price range:** C

producer: Maison Sichel
classification: Red table wine
grape variety: Cabernet Sauvignon and others
city or village: Margaux
Long-lived.

Brilliant red color and a full, rich bouquet. The wine is elegant, soft, and full—the finish is velvety. **price range:** C

producer: Henri & Simone Martin
classification: Château-bottled red table wine
grape variety: Cabernet Sauvignon (60%), Merlot (30%), and Petit-Verdot (10%)
city or village: St.-Julien-Beychevelle
château: Peymartin

This vineyard was created by the father of the present owner and "baptized" by M. Désiré Cordier, an old friend of the Martin family and founder of the Cordier firm, known the world over. At the time, M. Martin was mayor of St.-Julien-Beychevelle. M. Henri Martin is the grand Maître de l'Ordre du Commandérie du Bontemps de Médoc et Graves and is considered a leading authority in Bordeaux; he is most famous for elevating Château Gloria to status

worthy of some of the most famous classified-growth Médocs. St.-Julien wines are typically a little fuller than Margaux, and mature sooner than Pauillacs.

Fine bouquet; the wine is very soft, round, and subtle, with delicacy and fullness. **price range:** C

producer: Château Malescasse
classification: Château-bottled red table wine
grape variety: Cabernet Sauvignon and Merlot
city or village: Lamarque

A diagram of this château can be seen in Hugh Johnson's classic *World Atlas of Wine*.

Clear, brilliant deep red color and a woody and fruity bouquet of Cabernet. The wine has delicate varietal flavor, with some spice, and a berrylike flavor.
price range: B

producer: P. J. Mazeau
classification: Château-bottled red table wine
grape variety: Cabernet Sauvignon, Malbec, and Petit-Verdot
city or village: Listrac
château: Decorde

A full-bodied and robust wine with a rich ruby color and a well-developed bouquet.
price range: B

producer: P. J. Mazeau
classification: Château-bottled red table wine
grape variety: Cabernet Franc and Cabernet Sauvignon (50%), and Merlot (50%)
city or village: Listrac
château: Semeillan-Mazeau

The Listrac commune in the Haut-Médoc produces red wines that, without being of the very best class, remain very good wines. This one is the favorite wine of the

International Company of the Sleeping Car (!).

Deep ruby color and a pleasant bouquet. The wine is sinewy, full-bodied, and well-balanced; it is best appreciated when dining over a smooth roadbed.
price range: B

producer: M. G. Meffre
classification: Château-bottled red table wine
grape variety: Merlot and Cabernet Sauvignon
city or village: St.-Julien-Beychevelle
château: Glana La Rose

St.-Julien is a small community located in the heart of the Haut-Médoc between Margaux and Pauillac.

A strong bouquet and a very delicate taste. **price range:** B

producer: Mialhe
classification: Château-bottled red table wine
grape variety: Merlot and Cabernet
city or village: Margaux (Avensan)
1970 and 1971 vintages.

Deep red, almost opaque color; the bouquet has a slight cellar bouquet when the bottle is opened, but improves to a big, rich "nose" after a minute or so. The wine has a high acid/tannin ratio, with earthy, mouth-filling character. It suggests a Margaux and is long-lived. **price range:** B

producer: Mialhe
classification: Château-bottled red table wine

grape variety: Merlot and Cabernet
city or village: St. Seurin-de-Cadourne
château: Coufran

A fruity bouquet, showing bottle age; the wine tastes soft and supple, with an impression of low acidity. It is a very delightful Médoc that has St.-Estèphe character without the characteristic severity.
price range: B

producer: Prats Frères
classification: Château-bottled red table wine
grape variety: Cabernet and Merlot
city or village: St.-Estèphe

The château lies adjacent to the renowned Prats property of Château Cos d'Estournel, one of the greatest vineyards in Bordeaux, and has been the Prats' family home for generations.

Deep color; the wine is full-bodied, yet round and velvety. **price range:**

producer: Prats Frères
classification: Château-bottled red table wine
grape variety: Cabernet (66%) and Merlot (34%)
city or village: St.-Estèphe
château: Cos d'Estournel

Château Cos d'Estournel is one of the most important wine châteaux of Bordeaux. It was classified as a *deuxième cru* (second growth) in the 1855 classification of the Médoc and is considered by many to be the leading classified growth in St.-Estèphe. Its oriental façade has been a landmark in Bordeaux since it was constructed in the nineteenth century. The château was built essentially in Laotian style, with three pagodas on the roof indicating a strong Chinese influence. The exotic architecture was desired by the original owner, Louis Gaspard d'Estournel, to evoke images of faraway markets and reflect the fame of his wine.

Full, harmonious bouquet; the wine is well-balanced and has good body and great delicacy. Fine vintages yield a wine that can challenge any made in the Médoc.
price range: D

producer: Christian & Michel Querre
classification: Red table wine
grape variety: Cabernet Sauvignon and others
city or village: St.-Estèphe

Ruby color and a full bouquet. The wine is full, fruity, and delicate; it shows good breeding for a generic St.-Estèphe and is excellent value. **price range:** B

producer: R. Ollier
classification: Château-bottled red table wine
grape variety: Cabernet and Merlot
city or village: St.-Estèphe
château: Bonis

This wine develops bouquet and subtlety with prolonged bottle aging; only twenty-five hundred cases are produced each year.

Good clean color and a finely perfumed bouquet. The wine is full and fine, with roundness, good body, and a mellow finish. **price range:** B

producer: Baron Philippe de Rothschild, S.A.
classification: Château-bottled red table wine
grape variety: Cabernet Sauvignon, Cabernet Franc, and Merlot
city or village: Pauillac
château: Mouton-Rothschild

Officially rated *deuxième cru* (second growth) in the 1855 classification of the Médoc, Château Mouton-Rothschild became a *premier cru* (first growth) on June 22, 1973, by an official decree of the French Minister of Agriculture. "After discussion with all the necessary authorities," it was confirmed that the wines entitled to the classification "Premier Grand Cru Classé du Médoc" were, in alphabetical order, Châteaux Lafite-Rothschild, Latour, Margaux and Mouton-Rothschild, along with the Graves estate Château Haut-Brion. Wines of this quality develop subtleties that differ markedly from year to year, and experts can recognize classic vintages by the aroma alone.

Dark red, flawless color; a full, rich complex bouquet of cedar and black currants. The wine is big and generous, well-balanced, and gives a multitude of taste sensations. It should be served at room temperature—68 degrees F. **price range:** E

producer: Baron Philippe de Rothschild, S.A.
classification: Château-bottled red table wine
grape variety: Cabernet Sauvignon, Cabernet Franc, and Merlot
city or village: Pauillac
château: Mouton-Baron-Philippe

Château Mouton-Baron-Philippe, rated *cinquième cru* (fifth growth), used to be called Mouton d'Armailhacq before it was named for its owner, Baron Philippe de Rothschild, in 1956. Baron Philippe reserves a quantity of this wine every year to serve to his privileged guests at his home, Château Mouton-Rothschild. It is one of the finest château wines available.

Medium ruby-red color and a full, rich bouquet—a subtle and complex blend of eucalyptus and cedar in great vintages, typical of Pauillacs. On the palate the wine is medium-bodied and has a good finish. It should be served at room temperature—68 degrees F. **price range:** D

producer: Baron Philippe de Rothschild, S.A.
classification: Château-bottled red table wine
grape variety: Cabernet Sauvignon, Cabernet Franc, and Merlot
city or village: Pauillac
château: Clerc-Milon

Château Clerc-Milon was officially classified as a fifth growth (*cinquième cru*) in 1855. The tiny château was bought by Baron Philippe de Rothschild in 1970, and the percentage of grape varieties (*cépages*) are the same as his great Château Mouton-Rothschild; qualitatively, the wine very closely resembles Mouton. Usually very elegant, the wine will live for many years, further bottle aging developing the character and aromas that make Pauillac wines so famous.

Very dark ruby-red color; a rich and complex bouquet, with classic Cabernet aroma. On the palate the wine shows big body and is full and generous with plenty of tannin; it should be served at room temperature—68 degrees F. **price range:** D

producer: Baron Philippe de Rothschild, S.A.
classification: Red table wine
grape variety: Cabernet Sauvignon, Cabernet Franc, and Merlot
city or village: Pauillac

Baron Philippe de Rothschild Pauillac is a blended regional wine that, unlike the other Rothschild wines, can be drunk young—when three years old.

Good dark ruby-red color; the bouquet is refined, with pronounced Cabernet aroma. On the palate the wine is well-balanced, with big body and plenty of tannin; regional wines of this high quality offer good value without quality fluctuations from different vintages. The wine should be served at room temperature—68 degrees F. **price range:** C

producer: Ste. Anonyme du Château Prieuré-Lichine
classification: Château-bottled red table wine
grape variety: Cabernet Sauvignon and Merlot
city or village: Cantenac-Margaux
château: Prieuré-Lichine

Officially classified as a *troisième cru* (third growth) in the 1855 Médoc classification, Château Prieuré-Lichine is owned by Alexis Lichine, an American wine expert.

Clear, deep red color and a full, rich, and velvety bouquet. The wine is soft, relatively full-bodied, and is quick to mature for a Margaux; it often has a delicious taste. **price range:** C

producer: Schröder & Schÿler & Cie
classification: Château-bottled red table wine
grape variety: Cabernet and Merlot
city or village: Cantenac-Margaux
château: Kirwan

Château Kirwan is rated *troisième cru classé* (third classified growth) of Cantenac. Until recently, this wine was not château-bottled.

Medium-full ruby color and an elegant, perfumed bouquet characteristic of Margaux. The wine is dry, soft, and elegant, with good fruit. **price range:** C

producer: Pierre Saintout
classification: Château-bottled red table wine
grape variety: Cabernet Sauvignon (66%); Merlot, Malbec, and Petit-Verdot (33%)
city or village: St.-Julien
château: des Trois Canons

Château des Trois Canons has been owned by the Saintout family for over two centuries. The vineyards are situated on a gravel-clay soil, producing the very best wine. This parcel of land was already famous during the Hundred Years' War when the English army, which occupied this region, installed three cannons at this lookout point to stop the progression of the French army—thus giving the piece of land its name. The wine won gold medals in Paris in 1910 and 1955, and in Bordeaux in 1964 and 1970.

A fine, full-bodied wine with a remarkable bouquet. **price range:** B

producer: Société Civile du Château d'Agassac
classification: Château-bottled red table wine

grape variety: Cabernet and Merlot
city or village: Ludon
château: d'Agassac
Rated *cru bourgeois exceptionnel*, Château d'Agassac is owned by the same proprietor who owns Château Calon-Ségur to the north in St.-Estèphe.
Ruby color, clean flinty color, dry flavor, and an excellent value. **price range:** B

producer: Société Civile du Château Duplessis
classification: Château-bottled red table wine
grape variety: Cabernet and Merlot
city or village: Avensan-Moulis
château: Duplessis
Bright red color and a well-developed bouquet. The wine is dry and elegant.
price range: B

producer: Société Civile du Château Fourcas-Hosten
classification: Château-bottled red table wine
grape variety: Cabernet Sauvignon (45%), Merlot (45%), and Cabernet Franc and Petit-Verdot (10%)
city or village: Listrac
château: Fourcas-Hosten
Château Fourcas-Hosten is owned by a group of Americans, and the vinification of the wines is supervised by Émile Peynaud, dean of the Institute of Oenology at the University of Bordeaux. The vineyards went into full production in the fall of 1977. Although officially rated *cru bourgeois supérieur*, the wine is considered to be the equal of many more famous classified growths.
Brilliant red color and a fine bouquet. The wine is typically fine, though like any fine wine, its intensity depends on the vintage. **price range:** C

producer: Société Civile du Château Fourcas-Hosten
classification: Château-bottled red table wine
grape variety: Cabernet Sauvignon and Merlot

city or village: Listrac
château: Fourcas-Hosten
Château Fourcas-Hosten, although officially classified as *cru bourgeois supérieur*, is worthy of classified-growth status. The wine is vinified by M. Émile Peynaud, dean of oenology at the University of Bordeaux.
Red-violet color and a bouquet typical of wines from the Haut-Médoc. On the palate the flavor is good and long-lasting. **price range:** B

producer: Société Civile des Grands Crus Réunis
classification: Red table wine
grape variety: Cabernet Sauvignon and Merlot
city or village: Avensan-Moulis
château: Ville George
Château de Ville George is one of the six selected *cru bourgeois exceptionnels* (great growths).
A delicate bouquet, finesse with a velvety quality. **price range:** B

producer: Société Civile de Château Grand-Puy Ducasse
classification: Château-bottled red table wine
grape variety: Cabernet and Merlot
city or village: Pauillac
château: Grand-Puy Ducasse
A *grand cru classé* (classified great growth) in 1855, Château Grand-Puy Ducasse is officially rated *cinquième cru* (fifth growth).
Bright red color and a big, well-developed bouquet. The wine is dry and elegant. **price range:** C

producer: Société Civile du Château Lagrange
classification: Château-bottled red table wine
grape variety: Cabernet Sauvignon and Malbec

city or village: St.-Julien-Beychevelle
château: Lagrange
Château Lagrange was officially classified as a *troisième cru* (third growth) in the 1855 Médoc classification.
Clear red color and a full bouquet. The wine shows good body. **price range:** C

producer: Sociťé Civile du Château Larose-Trintaudon
classification: Château-bottled red table wine
grape variety: Cabernet Sauvignon, Cabernet Franc, and Merlot
city or village: St.-Laurent
One of the largest properties in the Haut-Médoc, Château Larose-Trintaudon is a sister château to Château de Camensac and is managed by M. Forner, who owns Camensac. It is officially rated as a *cru bourgeois supérieur*.
Rich red color and a characteristic, mature Cabernet bouquet. The wine is smooth, fruity, and early-maturing—it is excellent value. **price range:** B

producer: Société Civile des Vignobles du Château Bellegrave
classification: Château-bottled red table wine
grape variety: Cabernet and Merlot
city or village: Listrac
château: Bellegrave
Bright red color and a well-developed bouquet. The wine is dry and elegant.
price range: B

producer: Société Civile du Vignoble de Château Latour
classification: Château-bottled red table wine
grape variety: Predominantly Cabernet Sauvignon, with some Merlot and Malbec
city or village: Pauillac
château: Latour
Called "Les Forts de Latour" after the

ancient fortifications that border the property of Château Latour, this wine is the "second wine" of Château Latour and is produced from young vines that have not yet come into full maturity. Although young, the average age of the vines is considerably higher than four years—the minimum for French vines in superior districts like Bordeaux—and the wine possesses many of the same nuances of Château Latour, though to a slightly lesser extent.
Deep, solid red color and a full, classical bouquet. The wine is full, with beautiful structure, like a Château Latour.
price range: D

producer: Société Civile Immobilière La Tour Carnet
classification: Red table wine
grape variety: Cabernet Sauvignon, Merlot, Malbec, Petit-Verdot, and Cabernet Franc
city or village: St.-Laurent
château: La Tour Carnet
Château La Tour Carnet was classified in 1855 as a *grand cru* (great growth) of the Médoc, and all the wines are château-bottled. The vineyards that surround this old feudal castle constructed in the thirteenth century yield an elegant red wine with a bouquet reminiscent of violets.
Clear, deep red color and a fragrant bouquet suggesting violets. The wine is elegant, supple, and full-bodied—a firm, noble red wine. **price range:** D

producer: Société Civile du Vignoble de Château Latour
classification: Château-bottled red table wine
grape variety: Predominantly Cabernet Sauvignon, with some Merlot and Malbec
city or village: Pauillac
château: Latour
Officially classified as a *premier cru* (first growth) in the 1855 classification of the Médoc, Château Latour holds a position that is still unchallenged. Many knowledgeable oenophiles consider it the finest Claret, and it is clearly one of the world's greatest red wines. The estate has the uncanny ability to produce excellent wines in "off" vintages, when many of its rivals fail.
Quite deep, full majestic red color and a

splendid, complex, fragrant bouquet reminiscent of cedar. The wine is huge, full, and fruity; when mature, it displays a multitude of different flavors. **price range:** E

producer: Société Viticole de Château Lascombes
classification: Château-bottled red table wine
grape variety: Cabernet Sauvignon, Merlot, and Cabernet Franc
city or village: Margaux
château: Lascombes
Officially classified as a *deuxième cru* (second growth) in the 1855 Médoc classification, Château Lascombes was at one time owned by a group of American investors headed by the American wine expert Alexis Lichine.
Full bouquet typical of Margaux; the wine has great finesse, smoothness, and is quite full-bodied in great years. It tends to mature rapidly for a Margaux, but is long-lived. **price range:** C

producer: S. V. de St.-Estèphe
classification: Red table wine
grape variety: Cabernet and Merlot
city or village: St.-Estèphe
château: Faget
A good Claret from the St.-Estèphe area; only twenty-five hundred cases are produced each year.
Good clean color and a fine bouquet. The wine is pleasant, with elegant fullness.
price range: B

producer: Nicolas Tari
classification: Château-bottled red table wine

grape variety: Cabernet Sauvignon, Cabernet Franc, and Merlot
city or village: Labarde
château: Giscours
Officially rated *troisième cru* (third growth) in the 1855 classification of the Médoc, Château Giscours is considered by many experts to be among the best Margaux produced today. Though technically in the commune of Labarde, Labarde is officially entitled to the appellation "Margaux" under the law, and the wine is a representative Margaux. The 1972 Giscours is an acknowledged success in that uneven vintage, which speaks well of winemaster Pierre Tari—son of Nicolas Tari, and head of the Comité des Grands Crus Classés de Médoc.
Deep, dark, full color and a bouquet showing much complexity and finesse. The wine is dry, full-flavored, and develops added complexity with bottle aging.
price range: C

producer: J. P. Theron
classification: Château-bottled red table wine
grape variety: Cabernet Sauvignon and Merlot
city or village: Listrac
Classified as a *cru bourgeois supérieur*, the vineyard was replanted in part fifteen years ago, but retains a large proportion of vines twenty years of age and older.
Brilliant dark red color and a fine bouquet. The wine is round and soft, typical of Médocs, and is very fine.
price range: C

producer: Paul & Roger Zuger
classification: Château-bottled red table wine
grape variety: Cabernet (65%), Merlot (30%), and Petit-Verdot (5%)
city or village: Margaux
château: Malescot-St.-Exupéry
The estate was created in 1697 by Simon Malescot and was later owned by Count Jean-Baptiste de Saint-Exupéry (grandfather of the famous author) from 1827 to 1858. The Zuger family has owned the château since 1955. As required by the

Comité Interprofessionel des Grands Crus du Médoc, all the wines are château-bottled; and when quality is not up to standard the wines are declassified and simply sold as Margaux, not Malescot. This happened recently in 1963 and 1968.
Ruby-red color, which darkens with age, and a bouquet of raspberries in youth that changes to "black currants" later. The wine is long-lived, losing its youthful tannin and increasing its bouquet with bottle age; its qualities naturally depend on the vintage.
price range: C

MÉDOC

producer: Gilbey S.A.
classification: Château-bottled red table wine
grape variety: Cabernet and Merlot
city or village: St.-Yzans-de-Médoc
château: Loudenne
Château Loudenne was originally acquired by Walter and Alfred Gilbey—producers of the famed Gilbey's gin—in 1875 as a base from which to conduct their wine trade. The wine is produced under the direct supervision of Martin Bamford, English Master of Wine, and its superiority reflects the attention and detail given from the vine to the bottle.
Well-colored ruby hue, leaning toward garnet with age; a fine, soft, and medium-full bouquet, giving the added complexity of new wood. The wine is dry, complex, and full-flavored, with medium-full body. Generally acknowledged to be a wine of superior class to its official rating of *cru bourgeois*. **price range:** B

producer: Pierre Monge
classification: Château-bottled red table wine
grape variety: Cabernet Sauvignon, Cabernet Franc, Merlot, Malbec, and Petit-Verdot
city or village: Bégandan
This wine was not imported to the United States until 1972. The first vintage to appear in America was the 1967, a representative vintage of a good estate-bottled wine from one of the lesser-known districts in the Médoc.
Deep ruby color and a youthful bouquet of fresh raspberries that ages to a deeper

mellowness. Though the wine has harsh tannins when young, which overpower one initially, they mature roundly and the wine becomes highly respectable.
price range: C

producer: Prats Frères
classification: Red table wine
grape variety: Cabernet and Merlot
L'Île Margaux is the only island in the Gironde estuary that is officially considered part of the Médoc region. Domaine de l'Île Margaux is a popularly priced *Bordeaux supérieur* wine, typical of a good Margaux.
Medium red color; the wine has distinctive body and is light, fruity, and refreshing.
price range: B

producer: Quien & Co.
classification: Red table wine
grape variety: Cabernet Sauvignon and Merlot
An area that produces the well-known wines of the world-famous classified châteaux.
Light ruby color and an elegant bouquet. The wine is well-balanced and will improve with three or four years of bottle aging. **price range:** B

producer: Baron Philippe de Rothschild, S.A.
classification: Red table wine
grape variety: Cabernet Sauvignon, Cabernet Franc, and Merlot

Baron Philippe de Rothschild Médoc is a blended regional wine that, unlike some other Rothschild red wines, can be drunk young—when three years old.

Excellent medium-dark red color and a dlic
t bouquet typical of Médocs. The wine is well-balanced, with medium body; regional wines of this high quality offer good value without quality fluctuations from different vintages. The wine should be served at room temperature—68 degrees F.
price range: B

POMEROL

producer: Ardurat-Raynaud
classification: Château-bottled red table wine
grape variety: Merlot (50%), Cabernet Sauvignon (35%), and Malbec (15%)
city or village: Pomerol
château: Le Commandeur
This estate is one of the oldest in Pomerol. It is composed of two different growths: La Croix-de-Gay, and Le Commandeur, which were combined as a result of the expansion of the domaine. The vineyard has belonged to the same family for many generations and has always had the best care.

A fine, characteristically perfumed bouquet; the wine combines the body of a Burgundy with the fragrance of a Bordeaux. The fine qualities create a real pleasure on the palate. **price range:** B

producer: F. Ginestet
classification: Red table wine
grape variety: Merlot and Bouchet
The small vineyard area of Pomerol benefits from exceptional soil, and the wines are characterized by great quality and consistency.

Deep ruby color and a rich, fruity bouquet. The wine is full-flavored and rich, with great warmth. **price range:** C

producer: J. Bouldy
classification: Château-bottled red table wine
grape variety: Merlot and Bouchet
château: Bellegrave
Bright red color and an outstanding, elegant bouquet. **price range:** B

producer: M. Faisandier
classification: Château-bottled red table wine
grape variety: Cabernet and Merlot
city or village: Pomerol
A small Pomerol château, owned by a man who considers wine making an art.

Quite pronounced red color and a bouquet of violets. The wine is round and soft, a typical Pomerol. **price range:** C

producer: Mme. Lily Lacoste-Loubat & J.-P. Moueix
classification: Château-bottled red table wine
grape variety: Merlot and Bouchet
city or village: Pomerol
château: Petrus
Château Petrus, named for St. Peter the fisherman apostle, is the most famous Pomerol estate and the most expensive. It is owned jointly by Mme. Lily Lacoste-Loubat and Jean-Pierre Moueix; the former inherited the estate from Mme. Edmond Loubat, the name of whom is still featured on the label.

One of the world's truly greatest red wines. **price range:** E

producer: Marcel Bertrand
classification: Red table wine
grape variety: Merlot (70%) and Bouchet (30%)
château: Rouget
Rated *grand cru* (great growth), the vineyards are on the hilltop of Pomerol.

A traditional full-bodied wine with a deep topaz color. **price range:** D

producer: Mme. Lily Lacoste-Loubat
classification: Château-bottled red table wine
grape variety: Cabernet and Merlot
city or village: Pomerol
château: Latour-à-Pomerol
Château Latour-à-Pomerol is owned by the same proprietor that directs Château Petrus, Mme. Lily Lacoste-Loubat, who inherited it from her aunt, Mme. Edmond Loubat; this name is still indicated on the label. Though there is no official classification of Pomerol estates, Latour-à-Pomerol is considered unofficially to be one of the very finest Pomerol châteaux. The estate is run by Jean-Pierre Moueix, an important Pomerol proprietor, who makes the wine for Mme. Lacoste-Loubat and sells it along with wines from other outstanding Pomerol properties.

Deep, almost blackish-red color and a deep, scented bouquet reminiscent of truffles and violets. The wine is full, mellow, and silky, with a long finish.
price range: E

producer: C. Leymarie & Fils
classification: Château-bottled red table wine
grape variety: Merlot, Cabernet Franc, and Cabernet Sauvignon
city or village: Pomerol
château: Beauchêne
Deep red color and an elegant bouquet. The wine is very full and round, with a lot of flavor and generosity. **price range:** C

producer: Jean-Pierre Moueix & Cie.
classification: Château-bottled red table wine
grape variety: Merlot and Bouchet
city or village: Pomerol
château: Lagrange
Deep, almost purple-red color and a ripe, "roasted" bouquet. The wine is very rich and complete—a typical Pomerol, and a very good one. **price range:** C

producer: Christian & Michel Querre
classification: Red table wine
grape variety: Merlot and Bouchet
One of the good wines of Pomerol; very distinctive. Michel Querre also owns Château Patris, located a few kilometers away in St.-Émilion.

Dark red color and a splendid, powerful bouquet. The wine is full-bodied and velvety; it matures quickly but will perhaps not keep quite as long as a St.-Émilion.
price range: D

producer: Baron Philippe de Rothschild, S.A.
classification: Red table wine
grape variety: Merlot and Bouchet
Baron Philippe de Rothschild Pomerol is a blended regional wine that, unlike some other Rothschild red wines, can be drunk young—when three years old. The wines have great depth of color to the point of being brilliant. Their fruity character allows them to enhance almost every meal.

Beautiful dark crimson-red color and a big, rich classic aroma of Merlot. The wine is full-bodied, with a long finish; regional wines of this high quality offer good value without quality fluctuations from different vintages. The wine should be served at room temperature—68 degrees F.
price range: C

ST. ÉMILION

producer: M. Barret-Chariol
classification: Château-bottled red table wine
grape variety: Cabernet Sauvignon, Merlot, and Cabernet Franc
city or village: St.-Émilion
château: de Lescours

Château de Lescours, built in 1341, is one of the oldest châteaux in the Bordeaux region.

Clear, vibrant ruby-red color and a woody bouquet of Cabernet. The wine is full, rich, and fat, typical of St.-Émilions; it is an excellent wine displaying better characteristics than its appellation suggests. **price range:** B

producer: A. Bichot
classification: Red table wine
grape variety: Merlot and Cabernet
city or village: St.-Émilion

Rich ruby-red color and a fruity bouquet. The wine is tannic, full-bodied, and well-balanced; it ages well and goes well with red meat, prepared dishes, and cheese. **price range:** B

producer: Henri Bordas
classification: Château-bottled red table wine
grape variety: Cabernet Franc and Merlot
city or village: St.-Émilion
château: du Calvaire

Light ruby color and a bouquet with good fruit. The wine is round and supple, very pleasant to the taste when young, but it ages well and develops full maturity after five or six years of bottle aging.
price range: C

producer: Borie-Manoux
classification: Château-bottled red table wine
grape variety: Cabernet and Merlot
city or village: St.-Émilion
château: Trotte Vieille

Rated *premier grand cru classé* (first great classified growth) in 1955, Château Trotte Vieille is one of the most important St.-Émilion châteaux. The vineyards extend over some 25 acres on the slopes (*côtes*) of St.-Émilion; production averages some 60,000 bottles annually.

Rich red color and a bouquet with delicate fruitiness. The wine is dry and elegant. **price range:** C

producer: A. Bourricaud
classification: Château-bottled red table wine
grape variety: Merlot and Cabernet Franc
city or village: St.-Émilion
château: Tremblant

A good St.-Émilion from a single property.

Light red color and a very delicate bouquet. The wine is round and well-balanced. **price range:** B

producer: M. L. Brun
classification: Château-bottled red table wine
grape variety: Merlot, Cabernet Sauvignon, and Malbec
city or village: St.-Christophe-des-Bardes

A château-bottled St.-Émilion with good breed.

Very clean and pleasant aroma; the wine is smooth and round. **price range:** C

producer: Calvet
classification: Red table wine
grape variety: Bouchet and Merlot

The brand name Tauzia (after the name of a château owned by Calvet) was first introduced in 1925. The wine is given a sufficient period to mature in the bottle before being offered to the trade.

Full red color with tinges of brown on the edges and a fruity bouquet. The wine is fairly full-bodied and mature. **price range:** B

producer: R. Capdemourlin-Berthon
classification: Château-bottled red table wine
grape variety: Merlot and Bouchet
city or village: St.-Émilion
château: Balestard-La Tonnelle

Praised by the poet François Villon, whose work appears on the label, Château Balestard-La Tonnelle is officially rated as a *grand cru classé* (classified great growth) of St.-Émilion.

Deep red color and a ripe bouquet of Merlot—typical of well-made St.-Émilions. The wine is rich and harmonious, with sufficient tannin to age well; it is a fine, elegant St.-Émilion. **price range:** C

producer: Pierre Chariol
classification: Red table wine
grape variety: Cabernet Sauvignon, Merlot, and Malbec

city or village: St.-Émilion

A well-priced wine offering character and individuality.

Ruby-red color with some browning at the edges and a typically complex Bordeaux bouquet with good fruit. The wine has complexity, berrylike fruitiness, and is ready to drink when sold. **price range:** B

producer: Pierre Cartier & Fils
classification: Red table wine
grape variety: Merlot and Bouchet

Bright red color and a well-developed bouquet. The wine is fruity and dry.
price range: A

producer: P. Dangin
classification: Château-bottled red table wine
grape variety: Merlot and Cabernet Sauvignon
city or village: St.-Émilion
château: Bellegrave at Vignonet

A fairly supple example of an excellent château-bottled St.-Émilion.

Rich yet delicately perfumed bouquet; the wine is quite full-bodied.
price range: A

producer: F. Ginestet
classification: Red table wine
grape variety: Merlot and Bouchet

St.-Émilions have long been known as

the "Burgundies of the Bordeaux region," and F. Ginestet, producer of some of Bordeaux's finest wines, ships excellent regional St.-Émilions.

Deep garnet color and a full, round bouquet. The wine is full-bodied, round, and flavorful. **price range: B**

producer: Robert Giraud
classification: Château-bottled red table wine
grape variety: Merlot, Cabernet Franc, and Cabernet Sauvignon
city or village: St.-Émilion
château: Villemaurine

Officially classified as a *grand cru classé* (classified great growth) of St.-Émilion.

Brilliant dark red color and a rich, round bouquet. It is a typical St.-Émilion—smooth, full-bodied, soft, and generous.
price range: C

producer: Lurton Frères
classification: Château-bottled red table wine
grape variety: Merlot and Cabernet
city or village: St.-Émilion
château: Clos-Fourtet

Classified as one of the twelve *premier grands crus classés* (first great classified growths) of St.-Émilion, Clos-Fourtet is situated near the very center of St.-Émilion. The cellar, one of the district's showplaces, is dug out of the side of a hill.

Deep, full ruby color and a full bouquet typical of a fine St.-Émilion. On the palate the wine is fruity and robust.
price range: C

producer: Héritiers Jean Cap-de-Mourlin
classification: Château-bottled red table wine

grape variety: Merlot (60%), Cabernet Sauvignon (20%), and Cabernet Franc (20%)
city or village: St.-Émilion
château: Cap-de-Mourlin

Cap-de-Mourlin is one of the oldest and most respected of the St.-Émilion châteaux and is rated *grand cru classé* (classified great growth). The wine is often served at receptions at the Élysée Palace and at the Hotel Matignon; recently it was chosen to be the wine served to the U.S. astronauts at their reception in Paris.

Very well-developed bouquet reminiscent of truffles; the wine is rich in tannin but does not have astringency; it is a fine, full-bodied red wine distinguished by generosity combined with a great delicacy of flavor. **price range:** C

producer: Maison Sichel
classification: Red table wine
grape variety: Merlot and Cabernet

Can be drunk young; because of their softness, these wines are often referred to as the "Burgundies of the Bordeaux region."

Brilliant red color and a full, rich bouquet. The wine is round, soft, and stylish. **price range:** B

"Bronze is the mirror of the form; wine, of the heart."
—Aeschylus

producer: Pierre Jean
classification: Château-bottled red table wine
grape variety: Merlot, Cabernet, and Malbec
city or village: St.-Émilion
château: Trimoulet

A St.-Émilion *grand cru classé* (classified great growth), Château Trimoulet is a wine that has always been especially well received in the restaurant trade. Though it possesses excellent aging qualities, the wine is eminently enjoyable with as little as two years' bottle age.

Medium-deep ruby color and a delicate, dry bouquet. On the palate the wine is full and generous. **price range:** C

producer: A. Manoncourt
classification: Château-bottled red table wine
grape variety: Cabernet Sauvignon, Merlot, and Bouchet
city or village: St.-Émilion
château: Figeac

Chateau Figeac, classified *premier grand cru* (first great growth) in 1955, is closer in style to a Pomerol than a St.-Émilion. It enjoys superior soil near the Pomerol boundary, a situation reflected in the fullness of the wines.

Very beautiful color and a very personal, scented bouquet. The wine is generous and vigorous; it would go well with red meats, game, Roquefort cheese, and lamb.
price range: D

producer: C. Mazière
classification: Château-bottled red table wine
grape variety: Merlot and Malbec
city or village: St.-Émilion
château: Simard

The vineyard has been in continuous production since the eighteenth century.

Deep ruby color; the wine is soft and full, richer than a Médoc or a Graves, and finishes well. It is a favorite among Claret drinkers when dining on beef, fowl, or just a nibble of cheese. **price range:** B

producer: Prats Frères
classification: Château-bottled red table wine
grape variety: Merlot and Bouchet
city or village: St.-Émilion
château: Petit-Figeac

This property adjoins the great Château Figeac.

Full, soft flavor—a full-bodied soft red wine from the famous St.-Émilion region.
price range: B

producer: Charles Mestre-Guilhem
classification: Château-bottled red table wine
grape variety: Cabernet Sauvignon (10%), Merlot (75%), and Cabernet Franc (15%)
city or village: St.-Sulpice de-Faleyrens

This vineyard was taken over and improved by the last two generations of the present owners. It is managed according to ancestral traditions.

Fine, harmonious bouquet; the wine is fine, generous, and full-bodied. Its rich tannin assures long and happy life without disagreeable astringency. **price range:** B

producer: Christian & Michel Querre
classification: Red table wine
grape variety: Bouchet and Merlot
city or village: St.-Sulpice de-Faleyrens

Deep red color and an attractive bouquet. The wine becomes quite soft, velvety, and delicate with age, and its color deepens; it is well-balanced, high in alcohol, and good value for the money.
price range: C

producer: Quien & Co.
classification: Red table wine
grape variety: Merlot and Cabernet

One of the most popular Bordeaux wines in the United States.

Deep red color and very round, supple flavor. **price range:** B

producer: Louis Rapin
classification: Château-bottled red table wine
grape variety: Cabernet (Bouchet) and Merlot
city or village: Montagne–St.-Émilion
château: Maison Blanche
Brilliant dark red color and a fruity bouquet. The wine tastes soft, clean, and stylish. **price range:** B

producer: Baron Philippe de Rothschild, S.A.
classification: Red table wine
grape variety: Merlot and Cabernet
Baron Philippe de Rothschild St.-Émilion is a blended regional wine that, unlike some other Rothschild red wines, can be drunk young—when three years old. The wines have great depth of color to the point of being brilliant. Their fruity character allows them to enhance almost every meal.
Light crimson color and a full, rich Merlot aroma. The wine is full-bodied, with a good finish; regional wines of this high quality offer good value without quality fluctuations from different vintages. The wine should be served at room temperature—68 degrees F. **price range:** B

producer: A. Simon
classification: Red table wine
grape variety: Merlot, Cabernet Franc, and Cabernet Sauvignon
city or village: St.-Émilion
A true wine in the St.-Émilion style.

Reddish-brown color and a classic, fruity and individual Claret bouquet. The wine is soft, with excellent depth.
price range: A

producer: Société Civile du Château Laroque
classification: Château-bottled red table wine
grape variety: Merlot and Cabernet
city or village: St.-Christophe-des-Bardes
Rich bouquet; the wine is full-bodied, dry, and well-balanced. **price range:** B

producer: Société Civile du Château Montlabert
classification: Château-bottled red table wine
grape variety: Merlot, Cabernet Franc, and Cabernet Sauvignon
city or village: St.-Émilion
château: Montlabert
The main shareholders of this château are North Americans.
Brilliant red color and a very characteristic, fruity bouquet. The wine is soft, fruity, and very tasty; it is delicate and charming.
price range: C

producer: Société Civile Immobilière du Château Puyfromage
classification: Château-bottled red table wine
grape variety: Cabernet Sauvignon, Cabernet Franc, and Merlot
city or village: Saint-Cibard
Château Puyfromage was classified as a St.-Émilion from the establishment of the

property in 1574 until the classification of St.-Émilion in 1955. At that time, an arbitrary line was drawn defining the limits of the Appellation Contrôlée St.-Émilion, and the Puyfromage vineyards fell on the wrong side of the road. It must therefore bear the classification *Bordeaux supérieur*, although the wines have true St.-Émilion quality and character.
Deep ruby to garnet-red color and a fruity, warm bouquet. The wine is full-bodied, well-balanced and has great depth of flavor. It reaches maturity in three to five years, although it is able to continue improving with additional bottle age.
price range: B

producer: Valette
classification: Château-bottled red table wine
grape variety: Cabernet Sauvignon, Cabernet Franc, and Merlot
city or village: St.-Émilion
château: La Clusière
The vineyards of Château La Clusière are situated on the grounds of Château Pavie, and likewise produce wines of great quality. Both vineyards are owned by M. Valette; Château Pavie is one of the oldest and most renowned *premier grand cru classés* (first great classified growths) of St.-Émilion.
A particularly good bouquet and a typical flavor of a fine St.-Émilion, well-bred and with great class. **price range:** C

producer: L. Yerlès
classification: Château-bottled red table wine
grape variety: Merlot and Cabernet
city or village: Montagne–St.-Émilion
château: des Tours
A château-bottled wine from the largest vineyard in St.-Émilion. The château itself is a beautiful castle placed in the middle of the vineyard.
Light ruby color and a very round, supple flavor typical of St.-Émilion.
price range: B

producer: Valette
classification: Château-bottled red table wine
grape variety: Cabernet Sauvignon, Bouchet, Merlot, and Malbec
city or village: St.-Émilion
Situated on the hill of St.-Émilion, the vineyard has only a small production, but gives wines similar in many respects to Médoc in some years. It is close to the best St.-Émilions in quality.
Brilliant ruby-red color and a fine bouquet. The wine is soft and distinctive—a very high-class wine.
price range: C

producer: Valette
classification: Château-bottled red table wine
grape vareity: Merlot and Bouchet
city or village: St.-Émilion
château: Pavie
Château Pavie, rated *premier grand cru* (first great growth), is the largest *premier grand cru* in the region. The cellars lie beneath the slopes of St.-Émilion, and the wine has won three gold medals, two *Diplomes d'Honneur* at Liège and London, and the *Hors Concours* in Bordeaux in 1907.
A soft, full, and distinctly fruity Claret.
price range: C

producer: Vignobles Rollet S.A.
classification: Château-bottled red table wine
grape variety: Cabernet Sauvignon, Bouchet, Malbec, and Merlot
city or village: St.-Étienne
château: Roc St. Michel
A delicate bouquet, smooth texture, and fine breeding. The wine is sturdy, generous, and full; it finishes dry.
price range: B

GRAVES

producer: Jean Kressmann
classification: Red table wine
grape variety: Cabernet Sauvignon, Merlot, Malbec, and Petit-Verdot
city or village: Martillac
château: La Tour–Martillac

Some of the vines at Château La Tour–Martillac are the oldest in the area, producing very small quantities of wine but in the very highest class. The wines are not château-bottled but are bottled at the Kressmann facilities in Bordeaux, yet they are among the best red and white wines produced in Graves.

The color (like anything else) depends on the vintage, but it usually is very dark, and the bouquet extremely fine. The wine is full of flavor—packed, in great vintages—and is sound and of a very high class. **price range:** D

producer: Société des Grandes Graves
classification: White table wine
grape variety: Semillon and Sauvignon Blanc
city or village: Léognan

Brilliant very light gold color and a crisp, dry bouquet. The wine is dry, clean, and fruity; it should age well and is typical of a light Graves. **price range:** B

producer: Maison Sichel
classification: White table wine
grape variety: Sauvignon Blanc and Semillon
Should be drunk young.

Brilliant golden-yellow color and a flowery bouquet. The wine is dry, yet slightly sweet, and has a mellow flavor.
price range: B

producer: Pierre Cartier & Fils
classification: White table wine
grape variety: Semillon and Sauvignon Blanc

Bright clear color and a well-developed bouquet. The wine is quite dry.
price range: A

producer: Daniel Sanders
classification: Château-bottled red table wine
grape variety: Cabernet Sauvignon, Cabernet Franc, and Merlot
city or village: Léognan
château: Haut-Bailly

Château Haut-Bailly is officially classified as a *grand cru classé* (classified great growth) of Graves. It is one of the best châteaux of Graves.

Delicate, exceptional bouquet and flavor. **price range:** C

producer: Prats Frères
classification: Château-bottled white table wine
grape variety: Sauvignon Blanc and Semillon
château: Piron

Produced and bottled at the elegant Château Piron, owned by the Boyreau family for nearly three hundred years.
price range: B

producer: J. Guillemaud
classification: Château-bottled white table wine
grape variety: Semillon and Sauvignon Blanc
city or village: Léognan
château: Larrivet-Haut-Brion

The estate-bottled red and white wines of Château Larrivet-Haut-Brion are renowned for their outstanding breed. The estate is classified as a *grand cru* (great growth) of Graves.

Clear straw color and a fruity bouquet. On the palate the wine is dry, fruity, and delicate, with a dry finish and a charming softness. **price range:** C

producer: J. Guillemaud
classification: Château-bottled red table wine
grape variety: Cabernet Sauvignon, Merlot, and Malbec
city or village: Léognan
château: Larrivet-Haut-Brion

The estate-bottled wines of Château Larrivet-Haut-Brion are both red and white wines of outstanding breed.

Garnet color and a delicate, beautiful bouquet. The wine combines great finesse and suppleness.
price range: D

producer: Jean Ricard
classification: Château-bottled red table wine
grape variety: Cabernet Sauvignon, Merlot, and Malbec

city or village: Léognan (Domaine de Chevalier)

A classified great growth (*grand cru classé*) from Graves, Domaine de Chevalier is the only top Bordeaux château to be called a *domaine*. Both red and white wines are produced; the red is rich and elegant and commands a higher price than many classified Médoc growths; the white is dry and fruity, but is extremely rare. Estate-bottled.

Deep garnet color and a fruity bouquet. The wine tastes rich, fruity, and elegant and has an outstanding pedigree.
price range: E

producer: F. Ginestet
classification: White varietal table wine
grape variety: Sauvignon Blanc

The Sauvignon Blanc grape produces one of the most distinctive Bordeaux white wines.

Clear pale straw color and a pleasing, fruity bouquet. The wine is light, dry, and fruity. **price range:** A

producer: Alphonse Denis
classification: Red table wine
grape variety: Cabernet Sauvignon and Merlot
city or village: Mérignac

Attractive ruby color; leaves "legs" in the glass, a sign of good body. The wine is remarkably soft, is drier than a Médoc and more austere. It is highly recommended with game, lighter cuts of beef, and cheese (Camembert, Brie, Port-Salut, and aged Cheddar). **price range:** B

Truly great gastronomes are those who chart courses through pleasant places, cultivate kindred spirits along the way, and listen to the voice of experience in others.

producer: Société Civile du Château Bouscaut
classification: Château-bottled red table wine
grape variety: Cabernet Sauvignon, Cabernet Franc, Merlot, and Malbec
city or village: Cadaujac
château: Bouscaut

Classified *grand cru* (great growth) in 1953, Château Bouscaut is an outstanding Graves château that is now owned by a group of Americans. Each vintage is matured in new Limousin oak casks, which imparts an unmistakable flavor and balance to the wine.

Good color; full, supple, good fruit and color. Finishes well. **price range:** C

producer: Société Civile des Domaines Woltner
classification: Château-bottled red table wine
grape variety: Cabernet Sauvignon (60%), Merlot (30%), and Cabernet Franc (10%)
city or village: Pessac
château: La Mission-Haut-Brion

Château La Mission-Haut-Brion is among the most famous and prized of all Bordeaux wines. Vinification takes place in steel vats with glass linings, installed in 1951 and accounting for a remarkable increase in quality. At least two-thirds of the soil in the vineyard is stones, poor for other crops but superb for drainage and for vines. It was classified *grand cru* (great growth) in 1953.

An outstanding red Graves.
price range: E

producer: P. de Bethmann
classification: Château-bottled white table wine

grape variety: Semillon and Sauvignon Blanc
city or village: Léognan
château: Olivier

Classified *grand cru* (great growth) in 1953, Château Olivier is one of the most important Graves estates and is classified as a national monument by the government. The vineyard is composed of gravelly soil mixed with sand.

A Sauvignon aroma; dry. Should be served well-chilled. **price range:** C

producer: Baron Philippe de Rothschild, S.A.
classification: White table wine
grape variety: Sauvignon Blanc and Semillon

Baron Philippe de Rothschild Graves is a blended regional wine, named for the gravelly soil in the area.

Light golden-straw color and a delicate bouquet with a slight earthy aroma. On the palate the wine is light and dry, exceptionally smooth with a good finish. Regional wines of this high quality offer good value without quality fluctuations from different vintages. The wine should be served chilled after two or three hours in the refrigerator. **price range:** B

producer: Érik Bocké
classification: Château-bottled red table wine
grape variety: Cabernet Sauvignon (40%), Merlot (35%), Malbec (15%), and others
city or village: Léognan
château: Fieuzal

Planted in the most noble vines, Château Fieuzal is well known for the exceptional quality of its red wines, which are characteristically full-bodied. The wines have won many gold medals: the 1966 and the 1967 Fieuzal at the International Exposition in Ljubljana, Yugoslavia, and the 1970 and 1971 vintages at the International Oenological Contest at Milan in 1973.

A lovely Graves bouquet and an attractive, individual flavor. The wines combine body and exquisite finesse with highly developed bouquet. **price range:** C

producer: J. R. Parkington & Co. Ltd.
classification: White table wine
grape variety: Semillon, Sauvignon Blanc, and Muscadelle

Pale yellow color; a medium-dry white Graves. **price range:** B

producer: Société du Château Bouscaut
classification: Château-bottled white table wine
grape variety: Sauvignon Blanc and Semillon
city or village: Cadaujac
château: Bouscaut

A *grand cru classé* (classified great growth) of Graves, Château Bouscaut is owned by a group of Americans.

Its fresh flavor makes it perfect for white meats, fish, and mild cheeses.
price range: C

producer: M. E. Coste
classification: Château-bottled red table wine
grape variety: Cabernet Sauvignon, Merlot, and Malbec
city or village: Portets
château: de May

The grapes for this wine grow on gravelly soil, giving it rich texture and interesting fragrance.

Dark purple-red color and a full, rich, and "masculine" bouquet. The wine is dry, vigorous, and full-bodied, with good fruit and a long-lasting finish. **price range:** B

producer: Schröder & Schÿler & Cie
classification: Red table wine
grape variety: Cabernet Sauvignon and Merlot

The only branded red Graves wine sold in the United Kingdom.

Bright red color and a pleasant bouquet with a hint of fruit. The wine is firm, round, and well-made; it has a lingering aftertaste and is excellent value. **price range:** A

producer: Quien & Co.
classification: White table wine
grape variety: Sauvignon Blanc and Semillon

One of the most popular white wines of Bordeaux.

Straw-yellow color and a light bouquet. The wine is medium dry and quite smooth; serve chilled. **price range:** B

producer: A. Simon
classification: White table wine
grape variety: Sauvignon Blanc and Semillon

This wine is a Graves Moelleux (soft).

Pale yellow color and a rich lemony bouquet. The wine is full and medium dry; a good example of one of the best-known Bordeaux white wines. **price range:** A

CÉRONS

producer: J. L. Perromat
classification: Château-bottled white table wine
grape variety: Sauvignon Blanc and Semillon
château: de Ferbos

Château de Ferbos is located on the banks of the Garonne River at Cérons. The firm of F. Ginestet carefully selects and meticulously supervises the production of this château-bottled white Bordeaux.

A pale straw color and a fruity, dry bouquet. The wine is dry and fruity with a fresh, clean tay—a superior dry Cérons.
price range: B

producer: Christian & Michel Querre
classication: White table wine
grape variety: Semillon and Sauvignon Blanc

One of the principal vineyards in the Céronscmune, a small area located between Graves and Sauternes. The wine contains at least 12% alcohol by volume.

Golden color and a delicate bouquet. The wine is dry and full-bodied, rather high in alcohol. **price range:** B

SAUTERNES

producer: Comtesse de Vaucelles née Durieu de Lacarelle
classification: Château-bottled red table wine
grape variety: Cabernet and Folle-Noire
city or village: Langon
château: Filhot

"Pinaud du Rey" is a rare red wine produced on the estate of the Château de Filhot, famous for its white wine. The vineyard was restored in the eighteenth century by the Duroy family, and an old tower dat-

ing from this time still stands today. Using the inscription "Cru du Roy" or "Pinaud du Rey" (vineyard of the king) for advertisement, this old growth has the first-quality certificate for all Sauternes wines, first issued in 1672. The trademark Cru du Roy was transferred by marriage to Château Suduiraut in the commune of Preignac. After their last mention in the 1855 classification of Sauternes, in which Filhot was rated *deuxième cru* (second growth), the vineyard of Pinaud was destroyed by the Lur-Saluces family after the phylloxera. Some parts of the old vineyard are still planted in red vines, and can use this name that was developed for a later time. Though technically grown in Sauternes, there is no red-wine appellation *Sauternes* and so the wine must bear the appellation *Bordeaux*.

Light *clairette* color and a fresh bouquet The wine is young and fresh, rather rustic, and often with an exotic aftertaste.
price range: A

producer: Comtesse de Vaucelles née Durieu de Lacarelle
classification: Château-bottled white table wine
grape variety: Semillon, Sauvignon Blanc, and Muscadelle
city or village: Langon
château: Filhot

Classified as a *deuxième cru* (second growth) of Sauternes in 1855, Chateau Filhot derives its name from the family de Filhot, which seems to have originated the name "Sauternes" (or Sauterne, before 1800), with a large diffusion at Bordeaux of the label "Vin de Filhot—Sauterne"—instead of the old, admitted appellation "Vin de Langon"—after 1709. In the nineteenth century, the castle and vineyard were named Château de Sauternes by the family de Lur-Saluces; they were recently repaired by the de Lacarelle family.

18th century

C. I. Filbot 19th century

20th century

Rich gold color and a complex bouquet of grapes and Botrytis mold dominated by fruit. On the palate the wine is sweet, liquorous, and complex, yet the sweetness is juxtaposed by the complexity of flavors. The wine is rich and develops even more complexity with bottle aging. In Sauternes it is served with wild pigeons and other birds; in Paris it is served as an *apéritif* or *digestif*, or a dessert wine, with *foie gras*. In England it is served between meals as a feast wine. **price range:** C

producer: Comtesse de Vaucelles née Durieu de Lacarelle
classification: White table wine
grape variety: Semillon, Sauvignon Blanc, and Muscadelle
city or village: Langon

This wine is called "Cru de Saubade," after the *metairie* (farm) de Saubade that was a part of the old vineyards of the de Filhot family. The name applies to white wines entitled either to the appellation *Bordeaux* or *Bordeaux supérieur*, according to need in a particular vintage. The wines are typical Sauternes, although slightly less sweet and rich than a top growth such as Château Filhot (owned by the same proprietor).

Gold-yellow color and a Sauvignon aroma with a slight "burn" of Botrytis mold. On the palate the wine is sweet and rich, typical of a good Sauternes.
price range: B

producer: Comtesse de Vaucelles née Durieu de Lacarelle
classification: White table wine
grape variety: Semillon, Sauvignon, and Muscadelle
city or village: Langon
château: Filhot

Called "Cru de Verdoulet," this is the "dry Sauternes" produced by Château Filhot in years when a part of the production is declassified and not sold as Sauternes under the château label. In style it is close to a white Graves, but does not bear this name because it is a by-product of the primary production at Château Filhot. Maison Noble de Verdoulet is the former name of Château Filhot; since the wine is declassified, it cannot be called Sauternes and only bears the appellation *Bordeaux*.

Clear yellow color and a fruity bouquet owing to the Sauvignon and Muscadelle vines. The wine is dry, light, and full of fruit.
price range: A

producer: Hallgarten Frères
classification: White table wine
grape variety: Semillon and Sauvignon Blanc

Golden-yellow color and a very pronounced fruity bouquet. The wine is smooth, sweet, and has a long finish; it is beautifully balanced, being sweet but not cloying, and rich but finishing dry.
price range: B

producer: R. & C. Medeville
classification: White table wine
grape variety: Semillon, Sauvignon Blanc, and Muscadelle
city or village: Preignac
vineyard: Clos des Ramparts

A lusciously sweet wine that owes its natural sugar to the "noble rot."

Golden-yellow color and a very rich, full bouquet. The wine is lusciously sweet, fruity, and fat. **price range:** C

producer: Quien & Co.
classification: White table wine
grape variety: Semillon, Sauvignon Blanc, and Muscadelle

By all odds, the greatest sweet white wine of Bordeaux. It owes its fullness, natural sweetness, and high alcoholic content to the "noble rot" and by picking the grapes late in the harvest.

Golden-yellow color and a very rich, full bouquet. The wine is very sweet and luscious; though a dessert wine, it is also excellent as an aperitif. **price range:** C

producer: Quien & Co.
classification: White table wine
grape variety: Semillon, Sauvignon Blanc, and Muscadelle
city or village: Barsac
A wine very similar to a Sauternes, though it has a special bouquet and added fruit.
Golden-yellow color and a very distinguished bouquet. The wine is sweet, fat, full-bodied, and rich. **price range:** C

producer: C. Jouvet S.A.
classification: White table wine
grape variety: Semillon and Sauvignon Blanc
city or village: Barsac
A beautiful nectar with soft sweetness and a pleasant aroma.
Aromatic fragrance and sweet flavor typical of wines from this district.
price range: B

producer: Société Civile du Château de Rayne-Vigneau
classification: Château-bottled white table wine
grape variety: Sauvignon Blanc, Semillon, and Muscadelle
city or village: Bommes
château: Rayne-Vigneau
Château Rayne-Vigneau was rated a *premier cru* (first growth) of Sauternes in 1855.
Clear bright color and a well-developed bouquet. The wine has a luscious, sweet flavor. **price range:** C

producer: Maison Sichel
classification: White table wine
grape variety: Semillon and Sauvignon Blanc
Clear, brilliant golden color and a full, rich bouquet. The wine is luscious and fruity, with a long-lasting flavor; serve well chilled. **price range:** C

producer: Maison Sichel
classification: White table wine
grape variety: Semillon and Sauvignon Blanc
city or village: Barsac
Long-lived.
Clean, brilliant color and a full, rich, and aromatic bouquet. The wine is luscious and elegant. **price range:** B

producer: Prats Frères
classification: White table wine
grape variety: Sauvignon Blanc and Semillon
A rich, sweet, full-bodied, and fruity white wine. **price range:** B

producer: F. Ginestet
classification: White table wine

grape variety: Sauvignon Blanc and Semillon
Unique among French wines, the famous Sauternes are comparable only with the great German wines. Ginestet Sauternes is an exceptional regional Sauternes.
Golden color and a rich, sweet bouquet. The wine is sweet, rich, and full-bodied, yet not overpowering. **price range:** C

producer: Baron Philippe de Rothschild, S.A.
classification: White table wine
grape variety: Sauvignon Blanc and Semillon
Baron Philippe de Rothschild Sauternes is a blended regional wine from the district of Sauternes, long famous for its sweet white wines. The natural sweetness in this wine is developed by leaving the grape on the vine until it is actually overripe.
Golden, crystal-clear color and a delightfully complex aroma. On the palate the wine is lusciously sweet, with a very long aftertaste of ripe grapes. Regional wines of this high quality offer good value without quality fluctuations from different vintages. The wine should be served chilled after two or three hours in the refrigerator.
price range: C

producer: Office Viticole de Sauternes et Barsac
classification: White table wine
grape variety: Semillon, Sauvignon Blanc, and Muscadelle
city or village: Langon
"Terre Noble" Sauternes is sold by the local Vintners Union after being blended from a number of different properties. It often competes favorably with the many fine classified châteaux of Sauternes and Barsac, and the label can apply to wines from Sauternes, Barsac, or Barsac-Sauternes and still describe the same wine. The wine is sold principally in France, for a local group of connoisseurs.
Yellow-gold color and a complex bouquet with fruit and the characteristic "burn" of Botrytis mold. On the palate the

wine is liquorous—sweet and rich—and it finishes well
price range: B (recent vintages); C (old vintages)

producer: Vintners' Syndicate of Sauternes
classification: White table wine
grape variety: Semillon, Sauvignon Blanc, and Muscadelle
city or village: Langon
"Duc de Sauternes" is obtained by a blending of the wines contributed by all members of the Syndicate of Sauternes. A good average Sauternes, it serves mainly for general promotion of the region's wines.
Gold color and a complex bouquet with the "burn" of Botrytis mold. The wine is sweet and liquorous, typical of its kind.
price range: B

producer: André Jalbert
classification: Château-bottled white table wine
grape variety: Semillon, Sauvignon, and Muscadelle
château: Lamourette
A delightful wine with a special aroma, subtle bouquet, and a powerful body.
price range: B

producer: M. Lacoste
classification: White table wine
grape variety: Semillon and Sauvignon Blanc
city or village: Barsac
Golden color and a hint of honey in the bouquet. The wine is sweet, full-bodied, and has great finesse—a wine of distinction. **price range:** B

producer: Edmond Rolland
classification: Château-bottled white table wine
grape variety: Semillon and Sauvignon Blanc
city or village: Barsac
château: Coutet

Château Coutet was officially classified as a *premier cru* (first growth) of Barsac-Sauternes in 1855.

Slight straw-color and crystal-clear; the bouquet is fruity and fresh. The wine is semi-dry, with great fruit, and has a somewhat "piercing" quality; it shows great breeding and will hold its fruit for a long time.   **price range:** C

producer: Daniel Sanders
classification: Château-bottled white table wine
grape variety: Sauvignon Blanc, Semillon, and Muscadelle
city or village: Barsac
château: du Mayne

A rich, flavorful Barsac.

Light, delicate golden color and a delicate bouquet typical of Barsacs. The wine is liquorous and generous, sure to be appreciated.   **price range:** B

producer: Baron Philippe de Rothschild, S.A.
classification: White table wine
grape variety: Sauvignon Blanc and Semillon

Baron Philippe de Rothschild Barsac is a blended regional wine from the district of Barsac, long famous for its sweet white wines. The natural sweetness in this wine is developed by leaving the grape on the vine until it is actually overripe.

Golden crystal-clear color and a delightfully complex aroma. On the palate the wine is lusciously sweet, with a very long aftertaste of ripe grapes. Regional wines of this high quality offer good value without quality fluctuations from different vintages. The wine should be served chilled after three or four hours in the refrigerator.   **price range:** C

producer: D. Cordier
classification: Château-bottled white table wine
château: Lafaurie-Peyraguey

This white wine is sweet, produced by a classified first great vineyard of Sauternes.
price range: D

PREMIER CÔTES DE BORDEAUX

producer: P & C Armand
classification: Château-bottled white table wine
grape variety: Sauvignon Blanc and Semillon
city or village: Ste. Croix-du-Mont
château: La Rame

An excellent white dessert wine, moderately priced because it comes from a lesser-known area than the Sauternes—many of which it closely resembles.

Brilliant, viscous golden color and a grapey and complex bouquet with a honeylike richness. The wine has a pronounced Botrytis flavor, like a Sauternes, and is developed and viscous.
price range: B

producer: Robert Giraud
classification: Château-bottled rosé table wine

grape variety: Cabernet Sauvignon and Bourdut
city or village: Cadillac
château: de Cadillac

Clear, brilliant rosé color and a fresh, fruity bouquet. The wine is clean and dry, with good acidity and a fresh taste.
price range: B

producer: Robert Giraud
classification: Château-bottled white table wine
grape variety: Sauvignon Blanc, Semillon, and Muscadelle
city or village: Cadillac
château: de Cadillac

Clear straw color and a full, dry, and somewhat fruity bouquet. The wine is dry and crisp, with a good fruity flavor.
price range: B

producer: Héritiers Germe
classification: Château-bottled red table wine
grape variety: Cabernet Sauvignon and Merlot
château: Lamégo

A good Claret produced in a little-known area of Bordeaux.

Light red color and a delicate bouquet.
price range: B

producer: J. R. Parkington & Co.
classification: White table wine
grape variety: Semillon and Sauvignon Blanc

Full, rich bouquet; the wine is sweet and typical of the region.   **price range:** A

producer: A. Simon
classification: White table wine
grape variety: Semillon, Sauvignon Blanc, and Muscadelle
city or village: Ste. Croix-du-Mont

A very good alternative to Sauternes at a considerable saving.

Medium yellow color and a rich and fragrant bouquet. The wine is sweet and full, an excellent sweet dessert wine.
price range: A

CÔTES DE BOURG

producer: H. Auditeau
classification: Château-bottled red table wine
grape variety: Cabernet, Merlot, and Malbec
city or village: Bourg-sur-Gironde
château: Caruel

Château Caruel is among the best growths of the Côtes de Bourg. The firm of F. Ginestet carefully selects and meticulously supervises the production of this château-bottled wine.

A lovely deep red color and a floral bouquet. The wine is delicate, soft, and full-bodied, with a fine balance.
price range: B

producer: M. Bourdillas
classification: Château-bottled red table wine
grape variety: Cabernet Franc, Merlot, and Malbec

city or village: Lansac
château: Goujon

This wine, produced on the banks of the Gironde estuary, is very characteristic of the Côtes de Bourg area that lies just opposite the Médoc district.

Deep red color and a light bouquet that shows finesse. The wine is very round and supple. **price range:** B

producer: André Jalbert
classification: Château-bottled red table wine
grape variety: Cabernet Sauvignon, Malbec, and Cabernet Franc
city or village: Ste.-Eulalie
château: Tour de Terrefort

Full-bodied and well-balanced, the wine improves with age. **price range:** A

producer: A. Jaubert
classification: Château-bottled red table wine
grape variety: Cabernet, Merlot, and others
city or village: Bayon
château: La Crois de Millorit

Full, rich bouquet; a flavor similar to a more expensive red Bordeaux. **price range:** B

producer: Prats Frères
classification: Château-bottled red table wine
grape variety: Cabernet Franc and Merlot
château: Falfas

Château Falfas was constructed originally as a hunting lodge in the fourteenth century. All the wines are now bottled at the château.

An agreeable, full-bodied, and fruity Claret that matures well. **price range:** B

CÔTES DE BLAYE

producer: M. Bernard
classification: Château-bottled red table wine
grape variety: Cabernet, Merlot, and Malbec
city or village: St.-Martin-Lacaussade
château: Mazerolles

A good wine from the Premières Côtes de Blaye that gains in subtleties with age; only fifteen hundred cases are produced each year.

Deep red color and a rather fine bouquet. The wine is supple, delicate, and fruity. **price range:** B

producer: J. Bossuet
classification: Château-bottled red table wine
grape variety: Merlot, Cabernet, and Malbec
city or village: Lars
château: Peybonhomme

Clean red color, not dark; a light and fruity bouquet and a very agreeable supple fruity flavor—the wine is well-balanced. **price range:** B

producer: Mme. Pierre Dupuy
classification: Château-bottled red table wine

grape variety: Cabernet Sauvignon, Merlot, and Malbec
city or village: Blaye
château: Segonzac

Situated on the right bank of the Gironde River, near the town of Blaye, the 75 acres of Château Segonzac produce fragrantly rich, soft wines that are most appealing. Estate-bottled.

Clear light-ruby color and a fragrant bouquet. The wine tastes soft and rich and is well-balanced. **price range:** B

ENTRE-DEUX-MERS

producer: Prats Frères
classification: White table wine
grape variety: Sauvignon Blanc and Semillon

Fresh, delicate bouquet and a light, fruity flavor; the wine is quite dry. **price range:** B

producer: Quien & Co.
classification: White table wine
grape variety: Semillon, Sauvignon Blanc, and Muscadelle

A light, crisp dry wine; though it accompanies seafood well, it may also be served as an aperitif.

Very dry; should be served well chilled. **price range:** A

producer: M. Reigner
classification: Château-bottled red table wine

grape variety: Merlot, Cabernet, and Malbec
city or village: Pompignac
château: Malard

Clean dark red color and a neat, vinous bouquet. The wine is full and well-balanced, with that good strong Bordeaux taste. **price range:** A

producer: C. Garras
classification: Château-bottled red table wine
grape variety: Cabernet Franc, Merlot, and Cabernet Sauvignon
city or village: Frontenac
château: La Croix du Moulin

The part of the Entre-Deux-Mers that lies near the mouth of the Gironde contains the finest vineyards, which overlook the river banks. They are planted on gravelly ridges. The rest of the soil does not produce wine of any significance.

Well-balanced, elegant, with a delicate bouquet and fruity flavor. **price range:** A

producer: Société Civile du Château Guibon
classification: Château-bottled white table wine
grape variety: Sauvignon Blanc and Semillon
city or village: Daignac

Bright white color; light bouquet; and dry, fruity flavor. **price range:** A

"When they [wines] were good they pleased my sense, cheered my spirits, improved my moral and intellectual powers, besides enabling me to confer the same benefits on other people."
—George Saintsbury

OTHER BORDEAUX WINES

producer: Baron Philippe de Rothschild S.A.

classification: White table wine

grape variety: Sauvignon Blanc and Semillon

A blended Bordeaux regional wine, Mouton Cadet is produced by Baron Philippe de Rothschild, owner of Châteaux Mouton-Rothschild, Mouton-Baron-Philippe, and Clerc-Milon. Mouton Cadet is produced in large quantities and is sold in 108 different countries; it is the only branded Bordeaux wine sold in all 50 states in the United States. The dry white wine, Mouton Cadet Blanc Sec, is a fine counterpart to the red.

Brilliant light straw color and a fruity, refreshing aroma. The wine is light, quite dry and crisp, with a good finish. Branded wines displaying this high quality offer good value at reasonable prices and are a fine introduction to Bordeaux. The wine should be served chilled after two hours in the refrigerator. **price range:** B

producer: Baron Philippe de Rothschild S.A.

classification: Red table wine

grape variety: Cabernet Sauvignon, Cabernet Franc, and Merlot

A blended Bordeaux regional wine, Mouton Cadet is produced by Baron Philippe de Rothschild, owner of Châteaux Mouton-Rothschild. Mouton-Baron-Philippe, and Clerc-Milon. Mouton Cadet is produced in large quantities and is sold in 108 different countries; it is the only branded Bordeaux wine sold in all 50 states in the United States.

Clean, lively medium-red color and an elegant bouquet showing the classic aroma of Bordeaux. The wine is dry, smooth, and full-bodied; branded wines displaying this high quality offer good value at reasonable prices and are a fine introduction to Bordeaux. The wine should be served at room temperature—68 degrees F. **price range:** B

producer: Baron Philippe de Rothschild S.A.

classification: Rosé table wine

grape variety: Cabernet Sauvignon, Cabernet Franc, and Merlot

A blended Bordeaux regional wine, Mouton Cadet Rosé is produced by Baron Philippe de Rothschild, owner of Châteaux Mouton-Rothschild, Mouton-Baron-Philippe, and Clerc-Milon. Cadet Rosé is made in the classic French tradition of the first light squeezing of red grapes, and has just the right amount of dryness to make it ideal with all kinds of food.

Clean and lively rosé color with orange undertones; the bouquet is shy and fruity. On the palate the wine is light, crisp and refreshing; it should be chilled for two to three hours in the refrigerator prior to serving. **price range:** B

producer: Quien & Co.

classification: Red table wine

grape variety: Cabernet Sauvignon

A pleasant Bordeaux regional that can be drunk young.

Delicate bouquet. **price range:** A

producer: Quien & Co.

classification: White table wine

grape variety: Sauvignon Blanc

A pleasant regional wine with a typical Sauvigon flavor.

Light yellow color and a very dry flavor: to be drunk well chilled. **price range:** A

producer: Pierre Cartier & Fils

classification: Red table wine

grape variety: Cabernet and Merlot

Bright red color and a well-developed bouquet. The wine is dry. **price range:** A

producer: Pierre Cartier & Fils

classification: White table wine

grape variety: Semillon and Sauvignon Blanc

Clear color and a well-developed bouquet. The wine is dry. **price range:** A

producer: Pierre Cartier & Fils

classification: Red table wine

grape variety: Cabernet and Merlot

Bright red color and a well-developed bouquet. The wine is dry. **price range:** A

producer: Compagnie Girondine des Vins Mousseux

classification: White sparkling wine

grape variety: Blend

A *vin mousseux* (sparkling wine) bottled in Bordeaux by the makers of the largest-selling imported sparkling wine in the United Kingdom.

Pale straw-yellow color, with good sparkle and a light, fruity bouquet. The wine is crisp and dry, with balanced fruit. **price range:** B

producer: Société Civile du Château Canteloup

classification: Château-bottled red table wine

grape variety: Cabernet Sauvignon and Cabernet Franc

château: Canteloup

Light red color and a delicate bouquet. It is a typical, sound Claret. **price range:** B

producer: Findlater Mackie Todd

classification: Red table wine

grape variety: Cabernet, Merlot, and Malbec

An excellent nonvintage Bordeaux rouge, "Saint Mermion" is ready to drink when shipped. It is bottled by Findlater Mackie Todd in London; alcoholic strength: 11½% by volume.

Clear, bright ruby-red color and a vinous, well-balanced bouquet. The wine is clean, dry, and mature. **price range:** A

producer: Charles deRoy Père et Fils

classification: Red table wine

grape variety: Cabernet and Merlot

A red Bordeaux bottled in England.

Good red color and a clean, pleasant bouquet. The wine is fruity and dry; an excellent luncheon wine. **price range:** A

producer: Christian & Michel Querre
classification: Red table wine
grape variety: Cabernet Sauvignon and others
  Michel Querre is the owner of Châteaux Mazeyres in Pomerol and Patris in St.-Émilion. The overage from these two excellent vineyards are blended into his Bordeaux Supérieur.
  Light red color and an attractive bouquet. The wine is fruity and delicate.
price range: B

producer: Dourthe Frères
classification: White table wine
grape variety: Semillon and Sauvignon Blanc
  Delicate bouquet; the wine is dry, smooth, fruity, and delicate.
price range: B

producer: Maison Sichel
classification: Red table wine
grape variety: Cabernet Sauvignon
  A good everyday wine.
  Red-purple color and a characteristic varietal bouquet. The wine is full-bodied and has a long-lasting flavor.
price range: B

producer: G. Rozier
classification: Château-bottled red table wine
grape variety: Cabernet Sauvignon and Merlot
city or village: St.-Gervais
château: des Arras
  One of the first growths of St.-Gervais, Château des Arras was established in 1560. Estate-bottled, its wines are produced by traditional methods and have won a number of gold and silver medals.
  Clear light red color and a dry, delicate bouquet. The wine is fruity yet dry, with great finesse.   **price range:** C

producer: Daniel Querre
classification: Red table wine
grape variety: Cabernet, Merlot, and Malbec
  A good example of a red Bordeaux.
  Medium ruby-red color and a "peppery" bouquet. The wine is medium-bodied, with dominant tannin and acidity.
price range: B

producer: Prats Frères
classification: White table wine
grape variety: Sauvignon Blanc and Semillon
  A fresh, dry, and pleasant white wine that is modestly priced.   **price range:** B

producer: Louis Dubroca
classification: Red table wine
grape variety: Cabernet Sauvignon, Cabernet Franc, and Merlot
  "Saint Anac" is a generic wine from Bordeaux sold under the maiden name of the wife of Louis Dubroca, who founded the company in 1830. The wine was introduced officially on the U.S. market by Crosse & Blackwell Vintage Cellars in the fall of 1976 and was vinified under the supervision of Emile Peynaud, dean of the Bordeaux Oenological Institute.
  Dark red color and a fruity bouquet. The wine is soft, fruity, and well-balanced; it is still quite young upon release and can age further.   **price range:** A

producer: Société Civile du Château Guibon
classification: Château-bottled white table wine
grape variety: Sauvignon Blanc and Semillon
city or village: Daignac
  Clear color and a light bouquet. The wine is quite dry.   **price range:** A

producer: A. Simon
classification: Red table wine
grape variety: Cabernet Sauvignon, Cabernet Franc, and Merlot
  "Claret" originally meant a mixture of red and white wines, creating a rosé. Later, the word came to mean a light red wine typical of the Bordeaux region.
  Medium red color and a fruity, perfumed bouquet. The wine is full, soft, and interesting and finishes dry—a traditionally made Bordeaux of high quality.   **price range:** A

producer: Vicomte Louis de Pitray
classification: Château-bottled red table wine
grape variety: Cabernet, Merlot, and Malbec
district: Côtes de Castillon
city or village: Gardegan
château: Pitray
  At a recent tasting, Château Pitray 1962 was judged to be superior, both in terms of price and quality.
  Pronounced bouquet; rich, full-bodied, with beautiful finesse. The wine resembles a St.-Émilion.   **price range:** B

producer: Louis Dubroca
classification: White table wine
grape variety: Semillon and Sauvignon Blanc
district: Montravel
city or village: St.-Loubes
  Light gold color with green hues; a grapey bouquet. The wine is lively, dry, and slightly puckery owing to ample fruit acidity; it is an excellent aperitif and also goes well with seafood and fowl.
price range: A

producer: Margnat Frères
classification: Château-bottled red table wine
grape variety: Cabernet, Merlot, and Malbec
city or village: Tresses
château: Sénailhac
  Clear light red color and a tangy bouquet typical of Bordeaux. The wine is quite elegant.   **price range:** B

producer: M. Chatonnet
classification: Red table wine
grape variety: Cabernet Sauvignon, Cabernet Franc, and Merlot
district: Côtes de Castillon
city or village: St.-Magne-de-Castillon
A good light Claret, early to mature. Medium red color and a perfumed, fruity bouquet. The wine is smooth and well-balanced. **price range:** A

producer: Robert Giraud
classification: Red table wine
grape variety: Merlot, Cabernet Sauvignon, and Malbec
district: Cubzadais
city or village: St.-André-de-Cubzac
Very good value at the current price, especially the 1973 and 1974 vintages.
Dark ruby-red color and a full nose typical of a good Bordeaux. The wine is fruity, full-bodied, and smooth, with good acidity for aging. **price range:** A

producer: G. Martin
classification: Château-bottled red table wine
grape variety: Merlot and Bouchet
district: Lalande-de-Pomerol
A lesser-known château giving sound, attractive and early-maturing wines.
Rich red color and a warm bouquet of fruit and perfume. The wine is smooth and solid, flavorful, and has depth; it is good value. **price range:** A

producer: Mme. Veuve Peuchant
classification: Château-bottled red table wine
grape variety: Cabernet Sauvignon and Merlot
district: Côtes-Canon-Fronsac
city or village: Fronsac
Château: La Duchesse
Only twelve hundred cases are produced each year.
Deep red color and an assertive, rich bouquet. The wine is rich, aromatic, and full-bodied; as it is full of tannin, it rewards aging. **price range:** B

producer: Henri Tytell & Fils
classification: White table wine
region: Bordeaux
This dry white wine is good with seafood, and an excellent value. It has a light bouquet and straw color. **price range:** A

*"If all be true that I do think,
There are five good reasons
we should drink:
Good wine—a friend—or
being dry—
Or lest we should be by and
by—
Or any other reason why."*
—Henry Aldrich,
"Five Reasons for Drinking"

FRANCE, BURGUNDY

CHABLIS

producer: A. Bichot & Cie
classification: White table wine
grape variety: Pinot Chardonnay
Light cold color and a clean, delicate bouquet. The wine is dry, slightly acidic, and well-balanced; it is excellent with hors d'oeuvres, seafood, and white meat—serve chilled. **price range:** B

producer: Bouchard Aîné et Fils
classification: White table wine
grape variety: Chardonnay
city or village: Chablis
"Petit Chablis" is a wine to drink young, while it is still fresh.
Soft, golden color with greenish hues and a clean, fresh bouquet. The wine is dry, yet soft, and has a flinty tang; it is ideal with hors d'oeuvres (including shellfish), poultry, and particularly oysters, long considered its perfect accompaniment. **price range:** B

producer: Caves Renier
classification: White table wine
grape variety: Chardonnay
city or village: Chablis
Pale color and an astringent flavor. **price range:** B

producer: Chanson Père et Fils
classification: White table wine
grape variety: Chardonnay
city or village: Chablis
The palest and driest of all white Burgundies.

Pale color and a crisp, delicate bouquet. The wine has the characteristic flinty flavor of Chablis. **price range:** C

producer: R. d'Herville
classification: White table wine
grape variety: Chardonnay
city or village: Chablis
Light pale yellow color and a fresh, clean bouquet with some fruit. The wine is a typical Chablis—clean, astringent, but well-made. **price range:** B

producer: Joseph Drouhin
classification: White table wine
grape variety: Chardonnay
city or village: Chablis
A wine that shows what fine Chablis is all about, rated *premier cru* (first growth).
Pale, straw-shaded color with greenish tints and a clean, dry bouquet. The wine is dry, austere, almost "steely," but is fruity. **price range:** C

producer: C. Jouvet S. A.
classification: White table wine
grape variety: Chardonnay
city or village: Chablis
Chablis comes from a strictly delimited area comprising twenty communes that extend over an area rich in chalk.
Pale straw-yellow color and a delicate bouquet. The wine is dry, with a characteristic flinty flavor of Chablis. **price range:** C

producer: Leonard Kreusch Inc.
classification: White table wine
grape variety: Chardonnay
city or village: Chablis
Rated *grand cru* (great growth); estate-bottled.
Green-gold color. **price range:** C

producer: Alexis Lichine & Co.
classification: White table wine
grape variety: Chardonnay
city or village: Chablis
  Pale straw color and a delicate and fruity bouquet. The wine is crisp, dry, and fruity; very refreshing.   **price range:** B

producer: Albert Long-Depaquit
classification: White table wine
grape variety: Chardonnay
city or village: Chablis
  Rated *premier cru* (first growth).
  Flinty bouquet; the wine is crisp and dry.
price range: B

producer: Maison Sichel
classification: White table wine
grape variety: Pinot Chardonnay
city or village: Chablis
  Rated *premier cru* (first growth), this wine should be consumed young.
  Brilliant straw color and a deep, full bouquet. The wine is crisp, dry, and elegant.   **price range:** C

producer: B. B. Mason & Co., Ltd.
classification: White table wine
grape variety: Pinot Chardonnay
city or village: Chablis
  Chablis is a small region in northern Burgundy that produces one of the most popular dry white wines. "Petit Chablis" is

produced from the outermost vineyards in the district.
  Bright pale green color and a light, elegant bouquet. The wine is very dry and crisp.   **price range:** A

producer: Piat Père et Fils
classification: White table wine
grape variety: Pinot Chardonnay
city or village: Chablis
  Rated *premier cru* (first growth).
  Bright clear color and a pronounced bouquet. The wine is dry, with a flinty flavor typical of Chablis.   **price range:** B

producer: Albert Pic & Fils
classification: White table wine
grape variety: Chardonnay
city or village: Chablis
Vineyard: Blanchot
  The finest Chablis vineyards are classified *grand cru* (great growth) and are produced from only seven vineyards. "Blanchots" is a *grand cru;* this wine is estate-bottled, and it is quite rare. Albert Pic is the only exporter of Chablis to the United States who owns a part of all the *grand cru* vineyards.
  Brilliant color with a hint of green; a clean, fresh, and full bouquet. The wine is dry, with a flinty flavor; it is everything the finest authentic Chablis should be, being austerely dry, crisp, and with an unmistakable flinty flavor.   **price range:** C

producer: Albert Pic & Fils
classification: White table wine
grape variety: Chardonnay
city or village: Chablis
  Chablis is possibly the most renowned white wine in the world. There are many such wines on the market, which vary greatly in quality; therefore, the careful selection of a reputable shipper is of prime importance. Pic Chablis is a perfect example of this type of wine.
  Brilliant white color with tints of green and a clean, fresh bouquet. The wine tastes crisply dry, well-balanced, and has a pleasing touch of acidity.   **price range:** B

producer: Albert Pic & Fils
classification: White table wine
grape variety: Chardonnay
city or village: Chablis
vineyard: Bougros
  The Bougros vineyard is one of seven officially classified as *grand cru* (great growth) in Chablis, which usually produce the finest wines; since less than 250 acres are in production at any given time, the wines are quite rare. Albert Pic is the only exporter of Chablis to the United States who owns a portion of all seven *grand cru* vineyards.
  Brilliant clear color with a hint of green and a clean, fresh and full bouquet. The wine is dry and crisp, with a characteristic flinty flavor; it is everything an authentic Chablis should be: austerely dry, crisp, with a lovely and unmistakable flavor.
price range: C

producer: Albert Pic & Fils
classification: White table wine
grape variety: Chardonnay
city or village: Chablis
vineyard: Les Preuses
  Les Preuses is one of the seven finest vineyards in Chablis rated *grand cru* (great growth), which normally produce the finest wines.
  Brilliant clear color with a hint of green and a clean, fresh, and full bouquet. The wine is dry and crisp, with a lovely, unmistakable flinty flavor typical of an authentic *grand cru* Chablis; it is quite dry.
price range: C

producer: Albert Pic & Fils
classification: White table wine
grape variety: Chardonnay
city or village: Chablis
vineyard: Vaudésir
  Vaudésir is one of seven vineyards in Chablis officially rated *grand cru* (great growth), which normally produce the best wine.
  Brilliant clear color with a hint of green and a clean, fresh, and full flavor. The wine is quite dry and crisp, with the lovely and unmistakable flinty flavor of a fine, authentic Chablis.   **price range:** C

producer: Albert Pic & Fils
classification: White table wine
grape variety: Chardonnay
city or village: Chablis
vineyard: Grenouilles
  Grenouilles is one of seven vineyards in Chablis officially rated *grand cru* (great growth), which normally give the best wines.
  Brilliant clear color with hints of green and a clean, fresh, and full bouquet. The wine is dry and crisp, with the unmistakable flinty flavor of an authentic Chablis.
price range: C

producer: Albert Pic & Fils
classification: White table wine
grape variety: Chardonnay
city or village: Chablis
vineyard: Valmur
  Valmur is one of seven vineyards in Chablis officially rated *grand cru* (great growth), which normally produce the best wines.
  Brilliant clear color with a hint of green and a clean, fresh, and full bouquet. The wine is dry but not austerely so, with the unmistakable flinty flavor characteristic of an authentic Chablis.   **price range:** C

producer: Albert Pic & Fils
classification: White table wine
grape variety: Chardonnay
city or village: Chablis
vineyard: Les Clos
  Les Clos is one of seven vineyards in Chablis officially rated *grand cru* (great growth), which normally produce superior wines.
  Brilliant clear color with a hint of green and a clean, crisp, and full bouquet. The wine combines dryness and crispness with the characteristic flinty flavor of an authentic Chablis; its quality is unmistakable.
price range: C

producer: Poulet Père et Fils
classification: White table wine
grape variety: Chardonnay
city or village: Chablis
vineyard: Les Preuses

Only seven small Chablis vineyards are entitled to the highest-ranking appellation *grand cru* (great growth) and all produce wines of the highest class. Cistercian monks at the Abbey of Pontigny contributed greatly to the reputation of Chablis over three centuries. Poulet Père et Fils, *négociants-éleveurs* at Beaune, were established in 1767.

Fine, fruity bouquet; the wine is dry, light, and sinewy. A very fine wine and a great selection. **price range:** A

producer: Quien & Co.
classification: White table wine
grape variety: Chardonnay
city or village: Chablis

Chablis has been imitated in many countries, but its excellence has never been equaled. It is produced in the most northern part of Burgundy around the little village of Chablis.

Light yellow, almost greenish color, and a very fine, subtle bouquet.
price range: C

producer: A. Regnard & Fils
classification: White table wine
grape variety: Chardonnay
city or village: Chablis

The Montée de Tonnerre vineyard, rated *premier cru* (first growth), is a higher grade than Chablis. There are about two dozen classified growths, and Montee de Tonnerre is one of the exceptionally fine ones. The wine is estate-bottled.

Brilliant clear color with a hint of green and a clean and fresh bouquet. The wine is dry and crisp, with a clean flinty flavor. It is well-balanced and full-bodied.
price range: C

producer: A. Regnard & Fils
classification: White table wine
grape variety: Chardonnay
vineyard: Mont de Milieu

Officially rated *premier cru* (first growth), Mont de Milieu is one of about two dozen such vineyards in Chablis, which produce wines of a higher grade than ordinary Chablis. The wines from Mont de Milieu are especially fine.

Brilliant clear color with a hint of green and a clean, crisp bouquet. The wine is clean and crisp, with the flinty flavor of a good Chablis; it is quite well-balanced.
price range: C

producer: A. Regnard & Fils
classification: White table wine
grape variety: Chardonnay
city or village: Chablis
vineyard: Fourchaume

Officially rated *premier cru* (first growth), Fourchaume is one of about two dozen such vineyards in the commune of Chablis and perhaps the best-known of the *premiers crus*. These wines are usually of a much higher grade than ordinary Chablis.

Brilliant clear color with a hint of green and a clean, crisp bouquet. The wine is dry and crisp, with a flinty flavor characteristic of Chablis; it is full-bodied and quite well-balanced.
price range: C

producer: Thomas-Bassot
classification: White table wine
grape variety: Pinot Chardonnay
city or village: Chablis

The Maison Thomas-Bassot is' held in high esteem, both in the United States and abroad. Their high standards are famous and have been chronicled in books written by such notables as Harry Waugh and Peter Sichel. This regional Chablis is a fine example of a *négociant*'s (shipper's) wine.

Straw color and a clean, typical bouquet. The wine has great flavor and an excellent finish, showing the expertise of a shipper's selections.
price range: B

producer: Testut Frères
classification: White table wine
grape variety: Chardonnay
city or village: Chablis

Basic Chablis are honest wines that show the region's true characteristics; their nobler brethren *(premiers crus* and *grands crus)* are fuller and more complex.

Brilliant color with slight green tinges and a fine, delicate bouquet. The wine is dry, crisp, and refreshing—the ideal wine for shellfish. **price range:** B

producer: Testut Frères
classification: White table wine
grape variety: Chardonnay
city or village: Chablis

A *grand cru* (great growth) Chablis, the highest classification for this region. *Grands crus* Chablis tend to be long-lived; the 1967 is at its peak after a decade.

Brilliant color with greenish tinges and a pronounced yet delicate bouquet. The wine is full-flavored, superb, dry, and has a flinty flavor. It becomes rounded with age and is ideal with fish, or on its own, shared with a friend. **price range:** D

producer: Testut Frères
classification: White table wine
grape variety: Chardonnay
city or village: Chablis

Rated *premier cru* (first growth), among the most select wines of the Chablis region.

Brilliant color with green tinges and a fine, delicate bouquet. The wine is round and full, dry with a flinty flavor. It is an ideal wine with shellfish and fish.
price range: C

producer: Guy Robin
classification: White table wine

grape variety: Chardonnay
city or village: Chablis
Estate-bottled.

Pale green-gold color and an intense, fruity bouquet. The wine is dry, firm and stylish—a fine Chablis. **price range:** C

producer: A. Simon
classification: White table wine
grape variety: Chardonnay
city or village: Chablis

A good example of this much sought-after appellation.

Pale yellow color and a bouquet of light fruit. The wine is crisp, with the light flavor of Chardonnay, and has good acidity.
price range: B

CÔTE DE NUITS

producer: Jean Bonnardot
classification: Red table wine
grape variety: Pinot Noir
city or village: Villers-La-Faye

In 1973 the Hautes-Côtes about Nuits-St.-Georges enjoyed a fortnight's more sunshine than did the Côte d'Or, and produced some excellent wines.

Medium red color and an elegant "nose" typical of a good Burgundy. The wine is firm and fruity; it will soften and round out with bottle age. **price range:** B

producer: Pierre Bourée Fils
classification: Red table wine
grape variety: Pinot Noir
city or village: Gevrey-Chambertin

An excellent red Burgundy, made in small quantities by growers in the area. It is much sought after by wine lovers.

Lovely smooth bouquet typical of Pinot; the wine is beautifully balanced, with a long flavor. **price range:** C

producer: Claude Chonion
classification: Red table wine
grape variety: Pinot Noir
city or village: Chambolle-Musigny

An excellent wine from one of the most distinguished communes in the Côte de Nuits.

Very delicate bouquet; the wine's great vinosity lends power and spice to meat with white sauces, camembert cheese, and all delicately flavored dishes.
price range: E

producer: Claude Chonion
classification: Red table wine
grape variety: Pinot Noir
city or village: Gevrey-Chambertin

The 1971 vintage could still improve before reaching its peak.

Deep, clear ruby color and a fine, well-developed bouquet. The wine is strong-flavored, even, and round, combining force with finesse; it is superb when drunk with a first-class Roquefort.
price range: D

producer: Claude Chonion
classification: Red table wine
grape variety: Pinot Noir
city or village: Nuits-St.-Georges

The wines of Nuits-St.-Georges are less firm than the Gevrey-Chambertins, but have more body than those from Chambolle-Musigny. They mature early and hold their appeal for a considerable length of time.

Slightly amber, bright color, and a composite bouquet. The wine is round, full of vigor and force, and is very harmonious.
price range: D

producer: Claude Chonion
classification: Red table wine
grape variety: Pinot Noir
city or village: Vosne-Romanée

The wines from Vosne-Romanée (which

contains no less than seven *grands crus,* or great growths) are among the most prestigious in Burgundy and are among the world's finest.

Deep, clear color and a penetrating and subtle bouquet. The wine is light and elegant, with exceptional finesse; it would go well with venison, truffles or cheeses (except chèvre).
price range: D

producer: Comte Georges de Vogüé
classification: Red table wine
grape variety: Pinot Noir
city or village: Chambolle-Musigny
vineyard: Les Amoureuses

Rated *premier cru* (first growth), Les Amoureuses is one of the top Chambolle-Musigny vineyards and is bested only by Les Musigny and Bonnes-Mares. It always produces an especially delicate and fine red Burgundy, and, since the name means "women in love" in French, is aptly named.

Deep red color with a beautiful hue, and a full-scented bouquet reminiscent of violets. On the palate the wine is soft and gracious—wholly harmonious.
price range: E

producer: Comte Georges de Vogüé
classification: Red table wine
grape variety: Pinot Noir
city or village: Chambolle-Musigny
vineyard: Bonnes-Mares

Rated *grand cru* (great growth), Bonnes-Mares is the second-greatest vineyard in Chambolle-Musigny, after Musigny. It is produced by one of the most respected growers in Chambolle, the Comte Georges de Vogüé.

Deep, clear red color and a fine deeply scented bouquet. The wine is soft, generous, and silky-textured; a great Burgundy from the "master."
price range: E

producer: Comte Georges de Vogüé
classification: White table wine
grape variety: Chardonnay
city or village: Chambolle-Musigny
vineyard: Les Musigny

The rare white Musigny (Musigny Blanc) is produced from a small parcel of white vines in the great Musigny vineyard, and is likewise rated *grand cru* (great growth). It is one of the rarest Burgundies and is one of the world's scarcest and most sought-after wines.

Polished yellow-gold color, with shimmering green tints; a huge "nose" packed with complex subtleties. On the palate the wine is big, full, and dry; a real mouthful, with a faint "fat" quality.
price range: E

producer: Comte Georges de Vogüé
classification: Red table wine
grape variety: Pinot Noir
city or village: Chambolle-Musigny
vineyard: Les Musigny

Rated *grand cru* (great growth), Les Musigny is perhaps the singularly greatest red Burgundy, renowned for its great finesse and elegance. The reference "Cuvée Vieilles Vignes" indicates that the wine is produced predominantly from old vines, giving especially fine fruit and flavor.

Deep, rich rose and a huge, classic "nose" scented with violets and truffles. The wine is generous and full on the palate, with a "chewy" texture.
price range: E

producer: Domaine Arlaud
classification: Red table wine
grape variety: Pinot Noir
city or village: Gevrey-Chambertin
vineyard: Les Combottes

Domaine Arlaud produces a number of red wines of the very best class, of which his Les Combottes is typical.

A powerful bouquet; the wine is perfumed, powerful, and has a light aftertase of violets.
price range: C

producer: Domaine Arlaud
classification: Red table wine
grape variety: Pinot Noir
city or village: Morey-St.-Denis
vineyard: Clos de la Roche

Rated *grand cru* (great growth), the Clos de la Roche vineyard is one of the finest vineyards in Morey-St.-Denis and in the Côte d'Or. The Domaine Arlaud produces a number of red wines of very good quality, of which this Clos de la Roche is very typical.

A fine bouquet; the wine has robust body and a sensuous, delicate flavor.
price range: C

producer: Domaine Arlaud
classification: Red table wine
grape variety: Pinot Noir
city or village: Chambolle-Musigny

Rated *premier cru* (first growth), this is a typically fine Chambolle-Musigny from several leading vineyards. The Domaine Arlaud produces a number of very good red wines, of which this is representative.

A fine, delicately perfumed bouquet; the wine is rich in vinosity and is full and complex, with a good aroma.
price range: C

producer: Domaine Henri Gouges
classification: White table wine
grape variety: Pinot Blanc
city or village: Nuits-St.-Georges
vineyard: La Perrière

One of the rare white wine vineyards of the Côte de Nuits; estate-bottled. Officially the wine is rated *premier cru* (first growth).

Pale gold color and a fruity, intense bouquet. The wine is full-bodied, with intense varietal character.
price range: D

producer: Domaine Henri Lamarche
classification: Red table wine
grape variety: Pinot Noir
city or village: Vosne-Romanée
vineyard: La Grande Rue

The La Grande Rue vineyard lies directly behind Romanée-Conti, the most famous plot of land in Burgundy. It is officially rated *premier cru* (first growth).

Medium-to-deep red color and an intense, suave bouquet. The wine is soft, elegant, and slow to mature.
price range: E

producer: Joseph Faiveley
classification: Red table wine
grape variety: Pinot Noir
city or village: Premeaux
(Nuits-St.-Georges)
vineyard: Clos de la Maréchale

The Clos de la Maréchale vineyard, rated *premier cru* (first growth), is one of the leading growths of Premeaux but is entitled to the appellation *Nuits-St.-Georges* as the two communes adjoin. It is a wine of consistently high quality, from one of the most important producers of the Côte d'Or.

Deep, clear ruby color and a fine, perfumed bouquet. On the palate the wine is dry, soft, and full. **price range:** E

producer: L'Héritier-Guyot
classification: Red table wine
grape variety: Pinot Noir
city or village: Vougeot
vineyard: Clos de Vougeot

The vineyard of Clos de Vougeot is dominated by the massive château built in the fifteenth century by Cistercian monks. A select parcel of the vineyard is owned by L'Héritier-Guyot, and it produces one of the most distinguished wines of the Côte de Nuits. Estate-bottled.

Brilliant deep ruby color and a bouquet with distinct perfume—flowery and full, with a hint of violets. The wine is soft and velvety, slightly dry, and well-balanced. The finish lingers, which is characteristic of a well-made Clos de Vougeot.
price range: E

producer: Louis Jadot
classification: Red table wine
grape variety: Pinot Noir
city or village: Nuits-St.-Georges
vineyard: Les Boudots

Rated *premier cru* (first growth), the vineyard of Les Boudots produces wines of outstanding quality. This wine has great staying power and is estate-bottled.

Deep red color and a full, rich bouquet. This vigorous wine is a full, rich Burgundy. **price range:** E

producer: Louis Jadot
classification: Red table wine
grape variety: Pinot Noir
city or village: Vosne-Romanée

Within the commune of Vosne-Romanée, some of the most expensive wines in the world are produced.

Deep ruby color and a delicate, lingering bouquet. The wine is sturdy, full-bodied, and has the velvety richness of superior Vosne-Romanées combined with a characteristic delicacy. **price range:** E

producer: Louis Jadot
classification: Red table wine
grape variety: Pinot Noir
city or village: Gevrey-Chambertin
vineyard: Les Combottes

The Les Combottes vineyard, rated *premier cru* (first growth), adjoins the great Chambertin vineyard and likewise produces an outstanding red wine.

Deep red color and an unusually full, fruity bouquet. The wine is full-flavored and quite complex in great vintages.
price range: E

producer: Louis Jadot
classification: Red table wine
grape variety: Pinot Noir
city or village: Chambolle-Musigny/
Morey-St.-Denis
vineyard: Bonnes-Mares

Bonnes-Mares, one of the greatest red wine vineyards in the Côte de Nuits, is classified as a *grand cru* (great growth) and is divided between the adjoining communes of Chambolle (32 acres) and Morey (5 acres). The wines typically combine the delicacy of Chambolles with the more robust qualities of the Moreys; M. Jadot produces this wine only in the best vintages.

Deep red color and a rich, balanced bouquet. The wine is rich and full-bodied, a typically fine red Burgundy.
price range: E

producer: Louis Jadot
classification: Red table wine
grape variety: Pinot Noir
city or village: Chambolle-Musigny

The wines of Chambolle-Musigny typically combine the sturdiness of those produced farther north with the elegance of southern Côte de Nuits red wines.

Deep ruby-red color and a full bouquet. The wine is full-bodied yet delicate, combining strength and delicacy in a uniquely pleasing balance. **price range:** E

producer: Louis Jadot
classification: Red table wine
grape variety: Pinot Noir
city or village: Morey-St.-Denis
vineyard: Clos de la Roche

Officially rated *grand cru* (great growth), the Clos de la Roche vineyard extends over 38 acres in the commune of Morey-St.-Denis and is one of that commune's best. Its rich soil gives the wines great strength and longevity.

Deep garnet-red color and a big, lingering bouquet. The wine has a rich, full flavor characteristic of very great red Burgundies. **price range:** E

producer: C. Jouvet S.A.
classification: Red table wine
grape variety: Pinot Noir
city or village: Gevrey-Chambertin

An excellent red wine from a world-famous wine village.

Fragrant bouquet and a well-balanced, full-bodied flavor. Drink with red meats, game, and cheese. **price range:** E

producer: C. Jouvet S.A.
classification: Red table wine
grape variety: Pinot Noir
city or village: Nuits-St.-Georges

Well-balanced bouquet; an admirable, generous, and sturdy red Burgundy. Delightful with red meats and cheeses; serve at room temperature. **price range:** E

producer: Maison Sichel
classification: Red table wine
grape variety: Pinot Noir
city or village: Nuits-St.-Georges

Brilliant deep red color and a fruity, vinous bouquet. The wine is generous and quite full-bodied. **price range:** E

producer: Maison Sichel
classification: Red table wine
grape variety: Pinot Noir
city or village: Gevrey-Chambertin

One of the best-known red Burgundies. Brilliant ruby color and a deep, rich bouquet. The wine is big and powerful and has a smooth flavor. **price range:** E

producer: Moillard
classification: Red table wine
grape variety: Pinot Noir
city or village: Vosne-Romanée

Vosne-Romanées are typically fine wines with breeding, elegance and exceptional balance. **price range:** C

producer: Moillard
classification: Red table wine
grape variety: Pinot Noir
city or village: Gevrey-Chambertin

Deep, rich color and a fine bouquet. The wine is full-bodied and well-balanced, showing the art of judicious blending—a memorable wine from a great wine region.
price range: C

producer: J. Mommessin
classification: Estate-bottled red table wine
grape variety: Pinot Noir
city or village: Morey-St.-Denis
vineyard: Clos de Tart

The Clos de Tart vineyard, rated *grand cru* (great growth), was founded by a holy order and was originally called "Clos des Dames de Tart," after the sisters who tended it. It is one of the finest red Burgundies; total annual production ranges from 800 to 1,200 cases.

Dark red color and a very full bouquet. The wine is smooth and shows all the qualities for which Burgundies are famous.
price range: E

producer: Poulet Père & Fils
classification: Red table wine
grape variety: Pinot Noir
city or village: Flagey-Échezeaux

The vineyard lies between Clos Vougeot and Vosne Romanée, 79 acres in all with a total production of about 6,000 cases a year.

A top-class wine with subtlety, finesse, elegance, and full body.
price range: E

producer: Poulet Père & Fils
classification: Red table wine

grape variety: Pinot Noir
city or village: Vougeot

One of the smallest and most famous vineyards in France.

The wines of Clos Vougeot are usually rich yet supple and very soft. Their bouquet resembles the aroma of truffles. They have considerable elegance and a unique distinction.
price range: E

producer: Poulet Père & Fils
classification: Red table wine
grape variety: Pinot Noir
city or village: Vosne-Romanée

One of the giants of the wine world. Slightly lighter than its neighbor, Romanée Conti.

Rich, full of vinosity and breed.
price range: E

producer: Poulet Père & Fils
classification: Red table wine
grape variety: Pinot Noir
city or village: Chambolle

Musigny is one of the most ancient growths of Burgundy. Documents prove that it existed in the eleventh century. A grand wine.

Musigny is distinguished by a great delicacy derived from an exceptional finesse and a remarkable bouquet. **price range:** E

producer: Poulet Père & Fils
classification: Red table wine
grape variety: Pinot Noir
city or village: Gevrey

Produced by one of the oldest firms in Burgundy, which was established in 1747. Chambertin is another Burgundy "great."

Chambertin has a lively color and is full-bodied and vigorous. It combines an extraordinary richness with great finesse.
price range: E

producer: Poulet Père & Fils
classification: Red table wine
grape variety: Pinot Noir
city or village: Chambolle

This is the other outstanding vineyard of Chambolle. These wines rival those of Musigny and are very similar in style but with a little less elegance.

Soft, supple, with finesse and distinction. **price range:** E

producer: Quien & Co.
classification: Red table wine
grape variety: Pinot Noir
village: Nuits-St.-Georges

Deep red color and a very elegant, delicate bouquet. The wine is full-bodied and round; it is a great wine that will develop and improve by further bottle aging.
price range: C

producer: A. Simon
classification: Red table wine
grape variety: Pinot Noir
city or village: Côte de Nuits–Villages

Only five villages may sell part of their produce as Côte de Nuits–Villages.

Reddish-brown color and a well-developed bouquet with attractive Pinot perfume. The wine tastes smooth and rich.
price range: B

producer: Henri Rebourseau
classification: Red table wine
grape variety: Pinot Noir

city or village: Gevrey-Chambertin, Vougeot

The Domaines H. Rebourseau are in Chambertin, Hazy Chambertin, Charmé-Chambertin, Clos Vougeot; they were originally owned by General Rebourseau's mother's family and are now in the hands of the father and her son, Pierre.

This very powerful Burgundy is an overproduction of their various estates from Gevrey and Clos Vougeot and is bottled at their estate. **price range:** C

producer: Thomas-Bassot
classification: Red table wine
grape variety: Pinot Noir
village: Gevrey-Chambertin

Maison Thomas-Bassot is concerned less with embellishments on the labels than with making excellent wine. Although domaine-bottled, the wine does not display this classification on the label, which the producer is entitled to. It is produced from one of the finest holdings in Burgundy.

Deep red color and a fine bouquet typical of a Gevrey-Chambertin. The wine is full-flavored. **price range:** D

producer: Thomas-Bassot
classification: Domaine-bottled red table wine
grape variety: Pinot Noir
city or village: Gevrey-Chambertin
vineyard: Griotte-Chambertin

The Griotte-Chambertin vineyard is situated adjacent to the famous Chambertin vineyard and is likewise rated *grand cru* (great growth). The "clos" (section) is a monopole of the Maison Thomas-Bassot, and the wines are an exclusive of this firm. Annual production is approximately 30 *pièces* (barrels), equal to about 750 cases.

Deep red color and a bouquet full of fruity character. The wine is mouth-filling, with long length and finesse. It is truly superb, worthy of the finest cuisine.
price range: E

producer: Thomas-Bassot
classification: Red table wine
grape variety: Pinot Noir

city or village: Gevrey-Chambertin
vineyard: Ruchottes-Chambertin

The Clos des Ruchottes vineyard is located just above the Clos de Bèze vineyard in the commune of Gevrey-Chambertin, and is likewise rated *grand cru* (great growth). The small "clos" within the Ruchottes vineyard is a monopole of Thomas-Bassot, and no one else is entitled to use this name.

Deep red color and a fine bouquet full of Pinot character with obvious breeding. The wine combines flavor and finesse with a long finish; it is impeccably balanced, with all the characteristics that please the connoisseur. **price range:** E

producer: Thomas-Bassot
classification: Red table wine
grape variety: Pinot Noir
city or village: Chambolle-Musigny

This fine wine displays the great care lavished by a leading *négociant* (shipper) who possesses the latest oenological techniques.

Deep red color and a bouquet full of Pinot Noir character combined with the characteristic "nose" of Chambolle-Musigny. The wine fills the mouth and finishes well. **price range:** D

producer: Thomas-Bassot
classification: Red table wine
grape variety: Pinot Noir
village: Gevrey-Chambertin

Domaine-bottled, rated *premier cru* (first growth).

Deep red color and a strong, full bouquet. The wine literally fills the mouth, with an incredible lingering finish. An excellent bottle of wine. **price range:** D

producer: Thomas-Bassot
classification: Red table wine
grape variety: Pinot Noir
city or village: Gevrey-Chambertin
vineyard: Mazy-Chambertin

This domaine-bottled wine is as good as any in Gevrey-Chambertin.

Deep red color; the bouquet is full and rich—typical of its breed. The wine is big and strong, with finesse and a lingering finish. **price range:** D

CÔTE DE BEAUNE

producer: Jean Bachelet
classification: White table wine
grape variety: Chardonnay
city or village: Chassagne-Montrachet

Estate-bottled.

Pale gold color and a fruity bouquet showing great varietal character. The wine is suave, soft, and has a long finish; it is a fine example of a white Burgundy. **price range:** C

producer: Bachelet-Ramonet
classification: White table wine
grape variety: Chardonnay
city or village: Chassagne-Montrachet

Estate-bottled.

Pale gold color and a fruity bouquet showing varietal characteristics. The wine is elegant and graceful, with a long finish—it is a wine of style and grace. **price range:** C

producer: Baudrand & Fils
classification: Red table wine
grape variety: Pinot Noir
city or village: Chassagne-Montrachet

Clear, dark red color, and a full, vinous bouquet. The wine is rich, mellow, well-rounded, and fine. **price range:** C

producer: A. Bichot & Cie.
classification: Red table wine
grape variety: Pinot Noir

city or village: Beaune (Château de Mercey)

Fine red color and a powerful, fragrant bouquet. The wine is fruity and shows great finesse; it goes well with roast meat, furred and feathered game, and cheese.
price range: B

producer: Pierre Bitouzet
classification: Red table wine
grape variety: Pinot Noir
village: Savigny-les-Beaune

Estate-bottled.

Bright medium-dark red color and a fruity bouquet. The wine is round and pleasant, with good varietal character; it is medium-bodied. **price range:** C

producer: Bouchard Père & Fils
classification: Red table wine
grape variety: Pinot Noir
city or village: Gevrey-Chambertin

This Gevrey-Chambertin is dry and sturdy. **price range:** C

producer: Bouchard Père & Fils
classification: Red table wine
grape variety: Pinot Noir
city or village: Pommard

This wine is dry and full-bodied.
price range: E

producer: Chanson Père et Fils
classification: White table wine
grape variety: Chardonnay
village: Meursault

A full-bodied white Burgundy with elegance and finesse. **price range:** C

producer: Chanson Père et Fils
classification: Red table wine
grape variety: Pinot Noir
city or village: Beaune
vineyard: Clos des Marconnets

A round, full-bodied, and elegant red wine from a single vineyard.
price range: D

producer: Claude Chonion
classification: Red table wine
grape variety: Pinot Noir

A declassified wine (12% alcohol) made from vineyards that have exceeded the legal maximum production levels or that do not meet applicable standards to be sold under their own name. It is ready to drink when shipped but often repays extra bottle aging.

Light, clear ruby color and a round, pleasant bouquet. The wine if full-bodied yet preserves lightness and elegance.
price range: B

producer: B & J. M. Delaunay
classification: White table wine
grape variety: Pinot Chardonnay
city or village: Meursault

A generic Meursault by a top producer. This white Meursault is greenish; a brilliant white wine, full-bodied with a dry and mellow finish.
price range: B

producer: Charles DeRoy Père et Fils
classification: Red table wine
grape variety: Pinot Noir

city or village: Gevrey-Chambertin
vineyard: Chambertin–Clos de Bèze

Bottled in Beaune, this wine comes from one of the greatest *grand cru* (great growth) vineyards in Burgundy.

Good, deep color and a full, fruity bouquet. The wine is big and rich, with full body and plenty of character. A classic wine, it should continue to develop over the next few years and is excellent with game, red meat, and cheese. **price range:** E

producer: Domaine Henri Boillot
classification: White table wine
grape variety: Pinot Blanc
city or village: Meursault
vineyard: Les Genevrières

Les Genevrières is one of the best vineyards in Meursault, rated *premier cru* (first growth).

Clear color and a very fruity and fragrant bouquet. The wine is very big, but exquisite, and combines smoothness and finesse. **price range:** D

producer: Domaine Henri Boillot
classification: White table wine
grape variety: Pinot Blanc
city or village: Puligny-Montrachet
vineyard: Les Pucelles

Les Pucelles, rated *premier cru* (first growth), is one of the best vineyards of Puligny-Montrachet, and adjoins the great Montrachet vineyard.

Clean color and a purebred bouquet all its own. The wine is very big but smooth, with great finesse, and is full and fruity. **price range:** D

producer: Domaine Henri Boillot
classification: White table wine
grape variety: Pinot Blanc
city or village: Puligny-Montrachet

This relatively inexpensive wine is made from the surplus production of the Henri Boillot Domaine. Vineyards that exceed the maximum yield allowed by law are re-

quired to be declassified, and often their wines are excellent value.

Clear white color and a fruity bouquet. The wine is agreeable, delicate, and smooth, combining fruit with finesse. **price range:** B

producer: Domaine Henri Boillot
classification: White table wine
grape variety: Pinot Blanc
city or village: Meursault

Rated *premier cru* (first growth).

Clear color and a delicate and fruity bouquet. The wine is very pleasant and mellow, with a fruity fragrance. **price range:** C

producer: Domaine Henri Boillot
classification: Red table wine
grape variety: Pinot Noir
city or village: Volnay
vineyard: Les Chevrets

The Les Chevrets vineyards, also known as Chevret, is one of the leading plots in Volnay and is rated *premier cru* (first growth).

Ruby-red color and an ample bouquet. The wine is supple, silky, and distinguished by its finesse; it is a very well-balanced wine, with plenty of fruit. **price range:** D

producer: Domaine Henri Boillot
classification: Red table wine
grape variety: Pinot Noir
city or village: Beaune
vineyard: Les Épenottes

Rated *premier cru* (first growth), the Épenottes vineyard lies on the border between Beaune and Pommard and shares many characteristics of the Pommard-Épenottes vineyard.

Ruby-red color and a finely perfumed bouquet. The wine is soft, supple, and mellow; it is a big, well-structured wine, a solid thoroughbred. **price range:** D

producer: Domaine Henri Boillot
classification: Red table wine
grape variety: Pinot Noir
city or village: Pommard
vineyard: Les Rugiens

Pommard-Rugiens is one of the two best vineyards in Pommard, rated *premier cru* (first growth).

Ruby-red color and a full, perfumey bouquet. The wine is sturdy, rich, and distinctive, with plenty of fullness. **price range:** D

producer: Domaine des Comtes Lafon
classification: Red table wine
grape variety: Pinot Noir
city or village: Volnay/Meursault
vineyard: Les Santenots

The Santenots vineyard, rated *premier cru* (first growth), is actually located in Meursault. It produces the last great red Burgundy before the vineyards change to white grape varieties in the south. This wine is estate-bottled.

Brilliant light red color and a flowery bouquet. This perfectly balanced, soft, delicate and rich red wine combines fresh flavor with a long-lasting finish. **price range:** E

"Who prates of war or want after taking wine?"

— Horace

producer: Domaine des Comtes Lafon
classification: White table wine
grape variety: Chardonnay
city or village: Meursault
vineyard: Les Genevrières

Meursault is the capital of the slope of great white wines. Les Genevrières is rated *premier cru* (first growth), and this wine is estate-bottled.

Clear color with tints of green and a bouquet that suggests hazelnuts. The wine is round, soft, and dry. **price range:** E

producer: Domaine Joseph Matrot
classification: White table wine
grape variety: Chardonnay
city or village: Meursault

Estate-bottled.

Pale gold color and a slightly "earthy" bouquet typifying the grape variety. The wine is quite full-bodied—a first-class Meursault. **price range:** C

producer: Domaine Étienne Sauzet
classification: White table wine
grape variety: Chardonnay
city or village: Puligny-Montrachet

Estate-bottled.

Pale gold color and a fine bouquet showing the typical varietal style with a faint touch of oak. The wine is big, rich, and powerful **price range:** D

producer: Joseph Drouhin
classification: White table wine
grape variety: Chardonnay
city or village: Aloxe-Corton
vineyard: Corton-Charlemagne

The Corton-Charlemagne vineyard, rated *grand cru* (great growth), is one of the most outstanding white Burgundies.

Yellow-gold color and a full scent with an undertone of cinammon. The wine is dry, full, and expansive, with numerous complex flavors—it is a wine of extraordinary style and quality. **price range:** E

producer: Joseph Drouhin
classification: White table wine
grape variety: Chardonnay

city or village: Beaune
vineyard: Clos des Mouches

The only white wine entitled to the appellation Beaune, the rare white Clos des Mouches is produced from a small 6-hectare plot planted in white Chardonnay vines; because of its scarcity, it is consistently sought after. The vineyard is rated *premier cru* (first growth).

Pale gold color with shimmering highlights and a full, generous, and complex bouquet. The wine is dry, full, and classic.
price range: E

producer: Joseph Drouhin
classification: White table wine
grape variety: Chardonnay
city or village: Puligny-Montrachet
vineyard: Clos du Cailleret

Rated *premier cru* (first growth), the Clos du Cailleret vineyard borders the *grand cru* (great growth) vineyards of Le Montrachet and Chevalier-Montrachet.

Shimmering pale gold color and a very complex and distinguished bouquet. On the palate the wine is dry, complex, and full-flavored; an exceptionally fine wine that rivals the best white Burgundies.
price range: E

producer: Joseph Drouhin
classification: White table wine
grape variety: Chardonnay
city or village: Meursault

A classical Meursault rated *premier cru* (first growth).

Green-tinted, shimmering gold color and a deep-scented, nutty bouquet. The wine is dry, full, and powerful.
price range: D

producer: Joseph Drouhin
classification: Red table wine
grape variety: Pinot Noir
city or village: Volnay–Clos des Chênes

Rated *premier cru* (first growth), this is an excellent example of a good Volnay.

Light but positive clear color and a highly fragrant, perfumed bouquet. The wine is delicate and flavorful and has elegance and finesse.
price range: E

producer: Joseph Drouhin
classification: Red table wine
grape variety: Pinot Noir
city or village: Beaune
vineyard: Clos des Mouches

The Clos des Mouches vineyard, rated *premier cru* (first growth), is owned by a number of growers, but the principal owner is Joseph Drouhin. He holds 12 hectares of a parcel that borders the commune of Pomamrd to the South, planted equally in Pinot Noir and Chardonnay.

Clear, well-colored appearance; and a bouquet with distinct, generous Pinot fragrance. On the palate the wine is medium full, balanced, and perfumed—a wine for the true connoisseur of fine Burgundy.
price range: E

producer: Joseph Faiveley
classification: Red table wine
grape variety: Pinot Noir
city or village: Aloxe-Corton
vineyard: Le Corton (Clos des Cortons)

The Clos des Cortons vineyard, rated *grand cru* (great growth), has a single proprietor, Joseph Faiveley. Although it is an exceptional wine from the Côte de Beaune, it more closely resembles one from the Côte de Nuits to the north.

Deep, full red color and a rich bouquet. On the palate the wine is silky and powerful; a very exciting wine. **price range:** E

producer: Prince Florent de Merode
classification: Red table wine
grape variety: Pinot Noir
city or village: Pommard
vineyard: Clos de la Platière

Estate-bottled, officially rated *premier cru* (first growth).

Deep red color and a fruity bouquet typical of good Pommards. The wine is big, rich, ripe, and full-bodied.
price range: E

producer: Prince Florent de Merode
classification: Red table wine
grape variety: Pinot Noir
city or village: Aloxe-Corton
vineyard: Corton (Clos du Roi)

Estate-bottled, officially rated *grand cru* (great growth), the only red wine vineyard so designated in the Côte de Beaune.

Deep red color and a fruity bouquet reminiscent of cherries. The wine is big, rich, and deep—it is a very great Burgundy.
price range: E

producer: Louis Jadot
classification: White table wine
grape variety: Chardonnay
city or village: Puligny-Montrachet
vineyard: Chevalier-Montrachet "Les Demoiselles"

"Les Demoiselles" is a select portion of the famed Chevalier-Montrachet vineyard, rated *grand cru* (great growth) and surpassed only by the great Le Montrachet. The wine is estate-bottled by Maison Louis Jadot, one of the most respected producers of great Burgundies.

Golden color and an intense, clean bouquet. The wine is delicate and shows great finesse and breeding—it is one of the very greatest white Burgundies.
price range: E

producer: Louis Jadot
classification: White table wine
grape variety: Chardonnay
city or village: Puligny-Montrachet
vineyard: Le Montrachet

Rated *grand cru* (great growth), the vineyard of Le Montrachet is generally considered to be the greatest white Burgundy vineyard in the world.

Golden color and a pronounced, seductive bouquet. The wine is quite dry, with surprising depth. The bouquet is balanced by the richness and delicacy of the taste, and the finish lingers long after the wine is consumed. **price range:** E

producer: Louis Jadot
classification: White table wine
grape variety: Chardonnay
city or village: Savigny-les-Beaune

Usually known for its red wines, Savigny-les-Beaune also produces a small amount of white wines that are rapidly gaining the reputation they deserve.

Light straw color and a fragrant bouquet. The wine is crisp, fresh, and flavorful.
price range: C

producer: Louis Jadot
classification: Red table wine
grape variety: Pinot Noir
city or village: Beaune

Beaune wines are lighter and more delicate than other Burgundies, with a more subtle bouquet. Louis Jadot's regional Beaune is typical of the wines of this area.

A ruby color and delicate, subtle bouquet. The wine is dry, soft, and well-balanced. **price range:** C

producer: Louis Jadot
classification: Red table wine
grape variety: Pinot Noir
city or village: Beaune
vineyard: Clos des Ursules

The Clos des Ursules vineyard has been the property of the Jadot family since 1826. This rich red wine is slow to mature and is longer-lived than many other Beaune wines. Estate-bottled.

A deep rich color and a big bouquet. The wine is sturdy, rich, and full in flavor.
price range: E

producer: Louis Jadot
classification: Red table wine
grape variety: Pinot Noir
city or village: Aloxe-Corton
vineyard: Les Pougets

This fine estate-bottled red wine is a peer of the great red wines of the Côte de Nuits to the north.

Brilliant red color and a rich bouquet. The wine is suave, delicate, and full-bodied, with extraordinary suavity of flavor and matchless bouquet. **price range:** E

producer: Louis Jadot
classification: Red table wine
grape variety: Pinot Noir
city or village: Pommard

Pommard is probably the best-known name in Burgundy, and this wine is always in great demand.

Bright ruby color and a soft, fruity bouquet. The wine is well-balanced and velvety, with good flavor and bouquet. **price range:** E

producer: Louis Jadot
classification: White table wine
grape variety: Chardonnay
city or village: Puligny-Montrachet
vineyard: Chevalier-Montrachet "Les Demoiselles"

Louis Jadot is one of the few owners in the Chevalier-Montrachet who holds a plot called "Les Demoiselles," a carryover from an older vineyard that existed before Chevalier-Montrachet was officially classified as a *grand cru* (great growth) in 1936. M. Jadot holds only a few acres of choice land, making this wine quite rare indeed. Great white Burgundies like these have inspired many a song and poem; this wine is produced only in the best vintages.

Rich golden color and a luscious, fruity bouquet. The wine is full-bodied and fruity, possessing the rare finesse characteristic of great white Burgundies. **price range:** E

producer: Louis Jadot
classification: Red table wine
grape variety: Pinot Noir
city or village: Beaune
vineyard: Bressandes

Bressandes is considered one of the best vineyards in Beaune; rated *premier cru* (first growth), it gives outstanding red wines. This one is estate-bottled from one of the eleven Jadot properties and is produced only in the best vintage years.

Brilliant ruby-red color and a deep, fruity bouquet. The wine is soft, full of fruit, and has a fine depth of flavor; it is an outstanding Beaune. **price range:** E

producer: Louis Jadot
classification: Red table wine
grape variety: Pinot Noir
city or village: Volnay

Volnay wines are known for their freshness and perfectly balanced flavor: an old song says, "You can't be gay without drinking Volnay." Louis Jadot produces this wine only in the best vintage years.

Brilliant light red color and a perfumed, flowery bouquet. The wine is quite soft and delicate, a typical Volnay. **price range:** D

producer: Louis Jadot
classification: White table wine
grape variety: Chardonnay
city or village: Aloxe-Corton
vineyard: Corton-Charlemagne

Louis Jadot is one of the largest proprietors of this great vineyard, officially rated *grand cru* (great growth) and one of the finest in Burgundy. M. Jadot only produces this exceptional white Burgundy in the best vintages.

Pale golden color and a generous bouquet. The wine is rich, full-flavored, and "big," but is dry and combines richness with dryness. **price range:** E

producer: Louis Jadot
classification: Red table wine
grape variety: Pinot Noir
city or village: Beaune
vineyard: Les Theurons

The Les Theurons vineyard, officially rated *premier cru* (first growth), is one of the best in Beaune. Louis Jadot's holding in the vineyard is one of the eleven he owns in and around Beaune; M. Jadot produces this wine only in the best vintages.

Bright ruby-red color and a delicate, fruity bouquet. The wine has a fruity, velvety flavor characteristic of a superior Beaune. **price range:** E

producer: Louis Jadot
classification: Red table wine
grape variety: Pinot Noir
city or village: Beaune
vineyard: Boucherottes

The Boucherottes vineyard is a particular *climat* (land parcel) shared by the adjoining communes of Beaune and Pommard; under the laws of Appellation Contrôlée, wines produced from a specific commune must be labeled according to their region of production. Both sections are officially rated *premier cru* (first growth); Beaune Boucherottes is considered superior to many red Pommards (which are often overrated), and this wine is produced only in the best vintages.

Brilliant garnet-red color and a soft, fruity bouquet. The wine is soft, with a well-rounded, fruity flavor reflecting the grapes from which it is made. **price range:** E

producer: G. Kriter & Co.
classification: White sparkling wine
grape variety: Chardonnay, Pinot Blanc, and Aligote
city or village: Beaune

Kriter "Blanc de Blancs" is a blend of various white Burgundy wines. The wines are naturally fermented in the bottle and are bottled only in vintage years.

Light straw color and delicate bouquet. The wine is crisp, dry, and fairly full-bodied; it has delicate effervescence, and is lower in acidity than many other sparkling wines. **price range:** C

producer: Marquis de Laguiche
classification: White table wine
grape variety: Chardonnay
city or village: Chassagne-Montrachet

This wine is produced by one of the most important proprietors of the *grand cru* (great growth) Le Montrachet vineyard, and actually comes entirely from the *premier cru* (first growth) vineyard of Morgeot, although this fact is not mentioned on the label.

Polished pale gold color and a clear, full fragrance of classic white Burgundy. The wine is full, dry, and well-balanced, yet slightly austere; a beautiful white Burgundy. **price range:** D

producer: Marquis de Laguiche
classification: White table wine
grape variety: Chardonnay
city or village: Puligny- and Chassagne-Montrachet
vineyard: Le Montrachet

Considered to be the greatest dry white wine in the world, Le Montrachet is rated *grand cru* (great growth) and is produced by several different proprietors. The Marquis de Laguiche is the largest owner within the Montrachet vineyard, and the sale of his wine is entrusted to the Domaine Joseph Drouhin.

Polished bright gold color and a complex bouquet combining many subtle nuances. On the palate the wine shows outstanding balance with many different flavors; it is a classic Montrachet, a wine that inspired the saying by Alexandre Dumas: "It should be drunk kneeling, with one's head bared." **price range:** E

producer: Louis Latour
classification: Red table wine
grape variety: Pinot Noir
city or village: Aloxe-Corton
vineyard: Corton

Officially rated *grand cru* (great growth), this wine is sold under Louis Latour's proprietary label, Château Corton-Grancey.
price range: E

producer: Pierre Latour
classification: Red table wine
grape variety: Pinot Noir
city or village: Meursault
Wonderfully soft and with great finesse. The older wines (1950, '52, '53, 55) are proof of what age does for fine wines.
price range: E

producer: Lejay Lagoute
classification: Aperitif wine
grape variety: Pinot Chardonnay blended with some Cassis liqueur
city or village: Dijon
The late Canon Felix Kir gave the exclusive right to the use of his name to Maison Lejay Lagoute in 1951, when Kir was dean of representatives in the French National Assembly. This remarkable man was a member of the Resistance during World War II and later became mayor of Dijon. His favorite drink was a light white Burgundy flavored with a little Cassis, and as he was largely responsible for its tremendous popularity, it has now assumed his name: "Original Canon Kir." It is produced only by the firm of Lejay Lagoute.
Pink color, fruity bouquet, and sweet flavor.
price range: A

producer: Maison Jacquin en France
classification: White table wine
grape variety: Pinot Chardonnay
"Vin des Beaumonts," is made from nonappellation selections of wines from the Côte de Beaune and Mâcon districts of France.
Pale golden color and a pleasant fruity bouquet. The wine is dry and fresh.
price range: A

producer: Maison Sichel
classification: Red table wine
grape variety: Pinot Noir
city or village: Pommard
One of the best-known red Burgundies. Deep red color and a fruity, flowery bouquet. The wine is intense, with a well-rounded fruity flavor, and is quite full-bodied.
price range: E

producer: Maison Sichel
classification: White table wine
grape variety: Chardonnay
city or village: Meursault
Long-lived.
Brilliant golden color and a full, rich bouquet. The wine is round and elegant, stylish yet soft.
price range: D

producer: Patriarche Père et Fils
classification: White table wine
grape variety: Pinot Blanc
city or village: Beaune
Pale golden color and a refined bouquet. The wine is clean, with a crisp flavor.
price range: B

producer: Patriarche Père et Fils
classification: Red table wine
grape variety: Pinot Noir
city or village: Beaune
Ruby color and a bouquet with a generous hint of raspberries. The wine is soft and generous.
price range: B

producer: Poulet Père & Fils
classification: White table wine
grape variety: Pinot Chardonnay
city or village: Montrachet
The vineyards are situated on the lower slopes of the hillside.
This wine is dry, elegant, and vigorous with all of the qualities of a great wine. It has delicious bouquet and fruitiness.
price range: E

producer: Quien & Co.
classification: Red table wine
grape variety: Pinot Noir
city or village: Pommard
Deep red color and a very rich bouquet. The wine is robust, full-bodied, and well-balanced, with a lot of "sap"; ages well.
price range: E

producer: Guy Roulot
classification: White table wine
grape variety: Chardonnay
city or village: Meursault
This wine won a silver medal at the Paris Concours Générale.
price range: C

producer: Guy Roulot
classification: White table wine
grape variety: Chardonnay
city or village: Meursault
Guy Roulot regularly wins medals at the Paris Concours Générale for the best white wines of Meursault.
Straw color and a fruity, subtle bouquet. This soft, full, and rich white wine literally fills the mouth.
price range: C

producer: Guy Roulot
classification: White table wine
grape variety: Chardonnay
city or village: Meursault
This wine was selected as the best white Meursault in 1973 and received the award of the Confrérie des Chevaliers du Tastevin.
price range: C

producer: Guy Roulot
classification: White table wine
grape variety: Chardonnay
city or village: Meursault
vineyard: Charmes
Rated *premier cru* (first growth), this wine placed second in the famous Paris tasting held by British wine merchant Stephen Spurrier.
price range: C

producer: A. Simon
classification: Red table wine
grape variety: Pinot Noir
city or village: Cote de Beaune–Villages
Only sixteen villages are allowed to sell their wines as Cote de Beaune–Villages, either singly or as a blend.
Red color with brown edges and a bouquet with classic Pinot Noir perfume. The wine tastes soft and smooth.
price range: B

producer: Henri de Villamont
classification: Red table wine
grape variety: Pinot Noir
city or village: Savigny-les-Beaune
1971 vintage, a blend of wines from various vineyards in Savigny-les-Beaune. Henri de Villamont's cellars are located

right in the center of the village; hence the name "Le Village."

Red color, showing some maturity; the bouquet has a tart, earthy character and suggests violets. The wine is soft, big, and mouth-filling on the palate; it is a superb, satisfying example of a Savigny-les-Beaune. **price range: C**

producer: Veuve Ambal
classification: Red table wine
grape variety: Pinot Noir
city or village: Beaune
Ruby-red color with some browning at the edges and a full and elegant bouquet. The wine is velvety and supple, with good fruit and some wood—a fine Burgundy.
price range: C

producer: Michel Voarick
classification: White table wine
grape variety: Pinot Chardonnay
city or village: Aloxe-Corton
vineyard: Corton-Charlemagne
The Corton-Charlemagne vineyard is rated *grand cru* (great growth) and is one of the leading vineyards in Burgundy. Domaine Michel Voarick received a Medal of Honor for this wine; the domaine also produces a fine Corton-Languettes (*grand cru*), a Pernand-Vergelesses, an Aloxe-Corton and a Côte-de Beaune—Villages.

Fine, distinguished bouquet; the wine is complete, very harmonious, full, and aromatic. **price range: C**

MÂCONNAIS

producer: A. Bichot & Cie
classification: White table wine
grape variety: Pinot Chardonnay
city or village: Mâcon
Pale gold color and a clean, seductive bouquet. The wine is dry and has finesse; it accompanies seafood and fresh/salt-water fish. **price range: C**

producer: Bouchard Père & Fils
classification: Red table wine
grape variety: Gamay
district: Mâcon Supérieur
This is a dry, light red wine.
price range: B

producer: Bouchard Père & Fils
classification: White table wine
grape variety: Pinot Chardonnay
city or village: Pouilly-Vinzelles
This is a dry yet fruity white wine.
price range: B

producer: Cave Coopérative de Buxy
classification: Red table wine
grape variety: Pinot Noir (33⅓%) and Gamay (66⅔%)
city or village: Buxy
"Bourgogne Passetoutgrain" is a suble blend of Gamay and Pinot Noir grapes and represents only two or three percent of the appellation Bourgogne.

Fresh, fruity, light-bodied with a pleasant "nose" and a finish on the Gamay side.
price range: B

producer: Chanson Père et Fils
classification: White table wine
grape variety: Chardonnay
city or village: Mâcon
Mâcon blanc is a fruity yet dry white wine with a delicately subtle bouquet.
price range: B

producer: E. Chevalier & Fils
classification: White table wine
grape variety: Chardonnay
city or village: Charnay-les-Mâcon
A Mâcon blanc that matures quickly; good value for the money.
Light color and a fragrant bouquet. The wine is smooth and dry. **price range: A**

producer: E. Chevalier & Fils
classification: White table wine
grape variety: Chardonnay
city or village: Fuissé
A typically good Pouilly-Fuissé.
Slight yellow color and a fine bouquet. The wine has a fresh, fruity flavor.
price range: A

producer: Gaston Delorme
classification: White table wine
grape variety: Chardonnay
city or village: Vergisson
Fine, characteristic, and very distinguished bouquet; the wine is dry, racy, and fruity, with especially good balance.
price range: B

producer: Joseph Drouhin
classification: White table wine
grape variety: Chardonnay
"Laforet" is a blend of white wines produced in the Mâcon Villages district. It has been very well received in the restaurant trade in terms of its quality, and in blind tastings Laforet has scored well against many other wines of higher appellation and price.

Brilliant, shimmering pale straw color and a clean, full varietal bouquet. The wine is dry, medium-full-bodied, and quite fruity. **price range: B**

producer: Louis Jadot
classification: White table wine
grape variety: Chardonnay
The Appellation Contrôlée Pouilly-Fuissé applies only to wines produced in four communes in the central and best portion of the Mâconnais district. Pouilly-Fuissé is one of the best-known wines of France, and the demand always exceeds the supply.

Pale yellow color and a delicately fruity bouquet. This delicate, fine white wine combines richness and dryness.
price range: C

producer: Louis Jadot
classification: White table wine
grape variety: Chardonnay
The Appellation Contrôlée Mâcon Blanc Villages applies to wines produced in several communes situated around the villages of Mâcon. Louis Jadot's Mâcon Blanc Villages is one of his most popular white Burgundies.

Pale straw color and a fruity bouquet. The wine is delicate, clean, crisp, and dry.
price range: B

producer: Louis Jadot
classification: White table wine
grape variety: Chardonnay
The Appellation Contrôlée St.-Véran applies to vineyards located on chalky slopes that border the famous Pouilly-Fuissé. They produce a delicate, fruity white wine with a clean, fresh bouquet.

Pale straw color and a fruity bouquet. The wine is delicate and has a fruity, clean taste. **price range: B**

producer: C. Jouvet S.A.
classification: White table wine
grape variety: Chardonnay
city or village: Mâcon Villages

A fresh, light wine with a dry, crisp, and fruity flavor; delightful with cold cuts, seafood, and white meat. Serve well chilled.
price range: B

producer: C. Jouvet S.A.
classification: White table wine
grape variety: Chardonnay

Green-gold color and a fruity bouquet. The wine is soft and dry; serve chilled, with seafood and white meats. **price range:** C

producer: Jean LaCroix
classification: White sparkling wine
grape variety: Pinot Chardonnay
city or village: Mâcon

A *Bourgogne mousseux* (sparkling Burgundy) naturally fermented in the bottle by the *méthode champenoise,* and aged seven months in the bottle.

Full, bubbly appearance and a soft, creamy flavor. **price range:** B

producer: Edmond Laneyrie
classification: White table wine
grape variety: Chardonnay
city or village: Soluté

Estate-bottled.

Pale gold color and a fruity varietal bouquet. The wine is quite rich.
price range: C

producer: Maison Sichel
classification: White table wine
grape variety: Chardonnay

Should be drunk young.

Brilliant straw color and a fruity bouquet. The wine is "steely" but very fruity, and is quite dry. **price range:** C

producer: B. B. Mason & Co., Ltd.
classification: White table wine
grape variety: Pinot Chardonnay
city or village: Mâcon

Pale straw color and a light bouquet. The wine is dry, fresh, and very clean; it is good to quaff, and goes well with fish dishes.
price range: C

producer: Moillard
classification: White table wine
grape variety: Chardonnay

With the price of Pouilly-Fuissé increasing, Moillard has selected this wine to fill the need for a moderately priced white Burgundy that still retains the quality of a Pouilly-Fuissé.

A fruity, soft white wine. **price range:** B

producer: J. Mommessin
classification: White table wine
grape variety: Chardonnay
château: Pouilly

White Burgundies have been praised equally as the reds, although today production of red wine is more substantial than the white. One of the finest white Burgundies, Pouilly-Fuissé is growing in popularity as a very pleasant white wine.

The production of Château Pouilly is extremely limited: only 5,000 to 8,000 cases are produced annually. The demand for this wine is great, but only a limited quantity is available on the U.S. market.

Clear color; excellent bouquet; and smooth, fruity flavor. **price range:** B

producer: Pasquier-Desvignes, S.A.
classification: White table wine
grape variety: Chardonnay

"Marquisat White" retains its freshness and fragrance as you drink it, and is best when consumed young—before it is four years old. The Pasquier-Desvignes family has been producing wines on the estate of Le Marquisat continuously since 1420.

Clean, clear, light golden color and a fresh, fruity bouquet with a touch of oak. The wine is crisp, clean and well-balanced; it should be served chilled, after two or three hours in the refrigerator.
price range: B

producer: Poulet Père & Fils
classification: White table wine
grape variety: Pinot Chardonnay
city or village: Fuissé

Probably the most famous wine of Mâconnais.

The wine is dry, vigorous, and well-rounded, with a great bouquet.
price range: C

producer: Quien & Co.
classification: White table wine
grape variety: Pinot Chardonnay

One of the most popular white Burgundies.

Golden color and a strong and vigorous bouquet. The wine is very full, generously dry, and fresh—it can age well.
price range: C

producer: Marcel Robert
classification: White table wine
grape variety: Chardonnay

Clean, dry, and fresh bouquet; the wine is full-bodied and elegant, with a crisp flavor. **price range:** B

producer: Paul Sapin
classification: White table wine
grape variety: Chardonnay
city or village: Lancié

Pale gold color and an intense, fruity bouquet. The wine is dry, with medium body. **price range:** B

producer: A. Simon
classification: White table wine
grape variety: Chardonnay
city or village: Mâcon

A good alternative to Pouilly-Fuissé.

Pale yellow-green color and a light bouquet showing good fruit and acidity. The wine is dry, with good Chardonnay flavor—an excellent example of a dry white Burgundy. **price range:** A

producer: A. Simon
classification: Red table wine
grape variety: Pinot Noir and Gamay
city or village: Mâcon

An excellent value in Burgundy.

Garnet-red color and a young, fruity bouquet. The wine is soft and round-tasting. **price range: A**

producer: Thomas-Bassot
classification: White table wine
grape variety: Pinot Chardonnay

A fine example of a Pouilly-Fuissé, distributed by a leading *négociant-éléveur* (shipper) in Burgundy.

Clear color with tints of yellow and a typical bouquet. The wine displays good length. **price range: B**

producer: Thorin
classification: White table wine
grape variety: Pinot Chardonnay
city or village: Vergisson

Many people believe Pouilly-Fuissé to be the best white wine of southern Burgundy. The estate of the Château de France dates back to medieval times when the kings of France were at war with the dukes of Burgundy. **price range: C**

producer: Henri Tytell & Fils
classification: White table wine
grape variety: Chardonnay

An excellent substitute for Pouilly-Fuissé.

Straw color, a fragrant bouquet, and dry on the palate. **price range: B**

producer: Les Vignerons d'Igé
classification: White table wine
grape variety: Pinot Chardonnay
city or village: Igé

In 1971, 1972, and 1974 the Vignerons won medals for their wines.

A very full-bodied white Mâcon with class and character. **price range: B**

CÔTE CHALONNAISE

producer: Cave Cooperative de Buxy
classification: White sparkling wine
grape variety: Pinot Chardonnay
city or village: Buxy

A fine example of a sparkling Burgundy (*Bourgogne mousseux*) made by the *méthode champenoise*.

Clear color with fine sparkle and a clean, dry, and fresh bouquet. The wine is crisp, bone-dry, and fruity, with full bubbles.
price range: B

producer: Cave Cooperative de Buxy
classification: Red table wine
grape variety: Pinot Noir
city or village: Buxy

A fine example of an authentic Pinot Noir from a superb vintage, with a quality superior to what its modest appellation suggests.

Bright ruby-red color and a pungent, mature bouquet typical of Pinot Noir. The wine has an intense, mature flavor of the grape.
price range: B

producer: Joseph Faiveley
classification: Red table wine
grape variety: Pinot Noir
city or village: Mercurey
vineyard: Clos des Myglands

The Clos des Myglands, an exclusive of Joseph Faiveley, is a good example of the best red Burgundies produced outside the Côte d'Or and is similar to a fine Côte de Beaune red wine.

Medium-deep red color and an excellent Pinot fragrance showing good fruit. On the palate the wine is dry, soft, and flavorful.
price range: C

producer: R. d'Herville
classification: Red table wine
grape variety: Pinot Noir
city or village: Mercurey

Brilliant purple-red color and a soft, fruity, and well-aged bouquet with a hint of wood. The wine is rich and flavorful, with a slight spiciness. **price range: B**

producer: Marquis de Jouennes d'Herville
classification: Red table wine
grape variety: Pinot Noir
city or village: Mercurey

Château de Chamirey is one of the leading estates in the Mercurey district.

Clear purplish-red color and a bouquet with full varietal character. The wine is spicy and warm, with good richness.
price range: B

producer: Maison Sichel
classification: Red table wine
grape variety: Pinot Noir
city or village: Mercurey

Should be drunk young.

Light red, brilliant color, and a rich, perfumey bouquet. The wine is light, but satisfying and fruity. **price range: C**

BEAUJOLAIS

producer: Aujoux & Cie., S.A.
classification: Red table wine
grape variety: Gamay

city or village: Lacenas

This wine is produced on the estate of Château de Bionnay and is bottled in a special container with an informative little folder giving some details about the château.

Light red color and a pleasant, "special" bouquet resulting from the soil at Lacenas. The wine is delicate, very fruity, and has great finesse and vitality; it has a particular flavor and should be drunk young.
price range: B

producer: A. Bichot & Cie
classification: Red table wine
grape variety: Gamay
château: de Buffavent

Château de Buffavent is entitled to the appellation *Beaujolais Supérieur*.

Brilliant clear red color and a fruity bouquet. The wine is light, youthful, and fruity and goes well with meat and cheese; serve slightly chilled. **price range: B**

producer: Bouchard Aîné et Fils
classification: Red table wine
grape variety: Gamay
city or village: Fleurie

Fleurie is one of the nine *crus* (growths), which usually produce wine superior to a plain Beaujolais.

Fine bouquet; the wine is light, but fruity and fragrant. **price range: B**

producer: Bouchard Aîné et Fils
classification: White table wine
grape variety: Chardonnay

A white (*blanc*) Beaujolais is unusual, and it provides an interesting and pleasant alternative to many more famous white Burgundies.

Clear color with hints of gold and a fine, fruity bouquet. The wine is fresh, crisp, and pleasing. **price range: B**

producer: Château de Bussy
classification: Red table wine
grape variety: Gamay Noir à Jus Blanc
Rich red color and a fruity perfume in the bouquet. The wine has a refreshing acidity and is best quaffed rather than sipped. It should be drunk young, slightly chilled or at cool room temperature.
price range: C

producer: Chanson Père et Fils
classification: White table wine
grape variety: Chardonnay
A white Beaujolais.
Fruity bouquet; a delicate and dry white wine. **price range:** C

producer: Chanson Père et Fils
classification: Red table wine
grape variety: Gamay
city or village: Brouilly
A fruity, full-bodied, and full-flavored red wine. **price range:** B

producer: E. Chevalier & Fils
classification: Red table wine
grape variety: Gamay
city or village: Beaujeu St.-Étienne
Ruby-red color and a fragrant bouquet. The wine is light and fruity. **price range:** A

producer: A. Dherbey
classification: Red table wine
grape variety: Gamay
city or village: Villefranche-sur-Saône
Ruby-red color and a very fruity bouquet. The wine seems "a young lady" and is very charming. **price range:** B

producer: Joseph Drouhin
classification: Red table wine
grape variety: Gamay
The production of Beaujolais-Villages is restricted to only certain vineyards, which surpass plain Beaujolais in quality. The wine is an excellent example of good Beaujolais.
Clear ruby color and a fruity, zesty, and fresh bouquet. On the palate the wine is dry and very fruity. **price range:** B

producer: Louis Jadot
classification: Red table wine
grape variety: Gamay
city or village: Morgon
Morgon is the longest-lasting of the nine Beaujolais *crus* (growths). It is slightly less fruity than the other *crus*, but retains a distinct flavor and deep bouquet.
Brilliant ruby color and a distinctly deep bouquet. The wine is dry and flavorful.
price range: C

producer: Louis Jadot
classification: Red table wine
grape variety: Gamay
city or village: Fleurie
Fleurie is known as the "Queen of Beaujolais." It is the lightest and most deli-cate of the nine Beaujolais *crus* (growths), those districts that produce superior Beaujolais.
Brilliant ruby color and a fruity bouquet. The wine tastes fruity and silky.
price range: C

producer: Louis Jadot
classification: Red table wine
grape variety: Gamay
city or village: Moulin-à-Vent
In the hilly northern part of the Beaujolais district, nine villages produce red wines from the Gamay grape. These villages have been officially called *crus* (growths) and have their own distinct characteristics. Moulin-à-Vent is considered by many to be the finest *cru.*
Deep red color and a generous bouquet. The wine is rich and fruity, with distinct character of the Gamay grape. Moulin-à-Vent has more strength and depth than most Beaujolais, and improves with age.
price range: C

producer: Louis Jadot
classification: White table wine
grape variety: Chardonnay
Louis Jadot "Beaujolais Blanc" is pro-duced in limited quantities from a small area in the Beaujolais planted in Chardon-nay. Kobrand Corporation was the first im-porter to introduce this wine to the United States.
Pale yellow color and a fruity bouquet. This wine is agreeable, light, and fruity.
price range: B

producer: C. Jouvet S.A.
classification: Red table wine
grape variety: Gamay
Beaujolais-Villages wines are in a higher class than regular Beaujolais and are at their best when drunk young—within two years after they are made.
A fruity, full-bodied, and delightfully charming wine with fruity freshness and versatility. Serve either at cool room tem-perature or slightly chilled.
price range: B

producer: Leonard Kreusch Inc.
classification: Red table wine
grape variety: Gamay
An estate-bottled wine from the thirty-five Beaujolais-Villages.
Fruity. **price range:** A

producer: Château de Lacarelle
classification: Red table wine
grape variety: Gamay
city or village: St. Étienne-des-Ouillières
Owner of the vineyard of Château Lacarelle since the eighteenth century, the de Lacarelle family is also known for ren-ovating the vineyard of Château Filhot in Sauternes.
Bright red color and a fresh, flowery bouquet. The wine is characteristically light but perfect Beaujolais—rich and full of fruit. **price range:** B

producer: Princesse Lieven
classification: Red table wine
grape variety: Gamay
city or village: Morgon
Château de Bellevue is one of the lead-ing estates in Morgon.
Bright red color and a well-developed bouquet. The wine is dry. **price range:** B

*"Then a smile, and a glass,
and a toast, and a cheer
For all the good wine, and
we've some of it here."*
—Oliver Wendell Holmes

producer: Maison Sichel
classification: Red table wine
grape variety: Gamay

Should be drunk young.

Brilliant light red color and a fresh bouquet. The wine is light, appealing, and very fruity; it should be served slightly chilled. **price range:** B

producer: Moillard
classification: Red table wine
grape variety: Gamay
city or village: Brouilly
château: de la Valette

Brouilly is not a single township but a delimited area that includes five communes surrounding the famous hill of the Côte de Brouilly. Maison Moillard, the overseers of perfection in Burgundy, have attached their name to the Château de la Valette as a seal of quality.

Teases the taste buds into thinking it is a great growth of Burgundy **price range:** B

"The bottle you drank before must not make you regret the bottle to come."

—French proverb

producer: J. Mommessin
classification: Red table wine
grape variety: Gamay
city or village: Brouilly

Beaujolais-Villages comes from the five villages around Brouilly and twenty-eight others in the northern part of Beaujolais, which has superior soil and exposure.

Light red color and a fresh, fruity bouquet. The wine is fruity, smooth, and should be drunk young. **price range:** B

producer: Pasquier-Desvignes S. A.
classification: Red table wine
grape variety: Gamay

Perhaps the easiest to drink of all red wines, Beaujolais complements all meals. The Pasquier-Desvignes family has been producing wines on the estate of Le Marquisat continuously since 1420.

Light red, youthful color and a full, rich Gamay aroma. The wine is light and fruity on the palate, with good body and finish. It is best drunk after spending 30–40 minutes in the refrigerator, so that it approximates "cellar temperature." **price range:** B

producer: Pasquier-Desvignes S. A.
classification: Red table wine
grape variety: Gamay
city or village: Morgon

Grand cru (great growth) Beaujolais wines exhibit subtle differences that distinguish them from ordinary Beaujolais. The Pasquier-Desvignes family has been producing on the estate of Le Marquisat continuously since 1420.

Dark red color and a full, complex and rich aroma. The wine is long-lasting, though it drinks very well when young, and has a good finish. **price range:** C

producer: Pasquier-Desvignes S. A.
classification: Red table wine
grape variety: Gamay
city or village: Moulin-à-Vent

Grand cru (great growth) Beaujolais. Moulin-à-Vent is usually the sturdiest and best of the Beaujolais crus.

Medium-to-dark red color and a full, rich aroma. The wine has good fruit and great depth of flavor; although it drinks very well when young, it is long-lived.
price range: C

producer: Pasquier-Desvignes S.A.
classification: Red table wine
grape variety: Gamay
city or village: Fleurie

Grand cru (great growth) Beaujolais. Medium-to-dark red color and a full, rich Gamay aroma. The wine is fruity and full; although it is long-lived, it drinks very well when young. **price range:** C

producer: Pasquier-Desvignes S. A.
classification: Red table wine
grape variety: Gamay
city or village: Juliénas

Grand cru (great growth) Beaujolais. Medium red color and a light and fruity bouquet. The wine shows good balance and drinks very well when young; it is a joy to drink. **price range:** C

producer: Pasquier-Desvignes S. A.
classification: Red table wine
grape variety: Gamay
city or village: Brouilly

Grand cru (great growth) Beaujolais. Brouilly is usually one of the quickest of the Beaujolais crus to mature.

Flawless medium-red color and a big aroma. The wine is full and rich and drinks very well when young. **price range:** C

producer: Quinson Fils
classification: Red table wine
grape variety: Gamay

---

city or village: Fleurie

Officially a *grand cru* (great growth), Fleurie is typically one of the lightest and most luscious of the Beaujolais. This wine is estate-bottled. **price range:** B

producer: Paul Sapin
classification: Red table wine
grape variety: Gamay
city or village: Lancié

Purply-red color and a fruity bouquet. The wine is well-rounded and soft, in the pleasing style of Beaujolais.
price range: B

producer: Robert Sarrau
classification: Red table wine
grape variety: Gamay
city or village: Juliénas
château: des Capitans

The Château des Capitans is one of the older vineyards in the Julienas commune. It is always identified by a definite sharpness and nerve.

Deep garnet color and a fruity, mildly violet bouquet. The wine is light, crisp, and has a very pleasant, astringent aftertaste. It is a prime example of a Beaujolais from the commune of Juliénas. **price range:** B

producer: D. Stagnara
classification: Red table wine
grape variety: Gamay
city or village: Odenas

This domain originated under the reign of Louis XIV and has remained unchanged ever since. The vinification methods are traditional: the grapes are pressed by old wooden presses, and the wine is estate-bottled and unblended.

Typical, very well developed bouquet; the wine is fruity and tender, with suppleness and the typical Beaujolais lightness.
price range: B

producer: Thorin
classification: Red table wine
grape variety: Gamay Noir à Jus Blanc
The "Royal-Beaujolais" traditional cuvée is presented under the emblem of the provincial regiment created by "Le Roi Soleil" (Louis XIV) in 1685, which later became famous in the American Revolution when generals Rochambeau and Choiseul-Praslin joined forces against English General Cornwallis at the battles of Chesapeake and Yorktown (1781).
price range: B

producer: Thorin
classification: Red table wine
grape variety: Gamay Noir à Jus Blanc
city or village: Moulin-à-Vent
The Château des Jacques is among the oldest and most important estates in the Moulin-à-Vent district, the most famous part of the Beaujolais region. Many ancient documents held by the Thorin family refer to "Ager Thorinsis" in the ninth and tenth centuries. Beneath the picturesque *moulin* (windmill) near the town of Romanèche-Thorins is the celebrated château itself, which includes the domaines of Clos des Thorins, de la Roche, de Champ Decour, de Rochegres, du Grand Carquelin, and fifteen other vineyards. **price range:** B

producer: Thorin
classification: White table wine
grape variety: Chardonnay
city or village: La Chapelle de Guinchay
An unusual but excellent wine from the Beaujolais district (which produces red wines almost exclusively), "Beaujolais Blanc" has been acclaimed since 1643. It was here that the Baron Jehan de Franc always reserved for his personal use a cask "of the very best white wine."
price range: B

producer: Thorin
classification: Red table wine
grape variety: Gamay Noir à Jus Blanc
city or village: Fleurie
This Fleurie estate is called Château des Bachelards. **price range:** B

producer: Poulet Père & Fils
classification: Red table wine
grape variety: Pinot Noir
Blended under the guidance of the Poulet firm from various vineyards in Burgundy.
A charming red Burgundy that is ideal for everyday enjoyment. Distinctive "nose" and an inexpensive wine with finesse.
price range: A

producer: Poulet Père & Fils
classification: White table wine
grape variety: Pinot Chardonnay and Aligoté
An excellent everyday wine. Blended under the supervision of the Poulet firm.
Lightly dry, fresh, and fruity. A very pleasant wine. **price range:** A

"Fill ev'ry glass, for wine inspires us,
And fires us
With courage, love and joy.
Women and wine should life employ.
Is there ought else on earth desirous?"
—John Gay

FRANCE, RHONE

producer: A. Bichot & Cie.
classification: Rosé table wine
grape variety: Sereine
district: Tavel
Fruity bouquet and a fresh, fruity taste. The wine goes well with high-flavored foods and soft cheeses; should be served chilled. **price range:** C

producer: A. Bichot & Cie.
classification: Red table wine
grape variety: Syrah
district: Côtes-du-Rhône
Purple-red color and a bouquet reminiscent of violets. The wine is pleasant and harmonious and goes well with red meats and cheeses: it should be served at room temperature. **price range:** B

producer: Bouchard Père & Fils
classification: Red table wine
grape variety: Eleven varieties, predominantly Syrah
district: Châteauneuf-du-Pape
This Chateauneuf-du-Pape is dry and full. **price range:** D–E

producer: La Cave des Vignerons de Gigondas
classification: Red table wine

grape variety: Grenache
district: Gigondas
city or village: Vaucluse
Estate-bottled.
A brilliant deep ruby color and a big, fruity bouquet. The wine is deep-colored, warm, radiant, and full-bodied; favors aging. **price range:** B

producer: Chanson Père et Fils
classification: Red table wine
grape variety: Grenache, Syrah, and others
district: Côtes-du-Rhône
A ruby-red, hearty, robust, and full red wine from the Côtes-du-Rhône region.
price range: B

producer: Chapoutier & Cie.
classification: Rosé table wine
grape variety: Grenache and others
district: Avignon
city or village: Tavel
Generally consumed when young.
Elegant rosé color and a pleasing aroma. The wine is dry, fresh, and fruity and combines finesse and body to a degree rarely found in rosé wines. Serve chilled with all foods. **price range:** B

producer: Chapoutier & Cie.
classification: Red table wine
grape variety: Syrah, Grenache, and others
district: Southern Rhône
—Châteauneuf-du-Pape
city or village: Avignon
A celebrated, sturdy red wine with a high alcoholic content.
Deep crimson color; the wine is dry, full-bodied, and mellow. Serve at room temperature with all red meats and cheeses. **price range:** D

producer: Chapoutier & Cie.
classification: Red table wine
grape variety: Syrah
district: Northern Rhône
city or village: Tain-l'Hermitage

This wine is produced from a single extraordinary hillside. It is a very famous wine of the highest quality and is quite long-lived.

Deep red color and a pronounced bouquet. The wine is dry and full-bodied, with a soft finish; serve at cool room temperature to complement red meats, cheese, and game. **price range:** D

producer: Chapoutier & Cie.
classification: Red table wine
grape variety: Syrah
district: Northern Rhône
city or village: Tain-l'Hermitage

"M. de la Sizeranne" is an excellent example of the famous Hermitage wine at its very best. It is produced on just one extraordinary hillside from one of the finest portions of the Hermitage vineyard.

Deep red color and a rich, pronounced bouquet. The wine is dry, full-bodied, generous, and mellow, with a soft finish; it is very long-lived, and would be ideal with red meats, game, and cheeses.
price range: D

producer: Chapoutier & Cie.
classification: Red table wine
grape variety: Syrah, Grenache, and others
district: Southern Rhône —Châteauneuf-du-Pape
city or village: Avignon

Produced only in small quantities, "La Bernardine" is a fine example of the vigorous Châteauneuf-du-Pape wines and comes from one of the most select portions in Châteauneuf-du-Pape.

Deep crimson color and a full bouquet. The wine is dry, full-bodied, and lusciously mellow; it is fresh-tasting when consumed young. **price range:** D

producer: Chapoutier & Cie.
classification: Red table wine
grape variety: Blend
district: Côtes-du-Rhône Villages

Côtes-du-Rhône Villages is a limited appellation denoting wines of higher quality than those merely labeled Côtes-du-Rhône. This is further identified as "Cuvée Chapoutier."

Ruby color; the wine is dry, full-bodied, and flavorful, with a roundness and high alcoholic content. **price range:** B

producer: Chapoutier & Cie.
classification: White table wine
grape variety: Rousanne and Marsanne
district: Northern Rhône
city or village: Tain-l'Hermitage

The rare and unusual white Hermitage comes from a district celebrated for its full-bodied reds. It is a wine of definite character and is especially fresh and fruity when young, though it is quite long-lived.

Pale gold color and a pronounced bouquet. The wine is mellow and full-bodied without being sweet; it is excellent served chilled with seafood and hors d'oeuvres, but is also fine with all white meats and poultry. **price range:** D

producer: Chapoutier & Cie.
classification: White table wine
grape variety: Rousanne and Marsanne
district: Northern Rhône
city or village: Tain-l'Hermitage

The "Chante Alouette" is an especially fine white Hermitage wine from one of the most select portions of the Hermitage vineyards; it is quite long-lived.

Pale gold color and a rich bouquet. The wine is dry, full-bodied, and has a fine rich flavor; its pronounced, full flavor is excellent with seafood and all white meats. Serve well chilled. **price range:** D

producer: Chapoutier & Cie.
classification: Red table wine
grape variety: Syrah, with some Viognier
district: Northern Rhône—Côte-Rôtie
city or village: Ampuis

The Côte-Rôtie, or "roasted slope," is composed of vineyards planted on a series of narrow terraces on incredibly steep slopes. Cultivation is quite expensive, and production is very limited, but the wines have great distinction and finesse and are extremely long-lived.

Deep red color and a rich bouquet with a hint of raspberries and violets. The wine is dry, full-bodied, and has a lovely velvety finish. **price range:** E

producer: Chapoutier & Cie.
classification: Red table wine
grape variety: Blend
district: Côtes-du-Rhône

A pleasant, soft, and velvety table wine. Ruby color; the wine is dry, full-bodied, and velvety, with a delightful tang.
price range: B

producer: Chapoutier & Cie.
classification: White table wine
grape variety: Rousanne and Marsanne
district: Northern Rhône
city or village: St.-Joseph

Light flavor; a pleasant, good-quality white wine. Serve chilled.
price range: C

producer: Chapoutier & Cie.
classification: White table wine
grape variety: Rousanne and Marsanne

district: Northern Rhône
city or village: Crozes-Hermitage

A good quality, pleasant light wine not unlike Hermitage Blanc.

Pale gold color; the wine is dry and full-bodied. **price range:** C

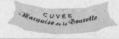

producer: Chapoutier & Cie.
classification: Red table wine
grape variety: Syrah (100%)
district: Northern Rhône
city or village: Crozes-Hermitage

A good-quality, pleasant red wine not unlike Hermitage.

A dry, full-bodied red wine.
price range: C

producer: Delas Frères
classification: Red table wine
grape variety: Syrah
district: Hermitage
city or village: Tain-l'Hermitage

"Cuvée Marquise de la Tourette" wine is produced by Delas Frères from a very small part of the famed Hermitage vineyard, one of the classic vineyards of France. Rare and always scarce, the wine is one of the longest-lived French wines.

Very deep, full ruby color, with fine robe; the bouquet is classic, with a "raspberry" aroma. The wine is mouth-filling, has great depth, and is long-lasting. It is a classic wine, very long-lived. **price range:** C

producer: Delas Frères
classification: White table wine
grape variety: Rousanne and Marsanne
district: Crozes-Hermitage
city or village: Tain-l'Hermitage

This white Crozes-Hermitage is an excellent example of the rare white wines of the Côtes-du-Rhône.

Brilliant pale straw color with shimmering gold tints; and a light, flowery and elegant bouquet. The wine is quite elegant, with plenty of fruit and depth.
price range: B

producer: Delas Frères
classification: Red table wine
grape variety: Syrah
district: Hermitage
city or village: Tain-l'Hermitage

Hermitage "St.-Christophe," produced only by Delas Frères, is named for the fabled chapel of St. Christope perched near the very top of the Hermitage slope, "the hill of the hermit." The chapel is built on the site of the Roman temple of Mercury, overlooking the village of Tain-l'Hermitage below.

Deep, full red color and a complex bouquet suggesting raspberry and violets. The wine is full and robust, with a lingering aftertaste; it is a classic Rhône wine that justifies its high reputation. **price range:** C

producer: Delas Frères
classification: Rosé table wine
grape variety: Grenache
district: Tavel
city or village: Tavel

Tavel is the most famous and perhaps the most interesting French rosé; this is an excellent example of a fine Tavel.

Diamond-bright rosé color and a light, fruity bouquet with lots of elegance. It is a delicious drinking wine—very elegant and fruity. **price range:** C

producer: Delas Fréres
classification: Red table wine
grape variety: Grenache, Syrah, Cinsault, and Clairette
district: Lower Rône—Châteauneuf -du-Pape

This fine Châteauneuf-du-Pape, "St.-Esprit," is one of the most popular Rhône wines. It often reaches over 14% alcohol, but at the same time possesses a balance of fruit and acidity seldom found in a Châteauneuf-du-Pape.

Deep, fine ruby-crimson color and a full, powerful and fruity "nose." The wine is fine, full-bodied, and classically Châteauneuf-du-Pape. **price range:** C

producer: Delas Frères
classification: Red table wine
grape variety: Syrah and Grenache
district: Côtes-du-Rhône

Delas Frères, founded in 1835, is one of the oldest and most important houses in the northern Côtes-du-Rhône. "Saint-Esprit" is their regional wine entitled to the Côtes-du-Rhône appellation.

Deep ruby color and a typically grapey bouquet with a slight peppery quality, typical of Rhône wines. On the palate the wine is full, round, and robust; it shows great class and maturity from wood aging, and is superior to many others entitled to this appellation. **price range:** B

producer: Delas Frères
classification: White table wine
grape variety: Marsanne and Roussanne
district: Hermitage
city or village: Tain-l'Hermitage

Produced in the northern Côtes-du-Rhône district, the rare white Hermitage is among the longest-lived of all dry French white wines. It is the best Rhône white wine, with slightly more fullness than a white Burgundy.

Full golden color and a full, flinty bouquet with plenty of fruit and balance. The wine is quite mouth-filling, with a rich, lingering finish. A classic, well-balanced white Hermitage. **price range:** C

producer: Delas Frères
classification: Red table wine
grape variety: Syrah
district: St.-Joseph
city or village: Tournon

Produced in several different communes within the northern Côtes-du-Rhône, St.-Joseph was the favorite wine of King Louis XII.

Deep ruby color and an elegant, flowery bouquet. On the palate the wine is full of fruit and finishes well; it is well-balanced, supple, and shows great distinction. A good value. **price range:** B

producer: Delas Frères
classification: Red table wine
grape variety: Syrah and Viognier
district: Côte-Rôtie
city or village: Ampuis

The Côte-Rôtie is probably the oldest vineyard in France, dating back to Roman times and even beyond. Very long-lived, the wines are representative of the classic reds of the northern Côtes-du-Rhône.

Deep, full ruby color showing great depth, and a huge, full bouquet. The wine is mouth-filling, with great class and body. **price range:** C

producer: Julien Devèze
classification: Red table wine
grape variety: Grenache (80%), Counoise (10%), Clairette, and others
district: Vaucluse—Châteauneuf-du-Pape
city or village: Avignon

Great and distinctive bouquet, and a very powerful, warm, and "fiery" wine. It has the sumptuous, distinctive flavor of a fine Châteauneuf-du-Pape. **price range:**

producer: A. Dherbey
classification: Red table wine
grape variety: Grenache, Syrah, and Mourvèdre
district: Southern Rhône —Châteauneuf-du-Pape

Dark red color; the wine is strong, full of subtlety, and has a sturdy body. It should be drunk "seriously," with red meats. **price range:** B

producer: Domaine Gerin
classification: Red table wine
grape variety: Syrah
district: Northern Rhône—Côte-Rôtie

Côte-Rôtie is the oldest of all the Côtes-du-Rhône vineyards. Domaine Gerin Côte-Rôtie won a gold medal in 1970.

Deep red color and a bouquet of violets. The wine is rich, elegant, and heady and shows breeding; it goes well with red meat and prepared dishes, games, and cheeses. **price range:** C

producer: Domaine de Mont-Redon
classification: Red table wine
grape variety: Grenache, Cinsault, Clairette, and Syrah
district: Châteauneuf-du-Pape
city or village: Avignon

Mont-Redon is one of the oldest and largest wine estates in France, dating from 1334. This wine is regarded as the "jewel" of Châteauneuf-du-Pape, and is estate-bottled.

A deep red color and a full, rich bouquet. This big, full-flavored, and robust wine is rich with an incomparable bouquet. **price range:** C

producer: Pierre Labeye
classification: Red table wine
grape variety: Grenache, Cinsault, and Syrah
district: Côteaux du Tricastin
city or village: Les Granges-Gontardes

The Côteaux du Tricastin is a large new vineyard area only granted Appellation Contrôlée status in the past few years. It already produces some of the best wines in the Rhône Valley, and as it matures it should compare favorably with many wines from more famous areas like Hermitage and Châteauneuf-du-Pape.

Bright medium-red color and a fragrant bouquet. The wine is full, round, fruity, and very well-balanced; it is a satisfying table wine showing depth and a pronounced style of its region. **price range:** C

producer: La Vieille Ferme
classification: Red table wine
grape variety: Syrah and Grenache
district: Côtes-du-Rhône
city or village: Jonquières

Unlike other Côtes-du-Rhône, La Vieille Ferme uses a generous portion of Syrah grapes in a blend to add strength.

Deep red color and a fruity bouquet. The wine is soft and velvety. **price range: A**

producer: Maison Sichel
classification: Red table wine
grape variety: Various
district: Southern Rhône—Châteauneuf-du-Pape
city or village: Avignon
Long-lived.
Brilliant deep red color and a full bouquet. The wine is full-bodied yet smooth, with a spicy flavor. **price range: B**

producer: B. B. Mason & Co., Ltd.
classification: Red table wine
grape variety: Grenache and Syrah
district: Côtes-du-Rhône
Ruby color and a fruity bouquet. The wine is soft and flavorful, with good body.
price range: B

producer: Jean Olivier
classification: Rosé table wine
grape variety: Grenache, Clairette, and Cinsault
district: Tavel
city or village: Tavel
Renowned for its pink color, this brilliantly clear wine is fermented just long enough to bring out its rosé color, a delicate process demanding perfect grapes. Château d'Aqueria is acclaimed as the finest rosé of France. Estate-bottled.
A true pink color and a fruity bouquet. The wine is clean, with dry crispness and a fruity roundness. **price range:** B

producer: Pascal Frères
classification: Red table wine
grape variety: Syrah
district: Côtes-du-Rhône
city or village: Vacqueyras
This wine won a gold medal at a tasting held at the Concours d'Orange.
Deep red color and a full, classic bouquet with some fruit. The wine is full-flavored and gutsy, with a long-lasting finish. It is worthy of its honor. **price range:** A

producer: Pascal Frères
classification: Red table wine
grape variety: Syrah
district: Côtes-du-Rhône
city or village: Vacqueyras
Deep red color; a fine and fruity bouquet. The wine has good flavor and fine balance, and fills the mouth; it is a worthy Côtes-du-Rhône, gutsy, and has a soft, lingering finish. **price range:** A

producer: Piat Père et Fils
classification: Red table wine
grape variety: Syrah, Grenache, and others
district: Southern Rhône—Châteauneuf-du-Pape
city or village: Avignon
Bright deep-red color and a developed bouquet. The wine is quite full-bodied.
price range: B

producer: Quien & Co.
classification: Red table wine
grape variety: Grenache, Syrah, and eleven others

district: Southern Rhône—Châteauneuf-du-Pape
This wine has been called the "Child of the Sun," since it grows in the sunniest part of France north of the Riviera.
Deep red color and a strong and full bouquet. The wine is robust, generous, and full-bodied; it is the perfect wine to accompany game or fancy food with sauce. **price range:** C

producer: Alexandre Rochette & Cie.
classification: Red table wine
grape variety: Syrah and Marsanne
district: Hermitage
city or village: Drôme
The firm of Rochette, established in 1898, is proprietor and shipper of the finest quality wines from the Côtes-du-Rhône with holdings in many vineyards in the 150-mile-long region.
Ruby-red color with a fruity and pronounced bouquet. On the palate the wine is full-bodied, velvety, and fruity; it is generous and mellow with a pleasing raspberrylike flavor and pronounced bouquet. **price range:** D

producer: Rosenheim/Hallgarten Wines, Ltd.
classification: Red table wine
grape variety: Blend
district: Côtes-du-Rhône
A nationally distributed Hallgarten-branded wine.
Light red color and a fruity bouquet. The wine is full-flavored and well-balanced, with a long finish. **price range:** B

producer: Charles Roux et ses Fils
classification: Red table wine
grape variety: Syrah, Grenache, Mouvèdre, Cinsault, and Viognier
district: Côtes-du-Rhône
city or village: Sablet
château: Trignon

Charles Roux is known for his devotion to the quality of wine he produces. His father was a pioneer in the process of carbonic maceration.
The wine is pleasant, soft, and full-bodied. **price range:** A

producer: A. Simon
classification: Red table wine
grape variety: Grenache, Syrah, and others
district: Southern Rhône—Châteauneuf-du-Pape
A total of thirteen different grape varieties are used for this wine, which adds complexity to their style.
Deep ruby-red color and a rich, vinous bouquet. The wine is firm, rich, and full-bodied—one of the classic Rhône wines.
price range: A

producer: Société les 3 Domaines
classification: Red table wine
grape variety: Thirteen varieties; 80% Grenache, Clairette, Syrah, and Cinsault
district: Châteauneuf-du-Pape
A typical sturdy red Châteauneuf with a fruity "nose." **price range:** C

producer: Société des Vignerons Producteurs Tavel (Gard)
classification: Rosé table wine
grape variety: Grenache, Cinsault, Clairette, Picpoul, and Carignan
district: Côtes-du-Rhône
city or village: Tavel
A favorite wine of Francis I and celebrated by the Renaissance poet Ronsard. Near Avignon, on the right bank of the Rhône River, the appellation Côtes-du-Rhône denotes the very best of rosé wines.
Ruby-colored with topazlike reflections that increase with age. It is heady, dry, fruity, and very elegant, with a light peppery flavor. **price range:** A

producer: Henri Tytell & Fils
classification: Red table wine
district: Côtes-du-Rhône

This ruby-red wine is dry to the palate, with a light bouquet.

This is a good substitute for higher-priced Beaujolais. **price range:** A

producer: Henri Tytell & Fils
classification: Red table wine
district: Châteauneuf-du-Pape

This is a full-bodied, robust wine of ruby color. It has a strong bouquet and is dry to the palate. **price range:** B

FRANCE, OTHER FRENCH WINES

producer: Amiral Conge
classification: Red table wine
grape variety: Carignan, Cinsault, and Grenache
region: Languedoc
district: Coteaux du Languedoc V.D.Q.S.
village: St.-Series

The owner of this château is a retired admiral who manages his vineyard with the precision one would expect from a man of his profession.

Bright ruby color and a fresh, herby bouquet. The wine is firm but easy to drink; one of the better Languedoc reds. It should be drunk fairly young. **price range:** A

producer: Les Vignerons de Chusclan
classification: White table wine
grape variety: Clairette, Rousane, Mourvèdre, and Viognier
city or village: Chusclan

"Côtes-du-Rhône Blanc" is produced from the five communes on the right bank of the Rhône River, north of Tavel and west of Orange, with Chusclan being the most important commune.

Greenish-yellow in color; dry, with a full body and a unique spicy bouquet.
price range: A

producer: Vincent
classification: Red table wine
grape variety: Grenache, Carignan, and Cinsault
district: Côtes-du-Rhône
city or village: Combes-Sabran

The attractive château on the property dates from the eighteenth century, entitling the wines to bear the appellation *mis en bouteille au château.*

Bright red color and a fruity bouquet. The wine is round and well-balanced, with good body; a typical wine from the Côtes-du-Rhône region. **price range:** B

producer: Louis Dubroca
classification: White table wine
grape variety: Sauvignon Blanc and Semillon
region: Bergerac
district: Montravel

This dry white wine comes from a region some 60 miles to the east of Bordeaux.

"Blanc de Blanc de Montravel" has been sold in the United States quite successfully since 1969, and is a best seller in the line of imported wines produced by Louis Dubroca, having gained very good consumer acceptance. The label shown is a new one used since the fall of 1976.

Pale yellow color and a fruity bouquet. The wine is fresh and crisp, a happy medium between the very dry white wines of the upper Loire Valley and the full-bodied whites of Burgundy. **price range:** A

producer: L'Héritier-Guyot
classification: Red table wine
region: Coteaux du Languedoc
district: Hérault (Faugères)
city or village: Béziers

A few selected wines from the Coteaux du Languedoc area have been classified V.D.Q.S. Faugères is the most renowned of these Hérault wines; a good example is produced and bottled by the highly reputed firm of L'Héritier-Guyot.

A rich ruby color and a full, rich bouquet. The wine is full-bodied and well-balanced. **price range:** A

producer: M. Christophe Jonquère d'Oriola
classification: Red table wine
grape variety: Carignan, Grenache, and Cinsault
region: Languedoc
district: Côtes du Roussillon V.D.Q.S.
city or village: Corneilla del Vercol

This château is owned by an old, established Catalan family famous in France as equestrian champions.

Dark, full red color and a fruity bouquet. The wine is firm, round, and easy to drink—a good example of a wine from the promising Roussillon area. **price range:** A

producer: G. Nissard
classification: Rosé table wine
grape variety: Grenache Gris
region: Gard
district: Costières du Gard V.D.Q.S.

This wine is made exclusively from the

---

unusual Grenache Gris, a pink grape. It can therefore be vinified like a red wine instead of being taken off the skins after twenty-four hours like most rosés, thus giving it a very smooth-tasting quality while retaining its lightness. It is sold in an unusual Camargue bottle.

Pale salmon color and a fragrant, herblike bouquet. The wine is very full-flavored and will stand up to full-flavored seafood or Paella. **price range:** A

producer: UNIDOR
classification: White table wine
grape variety: Muscadelle (80%), Semillon, and Sauvignon Blanc
region: Southwest *(Sudouest)*
district: Bergerac
village: Monbazillac

Bright, rich golden color and a full bouquet. The wine is sweet and luscious, very rich, and has a touch of honey to the taste. It can be drunk either as an aperitif or as a dessert wine and should be served chilled. **price range:** B

producer: UNIDOR
classification: White table wine
grape variety: Sauvignon Blanc (100%)
region: Southwest *(Sudouest)*
district: Bergerac
city or village: Bergerac

This wine should be drunk in its first year to appreciate its fresh flavor.

Pale color, with green tints, and a very fine, developed bouquet. The wine is dry and fruity, with the typical flinty taste of Sauvignon. **price range:** B

producer: UNIDOR
classification: White table wine
grape variety: Semillon, Sauvignon Blanc, and Muscadelle
region: Southwest *(Sudouest)*
district: Bergerac
city or village: Bergerac

A Bergerac "Blanc de Blancs" that should be drunk quite young.

Pale yellow color and a fine and delicate bouquet. The wine is dry and fruity, with a fresh taste. **price range:** B

Italy, one of the great wine countries of the world, produces red, white, and rosé table wines, as well as sparkling wine, aperitifs, and dessert wines. Almost every region provides enormous variety, and each wine is endowed with the individuality of the grower or owner of the estate and/or the company handling the final product. This abundance of "individualities" is responsible for the charm of Italian wines.

Grape varieties are distinctly Italian, as is the tradition of wine making in this Mediterranean country. Some Italian wines are produced from a single grape variety. Others are made from rigidly specified mixtures of grapes, which are by no means the same as blends of wine.

In discussing Italian wines, it is logical to treat each region as a separate entity, progressing geographically from one extreme of the country to another.

Piedmont This region is famous for the wines from three grapes: Nebbiolo, Barbera (reds), and Moscato (whites). *Barolo, Barbaresco,* and *Gattinara* are Nebbiolo grape wines; *Ghemme* is produced from a large proportion of Nebbiolo combined with other varieties. All require considerable aging and rank among Italy's greatest reds. All are named for the places in which they are grown, and these production areas are small. The Barbera grape, twenty times as common as the noble Nebbiolo, produces wines that generally are double-named, e.g., *Barbera d'Alba.* A fine Piedmontese grape, the Grignolino, is available only in limited quantity. The Dolcetto produces a dry red wine. The Freisa gives a dry red wine that is slightly sweet. The wine of these last three grape varieties usually has a geographical location following the name, e.g., *Grignolino d'Asti, Dolcetto d'Alba, Freisa de Chieri.* From the Moscato grape comes Italy's elegant sparkling wine, *Asti Spumante.* Some producers also use the Pinot grape to make this festive Italian delicacy.

Valle d'Aosta This is Italy's smallest region. Against a background of snowy Alps, grapes are grown high on hillsides. *Donnaz,* produced from Nebbiolo grapes, is the region's best-known wine. It is a smooth, full-bodied red that takes its name from a local town. The Petit Rouge grape, grown 2,000 feet above sea level, produces *Enfer d'Arvier,* the Aosta Valley's only D.O.C. wine besides Donnaz.

Lombardy This is the northernmost part of Italy. Among the Alps of Valtellina, 2,500 feet above sea level, the Nebbiolo grape is grown to produce a hardier red wine than that of Piedmont, but one that achieves real delicacy with aging. Small proportions of other grapes are sometimes added. Subdistrict names, e.g., *Sassella, Grumello, Inferno,* are often used. In the Oltrepò Pavese district, in the Pavia area, vigorous cooperatives and dedicated proprietors maintain a universally high level of quality control. Fine reds and whites are produced from Pinot and Riesling grapes, as well as from a number of Italian grapes. The wines of *Frecciarossa,* which is a brand name, have a high reputation. From the Lombard bank of Lake Garda, *Chiaretto,* a very pale red wine, has an unusual freshness and charm; and *Lugana,* a light, delicate white wine, has a pleasant fresh taste.

Veneto This is one of the largest producing regions, situated between Lake Garda and the Po and the Piave rivers. It is best known for the great trio of Veronese wines: *Valpolicella* and *Bardolino* (reds) and *Soave* (white). *Valpolicella,* from the largest district north of Verona, is a cherry-red wine with a gentle sweet smell and a nice trace of bitterness in the aftertaste. *Bardolino,* from the same grapes grown in lighter soils, is a lighter red with a refreshing touch of sharpness. *Soave,* perhaps Italy's most famous white wine, comes from a small hill district east of Verona. It is pale, dry, and very well-balanced, with a hint of floweriness. All wines represent place names. All are best drunk young and cool. A Veronese speciality is *Recioto,* made from the *recie* (ears), or outer bunches, of grapes, that have had the most sun. This is a heavier, sweeter wine. *Amarone* is a dry, rich, heavy red wine. The hills around the town of *Conegliano,* north of Venice, produce a white and fragrant wine from the Prosecco grape. Throughout the region a good deal of wine is made from Cabernet and Merlot grapes, resulting in some excellent reds, and Pinot and Tocai grapes are also widely grown. These will generally have an area name attached to the grape variety, e.g., *Cabernet di Pramaggiore, Merlot del Piave, Tocai di Lison.*

Trentino–Alto Adige This region lies in the Adige Valley, parts of which are almost entirely carpeted with vines. Wines of high quality are produced throughout. In the Trentino, or lower valley, the *Teroldego* grape gives its name to a quality wine. Other Trentino area wines include *Merlot, Cabernet, Pinot, Moscato,* and *Riesling.* A fine full rosé, *Casteller,* is also made around Trento. In the upper part, as the valley narrows towards Bolzano, the reds are soft and well-balanced, with a touch of bitterness. The most quality red wines are produced in the area of Lago di Caldaro, about 30 miles long. Best known of the other smaller areas is Santa Maddalena, east of Bolzano. The village of Terlano is a notable producer of white wines such as *Pinot Bianco* and *Riesling,* and Tramin produces a *Gewürztraminer.*

Friuli–Venezia Giulia This is the region in the extreme northeast of Italy and produces many quality wines from the three main areas of production: Colli Orientali del Friuli (eastern Friuli Hills wines), Grave del Friuli (western Friuli Hills wines), and Collio Goriziano (Gorizia Hills wines). The white, gray, and black Pinot grapes are cultivated in all three areas. The white makes a dry wine, faintly light in texture and color. The gray gives a more deeply colored white, while the black provides a smooth red wine of full body and flavor. The Cabernet grape makes a full red wine, harsh when young, but fine after several years in the bottle; and the Merlot grape yields a fine ruby-red wine. *Tocai,* a well-known Friuli white, is dry, yellowish-white, with a slightly bitter undertaste. *Verduzzo* is a full-bodied and slightly tannic white wine. The Riesling grape is also widely used to produce full-bodied white wines.

Liguria The narrow coastal strip of the Italian Riviera produces relatively little wine, but two areas are famous as wine-producing centers. One is Cinqueterre, or "five villages," between the cliffs and the sea, west of La Spezia, where some vineyards can be reached only by boat. The dry white wine produced here is full-flavored. A sweet white wine, made from sun-dried grapes, is luscious but rare. The second area, Dolceacqua, is famous for its elegant dry red wine.

Emilia–Romagna This area produces four wines of importance. *Lambrusco,* a unique dry, semi-sparkling red, comes from the grapes of the same name grown in the vicinity of Modena. Fragrant, fresh, and clean, *Sangiovese* is the grape used in the Romagna Hills to produce a full-bodied, well-balanced red wine whose bouquet is intensified by age. Near Forlì, Ravenna, and Bologna, the Trebbiano grape produces a dry, well-balanced white wine known as *Trebbiano di Romagna.* On the northern slopes of the Apennines, the *Albana* grape gives its name to a widely popular, light, fresh white wine.

Tuscany This is the home of Italy's *Chianti.* This wine is produced from a classic mixture of Sangiovese and Canaiolo (red) and Trebbiano and Malvasia (white) grapes. *Chianti* is made in two styles. The first is made for drinking young and fresh. It was traditionally put in the familiar straw-covered flask; today it is also marketed in other bottles. When young it is grapey, with a slight edge, and compulsively drinkable. The second Chianti style is left to mature three or more years in oak casks, thereby acquiring great power and delicacy. Known then as *Riserva,* it goes into Bordeaux-shaped bottles. A good *Riserva* will be full-bodied and fragrant and can reach a distinction, and sometimes a longevity, to match fine wines anywhere in the world. In the heart of the Chianti area is the Chianti Classico Zone, the original area of about a hundred square miles. There are six other major districts, each with its voluntary protecting *Consorzio* and distinctive neck label or seal. In Montepulciano, near Chianti country, the same grapes that produce Chianti yield a generous dry red wine, *Vino Nobile di Montepulciano,* which can be traced back as far as the fourteenth century. South of Siena, the small hill town of Montalcino produces a truly great red, *Brunello di Montalcino,* made from a variety of the Sangiovese grape. Even bigger and more fragrant than *Chianti Riserva,* it needs many years to mature. One Tuscan white wine deserves special mention. This is *Vernaccia di San Gimignano,* a dry wine of quality produced around the small hilltop town famous for its towers.

Marches This is the region on the Adriatic coast where the Verdicchio grape and the amphora-shaped bottle have made an easily recognizable, delightful white wine. The best known *Verdicchio* is from the Castelli di Jesi area, inland from Ancona. It has a pale straw color and fullness with a touch of austerity. Good *Verdicchios* are made in other districts, notably near Matelica. The Marches also has some good red wines, *Rosso Conero* and *Rosso Piceno,* both from the Montepulciano and Sangiovese grapes, *Rosso Conero* is a dry, robust wine, which ages nicely; *Rosso Piceno* is a soft, ruby-red wine.

Umbria This is another very small region. From Umbria comes a great white wine, *Orvieto* (from the town of the same name that is perched on its massive rock, out of which are carved the cellars where the wine matures). *Orvieto* is made both dry and *abboccato* (semi-sweet). The *abboccato* is the pride of the area. It is light and delicate. Dry *Orvieto* is well-balanced, with a flowery bouquet. Near Assisi is the tiny *Torgiano* area that produces a white and a red wine. The full red has a pleasant scent and a pronounced flavor and needs at least five years of aging. The white is quite dry, and can age beautifully for ten years.

Latium This is the region of Rome where internationally known white *Frascati* is grown. Strong and fragrant and with a flavor of golden grape skins, it is made in dry and *abboccato* styles. But *Frascati* is only one of the great Castelli Romani wines, made among the Roman castles in the Alban hills southeast of Rome. Others include *Colli Albani* and *Colli Lanuvini,* whites made from grapes grown on volcanic soil and matured in deep cellars. *Marino,* a red, white, and rosé wine, is a pleasant everyday wine. *Est! Est! Est!* resembles the Castelli Romani wines but comes from the slopes around Lake Bolsena. It is clear and dry, somewhat lighter than Frascati. The name Est! Est! Est! derives from a steward of a twelfth-century German bishop who was traveling to Rome. The steward was sent ahead by his master to mark the inns where good wine could be found, by chalking *Est* (This is it) on the door. At Montefiascone he was so enthusiastic he chalked *Est! Est! Est!* In the Aprilia district, between the Alban hills and the sea, *Trebbiano* (white) and *Sangiovese* and *Merlot* (red) grapes produce good-quality wines usually under the grape names, e.g., *Merlot di Aprilia.*

Abruzzo and Molise   These regions are on the Adriatic side of central Italy. Two grapes are used for the pleasant wines of these regions. The *Montepulciano d'Abruzzo* is a pale, very drinkable red wine. The white *Trebbiano d'Abruzzo* has a pleasant "nose" but is sometimes very sharp.

Campania   The reds and whites of Ischia. The best known is the dry, white *Lacryma Christi,* grown on the slopes of the volcano Vesuvius and distinguished by the added words *del Vesuvio.*

Apulia   One of the largest wine-producing regions of good-quality table wines. One of the best areas is Castel del Monte, inland between Bari and Foggia, where very drinkable red, white, and rosé wines are produced. The white is well-balanced and fresh; the red is dry and tannic; the rosé is dark and

fragrant. From the north of the region come *San Severo White,* a dry, highly alcoholic wine; and *San Severo Red,* produced from the reliable Montepulciano grape. *Torre Quarto* is a red produced in this area; farther south, *Locorotondo* white is produced.

Basilicata   The inland region with an extinct volcano, Vulture, on whose slopes grows the unusual Aglianico grape. A dry red *Aglianico del Vulture,* after a few years in the bottle, can be one of the best wines of southern Italy.

Calabria   The "toe" of the Italian peninsula. The wines of *Ciro* claim descent from those of the ancient Greek settlers. Dry *Ciro* is a big, robust wine. The white is full, flowery, and also dry.

Sicily   Here they have produced wine for over two hundred years, notably the dessert wine *Marsala.* A fortified wine, Marsala is produced in dry and sweet varieties, as well as in specially flavored versions. It is a superior dessert wine that has also achieved fame as a cooking ingredient. The slopes of Mount Etna, in strictly designated areas provide *Etna Red* and *Etna White.* The red is dry, robust and ruby-colored. The white is dry, fragrant, and well-balanced. *Regaleali* white and red are dry, warm, and smooth. *Corvo di Salaparuta* wines, from near Palermo, have been known outside the island for nearly 150 years. The red is fine and velvety with an interesting aroma. The white is fresh and full. A delicate pale white, *Platino,* is also produced. Named after the ancient Greek city of Segesta, both a red and white *Segesta* are well-balanced. In southern Sicily, *Draceno, Drepano,* and *Saturno* are produced.

Sardinia   Another island with pleasant wines. *Vernaccia, Cannonau,* and *Torbato* are the most popular.

HOW TO READ AN ITALIAN WINE LABEL

THE NAME   Italian wine names are often geographical, e.g., Chianti, Gattinara, Valpolicella. Sometimes a single commune gives its name to a wider district, or the name indicates the sole or principal grape variety used, e.g., Barbera, Verdicchio. If the grape is common it is further defined by a place name, e.g., Barbera d'Alba, Verdicchio dei Castelli de Jesi. And there are a few examples of purely historical names, such as Est! Est! Est!

THE PRODUCER'S NAME   Sometimes simply the name of the producer and the town; often they are prefixed with *produttori* (producers), *cantine* (cellars), *cantina sociale* (cooperative producer), *casa vinicola* (wine house), *tenuta* (estate).

D.O.C.   *Denominazione di Origine Controllata,* the national guarantee of genuineness, found on the main label over or under the wine name.

VINTAGES   On the main label or a shoulder label; *annata* means "year," and *vendemmia* means "vintage."

GROWER'S CONSORTIA SEALS   The seal label of a consortium still appears as a sign of careful control. This is printed on a strip of paper, usually at the top of the neck, across the edge of the foil cork cover. It may have a space for a bottle number, which indicates strictly limited production.

BOTTLING   Bottling usually takes place in or near the production area. This is indicated by the producers, e.g., *imbottigliato* (bottled) or *infiascato* (put in flasks) *or in zona stabilimento* (at the producer's premises).

DESCRIPTIVE WORDS   Words such as *extra, fine, selezionato* are forbidden by law. Under D.O.C. regulations, *vecchio* (old) *riserva* (reserve) guarantee aging.

CLASSICO   Used after the wine's name, e.g., Soave *Classico* means that the wine comes from the original heartland of a production area.

SUPERIORE   Soave Classico *Superiore* indicates that the wine has a slightly higher natural alcoholic content and, for some varieties, has been aged longer than the same wine without the *Superiore* designation.

THE MEANING OF CHIANTI CLASSICO

Chianti Classico (Classical Chianti) is that Chianti wine production, as defined by Italian Law, in which the Italian government has examined the vineyards in the Chianti Classico area and has admitted them for listing in the register of Chianti Classico. Only those vineyards that, due to the quality of their vines and the position of their land, are regarded as suitable for growing the very best grapes are registered.

Chianti Classico wine may be produced solely from grapes provided by vineyards listed in the register. In the Chianti Classico area, the production of grapes per acre of land allowed by the government is lower than the one allowed for other Chianti areas. As a consequence, the minimum alcoholic content of the Chianti Classico wine is higher (12%).

The "Black Rooster" is given only to Chianti Classico wine controlled by the technical departments of the Association of Classico Vineyards. It is the consumers' guarantee of a superior wine.

ITALY, EMILIA ROMAGNA

producer: A.V.F.F.-S.n.c.
classification: Red varietal table wine
grape variety: Lambrusco

Mazzoni Lambrusco is a fruity wine with an intense bouquet. To the eye, it is fresh and lively, with an effervescent sparkle. The wine can be enjoyed as soon as it is bottled, which is generally six months after the grape harvest.   **price range:** A

producer: Barone
classification: Red table wine
grape variety: Lambrusco
district: Lambrusco D.O.C.

Pleasant, fruity bouquet; a mellow, full-bodied, and mildly effervescent Lambrusco, soft and delicious.   **price range:** A

producer: Nando Cavalli & Figli
classification: Red sparkling wine
grape variety: Lambrusco
district: Lambrusco D.O.C.
city or village: Scandiano
Naturally fermented.
Deep red color and a fruity bouquet. The wine is slightly effervescent from natural fermentation and is best drunk chilled.
price range: A

producer: C.I.V.
classification: Red sparkling wine
grape variety: Lambrusco
district: Modena
A slight crackle makes Lambrusco one of the "fun wines" of today.
Clear red color and a fruity bouquet. The wine is semi-dry. **price range:** A

producer: C.I.V.
classification: Red sparkling wine
grape variety: Lambrusco
district: Lambrusco de Sorbara
city or village: Modena
A happy wine for pleasure without pretense, Lambrusco is an Italian wine for many American palates. **price range:** A

producer: Adolfo Donelli & Figlio
classification: Red table wine
grape variety: Lambrusco
district: Lambrusco D.O.C.
A Lambrusco of the *amabile* (sweet) type

that has achieved great popularity in America, though it is not widely consumed in Italy, Italians preferring a *secco* (dry) wine.
Ruby-red color and a plush, flowery bouquet. The wine is sweet and full, with a lingering flavor; it has an "attitude" and a high incidence of sparkle that continues even after bottling, especially if the grapes come from the Sorbara district, assures the wine of instant popularity. **price range:** A

producer: Florio
classification: Red table wine
grape variety: Chiefly Lambrusco
This is a fruity and pleasingly sweet red wine. Its slight sparkle and intense bouquet contribute to its jubilant character. **price range:** A

producer: Fratelli Folonari
classification: Red table wine
grape variety: Lambrusco
district: Lambrusco D.O.C.
city or village: Bologna–Sorbara
Folonari Lambrusco is one of the few Lambruscos in which the sparkle is achieved naturally by halting fermentation—not by adding carbon dioxide, as is the case with many wines of its type. It is a "fun" wine.
Purplish-red color; a fruity, grapey bouquet. The wine is slightly sparkling, or *frizzante*, and is very refreshing; it is fruity and quite full-bodied.
price range: B (2-liter bottle)

producer: Vinicola Logoluso
classification: Red table wine
grape variety: Lambrusco
district: Lambrusco di Sorbara D.O.C.
A light, fruity, and sweet red wine.
price range: A

producer: I. L. Ruffino
classification: Red sparkling wine
grape variety: Lambrusco Reggiano

ITALY, LATIUM

producer: Marchesi L. & P. Antinori
classification: White table wine
grape variety: Trebbiano
district: EST! EST! EST! D.O.C.
city or village: Montefiascone
A fruity, elegant dry white wine.
price range: B

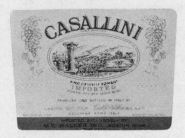

producer: Cantina Soc. Coop. "Colli Albani" s.r.l.
classification: Red table wine
This wine is dry and red.
price range: A

producer: Fattoria Pavan
classification: Red table wine
grape variety: Malvasia, Trebbiano, Bonvino, and Bellone

district: Lambrusco D.O.C.
The sparkle in this Lambrusco is produced by natural fermentation and produces a pink froth when the wine is served. A high sugar content is balanced by a high acidity.
Deep ruby-purple color with violet undertones and a strong, vinous, and very fruity bouquet with a characteristic fragrance. The wine is fruity, semi-dry, and harmonious. **price range:** A

This wine was essentially unknown in the United States before Rolar made it generally available. It is produced in accordance with ancient traditions of vinification. Estate-bottled.
A delightful, fine light table wine.
price range: B

producer: Fattoria Pavan
classification: White table wine
grape variety: Malvasia, Trebbiano, Bonvino, and Bellone
Estate-bottled.
Pale straw color and a delicate bouquet. The wine is dry, with a pleasant slight bitter touch. It is excellent with appetizers, soup, veal, poultry, cheese, and egg dishes; best served cold. **price range:** B

producer: Fontana Candida
classification: White table wine
grape variety: Malvasia Rosso
district: Frascati D.O.C.
city or village: Frascati
Fontana Candida Frascati is shipped in air-conditioned containers and is sold only when the new vintage is available. It is the freshest Italian wine available in America, and is easy for three people to drink at a single sitting. Always the latest vintage is available.
Very light, almost white in color, with light green hues, and a fruity, "peppery" bouquet. The wine is clean, dry, and low in acid; it is very easy to drink. **price range:** A

producer: Fratelli Polatti
classification: White table wine
grape variety: Nebbiolo
district: Valtellina
city or village: Sondrio

"Bianco di Montagna" is made from red Nebbiolo grapes grown in Lombardy, just east of Piedmont, in northern Italy. It has no regional Valtellina D.O.C. designation because it does not fit the category for red wines of this district, but it is grown in and around the Inferno, Sassella, and Valgella vineyards. The name of the wine is a proprietary brand belonging to Fratelli Polatti.

Green-gold color and a full, soft straw-like bouquet. The wine is full-bodied and dry and has a clean, crisp flavor. It is one of the more interesting and full-bodied white wines Italy has to offer. **price range:** B

producer: Masieri–San Carlo–Chiro
classification: Red table wine
grape variety: Chiavennasca (Nebbiolo)
district: Valtellina Superior D.O.C.
city or village: Chiuro

Ruby-red color with a characteristic persistent bouquet. The wine is dry and slightly tannic. **price range:** A

producer: Nino Negri
classification: White table wine
grape variety: Pinot, with a small quantity of Riesling
district: Valtellina
city or village: Sondrio

This very interesting white wine combines the complexity of the Pinot and the softness of Riesling. Alcohol 12.25% by volume.

Pale yellow color with greenish tinges; a delicate and fruity bouquet. The wine is dry, well-balanced, and has a pronounced aftertaste; a robust white wine.
price range: B

producer: Nino Negri
classification: Red table wine
grape variety: Nebbiolo
district: Valtellina D.O.C.
city or village: Sondrio

"Fracia" is produced exclusively by Nino Negri; 12.5% alcohol.

Ruby-red color, inclining to garnet; a deep, delicate, and fruity bouquet. The wine tastes dry and is characteristically tannic when young. **price range:** B

producer: Nino Negri
classification: Red table wine
grape variety: Nebbiolo
district: Valtellina D.O.C.
city or village: Sondrio

"Sfursat" is produced exclusively by Nino Negri. The grapes are picked during the harvest and are left to dry until the end of January, at which time they are crushed and fermented. The wine is then aged for at least three years—two in cask—before being sold. It is usually a big wine; with 14% alcohol.

Deep red color and an elegant bouquet, with lots of fruit. The wine is complex, dry, and has great depth; it is especially recommended for game and roasts.
price range: B

producer: Nino Negri
classification: Red table wine
grape variety: Nebbiolo
district: Valtellina (Inferno) D.O.C.
city or village: Sondrio

Ruby-red color, with pomegranate tinges; the bouquet is delicate and complex. The wine is quite dry and has a tannic finish; it is harmonious and reminds one of hazelnuts. It is a wine for roasted or grilled meats. **price range:** B

producer: A. Rainoldi
classification: Red table wine
grape variety: Nebbiolo
district: Valtellina (Inferno) D.O.C.
city or village: Sondrio

Inferno is the most robust of the wines from the Valtellina district, produced from vines that grow on the steep banks of the River Adda. The style of wines as regards bouquet, structure, and depth is similar to the wines of the Médoc but with a characteristic flavor of Nebbiolo.

Dark red color and a nutty, vinous, and woody bouquet. Valtellinas are tannic when young but develop a refined, gentle quality with three to five years' bottle age. This Inferno is medium-bodied, austere, and slightly intense in its youth.
price range: B

producer: A. Rainoldi
classification: Red table wine
grape variety: Nebbiolo
district: Valtellina (Sassella) D.O.C.
city or village: Sondrio

The characteristics of Sassella lie in between those of Inferno and Grumello: long life and intense, heady bouquet; full body; and refined Nebbiolo flavor.

Light ruby color and a direct, vinous bouquet that has some nut and wood character. The wine is medium-bodied and has good depth of flavor. **price range:** B

producer: A. Rainoldi
classification: Red table wine
grape variety: Nebbiolo
district: Valtellina (Grumello) D.O.C.
city or village: Sondrio

Grumello is a slightly lighter wine than Inferno or Sassella, but has more fruit and intensity. The style of wines as regards bouquet, structure, and depth is similar to the wines of the Médoc but with a characteristic flavor of Nebbiolo. The vineyards of the Valtellina district are in northern Italy, east of Piedmont, near Lake Como, on the steep banks of the River Adda.

Dark red color and a pungent, nutty bouquet. The wine is medium-bodied and slightly austere when young, and finishes well. It possesses clean Nebbiolo flavor and develops complexity and refinement with bottle age. **price range:** B

producer: A. Rainoldi
classification: Red table wine
grape variety: Nebbiolo
district: Valtellina (Valgella) D.O.C.
city or village: Sondrio

Valgella is a slightly lighter wine than the other Valtellinas, produced from vineyards on the steep banks of the River Adda. The style of wines as regards bouquet, structure, and depth is similar to the wines of the Médoc but with a characteristic flavor of Nebbiolo. The vineyards are in northern Italy, east of Piedmont, near Lake Como.

Dark red color and a soft, vinous bouquet that is gentle and refined. The wine has medium-light body and Nebbiolo flavor; it is vivacious and gently tannic when young, and shows delicate warmth, finesse, and complexity with further bottle aging.
price range: B

producer: I. L. Ruffino
classification: White table wine
grape variety: Trebbiano di Lugana
district: Lugana D.O.C.
village: Lugana

Lugana is produced only in small quantities and has an appealing personality. It should be drunk young to appreciate its freshness.

Light straw color with green reflections and a delicate, characteristic bouquet. The wine tastes dry and is medium-bodied, with a slightly "steely" finish.
price range: B

producer: Azienda Vinicola Castelfiora
classification: Red table wine
grape variety: Sangiovese, Canaiolo, Trebbiano, and Mamolo
district: Monte Conero (Rosso Conero D.O.C.)
city or village: Ancona
1971 Vintage.
Light ruby-red color and a delicate bouquet suggesting almonds. A subtle, superior wine with roasted and/or broiled meats, game, and lamb; serve slightly chilled. **price range:** B

"O thou invisible spirit of wine!"
—Shakespeare, *Othello*

producer: Azienda Vinicola Umani Ronchi
classification: White table wine
grape variety: Verdiso, Malvasia, and Trebbiano
district: Castelli di Jesi
city or village: Osimo Scalo
This wine is produced on the hillsides in the classic Verdicchio-producing zone overlooking the Adriatic Sea.
Light color with greenish overtones and a delicate bouquet. This fresh, crisp wine is a perfect complement to fish.
price range: A

producer: Cantina Sociale di Cupramontana
classification: White table wine
grape variety: Verdicchio
district: Verdicchio Classico dei Castelli di Jesi D.O.C.
city or village: Cupramontana
Delicate straw color with greenish hues; a delicate and fruity bouquet. This dry, well-balanced wine has a pleasant, astringent aftertaste; it can be enjoyed by itself or with antipasto and fish dishes.
price range: B

producer: Casa Vinicola Fratelli Tombolini
classification: White table wine
grape variety: Verdicchio
district: Verdicchio dei Castelli di Jesi Classico D.O.C.
city or village: Ancona
Won diploma and gold medal at the second Esposizione Bevande Europa (E.B.E.) in Milano, as the best of its type. Shipped in an amphora bottle.
Pale straw color and a full bouquet with a touch of austerity. The wine is full and dry.
price range: A

producer: Fazi-Battaglia
classification: White table wine
city or village: Ancona
This is a dry, light, pale gold wine.
This is the Verdicchio that is in the original and distinctive amphora bottle with the descriptive scroll attached to the neck.
price range: B

producer: Florio
classification: White varietal table wine
grape variety: Verdicchio
district: Castelli di Jesi
This is a delightfully dry, well-balanced wine of golden color.
The wine is bottled in an amphora-shaped bottle. **price range:** B

ITALY, PIEDMONT

producer: Luigi Calissano & Figli
classification: Red table wine
grape variety: Nebbiolo
district: Barolo D.O.C.
city or village: Alba
A "Riserva Speciale" Barolo that is softer and bigger than most others available in the United States. The wine was vinified "soft," especially for American, Swiss, and French palates. Luigi Calissano & Figli has three million bottles of Barolo from Murra, the largest library in Barolo, with the greatest supply of vintages, cuvées, and quality.
Red, almost opaque color, with some red-brown hues; a bouquet of violets, tar, and earth. The wine is big, mouth-filling with high acidity—it wears well after a few sips. **price range:** B

producer: Cantina Sociale Canelli
classification: White varietal table wine
grape variety: Muscat (Moscato)
district: Asti
city or village: Canelli
This particular wine is produced by one of Asti's oldest *cantinas* (producers), and although it is generally not known in America, it ranks with the best Muscats from other areas.
Clear, sparkling straw color and a sweet Muscat bouquet. The wine is semi-dry, sprightly, and has a lingering aftertaste.
price range: B

producer: Cantina Sociale Vallebelbo
classification: White table wine
grape variety: Moscato d'Asti
district: Asti
city or village: S. Stefano Belbo
This still wine is the nonsparking version of the much better-known Asti Spumante. It has the lowest alcoholic content of any quality still wine produced in this region.
Pale clear color and a light, flowery, and grapey bouquet. The wine has a slight *petillant* (crackling) quality and is quite sweet and refreshing. **price range:** A

producer: Cantina "Terre del Barolo"
classification: Red table wine
grape variety: Nebbiolo
district: Nebbiolo d'Alba D.O.C.
city or village: Roddi, Diano, and Grinzane
Dark ruby-red color and an austere, aromatic bouquet. Though rough at first, the wine softens after three years.
price range: B

producer: Cantina "Terre del Barolo"
classification: Red table wine
grape variety: Nebbiolo
district: Barolo D.O.C.
city or village: Barolo
Deep red color and a bouquet of violets and/or tar; when aged, of faded roses. This velvety, full-bodied wine has a dry, almost austere taste, but it is rich and harmonious.
price range: B

producer: Cantina "Terre del Barolo"
classification: Red table wine
grape variety: Barbera
district: Barbera d'Alba D.O.C.
city or village: Monforte and La Morra
Ruby-red color and a bouquet similar to a Barolo, like violets. The wine is full-bodied and robust with a slight earth flavor—dry, genuine, and strong.
price range: B

producer: Cantina "Terre del Barolo"
classification: Red table wine
grape variety: Dolcetto
district: Dolcetto d'Alba D.O.C.
city or village: Diano d'Alba and Grinzane
A typical Piedmontese wine.
A bouquet of violets and a very slightly sweet *amabile* taste characteristic of Dolcetto. **price range:** B

producer: Pi. Gi. Pi. Castagnole Lanze
classification: Red sparkling wine

A sparkling wine that comes with a reusable cap right on the bottle. After removing the cork, the bottle can be resealed over and over. The wine contains 9% alcohol by volume.

Clear, bright red color; a bubbly, big, fruity "take anywhere" wine. **price range: A**

"Taste cannot be controlled by law." —Thomas Jefferson

producer: Pi. Gi. Pi. Castagnole Lanze
classification: White sparkling wine

A sparkling wine that comes with a reusable cap right on the bottle. After removing the cork, the bottle can be resealed over and over. The wine contains 9% alcohol by volume.

A big, fruity Asti Spumante-type wine; being bubbly, it is a wine for all life styles, but is not a "pop" wine. **price range: A**

producer: Cossano Belbo
classification: White sparkling wine
grape variety: Muscat Cavelli
district: Asti
city or village: Cossano Pielbo

This deep yellow Asti Spumante has a distinct Muscat "nose," with a slight bouquet of yeast. To the palate it is slightly sweet, with the distinct flavor of the Muscat grape. **price range: A**

producer: Cossano Belbo
classification: Red varietal sparkling wine
grape variety: Lambrusco
district: Asti
city or village: Cossano Belbo

This deep red sparkling wine is fruity and slightly sweet. **price range: A**

producer: Duretto & Co.
classification: White sparkling wine
grape variety: Moscato
district: Asti Spumante D.O.C.
city or village: Cossano Belbo

This Asti Spumante is mainly exported to the United Kingdom.

Light yellow color and a sweet Muscat aroma. The wine is sparkling and fruity and is suitable for any occastion—it is particularly good with sweets. **price range: B**

producer: F.lli Gancia & Cia.
classification: Red sparkling wine
grape variety: Nebbiolo

This light, semi-sweet, clean-tasting wine has a delicate bouquet. It is a delight with any entrée, roast or game.

The wine is bottle-fermented and should be served well-chilled. **price range: C**

producer: F.lli Gancia & Cia.
classification: White sparkling wine
grape variety: Moscato de Canelli
city or village: Asti

This bright, clear, pale gold sparkling wine has a semi-sweet taste and a distinctive, aromatic bouquet. It is delicious with any course in a meal or, with a dash of

bitters and an orange slice, makes a splendid cocktail.

The wine has the taste of "icy grapes" and is less sweet than most other Asti Spumantes, making it extremely pleasant to the American palate. **price range: C**

producer: Florio
classification: White sparkling wine
grape variety: Moscato
district: South of Turin
city or village: Asti

This is a sweet, light wine, delightful with sweets or fruits. It has a country-fresh aroma and a beautiful straw-colored sparkle. **price range: C**

producer: Fontanafredda
classification: Red table wine
grape variety: Nebbiolo
district: Barolo D.O.C.
city or village: Barolo

Sold always with a vintage date.

Deep ruby color and a full bouquet. The wine is dry, full-bodied, and tannic; it goes well with red meat, prepared dishes, game, and cheese. Serve at room temperature. **price range: C**

producer: Fontanafredda
classification: White sparkling wine
grape variety: Moscato
district: Asti Spumante D.O.C.
city or village: Asti

Naturally fermented in the bottle.

Very pale, fresh gold color and a good Moscato bouquet. The wine is semi-dry on the palate. **price range: B**

producer: Francesco Cinzano & Cia.
classification: White sparkling wine

grape variety: Pinot Bianco and Pinot Grigio (Pinot Gris)
district: Torino

"Cinzano Brut Reserve Spumante" is made only in selected years although a vintage date is not specified. It is produced only in limited quantities and carries the designation Denominazione di Origine *Semplice* (simple).

Light straw color and a pleasant, clean bouquet. The wine is dry, well-balanced, and light-bodied; it has a good aftertaste. **price range: C**

producer: Franco
classification: Red table wine
grape variety: Nebbiolo
district: Barolo D.O.C.

This wine is aged in oak casks.

A pomegranate red color, taking on slightly orange reflections. The bouquet is rich, recalling the aroma of violets and roses. The wine is dry, rich, and full-bodied—vigorous yet harmonious. It is an exquisite wine for red meat, roasts, and all game. Open the bottle several hours before serving at room temperature. **price range: C**

producer: Franco
classification: Red table wine
grape variety: Nebbiolo
district: Barbaresco D.O.C.

This wine is aged in oak casks.

Orange-tinted pomegranate-red color and a characteristic ethereal bouquet. The wine is full and dry, with a vigorous flavor; it is excellent with roasts, smoked meats, venison, and liver pâté. Uncork several hours before serving at room temperature. **price range: C**

producer: Franco
classification: Red varietal table wine
grape variety: Nebbiolo

A table wine suitable for general use. Seductive ruby-red color and a gentle bouquet. The wine is fresh and dry; be sure to uncork it at least one hour before serving at room temperature. **price range: B**

producer: Franco
classification: Red varietal table wine
grape variety: Dolcetto

Clear ruby-red color; the wine has a subtle fresh taste, is dry and light, with low acidity. It is a superior table wine that is most pleasant with sausages, salami, and smoked meats. Be sure to uncork the bottle at least one hour before serving at room temperature. **price range: B**

producer: Franco
classification: Red varietal table wine
grape variety: Barbera

The wine is aged in oak casks and may contain sediment; if so, decanting is required.

Pomegranate-red color and an excellent bouquet. The wine is dry, rich, and full-bodied; it is most appropriate with roasts. Be sure to open the bottle several hours before serving at room temperature. **price range: B**

producer: Franco
classification: Red varietal table wine
grape variety: Grignolino

Grignolino wines are produced in a very limited quantity and are suitable for moderate aging.

Beautiful light ruby-red color and a pleasing bouquet reminiscent of roses. The wine is dry, with an almost imperceptible but agreeable bitter touch. It is light, fine, and harmonious; it will enhance any meal, yet is particularly appropriate with fowl. Be sure to let the wine breathe at least one hour before serving at room temperature. **price range: B**

producer: Franco
classification: Red varietal table wine
grape variety: Barbera
district: Barbera d'Asti D.O.C.
city or village: Near Asti

Suitable as a universal table wine.

Beautiful pomegranate-red color deepening with age; a noble and generous wine of dry and harmonious taste. Uncork the bottle at least one hour before serving at room temperature. **price range: B**

producer: Franco
classification: White sparkling wine
grape variety: Muscat
district: Asti Spumante D.O.C.
city or village: Asti

A welcome guest at parties and festive occasions.

Light color and a fragrant bouquet. The wine is sweet and delightful, with long-lasting froth. It should be served very cold, about 40 degrees F. **price range: B**

producer: Franco
classification: Red table wine
grape variety: Nebbiolo (Spanna)
district: Novara Hills
city or village: Near Vercelli

Produced in limited quantities, this wine is suitable for aging.

Bright ruby color, becoming brick red with time and then turning to a clear orange. The bouquet suggests roses and violents when mature. The wine is smooth, well-balanced, and full; Spanna is preferred by some to Barolo, being lighter and more delicate. It is excellent with roasts and game; aerate for at least one hour at room temperature before serving. **price range: B**

producer: Franco
classification: White sparkling wine
grape variety: Pinot Bianco (Pinot Blanc)
Brut Spumante
Naturally fermented.

Tiny bubbles and a delicate bouquet. The wine is dry and superbly refined, a perfect complement to festive dining. Should be served cold, about 40 degrees F. **price range: C**

producer: Guido Giri
classification: Red varietal table wine
grape variety: Dolcetto
district: Dolcetto d'Alba D.O.C.
city or village: Cuneo

Brilliant red color and a fresh, intense bouquet. The wine is dry and is excellent with all kinds of food. **price range: B**

producer: Guido Giri
classification: Red varietal table wine
grape variety: Barbera
district: Barbera d'Alba D.O.C.
city or village: Cuneo

Deep red color and an intense bouquet typical of Barbera. Very dry, this is an excellent wine to be served with all kinds of food. **price range: B**

producer: Guido Giri
classification: Red varietal table wine
grape variety: Nebbiolo
district: Nebbiolo d'Alba D.O.C.
city or village: Cuneo

This wine is made from the same grapes as Barolo and Barbaresco; in comparison, however, it is much lighter.

Ruby-red color and an intense varietal bouquet. Very dry, this wine is excellent with all meats, especially so with cheese. **price range: B**

producer: Guido Giri
classification: Red varietal table wine
grape variety: Grignolino
district: Grignolino d'Alba D.O.C.
city or village: Cuneo

Grignolino wines are characteristically light in color; this is the lightest of their wines.

Clear, red color and a delicate but intense bouquet. Quite dry, this wine is excellent with meats, fish, and chicken but can be served with all foods because of its delicate and full body. **price range: B**

producer: Guido Giri
classification: Red table wine
grape variety: Nebbiolo
district: Barolo D.O.C.
city or village: Cuneo

The life of this superior red wine depends on the quality of the vintage.

Red color, with orange tinges, and a very intense Nebbiolo bouquet. The wine is very dry, full, and round; it would be excellent with roasts and game. **price range: C**

producer: Guido Giri
classification: Red table wine
grape variety: Nebbiolo
district: Barbaresco D.O.C.
city or village: Cuneo

Barbaresco differs from Barolo chiefly in aroma, which in the former is more delicate. The life of this superior wine depends on the quality of the vintage.

Red color, with orange tinges, and a very intense bouquet. The wine is very dry, full, and round; it would be excellent with roasts and game. **price range: C**

producer: I.R.V.A.S. S.p.A.
classification: Sparkling wine
city or village: Asti

This is a naturally fermented, sweet sparkling wine. **price range: A**

producer: Italivini Ltd.
classification: White sparkling wine
grape variety: Pinot Bianco
district: Cuneo
city or village: Canale

This unusually dry sparkling wine is produced by the *cuve close* method, and is fermented slowly for about eight weeks. It is sealed with a natural cork closure.

Light straw color and a bouquet characteristic of Pinot. The wine is dry and does not have the typical aftertaste of so many Italian sparkling wines. **price range: B**

producer: Italivini
classification: White sparkling wine
grape variety: Moscato
district: Cuneo
city or village: Canale

This medium sweet sparkling wine is produced by the *cuve close* method, with slow fermentation lasting about eight weeks. It is sealed with a natural cork closure.

Straw color and a Muscat bouquet. The wine is medium sweet, with the typical taste of the grape, and is well-balanced. **price range: B**

producer: L.C.&F. S.p.A.
classification: White sparkling wine
grape variety: Moscato d'Asti
district: Asti Spumante D.O.C.
city or village: Alba

Ready to drink when shipped.

Straw color and an aromatic bouquet. It is a fragrant, sweet sparkling dessert wine. **price range: B**

producer: Martini & Rossi
classification: White sparkling wine
grape variety: Moscato
district: Asti Spumante D.O.C.
city or village: Chieri
price range: B

producer: G. & F. Orsolani
classification: White sparkling wine
grape variety: Moscato
district: Asti Spumante D.O.C.
price range: B

producer: Torre dei Conti
classification: White sparkling wine
grape variety: Moscato
district: Asti Spumante D.O.C.
city or village: Canelli

Yellow color and a sweet bouquet. The wine is soft and delicious on the palate, and although sweet, does not leave an aftertaste like so many other Spumantes. It is extremely good when consumed well chilled, either by itself or with desserts. **price range: B**

producer: A. Vallana & Figlio
classification: Red table wine
grape variety: Nebbiolo (Spanna)
district: Gattinara D.O.C.
city or village: Maggiora

Cantina del Camino is the fourth finest of the six wine estates owned by Vallana in and around the township of Gattinara. Vallana, recognized throughout the world as one of the finest producers of Gattinara, prefers to call his wines "Spanna," according to the local name for the Nebbiolo in the Novara Hills district. Although almost all the Vallana estates are within the Gattinara D.O.C. zone, Spanna has not yet received a D.O.C. classification, and hence these wines are not sold under the D.O.C. seal.

Medium-dark ruby color and a soft, well-perfumed bouquet that is typical of Nebbiolo wines. The wine has medium body, medium tannin, and tastes soft with good fruit. It is warm and quite gentle on the palate and has a lovely berry aroma and flavor. **price range: B**

producer: A. Vallana & Figlio
classification: Red table wine

grape variety: Nebbiolo (Spanna)
district: Gattinara D.O.C.
city or village: Maggiora

Cinque Castelli is one of the six estates owned by Vallana in the township of Gattinara, and is the lightest of the Spannas produced by A. Vallana. Vallana is recognized throughout the world as one of the finest producers of Spanna/Gattinara.

Medium ruby color and a bouquet with medium intensity and good Nebbiolo character. The wine is medium-bodied and soft, with moderate tannin, notable Gattinara character, and a lingering finish. **price range: B**

producer: A. Vallana & Figlio
classification: Red table wine
grape variety: Nebbiolo (Spanna)
district: Gattinara D.O.C.
city or village: Maggiora

San Lorenzo is Vallana's third-finest estate among the six he owns in and around the township of Gattinara. It is a straightforward wine with slightly less "tar" than Montalbano, and has long aging possibilities. Vallana is recognized throughout the world as one of the finest producers of Gattinara and Spanna.

Dark ruby color and a rich, soft, elegant bouquet. The wine is full-bodied and sturdy, with medium tannin; soft and harmonious. **price range: B**

producer: A. Vallana & Figlio
classification: Red table wine
grape variety: Nebbiolo (Spanna)
district: Gattinara D.O.C.
city or village: Maggiora

Campi Raudii is Vallana's finest estate among the six he owns in and around the township of Gattinara. It is the finest Gattinara in its style, and perhaps the most-prized wine produced in Italy. It is superbly balanced, whether five, ten, or twenty years old, and is exceptionally long-lived.

A very dark ruby-red color and a rich, intense, and complex bouquet suggesting cherries. The wine is thick, big, complex, and very powerful. **price range: B**

producer: A. Vallana & Figlio
classification: Red table wine
grape variety: Nebbiolo (Spanna)
district: Gattinara D.O.C.
city or village: Maggiora

Traversagna is Vallana's second-finest wine estate among the six he owns in and around the township of Gattinara.

Very dark ruby color and a rich, intense tarry bouquet. The wine has huge body and is quite tannic, intense, and woody. It is an austere-styled Spanna, becoming mellow with appropriate wood aging.
price range: B

producer: A. Vallana & Figlio
classification: Red table wine
grape variety: Nebbiolo (Spanna)
district: Gattinara D.O.C.
city or village: Maggiora

Montalbano is one of the six estates owned by Vallana, who has received fifty gold medals and honorable mentions at international exhibitions held throughout Europe.

A very dark ruby color and a bouquet suggesting rich raspberries—slightly pungent and earthy. The wine is big, chewy, and mouth-filling, with roundness and good fruit. It is a masculine wine with intense flavor.
price range: B

bodied and soft, a supreme example of the finest estate-bottled Chianti Classicos.
price range: C

producer: Marchesi L. & P. Antinori
classification: Red table wine
grape variety: Sangiovese, Canaiolo, Malvasia, and Trebbiano
district: Chianti Classico D.O.C.

An estate-bottled Chianti Classico from Antinori's Santa Cristina estate.

A full-flavored, bold red wine.
price range: B

producer: Marchesi L. & P. Antinori
classification: White table wine
grape variety: Trebbiano and Malvasia

"Bianco di Toscana," a white Tuscan table wine.

A dry, golden, and full-bodied white wine.
price range: B

producer: Marchesi L. & P. Antinori
classification: White table wine

A light, fruity, and medium dry white wine shipped in a unique fish-shaped bottle.
price range: B

producer: Bertolli-Alivar S.p.A.
classification: Red table wine

grape variety: Sangiovese, Canaiolo, Malvasia, and Trebbiano
district: Chianti D.O.C.

Brilliant red color and fruity bouquet. A dry and tart red wine.   **price range:** B

producer: Bertolli-Alivar S.p.A.
classification: Red table wine
grape variety: Sangiovese, Canaiolo, Malvasia, and Trebbiano
district: Chianti Classico D.O.C.

Medium red color and a flowery bouquet. The wine is dry and tart.
price range: B

producer: Buitoni
classification: Red table wine
grape variety: Sangiovese, Canaiolo, and Trebbiano
district: Chianti Classico Riserva D.O.C.
city or village: Greve
price range: B

ITALY, TUSCANY

producer: Marchesi L. & P. Antinori
classification: Red table wine
grape variety: Sangiovese, Canaiolo, Trebbiano, and Malvasia
district: Chianti Classico D.O.C.

A superior Chianti Classico, estate-bottled.

Generous bouquet and soft, full-bodied flavor.   **price range:** B

A superior white table wine, estate-bottled.

Generous bouquet and soft, full-bodied flavor.   **price range:** B

producer: Marchesi L. & P. Antinori
classification: White sparkling wine
grape variety: Trebbiano and Malvasia

Produced on the estates of the Marchesi Antinori and renowned in Italy as a top-quality sparkling wine.   **price range:** C

producer: Marchesi L. & P. Antinori
classification: Red table wine
grape variety: Sangiovese, Canaiolo, Trebbiano, and Malvasia
district: Chianti Classico D.O.C.

A superior Chianti Classico, reserved from the best grades of Villa Antinori Chianti and aged in bottle for an additional five years.

Generous bouquet; the wine is full-

producer: Marchesi L. & P. Antinori
classification: White table wine
grape variety: Sangiovese, Canaiolo, Malvasia, and Trebbiano

producer: Buitoni
classification: Red table wine
grape variety: Sangiovese, Canaiolo, and Trebbiano
district: Chianti D.O.C.
city or village: Greve
price range: B

producer: Cantina Ponte Vecchio
classification: White table wine
grape variety: Trebbiano and others
district: Chianti
city or village: Rufina

The cellars of the Ponte Vecchio Cantina have been in the family of the present owner, Carlo Bellini, for many generations.

Slight straw color and an aromatic bouquet. The wine is semi-dry and should be served cold with fish or broiled meat.
price range: B

producer: Cantina Ponte Vecchio
classification: Red table wine
grape variety: Sangiovese, Malvasia, Canaiolo, and Trebbiano
district: Chianti D.O.C.
city or village: Rufina

The Cantina Ponte Vecchio produces some of the best Chianti wines. The vineyards are situated in hilly country composed essentially of marl, and this particular physical-chemical combination gives particular kinds of grapes that are transformed into superior wine by art handed down from generation to generation. The Bellini firm originated many years ago and was one of the first members of the Consorzio Chianti Putto, created in 1927 in order to promote genuine Chianti wines and protect them from imitators.

Ruby-red color, turning to brick-red with age, and an intense aroma. The wine is dry, slightly sapid, and tannic; it is suitable for every kind of meat or game, and for the gourmet. It should be served at room temperature.
price range: B

producer: Luigi Cappellini (Verrazzano)
classification: Red table wine
grape variety: Sangiovese, Canaiolo, and Trebbiano
district: Chianti Classico D.O.C.
city or village: Greve

This estate-bottled wine is produced on the same estate where Giovanni da Verrazzano, the great explorer, was born. The castle is still part of the château and win-

ery. The wine is bottled only in Bordeaux-shaped bottles and has about 12.5% alcohol.

Lively ruby-red color and a characteristically fruity bouquet reminiscent of violets. The wine is harmonious, dry, well-balanced, and slightly tannic.
price range: B

producer: Casa Vinicola dei Conti Serristori
classification: Red table wine
grape variety: Sangiovese, Trebbiano, Canaiolo Nero, and Malvasia
district: Chianti Putto D.O.C. (Colli Fiorentini)
city or village: S. Andrea in Percussina

The vineyard was established and is still owned by the Serristori family, descendents of Niccolò Machiavelli.

Ruby-red color and a fruity bouquet. This light and fragrant red wine is made to be consumed young, but it has sufficient body to mellow with age.
price range: B

"Bronze is the mirror of the form; wine, of the heart."
—Aeschylus

producer: Casa Vinicola dei Conti Serristori
classification: White table wine
grape variety: Trebbiano Toscano and Greco
district: S. Casciano Val di Pesa
city or village: S. Andrea in Percussina

The vineyards and property were established by the scholar Niccolò Machiavelli in the fifteenth century, and the property has been in continuous production ever since. Previously called White Chianti, Bianco Toscana is now the official name for the regional white wine of Tuscany.

Straw color and a delicate, fragrant bouquet. The wine is dry, with distinctive fruitiness, and has sufficient character to be recommended as an aperitif and to be served with poultry, fish, and pasta.
price range: B

producer: Chianti Melini, S.A.
classification: Red table wine
grape variety: Sangiovese, Canaiolo, Malvasia, and Trebbiano
district: Chianti D.O.C.

Ruby color and a full bouquet. The wine is earthy; not as full-bodied as one might expect.
price range: B

producer: Chianti Melini S.A.
classification: Red table wine
grape variety: Sangiovese, Canaiolo, Trebbiano, and Malvasia
district: Chianti Classico D.O.C.

A superior Chianti demonstrating the great improvement in the quality of Italian wines.

Ruby color and a fruity bouquet. The wine is fruity, with an earthy finish.
price range: B

producer: Chianti Melini S.A.
classification: White table wine
grape variety: Trebbiano and Malvasia

Called "Bianco Toscana" instead of White Chianti, the latter name no longer being permitted under D.O.C. regulations.

Clear limpid color and a delicate bouquet. The wine is light and dry, with just a touch of body.
price range: B

producer: Coli
classification: Red table wine
grape variety: Sangiovese and Canaiolo (red); Trebbiano and Malvasia (white)
district: Chianti Classico D.O.C.

city or village: Val di Pesa–San Casciano

The area of production for this wine is in the northwestern corner of the Chianti Classico region.

Deep garnet-red color and a casky, violet bouquet. The wine is medium light and brisk, with a most agreeable astringency—it is an exceptionally fine example of one of the world's best wine types.
price range: B

producer: Creazzo—Vi.Co. Certaldo
classification: Red table wine
grape variety: Sangiovese, Canaiolo, Trebbiano Toscano, and Malvasia
district: Chianti Putto D.O.C.

This Chianti Putto D.O.C. is the nearest Chianti in taste and body to the Classico. It bears an infant's picture on the bottle neck. It is not as full-bodied as a Classico (black rooster seal) however, its velvety finish makes it more pleasant for everyday drinking.

Dark bright-red color and a deep, flowery vinous bouquet. The wine is dry and pleasantly balanced, with a velvety finish.
price range: A

producer: Exportvini Toscana S.A.S.
classification: Red table wine
grape variety: Sangiovese

This regional Tuscan wine is produced from grapes grown within the region. The wine is aged twelve months in wood before bottling and is ideal after a year or so. It contains 11½% alcohol by volume.

Clear bright red color and an intense fruity bouquet. The wine is dry, medium-bodied, and very easy to drink.
price range: A

producer: Fattoria Carpineto
classification: Red table wine

grape variety: Sangiovese, Trebbiano, Malvasia, and Canaiolo
district: Chianti Classico D.O.C.
city or village: Greve

Ruby-red color, tending to garnet with age. The bouquet is intense but delicate, and the wine is slightly tannic and dry. It would be perfect to accompany meat-based dishes and should be uncorked an hour or two before serving at room temperature. **price range:** B

producer: Fattoria di Nozzole
classification: Red table wine
grape variety: Sangiovese, Canaiolo, Trebbiano, Malvasia, and Colorino
district: Chianti Classico D.O.C.
city or village: Greve

Nozzole Chianti is available only in outstanding vintages and is produced in the best part of the strictly defined Chianti region. It is bottled in a Bordeaux-style bottle reserved only for the finest Chianti Classico. The term "Riserva" certifies that the wine has aged for a minimum of three years in oak casks. Nozzole has been a renowned name for Chianti for over seven hundred years, and the wines are estate-bottled.

Deep ruby-red color and a big, mellow bouquet. The wine is elegant, velvety, full-flavored, and characteristically full-bodied Chianti. **price range:** B

producer: Florio
classification: Rosé table wine

This is a fresh, fruity rosé wine of delicate pink color. To the palate it is fresh and light. **price range:** A

producer: Florio
classification: Red table wine
district: Chianti

The wine is shipped in a straw-covered bottle called a *fiasco.*

This dry, full-bodied wine is bursting with a clean, fresh, zesty taste. It is ruby in color. It should be drunk with Italian food and red meats. **price range:** B

producer: Florio
classification: Red table wine
grape variety: Chiefly San Gioveto and Cannaiolo
district: Chianti Classico

The wine comes in a straight bottle without straw wrapping, carrying on its neck the seal of the producers' association, the "Marca Gallo," a white cock on a black target.

This dry, full-bodied wine has a velvety texture and a deeply fragrant bouquet. It is a greatly superior and decidedly different Chianti, enjoyed by connoisseurs for its aged, hearty flavor. The wine should be drunk with red meats and pasta. **price range:** B

producer: Fratelli Folonari
classification: Red table wine
grape variety: Sangiovese, Canaiolo, Trebbiano, and Malvasia
district: Chianti D.O.C.
city or village: Brescia

This wine is available only in 1.50-liter (50.7 oz.) bottles and is priced nationally at under $4. For the price, it is one of the best values in Chianti.

Dark red color and a refreshing bouquet; the wine is light, fruity, and slightly piquant. Serve chilled. **price range:** B

producer: Riccardo Giunti & Figli
classification: White table wine
grape variety: Trebbiano and Malvasia
district: Chianti
city or village: Poggibonsi

A well-balanced dry white wine produced in the Chianti district but not entitled to a D.O.C.

Straw color and a limited bouquet. The wine is dry, with an "almond" finish; it is well-balanced and should be served slightly chilled with hors d'oeuvres or fish. **price range:** B

producer: Machiavelli
classification: Red table wine
grape variety: Sangiovese, Trebbiano, Canaiolo Nero, and Malvasia
district: Chianti Classico D.O.C.
city or village: S. Andrea in Percussina

The property and vineyards were established by the scholar Niccolò Machiavelli in the fifteenth century and have been in continuous production ever since. The Machiavelli home is preserved and has been designated a national monument.

Ruby-red color, turning to garnet with age, and a strong bouquet of violets, becoming delicate with bottle age. The wine is dry, full-bodied, and slightly tannic, becoming velvety with age. It is a complex wine whose character improves and mellows when allowed to age. **price range:** B

producer: Machiavelli
classification: White table wine
grape variety: Trebbiano Toscano and Greco
district: S. Casciano Val di Pesa
city or village: S. Andrea in Percussina

The vineyards and property were established by the scholar Niccolò Machiavelli in the fifteenth century, and the property has been in continuous production ever since. Bianco Toscano, previously called White Chianti, is now the official name for the regional white wine of Tuscany.

Straw color and a delicate, fragrant bouquet. The wine is dry, with distinctive fruitiness, and has sufficient character and body to be drunk with generously seasoned foods. **price range:** A

producer: Masieri—A.G.C. Gaiole in Chianti
classification: Red table wine
grape variety: Sangiovese, Canaiolo, Trebbiano Toscano, and Malvasia
district: Chianti Classico D.O.C.
city or village: Gaiole in Chianti

Dark ruby-red color with a deeply vinous bouquet suggestive of violets. The wine is dry, sapid, full, and slightly tannic. **price range:** A

"If God forbade drinking would He have made wine so good?"
—Cardinal Richelieu

producer: Melini
classification: Red table wine
grape variety: Sangiovese, Canaiolo, Trebbiano, and Malvasia
district: Chianti Classico D.O.C.
city or village: Siena

A superior "Riserva" Chianti comparable to a well-made Bordeaux. It is soft and subtle, capable of standing with the best red wines of Europe.

Red color with brownish hues; some earthy character in the bouquet from bottle aging. The wine is clean and full, with probably the best example of finesse possible in Italian wines. **price range:** B

producer: Melini
classification: Red table wine
grape variety: Sangiovese, Canaiolo, Trebbiano, and Malvasia
district: Chianti Classico D.O.C.
city or village: Siena

Now available in fifths.

Light ruby color with good depth; a fresh, tingly yet earthy bouquet. A delightful, easy-to-drink wine; excellent, with a slight bite. A fine example of Chianti as enjoyed by the Florentines. **price range:** B

producer: Renzo Oliveri, Tenuta Palazzo al Bosco
classification: Red table wine
grape variety: Sangiovese, Canaiolo, Trebbiano, and Malvasia
district: Chianti Classico D.O.C.
city or village: La Romola

The vineyards that comprise Palazzo al Bosco contain a high percentage of older vines; approximately 60% are twelve years old or older. It is a well-established fact in the wine-growing world that grape vines produce wines with more character as the vines age, and adapt themselves to their particular site. The vineyards are tended and the wines are made according to the strict regulation of the Consorzio Vino Chianti Classico. All wines are sold in numbered bottles, which are registered with the Consorzio.

When young (two to three years old), this wine is a brilliant clear ruby. As it ages, the wine deepens in shading and depth of flavor. The aroma develops with proper aging, changing from the fresh fruity aroma to a deep winey bouquet that is characteristic of fine-quality red wines. To the palate the wine is completely dry, full-bodied, and full-flavored. **price range:** B

producer: Renzo Olivieri, Tenuta Palazzo al Bosco
classification: White table wine
grape variety: Trebbiano and Malvasia
district: Firenze
city or village: La Romola

"Bianco Secco" comes from the Chianti district and is made from two of the grape varieties used in the production of red Chianti, but it is not allowed to be called White Chianti as only red wines can be called Chianti under D.O.C. regulations.

Clear, paper-white color and a very crisp, fresh bouquet. The wine is full-flavored, extremely dry and refreshing, with no hint of sweetness. It is excellent with all fish, seafood, poultry, white meats, and sharp cheeses. **price range:** A

producer: Pandolfini
classification: Red table wine
grape variety: Sangiovese and Canaiolo
district: Chianti Classico D.O.C.
city or village: Panzano

A good substitute for higher-priced wines without any sacrifice in quality.

Ruby color, a soft bouquet, and a dry taste. **price range:** A

producer: I. L. Ruffino
classification: Red table wine

"Il Magnifico" was created by Ruffino in honor of Lorenzo de Medici. Lorenzo was head of the famous Medici family during the height of the Italian Renaissance. It is not a D.O.C. wine, and so bears the Denominazione di Origine *semplice* (simple).

Ruby-red color, turning brown with age, and a delicate, pleasant bouquet. The wine is semi-dry, soft, and mellow; a low acidity adds softness to the wine, and slight chilling before serving allows the wine to be properly enjoyed. **price range:** B

producer: I. L. Ruffino
classification: Red table wine
grape variety: Sangiovese (c. 65%), Canaiolo, Malvasia, Trebbiano, and Colorino
district: Chianti D.O.C.

"Riserva Ducale Gold" is produced only in the best vintage years. Skilled pickers select the grapes by hand, and the wine is later bottled after many years of aging in small casks. A high amount of tannin assures long life to the wine.

Brilliant ruby color, turning to brick-red with age; an intense, rich bouquet with a fragrance of violets. The wine is dry, harmonious, and full-bodied; it is particularly stylish and has a long aftertaste. **price range:** D

producer: I. L. Ruffino
classification: Red table wine
grape variety: Sangiovese (c. 65%), Canaiolo, Trebbiano, Malvasia, and Colorino
district: Chianti D.O.C.

"Riserva Ducale" was the favorite wine and source of inspiration to the supreme creative art of the Italian musical genius Giuseppe Verdi. *Riserva* means that by law the wine must remain three years in cask prior to bottling. A high alcoholic strength of 13% and ample tannin assures long life to the wine.

Deep ruby-red color with brown overtones when aged, and a bouquet with intense vinosity—often a rich smell of violets is detected. The wine is clean, harmonious, and soft, with a lingering finish. **price range:** B

producer: I. L. Ruffino
classification: Red table wine
grape variety: Sangiovese (c. 65%), Canaiolo, Trebbiano, and Malvasia
district: Chianti D.O.C.

Chianti Ruffino D.O.C. is marketed when it is two or three years old to assure freshness and characteristic bouquet. The *governo* system of adding a little concentrated grape must to the new wine adds a slight sparkle and freshness to the wine. Recently Ruffino discontinued the use of *fiaschi* (straw-covered bottled) for its Chianti and substituted a new bottle and label for export.

Limpid ruby-red color and a vinous bouquet with characteristic fragrance of young Chianti. The wine is dry, harmonious, and velvety. **price range:** B

producer: I. L. Ruffino
classification: Rosé table wine
grape variety: Blend of red varieties

This is the largest-selling rosé in Italy; it is sold without a vintage date. It must be drunk very young to appreciate its freshness.

Rose to onion-skin color and a pleasant bouquet of moderate intensity. The wine is fresh and slightly fruity; it is medium-bodied and has sufficient acidity to balance its sweetness. **price range:** B

producer: Aldobrando Saccardi
classification: Red table wine
grape variety: Sangiovese and Canaiolo
district: Chianti Classico D.O.C.
city or village: Firenze

The 1973 vintage (non-*Riserva*) was a gold-medal winner at the Lega del Chianti in Castellina for the best Chianti Classico of the 1973 vintage. The family dates back to the fifteenth century, and a monastery on the estate was established in the fourteenth century. The wine was formerly sold only in bulk to other producers and exported to the United States under different names.

Strong, typical bouquet; the wine has good flavor and great depth. In the vintage, the finest of its type. **price range:** B

producer: Aldobrando Saccardi
classification: Red table wine
grape variety: Sangiovese and Canaiolo
district: Chianti Classico D.O.C.
city or village: Firenze

The 1972 Chianti Classico Riserva was awarded a gold medal in the Lega del Chianti gradings. The wine was formerly sold in bulk to major name brands that appear in the United States.

Full, rich bouquet; the wine has good length and a typical flavor. A great bottle of Chianti. **price range:** C

producer: S.E.V.A. S.p.A. Greve
classification: Red table wine
grape variety: Sangiovese, Malvasia, and Trebbiano

This bright ruby-red wine is the best-known and most widely imported product of the Tuscan vineyards. It is dry, intense, smooth, and vivacious, with a lively bouquet.

The bottles for the wine are covered in wicker. **price range:** A

ITALY, TUSCANY

producer: Tenuta di Vicchiomaggio S.R.L.
classification: Red table wine
grape variety: Sangiovese, Canaiolo, Trebbiano Bianco, and Malvasia
district: Chianti Classico D.O.C.
city or village: Greve

Estate-bottled, 1971 vintage. The wine is bottle-aged prior to shipment. At the annual tasting of Chianti Classicos in 1976, this wine was chosen by the commission of experts as "best of its type."

A ruby color acquiring golden overtones with age. The bouquet is robust and pronounced; the wine is piquant and dry on the palate. It is suitable for all types of Italian cuisine (with the exception of fish and shellfish); open bottle one hour before serving. **price range:** A

producer: I. L. Ruffino
classification: White table wine
grape variety: Trebbiano Toscana (50–60%), Verdello, Grechetto, and Malvasia
district: Orvieto D.O.C.
city or village: Orvieto

Orvieto comes in two types: *secco* (dry) and *abboccato* (semi-dry); this one is *abboccato*. It is one of the most well-known white wines in Italy, and is starting to be appreciated in the United States.

Light straw color and a very typical, delicate bouquet. The wine is semi-dry, pleasant, and soft, with medium body and good finish. **price range:** B

producer: I. L. Ruffino
classification: White table wine
grape variety: Trebbiano Toscana, Verdello, Malvasia, and Grechetto
district: Orvieto D.O.C.
city or village: Orvieto

Most of the Orvieto district—especially the district surrounding the town of Orvieto—is characterized by the presence of *tufo* soil, giving the grapes (and the wine) a particularly pleasant acidity and slightly bitter aftertaste characteristic of Orvieto wines. This is a *secco* (dry) Orvieto.

Light straw color and a delicate, pleasant bouquet. The wine is dry, with medium body and a faint bitter finish. It is recognized as one of the better Italian wines, with a pleasantly refreshing character. Serve chilled. **price range:** B

ITALY, UMBRIA

producer: Marchesi L. & P. Antinori
classification: White table wine
grape variety: Malvasia and Trebbiano
district: Orvieto D.O.C.

A fruity, fresh white wine with a delightful flavor and slightly bitter undertone.
price range: B

producer: Bertolli-Alivar S.p.A.
classification: White table wine
grape variety: Trebbiano and Malvasia
district: Orvieto D.O.C.

Brilliant straw color and a fruity bouquet. The wine is very dry *(secco)*.
price range: B

producer: Florio
classification: White table wine
city or village: Township of Orvieto

This is a full-bodied dry wine with a delicate bouquet. It is surprisingly ample, brimming with a fresh, fruity taste.

The wine is shipped in a straw-covered, broad-based flask called a *pulcianella*.
price range: B

producer: Fattoria Carpineto
classification: White table wine
grape variety: Trebbiano, Verdello, Procanico, and Greco
district: Orvieto D.O.C.

One of Italy's most important wines. Pale straw color with golden reflections and a typical delicate aroma. The wine is superior, dry, and has a delightful acidulous aftertaste. It is most highly recommended with fish, as it is refreshing and harmonious. It is best drunk cold.
price range: A

producer: Papini
classification: White table wine
grape variety: Trebbiano, Verdello, and Malvasia
district: Orvieto Secco D.O.C. (Classico)
city or village: Orvieto

Pale gold color and a delicate bouquet. The wine is smooth, with well-balanced flavor; serve well chilled as an excellent accompaniment to antipasto, fish, shellfish, and white meats. **price range:** B

ITALY, VENETO

producer: Agricola Masi S.A.
classification: Red table wine
grape variety: Corvina, Molinara, Negrara, and Rondinella
district: Verona—Valpolicella Classico D.O.C.
city or village: Sant'Ambrogio

A ruby-red color and a fragrant, fruity bouquet. This velvety wine is rather light in alcohol and body. **price range:** A

producer: Agricola Masi S.A.
classification: Red table wine

grape variety: Corvina, Negrara, and Molinara
district: Verona—Bardolino Classico Superiore D.O.C.
city or village: Bardolino

Ruby-red color and a delicate bouquet. This light, fruity wine has a dry and pleasing taste, at times pungent. **price range:** A

producer: Agricola Masi S.A.
classification: Red table wine
grape variety: Corvina, Molinara, Rondinella, and Dindarella
district: Verona
city or village: Valpolicella D.O.C.

A "Recioto della Valpolicella" made from partially dried, selected grapes, stronger and more costly than regular Valpolicella. This is an *amarone* Recioto, in which the higher sugar content is used up in fermentation, producing a dry wine.

Deep garnet-red color and a solid, rounded bouquet. A soft wine that goes well with almost everything except fish.
price range: C

producer: Agricola Masi S.A.
classification: White table wine
grape variety: Garganega and Trebbiano
district: Verona—Soave Classico Superiore D.O.C.
city or village: Soave

A pale straw color with a tint of greenish highlights; the bouquet has a slight aroma of almonds. This light wine is clean and fresh, dry without being acid.
price range: A

producer: Agricola Masi S.A.
classification: Red table wine
grape variety: Corvina, Rondinella, Molinara, and Dindarella
district: Verona
city or village: Valpolicella D.O.C.

A "Recioto della Valpolicella" made from partially dried, selected grapes, stronger and more costly than regular Valpolicella.

Dark garnet-red color and a bouquet of violets and roses. The wine is delicious and sweet on the palate and is very delightful at the end of a meal, slightly chilled. It should be classified as "luscious."
price range: C

producer: Agricola Masi S.a.S.
classification: White table wine
grape variety: Garganega and Trebbiano
district: Verona

A "Recioto Bianco," a white wine made from partially dried grapes. Very small quantities are available, and this is probably the only one in the United States.

Amber-yellow color and a bouquet with a definite smell of cherry blossoms. The wine has a sweet, soft warm flavor, with a slightly bitter aftertaste.
price range: E

producer: Marchesi L. & P. Antinori
classification: Red table wine
grape variety: Molinara, Negrara, Rondinella, and Corvina
district: Valpolicella D.O.C.

Ruby-red color and a soft, delicate bouquet. The wine has a slight bitter flavor.
price range: A

producer: Marchesi L. & P. Antinori
classification: White table wine
grape variety: Trebbiano and Garganega
district: Verona—Soave D.O.C.
city or village: Soave

A pleasant, light, and fairly dry white wine.
price range: A

producer: Marchesi L. & P. Antinori
classification: Red table wine
grape variety: Corvina, Negrara, Rondinella, and Molinara
district: Bardolino D.O.C.

A delicate, medium-bodied red wine with a light ruby color.
price range: A

producer: Azienda Agricola Santa Sofia
classification: Red table wine
grape variety: Corvina, Molinara, and Rondinella
district: Verona—Valpolicella Classico D.O.C.

A "Recioto della Valpolicella," a full-bodied red wine made from partially dried grapes. The term *amarone* indicates that the wine is fermented dry.

Deep ruby-red color and a particularly characteristic bouquet. The wine is full, warm, and velvety; it is very good with roasted meat, and particularly so with venison.
price range: D

producer: Azienda Agricola Santa Sofia
classification: Red table wine
grape variety: Corvina, Molinara, and Rondinella
district: Verona—Valpolicella Classico D.O.C.

Dark ruby-red color and a characteristic delicate bouquet. The wine tastes soft, velvety, and a little bitter. It is a very good wine for all red meat dishes.
price range: A

producer: Bertani
classification: Red table wine
grape variety: Corvina and Negrara
city or village: Valpolicella

This is a very rich, full-bodied wine of deep ruby color.

The grapes for this wine are from the ears of the vine, which are more exposed to the sun than the other parts. Therefore they mature more rapidly.
price range: D

producer: Bertani
classification: Red table wine
grape variety: Corvina, Negrara, and Molinara
city or village: Valpolicella

This is a very rich, very dry wine with a delicate aroma of bitter almonds. It is of ruby-red color.
price range: B

producer: Bertani
classification: Red table wine
grape variety: Corvino, Negrara, and Molinara
city or village: Bardolino

This light, fresh, fruity wine has a delicate bouquet and is slightly tart.
price range: B

producer: Bertani
classification: White table wine
grape variety: Trebbiano
city or village: Soave

This wine is very dry, slightly acidic, with a pleasant bouquet and greenish highlights in its light straw color.
price range: B

producer: Bertolli-Alivar S.p.A.
classification: White table wine
grape variety: Garganega and Trebbiano
district: Soave D.O.C.
city or village: Soave

Light straw color and a fruity bouquet. The wine is light, dry, fruity, and of excellent quality.
price range: B

producer: Biscardo S.A.
classification: Red table wine
grape variety: Corvina, Rondinella, Molinara, and Negrara
district: Verona—Valpolicella D.O.C.
A classic Veneto wine.
Bright mid-raspberry color and a light bouquet with inviting fruit. The wine is well-balanced, fruity, supple, and medium dry. **price range:** A

producer: B.V.B.
classification: White table wine
grape variety: Garganega and Trebbiano
district: Verona
Pale straw color; the wine is light, clean, and dry. **price range:** A

producer: B.V.B.
classification: Red table wine
grape variety: Corvina, Molinara, Negrara, and Rondinella
district: Verona
A fragrant and fruity red wine.
price range: A

producer: Cantina Sociale de Soave
classification: White table wine
district: Verona

producer: Cantina Sociale de Soave
classification: Red table wine
district: Verona
city or village: Valpolicella
This ruby-red wine is dry and soft, with a light bouquet. **price range:** A

city or village: Soave
This straw-colored wine is dry and has a light bouquet. **price range:** A

producer: Creazzo—P.B.F. Marano di Valpolicella
classification: White table wine
grape variety: Garganega and Trebbiano di Soave
district: Soave Classico Superiore D.O.C.
city or village: Marano
Pale yellow-straw color and a very light flowery bouquet. The wine is dry, round, and has a pleasant little "bite" on the tongue. **price range:** A

producer: Deroà S.R.L.
classification: White table wine
grape variety: Pinot Bianco
district: Treviso—Vini del Piave D.O.C.
city or village: Oderzo
A typical wine of the Piave River Valley, very popular.
Clear color with green-watery hues and a delicate but persistent bouquet. The wine is mellow, harmonic, and has well-balanced acidity and a "bread crust" taste. It is quite dry. **price range:** A

producer: Deroà S.R.L.
classification: White table wine
grape variety: Grappariol (100%)
district: Treviso—Piave Valley
city or village: Oderzo
Deroà is a leading producer in the Piave Valley.
Light, transparent, and brilliant color, and a "prickly," flowerlike bouquet. The wine is light but smooth and piquant; full of harmony, like many Deroa wines.
price range: A

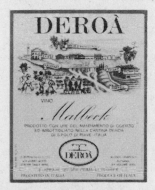

producer: Deroà S.R.L.
classification: Red table wine
grape variety: Malbeck (100%)
district: Treviso—Piave Valley
city or village: Oderzo
The Malbec grape is native to Bordeaux but also grows beautifully in the Piave Valley (where it is called Malbeck), where it has been planted since the 1920s.
Ruby-red, brilliant color and an herblike bouquet typical of the grape variety. The wine has a slight cherry flavor and is herby; it finishes bitter and is dry.
price range: A

producer: Deroà S.R.L.
classification: Red table wine
grape variety: Pinot Rosso (60%), Cabernet Sauvignon(40%)
district: Treviso
city or village: Tempio

A very happy marriage between the Pinot Noir and the Cabernet Sauvignon.
Pale ruby-red color and an elegant bouquet. The wine is smooth and dry, with good body. **price range:** A

producer: Deroà S.R.L.
classification: Rosé table wine
grape variety: Raboso (100%)
district: Treviso
city or village: Maserada sul Piave
Cherry-colored, with different hues, and a winey bouquet reminiscent of raspberries. The wine is full and elegant, with balanced acidity, and is quite dry and fresh—excellent with grilled fish or soups.
price range: A

producer: Deroà S.R.L.
classification: Red table wine
grape variety: Cabernet (95%) and Merlot (5%)
district: Treviso
city or village: Maserada sul Piave
Under D.O.C. regulations, a wine can only be called "Riserva" after the second year following the grape harvest; e.g., grapes gathered in October 1976 can only be sold as Riserva after January 1, 1979.
Ruby-red color with grainy hues, and an herby, tarry bouquet characteristic of Cabernet. The wine is dry and slightly tannic, typical of red wines from the Piave area, and is excellent with all roasts except pork. **price range:** A

producer: Deroà S.R.L.
classification: Red table wine
grape variety: Pinot Rosso (100%)
district: Treviso
city or village: Maserada sul Piave
A "Gran Riserva" made of selected grapes and special vintages.

Pale ruby-red color and a complex bouquet that diminishes with age. The wine is characteristically mellow and quite dry. **price range: A**

producer: Deroà S.R.L.
classification: Red table wine
grape variety: Cabernet (95%) and Merlot (5%)
district: Treviso
city or village: Maserada sul Piave

Ruby-red color with grainy hues and an herblike bouquet suggestive of tar, which is characteristic of Cabernet. The wine is dry, slightly tannic, and well-structured; it is excellent with all roasts (except pork) and is typical of a Piave Valley wine. **price range: A**

producer: Deroà S.R.L.
classification: Red table wine
grape variety: Merlot (95%) and Cabernet (5%)
district: Treviso
city or village: Maserada sul Piave

Ruby-red color and an herblike bouquet typical of Merlot. The wine is dry, well-balanced with tannin, and finishes slightly bitter; it is an excellent wine from the Piave region and should be drunk with all pasta dishes and roasts. **price range: A**

producer: Deroà S.R.L.
classification: Red table wine
grape variety: Merlot (95%) and Cabernet (5%)

district: Treviso
city or village: Maserada sul Piave

Under D.O.C. regulations, a wine can only be called "Vecchio" after the second year following the grape harvest; e.g., the grapes gathered in October 1976 can only apply to wines sold after January 1, 1979. This wine is rounder on the palate than our "non-Vecchio."

Ruby-red color and an herblike bouquet typical of Merlot. The wine is dry, well-balanced in tannin, and finishes slightly bitter; it is an excellent wine from the Piave region and should be drunk with all pasta dishes and roasts. **price range: A**

producer: Deroà S.R.L.
classification: White table wine
grape variety: Verduzzo
district: Treviso
city or village: Maserada sul Piave

A typical wine of the Piave Valley, to be drunk young.

Very clear, light straw color and a bouquet suggestive of yeast, like Champagne. The wine is dry, slightly tannic, and winey; it is excellent with fish dishes made with light sauces. **price range: A**

producer: Deroà S.R.L.
classification: White table wine
grape variety: Blend of Riesling and Pinot Blanco
district: Treviso
city or village: Maserada sul Piave

Pale straw color with green hues and a bouquet suggestive of "Ginestra" flowers. The wine is amiable with a slight Muscat flavor, and very fine; it is excellent as an aperitif or after a meal, but its flavor might be too pronounced to accompany a meal. **price range: A**

producer: Deroà S.R.L.
classification: Rosé table wine
grape variety: Pinot Nero
district: Treviso
city or village: Maserada sul Piave

Pale rosé color and a bouquet reminiscent of roses. The wine is amiable, with a dry finish; it is a beautiful summer drink, to serve either as an aperitif or as a thirst quencher. Should be drunk young, especially with cakes. **price range: A**

producer: Deroà S.R.L.
classification: Red table wine
grape variety: Raboso
district: Treviso
city or village: San Polo di Piave

Obtained from slightly dried Raboso grapes from a single vineyard.

Ruby-red color suggestive of an Oloroso Sherry; oaky bouquet. The wine is semi-sweet, or *abboccato;* it would be fine drunk on a snowy day in front of a fire, or as a dessert wine. **price range: B**

producer: Deroà S.R.L.
classification: Red table wine
grape variety: Cabernet
district: Treviso
city or village: Laviada Ponte di Piave

A rare, very full-bodied wine produced from a single vineyard.

"Black" color and an herblike bouquet of Cabernet Sauvignon. The wine is semi-dry, or *abboccato,* and has a tannic aftertaste. **price range: A**

producer: Deroà S.R.L.
classification: White table wine
grape variety: Verduzzo
district: Udine
city or village: Ramandolo

The name "Ramandolo" was given after the town of the same name, where Verduzzo grapes are grown. The soil there gives the wine its particular flavor.

Golden-yellow color with amber hues and a strong, warm bouquet reminiscent of violets. The wine is amiable but has a dry finish and is slightly tannic; it is a dessert wine and should be drunk young. **price range: B**

producer: Deroà S.R.L.
classification: White sparkling wine
grape variety: Grappariol
district: Treviso
city or village: Maserada sul Piave

Obtained solely from Grappariol grapes, this wine obtains its sparkle via the *méthode champenoise* but it is not disgorged: it is sold with the sediment still in the bottle. It should be drunk very young and is made exclusively by Deroà.

Pale yellow, almost white color, and a

fruity bouquet. The wine is dry, fresh and elegant, with a faint yeast flavor; it should be served very cold, and is excellent with oily or fried fish. **price range: B**

producer: Deroà S.R.L.
classification: White sparkling wine
grape variety: Pinot Bianco (100%)
district: Treviso
city or village: Maserada sul Piave

A sparkling *(spumante)* wine produced by the *cuve close,* or Charmat, process.

Slight pale green color and a flowery bouquet. The wine is fresh, bubbly, and has a yeasty flavor; serve with any dish or alone as an aperitif. **price range: B**

producer: Deroà S.R.L.
classification: Rosé sparkling wine
grape variety: Pinot Noir (100%)
district: Treviso
city or village: Maserada sul Piave

Made from Pinot Noir grapes vinified rosé via the *cuve close,* or Charmat, process.

Pale rose color and a fruity bouquet. The wine is clean, fresh, and dry, with good acidity; it is an excellent accompaniment to any dish, either after meals or as an aperitif. **price range: A**

producer: Deroà S.R.L.
classification: Red table wine
grape variety: Cross (hybrid) between Cabernet and Prosecco
district: Treviso
city or village: Maserada sul Piave

The headmaster of the school of oenology in Conegliano, Veneto, M. Manzoni, created this hybrid at the first and foremost school of its kind in Italy. Good results depend on the clay soil in which the grapes are grown.

Ruby-red color and an intense yet delicate bouquet. The wine is dry and full-bodied, slightly tannic, and should be drunk young. **price range: A**

producer: Deroà S.R.L.
classification: White table wine
grape variety: Pinot Grigio (Pinot Gris)
district: Treviso
city or village: Oderzo and Mottia

Although sold as a white wine, this must not be confused with an ordinary white: when vinified, the wine acquires many different hues—the more smoky the color, the better the wine.

Smoky appearance and a strong, fragrant "bread crust" aroma. The wine is dry, full-bodied, and has a strong perfume; it should be drunk young, as an aperitif, and is excellent with "Risotti," fish with sauces, hors d'oeuvres, and white meals. **price range:** A

producer: Deroà S.R.L.
classification: White table wine
grape variety: Pinot Grigio (Pinot Gris)
district: Treviso
city or village: Maserada sul Piave

Smoky color and a "bread crust" bouquet—full and fragrant. The wine is dry and full-bodied; it should be drunk young as an aperitif or with fish in sauces or hors d'oeuvres. **price range:** A

producer: Deroà S.R.L.
classification: White table wine
grape variety: Traminer
district: Treviso
city or village: Maserada sul Piave

One of the great white wines.

Straw-yellow color and an exotic bouquet of fruits and banana. The wine is warm, velvety, and smooth; as it is full-bodied, it is excellent with smoked salmon or grilled trout. **price range:** A

producer: Deroà S.R.L.
classification: Red table wine
grape variety: (Merlot (95%) and Cabernet (5%)
district: Treviso
city or village: Maserada sul Piave

Made from selected grapes and specific vintages.

Ruby-red color and an herblike bouquet typical of Merlot. The wine is dry, well-balanced with tannin, and slightly bitter; it is an excellent example of a Piave wine and should be drunk with all pasta dishes and roasts. **price range:** B

producer: Deroà S.R.L.
classification: Red table wine
grape variety: Cabernet (95%) and Merlot (5%)
district: Treviso
city or village: Maserada sul Piave

A typical wine from the Piave Valley, made from selected grapes and particular vintages.

Ruby-red color with grainy hues and an herblike bouquet with the tarry characteristic of Cabernet. The wine is dry, slightly tannic, and well-structured; it is excellent with all roasts except pork. **price range:** B

producer: Deroà S.R.L.
classification: White table wine
grape variety: Müller-Thurgau (cross between Riesling and Sylvaner)
district: Treviso
city or village: Maserada Sul Piave

This is a well-balanced wine, fresh and dry to the palate.

This wine is completely different from the Müller-Thurgau wines grown in other countries, for instance, Germany. The vines were created by a crossing made by an Austrian professor, Dr. Müller. A crossing is not a graft. **price range:** below A

producer: Deroà S.R.L.
classification: White table wine
grape variety: Tocai Italico
district: Treviso
city or village: Maserada sul Piave

The Italian Tocai is a completely different kind of grape than the Tocai (Tokay) of Hungary. In the Piave Valley it gives a high-quality wine.

Lemon-yellow color and a light and delicate bouquet suggestive of wild flowers. The wine is light, velvety, and dry, with a slightly bitter aftertaste; it should be drunk very young and is excellent with fish, soups, and other dishes. **price range:** A

producer: Deroà S.R.L.
classification: White table wine
grape variety: Müller-Thurgau
district: Treviso
city or village: Maserada Sul Piave

This Müller-Thurgau is obtained through selected grapes. The alcohol content is higher than that of the basic Müller-Thurgau.

This wine is excellent with the best fine fish, crustaceans and mussels, being well-balanced, fresh, and dry to the palate. It has a thin bouquet and lovely straw-yellow color. **price range:** A

producer: Deroà S.R.L.
classification: White table wine
grape variety: Riesling Italico
district: Treviso
city or village: Maserada Sul Piave

This is a dry Riesling with a fragrant, mellow bouquet. It has green hues to its pale gold color and should be drunk with bouillons, fish, or as an aperitif.

This wine is made from selected grapes. **price range:** A

producer: Deroà S.R.L.
classification: Red table wine
grape variety: Raboso
district: Treviso
city or village: Maserada Sul Piave

This is typical of the wines of east Venice, in the Piave region. It is full-bodied and very dry, with the tannin content well-balanced. Its scent is that of a Morello cherry, and its color a strong ruby red. Excellent with roast pork.

The wine should last over twenty years, and respond well to aging in the bottle. **price range:** below A

producer: Deroà S.R.L.
classification: White table wine
grape variety: Riesling Italico
district: Treviso
city or village: Maserada Sul Piave

This wine has the characteristic palate of the Riesling grape, with a mellow, fragrant bouquet. **price range:** below A

producer: Deroà S.R.L.
classification: Red table wine
grape variety: Raboso
district: Treviso
city or village: Maserada Sul Piave

This strong, ruby-colored wine is full-bodied and very dry. This is part of Deroà's "Gran Riserva" line, made of selected grapes and particular vintages.

The wine should respond well to bottle aging of up to twenty years. **price range:** below A

producer: F.lli Gancia & Cia.
classification: Red table wine
grape variety: Corvina, Negrara and Molinara
district: Valpolicella, near Verona

The wine has great character and excellent body. It is quite robust and ages extremely well. When it reaches maturity at about three years, Valpolicella is considered one of the best Italian red wines.
price range: A

producer: F.lli Gancia & Cia.
classification: Red table wine
district: Verona

This brilliant light red wine is delicate and fresh to the palate. It goes well with all foods and requires little aging.
price range: A

> *"O thou invisible spirit of wine!"*
> —Shakespeare, *Othello*

producer: F.lli Gancia & Cia.
classification: White table wine
grape variety: Garganega, Trebbiano
city or village: Soave

This is the queen of Italian white wines, famous since the days of Caesar. It is crisp, light, and fresh, with a delightful bouquet. It should be served well chilled with fish and light meats.
price range: A

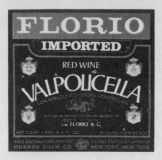

producer: Florio
classification: Red table wine
grape variety: Corvina, Molinara, Negrara, and Rondinella
district: Northwest of Verona—Valpolicella

This is a delicate, light, fruity wine, remarkable for its subtlety and breed. Its soft, mellow flavor is complemented by a fragrant bouquet.

The wine should be served at cool room ("cellar") temperature.
price range: B

producer: Florio
classification: Red table wine
grape variety: Primarily Corvina, Negrara, and Molinara
district: Eastern shore of Lake Garda
city or village: Bardolino

This wine is lighter than, but deliciously close to, a Valpolicella. It has a scintillating, soft, fresh taste; a subtle bouquet; and is of a clear, light ruby-red color.
price range: B

producer: Florio
classification: White table wine
grape variety: Garganega, Trebbiano, and some Riesling
district: East of Verona, on the foothills of the Alps
city or village: Soave

This is a light, clean wine with very little acidity. Its pale golden color and excellent bouquet contribute to the excellence of this velvety wine.

The wine is shipped in tall green bottles, like Alsatian wines.
price range: B

producer: Fratelli Folonari
classification: White table wine
grape variety: Garganega and Trebbiano
district: Verona
city or village: Soave

This wine is available only in 2-liter (67 oz.) bottles. It is one of the better white wines of Italy and is an American favorite.

Pale straw color and a fruity bouquet. The wine tastes light and fresh; it is dry, with a soft finish. Serve chilled.
price range: B

> *May our wine brighten the mind and strengthen the resolution.*

producer: Fratelli Folonari
classification: Red table wine
grape variety: Corvina, Negrara, and Molinara
district: Verona—Bardolino D.O.C.

This wine is available only in 2-liter (67 oz.) bottles. It is often called the "Italian Beaujolais."

Light red color and a fruity, fresh bouquet. The wine tastes lively and fruity; it is charming, pleasant, and easily drinkable.
price range: B

producer: Fratelli Folonari
classification: Red table wine
grape variety: Corvina, Molinara, Negrara, and Rondinella
district: Verona

This wine is imported only in 2-liter (67 oz.) bottles. It is ready to drink when shipped.

Ruby-red color and a fruity, fragrant bouquet. The wine tastes soft, velvety, and is light in alcohol—a delightful and distinguished red wine.
price range: B

producer: Italvini
classification: Rosé table wine
grape variety: Lagrein
district: Verona
city or village: Negrar

This wine is also available in *rosso* (red) and *bianco* (white).

Light rose color and a "plain" bouquet. The wine is medium dry and pleasant, not too dry, and well-balanced; it is excellent with smoked meats and is an ideal party or picnic wine. Serve slightly chilled.
price range: A

producer: Lagriavivi
classification: White table wine
grape variety: Riesling

The Trentino is a mountainous region located immediately north of the city of Verona. It is particularly famous for its delicate, fruity, and dry white wines made from grapes that grow on vineyards along the entire range of medium and lower slopes on the Dolomite Mountains.

Green-tinged color and a particularly delicate bouquet. The wine combines subtle freshness with harmonious flavor; it will enchant many a discerning palate, and, when chilled, is an ideal summer wine.
price range: A

producer: Lamberti
classification: Red table wine
grape variety: Corvina, Rondinella, and Molinara
district: Valpolicella D.O.C.

This is a "Recioto della Valpolicella" made from grapes that have been more exposed to the sun than regular Valpolicella. The grapes are selected and allowed to dry after the harvest, then pressed by the end of December. Normally Reciotos are sweet, but the term *amarone* means that the sugar in the wine is fermented dry, making it more versatile. The wine contains 14% alcohol.

Very deep pomegranate-red color and a deep and elegant bouquet showing a lot of fruit. The wine is dry, full-bodied, velvety, and harmonious; a big wine that is perfect with game and roasts. **price range: C**

producer: Lamberti
classification: Red table wine
grape variety: Corvina Veronese, Rondinella, Molinara, and Negrara
district: Bardolino Classico Superiore D.O.C.

Light ruby-red color and a very pleasant and fruity bouquet. The wine is delicately dry and very fresh; because it is not too strong, it is well-suited to fish dishes, fowl, veal, and by itself. **price range: B**

producer: Lamberti
classification: White table wine
grape variety: Garganega and Trebbiano di Soave
district: Soave Classico Superiore D.O.C.
city or village: Soave

Straw-yellow color, with a greenish hue, and a delicate bouquet. The wine is dry, well-balanced, and harmonious, with a soft, lingering aftertaste. **price range: B**

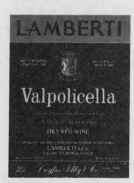

producer: Lamberti
classification: Red table wine
grape variety: Corvina, Rondinella, and Molinara
district: Valpolicella Classico Superiore D.O.C.

Valpolicella is fuller and more complex than Bardolino, although the two regions adjoin and the grape varieties are identical. This wine has 12% alcohol.

Ruby-red color of medium intensity and a delicate bouquet with a slight aroma of almonds. The wine is dry, full, velvety, and harmonious; it would go well with lean roasts. **price range: B**

producer: Masieri—P.B.F. Marano di Valpolicella
classification: White table wine
grape variety: Garganega and Trebbiano di Soave
district: Soave Classico Superiore D.O.C.
city or village: Marano

Straw-yellow color and a very delicate, light bouquet. The wine is dry, with a pleasant bitter finish. **price range: A**

producer: Masieri—P.B.F. Marano di Valpolicella
classification: Red table wine
grape variety: Corvina Veronese, Rondinella, and Molinara Negrara
district: Bardolino Classico Superiore D.O.C.
city or village: Marano

Pale ruby color and a delicately vinous bouquet. The wine has a dry, slightly bitter taste. **price range: A**

producer: Masieri—P.B.F. Marano di Valpolicella
classification: Red table wine
grape variety: Corvina Veronese, Rondinella, and Molinara

---

district: Recioto della Valpolicella Amarone D.O.C.
city or village: Marano

This is a "Recioto Valpolicella" made from partially dried grapes. Flavius Magnus Aurelius Cassiodorus Sanator (A.D. 490–585), an historian in the time of Theodoric, described this wine (then called *acinatico*) as "of regal color, of pure taste, of unbelievable suavity, fleshly liquid, not only a drink, but also a food!"

Deep garnet color and an intensely vinous, pleasant bouquet. The wine is warm, smooth, and full-bodied, with an elegant finish. **price range: C**

producer: Masieri—P.B.F. Marano di Valpolicella
classification: Red table wine
grape variety: Corvina Veronese, Rondinella, and Molinara
district: Valpolicella Classico Superiore D.O.C.
city or village: Marano

Ruby-red color and a delicate, vinous bouquet reminiscent of bitter almonds. The wine is dry, with a velvety finish. **price range: A**

producer: S.A. Mirafiore
classification: Red table wine

This is the country wine of the farmer and gentleman. Its full body is anticipated by its deep red color. It receives a minimum of two years' aging, but is best after five years. **price range: C**

producer: Palanca
classification: White table wine
grape variety: Garganega and Trebbiano

---

district: Soave D.O.C.

One of Italy's finest white wines; suitable for moderate aging.

Shining straw color and a delightful bouquet. The wine is fresh, dry, and harmonious with an aftertaste often reminiscent of almonds. It is a great wine for hors d'oeuvres, soups, egg, and fish dishes. Served chilled. **price range: A**

producer: Palanca
classification: Red table wine
grape variety: Corvina, Rondinella, and Molinara
district: Verona—Bardolino D.O.C.

Ruby-red color; the wine has a delicate, fresh, dry taste with a pleasant hint of bitterness. It is particularly appropriate with rice, pasta, fish, fowl, and egg dishes. Serve cool, about 61 degrees F. **price range: A**

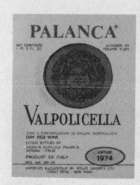

producer: Palanca
classification: Red table wine
grape variety: Corvina, Rondinella, Molinara, and Rossignola
district: Verona—Valpolicella Classico D.O.C.

Suitable for prolonged aging.

Ruby color, turning to pomegranate with age, and a pleasantly delicate bouquet recalling bitter almonds. The wine is dry, but soft and well-balanced, and is a great wine for lean roasts, liver, and hearty dishes in general. **price range: A**

producer: Pastrengo
classification: Red table wine
district: Verona

Clear red color and a good bouquet. The wine is fruity but does not have much body; nevertheless, it is a first-class value. **price range: A**

producer: I. .L Ruffino
classification: Red table wine
grape variety: Corvina (chief variety), Rondinella, and Molinara
district: Valpolicella Classico Superiore D.O.C.

The *governo* system of adding a little concentrated grape must to the wine is used for this Valpolicella to assure greater roundness and more alcohol.

Ruby-red color with brown tints when well-aged; a vinous, fragrant bouquet with pronounced "almond" characteristics. The wine is dry and soft, with a long finish.
price range: B

*"Die I must, but let me die
drinking in an inn!
Hold the wine-cup to my lips
sparkling from the bin!
So, when angels flutter down
to take me from my sin,
'Ah, God have mercy on this
sot,' the cherubs will begin."*
—Walter Map

producer: I. L. Ruffino
classification: Red table wine
grape variety: Corvino Veronese (50–60%), Rondinella, Molinara, and Negrara
district: Verona—Bardolino Classico Superiore D.O.C.
city or village: Bardolino

Ruby-red, medium-light color and a delicate, pleasant bouquet. The wine is dry and sapid, harmonious with a slight bitter aftertaste. It is well-balanced and charming, with a pleasantly appealing flavor.
price range: B

producer: I. L. Ruffino
classification: White table wine
graparlety: Garganega (70–90%) and Trebbiano di Soave (10–30%)
district: Verona—Soave Classico Superiore D.O.C.
city or village: Soave

A wine with a pleasant personality, quite popular in the United States.

Light straw color with some greenish tones and a delicate, vinous, and slightly fruity bouquet. The wine is dry, medium-bodied, and has a slight bitter aftertaste.
price range: B

producer: S.P.A.L.
classification: Red table wine
grape variety: Merlot
district: Veronese Hills

Bottled only in double liters. Exceptional value.

Ruby-red color and a fruity bouquet. A smooth wine, ready to drink when shipped.
price range: B

producer: S.P.A.L.
classification: White table wine
grape variety: Garganega and Trebbiano
district: Veronese Hills

Bottled only in double liters. Exceptional value.

Straw color and a delicately fragrant bouquet. A soft wine, ready to drink when shipped. **price range:** B

producer: Tommasi
classification: White table wine
grape variety: Garganega and Trebbiano
district: Verona—Soave Classico D.O.C.

The grapes for this wine are cultivated and vinified by traditional methods. The wine is suitable for moderate aging.

Shining straw color and a delightful bouquet. The wine is fresh, dry, with harmonious flavor and a characteristic aftertaste reminiscent of almonds. It is a great wine for hors d'oeuvres, soups, egg, and fish dishes. Should be chilled about about 52 degrees F. **price range:** B

producer: Tommasi
classification: Red table wine
grape variety: Corvina, Rondinella, and Molinara
district: Verona—Bardolino Classico D.O.C.

The grapes for this wine are cultivated and vinified by traditional methods. The wine is suitable for moderate aging.

Ruby-red color; the wine has a delicate, fresh, dry taste with a hint of pleasant bitterness. It is a particularly appropriate wine with rice, pasta, fish, fowl, and egg dishes. Serve cool. **price range:** B

*"Wine is light, held together
by water."* —Galileo

producer: Tommasi
classification: Red table wine
grape variety: Corvina, Rondinella, Molinara, and Rossignola
district: Verona—Valpolicella Classico D.O.C.

One of Italy's best red wines, suitable for prolonged aging.

Ruby-red color, turning to pomegranate with age, and a pleasantly delicate and characteristic bouquet that recalls bitter almonds. The wine is dry but soft and well-balanced. It is a great wine for lean roasts, liver, and hearty dishes in general. Serve at room temperature, after allowing the wine to breathe for at least one hour before serving. **price range:** B

producer: Tommasi
classification: Red table wine
grape variety: Corvina, Rondinella, and Molinara
district: Verona—Recioto della Valpolicella Amarone D.O.C.

This is a "Recioto Valpolicella" made from grapes selected only from the top and sides of the bunch, which are left to dry on trays before vinification according to traditional methods. It is later aged in Yugoslav oak casks.

Deep pomegranate-red color and a rich, intense bouquet. The wine is dry, round, and velvety, with mouth-filling harmony of bouquet and body. This exceptional wine is well-suited to game and roasts in general and is one of the world's finest red wines. Serve at room temperature.
price range: C

The production of German wine falls into three categories—table wine, quality wine, and specially graded quality wine—that make it easy for you to select according to your personal needs and desires. The categories can be described as follows:

Table Wine (Tafelwein)   Table wines are light, pleasant wines, consumed mainly in Germany itself; they are produced from approved grape varieties in the Mosel, Rhein, Main, Neckar, and Oberrhein.

Quality Wine (Qualitätswein)   Quality wine has more body than table wine. It is also made from approved grape varieties. Wines in this category must come exclusively from one of the eleven Designated Regions. Official government panels of experts taste and analyze all quality wines before giving them a control number. This ensures that the wines conform to special requirements set up to monitor that quality.

Specially Graded Quality Wines (Qualitätswein mit Prädiket)   This is the highest category of German wine. All specially graded quality wines must be produced from approved grape varieties; each one of the wines that fall in this category is checked for the time of its vintage, the method by which it has been harvested, and the degree of ripeness of the grapes. In addition to the control number, a declaration of the grade must appear on the label. Five grades have been set up within this category. They are:

Kabinett   An elegant, fully ripened wine, harvested at the normal time. "Normal" in Germany as a rule means October, a time when the grapes in the rest of Europe have long since been plucked. It is this lengthy, slow-ripening time that gives rise to the unique characteristics of German wines.

Spätlese   These wines come from grapes harvested after the normal picking period. They are distinguished by a special elegance and ripeness and are appealingly round and delicious.

Auslese   Wines produced from fully ripe grapes that are specially sorted and pressed separately. Auslese wines reveal their elegance through their full bouquet and are unquestionably produced on special occasions.

Beerenauslese   This indicates wines of exceptional quality. The wine is made from ripe and overripe berries, separated by hand. The result is a luscious, sweet, and truly noble wine with a flowerlike aroma.

Trockenbeerenauslese   This is the grade that represents the crowning achievement in German viticulture—a wine of the finest quality. Only grapes shriveled like raisins are pressed for this wine, which offers significant characteristics in both appearance and taste.

The best understanding of German wines comes from a comprehension of the structure of the eleven Designated Regions in which they are produced. The history of these great wines is long and detailed, but the vital facts have been consolidated in a useful little booklet called *A Short Guide to German Wines*. A wide variety of wine is available from these eleven regions and each officially designated territory consists of two or more districts; each district consists of several villages or parishes that form a geological or climatic unity. Within each village there can be a number of individually owned vineyards. Precise definitions of what constitutes a village, a district, and a region are strictly controlled by the German government; these definitions are evident on the various wine labels. The eleven Designated Regions are:

Baden   About a dozen different wines come from Baden. A few of them are the full-bodied *Ruländer;* the light, aromatic *Gutddel;* the spicy *Kaiserstühl* wines growing in the heat-retaining volcanic soils; the potent wines of Lake Constance; and the popular *Weissherbst.* Baden is the southernmost wine region, on the right bank of the Rhine. It is located between Lake Constance and Heidelberg and includes the districts of Lake Constance, Markgraflerland, Kaisersthül-Tuniberg, Breisgau, Ortenau, Badishe Bergstrasse/Kraichgau, Badisches Frankenland.

Rheinpfalz   Known historically as the "Wine Celler of the Holy Roman Empire" the Palatinate is the most thickly forested of the German wine regions. There is plenty to suit every taste here—from the mild, fresh wines made from Sylvaner and Müller-Thurgau grapes to the piquant varieties that flourish in the loam of the Oberhaard. *Traminer, Muskateller,* and *Ruländer* are also produced here.

Württemberg   Strong-tasting white wines are the classic Württemberg speciality, but wines from this region are seldom encountered ouside their locality; you will have to seek them out. The Tröllinger vine is typical of the region. Red grapes are especially abundant, making it possible to produce *Early and Late Burgundy, Black Riesling,* and *Limberger* in this region.

Franken   Along the River Main, Sylvaner vineyards produce robust, earthy, and dry "manly" wines, while the Müller-Thurgau grape produces piquant wines. Franconian wine is sold in flagon-shaped bottles called *bocksbeutels.* Cultivation in Franken, which stretches from the Steigerwald to the other side of the Spessart, is confined to Steigerwald, Maindreieck, and Mainviereck, the warmest parts of the region.

Rheinhessen   The provinces of Bingen, Nierstein, and Wonnegau are the districts of the Rhenish Hesse. The wines originate on the left bank of the Rhine, in the areas of Worms, Mainz, Bingen, and Alzey. Inasmuch as the soils vary considerably, Rhenish Hesse produces both wholesome table wines and top-quality vintages. It was in this ancient country, in 1404, that the Riesling vine was first given its name. In addition to Riesling, Silvaner, Müller-Thurgau, Scheurebe, Siegerrebe, and Kanzlerrebe are found in Hesse. The Morio-Muskat is also present but somewhat rarer, since it comes from a new breed of vine. Red wines grow here: fine, spicy *Spätburgunder* and a light dinner wine, *Portugieser.*

Hessische Bergstrasse   This small wine region contains the districts of Starkenburg and Unstadt. During the springtime, the area around the magnificent medieval town of Heppenheim is alive with blossoming fruit trees and the quivering green vines that produce strong, tangy local *Riesling.*

Rheingau   The slopes of this region lie between Rheinkne and Taunushöhen. The district is known as Johannisberg. In the Rheingau, chestnuts, almonds, and figs flourish in the open, so it is not at all surprising that the Riesling grape develops true perfection in this favorable climate. The Rheingau is protected from the harsh weather by the Taunus Hills, and the Rhine River adds to the region's ideal situation by reflecting the sun's rays onto the vineyards. *Rheingau Riesling* is distinguished for its spicy elegance and fruity taste. It is a wine for connoisseurs.

Nahe   Kreuznach and Böckelheim, protected from the wind by the Soonwald Heights, are the districts of the Nahe region. Most of the typical vineyards grow along the middle Nahe and Alsenz. Riesling, Silvaner, and Müller-Thurgau are the most common varieties of grape, from which growers create wines of all grades, from light table wines to the finest vintages.

Mittelrhein   The middle Rhine is a spectacular region crowned with old castles. Terraced vineyards stretch along the right bank of the Rhine from the mouth of the Nahe to the Siebengebirge. The luscious fruits from the districts of Bacharach, Rheinburgengau, and Siebengebirge produce a local *Riesling* full of character that is lively and dry.

Mosel–Saar–Ruwar   Some of the steepest wine terraces in the world are located along the Mosel River and its tributaries, the Saar and Ruwar. Exhilarating, fragrant, and delicate wines are made here from the Riesling grape that grows on the steep southern slopes below Trier. The high-class fruity wines that come from the area along the Aar are rightly reknowned. Between the protective hills of the Hunsrück, the Mosel meanders toward the Rhine forming a climatic unit with the Saar and Ruwer that benefits all the vines of the districts of Zell-Mosel, Bernkastel, Saar-Ruwer, and Upper Mosel.

Ahr   This northernmost wine region of Germany is also the smallest and is noted for excellent red wines. The vines of the region ripen only because gravel and volcanic rock, which make up the soil, are able to store warmth during the day and release it at night. This rare natural process gives the red *Spätburgunder* wine its fine, velvety-soft character. The Ahr owes its reputation to this fine wine. One of the biggest red-wine areas in all Germany lies in the lower Ahr, on the slopes of the Eifel, in the district of Walporzhiem-Ahr.

HOW TO READ A GERMAN WINE LABEL

RHEINHESSEN The *region* from which the wine comes. Consult section on Germany for list of the eleven Designated Regions.

197– The vintage or *year* when the wine was made.

WINZERDORFER The village from which the wine comes. Here, the hypothetical village is *Winzerdorf*. It becomes the name of wine by adding an "er" at the end. (A New York wine would become a New York*er* and a London wine a London*er*).

REBBERG The vineyard *Rebberg*, surrounding Winzendorf, where grapes for the production of the wine have been grown.

RIESLING The *variety of grape* used to make the wine.

WEINKELLEREI The name of the producer or shipper.

A.P. NR. 438482281073 *Official quality testing number,* given by the government to wines passing rigid examination. Found only on quality wines. Consult section on Germany for details.

QUALITÄTSWEIN Refers to category of wine in bottle. Here, a *Qualitätswein*.

RHEINHESSEN

1971er
WINZERDORFER
REBBERG
RIESLING

Weinkellerei XYZ

A.P. Nr. 438482281073
QUALITATSWEIN

GERMANY, MOSEL

producer: Blum & Haas
classification: White table wine
grape variety: Riesling
grade: Qualitätswein mit Prädikat—Spätlese
city or village: Bernkastel
Fine Riesling bouquet; the wine is fruity and full-flavored, showing the typical finesse of a Spätlese. **price range:** B

producer: Deinhard & Co.
classification: White table wine
grade: Qualitätswein b.A.
city or village: Bernkastel (Bereich)
Deinhard "Green Label" is delightfully crisp, yet soft and delicious.
price range: B

producer: Deinhard & Co.
classification: White table wine
grade: Qualitätswein b.A.
city or village: Bernkastel
Fragrant, full-bodied, and rich wine.
price range: C

producer: Deinhard & Co.
classification: White table wine
grade: Qualitätswein b.A.
city or village: Zell (Bereich)
"Forellenwein" (trout wine) is pleasant, light, and dry, with a sprightly tang.
price range: B

producer: Deinhard & Co.
classification: White table wine
grape variety: Riesling
grade: Qualitätswein mit Prädikat—Kabinett
city or village: Bernkastel
vineyard: Doktor (Einzellage)
From the famous Doktor vineyard, one of the greatest in the Mittel-Mosel.
Elegant bouquet; the wine is rich and full-bodied. **price range:** E

producer: Peter Dören, Weingut
classification: White table wine
grape variety: Riesling
grade: Qualitätswein b.A.

city or village: Fankel
vineyard: Rosenberg (Einzellage)
Green-yellow color and a pleasant bouquet. The wine is round, soft, and dry, with a light, delicate flavor: a well-made dry wine. **price range:** A

producer: Export-Union Deutscher Weingüter
classification: White table wine
grape variety: Riesling
grade: Qualitätswein b.A.
city or village: Zell
vineyard: Schwarze Katz (Grosslage)
The master blenders at Export Union see to it that the "Black Cat of Zell" remains a purebred, producing the same quality regardless of the vintage.
The wine is slightly drier than a Liebfraumilch, but has the same clean finish. It is a "fun" wine, and a fine companion at all times. **price range:** B

producer: Felix Faber
classification: White table wine
grape variety: Riesling
grade: Qualitätswein b.A.
city or village: Zell
vineyard: Schwarze Katz (Grosslage)
Brilliant light straw color and a flowery bouquet. The wine is tart and fruity to the taste. **price range:** B

producer: Arthur Hallgarten GmbH
classification: White table wine
grape variety: Riesling
grade: Qualitätswein b.A.
city or village: Bernkastel
vineyard: Kurfürstlay (Grosslage)
Sold under the Moselgold brand label, this wine has national distribution in the United Kingdom.
Pale color and a varietal bouquet. The wine is medium dry, with a full flavor; it is excellent either as an aperitif or as an accompaniment to the main course.
price range: B

producer: Arthur Hallgarten GmbH
classification: White table wine
grape variety: Riesling
grade: Qualitätswein b.A.
city or village: Zell
vineyard: Schwarze Katz (Grosslage)

Distributed in t. e United Kingdom under the Keller Katz (cellar cat) label.

Pale color and a pronounced Riesling bouquet. The wine is well-balanced and medium dry, an excellent all-purpose wine. **price range:** B

producer: Carl Jos. Hoch
classification: White table wine
grape variety: Riesling
city or village: Bernkastel

Bright green color and a grapey bouquet. The wine is medium dry and fruity. **price range:** B

producer: Fritz Hübinger
classification: White table wine
grape variety: Riesling
grade: Qualitätswein mit Prädikat
city or village: Zeltingen

This is Bauer & Foss's best-selling German wine. It is praised at many tastings for its quality and competitive price.

Light gold color and a fresh, fruity bouquet. The wine is light, clean, and refreshing, with a delightful flavor. **price range:** A

producer: Fritz Hübinger
classification: White table wine
grape variety: Riesling

grade: Qualitätswein mit Prädikat
city or village: Zell

The vineyards from which this wine comes lie in one of the lesser parts of the Mosel, but in good years the best vineyards come into their own, like those in the nearby Saar-Ruwer district.

Full gold color and a fresh, clean varietal bouquet. The wine is well-balanced and has a long finish—a rare treasure from the Zell area. **price range:** C

producer: Hermann Kendermann
classification: White table wine
grape variety: Riesling
grade: Qualitätswein b.A.
city or village: Piesport
vineyard: Goldtröpfchen (Einzellage)

This wine is possibly the most popular of its kind shipped from Germany.

Clear gold color and a fruity, crisp bouquet. The wine is crisp, delicate, and refreshing; medium dry, it is one of the most delicious of Riesling wines and is exquisite with all meals. **price range:** B

producer: Hermann Kendermann
classification: White table wine
grape variety: Riesling
grade: Qualitätswein b.A.

Made from the most noble grape in Germany.

Pale golden color and a fruity, fresh bouquet. The wine is light, medium dry, with typical Riesling flavor; it is perfect as an aperitif. **price range:** B

producer: A. J. Koenen, Ltd.
classification: White table wine
grape variety: Riesling
grade: Qualitätswein b.A.
city or village: Zeltingen-Rachtig
vineyard: Münzlay (Grosslage)

Pale color with tints of green and a refreshing Riesling bouquet. The wine is dry and fresh, with a "slatey" quality reflecting

the soil from which the grapes are grown; it is excellent on its own or a fine accompaniment to fish dishes. **price range:** B

producer: A. J. Koenen Ltd.
classification: White table wine
grape variety: Riesling
grade: Qualitätswein b.A.
city or village: Piesport
vineyard: Treppchen (Einzellage)

Pale, light color with green tints and a crisp, fresh bouquet. The wine is crisp, dry, and elegant—it is perfect on its own, when slightly chilled, or as an excellent companion with fish dishes. **price range:** B

producer: A. J. Koenen Ltd.
classification: White table wine
grape variety: Riesling
grade: Qualitätswein b.A.
city or village: Cröv
vineyard: Nacktarsch (Grosslage)

"Cröver Nacktarsch" (naked bottom) is well known because of its amusing label that shows a little boy being spanked, with his pants down, for drinking in the wine cellar.

Pale color with tints of green and a delicate varietal bouquet. The wine is fresh, with a slight sparkle, or "spritz," and is quite dry. **price range:** B

producer: A. J. Koenen Ltd.
classification: White table wine
grape variety: Riesling
grade: Qualitätswein mit Prädikat
city or village: Piesport
vineyard: Goldtröpfchen (Einzellage)

The Goldtröpfchen vineyard is an *Einzellage* (single vineyard) admirably exposed on the slate soil above the village of Piesport. Although perhaps not as full-flavored as Rhine wines, Piesporters typify the delightful character of Mosels and are known as "the queens of the Mosel."

Very pale straw color, with a sparkle of green, and a light, fragrant bouquet. The wine is delicate, with balanced acidity, and is neither totally sweet nor fully dry. **price range:** C

producer: A. J. Koenen Ltd.
classification: White table wine
grape variety: Elbling, Müller-Thurgau, and Riesling
grade: Tafelwein (Moselblümchen)

Light pale color and a fresh, youthful bouquet. The wine tastes fruity, well-balanced, and is dry and pleasant—an excellent table wine. **price range:** A

producer: Leonard Kreusch Inc.
classification: White table wine
grape variety: Riesling
grade: Qualitätswein b.A.
city or village: Zell
vineyard: Schwarze Katz (Grosslage)
price range: A

producer: Leonard Kreusch Inc.
classification: White table wine
grape variety: Riesling
grade: Qualitätswein b.A.
city or village: Zeltingen
vineyard: Himmelreich (Einzellage)

Very sturdy.
price range: A

producer: Leonard Kreusch Inc.
classification: White table wine
grape variety: Riesling
grade: Qualitätswein b.A.
city or village: Erden

Spicy & delicate.
price range: A

producer: Leonard Kreusch Inc.
classification: White table wine
grape variety: Riesling
grade: Qualitätswein b.A.
city or village: Cröv
vineyard: Nacktarsch (Grosslage)
price range: A

producer: Leonard Kreusch Inc.
classification: White table wine
grape variety: Riesling and others
grade: Qualitätswein b.A.
price range: A

producer: Leonard Kreusch Inc.
classification: White table wine
grape variety: Riesling
grade: Qualitätswein b.A.
city or village: Bernkastel
price range: A

producer: Leonard Kreusch Inc.
classification: White table wine
grape variety: Riesling
grade: Qualitätswein b.A.
village: Piesport
price range: A

producer: Leonard Kreusch Inc.
classification: White table wine
grape variety: Riesling
grade: Qualitätswein b.A.
city or village: Piesport
price range: A

producer: Leonard Kreusch Inc.
classification: White table wine
grape variety: Riesling
grade: Qualitätswein mit
  Prädikat—Kabinett
city or village: Wehlen
vineyard: Sonnenuhr (Einzellage)
  Sonnenuhr means "sundial" in German. A flowery, well-balanced white Mosel wine. **price range:** B

producer: J. Lauerburg
classification: White table wine
grape variety: Riesling
grade: Qualitätswein b.A.
city or village: Bernkastel
vineyard: Badstube (Grosslage)
  This wine was formerly called either "Doktor" or "Bratenhöfchen," but the wines are now sold separately.
  Clear color and a flowery bouquet. The wine is dry and very appealing; a typically fine and delightful Mosel from a much-respected wine village. **price range:** C

producer: J. Lauerburg
classification: White table wine
grape variety: Riesling

grade: Qualitätswein mit
  Prädikat—Kabinett
city or village: Bernkastel
vineyard: Doktor (Einzellage, but
  boundaries still in litigation)
  The 1971 vintage has a label that still shows the combined vineyards *(Einzellagen)* of Doktor and Bratenhöfchen, but under the 1971 German Wine Law the output from the two vineyards cannot be combined and sold under these two names.
  Light golden color and an elegant, flowery bouquet. The wine is light, yet refreshing and firm. A beautiful, classic, and fine Mosel wine. **price range:** E

producer: J. Lauerburg
classification: White table wine
grape variety: Riesling
grade: Qualitätswein b.A.
city or village: Bernkastel
vineyard: Bratenhöfchen (Einzellage)
  Lauerburg is one of the most respected wine producers in the Mittel-Mosel district. He is a co-owner of the famous Doktor vineyard in Bernkastel.
  Clear light color and a flowery bouquet. The wine is intriguing and pleasingly fresh: an ideal summer wine. It should be drunk young.
price range: C

producer: Jacob Loesch
classification: White table wine
grape variety: Riesling
city or village: Piesport
  Piesport is one of the smallest wine villages in the Mosel valley, yet possibly the most famous. The vineyards extend over 120 acres of rocky soil facing due south.
  Fragrant, fruity bouquet; the wine has a delicate flavor that retains a degree of acidity, characteristic of a good Mosel, making it particularly suitable to accompany fish.
price range: C

producer: Madrigal Weinexport GmbH
classification: White table wine

grape variety: Riesling
grade: Qualitätswein b.A.
city or village: Zell
vineyard: Schwarze Katz (Grosslage)
  "Zeller Schwarze Katz" (black cat of Zell) is one of the most famous German wines. Officially classified as a composite vineyard, or *Grosslage*, the Schwarze Katz vineyard lies around Zell, and the vines are planted on the steep slopes of the Mosel River valley. All must be tended by hand, according to an old adage: "Where the plow can go, no vine should grow."
  Pale gold color and a flowery bouquet. The wine is light, crisp, and has a pleasing touch of acidity. **price range:** B

producer: Madrigal Weinexport GmbH
classification: White table wine
grape variety: Riesling
grade: Qualitätswein b.A.
city or village: Piesport
vineyard: Treppchen (Einzellage)
  Pale gold color and a delicately fragrant bouquet. The wine is refreshingly crisp and dry. **price range:** B

producer: Madrigal Weinexport GmbH
classification: White table wine
grape variety: Riesling
grade: Qualitätswein b.A.
city or village: Bernkastel (Bereich)
  "Bereich Bernkasteler Riesling" is produced from several villages within the Bernkastel *Bereich* (subregion).
  Pale gold color and a flowery, fragrant bouquet. The wine is refreshing, dry, and fruity. **price range:** B

producer: Ludwig Neuhaus
classification: White table wine
grape variety: Riesling
grade: Qualitätswein b.A.
city or village: Zell
vineyard: Schwarze Katz (Grosslage)
  "Neuhaus Zeller Schwarze Katz" is very

representative of its origin. The firm also ships Moselblümchen and May Wine at similar prices.

Light golden color and a varietal bouquet. The wine is clean and dry, a typical Mosel. **price range: A**

producer: Pfarrkirche St. Michel
classification: White table wine
grape variety: Riesling
grade: Qualitätswein mit Prädikat—Spätlese
city or village: Graach
vineyard: Himmelreich (Einzellage)

The Himmelreich *Einzellage* is the best-known Graach vineyard. It lies on a very steep slope facing south.

Green-yellow color and a fine, flowery bouquet. The wine has fine Riesling character, with well-balanced acidity. **price range: B**

producer: Pfarrkirche St. Michel
classification: White table wine
grape variety: Riesling
grade: Qualitätswein mit Prädikat—Kabinett
city or village: Bernkastel
vineyard: Badstube (Grosslage)

The Badstube *Grosslage* is a composite vineyard including five different vineyards on a south-facing slope in Bernkastel.

Green-yellow color and a fine bouquet. The wine shows excellent breeding and is fine and fruity. **price range: B**

producer: Franz Reh & Söhn
classification: White table wine
grape variety: Riesling, Silvaner, and Müller-Thurgau
grade: Qualitätswein b.A.
city or village: Bernkastel (Bereich)

"Klosterprinz" comes from the *Bereich* (district) of Bernkastel and is a blend of wines from better vineyards.

Pale straw-lemon color and a light, refreshing, and fruity Riesling bouquet. The wine is light, well-balanced with fruit and acidity, and medium sweet; serve lightly chilled. **price range: A**

producer: Adolf Rheinart
classification: White table wine
grape variety: Riesling
grade: Qualitätswein mit Prädikat—Spätlese
city or village: Ockfen
vineyard: Bockstein (Einzellage)

The Bockstein is the leading *Einzellage* in Ockfen, and one of the most famous in the entire Saar district. Saar wines are distinguished by their racy acidity, which often gives them a "steely" quality in middling vintages but contributes unsurpassed balance in great vintages. Adolf Rheinart Erben is one of the leading proprietors in the Bockstein vineyard.

Green-yellow color and an elegant, grapey bouquet. The wine is somewhat "steely" but very elegant. **price range: C**

producer: Rosenberg Weinkellerei GmbH
classification: White table wine
grape variety: Riesling
grade: Tafelwein (table wine)
city or village: Bernkastel

The producing winery has been under the control of the same family for over three and a half centuries.

A light, refreshing white wine, highly enjoyable with or without food. **price range: A**

producer: Rosenberg Weinkellerei GmbH
classification: White table wine
grape variety: Riesling
grade: Qualitätswein b.A.
city or village: Zell
vineyard: Schwarze Katz (Grosslage)

The producing winery has been under the control of the same family for over three and a half centuries.

A wine as charming as the area from which it comes. **price range: A**

producer: Schlosskelerei Lichtenthäler GmbH
classification: White table wine
grade: Qualitätswein b.A.
city or village: Zell
vineyard: Schwarze Katz (Grosslage)

A dry yet fruity Mosel wine. **price range: A**

producer: Gustav Adolf Schmitt
classification: White table wine
grape variety: Riesling
city or village: Bernkastel (Bereich)

"Bereich Bernkastel Riesling Vintage Dance" is a typically light, refreshing Mosel.

Pale almond, water-white color and a light, fruity bouquet. The wine is medium dry, with balanced acidity. **price range: A**

producer: Gustav Adolf Schmitt
classification: White table wine
grape variety: Traditional varieties of Mosel Valley

Pale almond, water-white color and a fruity bouquet. The wine is medium dry, with good acidity—an attractive light regional Mosel. **price range: A**

producer: Gustav Adolf Schmitt
classification: White table wine
grape variety: Riesling
grade: Qualitätswein b.A.
city or village: Zell
vineyard: Schwarze Katz (Grosslage)

The "Zeller Schwarze Katz" (black cat of Zell) is one of the best-known German wines, and like "Niersteiner Gutes Domtal," comes from a composite vineyard, or *Grosslage.*

Clear yellow color and a very fruity, fresh bouquet. The wine has balanced sweetness and acidity and shows the typical character of a light Riesling from the Mosel. It is suitable for any kind of light food, such as seafood or poultry. **price range: A**

producer: H. J. Schneider
classification: White table wine
grape variety: Riesling
grade: Qualitätswein mit Prädikat
city or village: Piesport

Though this wine is not estate-bottled, it is superior to many estate-bottlings *(Erzeugerabfüllungen),* and the vintage was as successful as 1971.

Golden color and a rich, fruity bouquet. The wine has good body and is well-balanced with a long finish. **price range: C**

producer: H. Sichel Söhne
classification: White table wine
grape variety: Riesling
grade: Qualitätswein b.A.
city or village: Piesport
vineyard: Michelsberg (Grosslage)

Light straw color and a fresh, fruity bouquet. The wine is crisp, refreshing, and should be drunk young; a good summer wine. **price range: B**

producer: H. Sichel Söhne
classification: White table wine
grape variety: Riesling
grade: Tafelwein (table wine)

Light color and a youthful bouquet; a good summer wine that should be drunk young. **price range: B**

producer: H. Sichel Söhne
classification: White table wine
grape variety: Riesling
grade: Qualitätswein b.A.
village: Bernkastel (Bereich)
  Light color and a fresh, fruity bouquet.
The wine is crisp and refreshing, an ideal
summer wine; it should be drunk young.
price range: B

producer: H. Sichel Söhne
classification: White table wine
grape variety: Riesling
grade: Qualitätswein b.A.
city or village: Zeltingen
vineyard: Münzlay (Grosslage)
  Light straw color and a fresh bouquet.
The wine is fruity and appealing, a delightful summer wine; it should be drunk young.
price range: B

---

*"Who prates of war or want
after taking wine?"*
          —Horace

producer: H. Sichel Söhne
classification: White table wine
grape variety: Riesling
grade: Qualitätswein mit
  Prädikat—Kabinett
city or village: Piesport
vineyard: Goldtröpfchen (Einzellage)
  A youthful, typical specimen of a fine
vineyard that has made this region famous.
  Clear yellow color and a flowery
bouquet. The wine is very fresh, with a
spicy flavor.   **price range:** C

producer: H. Sichel Söhne
classification: White table wine
grape variety: Riesling
grade: Qualitätswein mit
  Prädikat—Spätlese
city or village: Piesport
vineyard: Goldtröpfchen (Einzellage)
  A fine example of a popular Mosel wine.
Light straw color and a flowery bouquet.
The wine is crisp and appealing.
price range: C

---

*"Wine rejoices the heart of
man, and joy is the mother of
all virtue."*
          —Goethe

producer: H. Sichel Söhne
classification: White table wine
grape variety: Riesling
grade: Qualitätswein b.A.
city or village: Zell
vineyard: Schwarze Katz (Grosslage)
  Light color and a flowery bouquet. The
wine is very sprightly and fruity and is best
when drunk young.   **price range:** B

producer: Steigenberger
classification: White table wine
grape variety: Riesling
grade: Qualitätswein b.A.
city or village: Piesport
vineyard: Treppchen (Einzellage)
  Shipped in a green bottle.
  Delicate fragrance and a piquant, fruity
flavor characteristic of a good Piesporter.
price range: B

producer: Steigenberger
classification: White table wine
grape variety: Riesling
grade: Qualitätswein b.A.
city or village: Bernkastel (Bereich)
  Made from one of the greatest white wine
grapes and shipped in a green bottle.
  Delicate bouquet; the wine is full-bodied
and fruity.   **price range:** A

producer: Teitel & Co.
classification: White table wine
grade: Tafelwein (table wine)
  Clear straw color and a fruity bouquet.
The wine is semi-dry and has a pleasant
taste; serve chilled.   **price range:** A

producer: Teitel & Co.
classification: White table wine
grape variety: Riesling
grade: Qualitätswein b.A.
village: Bernkastel (Bereich)
  Clear straw color and a fruity bouquet.
The wine is semi-dry.   **price range:** A

producer: Teitel & Co.
classification: White table wine
grade: Qualitätswein b.A.
city or village: Zell
vineyard: Schwarze Katz (Grosslage)
  Straw color and a fruity bouquet. The
wine is semi-dry and full-bodied, with a
pleasant flavor; serve chilled.
price range: A

producer: Freiherr von Schorlemer
classification: White table wine
grape variety: Riesling
grade: Qualitätswein mit
  Prädikat—Kabinett
city or village: Brauneberg
vineyard: Kurfürstlay (Grosslage)
  Brauneberg is one of the most famous
villages in the Mosel, and it usually produced very good wines. The vineyards are
particularly well exposed to the sun, and
the grapes grow on the slate soil that occurs throughout the river valley.
  Clear color and a full, flowery, and ripe
bouquet. The wine is rich, well-balanced,
and has a long finish.   **price range:** A

producer: Freiherr von Schorlemer
classification: White table wine
grape variety: Riesling
grade: Qualitätswein mit
  Prädikat—Spätlese
city or village: Brauneberg
vineyard: Juffer (Einzellage)
  Juffer is the most famous Brauneberg
Einzellage, and the wines have a
worldwide reputation; they are especially
good in great vintages like 1971 and 1975.
  Clear, bright color and a rich, powerful
bouquet. The wine is big, full of fruit and
ripeness.   **price range:** B

---

producer: Freiherr von Schorlemer
classification: White table wine
grape variety: Riesling
grade: Qualitätswein mit
  Prädikat—Kabinet
city or village: Wintrich
vineyard: Ohligsberg (Einzellage)
  Ohligsberg is considered to be one of
Wintrich's best *Einzellagen.* The vineyard
was replanted five years ago, and it now
produces very good wine, especially in the
1973 vintage. Stephan von Schorlemer is
the only member of the family who still
owns and vinifies wines from his own vineyards.
  Clear, bright color and a soft, flowery
bouquet. The wine is robust, spicy, and full
of flavor; it is rather dry but has real Mosel
Riesling character and should have a good
shelf life.   **price range:** B

producer: Franz Weber
classification: White table wine
grape variety: Riesling
grade: Qualitätswein b.A.
city or village: Piesport
vineyard: Goldtröpfchen (Einzellage)
   Clear color and a light bouquet. The wine is semi-sweet. **price range:** A

producer: Franz Weber
classification: White table wine
grape variety: Riesling
grade: Tafelwein (table wine)
   Bright clear color and a light bouquet. The wine is semi-sweet. **price range:** A

producer: Franz Weber
classification: White table wine
grape variety: Riesling
grade: Qualitätswein b.A.
city or village: Zell
vineyard: Schwarze Katz (Grosslage)
   Clear color and a light, flowery bouquet. The wine is fruity, with a clean, crisp flavor. **price range:** A

producer: Franz Weber
classification: White table wine
grape variety: Riesling

---

grade: Qualitätswein b.A.
city or village: Bernkastel
vineyard: Kurfürstlay (Grosslage)
   Bright, clear color and a light bouquet. The wine is medium sweet.
price range: A

producer: Franz Weber
classification: White table wine
grape variety: Riesling
grade: Qualitätswein b.A.
city or village: Cröv
vineyard: Nacktarsch (Grosslage)
   Bright, clear color and a light bouquet. The wine is medium sweet. **price range:** A

producer: A. Weigand
classification: White table wine
grape variety: Elbling and Riesling
grade: Tafelwein (table wine)
   A reasonable, low-priced table wine—very drinkable and good value.
   Very pale green-gold color and a light, fresh, and earthy bouquet. The wine is medium dry, light, and has a slight sharpness. **price range:** A

producer: Weingut Louis Guntrum
classification: White table wine
grape variety: Riesling
grade: Qualitätswein b.A
city or village: Zell
vineyard: Schwarze Katz (Grosslage)
   When young, Mosel wines often have a slight sparkle, or "spritz" giving freshness and character.
   Pale greenish color and a lively, fragrant bouquet. The wine is fruity and semi-dry, with an invigorating fragrance; it is light in body and low in alcohol, making it excellent with fish or hors d'oeuvres.
price range: B

producer: Weingut Louis Guntrum
classification: White table wine
grape variety: Riesling
grade: Qualitätswein b.A.
village: Piesport
vineyard: Michelsberg (Grosslage)
   Soft green color and a fragrant, fruity, and delicate bouquet. The wine is light-bodied, semi-dry, and well-balanced, with an invigorating freshness resulting from its low alcoholic content. It is ideal with fish, hors d'oeuvres, or by itself.
price range: B

producer: Weingut Math. Hess-Becker
classification: White table wine
grape variety: Riesling
grade: Qualitätswein mit
   Prädikat—Spätlese—Eiswein
city or village: Fankel
vineyard: Rosenberg (Einzellage)
   Something special for the connoisseur, an *Eiswein* is pressed from partially frozen grapes picked very late in the growing season. They may or may not be affected by *Edelfaule (Botrytis cinerea).*
   Full, elegant gold color and a rich, noble bouquet. The wine is full and noble, with luscious natural sugar. **price range:** E

producer: Weingut Math. Hess-Becker
classification: White table wine
grape variety: Riesling
grade: Qualitätswein mit
   Prädikat—Auslese
city or village: Bruttig
vineyard: Götterlay (Einzellage)
   Auslesen wines are made from selected bunches of extra ripe grapes that have grown under particularly ideal conditions. Because of their sweetness and high price, they are wines for special occasions.
   Elegant golden color and a deep, fruity bouquet. An exceptionally great wine.
price range: C

producer: Weingut Math. Hess-Becker
classification: White table wine
grape variety: Riesling
grade: Qualitätswein mit
   Prädikat—Spätlese
city or village: Fankel
vineyard: Rosenberg (Einzellage)
   A characteristic *Spätlese* (late-picked) wine from the Mosel.
   Elegant and appealing gold color and a fruity bouquet. A delightful wine of elegance and finesse. **price range:** B

producer: Weingut Math. Hess-Becker
classification: White table wine
grape variety: Riesling
grade: Qualitätswein mit
   Prädikat—Kabinett
city or village: Fankel
vineyard: Rosenberg (Einzellage)
   Delightfully refreshing green-gold color and a pleasant bouquet. The wine is dry, with a slight "spritz," or effervescence; a wine for any occasion. **price range:** B

producer: Weingut Math. Hess-Becker
classification: White table wine
grape variety: Riesling and Silvaner
grade: Qualitätswein b.A.
city or village: Ellenz
vineyard: Goldbäumchen (Grosslage)
   Appealing green-gold color and a delicate bouquet. The wine is pleasantly soft and dry, with a slight degree of "spritz"; it is light and delicate. **price range:** A

producer: Weingut Math. Hess-Becker
classification: White table wine

grape variety: Riesling
grade: Qualitätswein b.A.
city or village: Zell
vineyard: Schwarze Katz (Grosslage)
Green-gold color and a pleasant, crisp bouquet. The wine is light, dry and pleasant, with some "spritz." **price range:** A

producer: Winzerverein
classification: White table wine
grape variety: Riesling
grade: Qualitätswein mit
Prädikat—Kabinett
city or village: Wintrich
vineyard: Stephanslay
Clear, bright color and a strong, fruity bouquet. The wine is fruity and robust, with a pleasing dryness; everybody likes this type of wine because of its good balance and fine acidity. It has all the virtues of a good Mosel wine. **price range:** B

producer: Winzerverein
classification: White table wine
grape variety: Riesling
grade: Qualitätswein mit
Prädikat—Spätlese
city or village: Wintrich
vineyard: Grosser Herrgott (Einzellage)
Wintrich wines have all the glamour one looks for in a good Mosel. The name *Grosser Herrgott* means "great and good lord." 1971 and 1975 were outstanding vintages in Germany.
Clear, bright color and a fine ripe bouquet. The wine is fragrant and fruity, very big and satisfying, but needs about two years to develop fully. Its pleasant acidity and good alcoholic content make a long shelf life possible. **price range:** B

GERMANY, RHEINPFALZ

producer: Dolamore
classification: White table wine
grade: Qualitätswein b.A.
Although this is not stated on the label, "College Hock" is a Qualitätswein from the Rheinpfalz area. **price range:** A

producer: Dr. Wolf Fleischmann
classification: White table wine
grape variety: Riesling
city or village: Bad Dürkheim
vineyard: Feuerberg (Grosslage)
Pale gold color and a spicy, true Riesling bouquet. The wine is dry but has a faint touch of sweetness; it is very fruity and excellent. **price range:** B

producer: Cark Jos. Hoch
classification: White table wine
city or village: Neustadt
Bright golden color and a flowery bouquet. The wine is medium dry and full-flavored. **price range:** B

producer: Fritz Hübinger
classification: White table wine
grape variety: Silvaner and Morio-Muskat
grade: Qualitätswein mit Prädikat
bereich: Südliche Weinstrasse
This wine is blended to maintain consistent quality; high-quality corks are used to assure long shelf life.
Light gold color and a bouquet suggesting peaches or apples. The wine is light and fresh-tasting, with a touch of sweetness; it is very good value. **price range:** A

producer: Fritz Hübinger
classification: White table wine
grape variety: Morio-Muskat and Silvaner
grade: Qualitätswein mit
Prädikat—Kabinett
city or village: Mailkammer
The grapes for this wine were produced by several local growers.
Straw color and a fruity bouquet. The wine is light, with a slight sweetness, and has a pleasant finish. It is superior to many Liebfraumilchs, which are blended regional wines. **price range:** A

producer: A. J. Koenen Ltd.
classification: White table wine
grape variety: Riesling
grade: Qualitätswein b.A.
city or village: Forst
vineyard: Schnepfenflug (Einzellage)
Clean, light straw color and a bouquet with characteristic Riesling fragrance that has the spicy quality of Rheinpfalz wines. The wine is clean, smooth, well-balanced, and dry; it is excellent with any meal, providing the dish is not too spicy.
price range: B

producer: Leonard Kreusch Inc.
classification: Red table wine
grape variety: Portuguiser and others
grade: Qualitätswein b.A.
city or village: Bad Dürkheim
vineyard: Feuerberg (Grosslage)
price range: A

producer: Palatia-Weinkellerei
classification: White table wine

grape variety: Silvaner (34%),
Müller-Thurgau (37%), Portuguiser (5%), and Riesling (6%)
grade: Qualitätswein b.A.
A wine of fine quality, currently produced by a small family now in its seventh generation.
Magnificent golden hue and a fruity, fragrant, and soft bouquet. The wine has a rich taste of the grape and finishes cleanly; it is a light wine that will enhance all entrées. Serve slightly chilled.
price range: B

producer: St. Ursula Weinkellerei
classification: White table wine
grape variety: Riesling
grade: Qualitätswein mit
Prädikat—Kabinett
city or village: Deidesheim
vineyard: Hofstück (Grosslage)
A successful selection made from 106 different *Prädikat* (unsugared) wines. It is low in alcohol (8–9%), and has about 2 degrees natural sugar.
Light straw-gold color and a very fruity bouquet. The wine has a rich flavor and is clean. **price range:** B

producer: St. Ursula Weinkellerei
classification: White table wine
grape variety: Riesling and Silvaner
grade: Qualitätswein b.A.
A very popular wine comparing competitively with more expensive wines of its type. It is selected only in the best vintages and is not cloyingly sweet.
Light gold color with glints of green and a very fruity Riesling bouquet. The wine is extremely clean, low in acid and alcohol, with a good fruity character.
price range: A

producer: H. Sichel Söhne
classification: White table wine
grape variety: Riesling

grade: Qualitätswein mit
Prädikat—Spätlese
city or village: Forst
vineyard: Jesuitengarten (Einzellage)
Golden-yellow color and a flowery
bouquet. The wine is very rich and appealing; a great, elegant specimen of the
world-renowned Rheinpfalz region.
price range: E

producer: H. Sichel Söhne
classification: White table wine
grape variety: Riesling
grade: Qualitätswein mit
Prädikat—Kabinett
city or village: Deidesheim
Deidesheim is an important wine town
located south of Bad Dürkheim.
Full, rounded bouquet and an agreeable
flavor. **price range:** B

producer: Weinkellerei von
Bassermann-Jordan
classification: White table wine
grape variety: Riesling
grade: Qualitätswein mit
Prädikat—Kabinett
city or village: Deidesheim
vineyard: Paradiesgarten (Einzellage)
The Rheinpfalz region has been producing wine for over two thousand years.
Named for the Palatine Hills in Rome, the
first residence of the Roman emperors, the
area was once called "the Wine Cellar of
the Holy Roman Empire." The
Bassermann-Jordan family have been
wine makers for over 250 years and are
largely responsible for the fame of Palatinate wines. All the wines are estate-bottled
(Erzeugerabfüllung).
Pale golden color and a "steely"
bouquet. The wine is fragrant, clean, and
has a delicious taste. **price range:** C

GERMANY, NAHE AND FRANKEN

producer: Deinhard & Co.
classification: White table wine
grade: Qualitätswein b.A.
city or village: Schloss Böckelheim
(Bereich)
Soft bouquet; well-balanced, fruity
flavor. **price range:** B

producer: Arthur Hallgarten GmbH
classification: White table wine
grape variety: Blend
grade: Qualitätswein b.A.
Sold under the Steingarten brand name
used by Hallgarten, in the squat
bocksbeutel flask.
Pale color and a fruity bouquet. The wine
is bone-dry, but retains a fruity character,
like many Franken weins. **price range:** B

producer: Leonard Kreusch Inc.
classification: White table wine
grape variety: Riesling
grade: Qualitätswein b.A.
city or village: Rüdesheim
vineyard: Rosengarten (Grosslage)
Big and full-bodied.
price range: A

producer: H. Sichel Söhne
classification: White table wine
grape variety: Riesling
grade: Qualitätswein b.A.
village: Schloss Böckelheim (Bereich)
Golden color and a fresh, youthful
bouquet. The wine is light and flowery.
price range: B

producer: Burgkellerei GmbH
classification: White table wine
grade: Qualitätswein b.A.
district: Liebfraumilch
Pale white color and a fruity bouquet.
The wine is light, semi-dry, and crisp;
serve chilled. **price range:** A

producer: Deinhard & Co.
classification: White table wine
grade: Qualitätswein b.A.
district: Liebfraumilch
Rich bouquet; full-bodied, round flavor.
price range: C

producer: Deinhard & Co.
classification: White table wine
grade: Qualitätswein b.A.
district: Liebfraumilch
Pleasing fruity bouquet; the wine is soft,
round, and well-balanced. **price range:** B

producer: Export-Union Deutscher
Weingüter
classification: White table wine

GERMANY, RHEINHESSEN

grape variety: Riesling
grade: Qualitätswein b.A.
district: Liebfraumilch
"Wedding Veil Liebfraumilch" is refreshingly fruity in its youth.
A good semi-sweet white wine with a
subtle flavor and rich body. It may be
served any time of day or evening with
most foods, chilled but not iced.
price range: B

producer: Export-Union Deutscher
Weingüter
classification: White table wine
grape variety: White varieties flavored with
woodruff herbs
grade: Tafelwein (table wine)
May Wine flavored with woodruff.
price range: B

producer: Felix Faber
classification: White table wine
grape variety: Silvaner and Riesling
grade: Qualitätswein b.A.
district: Liebfraumilch
Light straw color and a fruity bouquet.
The wine is light-bodied, with a fruity
flavor. **price range:** B

producer: Felix Faber
classification: White table wine
grape variety: Silvaner and Riesling
grade: Qualitätswein b.A.
district: Liebraumilch

Brilliant light straw color and a fruity bouquet. The wine is light-bodied, with a fruity flavor. **price range:** B

producer: Felix Faber
classification: White table wine
grape variety: Silvaner and Riesling
grade: Qualitätswein b.A.
district: Liebfraumilch

Brilliant light straw color and a fruity bouquet. The wine is light-bodied, with a fruity flavor. **price range:** B

producer: Findlater Mackie Todd & Co. Ltd.
classification: White table wine
grape variety: Riesling, Silvaner, Müller-Thurgau, and others
grade: Qualitätswein b.A.
district: Liebfraumilch

This Liebfraumilch is bottled in the Rhine region by the suppliers; it contains 11% alcohol by volume.

Pale straw color and a smooth, fruity bouquet. The wine is round, pleasing, and medium dry; it is a typical Liebfraumilch, with good light body and flavor.
price range: B

producer: Gartenhaus
classification: White table wine
grape variety: Müller-Thurgau
grade: Qualitätswein b.A.
district: Liebfraumilch

Light golden, crystal-clear color and a very pronounced bouquet. The flavor is typical of Müller-Thurgau; suggesting Muscat, it is a very pleasant, light dry wine that finishes cleanly. **price range:** A

producer: Arthur Hallgarten GmbH
classification: White table wine
grape variety: Blend
grade: Qualitätswein b.A.
city or village: Nierstein
vineyard: Gutes Domtal (Grosslage)

A regional Niersteiner with national distribution in the United Kingdom; one of the leading brands in Britain.

Pale color and a light and delicate bouquet. The wine is full-flavored and shows great length. **price range:** A

producer: Arthur Hallgarten GmbH
classification: White table wine
grape variety: Blend
grade: Qualitätswein b.A.
grape variety: Liebfraumilch

Sold under the "Kellergeist" (cellar spirit) label in the United Kingdom.

Pale color and a light, delicately grapey bouquet. The wine is very fruity and well-balanced; a quality wine representing good value for the money. **price range:** A

producer: Ernst Jungkenn
classification: White table wine
grape variety: Silvaner, Müller-Thurgau, and Riesling
grade: Qualitätswein b.A.
district: Liebfraumilch
city or village: Oppenheim

Most of the wines that the Jungkenn Winery uses come from their own cellars. The family crest dates back to 1553, and the Jungkenns have been in the wine business since 1653. This is an excellent example of a Liebfraumilch from the Rheinhessen district and shows the character that can be obtained from the Silvaner grape.

Pale gold color and a fruity—slightly spicy—bouquet. The wine is clean, soft, and slightly sweet; finishes well.
price range: A

producer: Ernst Jungkenn
classification: White table wine
grape variety: Silvaner, Riesling, and Müller-Thurgau
grade: Qualitätswein b.A.
city or village: Oppenheim
vineyard: Krötenbrunnen (Grosslage)

The Jungkenn family have been growers and merchants in this district for over four hundred years.

A medium-dry Rhine wine.
price range: B

"O thou invisible spirit of wine! if thou hast no name to be known by, let us call thee devil."
—Shakespeare, *Othello*

producer: Ernst Jungkenn
classification: White table wine
grape variety: Silvaner and Müller-Thurgau
grade: Qualitätswein b.A.
city or village: Oppenheim

Pale gold color and a fruity—slightly spicy—bouquet. The wine is slightly sweet, and has a tart finish; an excellent wine for the price. **price range:** A

producer: Hermann Kendermann
classification: White table wine
grape variety: Silvaner and Müller-Thurgau
grade: Qualitätswein b.A.
district: Liebfraumilch

Liebfraumilch is one of the largest-selling white wines exported from Germany. "Black Tower" is a superior Liebfraumilch.

Pale color and a fruity bouquet. The wine is medium dry and very refreshing; it is perfect with a meal or by itself, as an aperitif. **price range:** A

producer: A. J. Koenen Ltd.
classification: Red table wine
grape variety: Portuguiser
grade: Qualitätswein b.A.
city or village: Ingelheim

This light red wine *(Rotwein)* is made from the Portuguiser grape, a red grape grown in Germany that has nothing to do with Portugal. In Germany, red wines tend to be much lighter than those from more southern countries; they are cheerful, light, and low in alcohol, but are quite easy to drink.

Pale red color and a clean, grapey bouquet. The wine is light to the taste but balanced. **price range:** B

producer: A. J. Koenen Ltd.
classification: White table wine
grape variety: Riesling
grade: Qualitätswein b.A.

Any Liebfraumilch must be a *Qualitätswein* from the authorized regions *(Anbaugebiete)* in the Rhine area: Rheinhessen, Rheingau, Mittelrhein, Rheinpfalz (Palatinate), and Nahe. This Liebfraumilch is sold under the trade name Lorelei.

Clean light straw color and a fruity, fresh bouquet. The wine is balanced and pleasant, with a fine finish. **price range:** B

producer: A. J. Koenen Ltd.
classification: White sparkling wine
grape variety: Blend
grade: Prädikatsekt

A *Prädikatsekt* (sparkling wine with special attributes) produced by the *méthode champenoise.*

Pale and a fresh, lively, and decidedly fruity bouquet. The wine is clean and well-balanced, an ideally refreshing wine for celebrations. It can be taken before lunch or as an aperitif, for a refreshing change. **price range:** B

producer: A. J. Koenen Ltd.
classification: White table wine
grape variety: Riesling
grade: Qualitätswein b.A.
city or village: Nierstein
vineyard: Gutes Domtal (Grosslage)
Light straw color and a crisp, firm Riesling bouquet. The wine is clean, fruity, and well-balanced. **price range:** B

producer: A. J. Koenen Ltd.
classification: White table wine
grape variety: Riesling
grade: Qualitätswein b.A.
city or village: Oppenheim
vineyard: Krötenbrunnen (Grosslage)
Bright light straw color, and a clean, "noble" bouquet. The wine is dry, well-balanced, and has a delightful fruity quality—it is excellent with all meals except those that are highly spiced.
price range: B

producer: Leonard Kreusch Inc.
classification: White table wine
grape variety: Riesling blend
grade: Qualitätswein b.A.
price range: A

producer: Leonard Kreusch Inc.
classification: White table wine
grape variety: Riesling

grade: Qualitätswein b.A.
city or village: Oppenheim
vineyard: Krötenbrunnen (Grosslage)
Soft and fruity. **price range:** A

producer: Leonard Kreusch Inc.
classification: White table wine
grape variety: Riesling
grade: Qualitätswein b.A.
city or village: Nierstein
vineyard: Gutes Domtal (Grosslage)
Soft, delicate, and full-bodied.
price range: A

producer: Jacob Loesch
classification: White table wine
grape variety: Riesling
grade: Qualitätswein b.A.
district: Liebfraumilch
Liebfraumilch is certainly one of the best-known wine names. It originally referred to a few acres of vineyard around the Liebfrauenstift vineyard in Worms, but now applies to regional wines produced in a much larger area.
Full, naturally sweet bouquet; the wine is light and fruity, with a touch of acidity and sweetness; an ideal quaffing wine.
price range: C

producer: Jacob Loesch
classification: White table wine
grape variety: Riesling
grade: Qualitätswein b.A.
city or village: Nierstein
vineyard: Gutes Domtal (Grosslage)
Pleasantly fragrant bouquet; the wine is light and refreshing, with a touch of sweetness that makes it easy to drink. It goes well with cold meats, fish, or poultry and can be drunk throughout the meal. **price range:** C

producer: Madrigal Weinexport GmbH
classification: White table wine
grape variety: Riesling
grade: Qualitätswein b.A.
district: Liebfraumilch
A great number of regional Liebfraumilch wines are sold on the American market. For this reason, the integrity of the producer is of great importance. Madrigal Liebfraumilch is carefully selected and bottled in the Rhine district and is sold nationally in the United States.
Pale gold color and a fruity bouquet. The wine is medium dry and delicate, with good depth of flavor. **price range:** B

producer: Madrigal Weinexport GmbH
classification: White table wine
grape variety: Riesling
grade: Qualitätswein b.A.
city or village: Nierstein
vineyard: Gutes Domtal (Grosslage)
A fine example of a Rheinhessen wine from a composite vineyard, or *Grosslage.*
Pale gold color and a delicate, fruity bouquet. The wine is soft, round, and full-bodied, with great elegance.
price range: B

producer: Ludwig Neuhaus
classification: White table wine
grape variety: Müller-Thurgau
grade: Qualitätswein b.A.
district: Liebfraumilch
Light golden color and a very pronounced bouquet. The wine has a slight Muscat flavor; it is a very pleasant, light dry white Rhine wine that finishes cleanly.
price range: A

producer: Roll-Bootz
classification: White table wine
grape variety: Traminer
grade: Qualitätswein mit Prädikat—Spätlese
city or village: Dittelsheim
Clear golden color and a fragrant bouquet. The wine is well-balanced, with a spicy varietal flavor.
price range: B

producer: Roll-Bootz
classification: White table wine
grape variety: Silvaner
grade: Qualitätswein mit Prädikat
city or village: Dittelsheim
Clear golden color and a fragrant, flowery bouquet. The wine is medium dry, with a luscious fruity flavor. **price range:** C

producer: Roll-Bootz
classification: White table wine
grape variety: Morio-Muskat and Huxelrebe
grade: Qualitätswein mit Prädikat
city or village: Dittelsheim
Clear, bright golden color and a fragrant bouquet. The wine is well-balanced and medium sweet; a delightful all-purpose wine. **price range:** B

producer: Roll-Bootz
classification: White table wine
grape variety: Silvaner

grade: Qualitätswein mit
Prädikat—Auslese
city or village: Dittelsheim
Brilliant golden color and a flowery bouquet. The wine is noble, fully ripe, and well matured; an excellent dessert wine.
price range: C

producer: Roll-Bootz
classification: White table wine
grape variety: Silvaner
grade: Qualitätswein mit
Prädikat—Spätlese
city or village: Dittelsheim
Clear pale golden color and a delicate fruity bouquet. The wine is medium dry and well balanced.
price range: B

producer: Roll-Bootz
classification: Red table wine
grape variety: Portuguiser
grade: Qualitätswein b.A.
city or village: Dittelsheim
Fresh, light red color, and a fruity bouquet. The wine is pleasant and fruity, a fine everyday wine.
price range: B

producer: Roll-Bootz
classification: White table wine
grape variety: Silvaner
grade: Qualitätswein mit
Prädikat—Spätlese
city or village: Dittelsheim
Roll-Bootz wines have been produced by the family for over two hundred years in the small village of Dittelsheim in the Rheinhessen. The wines are in limited production but have won many prizes.
Clear golden color and a delicate, fruity bouquet. The wine is luscious and medium sweet; a special occasion wine.
price range: B

producer: Roll-Bootz
classification: White table wine
grape variety: Siegerrebe
grade: Qualitätswein mit
Prädikat—Spätlese
city or village: Dittelsheim
Clear golden color and a fruity bouquet. The wine is medium dry and well-balanced.
price range: C

producer: Roll-Bootz
classification: White table wine
grape variety: Müller-Thurgau
grade: Qualitätswein mit
Prädikat—Spätlese
Clear pale gold color and a fruity bouquet. The wine is well-balanced, with pronounced varietal flavor and some residual sugar.
price range: B

producer: Roll-Bootz
classification: White table wine
grape variety: Silvaner
grade: Qualitätswein b.A.
city or village: Dittelsheim
Clear, bright golden color and a flowery bouquet. The wine is robust and full-bodied; an excellent table wine.
price range: B

producer: Rosenberg GmbH
classification: White table wine
grape variety: Silvaner

grade: Qualitätswein b.A.
district: Liebfraumilch
The producing winery has been under the control of the same family for over three and a half centuries.
A wine for all seasons and situations.
price range: A

producer: Schlosskelerei Lichtenthäler GmbH
classification: White table wine
grade: Qualitätswein b.A.
district: Liebfraumilch
A light, fruity white Rhine wine.
price range: A

producer: Gustav Adolf Schmitt
classification: White table wine
grape variety: Blend
grade: Qualitätswein b.A.
district: Nierstein (Bereich)
Pale yellow color and a pronounced fruity, grapey bouquet. The wine is medium dry and of good quality.
price range: A

producer: Gustav Adolf Schmitt
classification: White table wine
grape variety: Sylvaner, Müller-Thurgau, and others
grade: Qualitätswein b.A.
district: Liebfraumilch
Pale yellow color and a fruity bouquet. The wine is medium dry, light, and pleasant; good value.
price range: A

producer: Gustav Adolf Schmitt
classification: White table wine
grape variety: Silvaner and Müller-Thurgau
grade: Qualitätswein b.A.
district: Liebfraumilch

Liebfraumilch is one of the most popular German wines. It can legally come from the Rheinhessen, Rheinpfalz (Palatinate), Mittelrhein, Rheingau, and Nahe districts; but the best originate in Rheinhessen.
Clear color and a fresh, flavorful bouquet. The wine is full, harmonious, and well-balanced; it is suitable with any kind of food or occasion, and should be chilled to about 50 degrees F.
price range: A

producer: Gustav Adolf Schmitt
classification: White table wine
grape variety: Silvaner and Müller-Thurgau
grade: Qualitätswein b.A.
city or village: Nierstein
vineyard: Gutes Domtal (Grosslage)
Niersteiner Gutes Domtal is the largest vineyard site in Rheinhessen, officially classified as a composite vineyard or *Grosslage*. Niersteiners rank with the best wines from the Rhine district.
Clear light color and a fresh bouquet. The wine is full, flavorful and harmonious; it is a fruity wine that can be drunk on any occasion.
price range: B

producer: Gustav Adolf Schmitt
classification: White table wine
grape variety: Riesling
grade: Qualitätswein mit
Prädikat—Spätlese
city or village: Nierstein
vineyard: Pettenthal (Einzellage)
The Pettenthal vineyard is one of the best single sites *(Einzellagen)* in Nierstein. It is located on the Rhine front and has a unique red soil that gives the grapes outstanding ripeness.
Yellow to deep yellow color and a very fruity bouquet with a suggestion of almonds or peaches. The wine is well-balanced with sweetness and acidity and has a fine finish. It is a delicious wine for the connoisseur and should be drunk on special occasions.
price range: C

producer: Gustav Adolf Schmitt
classification: White table wine

grape variety: Riesling and Silvaner
grade: Qualitätswein b.A.
city or village: Nierstein
vineyard: Gutes Domtal (Grosslage)
Nierstein is an important wine town in the Rheinhessen district, and its wines are noted for their bouquet, among the most pronounced of the Rheinhessens.
Light yellow color and a full bouquet. The wine is smooth and mild—a fine Niersteiner. **price range: B**

producer: G. K. L. Schmitt
classification: White table wine
grape variety: Riesling
grade: Qualitätswein b.A.
city or village: Nierstein
vineyard: Gutes Domtal (Grosslage)
Clear color and a pronounced bouquet. The wine is semi-dry. **price range: A**

producer: G. K. L. Schmitt
classification: White table wine
grape variety: Riesling and Silvaner
grade: Qualitätswein mit Prädikat—Kabinett
city or village: Nierstein
vineyard: Spiegelberg (Grosslage)
Bright, clear color and a pronounced bouquet. The wine is semi-dry.
price range: A

producer: G. K. L. Schmitt
classification: White table wine
grape variety: Riesling and Silvaner
grade: Qualitätswein mit Prädikat—Kabinett
city or village: Nierstein
vineyard: Auflangen (Grosslage)
Bright, clear color and a full bouquet. The wine is semi-dry and fruity.
price range: A

producer: G. K. L. Schmitt
classification: White table wine
grape variety: Riesling
grade: Qualitätswein b.A.
city or village: Nierstein
vineyard: Heiligenbaum (Einzellage)
Clear color and a light bouquet. The wine is semi-dry. **price range: A**

producer: G. K. L. Schmitt
classification: White table wine
grape variety: Riesling and Silvaner
grade: Qualitätswein b.A.
city or village: Nierstein
vineyard: Fritzenhölle (Einzellage)
Clear color and a light bouquet. The wine is semi-dry. **price range: A**

producer: G. K. L. Schmitt
classification: White table wine
grape variety: Scheurebe
grade: Qualitätswein mit Prädikat—Kabinett
city or village: Nierstein
vineyard: Bildstock (Einzellage)
Clear color and a pronounced bouquet. The wine is dry, with a spicy flavor.
price range: A

producer: G. K. L. Schmitt
classification: White table wine

grape variety: Riesling
grade: Qualitätswein mit Prädikat—Kabinett
city or village: Nierstein
vineyard: Paterberg (Einzellage)
Clear color and a light bouquet. The wine is semi-dry. **price range: A**

producer: G. K. L. Schmitt
classification: White table wine
grape variety: Riesling
grade: Qualitätswein mit Prädikat—Spätlese
city or village: Nierstein
vineyard: Rehbach
Clear, bright color and a pronounced bouquet. The wine is semi-sweet, with good flavor. **price range: A**

producer: G. K. L. Schmitt
classification: White table wine
grape variety: Riesling
grade: Qualitätswein mit Prädikat—Kabinett
city or village: Nierstein
vineyard: Hipping
Clear color and a full bouquet. The wine is semi-dry and well-balanced.
price range: A

producer: G. K. L. Schmitt
classification: White table wine
grape variety: Ruländer
grade: Qualitätswein mit Prädikat—Spätlese
city or village: Nierstein
vineyard: Rosenberg (Einzellage)
Clear golden color and a full, pronounced bouquet. The wine is semi-dry and full flavored.
price range: A

producer: G. K. L. Schmitt
classification: White table wine
grape variety: Riesling
grade: Qualitätswein mit Prädikat—Spätlese
city or village: Oppenheim
vineyard: Reisekahr (Einzellage)
Clear color and a full bouquet. The wine is semi-sweet, with good flavor.
price range: A

producer: G. K. L. Schmitt
classification: White table wine
grape variety: Riesling
grade: Qualitätswein mit Prädikat—Spätlese
city or village: Nierstein
vineyard: Bergkirche (Einzellage)
Clear color and a pronounced bouquet. The wine is semi-dry, with a soft flavor.
price range: A

producer: G. K. L. Schmitt
classification: White table wine
grape variety: Silvaner
grade: Qualitätswein mit Prädikat—Spätlese
village: Nierstein
vineyard: Paterberg (Einzellage)
Clear, bright color and a fine bouquet. The wine is semi-dry. **price range: A**

producer: G. K. L. Schmitt
classification: White table wine
grape variety: Silvaner

grade: Qualitätswein b.A.
city or village: Oppenheim
vineyard: Schloss (Einzellage)
Clear, bright color and a light bouquet. The wine is semi-dry and quite soft.
price range: A

producer: Franz-Karl Schmitt
classification: White table wine
grape variety: Riesling
grade: Qualitätswein mit Prädikat—Auslese
city or village: Nierstein
vineyard: Hipping (Einzellage)
Golden color and a rich, flowery bouquet. The wine is full and appealing—one of the Rheinhessen's finest wines, produced by a well-respected grower.
price range: E

producer: Franz-Karl Schmitt
classification: White table wine
grape variety: Silvaner and Müller-Thurgau
grade: Qualitätswein b.A.
city or village: Nierstein
vineyard: Patersberg (Einzellage)
Golden-yellow color and a full, flowery bouquet. The wine is broad and rich; a fine example of a Rheinhessen wine.
price range: C

producer: H. Sichel Söhne
classification: White sparkling wine
grape variety: Riesling
grade: Sekt
district: Rheingau
"Sparkling Blue Nun" is a German sparkling wine (*Sekt*) made via the *méthode champenoise* and fermented in the bottle. It is also available in magnum sizes.
Bubbly white color and a fresh bouquet. The wine is lovely and refreshing and should be drunk young. **price range:** C

producer: H. Sichel Söhne
classification: White table wine
grape variety: Silvaner and Müller-Thurgau
grade: Qualitätswein mit Prädikat—Auslese
city or village: Mainz
vineyard: St. Alban (Grosslage)
This wine was formerly sold as Liebfraumilch Auslese.
Light golden color and a full, fruity bouquet. The wine is luscious and elegant—a very fine Rheinhessen wine, suitable for dessert. **price range:** C

producer: H. Sichel Söhne
classification: White table wine
grape variety: Silvaner and Müller-Thurgau
grade: Qualitätswein b.A.
city or village: Nierstein (Bereich)
Light golden color and a fresh, flowery bouquet. The wine is fruity and appealing—a good Rheinhessen.
price range: B

producer: H. Sichel Söhne
classification: White table wine
grape variety: Riesling, Silvaner, and Müller-Thurgau
grade: Qualitätswein b.A.
district: Liebfraumilch
The "peer" among Liebfraumilch, "Blue Nun" is a much-loved Rhine wine that has achieved world renown. Almost 1.5 million cases are sold annually throughout the world; the wine is also available in magnums and splits.
Light golden color and a flowery bouquet. When drunk young, it is at its best and is refreshingly appealing.
price range: B

producer: Steigenberger
classification: White table wine
grade: Qualitätswein b.A.
district: Liebfraumilch
A very popular Rhine wine, shipped in a brown bottle.
Soft, mellow flavor, with a touch of natural sweetness. **price range:** A

producer: Josef Steinbach
classification: White table wine
grape variety: Riesling
grade: Qualitätswein b.A.
district: Liebfraumilch
M. S. Walker imports a whole line of fine German wines: Liebfraumilch, May Wine, Piesporter, Moselblümchen, Zeller Schwarze Katz, and so forth.
Soft, spicy bouquet. **price range:** A

producer: Teitel & Co.
classification: White table wine
grape variety: Riesling
grade: Qualitätswein mit Prädikat—Kabinett
city or village: Oppenheim
vineyard: Krötenbrunnen (Grosslage)
Pale straw color and a light bouquet. The wine is semi-dry. **price range:** A

producer: Franz Weber
classification: White table wine
grape variety: Silvaner

grade: Qualitätswein b.A.
district: Liebfraumilch
Bright, clear color and a light, fruity bouquet. The wine is medium sweet.
price range: A

producer: Franz Weber
classification: Red table wine
grape variety: Spätburgunder
grade: Qualitätswein b.A.
city or village: Ingelheim
Light red color and a fair bouquet. The wine is semi-dry. **price range:** A

producer: Franz Weber
classification: White table wine
grape variety: Riesling
grade: Qualitätswein b.A.
city or village: Oppenheim
vineyard: Krötenbrunnen (Grosslage)
Bright, clear color and a light bouquet. The wine is medium sweet.
price range: A

producer: Franz Weber
classification: White table wine
grape variety: Riesling
grade: Qualitätswein b.A.
city or village: Nierstein
vineyard: Gutes Domtal (Grosslage)
Bright, clear color and a light bouquet. The wine is medium sweet.
price range: A

producer: Michel Weber
classification: White table wine
grape variety: Riesling
grade: Qualitätswein b.A.
district: Liebfraumilch

One of the better Liebfraumilchs on the market, and competitively priced. Because of the many Webers producing German wines, many "sister" brand names are used to distinguish between them, such as "Raymond Neuerberg," which appears on this wine.

Clean straw color and a light, flowery bouquet of youth. The wine is refreshing, with a light sweetness and a touch of pleasant acidity. **price range: A**

producer: Weingut Erath
classification: White table wine
grape variety: Scheurebe, Silvaner, and Riesling
grade: Qualitätswein b.A.
district: Liebfraumilch

An admixture of the recently developed Scheurebe grape gives this wine its unique flavor. It is available in 23-oz. and 50.7-oz. sizes.

Brilliant clear color and a fresh, fruity bouquet. The wine is delightfully fresh, with a slight touch of sweetness, and is one of the better *Qualitätsweine* available. **price range: A**

producer: Weingut Louis Guntrum
classification: White table wine
grape variety: Silvaner and Müller-Thurgau
grade: Qualitätswein mit Prädikat—Kabinett
city or village: Oppenheim
vineyard: Schloss (Einzellage)

The Müller-Thurgau, widely grown in the Rheinhessen, is a cross between the Riesling and the Silvaner.

Clear golden color and a fine bouquet. The wine has a slight Muscat (flowery) flavor, benefitting from the blend of Silvaner and Müller-Thurgau grapes. **price range: B**

producer: Weingut Louis Guntrum
classification: White table wine
grape variety: Müller-Thurgau
grade: Qualitätswein mit Prädikat—Kabinett
city or village: Nierstein
vineyard: Spiegelberg (Grosslage)

Clear golden color and a clean, fruity bouquet. The wine has a fresh, flowery flavor; it is excellent with the starter course or with fish. **price range: B**

producer: Weingut Louis Guntrum
classification: White table wine
grape variety: Morio-Muskat
grade: Qualitätswein b.A.
city or village: Mainz
vineyard: Domherr

The Morio-Muskat grape is a cross between Silvaner and Weisser Burgunder; it is named for Peter Morio, who first cultivated it.

Clear golden color and a pronounced bouquet typical of the variety. The bouquet carries into the flavor, making the wine an unusually appealing specialty suitable for spicy foods. **price range: B**

producer: Weingut Louis Guntrum
classification: White table wine
grape variety: Müller-Thurgau
grade: Qualitätswein mit Prädikat—Kabinett
city or village: Oppenheim
vineyard: Schloss (Einzellage)

A producer-bottled wine (*Erzeuger-abfüllung*) of high quality at a reasonable price.

Light golden color and a flowery, delicate bouquet. The wine is full-bodied, semi-dry, and well balanced with fruit and acidity; one can taste the natural sweetness of the grapes in the wine. **price range: B**

producer: Weingut Louis Guntrum
classification: White table wine
grape variety: Silvaner
grade: Qualitätswein b.A.
district: Liebfraumilch
city or village: Nierstein

Germany is noted for Liebfraumilch; this high-quality wine is offered at a very reasonable price.

Light golden color and a flowery bouquet. The wine is fruity and semi-dry; it is a fine, well-balanced, and delightful Liebfraumilch. **price range: A**

producer: Weingut Math. Hess-Becker
classification: White table wine
grape variety: Riesling
grade: Qualitätswein b.A.
district: Liebfraumilch
city or village: Siefersheim

Very fine Liebfraumilch.

Elegant golden color and a fruity bouquet. The wine is very fruity and pleasant. **price range: A**

producer: Deinhard & Co.
classification: White table wine
grape variety: Riesling
grade: Qualitätswein mit Prädikat—Auslese
city or village: Oestrich
vineyard: Lenchen (Einzellage)

From the famous Lenchen vineyard, owned by Deinhard.

Rich bouquet; the wine is very full-bodied and fruity. **price range: E**

producer: Weinkellerei Wollersheim GmbH
classification: White table wine
grape variety: Blend
city or village: Koblenz

Made from grapes grown exclusively in Germany.

Light gold color and a fruity, fragrant bouquet. The wine is sweet and is excellent with many dishes. **price range: A**

producer: Zentralkellerei
classification: White table wine
grape variety: Silvaner, Müller-Thurgau, and Riesling
grade: Qualitätswein b.A.
district: Liebfraumilch

Pale golden color and a "succulent" bouquet. The wine is semi-dry and mild, with a delicious fruity flavor; it is a superior Liebfraumilch, with perfect balance. **price range: A**

GERMANY, RHEINGAU

producer: Gartenhaus
classification: White table wine
grape variety: Riesling
grade: Qualitätswein b.A.
city or village: Johannisberg (Bereich)

Light golden color and a varietal bouquet. The wine is dry and appealing; it is very good with shellfish and white meat. **price range: A**

producer: Henkell & Co.
classification: White sparkling wine
grape variety: Riesling
grade: Prädikatsekt
city or village: Wiesbaden

Henkell & Co. is the world's largest producer of sparkling wine; yearly production exceeds five million cases. The wines are produced via the *méthode champenoise*, as in Champagne, but an agreement between Germany and France prohibits calling German sparkling wine "Champagne."

Clear white color, with sparkle and a full bouquet. The taste is excellent, comparable to fine French sparkling wine.

price range: C

producer: A. J. Koenen Ltd.
classification: White table wine
grape variety: Riesling
grade: Qualitätswein b.A.
city or village: Johannisberg
vineyard: Erntebringer (Grosslage)

Clear pale gold color and a full varietal bouquet. The taste, like the bouquet, shows the characteristic style of a Rheingau Riesling; depending on the vintage and the producer, the wines typically have a noble and elegant quality.

price range: B

producer: A. J. Koenen Ltd.
classification: White table wine
grape variety: Riesling
grade: Qualitätswein mit Prädikat—Spätlese
city or village: Johannisberg
vineyard: Erntebringer (Grosslage)

Rheingaus are considered by many to be the greatest of all German wines. The other famous wine district, Mosel-Saar-Ruwer, likewise produces outstanding Riesling wines, but in style they are quite different—generally lighter and more delicate. It is often said that Rheingaus are the "kings" of German wines and Mosels the "queens," but both derive their nobility from Riesling. Great vintages like 1971 and 1976 allow the noble *Auslesen* (selected picking) wines to be made.

Clear pale gold color and an elegant and characteristic Riesling bouquet. This elegance carries through to the flavor, which hints at sweetness but does not finish sweet.

price range: B

producer: Leonard Kreusch Inc.
classification: White table wine
grape variety: Riesling
grade: Qualitätswein b.A.
city or village: Johannisberg
vineyard: Erntebringer (Grosslage)

Balance and depth of character.

price range: A

producer: Richard Nagler
classification: White table wine
grape variety: Riesling
grade: Qualitätswein mit Prädikat—Kabinett
city or village: Rüdesheim
vineyard: Burgweg (Grosslage)

The Burgweg *Grosslage* is a composite vineyard composed of a number of different *Einzellagen* in Rüdesheim and neighboring Geisenheim. In sunny years it produces *Spätlesen* and *Auslesen* that would tend to be sweeter and richer (but more expensive) than this *Kabinett*.

Golden-yellow color and a strong, spicy bouquet carrying into the flavor. The wine is full and finishes dry.

price range: B

producer: Richard Nagler
classification: White table wine
grape variety: Riesling
grade: Qualitätswein mit Prädikat—Spätlese
city or village: Winkel
vineyard: Honigberg (Einzellage)

This vintage produced outstanding Riesling wines in the Rheingau.

Yellow-white color and a long-lasting, fruity bouquet. The wine has good fruit and full body; it is a beautiful wine with a long-lasting finish.

price range: B

producer: Gustav Adolf Schmitt
classification: White table wine
grape variety: Riesling
grade: Qualitätswein b.A.
city or village: Johannisberg (Bereich)

A fine example of a typical Rheingau Riesling wine, this fruity and fresh wine comes from *Bereich* Johannisberg, which produces some of the most popular Rheingau wines. The wines keep very well in most vintages.

Clear yellow color and a very fruity, fresh bouquet. The wine's residual sugar is in harmony with its fine natural acidity. It should be drunk with poultry, seafood, or veal.

price range: A

producer: H. J. Schneider
classification: White table wine
grape variety: Riesling
grade: Qualitätswein mit Prädikat—Kabinett
city or village: Geisenheim

A few years extra bottle age improves the quality of this wine, produced from a vineyard leased to H. J. Schneider.

Golden color and a typical bouquet of Riesling. The wine is full-bodied and elegant, with a fresh taste.

price range: B

producer: H. Sichel Söhne
classification: White table wine
grape variety: Riesling
grade: Qualitätswein mit Prädikat
city or village: Kiedrich

One of the Rheingau's finest vineyards.
Golden color and a full, aromatic bouquet. The wine is fruity and very appealing.

price range: D

producer: H. Sichel Söhne
classification: White table wine
grape variety: Riesling
grade: Qualitätswein b.A.
city or village: Hochheim (Bereich Johannisberg)

The word "hock" is said to have derived from Hochheim, and it is now a household word throughout the world. Though it is called "Bereich Hochheim," it is located in the *Bereich* Johannisberg, of which Hochheim is a part.

Light golden color and a fresh, appealing bouquet. The wine is agreeable and appetizing—a fine example of a Hochheimer.

price range: C

producer: Steigenberger
classification: White table wine
grape variety: Riesling
grade: Qualitätswein b.A.
city or village: Johannisberg
vineyard: Erntebringer (Grosslage)

An elegant wine, shipped in a brown bottle.

Marvelous bouquet; the wine is full-bodied, with a piquant flavor.

price range: B

producer: Graf von Schönborn
classification: White table wine
grape variety: Riesling
grade: Qualitätswein mit Prädikat—Spätlese
city or village: Erbach
vineyard: Marcobrunn (Einzellage)

"Erbacher Marcobrunn," formerly called "Marcobrunner," is one of the Rheingau's best-known wines.

Rich golden color and a full, fine bouquet. The wine is rich, semi-sweet, and full-bodied.

price range: D

producer: Graf von Schönborn
classification: White table wine
grape variety: Riesling
grade: Qualitätswein mit Prädikat—Kabinett
city or village: Geisenheim
vineyard: Schlossgarten (Einzellage)

Golden color and a rich, elegant bouquet. The wine is appealing, with a fresh, stylish flavor; it is a great, racy Rheingau from a world-famous producer.
price range: C

producer: Franz Weber
classification: White table wine
grape variety: Riesling
grade: Qualitätswein b.A.
city or village: Johannisberg
vineyard: Erntebringer (Grosslage)

Clear color and a light bouquet. The wine is medium sweet. **price range:** A

producer: Franz Weber
classification: White table wine
grape variety: Riesling
grade: Qualitätswein b.A.
city or village: Rüdesheim
vineyard: Burgweg (Grosslage)

Bright clear color and a light bouquet. The wine is medium sweet. **price range:** A

producer: Weingut Hof Sonneck
classification: White table wine
grape variety: Riesling
grade: Qualitätswein mit Prädikat—Kabinett
city or village: Johannisberg
vineyard: Holle

The grapes for this wine were harvested on October 28, 1975 at 81 degrees Oechsle. The vineyards are located on sandy loam soil on the southwestern slopes of Johannisberg, and the distance between the rows of vines is 3.20 meters.

Light golden color and a beautiful fruity bouquet. The wine is round and well-balanced, with fine acidity and predominant Riesling character and flavor.
price range: B

producer: Weingut Hof Sonneck
classification: White table wine
grape variety: Riesling
grade: Qualitätswein mit Prädikat—Auslese-Eiswein
city or village: Johannisberg
vineyard: Goldatzel (Einzellage)

This unusual and rare wine is an *Eiswein*, made from grapes that were harvested while still partially frozen. The grapes were collected on December 22, 1975 when the temperature was minus 7 degrees C. In 1976 this wine won the silver medal of the Deutsche Landwirtschafts-Gesellschaft.

Deep gold color and an elegant and spicy bouquet. The wine has outstanding ripeness and a pronounced spicy sweetness—an excellent wine.
price range: E

producer: Weingut Hof Sonneck
classification: White table wine
grape variety: Riesling
grade: Qualitätswein mit Prädikat—Beerenauslese
city or village: Johannisberg
vineyard: Holle (Einzellage)

The grapes for this wine were harvested at 131 degrees Oechsle from old vines within the Holle vineyard. The grapes were shriveled on the vine, and when pressed gave only a very small yield with a high sugar content. This wine received the medal awarded by the Deutsche Landwirtschafts-Gesellschaft in 1973.

Golden color and a strong, rich bouquet typical of grapes affected by Botrytis. The wine is very big, rich, and beautiful, showing noble elegance and outstanding quality.
price range: E

producer: Weingut Hof Sonneck
classification: White table wine
grape variety: Riesling
grade: Qualitätswein mit Prädikat—Spätlese
city or village: Johannisberg
vineyard: Mittelholle (Einzellage)

The grapes used for this wine were harvested at 90 degrees Oechsle, and came from the southern slopes of the Johannisberg Weinbauort. *Spätlese* wines were first made (as such) by the monks at Schloss Johannisberg in 1775, and a monument near the Schloss attests to this fact.

Golden-yellow color and a particularly rich and strong bouquet.. The wine is full-bodied and big, with good fruit and elegance—a beautiful wine.
price range: C

Although Spain produces many wines, the two most important are Sherry and Rioja. Sherry, which derives its name fromt the town of Jerez de la Frontera, is produced in the southwestern part of Spain between the Guadalete and the Guadalquivir rivers. The best vineyards lie in the chalky white soils, called "Albariza soils," of the hillsides west and north of Jerez. The vines grown on the sand and clay found elsewhere in the region produce only second-class wines used chiefly for blending.

The Palamino grape used in the making of Sherry grows best in the Jerez superior zone, and after the juice is expressed from these grapes, it is stored in oak casks. Throughout the winter fermentation takes place; little by little, the action diminishes. In the spring "flor," a white film, often shows on the surface of the wine. This phenomenon, which does not always occur, is extremely important because the musts that are responsible for the flor are essential to the development of the pale, dry wines called "Fino," the best of the Sherries.

Oloroso-style Sherry results from the action of the spent yeasts. As they fall to the bottom of the casks, they leave the wine in contact with the air in such a manner that the oxygen causes the wine to become darker in color, richer in flavor, and more deeply aromatic. The Sherry is then fortified slightly with Brandy before it is finally racked in clean casks.

The essence of making fine Sherry consists of controlling and enhancing the natural qualities of the wines while they develop. Sherries are guided in this development by the Solera system, a process of slowly introducing new wine into row upon row of casks containing Sherries of increasing age. Each year, after the vintage, every cask of Sherry-in-the-making is classified as either Fino or Oloroso, the two basic dry types of Sherry. Various classifications of Sherry are:

Fino   This Sherry can be dry or very dry; it is pale, light, and very aromatic.

Amontillado   This Sherry is made by preselecting special Fino, which ages and gains color in the cask. Amontillado is not as dry as Fino but fuller in color and body.

Manzanilla   This is the palest of the Fino because the vineyards are close to the port of Sanlucar de Barrameda, and the wine matures in bodegas there. Closeness to the sea gives these wines a salty tang.

Oloroso   Wines classified as Oloroso are usually sweetened Sherries. They are generally darker, heavier, and fuller than Fino.

Cream Sherry   Sherries so designated are golden in color and are made from heavily sweetened Oloroso.

Spain's second great wine class is Rioja. It takes its name from the Rio Oja, a quiet mountain stream that flows into the Ebro River. The Ebro contributes to the quality of Rioja just as the Garonne contributes to the quality of Bordeaux, nourishing the river banks and the mountainsides covered with vines, irrigating the soil, and sweetening the climate. These famous vines make the best table wines of Spain.

Rioja is grown in a region divided into three zones, each of which differs in soil and climate. Grapes grown in the Rioja Alta and Rioja Alavesa produce medium-strength table wines; the wines of Rioja Baja develop a higher alcohol content. Rioja may be made from grapes grown in a single zone or from any combination of grapes grown in the three zones.

Grapes used for making Rioja are the Tempranillo, Graciano, Mazuelo, Garnacha, Malvasia, and Viura. The definitive character of Rioja wines comes from the way in which they are permitted to age and mature in barrels of American oak for at least two years before being bottled. Dark red Rioja is full-bodied and can be identified by the word "tinto" on the label. "Clarete" Rioja is lighter in color and character and is a softer red wine. Rioja white wine, called "blanco," ranges from dry to sweet. "Rosado" Rioja is a rosé wine that ranges from dry to semisweet.

The Rioja seal is a consumer's guarantee of quality. It not only proves that the wine originated in Rioja but also that it has been tested and approved by the Rioja Wine Control Board, meeting standards that have been adhered to for more than four centuries in Rioja, Spain.

SPAIN, RIOJA

producer: AGE Bodegas Unidas S. A.
classification: White table wine
grape variety: Viura
district: Logroño
city or village: Fuenmayor
This is a soft, fruity wine of golden color, clean and brilliant, with the correct bouquet of ripe grapes. It is very similar to the French Sauternes wines, for it is quite sweet.   **price range:** A

producer: AGE Bodegas Unidas S. A.
classification: Red table wine

grape variety: Graciano and Mazuela
district: Navarre
city or village: Haro
"Siglo Rioja" is wood-aged and always sold with a vintage date. It is bottled in an unusual flask covered with burlap.
Deep ruby color and a "raspberry" bouquet showing good breeding. The wine is well-balanced, with good tannin and aging qualities; it goes well with red meat, game, and cheese.   **price range:** A

producer: AGE Bodegas Unidas S. A.
classification: Red table wine
grape variety: Tempranillo, Mazuelo, and Garnacha (Grenache)
district: Logroño
city or village: Fuenmayor
This is a mellow, perfectly balanced ruby-red wine. Its bouquet is robust and rich. The wine has character and should improve with bottle age.
The unique package is easy to identify: a "burlap," which makes this wine easy to find all over the world.   **price range:** B

producer: Bodegas Bilbainas
classification: Red table wine
grape variety: Tempranillo and Garnacha
district: Navarre—Rioja Alta
city or village: Haro
Deep red color and a grapey bouquet. The wine is smooth-tasting.   **price range:** B

producer: Bodegas Bilbainas
classification: Red table wine
grape variety: Tempranillo
district: Navarre—Rioja Alta
city or village: Haro
A *Reserva* Rioja.
Deep, rich red color and a strong,

grapey bouquet. The wine is smooth-tasting, with balanced acidity.
price range: C

producer: Bodegas Bilbainas
classification: White table wine
grape variety: Tempranillo and Garnacha
district: Navarre—Rioja Alta
city or village: Haro
Floral bouquet; the wine is smooth-tasting.   **price range:** B

producer: Bodegas Bilbainas
classification: Red table wine
grape variety: Tempranillo

district: Navarre—Rioja Alta
city or village: Haro
A *Reserva* Rioja.
Deep, rich red color and a floral bouquet. The wine combines smooth body with strong flavor. **price range:** C

producer: Bodegas Bilbainas
classification: Red table wine
grape variety: Tempranillo
district: Navarre—Rioja Alta
city or village: Haro
This wine is very typical of a good Rioja, an area whose excellent wines justify its reputation as one of Spain's finest wine districts.
Rich, deep red color and a strong bouquet. The wine has the earthy, somewhat acidic taste characteristic of young Riojas, and it should have excellent aging potential. **price range:** B

producer: Bodegas Bilbainas
classification: Red table wine
grape variety: Tempranillo
district: Navarre—Rioja Alta
city or village: Haro
A Rioja *Vendimia Especial* (harvest special), made only in exceptional vintages.
Deep red color with amber tinges and a rich bouquet. A full-bodied Rioja.
price range: C

producer: Bodegas Gurpequi
classification: White table wine
grape variety: Malvasia and others
A good example of the excellent white wines produced in this area of Spain.
Pale straw color and a fresh, grapey bouquet. The wine is crisp and dry, with a good grapey flavor; it displays elegance and finesse normally found in wines of a much higher price. **price range:** A

producer: Bodegas Bilbainas
classification: White table wine
grape variety: Garnacha
district: Navarre—Rioja Alta
city or village: Haro
Very pale yellow color and a floral bouquet. The wine is light but fruity.
price range: A

producer: Bodegas Bilbainas
classification: Red table wine
grape variety: Temparillo
district: Navarre—Rioja Alta
city or village: Haro
This smooth, slightly acidic wine is of deep red color and has a very grapey bouquet. **price range:** A

producer: Bodegas Bilbainas
classification: White table wine
grape variety: Garnacha and Tempranillo
district: Navarre—Rioja Alta
city or village: Haro
Deep yellow color and a floral bouquet. The wine is strong-tasting, with a "woody" flavor. **price range:** A

producer: Bodegas Bilbainas
classification: Red table wine
grape variety: Tempranillo
district: Navarre—Rioja Alta
city or village: Haro
A three-year-old nonvintage wine blended from supplies left over from the harvest.
Light red color and a light, floral bouquet. The wine is light-bodied.
price range: A

producer: Bodegas Gurpequi
classification: Rosé table wine
grape variety: Garnacha and others
Medium rosé color and a delicate, pleasantly scented bouquet. The wine is medium dry, with a delicate flavor; it is a most attractive rosé of great finesse.
price range: A

producer: Bodegas Gurpequi
classification: Red table wine
grape variety: Garnacha and others
Typical of the good red Rioja wines, and justifying their growing popularity.
Medium-full garnet-red color and a deep fruity bouquet. The wine is soft and has attractive fruit. **price range:** A

producer: Bodegas Faustino Martinez
classification: Red table wine
grape variety: Garnacha and Tempranillo
district: Navarre
city or village: Álava-Oyón
This fine red Rioja is aged in wood for ten years.
Tawny color and a flowery bouquet. The wine is soft and round, displaying the fine character of a well-aged Rioja.
price range: D

producer: Bodegas Faustino Martinez
classification: White table wine
district: Navarre
city or village: Álava-Oyón

Rioja is one of Spain's most famous wine districts, particularly noted for its red wines. This is a white Rioja.
Bright pale golden color and a delicate bouquet. The wine is light and dry, with a fruity taste. **price range:** A

producer: Bodegas Faustino Martinez
classification: Red table wine
grape variety: Garnacha and Tempranillo
district: Navarre
city or village: Álava-Oyón
Rioja is one of the best wine areas in Spain, particularly for red wine.
Ruby color and a flowery bouquet. The wine is medium dry and full-flavored—good quality for the price. **price range:** B

producer: Bodegas del Romeral
classification: Red table wine
grape variety: Tempranillo and Graciano
district: Logroño
city or village: Fuenmayor
This dry, crimson-colored wine has a rich, full bouquet and a gleam in its appearance. It has a natural wood taste. The wine is appreciated by gourmets as the perfect accompaniment to distinguished dinners.
The wine comes in an elegant package: a Bordeaux bottle dressed with a wire net to distinguish this from other wines.
price range: E

producer: Marqués de Cáceres
classification: Red table wine
grape variety: Tempranillo and Garnacha
district: Navarre
city or village: Cenicero
This wine is produced only from grapes grown in the Rioja Alta (upper Rioja). Vinification takes place under the supervision of Emile Peynaud, world-renowned oenologist at the University of Bordeaux.

Dark red color and a fruity bouquet with a touch of oak. The wine is soft, with a faint "spicy" flavor and a long finish.

price range: A

producer: de la Torre y Lapuerta S. A.
classification: Red table wine
grape variety: Garnacha and Graciano
district: Logroño
city or village: Alfaro

The wine was aged in American oak casks for nine years and in the bottle for two years. It is made especially for red meats, game, or venison. This wine has been awarded the grand prize of the International American Club Federation and a gold medal in Yugoslavia.

This vintage wine is smooth to the palate, with a well-balanced, delicate bouquet. In appearance, it is limpid red.

price range: E

producer: Herederos del Marqués de Riscal
classification: Red table wine
grape variety: Garnacha and Tempranillo
district: Navarre
city or village: El Ciero

The firm was founded over one hundred years ago. The Marqués de Riscal wines are internationally renowned and are sold in over one hundred different countries.

price range: B

producer: R. Lopez de Heredia S. A.
classification: Red table wine
grape variety: Garnacha and Tempranillo

district: Navarre
city or village: Haro

This is Spain's only estate-bottled wine from the Rioja. All the bottles come with a *diploma de garantia* as a certificate of their authenticity. "Vina Tondinia" is a claret-type Rioja and is shipped in a Bordeaux-shaped bottle, after aging for a minimum of eight years. It is one of the finest Riojas in its class and offers both excellent value and great quality.

Ruby-red color, with touches of gold, and an extremely fine bouquet. The wine is dry, smooth, and well-developed; it should be drunk at room temperature.

price range: C

producer: R. Lopez de Heredia S. A.
classification: Red table wine
grape variety: Garnacha and Tempranillo
district: Navarre
city or village: Haro

Spain's only estate-bottled Rioja wine; all the bottles come with a *diploma de garantia,* certifying authenticity of origin. The firm was founded in 1877 and is one of the most respected producers in the Rioja district; this Burgundy-type wine is shipped in a similarly shaped bottle and is stored for at least eight years prior to shipment.

Big aroma; the wine has a full taste and is dry, smooth, and well-developed. Because of its great body, it is best with roasts and should be drunk at room temperature.

price range: C

"Wine is the intellectual part of the meal; meats are merely the material part."
— Alexandre Dumas

producer: R. Lopez de Heredia S. A.
classification: Red table wine
grape variety: Garnacha and Tempranillo
district: Navarre
city or village: Haro

Spain's only estate-bottled wine from Rioja. All the bottles come with a *diploma de garantia,* attesting to their authenticity and origin. This Bordeaux-type wine is shipped in a Claret-shaped bottle.

Ruby-red color and a full aroma. The wine is dry, smooth and well-developed, with vivacity; it goes well with all meats and poultry, and is a great wine for the price.

price range: A

producer: R. Lopez de Heredia S. A.
classification: White table wine
grape variety: Blend
district: Navarre
city or village: Haro

Spain's only estate-bottled wine from Rioja; all the bottles come with a *diploma de garantia* attesting to their authenticity of origin. This Bordeaux-type wine is aged for at least six years prior to shipment and is bottled in a Claret-shaped bottle.

Natural deep-amber color and a highly developed bouquet. The wine is dry and fine; it should be drunk fresh but never iced, as this would dull the aroma and flavor. It is exceptional value.

price range: A

producer: Federico Paternina
classification: Red table wine
grape variety: Tempranillo and Garnacha
district: Rioja Alta
city or village: Haro

A youthful red Rioja containing 12% alcohol by volume.

Light, bright-red color, and a smooth bouquet full of fruit and character. The wine is fresh, young, and clean, an ideal accompaniment for red or white meats.

price range: A

producer: Federico Paternina
classification: Red table wine
grape variety: Tempranillo and Garnacha
district: Rioja Alta
city or village: Haro

A *Reserva* Rioja aged approximately six years in wood and decanted prior to bottling so that no sediment appears. It is ready to drink when shipped.

Deep, bright-red color, and a fine, delicate bouquet. The wine is distinguished and full-bodied; it is an excellent accompaniment to roasts, red meats, and game.

price range: B

producer: Federico Paternina
classification: Red table wine
grape variety: Tempranillo and Garnacha
district: Rioja Alta
city or village: Haro

An excellent wine approximately ten years old, sold as a *Reserva.* It contains 12% alcohol by volume and is presented with wire netting around the bottle.

Deep red color and a penetrating bouquet. The wine's originally tannic body is replaced by finesse, and the wine shows breeding and quality typical of older Riojas.

price range: C

producer: Federico Paternina
classification: Rosé table wine
grape variety: Garnacha, Tempranillo, and Graciano
district: Rioja Alta
city or village: Haro

A wine sold when approximately four years old, containing 13% alcohol by volume.

Bright rosé color with medium depth and a fruity bouquet. The wine is dry, refreshing, and full of flavor; it is an ideal accompaniment to hors d'oeuvres, shellfish, fish, and mild cheeses. Serve cold.

price range: A

producer: Federico Paternina
classification: White table wine
grape variety: Malvasia and Garnacha
district: Rioja Alta
city or village: Haro

A very popular dry white wine containing 12% alcohol by volume. It is sometimes labeled "Blanco Seco" instead of "Banda Dorada" and is excellent value for the price.

Light white color and a full bouquet. The wine is light, fresh, and crisply dry; it is good with hors d'oeuvres, fish, and shellfish.

price range: A

producer: Federico Paternina
classification: Red table wine
grape variety: Tempranillo and Garnacha
district: Rioja Alta
city or village: Haro

A rare, select *Reserva* Rioja with great distinction. Its high cost is in relation to the long years it has spent aging in cask prior to being shipped.

Deep, dark color, showing extensive aging, and an exquisite bouquet. The wine is very delicate. **price range:** E

producer: Federico Paternina
classification: White table wine
grape variety: Malvasia and Garnacha
district: Rioja Alta
city or village: Haro

An extra dry white wine, approximately six years old (when shipped) and containing 12% alcohol by volume.

Light pale yellow color and a clean, fragrant bouquet. The wine is dry and mature; it is good with hors d'oeuvres, oysters, and the like. **price range:** B

producer: Federico Paternina
classification: White table wine
grape variety: Malvasia and Garnacha
district: Rioja Alta
city or village: Haro

An excellent aged white Rioja approximately; eight years old (when shipped), presented with wire netting around the bottle. It is extra dry and has great distinction.

Pale-yellow color and a fine, delicate bouquet. It is a very good accompaniment to fish, oysters, and the like.

price range: C

producer: Averys of Bristol Ltd.
classification: Fortified wine
grape variety: Palomino and Pedro Ximenez
region: Andalucía
city or village: Jerez de la Frontera
Pale dry Sherry. **price range:** C

producer: John William Burdon
classification: Fortified wine
grape variety: Palomino and Pedro Ximenez
region: Andalucía
village: Jerez de la Frontera

The Burdon *bodegas* were founded in 1821 by John W. Burdon, an Englishman. The *bodegas* were granted the royal warrant by King Alfonso XIII of Spain to be suppliers of Sherry to the Spanish royal family, an honor commemorated by a red and gold tassel on every bottle of Burdon's Sherry.

Pale straw-lemon color and a lovely bouquet of nuts and fruit. The wine is crisp, dry, and has good length, it is a balanced, well-made dry Sherry. **price range:** B

SPAIN, SHERRY

producer: Averys of Bristol Ltd.
classification: Fortified wine
grape variety: Palomino and Pedro Ximenez
region: Andalucía
city or village: Jerez de la Frontera
The perfection of a rich, sweet Amoroso Sherry. **price range:** D

producer: Averys of Bristol Ltd.
classification: Fortified wine
grape variety: Palomino and Pedro Ximenez
region: Andalucía
city or village: Jerez de la Frontera
Finest golden Amoroso Sherry.
price range: C

producer: Averys of Bristol Ltd.
classification: Fortified wine
grape variety: Palomino
region: Andalucía
city or village: Jerez de la Frontera
A powerful, full-bodied, and flavorful Sherry. **price range:** C

May our wine brighten the mind and strengthen the resolution.

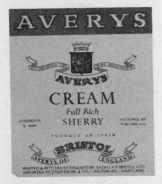

producer: Averys of Bristol Ltd.
classification: Fortified wine
grape variety: Palomino and Pedro Ximenez
region: Andalucía
city or village: Jerez de la Frontera
Pale color; the wine has a full, sweet flavor. **price range:** D

producer: Averys of Bristol Ltd.
classification: Fortified wine
grape variety: Palomino
region: Andalucía
city or village: Jerez de la Frontera
An exquisite, very dry Fino Sherry.
price range: C

producer: Averys of Bristol Ltd.
classification: Fortified wine
grape variety: Palomino
region: Andalucía
city or village: Jerez de la Frontera
Medium smooth, nutty flavor.
price range: C

producer: Croft & Co., Ltd.
classification: Fortified wine
grape variety: Palomino
region: Andalucía
city or village: Jerez de la Frontera
A dry, delicate Fino Sherry.
price range: B

producer: Croft & Co., Ltd.
classification: Fortified wine
grape variety: Palomino
region: Andalucía
city or village: Jerez de la Frontera
A medium-dry Amontillado Sherry.
price range: B

producer: Croft & Co., Ltd.
classification: Fortified wine
grape variety: Palomino and Pedro Ximenez
region: Andalucía
city or village: Jerez de la Frontera
A sweet, dark Oloroso Sherry.
Can be drunk either as an aperitif or after a meal. **price range:** B

producer: Croft & Co., Ltd.
classification: Fortified wine
grape variety: Palomino and Pedro Ximenez
region: Andalucía
city or village: Jerez de la Frontera
"Croft Original" is a blend of Fino, Amontillado, and Oloroso Sherries. It is therefore a unique pale Cream Sherry, as its name implies. **price range:** C

producer: Cuvillo
classification: Fortified wine
grape variety: Palomino and Pedro Ximenez

region: Lower Andalucía
city or village: Jerez de la Frontera
"Cuvillo Oloroso" is a rich, fruity Sherry that can be best appreciated as a liqueur at the end of a meal. Its fragrant, full-bodied bouquet and rich, deep amber color complement the glowing sensation it gives to the palate.
The oldest Solera in the blend can be calculated to be of some sixty-five years of age; the average age of the final blend would be twenty-five years.
price range: B

producer: Delage
classification: Fortified wine
grape variety: Palomino and Pedro Ximenez
region: Andalucía
city or village: Jerez de la Frontera
Delage also produces Oloroso, Cream, Fino, and Manzanilla Sherries. This one is an Amontillado.
Clear amber-gold color and a very pronounced bouquet. The wine is dry—an outstanding Sherry. **price range:** B

producer: Fernando A. de Terry
classification: Fortified wine
grape variety: Palomino
region: Andalucía
city or village: Puerto de Santa Maria
"Camborio Sherry" is named for a famous Spanish poet. It is aged under a blanket of flor yeast, giving the wine a characteristic fragrance and freshness.
Light golden color and a fresh, interesting fragrance. The wine is light and dry, with a delicate acidity; it is an excellent accompaniment to all seafoods, and it also adds an inimitable flavor when used in cooking meat dishes. **price range:** B

producer: Fernando A. de Terry
classification: Fortified wine

grape variety: Palomino and Pedro Ximenez
region: Andalucía
city or village: Puerto de Santa Maria
This Cream Sherry is produced from blends of good Oloroso and Pedro Ximenez, aged through the Solera system for a number of years to achieve an optimum blend of wines of different vintages. For generations, the de Terry family has bred prized Spanish horses, whose ancestry can be traced in the horses of the Lippenzaner Riding School in Vienna.
Golden-brown color and a rich bouquet. The wine is full-bodied, sweet, and mellow; it was created for a discriminating palate and is especially appealing as a dessert wine. **price range:** B

producer: Diez Hermanos
classification: Fortified wine
grape variety: Palomino
region: Lower Andalucía
city or village: Jerez de la Frontera
This is a Sherry that suits a person who prefers the sharply defined bouquet and taste of a dry Sherry but savors a softening touch of finesse. It is clean and medium dry, with a pleasantly round bouquet. This wine is universally popular with all Sherry lovers. **price range:** B

"To everything there is a season, and a time to every purpose . . ." —Ecclesiastes

---

producer: Diez Hermanos
classification: Fortified wine
grape variety: Palomino and Pedro Ximenez
region: Andalucía
city or village: Jerez de la Frontera
A medium-sweet Amontillado Sherry that is universally accepted by all Sherry drinkers. It has increased in popularity over the years.
Light golden color and a fragrant bouquet. The wine is medium sweet and

has a good nutty flavor; it keeps its freshness and does not overpower the palate.
price range: B

producer: Diez Hermanos
classification: Fortified wine
grape variety: Palomino
region: Lower Andalucía
city or village: Jerez de la Frontera
This is a wonderful Fino of very dry character, which leaves the palate clean and fresh. It is extremely delicate, with a fine bouquet. This is one of the finest Finos on the market today. **price range:** B

producer: Pedro Domecq
classification: Fortified wine
grape variety: Palomino
region: Andalucía
city or village: Jerez de la Frontera
"Double Century" dry Sherry is the perfect accompaniment to a light lunch.
Light golden color; the Sherry is medium dry, with a nutty flavor. **price range:** B

producer: Pedro Domecq
classification: Fortified wine
grape variety: Pedro Ximenez
region: Andalucía
city or village: Jerez de la Frontera
"Viña No. 25" is a very sweet dessert Sherry, with a full aroma and flavor.
Very dark brown color and a slight hint of raisins in the bouquet. The wine is very sweet and full-bodied, a fine sweet Oloroso Sherry. **price range:** B

producer: Pedro Domecq
classification: Fortified wine
grape variety: Palomino
region: Andalucía
city or village: Jerez de la Frontera
  "La Ina" dry Sherry is recognized as one of the world's finest aperitifs. It should be drunk very fresh and is best enjoyed chilled, as in Spain.
  Very pale straw color and a delicate, pungent bouquet. The wine is dry and has a refreshing "bite."   **price range:** C

producer: Duff Gordon & Co.
classification: Fortified wine
grape variety: Palomino
region: Andalucía
city or village: Puerto de Santa Maria
  A very rich Oloroso Sherry.
  Rich golden-brown color; the wine is almost as sweet as a Cream Sherry.
  price range: B

producer: Duff Gordon & Co.
classification: Fortified wine
grape variety: Palomino
region: Andalucía
city or village: Puerto de Santa Maria
  A Fino Sherry.
  Light straw color; the wine is very light and dry, smoother than most Fino Sherries. Serve chilled, before dinner, or with appetizers like shrimp, cheese, and the like.
  price range: C

producer: Findlater Mackie Todd & Co. Ltd.
classification: Fortified wine
grape variety: Palomino
region: Andalucía
city or village: Jerez de la Frontera
  A light, dry Fino Sherry matured in oak casks for three years and containing 18% alcohol by volume.
  Pale straw color and a sharp, fine flor bouquet. The wine is dry, light, and has fine crispness; it is clean and dry Fino Sherry, *the* classic aperitif.   **price range:** B

producer: Pedro Domecq
classification: Fortified wine
grape variety: Palomino and Pedro Ximenez
region: Andalucía
city or village: Jerez de la Frontera
  "Celebration Cream" Sherry is a full-bodied Sherry suitable for any time, any place.
  Dark golden color and a full-bodied, mellow flavor.   **price range:** C

producer: Duff Gordon & Co.
classification: Fortified wine
grape variety: Palomino
region: Andalucía
city or village: Puerto de Santa Maria
  "El Cid," a superior dry Sherry.
  Very pale light straw color; as the wine is very dry, it should be served chilled or on the rocks as an aperitif.   **price range:** C

producer: Duff Gordon & Co.
classification: Fortified wine
grape variety: Palomino
region: Andalucía
city or village: Puerto de Santa Maria
  Amontillado Sherry.
  Amber color; the wine is semi-dry and should be consumed before dinner as an aperitif or cocktail beverage, either straight or on the rocks.   **price range:** C

producer: Findlater Mackie Todd & Co. Ltd.
classification: Fortified wine
grape variety: Palomino and Pedro Ximenez
region: Andalucía
city or village: Jerez de la Frontera
  "Findlater's Cream" is a sweet Oloroso Sherry matured in oak casks for over three years, containing 18% alcohol by volume.
  Dark golden-amber color and a full, rich, and fragrant bouquet. The wine is smooth, sweet, and pleasing; it is a classic Cream Sherry—sweet but not heavy.
  price range: B

producer: Duff Gordon & Co.
classification: Fortified wine
grape variety: Palomino
region: Andalucía
city or village: Puerto de Santa Maria
  Medium-dry Sherry.
  Rich, golden-brown color; the wine is suitable either straight or on the rocks.
  price range: B

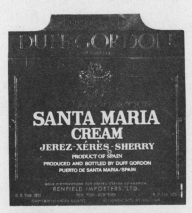

producer: Duff Gordon & Co.
classification: Fortified wine
grape variety: Palomino and Pedro Ximenez
region: Andalucía
city or village: Puerto de Santa Maria
  "Santa Maria" is a superior select Cream Sherry.
  Rich, golden-brown color; because of the wine's natural sweetness, it should be drunk after dinner in place of Cognac or cordials.   **price range:** C

producer: Findlater Mackie Todd & Co. Ltd.
classification: Fortified wine
grape variety: Palomino and Pedro Ximenez
region: Andalucía
city or village: Jerez de la Frontera
  "Dry Fly" is an Amontillado Sherry matured for three years in oak casks and containing 18% alcohol by volume.
  Brilliant amber color and a round, nutty bouquet with some "bite." The wine is full, medium sweet and soft, with a winery flavor; it makes a fine aperitif.
  price range: B

producer: M. Gil Galán S.A.
classification: Fortified wine
grape variety: Palomino
region: Andalucía
city or village: Jerez de la Frontera
  An Amontillado Sherry produced by the Solera system and aged in oak casks.
  Golden color; the wine has a nutty flavor and is medium dry, showing the tempering influence of age.   **price range:** B

producer: M. Gil Galán S.A.
classification: Fortified wine
grape variety: Palomino and Pedro Ximenez
region: Andalucía
city or village: Jerez de la Frontera
A Cream Sherry produced via the Solera system and aged in oak casks.
Dark golden color and a rich, flowery bouquet. The wine is full, rich, and smooth—a fine sweet fortified wine.
price range: B

producer: M. Gil Galán S.A.
classification: Fortified wine
grape variety: Palomino
region: Andalucía
city or village: Jerez de la Frontera
A dry Fino Sherry showing the character of wine produced via the action of flor yeast.
Pale straw color and a characteristic Fino Sherry bouquet. The wine is dry, but not harsh-tasting. **price range:** B

producer: Gonzalez Byass
classification: Fortified wine
grape variety: Pedro Ximenez
region: Andalucía
city or village: Jerez de la Frontera
A sweet Oloroso Cream Sherry.
Dark golden color and a full, rich bouquet. The wine is smooth, luscious, and long-lived. **price range:** C

producer: Gonzalez Byass
classification: Fortified wine
grape variety: Palomino
region: Andalucía
village: Jerez de la Frontera
A medium-dry Amontillado Sherry.
Bright amber color and a lightly pungent bouquet. The wine is mild, full-flavored, and dry. **price range:** B

> *"Give me a bowl of wine.*
> *In this I bury all*
> *unkindness."*
> —Shakespeare, *Julius Caesar*

producer: Gonzalez Byass
classification: Fortified wine
grape variety: Palomino
region: Andalucía
city or village: Jerez de la Frontera
Amontillado Sherry.
Amber color and a light, pungent bouquet. The wine is mild, yet full and dry, with a pleasant nutty flavor.
price range: C

producer: Gonzalez Byass
classification: Fortified wine
grape variety: Palomino
region: Andalucía
city or village: Jerez de la Frontera/Sanlucar de Barrameda
"Tio Pepe" is the driest and noblest of all Sherries.
Very pale color and a delicate bouquet. The wine is light-bodied but very subtle.
price range: C

producer: Gonzalez Byass
classification: Fortified wine
grape variety: Pedro Ximenez
region: Andalucía
city or village: Jerez de la Frontera
A sweet Oloroso Sherry.
Dark golden color and a savory, full, and rich bouquet. The wine is very smooth and satisfying. **price range:** B

producer: A. Parra Guerrero
classification: Fortified wine
grape variety: Palomino
region: Andalucía
city or village: Jerez de la Frontera/Sanlucar de Barrameda
A Manzanilla Sherry normally deteriorates in bottle, so this wine should be consumed as soon as possible after purchase.
Pale golden color; the wine is a typical Manzanilla and has the "salty" tang typical of wines from that region. **price range:** B

producer: A. Parra Guerrero
classification: Fortified wine
grape variety: Palomino
region: Andalucía
city or village: Jerez de la Frontera
A Fino Sherry produced from the family vineyards of La Perla de Pappaluna, Vin Reál, and Santa Maria de Gracia.
Very pale color and a flowery, herb like

bouquet with the characteristic Fino tang. The wine is crisp and dry, a Fino for the connoisseur. **price range:** B

producer: A. Parra Guerrero
classification: Fortified wine
grape variety: Palomino
region: Andalucía
city or village: Jerez de la Frontera
It is rare to encounter an entirely natural Oloroso Sherry—usually these wines are sweetened to make Amorosos or rich Olorosos.
Golden-brown color and a mature, full bouquet. The wine is dry and full-bodied, without any harshness; it will appeal not only to those who like dry wines, but to those who are sometimes put off by the extreme dryness of Fino Sherries.
price range: B

producer: A. Parra Guerrero
classification: Fortified wine
grape variety: Pedro Ximenez, Palomino, and Muscat
region: Andalucía
city or village: Jerez de la Frontera
Most Cream Sherries are produced on heavier soils in the Sherry district; this one comes exclusively from the finest *albariza* (white chalk) soils, giving it elegance and style. The name recalls the way Sherries used to be shipped to the East Indies and back, the motion and heat of the sea voyage improving the wines in the process.
Rich brown color and a flowery, grapey bouquet. The wine is smooth and rich-flavored, but only medium sweet: it will appeal to those who usually dislike sweeter Sherries. **price range:** B

producer: A. Parra Guerrero
classification: Fortified wine
grape variety: Palomino
region: Andalucía
city or village: Jerez de la Frontera
A dry Amontillado Sherry.
Pale golden-yellow color and a bouquet with Fino character—though slightly softer style. The wine has sufficient body and is not too dry; extra alcohol makes it rounder and fuller. **price range:** B

producer: A. Parra Guerrero
classification: Fortified wine
grape variety: Palomino and others
region: Andalucía
city or village: Jerez de la Frontera
This wine comes from a Solera established in the first half of the nineteenth century, giving a style of a previous age.
Concentrated golden-brown color and an aroma of a very old Fino. The wine is full on the palate, as a very old Oloroso should be; it can be served at the end of the meal, in place of Cognac.
price range: C

producer: Jarvis Halliday & Co. Ltd.
classification: Fortified wine
grape variety: Palomino and Pedro Ximenez
region: Andalucía
city or village: Jerez de la

Frontera—Sanlucar de Barrameda
A Manzanilla Sherry, this wine won a gold medal and diploma for excellence at the British Bottlers' Institute judging of open Sherry competition at the Brewers' Exhibition in London in 1976.
Pale gold color and a light, fragrant and distinguished bouquet. The wine is dry, crisp and clean, with the slightly salty flavor typical of a good Manzanilla. It is ideal as an aperitif or as an accompaniment to consommé. **price range:** B

producer: Jarvis Halliday & Co. Ltd.
classification: Fortified wine
grape variety: Palomino and Pedro Ximenez
region: Andalucía
city or village: Jerez de la Frontera
This excellent dessert wine was the winner of a gold medal and diploma for distinction in its class (Cream Sherry) in the open competition held by the British Bottlers' Institute at the Brewers' Exhibition in London, 1976.
Tawny-gold color and a pungent and distinguished bouquet. The wine is full, rich, and sweet—to be well-received by those who like sweet wines.
price range: B

producer: John Harvey & Sons
classification: Fortified wine
grape variety: Palomino and Pedro Ximenez
region: Andalucía
city or village: Jerez de la Frontera
A full, sweet, Oloroso Sherry.
Amber color and a typical Oloroso bouquet. The wine is full and sweet.
price range: C

producer: John Harvey & Sons
classification: Fortified wine
grape variety: Palomino and Moscato

region: Andalucía
city or village: Jerez de la Frontera
A semi-dry aperitif Sherry.
Clear color and a semi-dry flavor.
price range: C

producer: John Harvey & Sons
classification: Fortified wine
grape variety: Palomino
region: Andalucía
city or village: Jerez de la Frontera
An extra dry Fino Sherry.
Clear color; the wine is quite light, a fine Fino. **price range:** C

producer: John Harvey & Sons
classification: Fortified wine
grape variety: Palomino
region: Andalucía
city or village: Jerez de la Frontera
An elegant aperitif wine made from aged Solera wines.
Golden color, semi-dry flavor.
price range: C

producer: John Harvey & Sons
classification: Fortified wine
grape variety: Palomino and Pedro Ximenez
region: Andalucía
city or village: Jerez de la Frontera
A sweet, luscious Oloroso Sherry known the world over.
Amber-gold color and a fine bouquet. The wine is sweet and luscious—a truly superior Cream Sherry. **price range:** D

producer: James Hawker & Co., Ltd.
classification: Fortified wine
grape variety: Palomino and others
region: Andalucía
city or village: Jerez de la Frontera
An original classic Cream Sherry of great distinction and noble background, one of the greatest of its type on the market. Hawker Sherry was given to toast the voyage of *Mayflower II* (1957) on both sides of the Atlantic.
Rich sunlit amber color and a round, full, and refined bouquet. The wine is clean, sweet without being cloying, and finishes to perfection. **price range:** C

producer: James Hawker & Co., Ltd.
classification: Fortified wine
grape variety: Palomino and others
region: Andalucía
city or village: Jerez de la Frontera
Possibly the most popular of the Hawker Sherries, this pale dry light Amontillado is shipped to Boston and the New England states, where it suits the climate and the clientele. It is bottled, shipped, and sold by Hawker's of Plymouth, England, one of that country's oldest wine shippers.
Pale golden color and a delicate, gentle, and distinguished bouquet. The wine is fresh and light and is especially enjoyable when drunk fresh. **price range:** B

producer: James Hawker & Co., Ltd.
classification: Fortified wine
grape variety: Palomino and others
region: Andalucía
city or village: Jerez de la Frontera
The Hawker offices are situated on the quay in Plymouth harbour, England, from where the Virginia settlers sailed in 1558, and later Drake (1588) and the *Mayflower* Pilgrims (1620). Because of this, the wines are preferred over all others by the Pilgrim Society of Plymouth, Massachusetts, founded in 1818. Colonel John Hawker was the first American consul to England in 1790. This pale, light, and dry Sherry is especially blended for the American taste.

Pale golden color and a delicate, distinguished, and refined bouquet. The wine is medium dry, delicate, and fresh; a Sherry of classic style and reputation.
price range: B

producer: Emilio M. Hidalgo
classification: Fortified wine
grape variety: Palomino
region: Andalucía
city or village: Jerez de la Frontera
Emilio Hidalgo is one of the smaller Sherry producers, but he is among the oldest and most respected: the wines have been sold on the Continent and exported to England for many generations. They were first exported to the United States in 1973. This wine is a high-quality Cream Sherry.
Burnt amber to deep gold color and a full, nutty bouquet with clean pungency. The wine is very full-bodied, with sweetness in the bouquet carrying into the flavor and terminating with a mild, clean quality.
price range: B

producer: Marqués del Roncal
classification: Fortified wine
grape variety: Palomino and others
region: Andalucía
city or village: Jerez de la Frontera
Pale dry cocktail Sherry.
Light straw color and a dry, clean bouquet. The wine is completely dry but has a crisp, pleasant aftertaste.
price range: A

producer: Marqués del Roncal
classification: Fortified wine
grape variety: Palomino and others
region: Andalucía
city or village: Jerez de la Frontera
Rich Cream Sherry. The *bodega* for this Sherry was established in 1765.

Thick brown, syrupy color and a light, sweet bouquet. The wine is medium sweet, with a full, long-lasting flavor. Great value for the money.
price range: A

producer: Marqués del Roncal
classification: Fortified wine
grape variety: Palomino and others
region: Andalucía
city or village: Jerez de la Frontera
Medium-sweet, nutty Sherry.
Golden, syrupy color and a nutty, clean bouquet. The wine has a "bittersweet almond" flavor.
price range: A

producer: Rutherford, Osborne, and Perkins Ltd.
classification: Fortified wine
grape variety: Palomino and Pedro Ximenez
region: Andalucía
city or village: Jerez de la Frontera
This Amontillado Sherry could perhaps be called "Amontillado Pasado," as it has all the qualities and characteristic of an old wine with the charm of a younger one.
Clear golden color; the wine has a nutty but dry taste.
price range: B

producer: Sánchez Romate
classification: Fortified wine
grape variety: Palomino
region: Andalucía
city or village: Jerez de la Frontera
Pale dry Sherry.
price range: A

producer: Sánchez Romate
classification: Fortified wine
grape variety: Palomino
region: Andalucía
city or village: Jerez de la Frontera
Dry Amontillado Sherry.
Pale amber color; the wine is dry.
price range: A

producer: Sánchez Romate
classification: Fortified wine
grape variety: Palomino
region: Andalucía
city or village: Jerez de la Frontera
Cocktail Sherry.
price range: A

"Wine and women will make men of understanding to fall away." —Ecclesiasticus 19:2

producer: Sánchez Romate
classification: Fortified wine
grape variety: Palomino
region: Andalucía
city or village: Jerez de la Frontera
Cream Sherry.
price range: A

producer: Sánchez Romate
classification: Fortified wine
grape variety: Palomino
region: Andalucía
city or village: Jerez de la Frontera
Golden Sherry.
price range: A

producer: Savory & James Ltd.
classification: Fortified wine
grape variety: Palomino, Mantuo, and Canocaza
region: Andalucía
city or village: Jerez de la Frontera
A magnificent compromise between a dry Fino and a rich Cream Sherry is this medium-dry Amontillado.
Dark amber color and a full, nutty bouquet. The wine is semi-dry, medium-bodied, and mellow.
price range: B

producer: Savory & James Ltd.
classification: Fortified wine
grape variety: Palomino and Pedro Ximenez
region: Andalucía
city or village: Jerez de la Frontera
A deluxe Cream Sherry made from a well-aged Solera.
Ruby color and a nutty, rich bouquet. The wine is velvety, luscious, and creamy, with full body and a clean after-taste. The wine is full of character and flavor.
price range: B

producer: Savory & James Ltd.
classification: Fortified wine
grape variety: Palomino, Mantuo, and Canocaza
region: Andalucía
city or village: Jerez de la Frontera
A dry, delicate Fino Sherry.
Pale golden color and a delicate, slightly nutty bouquet. The wine is light, fine, and well-balanced, with a mildly piquant flavor. **price range:** B

producer: Williams & Humbert Ltd.
classification: Fortified wine
grape variety: Pedro Ximenez
region: Andalucía
city or village: Jerez de la Frontera
"Walnut Brown" Sherry was first shipped in 1919. It is a full-bodied, Sweet Oloroso Sherry that some people prefer to Port.
Clear dark brown color and a very fruity, almost raisinlike bouquet. The wine is full-bodied, fruity, and sweet—a first-class dessert wine. **price range:** B

producer: Williams & Humbert Ltd.
classification: Fortified wine
grape variety: Palomino
region: Andalucía
city or village: Jerez de la Frontera
"Palo Cortado" is a full-bodied dry Oloroso Sherry. The Solera that produces it has only a limited production, and the wines are without parallel.
Very deep gold color giving the impression that the wine is sweet; the bouquet shows that marked "essence of Sherry," and in flavor the wine is bone-dry, with an excellent, lingering finish. It is one of the most remarkable Sherries on the market, a wine for the connoisseur. **price range:** C

producer: Williams & Humbert Ltd.
classification: Fortified wine
grape variety: Palomino
region: Andalucía
city or village: Jerez de la Frontera
"Sack" was used in Shakespeare's time (and before) to designate the wines of Jerez, which were often shipped rather sweet to meet the taste of the times. The term "Dry Sack" was coined to indicate that this medium-dry Sherry was a drier wine than the original "sack," and the wine was first shipped in 1905. Dry Sack, therefore, is a medium-dry Amontillado Sherry, not too dry or too sweet.
Clear golden color and a full bouquet. The wine is full-bodied and finishes well—a typically fine Amontillado Sherry. **price range:** B

producer: Williams & Humbert Ltd.
classification: Fortified wine
grape variety: Palomino
region: Andalucía
city or village: Jerez de la Frontera
The Pando Solera was first set up by Williams & Humbert before the turn of the century, and "Pando Fino Sherry" was first shipped in 1878. It is a fairly full-bodied Fino, sturdier than many others of its type.
Very light pale gold color and a classic Fino bouquet. The wine is very dry, fuller-bodied than some other Finos, and particularly enjoyable as an aperitif. **price range:** B

producer: Williams & Humbert Ltd.
classification: Fortified wine
grape variety: Palomino
region: Andalucía
city or village: Jerez de la Frontera
After the wine is first made, some casks display a yeast-like growth known as "flor," which collects on the surface and extracts some of the remaining sugar while giving the wine a fresh and "living" fragrance. Only those casks that develop flor yeasts will be used in making Fino Sherry.
Pale straw color and a light and fruity bouquet. The wine is delicately dry, light, and crisp, suitable for use as an aperitif or with seafood. It should be served well chilled, like all Finos, as this accentuates both flavor and bouquet. **price range:** B

producer: Williams & Humbert Ltd.
classification: Fortified wine
grape variety: Pedro Ximenez
region: Andalucía
city or village: Jerez de la Frontera
This sweet dessert Sherry is made from grapes that have dried in the sun until they are almost raisins. The juice has a very high sugar content, which results in quite a lot of unresolved sugar in the wine; brandy is then added to stop fermentation before all the sugar has been converted into alcohol. The wine is then left to age via the Solera system in the usual way.
Rich brown color and a heavy, intense, and fruity bouquet. The wine is sweet, smooth, and full-bodied, with a slight nutty flavor; this rich old dessert wine is excellent as a liqueur or as an alternative to Port. It should be served at room temperature or slightly chilled. **price range:** B

producer: Williams & Humbert Ltd.
classification: Fortified wine
grape variety: Palomino
region: Andalucía
city or village: Jerez de la Frontera
"Dos Cortados" is a very special Sherry. Out of thousands of butts of new Sherries, only a few are selected to mature in a special Solera, and production is quite limited. The Solera is over one hundred years old, and the casks are made from American white oak, from which the wines get their characteristic woody bouquet.
Pale amber color and a strong, rich, and "woody" bouquet. The wine is dry, smooth, and full-bodied, with a slight almond flavor; it is a well-matured Oloroso Sherry that is excellent as an aperitif. It should be served very slightly chilled or at room temperature. **price range:** D

producer: Williams & Humbert Ltd.
classification: Fortified wine
grape variety: Palomino and Pedro Ximenez
region: Andalucía
city or village: Jerez de la Frontera
This very old Amontillado Sherry is made from an unusual blend of Amontillado with a small amount of sweet (cream) Sherry. The Soleras used for this wine are extremely old.
Golden-amber color and a full-bodied, rich bouquet with a slight fragrance of almonds. The wine is rich and full-bodied, with a smooth almondy taste; it is excellent as a late-morning or general aperitif and should be served at room temperature. **price range:** C

producer: Williams and Humbert Ltd.
classification: Fortified wine
grape variety: Palomino and Pedro Ximenez
region: Andalucía
city or village: Jerez de la Frontera
Williams & Humbert Cream Sherry is a blend of Oloroso (made from Palomino grapes) and sweet Sherry (made from Pedro Ximenez grapes).
Dark amber color and a mellow, heavily fruity bouquet. The wine is sweet, smooth, and creamy; this Oloroso Sherry is suitable for any time of day, especially with dessert or cheese. It is normally served at room temperature, but is quite refreshing if served chilled or on the rocks in summer. **price range:** B

"So Life's year begins and closes;
Days though shortening still can shine.
What though youth gave love and roses,
Age still leaves us friends and wine."

—Thomas Moore,
"Spring and Autumn"

producer: Amigó Hermanos
classification: White table wine
grape variety: Parellada and Macabeo
region: Catalonia
district: Tarragona
city or village: Cornudella
Brilliant straw color.
price range: A

producer: Amigó Hermanos
classification: Rosé table wine
grape variety: Garnacha
region: Catalonia
district: Tarragona
city or village: Cornudella
Brilliant light red color with orange tint and a fruity bouquet. **price range:** A

producer: Bodegas El Morano
classification: Flavored Wine
region: Tarragona
Fruity bouquet and flavor—an excellent party wine. **price range:** A

producer: Codorniu
classification: White sparkling wine
region: Catalonia
district: Villafranca de Pañades
city or village: San Sadurni de Noya

Codorniu is the largest producer of bottle-fermented (*méthode champenoise*) sparkling wines in the world, and the firm owns the biggest cellars in the Catalonia district. The area is beginning to be better known as a wine district, its specialty being sparkling wines. This *brut* (dry) wine is a good alternative to a more expensive French Champagne and has much of the same elegance.

Pale color, with small bubbles, and a clean, crisp bouquet. The wine is very dry and fresh-tasting, with a lingering finish; it has surprising dryness and delicacy.
price range: C

producer: Compañia de Los Vinos Generosos
classification: Red table wine
grape variety: Blend
region: Tarragona
The Tarragona region produces a red wine that is markedly superior to many *vin ordinaires*. It is quite acceptable as a carafe wine, when served with dinner; the company that produces this wine recently built an entire new winery on the scale of much larger ones in America, and such resources aim to compete with the "jug" wines produced in California.

Clear deep garnet color and a full, flowery bouquet. The wine is full-bodied and full-flavored. **price range:** A

producer: Compañia de Los Vinos Generosos
classification: Flavored red wine
grape variety: Blend of wine and fruit juices
region: Tarragona
This Sangria owes its excellence to a base wine, which is essentially a superior grade to many everyday red wines consumed in Spain. The level of citrus juices introduced into the blend is carefully controlled, making it a lighter Sangria than many of its type.

Light red color and a bouquet showing the citrus additives. The wine is sweet, with a fruity taste, and is best served chilled.
price range: A

producer: Conde de la Cortina
classification: Fortified wine
grape variety: Pedro Ximenez
region: Andalucía
district: Córdoba
city or village: Montilla-Moriles
Montilla wines are produced in a region east of Jerez. Mainly Pedro Ximenez grapes are grown, and the wines are usually shipped unfortified—though they are legally classed and taxed as fortified wines. This is a cream (sweet) Montilla.

Dark golden color; the wine has a rich, full flavor similar to Sherry, but a style all its own. **price range:** B

producer: Conde de la Cortina
classification: Fortified wine
grape variety: Pedro Ximenez
region: Andalucía
district: Córdoba
city or village: Montilla-Moriles
Montilla is a wine region located east of Jerez in Andalucíia, where mainly Pedro Ximenez grapes are grown. Although this wine is called "Amontillado," the term originally arose in the Sherry district to describe wines that began to take on a "Montilla-ed" character. Most Montillas are shipped unfortified, their high alcoholic content resulting from totally natural fermentation, although they are both classified and taxed as a fortified wine.

Golden color, and a flavor similar to Sherry—medium dry, like an Amontillado Sherry. **price range:** B

producer: Conde de la Cortina
classification: Fortified wine
grape variety: Pedro Ximenez
region: Andalucía
district: Córdoba
city or village: Montilla-Moriles
A Fino Montilla.
Pale straw color; dry and crisp taste.
price range: B

producer: Cruz Garcia Lafuente
classification: Red Flavored table wine
variety: Red wine and citrus flavors
region: Alto Ebro
district: Logroño
city or village: Fuenmayor
This is a sweet Sangria with a fruity bouquet and clean appearance.
Sangria is the typical and original recipe of blending red wine with natural fruit juice, famous all over the world. **price range:** A

producer: Freixenet S. A.
classification: White sparkling wine
grape variety: Macabelo, Parellada, and Xarel-lo
region: Catalonia
district: Barcelona
city or village: San Sadurni de Noya
Bottle-fermented, vintage-dated, and shipped in exclusive frosted bottles. A *brut* sparkling wine. **price range:** B

producer: Freixenet S. A.
classification: White sparkling wine
grape variety: Xarel-lo, Macabelo, and Parellada
region: Catalonia
district: Barcelona
city or village: San Sadurni de Noya
A *brut* (dry) sparkling wine fermented via the *méthode champenoise* and given a vintage date. It is shipped in an exclusive frosted bottle. **price range:** B

producer: Garrigós
classification: Rosé table wine
region: Valencia
price range: A

producer: Garrigós
classification: Red table wine
region: Valencia
Brilliant deep red color; the wine is dry and full-bodied. **price range:** A

producer: Garrigós
classification: White table wine
region: Valencia
Brilliant color and a fruity, distinct flavor.
price range: A

producer: Marqués de Humberto e Hijos
classification: White table wine
grape variety: Airen
region: La Mancha
district: Valdepeñas
city or village: Manzanares
Clear straw color and a fresh, fruity bouquet. The wine is clean and dry, with a short aftertaste. **price range:** A

producer: Marqués de Humberto e Hijos
classification: Red table wine
grape variety: Cencibel
region: La Mancha
district: Valdepeñas
city or village: Manzanares
Ruby-red color and a big, fruity bouquet. The wine is dry, with a long aftertaste.
price range: A

producer: Leonard Kreusch
classification: Red table wine
grape variety: Garnacha and others
region: Catalonia
district: Tarragona
city or village: Tarragona
price range: A

producer: Leonard Kreusch
classification: White table wine
grape variety: Garnacha and others
region: Catalonia
district: Tarragona
city or village: Tarragona
price range: A

producer: Raymat S. A.
classification: White sparkling wine

region: Catalonia
district: Barcelona
A *Reserva* sparkling wine made via the *méthode champenoise*.
Brilliant straw color and a grapey bouquet. The wine is fruity, with residual sugar. **price range:** B

producer: Sant'yago Vinicola Alavesa
classification: Flavored wine
region: Northern Spain
city or village: La Bastida
For years, Yago Sangria has been the nation's leading imported wine.
Bright red color and a fruity bouquet. The wine is sweet and is best served chilled, over ice. **price range:** A

producer: Sant'Yago Vinicola Alavesa
classification: Flavored wine
region: Northern Spain
city or village: La Bastida
Unique in the U.S. marketplace, this wine was introduced to the East Coast in August 1975 and distributed nationally by March 1976.
Bright clear color and a fruity bouquet. The wine is sweet and is best served chilled, over ice. **price range:** A

producer: Vicente, Suso y Pérez S. A.
classification: Red table wine
grape variety: Garnacha
region: Aragon
district: Cariñena
city or village: Cariñena
This wine is sold in twenty-six countries throughout the world.

Nice ruby color and a fruity, intense bouquet showing elegance and depth. The wine is nicely balanced, well-constructed, and satisfying—its rich, complex flavors linger long on the palate. **price range:** A

producer: Vicente, Suso y Pérez S. A.
classification: Red table wine
grape variety: Garnacha
region: Aragon
district: Cariñena
city or village: Cariñena
Beautiful ruby color and a full, spicy bouquet showing the effects of wood aging. The wine has lots of fruit and sufficient acid and tannin to improve for many years; it is a mouth-filling, powerful wine acknowledging the benefits of aging.
price range: A

producer: Vicente, Suso y Pérez S. A.
classification: Flavored wine
variety: Garnacha wine and natural fruit juices
region: Aragon
district: Cariñena
city or village: Cariñena
This is one of Spain's finest Sangrias, made from a perfect balance of Garnacha wine with natural fruit juices.
Deep ruby-red color and a very fruity bouquet. The wine is very pleasant and refreshing; serve chilled for a delicious "anytime" beverage. **price range:** A

producer: Vicente, Suso y Pérez S. A.
classification: Red table wine
grape variety: Garnacha, Bobal, and Crujidera
region: Province of Zaragoza
district: Ebro River Valley
city or village: Cariñena
The wine is aged for a minimum of four years in oak casks. It won the International Quality Trophy in 1974, the gold medal at the Exposition Internationale de Paris in 1926, the gold Medal at the Exposición de Vinos de Barcelona in 1928, and the 1974 Golden Dyonisses. A unique package for a unique wine.
This wine will grace any table, enhance an entrée of beef or fowl. It is hearty, robust, and full-flavored with a velvety finish and mellow, fruity bouquet. **price range:** B

Although Portugal produces many wines, it is best known by wine lovers for its greatest contributions to the world, Port (*Porto*) and Madeira. The glass of Port that has been an English institution for centuries is actually exported to the United Kingdom from a town called Oporto in Portugal.

Port is a slightly sweet wine with a heavy, rich flavor. Color may vary with type from tawny to dark red.

Vintage Port   This is a wine made from grapes grown in exceptionally good harvests. Like French wines, Ports are only accorded the vintage mark in years when the development of the grapes is considered to be perfect.

Tawny Port   This is a natural blend of wines taken from several vintages.

Ruby Port   This is Tawny Port to which a younger wine has been added to give freshness and color.

Madeira comes from the island of the same name. Famous for nearly four hundred years, this wine was much favored in America during colonial days. A fine wine, amber in color and somewhat sweet, it is the best known of all fortified wines. Madeira can vary in type and color from very dry to very sweet and from pale straw to amber.

Malmsey   This name means a thicker, luscious, sweeter wine.

Verdelho   Lighter and gentler than Malmsey with a smokier and less sweet taste.

Boal or Bual   Often referred to as "buttery" in its aroma because of its full delicious taste.

Sercial   This Madeira is dry and full, with a pleasant sharp taste.

One hundred and sixty-three years before France set up its system of *Appellations Contrôlées*, designating its best wines, Portugal established the *Denominacão de Origem*. Originally founded to protect the reputation of Port, the Denominacão and attendant controls on growing, production, area of origin, volume, aging, taste, and chemical analysis have been expanded to cover eight winegrowing areas. The principal ones are Douro (Porto), Minho (Vinho Verde), Setubal, Bucelas, Dão, Colares, and Madeira.

One of the most important identifications on Portugal's best wines is a seal that stretches across the cork, certifying that the contents of the bottle have passed an exhaustive series of government inspections. (Port alone must pass thirty-three separate tests.)

PORTUGAL, MADEIRA

producer: Cossart Gordon & Co.
classification: Fortified wine
grape variety: Sercial
village: Funchal
A pale light Madeira made from the Sercial grape.
Very pale color; the wine is dry, light, and graceful; serve chilled as an aperitif or with hors d'oeuvres, canapes, soups, or cheeses.   **price range:** B

producer: Cossart Gordon & Co.
classification: Fortified wine
city or village: Funchal
Dark golden color; the wine has a nutty, mellow flavor. Serve at room temperature with hors d'oeuvres, canapés, or cheeses.
price range: B

producer: Cossart Gordon & Co.
classification: Fortified wine
grape variety: Blend

city or village: Funchal
"Rainwater" Madeira, named for its color, is a light, dry Madeira.
Very pale color and a good bouquet. The wine is dry, very light, and has a slightly tart finish; it is excellent as an aperitif when served chilled.   **price range:** C

producer: Cossart Gordon & Co.
classification: Fortified wine
grape variety: Boal (Bual)
city or village: Funchal
Golden color; the wine is sweet, rich, and full-flavored. Serve at room temperature, either as an excellent after-dinner drink or with desserts, fruits, and cheeses.
price range: D

producer: Henriques & Henriques
classification: Fortified wine
grape variety: Sercial
A dry cocktail Madeira made from the Sercial grape.
Clear light amber color and a nutty bouquet showing light caramelization. The wine is fruity, with a "cooked" flavor from the *estufa* process; an excellent Madeira.
price range: B

producer: Rutherford & Miles
classification: Fortified wine

grape variety: Verdelho

Verdelho is one of the greatest Madeiras. Golden color and a full bouquet. The wine is full-bodied, fruity, and finishes dry.

price range: B

"Like the best wine . . . that goeth down sweetly, causing the lips of those that are asleep to speak."
—Song of Solomon 7:9

producer: Rutherford & Miles
classification: Fortified wine

The Rutherford family started business in Madeira in 1814, and later joined with the Miles family, shippers of Madeira since 1860.

Golden-brown color and a full bouquet. The wine has a slight "burned" flavor as a result of the *estufa* process, which caramelizes the wine somewhat, and has a dry, fruity finish. **price range:** B

"I love everything that's old: old friends, old times, old manners, old books, old wine." —Oliver Goldsmith

---

PORTUGAL, PORTO (PORT)

producer: A. A. Cálem & F. Lda.
classification: Fortified wine
grape variety: Verdelho and Rabigato
district: Alto Douro (Port Zone)
city or village: Vila Nova de Gaia

A White Port.

Full bouquet and dry flavor.
price range: B

producer: Rutherford & Miles
classification: Fortified wine
grape variety: Sercial

Sercial is normally the driest of the Madeiras; this one is fuller than most, but still has the typical flavor of Sercial and finishes dry.

Pale gold color and a delicate bouquet. The wine is dry and has good body.
price range: B

producer: Rutherford & Miles
classification: Fortified wine
grape variety: Sercial and Verdelho

"Rainwater" is made from a blend of Sercial and Verdelho and has always been very popular in the United States.

Golden color and a characteristic Madeira bouquet. The wine combines full body with a dry finish. **price range:** B

producer: Cockburn Smithes & Co. Ltd.
classification: Fortified wine

---

grape variety: Tinta varieties
district: Alto Douro
city or village: Vila Nova de Gaia

"Cockburn's Aldouro Port" is a Tawny Port that has spent a long time "in oak" (in cask), and is therefore lighter than Ruby Port.

Light red color with brownish tinges; the wine is medium dry and has special elegance and distinction. **price range:** C

producer: Cockburn Smithes & Co. Ltd.
classification: Fortified wine
grape variety: Tinta varieties
district: Alto Douro
city or village: Vila Nova de Gaia

Cockburn's "No. 25" is a Ruby Port of medium sweetness.

Dark ruby color; the wine is medium sweet, light, and fruity, with plenty of richness and body. **price range:** C

producer: Croft & Co. Ltd.
classification: Fortified wine
grape variety: Port varieties
district: Alto Douro
city or village: Vila Nova de Gaia

"Croft Fine Ruby" is a typical Ruby Port. Dark color; the wine is robust, yet smooth, with a fine bouquet.
price range: B

producer: Croft & Co. Ltd.
classification: Fortified wine
grape variety: Port varieties
district: Alto Douro
village: Vila Nova de Gaia

Vintage Port, 1970. This is a true Vintage Port bottled after two years in wood. Ideally, it should not be consumed until ten or fifteen years after the vintage, or even more—depending on the concentration of the wine. **price range:** E

producer: Croft & Co. Ltd.
classification: Fortified wine
grape variety: Port varieties
district: Alto Douro
city or village: Vila Nova da Gaia

"Croft Distinction" is a fine ten-year-old Tawny Port matured in cask.
price range: C

producer: Croft & Co. Ltd.
classification: Fortified wine
grape variety: Port varieties
district: Alto Douro
city or village: Vila Nova de Gaia

"Croft Three Diamonds Tawny" is a delightful, light Tawny Port.
price range: B

producer: Findlater Mackie Todd & Co. Ltd.
classification: Fortified wine
grape variety: Blend of Tintas
district: Alto Douro
village: Vila Nova de Gaia

Bottled by Findlater's in London after maturing in oak for three years. Alcoholic strength: 20% by volume.

Full ruby-red color and a full and winey bouquet. The wine is smooth, full-bodied, fruity, and sweet; it is a typical Port, ideal as a dessert wine. **price range:** C

producer: Findlater Mackie Todd & Co. Ltd.
classification: Fortified wine

grape variety: Various Tintas
district: Alto Douro
village: Vila Nova de Gaia

"Old Theophilus" is a light Tawny Port bottled by Findlater's in London after maturing in oak for over three years. It contains 20% alcohol by volume.

Light red color with brown tinges and a rich, mature, and pleasing bouquet. The wine is sweet, fruity, and light; it is eminently suitable either as an aperitif or as a dessert wine. **price range:** C

producer: Guimaraens Vinhos S.A.R.L.
classification: Fortified wine
grape variety: Touriga, Bastardo, Mourisco, Tinta Cão, and Tinta Francisca
district: Alto Douro
village: Vila Nova de Gaia

This wine is a blend of Ports, made from a formula that has not changed since 1822. Every bottle is numbered and registered at the winery, reflecting extreme care and meticulous handling, and bears the signature of a fine Port producer.

Deep ruby-red color and a fruity, full bouquet. The wine creates a symphony of taste sensations, reflecting the history of the Port trade, which dates back to the sixteenth century. **price range:** B

producer: John Harvey & Sons
classification: Fortified wine
grape variety: Port varieties
district: Alto Douro
village: Vila Nova de Gaia

"The Director's Bin" is an elegant old cask-aged Port.

Pale tawny-red color; a rich, sweet red wine. **price range:** E

producer: John Harvey & Sons
classification: Fortified wine
grape variety: Port varieties

district: Alto Douro
village: Vila Nova de Gaia

"Hunting Port" is a cask-matured Port. Tawny-red color; a sweet, full-bodied dessert wine. **price range:** C

producer: John Harvey & Sons
classification: Fortified wine
grape variety: Port varieties
district: Alto Douro
village: Vila Nova de Gaia

A rich, sweet dessert wine.
price range: C

producer: Quinta do Noval
classification: Fortified wine
grape variety: Touriga, Tinta Francisca, Mourisco, and others
district: Alto Douro
village: Vila Nova de Gaia

This is a true Vintage Port from one of the few producers that sells the wines unblended from a single estate or *quinta*. It is bottled two years after the vintage is declared and will continue to improve for about fifteen years after bottling.

Ruby-red color and a fruity bouquet. The wine is a typically fine Vintage Port—full and rich—and will prove to be long-lived.
price range: B

producer: Warre & Ca. Lda.
classification: Fortified wine
grape variety: Blend
district: Alto Douro
village: Vila Nova de Gaia

"Very Finest Old Tawny" is a wine of exceptional quality and age. It is produced by a company that has been producing Ports for over three hundred years.

Light tawny color and a bouquet showing great age and exceptional quality. The wine is medium sweet, but aging gives it an exquisite dry finish; it is a superb after-dinner wine, with cheese and/or nuts.
price range: B

producer: Warre & Ca. Lda.
classification: Fortified wine

PORTUGAL, OTHER PORTUGUESE WINES

producer: João T. Barbosa Lda.
classification: White table wine
grape variety: Aronto, Cercial, Fernao Pires, and others
region: North-central Portugal
district: Dão (Região Demarcada)
city or village: Viseu

The Dão region is one of the most appreciated wine regions in Portugal. It produces some of the best wines of that country; this is an example of a typical good quality Dão wine bottled in the United Kingdom.

Light golden color and a full, flinty, and earthy bouquet. The wine is dry, smooth, and full-bodied with good balance.
price range: A

producer: João T. Barbosa Lda.
classification: White table wine
region: Estremadura
district: Santarem
city or village: Rio Maior

A typical dry white Portuguese white of reasonably good quality, very pleasant for everyday drinking.

Light straw color and a very fresh, light, and fruity bouquet. The wine is light and soft, with very dry and mellow flavor.
price range: A

grape variety: Blend
district: Alto Douro
village: Vila Nova de Gaia

"Vintage Character Porto" is a superb blend of Port wines with the general characteristics of a Vintage Port, but because it matures in wood and not in bottle, it does lack a bottle bouquet and does not throw a deposit.

Light ruby color with tawny tinges and a bouquet characteristic of a Vintage Port. The wine is full and fruity, with a fine finish; it is to be drunk in lieu of a Vintage Port either for economy or when decanting a Vintage Port is impracticable. We recommend that it be enjoyed at midmorning with a biscuit. **price range:** B

producer: João T. Barbosa Lda.
classification: Red table wine
grape variety: Alfronheiro, Carnaucha, Alvorelita, and others
region: North-central Portugal
district: Dão
city or village: Viseu

The Dão region, one of the few in Portugal that have been officially demarcated according to quality, is one of the best regions for red table wines. This wine is aged in cask and then bottled in the United Kingdom.

Very dark red color with brown edges and a pleasant earthy bouquet. The wine is mellow, dry, and smooth-tasting, maturation mellowing its full body.
price range: A

producer: Caves Aliança, Vinícola de Sangalhos
classification: Rosé table wine
region: Northern Portugal
district: Douro River
city or village: Sangalhos

Demi-sec (semi-sweet), sparkling up to the legal limits of still wines. The wine is shipped in an exclusive heart-shaped bottle, and carries a vintage date.
price range: A

producer: Caves Campo
classification: Rosé table wine
region: Douro River Valley
A natural rosé wine, not produced—as are many inexpensive roseés—from a blend of red and white wines. It contains 12% alcohol by volume.
Clean, crisp, and full-bodied, with a hint of sweetness. **price range:** A

producer: Caves Nacionales Lda.
classification: Rosé table wine
grape variety: Tinta Pinheira
region: Northern Portugal
district: Minho
city or village: Viana do Castelo
To be drunk young; maderizes after four or fives years in the bottle.
Slightly sparkling rosé color and a pleasant bouquet. The wine is light, fresh, and excellent; serve cold with virtually any dish. **price range:** A

producer: Costa do Sol
classification: Rosé table wine
region: Sai
city or village: Sangalhos
This is a soft, mellow rosé wine.
price range: A

producer: José Maria de Fonseca
classification: Rosé sparkling wine
region: Lisbon
A dry, sparkling rosé table wine.
price range: B

producer: José Maria de Fonseca
classification: Rosé table wine
region: Lisbon
A dry, soft, and smooth rosé table wine called "Vinya." **price range:** A

producer: José Maria de Fonseca
classification: Red sparkling wine
region: Lisbon
A semi-dry, full-bodied sparkling rosé wine. **price range:** B

producer: José Maria de Fonseca
classification: White sparkling wine
region: Lisbon
Fragrant bouquet, the wine is semi-dry.
price range: B

producer: Guimaraens—Vinhos S.A.R.L.
classification: Rosé table wine
region: Northern Portugal
Guimaraens (Fonseca) is now in the fifth generation of producing this private reserve wine. Each bottle is numbered and registered at the winery, and bears the signature of Bruce Fonseca, assuring the wines' exceptional quality. Though the wine does not bear an estate-bottled designation, it deserves it.
Brilliant rosé color and a fruity bouquet. The wine is semi-dry, without the cloying sweetness that is synonymous with many rosés, and finishes cleanly.
price range: A

producer: Real Companhia Vinícola
classification: Rosé table wine
grape variety: Same used for making Port

region: Douro River Valley
"Lagosta Rosé" is aged a year in wood, unique among Portuguese rosés, which is why it is sturdier and has a deeper, more complex flavor than others of its type.
price range: A

producer: Real Companhia Velha
classification: Rosé table wine
grape variety: Grenache
A light, semi-sweet rosé.
price range: A

producer: Soc. Agricola da Quinta de Aveleda
classification: White table wine
grape variety: Loureiro, Azal, Malvasia, Pedernao, and Douradinah
region: Minho
district: Vinho Verde
Produced at the Aveleda estate, one of the most beautiful vineyard sites. This type of "Vinho Verde" has always charmed thousands of tourists who have visited Portugal, and this example is one of the best of its type.
Light shimmering pale straw color, with tints of green, and a clean, fruity bouquet. The wine is medium dry, light, and refreshing, with a slight effervescence, and has a clean finish. **price range:** A

producer: Soc. Comercial dos Vinhos de Mesa de Portugal Lda.
classification: Rosé table wine
region: Douro River Valley
"Mateus Rosé" is the most popular imported wine sold in the United States. It is produced at the beautiful Mateus Palace.
Clear pink color, with amber highlights, and a clean, fruity bouquet. The wine is medium dry and medium-bodied, with fine fruit and style—it is an excellent wine with unique versatility. **price range:** A

producer: Soc. Comercial dos Vinhos de Mesa de Portugal Lda.
classification: White table wine
grape variety: Semillon, Arinto, Doña Bianca, and Malvasia Fina
region: Douro River Valley
An all-purpose white wine.
Pale straw color and a clean, fruity bouquet. The wine is medium dry, very fruity, and excellent. **price range:** A

"Wine is wont to show the mind of man." —Theognis

producer: Vinicola do Vale do Dão Lda.
classification: Red table wine
grape variety: Touriga, Alvaralhao, Tinta Carvalha, and Cabernet Sauvignon
region: North-central Portugal
district: Dão
city or village: Viseu
The grapes for this wine are cultivated from steep granitic slopes, which are quite difficult to work.
Deep ruby color and a full, slightly earthy bouquet. The wine is dry, full-bodied, and generous; its quality is superior to many other wines of similar price.
price range: A

producer: Vinicola do Vale do Dão Lda.
classification: White table wine
grape variety: Arinto, Doña Branca, Bacelo, Cerceal, Ancruzado, and Semillon
region: North-central Portugal
district: Dão
city or village: Viseu
An exceptional white wine that is often compared to the white Hermitage of France.
Pale gold color and a full, aromatic bouquet. The wine is dry, fruity, and generous. **price range:** A

Long before the Christian faith was brought to English shores, even before the Romans taught the Britons the rudiments of agriculture and the process of brewing beverages from grain, a native "honey wine" was drunk by the inhabitants. This wine was called *Mead* and is probably as old and possibly older than grape wine. Mead, like wine, can be easily recognized in a number of ancient languages. *Miod* was the name the Danes gave to their honey drink, while the Welsh called it *Medd*.

From references that have survived, it can be seen that the earliest forms of Mead were made by merely adding warm water to honey. Natural yeast, floating in the air or picked up from flowers, caused the brew to ferment and turn into a type of "near beer." This frothy, murky beverage was sweet to the taste when young, but as the fermentation continued and converted the sugar into alcohol, the drink became progressively stronger and drier.

In Cornwall, the traditional home of Mead, it is often referred to as the "honeymoon drink." The name goes back to the Hammurabic Babylonian Law of 2000 B.C. which stipulated that "at the wedding feast wine of the bee is to be drunk and for a lunar month following the wedding, the bridegroom is to be given as much honey and honey wine as he needs by the bride's family." The lunar month being measured by the moon, "honeymonth" or "honeymoon" figured in the vocabulary of many languages. Cornish honey wine, Mead, is made from fermented honey fortified with French brandy to about the same strength as a good-quality Sherry.

The winegrowing skill came to England via the Roman legionnaires and was further supplemented by the arrival of the Saxons and Normans, who used wine especially for religious purposes. The county of Essex, at the time of the *Domesday Book,* was a favored area for growing grapes. Henry II's marriage to Eleanor of Aquitaine brought the vineyards of Bordeaux under English jurisdiction, and preference was given to wines that came from across the Channel. A gradual decline in English wine production was the result. Further declines ensued as climatic changes during the Middle Ages made the British Isles less hospitable to the growing of vines, and English viticultural and wine-making activities, principally under the auspices of the Church, received a death blow when Henry VIII ordered the dissolution of monastic communities.

Various attempts were made to produce wines on a commercial scale during the years that followed, but winegrowing did not become a serious venture again in England until after World War II. At that time, the advent of early ripening grape varieties, bred specifically for cultivation in the northern regions of Germany and France, made the revivification of viticulture possible.

Currently, the vineyards of England are to be found comparatively close to the locations of the vineyards of medieval times. The principal grapes planted are the Müller-Thurgau (often described as Riesling Sylvaner) and Seyval Blanc, the official E.E.C. name for Seyve Villard.

producer: Adgestone Vineyard
classification: White table wine
grape variety: Müller-Thurgau, Reichensteiner, and Seyval Blanc
region: Hampshire
district: Isle of Wight
city or village: Adgestone
Light straw color and a pronounced bouquet. The wine is clean, grapey, and has good acidity; it can be favorably compared to a German wine.
price range: B

producer: B. T. Ambrose
classification: White varietal table wine
grape variety: Müller-Thurgau
region: Suffolk
district: Upper Stour Valley
city or village: Cavendish
This is the first large commercial vineyard in Suffolk's Stour River valley region since the Roman era. The wines have won many prizes held nationally.
Fruity bouquet; the wine is clean, mellow, and pleasant—a distinctive, impressive wine for all occasions.
price range: B

producer: J. G. & I. M. Barrett (Felstar Wines)
classification: White table wine
grape variety: Müller-Thurgau and Sieger
region: East Anglia
city or village: Crick's Green
This wine is a blend of two grape varieties grown on a 10.5 acre vineyard situated between the two known sites of Domesday vineyards. The wine is one of eight varieties marketed under the Felstar label and is estate-bottled.
Light straw-gold color and a full, aromatic bouquet suggestive of Muscat. The wine is clean and finishes slightly sweet; ideal for social drinking.
price range: B

producer: Robert & Ann Blayney—Blayney Vineyards
classification: White table wine
grape variety: Müller-Thurgau, Huxelrebe, and Reichensteiner
region: Channel Islands
district: Jersey
city or village: St. Mary
This is the only wine produced in the Channel Islands. The vineyard covers 5 acres around the eighteenth-century granite house depicted on the label. There is as yet no classification for wines produced in the British Isles, but this one would qualify for a quality rating. The inherent deep fragrance of Huxelrebe enhances the qualities of Müller-Thurgau.
Green-gold color and a rich, fragrant bouquet. The wine is dry, grapey, and fresh, with a pleasant clean aftertaste. It is very popular as a partner with the abundant seafood of the Channel Islands.
price range: B

producer: Lower Bowden Estates Ltd.
classification: White table wine
grape variety: Müller-Thurgau and Seyve-Villard
region: Berkshire
district: Thames Valley

city or village: Pangbourne
Clear amber color and a fruity bouquet. The wine is dry. **price range:** B

producer: Bruce Hole
classification: White table wine
grape variety: Müller-Thurgau and Seyval Blanc
region: Berkshire
district: Thames Valley
city or village: Bradfield
The 4.5-acre vineyard is planted on south-facing ground in the valley of the Pang, a tributary of the Thames. The Romans first established vineyards in this district. Bruce Hole's first vintage was 1975.
Pale straw color and a fruity bouquet. The wine is dry, robust, and pleasantly fresh, with a powerful finish.
price range: B

producer: Capper/Merrydown Wine Co.
classification: White table wine
grape variety: Müller-Thurgau
region: West Midlands
district: Worcester
city or village: Suckley
This is one of the most northern of the English vineyards. The area has a history of wine making dating to Roman times, and more recently, in the monastic period, ending in 1537. The area is rolling, unbroken country with many small valleys and streams; fruit and hops grow in profusion.
Bright pale yellow color and a fruity bouquet. The wine is crisp and fresh, with the typical character of better English wines. **price range:** B

producer: Cherrybank Estates
classification: White varietal table wine
grape variety: Müller-Thurgau
region: East Anglia
district: Suffolk
city or village: Otley

The year 1975 marks the first vintage from this vineyard and winery, and it gave very pleasing results. The vineyard is situated on a gentle southwestern slope on the Finn Valley, overlooking a prehistoric fortification.

Clear, light golden color and an invigorating, fruity bouquet. The wine is fruity and full-bodied, with a slight sparkle; it is nicely balanced, very suitable for drinking with foods (especially good with fish), or as an aperitif. **price range:** B

producer: Cornish Mead Co. Ltd.
classification: Mead
grape variety: Honey (fermented honey fortified with French brandy)
region: Cornwall
district: Penzance
city or village: Newlyn

Mead is probably the oldest known alcoholic beverage. In some countries it is believed to be an aphrodisiac.

Full honey color and a floral fragrance suggestive of mimosa or eucalyptus. The wine is sweet and round.
price range: B

producer: Suffolk Vineyards Ltd.
classification: White varietal table wine
grape variety: Müller-Thurgau
region: East Anglia
district: Suffolk
city or village: Bruisyard

This is the first wine from this vineyard, which was started from scratch in 1971. It contains 11.5% alcohol by volume.

Pale bright color and a fresh bouquet. The wine is clean, light, and has freshness, but also has the tannin for keeping qualities. **price range:** B

producer: Flexerne Fruit Farm Ltd.
classification: White table wine
grape variety: Müller-Thurgau

region: Southern England
district: East Sussex
city or village: Newick

Flexerne Fruit Farm's wine was voted third place in the "English Wine of the Year" competition held at Christies, London, in 1975.

Pale green-straw color and a rich, full, and penetrating bouquet. The wine is well-made, with good fruit and body; a really nice, quality wine.
price range: B

producer: Fuller-Roope Vineyard
classification: White table wine
grape variety: Müller-Thurgau
region: East Anglia
district: Suffolk
city or village: Wickhambrook

The Vineyard covers 5 acres on a southern slope 400 feet above sea level, on clay soil. It is not far from the site of an ancient Benedictine monastery, Bury St. Edmunds, whose vineyard flourished until it was destroyed at the time of the Reformation. The Roope family were maternal ancestors of the Fuller family, and were in the wine trade with Portugal for four hundred years. The first vintage from this vineyard was 1975.

Very pale gold color with green tints and a flowery bouquet. The wine is deliciously unique—neither too dry nor too sweet—and has the special "Spätlese" quality with captivating charm. **price range:** B

producer: J. C. C. Hinchliffe
classification: White table wine
grape variety: Müller-Thurgau, Seyval Blanc, and Reichensteiner
region: East Sussex
district: Lewes
city or village: Plumpton Green

This wine is naturally fermented to completion, and is therefore dry. A medium-sweet wine can be made by withdrawing the sweet reserve at an early stage in fermentation, and later blending it with a dry wine prior to sterile bottling.

Pale gold color and a slightly fruity bouquet. The wine is similar to a Hock.
price range: B

producer: Kentish Vineyards
classification: White varietal table wine
grape variety: Müller-Thurgau
region: Kent
city or village: Nettlestead

Grown in one of the first commercial vineyards in England since the Reformation, near the site of some old Roman vineyards.

Pale gold color and a distinctive, fruity bouquet. The wine is light, medium dry, and combines distinctive character with a pleasing bouquet. **price range:** B

producer: Lamberhurst Vineyards
classification: White varietal table wine
grape variety: Seyve-Villard
region: Kent
district: Tunbridge Wells
city or village: Lamberhurst

The grapes for this wine are grown in Kent, "the Garden of England." The wine is fermented in a modern cellar under the supervision of a qualified wine maker from Germany. The priory dates back to the fourteenth century and was originally owned by the Prior of Leeds, where the monks wore black habits and produced communion wine.

Clear color and a fruity bouquet. The wine is clean, semi-dry, and smooth, outstanding for its variety. It is ideal for those who prefer a mild white wine.
price range: B

producer: Lamberhurst Vineyards
classification: White varietal table wine
grape variety: Müller-Thurgau (Riesling and Sylvaner)
region: Kent
district: Tunbridge Wells
city or village: Lamberhurst

Clear golden color and a distinctive, fruity varietal bouquet. The wine is dry but smoothtasting, and were it not for EEC regional control regulations, it would qualify as a "quality wine," suitable for dessert use. **price range:** C

producer: P & A Latchford
classification: White varietal table wine
grape variety: Müller-Thurgau (Riesling and Sylvaner)
region: Hertfordshire
city or village: Firthsden

Firthsden is one of England's new vineyard areas, and vines were planted in 1971.

Pronounced but delicate Muscat bouquet; the wine is crisp and fruity.
price range: B

producer: Merrydown Wine Co. Ltd.
classification: White table wine
grape variety: Müller-Thurgau and Seyval Blanc
region: Suffolk
district: Ipswich
city or village: Woodbridge

One of a number of new English vineyards that grows largely Riesling varieties, producing quality wines.

Hock type, dry. **price range:** B

producer: Merrydown Wine Co. Ltd.
classification: White table wine
grape variety: Blend

Pale color—typical of white wines of European origin—and a fresh, fruity bouquet. The wine is dry, light-bodied, and fruity, with distinctive character, like a Loire or Rhine wine. **price range:** B

producer: Merrydown Wine Co. Ltd.
classification: White table wine
grape variety: Müller-Thurgau,

Seyve-Villard, Reichensteiner, and Huxelrebe
region: Kent
city or village: West Peckham
This small vineyard has been newly planted in an area used several centuries ago for vineyards. The first wine was made in 1974.
Light color and a good, fresh bouquet. The wine is pleasant, refreshingly dry, and fruity, and has a delicate flavor; it is well-suited as an aperitif or with light meats or fish. **price range: B**

producer: Paget Brothers
classification: White table wine
grape variety: Müller-Thurgau and Reichensteiner
region: Sussex
district: South Downs
city or village: Singleton
It is thought that the Romans grew grapes at nearby Charlton, as the area has all the characteristics of a perfect vineyard: reasonably sheltered, not too steep slopes, a good exposure to the morning sun, silt-clay/loam soil overlying a bed of chalk, and a climatic environment in which the vine can flourish.
Grapey bouquet; the wine is dry, full-bodied, firm, and well-balanced.
price range: B

producer: Gillian Pearkes, Yearlstone Vineyard
classification: White varietal table wine
grape variety: Chardonnay
region: Devon
district: Exe River valley
city or village: Bickleigh
The Yearlstone Vineyard is situated on a steep slope facing due south, overlooking the River Exe, Devon's main waterway. It covers an area of 1.5 acres and occupies one of the most perfect sites in all England for vines. Four grape varieties are grown (Chardonnay, Siegerrebe, Madeleine Angevine, and Triomphe d'Alsace) for the main production, but over one hundred other varieties from Germany, Alsace, Austria, and Russia are grown experimentally on an additional half-acre, in search of the right grape variety for the English climate.
Pale gold color and a very fresh, flinty bouquet of spring flowers. The wine is clean, crisp, and has depth—the flavor is fruity and well-balanced.
price range: B

producer: C. P. & N. Reece
classification: White table wine
grape variety: Riesling and Sylvaner
region: East Anglia
district: Cambridgeshire
city or village: Gamlingay
One of a growing number of English vineyards, planted in 1970. The land rises 200 feet above sea level; the output now reaches 12,000 bottles annually, all made and bottled at the vineyard.
Light gold color with a touch of green and a flowery bouquet. The wine is semi-dry and balanced and can be drunk with meals. **price range: A**

producer: W. M. Rook Ltd., Stragglethorpe Vineyard
classification: White table wine
grape variety: Müller-Thurgau and Seyval Blanc
region: Lincoln
district: Lincoln
city or village: Stragglethorpe
Stragglethorpe Vineyard is one of the earliest English vineyards presently in production to be planted (1964). The first vintage was in 1967. This is probably the most northerly vineyard in Europe, located above the 53 degree parallel. The wines are single-vineyard wines.
Light gold color; the wine is dry.
price range: B

producer: Norman J. Sneesby/Isle of Ely Vineyard
classification: White table wine
grape variety: Müller-Thurgau
region: East Anglia
district: Cambridgeshire
city or village: Wilburton
One of the more recent English vineyards, planted in 1972. This excellent site produces good wine even in poor growing seasons. Grapes were grown on the site of Isle of Ely Vineyard in medieval times by

the monks of Ely. The wine contains about 11% alcohol by volume.
Pale golden color and a flowery, full bouquet. The wine is clean, full-flavored, and well-balanced, with a refreshing acidity. **price range: B**

producer: Stone's
classification: Fruit wine
variety: Currants flavored with ginger
Stone's ginger wine can be traced back in England to 1740. Today it is popular in Australia, New Zealand, and Jamaica, as well as the United States. The British enjoy it neat in a Sherry glass, but to the American palate we recommend the "Stone Head": 1/3 Stone's, 2/3 cold beer, and lots of ice.
Dark color and an extremely pronounced bouquet. The wine is strong-flavored.
price range: A

producer: B. H. Theobald, Westbury Vineyard
classification: White table wine
grape variety: Müller-Thurgau and Pinot
region: Berkshire
city or village: Purley
The Westbury vineyard in the Thames Valley produces some fine English wines.
Exquisite bouquet; the wine is clean, with a long-lasting flavor.
price range: C

producer: Wootton Wines
classification: White varietal table wine
grape variety: Müller-Thurgau
region: Somerset County
district: Mendip Hills
city or village: North Wootton
This 4-acre vineyard was planted in 1971 in the foothills of the Mendips. The

county of Somerset produces some excellent white wines.
Pale yellow-green color and a fruity bouquet. The wine is elegant, with a rounded flavor and a slight sparkle, giving it great charm. **price range: B**

producer: Moussec Ltd.
classification: White sparkling wine
grape variety: Blend
The largest-selling sparkling wine in Britain, made from a skillful blend of imported grape juice concentrate.
Light pale straw color, with good bubbles, and a light, invitingly fruity bouquet. The wine is medium dry, light, and tastes fruity. **price range: A**

producer: Coleman & Co. Ltd.
classification: Fortified wine
A long-established blend of imported grape-juice concentrate, with well-known tonic properties.
Deep red color and a rich, fruity bouquet. The wine is supple, with a fruity style.
price range: A

Grape cultivation began in Australia after Captain Arthur Phillip brought vine cuttings with him from England when he founded the colony of New South Wales in January 1788. But the pioneer who was primarily responsible for the establishment of the Australian wine trade was a young Scot named James Busby. This enterprising youth selected 20,000 cuttings from 678 varieties that he imported from France, Spain, Portugal, Palestine, Syria, Arabia, and Persia.

Today, most Australian vineyards concentrate on grapes similar to those cultivated in Europe, and the names given to Australian wines are principally generic—Claret, Burgundy, Sauterne, Moselle, and so on. Other Australian wines are produced under local district names, for example, Barossa and Coonawarra. Still others carry varietal names, such as Cabernet, Riesling, or Shiraz. Sometimes two varietal names are used in labeling a wine. Australia's better-known wine-making areas are:

Hunter Valley This is the oldest and best-known district; both red and white table wines are produced.

Murrumbidgee Valley This is the most important New South Wales wine-producing area; table, aperitif, and dessert wines are made.

Murray Valley Although this region has been closely identified with Sherry production in the past, there has been a recent concentration on the making of wines for the table.

Southern Wales This area has been producing good wines for more than one hundred years.

Coonawarra The most southerly vineyards in Australia are found in this district. Table wines constitute the main effort of wine makers from this part of Australia.

Rutherglen–Corowa Wines are of outstanding reputation when they come from this principle winegrowing area even though production has been reduced in recent times.

Great Western The district of Victoria gives us a wide variety of wines.

Tahbilk This area lies about 75 miles north of Melbourne and yields high-quality red and white table wines.

Barossa Valley This is one of the chief winegrowing regions of Australia, from which several notable wines come.

Clare–Watervale Exposure to the elements, on rolling hills and steep slopes that mount as high as 2,000 feet above sea level, make the varied wines from this area hearty.

Adelaide Metropolitan Although urbanization is slowly encroaching on the agricultural territory, many vineyards can still be found close to the city and produce some fine Sherries and table wines.

Swan Valley This is the chief viticultural center of western Australia. Long, hot summers favor the growth of grapes with high sugar content. Full-bodied wines are the result.

Some of the leading varietal wines of Australia are:

Rhine Riesling Because of the excellence of these wines, the grapes for their production are grown in most districts of Australia, especially South Australia, Hunter and Riverina (Murrumbidgee and Murray). In most of the South Australia area the wines have a very strong varietal "nose" and a very spicy flavor. In the Hunter district the varietal "nose" is much less dominant, though the wine has more vinosity.

Cabernet Sauvignon These vines grow very well in the nonirrigated areas of Australia, but they produce small harvests of wine with tremendous character that is usually blended with *Shiraz* and sold under a *Cabernet Shiraz* label. With the increase of plantings in the Riverina area and other places, 100% *Cabernet* is becoming more available.

Some of the important grape varieties used in the making of Australia's finest wines are:

Doradillo This grape is widely used for the production of Australia's Sherries.

Traminer This famous grape variety from Germany and Alsace produces well in Australia.

Hermitage or Black Shiraz This grape produces the main varietal table wine enjoyed "down under." These grapes are to be found extensively in all wine-producing regions.

Trebbiano White Hermitage This is the famous Trebbiano of Italy, which is also called *White Shiraz* in Australia. This grape variety produces a range of wines, from good full round whites to fruity wines with a light, pleasant flavor, all depending upon the geology of the place in which they are grown.

Palomino This is the world's greatest Sherry grape and is used almost exclusively for the production of Australia's fine Sherries.

Frontignac These grapes are used and much valued as the base of Muscat wines with rich flavor.

Grenache This is the grape grown most profusely in Australia for the production of rosé and Port wines.

Carignane This grape produces wine that is widely used for blending in Australia.

Lexia–Gordo Blanco These grapes, also known as *Muscat of Alexandria*, are used to the greatest degree for the making of Muscatel and Sweet Sherry.

Hunter River Riesling/Semillon This grape, known in Australia by both its names, is favored for cultivation in New South Wales to a greater degree than it is in other states.

Chardonnay In Australia this grape produces a good, balanced wine with a distinctive bouquet and fruity flavor.

AUSTRALIA, NEW SOUTH WALES

producer: Elliot's Wines Pty. Ltd.
classification: White table wine
grape variety: Semillon
district: Hunter River Valley
city or village: Pokolbin
 A light fruity wine with a firm acidity. Clear green-gold color and a bouquet showing Semillon character. The wine is light and fruity. **price range:** A

producer: Elliott's Wines Pty. Ltd.
classification: Red table wine
grape variety: Shiraz (90%) and Cabernet (10%)
district: Hunter River Valley
city or village: Pokolbin
 Clear, dark red color with tinges of purple, and a fruity bouquet. The wine combines full fruit flavor with a hint of Cabernet.
price range: A

*"Let us drink the juice divine,
The gift of Bacchus, god of wine."*
  —Anacreon

producer: Elliot's Wines Pty. Ltd.
classification: White table wine
grape variety: Trebbiano and Semillon
district: Hunter River Valley
city or village: Pokolbin
 Green-gold color and a fruity bouquet. The wine is light and fruity, with a firm acid finish. **price range:** A

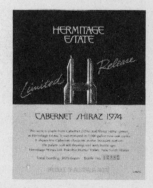

producer: Hermitage Wines Ltd.
classification: Red table wine
grape variety: Cabernet (52%) and Shiraz (48%)
district: Hunter River Valley
city or village: Pokolbin
 The grapes for this wine were harvested at 11.5 degrees Baumé and 6.98 g./ml. acidity. The wine was matured in 1000-gallon oak casks.
 Clear, deep red color, and a strong bouquet with Cabernet evident. The wine has fine acid/fruit balance, and will develop for many years. **price range:** B

producer: Hermitage Wines Ltd.
classification: White table wine
grape variety: Semillon
district: Hunter River Valley
city or village: Pokolbin

The grapes for this wine were harvested at 11 degrees Baumé, fermented for 9 days and matured in 100-gallon oak casks prior to bottling. It is sold as "Hunter River Riesling."

Clear green-gold color and a fruity bouquet with some wood elements. The wine is clean and shows good balance between fruit and acid; it is a typical dry white wine from the Hunter Valley area.
price range: A

producer: Hermitage Wines Ltd.
classification: Red table wine
grape variety: Shiraz
district: Hunter Valley
city or village: Pokolbin

This wine was made from fine Shiraz grapes grown on red volcanic soil.

Clear, deep red color, and a strong bouquet of fruit and oak. The wine has fine balance of fruit, tannin, and acid, complemented by maturation in new oak casks; it will take many years to reach its peak.
price range: A

producer: Hermitage Wines Ltd.
classification: Red table wine
grape variety: Shiraz
district: Hunter River Valley
city or village: Pokolbin

Fermented in Swiss-designed rotovat fermenters, which accelerate color extraction.

Clear deep color and a typical fruity character. The wine is soft, with good

---

Shiraz fruit, and is well-balanced; it is well-balanced for future development but is also good for present drinking.
price range: A

producer: Hermitage Wines Ltd.
classification: White table wine
grape variety: Semillon
district: Hunter River Valley
city or village: Pokolbin

A typical white wine from the Hunter Valley that benefits from bottle maturation. The grapes are grown on alluvial loam soil.

Clear green-gold color and a fruity bouquet.
price range: A

producer: McWilliam's Wines Pty. Ltd.
classification: Red table wine
grape variety: Hermitage
district: Lower Hunter River Valley
city or village: Pokolbin

McWilliam's has adopted the policy of distinguishing their Mount Pleasant table wines by giving them names from royalty: male names for whites, female names for reds. So this wine is called "Philip Hermitage" instead of being given a private bin number.

Brick-red color and a vinous bouquet with a touch of oak. The wine is soft, well-balanced, dry, and smooth, with a complex aroma and flavor.
price range: B

producer: McWilliam's Wines Pty. Ltd.
classification: Red table wine
grape variety: Cabernet Sauvignon (over 50%) and Shiraz
district: Riverina

This wine was matured in small oak casks prior to bottling. The dominant aroma of Cabernet blends admirably with the mellow roundness of Shiraz to yield a wine with good color and excellent balance.

Deep red color and a complex aroma of fruit and oak. On the palate the wine is mellow, round, and fruity.
price range: A

producer: McWilliam's Wines Pty. Ltd.
classification: Fortified wine
grape variety: Hermitage
district: Riverina

A rich, fruity Port wine with the flavor of sun-ripened grapes.

Ruby-red color and a fresh, fruity bouquet. The wine has a sweet, fruity taste.
price range: A

producer: McWilliam's Wines Pty. Ltd.
classification: Red sparkling wine
grape variety: Blend
district: Riverina

This light red sparkling wine is produced by the *charmat* (bulk) process and retains a touch of sweetness.

Light red color and a fruity bouquet. The wine has a fruity flavor and tastes slightly sweet.
price range: A

producer: McWilliam's Wines Pty. Ltd.
classification: White sparkling wine
grape variety: Semillon
district: Riverina

This wine is bottle fermented by the traditional *méthode champenoise*.

Pale straw color and a fresh, fruity bouquet. The wine is crisp and clean, medium dry, and has a good effervescent sparkle.
price range: B

producer: McWilliam's Wines Pty. Ltd.
classification: White table wine
grape variety: Hunter River Riesling (Semillon)
district: Lower Hunter River Valley
city or village: Pokolbin

McWilliam's has adopted the policy of distinguishing their Mount Pleasant table wines by giving them names from royalty instead of using bin numbers: male names for reds, and female names for whites. Thus, this wine is called "Elizabeth Riesling."

Pale gold color with a touch of green and a dominant bouquet with district character and vinosity. On the palate the wine is full and round, with excellent balance, and shows many characteristics of a white Burgundy.
price range: B

producer: McWilliam's Wines Pty. Ltd.
classification: Red varietal table wine
grape variety: Cabernet Sauvignon
district: Riverina

After fermentation, this wine received approximately two years' aging in small oak casks before bottling.

Brick-red color and a complex aroma of Cabernet fruit and oak wood. Made in the Claret style, the wine has a pronounced varietal aroma and flavor; it shows good balance and has a firm, tannic finish.
price range: A

producer: McWilliam's Wines Pty. Ltd.
classification: Fortified wine
grape variety: Palomino
district: Riverina

This dry Fino Sherry was matured in oak hogsheads under the influence of flor yeast for a minimum of two years.

Brilliant clear pale-straw-yellow color and a typical flor (aldehyde) aroma. The wine is crisp, dry, and tangy, with a subtle taste of oak and flor character.
price range: A

producer: McWilliam's Wines Pty. Ltd.
classification: White varietal table wine
grape variety: Rhine Riesling
district: Riverina

This dry Rhine Riesling was produced by controlled-temperature fermentation and was bottled very early without any wood aging.

Pale straw color with greenish tinges and a dominant varietal aroma. The wine has a very crisp, spicy flavor; it is delicate, with excellent acid balance.
price range: A

producer: McWilliam's Wines Pty. Ltd.
classification: White varietal table wine
grape variety: Traminer
district: Riverina

This wine was produced by controlled-temperature fermentation and was bottled very early without any wood aging.

Pale gold color and a spicy, aromatic bouquet typical of Traminer. The wine is fruity, full, spicy, and flavorful.
price range: A

producer: McWilliam's Wines Pty. Ltd.
classification: White varietal table wine
grape variety: Chardonnay
district: Riverina

This Chardonnay was produced by controlled-temperature fermentation and was bottled very early without any wood aging.

Pale golden color and a distinctive, pleasing bouquet. The wine has a crisp, fruity flavor and good balance; it is full-bodied, fruity dry table wine.
price range: A

producer: McWilliam's Wines Pty. Ltd.
classification: White varietal table wine
grape variety: Rhine Riesling
district: Riverina

The Rhine Riesling grapes used for this wine are allowed to remain on the vine until they become very ripe. This gives the wine its pleasant rich aroma and luscious fruity flavor. It is a "late harvest" Rhine Riesling, differing from our other Riesling through a slight touch of sweetness.

Pale gold color and a spicy, aromatic bouquet. The wine is rich and fruity, with a slight touch of sweetness.
price range: A

producer: McWilliam's Wines Pty. Ltd.
classification: Rosé varietal table wine
grape variety: Cabernet Sauvignon
district: Riverina

This fresh, fruity rosé wine was made entirely from Cabernet Sauvignon grapes and has a slight touch of effervescence.

Brilliant clear rosé color and a clean, fruity bouquet. The wine is quite fruity, with a firm finish.
price range: A

producer: Penfolds Wines Pty. Ltd.
classification: Red table wine
grape variety: Shiraz
district: Hunter River Valley
vineyard: Dalwood estate

Deep red color and a fruity bouquet with a hint of wood. The wine has a pleasant

mature wood flavor; it is a good quality wine that will improve with more bottle age.
price range: B

producer: Penfolds Wines Pty. Ltd.
classification: Red table wine
grape variety: Shiraz and Mataro
district: Hunter and Barossa valleys

A "Burgundy" of consistently high quality, made in an easy-to-drink style.

Deep Burgundy-red color and a subtle, fruity bouquet. The wine tastes smooth and is full-bodied.
price range: B

AUSTRALIA, SOUTH AUSTRALIA

producer: Angove's Pty. Ltd.
classification: Red table wine
grape variety: Shiraz and Mataro
district: Riverland
city or village: Renmark

Angove's "Burgundy" is a full-bodied red wine with good acid/tannin balance.

Excellent bouquet and taste; the wine is dry, soft, and delicious, with a fine finish.
price range: B

producer: Angove's Pty. Ltd.
classification: Fortified wine
grape variety: Pedro Ximenez
district: Riverland
city or village: Renmark

One of the finest Flor Sherries produced in Australia, Angove's takes up to five years to produce.

Straw color; excellent bouquet and flavor.
price range: C

producer: Penfolds Wines Pty. Ltd.
classification: White table wine
grape variety: Semillon
district: Hunter River Valley

Made in one of Australia's foremost white wine regions, this white "Burgundy" ages and softens well with bottle maturation.

Light golden color and a bold, full, and fruity bouquet. The wine is clean, soft, and well-balanced, with a fruity flavor.
price range: B

producer: Angove's Pty. Ltd.
classification: White varietal table wine
grape variety: Rhine Riesling
district: Riverland
city or village: Renmark

This dry Australian Riesling is called "Bookmark," a name that derives from an original station property in the Renmark area. The wine is produced under strictly controlled conditions.

Straw color and a delicate bouquet. The wine is light, delicate, and dry and has a crisp, clean acidity.
price range: B

producer: Angove's Pty. Ltd.
classification: Red table wine
grape variety: Cabernet Sauvignon and Shiraz

district: Riverland
city or village: Renmark

The Australian Claret is called "Tregrehan," the name of which derives from a small town in Cornwall, England, from where an ancestor of the Angove family originated.

Excellent bouquet and flavor; the wine is styled light and dry, with pleasing bouquet and crisp finish.   **price range:** B

producer: Barossa Co-operative Winery Ltd. ("Kaiser Stuhl")
classification: Rosé varietal table wine
grape variety: Grenache
district: Barossa Valley
city or village: Nuriootpa

Our Kaiserstuhl rosé has won many gold medals in Australian and international competition.

Brilliant pink color and a flowery, fruity varietal bouquet. The wine is pleasant and refreshing, with good color, flavor, and all-around balance.   **price range:** B

producer: Barossa Co-operative Winery Ltd. ("Kaiser Stuhl")
classification: White varietal table wine
grape variety: Rhine Riesling
district: Barossa Valley
city or village: Nuriootpa

This Rhine Riesling is produced in the "late harvest" style. Certain grapes are left on the vine for additional ripeness, and are then taken to temperature-controlled cellars where the wine is cold-fermented. This process allows a very flowery "nose" rich in esters, a great deal of flavor, and some agreeable residual natural sugar in the wine. A "Gold Ribbon Riesling Spätlese."

Light straw color and a typical bouquet of a fine Rhine Riesling wine. On the palate the wine is fruity and very refreshing.
price range: B

producer: Barossa Co-operative Winery Ltd. ("Kaiser Stuhl)
classification: Red varietal table wine
grape variety: Cabernet Sauvignon
district: Barossa Valley
village: Nuriootpa

This fine Cabernet Sauvignon comes from vineyards that yield 2.1 tons per acre. It is matured in French Nevers oak for added complexity.

Brilliant deep ruby-red color and a fine varietal bouquet. The wine is complex with lots of fruit; a typical, well-made Cabernet Sauvignon.   **price range:** B

producer: Barossa Co-operative Winery Ltd. ("Kaiser Stuhl")
classification: White sparkling wine
grape variety: White Hermitage, Tokay, and Semillon
district: Barossa Valley
city or village: Nuriootpa

"Gold Seal Special Cuvée Vintage Brut Champagne" is bottle-fermented in the traditional *méthode champenoise* and left on the yeast for no less than two years. After disgorging, it is transferred, using the Star method, before being sold.

Brilliant light gold color and a clean, yeasty bouquet. On the palate the wine is dry and refreshing.   **price range:** C

producer: Barossa Co-operative Winery Ltd.
classification: Red varietal table wine
grape variety: Cabernet Sauvignon
district: Barossa Valley

This wine is made in the Australian style, slightly bitter but not astringent. It has some wood aging and a distinctive Cabernet aroma.   **price range:** A

producer: Barossa Co-operative Winery Ltd.
classification: White varietal table wine
grape variety: Johannisberg Riesling (100%)
district: Barossa Valley
city or village: Eden Valley

This brilliant medium yellow wine has a fruity and distinct scent and some residual sweetness in its taste.   **price range:** A

producer: Barossa Co-operative Winery Ltd.
classification: White table wine
grape variety: Johannisberger Riesling
district: Barossa Valley

This is a dry, distinct Johannisberger Riesling with a fruity, distinct bouquet and brilliant light yellow appearance.
price range: A

producer: Barossa Co-operative Winery Ltd.
classification: Rosé varietal table wine
grape variety: Grenache
district: Barossa Valley

This is a light, fruity, slightly orange-colored wine with some residual sugar and a fruity bouquet.   **price range:** A

producer: Barossa Co-operative Winery Ltd.
classification: Red varietal table wine
grape variety: Petite Sirah
district: Barossa Valley

This is a brilliant red, dry, fruity Petite Sirah.   **price range:** A

producer: Barossa Co-operative Winery Ltd. ("Kaiser Stuhl")
classification: White varietal table wine
grape variety: Frontignan
district: Barossa Valley
village: Nuriootpa

This is a light golden wine of muscatey bouquet. It is luscious and semi-sweet, typical of the late picking. The wine is produced by temperature-controlled fermentation and is fermentation-arrested before all the sugar is converted. This is a superior-quality wine.

The white ribbon means that the wine is a late-picked wine.   **price range:** B

producer: Barossa Co-operative Winery Ltd. ("Kaiser Stuhl")
classification: White varietal table wine
grape variety: Rhine Riesling
district: Barossa Valley
city or village: Eden Valley

The grapes for this wine are picked late but still retain good, fresh acid. The wine is dry, with a good, clean finish and well-balanced acid. The bouquet is flowery and typical of the grape variety.

The green ribbon denotes the dry style with very little or no residual sugar or sweetness. The wine is temperature-controlled while it is fermenting.
price range: B

producer: G. Gramp & Sons Pty. Ltd.
classification: White table wine
district: Barossa Valley
This wine is distinctly fruity on account of the natural sugar retained during fermentation. **price range:** B

producer: G. Gramp & Sons Pty. Ltd.
classification: Red table wine
grape variety: Cabernet Sauvignon (60%) and Hermitage (40%)
district: Barossa Valley
This full-bodied, robust wine has a soft tannin finish. It is one of Australia's premium red table wines.
The wine has won gold medals in many Australian and international wine shows.
price range: B

producer: G. Gramp & Sons Pty. Ltd.
classification: White table wine
grape variety: Rhine Riesling (100%)
district: Barossa Valley
This clean, crisp, slightly acidic wine is among the best of Australia's table wines. it has a pronounced yet delicate Riesling grape fragrance.
The wine has won gold medals in many Australian and international wine shows.
price range: B

producer: G. Gramp & Sons Pty. Ltd.
classification: Red table wine

grape variety: Hermitage, Grenache, and Mataro
district: Barossa Valley
This fruity red wine is medium-bodied, with a pleasant softness.
price range: B

producer: Thomas Hardy & Sons, Ltd.
classification: Red varietal table wine
grape variety: Shiraz
district: Barossa Valley
city or village: Adelaide
The Shiraz grape from which this wine is made is one of the most widely used red grape varietles throughout Australia. Thomas Hardy & Sons has developed a high degree of expertise in wine making in the 140 years the family has been in business.
Clean ruby color and a soft, light flowery bouquet. The wine is even, with light body and tannin, and is reminiscent of a good Bordeaux: it shows the present state of the art of vinification in Australia.
price range: A

producer: F. F. Osborn & Sons Pty. Ltd.
classification: Red table wine
grape variety: Shiraz
district: Southern Hills
city or village: McLaren Vale
Deep red color and a varietal bouquet showing fruit and bottle age. The wine is round and fruity, with a firm finish.
price range: A

producer: F. E. Osborn & Sons Pty. Ltd.
classification: Red table wine
grape variety: Shiraz & Grenache
district: Southern Hills
city or village: McLaren Vale
The vineyards owned by F. E. Osborn & Sons Pty. extend over 170 acres, giving a total yield of 450 tons of grapes. Osborn wines have a distinctly unique style com-

bining regional influences with varietal characteristics; after aging in wood for two to three years, the wines are bottled by d'Arenberg Wines Pty. Ltd. and then aged for two more years prior to sale. This wine is called "Burgundy."
Rich red color and a varietal bouquet showing fruit and bottle aging. On the palate the wine is round, fruity, and has a firm finish.
price range: A

producer: F. E. Osborn & Sons Pty. Ltd.
classification: Red varietal table wine
grape variety: Cabernet Sauvignon
district: Southern Hills
city or village: McLaren Vale
Deep red color and a varietal bouquet with fruit resulting from lengthy bottle age. The wine is round, fruity, and has a firm finish.
price range: B

producer: F. E. Osborn & Sons Pty. Ltd.
classification: Red varietal table wine
grape variety: Shiraz
district: Southern Hills
city or village: McLaren Vale
The Osborn wines have a distinct, unique style combining regional influences with varietal characteristics.
Deep red color and a varietal bouquet showing bottle age. The wine is round, fruity, and has a firm finish.
price range: B

producer: F. E. Osborn & Sons Pty. Ltd.
classification: Red table wine
grape variety: Shiraz and Grenache
district: Southern Hills
city or village: McLaren Vale
The Osborn wines have a distinct, unique style combining regional influences with varietal characteristics.
Rich red color and a bouquet showing varietal characteristics, fruit, and bottle age. The wine is round and fruity, with a firm finish.
price range: B

producer: F. E. Osborn & Sons Pty. Ltd.
classification: Red varietal table wine
grape variety: Cabernet Sauvignon and Shiraz
district: Southern Hills
city or village: McLaren Vale
The Osborn wines have a distinct, unique style combining regional influences with varietal characteristics. This wine is sold under its varietal name and is made in the Claret style.
Deep red color and a bouquet showing varietal characteristics, fruit, and bottle age. The wine is round and fruity, with a firm finish.
price range: B

producer: F. E. Osborn & Sons Pty. Ltd.
classification: White table wine
grape variety: Palomino
district: Southern Hills
city or village: McLaren Vale
The Osborn wines have a distinct, unique style combining regional influences with varietal characteristics. "White d'Arenberg" is a dry white Burgundy-type wine that is a consistent award-winer.
Pale straw color and a fruity varietal nose. The wine is full-bodied and satisfying; round, fruity, with a firm finish.
price range: A

producer: F. E. Osborn & Sons Pty. Ltd.
classification: White varietal table wine
grape variety: Rhine Riesling and Frontignac
district: Southern Hills
city or village: McLaren Vale
The Osborn wines have a distinct, unique style combining regional influences with varietal characteristics. This wine is made of 85% Rhine Riesling and is marketed under this varietal name; however, a blend of 15% Frontignac has been included for added complexity.
Pale straw color and a fruity varietal bouquet. The wine is dry, round, and fruity, with a firm finish. **price range:** A

producer: F. E. Osborn & Sons Pty. Ltd.
classification: Fortified wine
grape variety: Palomino
district: Southern hills
city or village: McLaren Vale

A medium-dry Sherry of the Amontillado type, this wine is produced in the true aged Sherry style.

Pale amber color and a slight rancio bouquet suggesting flor yeast. The wine has a round, nutty flavor; it is full-bodied, with a dry finish. **price range:** B

"Never did a great man hate good wine." — Rabelais

producer: F. E. Osborn & Sons Pty. Ltd.
classification: Fortified wine
grape variety: Grenache and Shiraz
district: Southern hills
city or village: McLaren Vale

Typical of the area, this big, full-bodied "Tawny Port" is aged for many years in small wood casks.

Tawny color and a rich rancio bouquet. The wine is nutty, full-bodied, and has a dry finish. **price range:** B

producer: F. E. Osborn & Sons Pty. Ltd.
classification: Fortified wine
grape variety: Shiraz
district: Southern Hills
city or village: McLaren Vale

This special sweet red fortified wine is sold as a Vintage Port. Typical of its district and the informing grape variety, it was awarded Champion Trophy at the 1975 Brisbane Show in open class competition.

Deep red color and a varietal bouquet with full fruit. The wine is rich and sweet on the palate, with a long, dry finish.
price range: B

producer: Penfolds Wines Pty. Ltd.
classification: Fortified wine
grape variety: Shiraz
district: Barossa Valley
city or village: Coonawarra

This Tawny Port is a blend of old wines drawn from Australia's leading grape-growing areas.

Deep red color; the wine tastes smooth, mellow, and sweet; ideal with dessert.
price range: B

producer: Penfolds Wines Pty. Ltd.
classification: Red table wine
grape variety: Shiraz
district: Barossa Valley
city or village: Coonawarra

Bright red color and a pleasant, aromatic mixture of oak and fruit in the bouquet. The wine is medium-bodied, clean, fruity, and flavorsome; it is tremendously appealing and distinctive when young because of its superb balance and fruit, but also ages well. **price range:** C

producer: Penfolds Wines Pty. Ltd.
classification: White table wine
grape variety: Semillon and Rhine Riesling
district: Barossa Valley

The 1975 vintage of this Hock, which is currently available, won two bronze medals at an early showing in 1976 at shows in Sydney and Brisbane. For a readily available commercial wine, this was a great achievement.

Pale straw color and a clean, pleasant bouquet. The wine is delicate and well-balanced, with a pleasant amount of fruit showing through; it is clean, with all its elements in harmony. **price range:** B

producer: Penfolds Wines Pty. Ltd.
classification: Red table wine
grape variety: Shiraz
district: Barossa Valley
city or village: Auldana

"St. Henri" Shiraz is made from specially selected Shiraz grapes. This fact, combined with the extensive wood aging that the wines undergo, results in a wine of consistently high quality, though the amount produced is restricted.

Deep crimson color and a bouquet with a large dose of fruit and oak. The wine has full fruit flavor and, through its tannin, an astringent finish; it is a truly delightful Claret, one of Australia's great red wines.
price range: C

producer: Penfolds Wines Pty. Ltd.
classification: Red table wine
grape variety: Shiraz
district: Barossa Valley
city or village: Kalimna

The wine makers at Penfold have aimed at achieving a high-quality dry red wine. For this Claret, special attention is given to grape selection, wood maturation, and bottling so that quality is ensured.

Deep red color; the wine combines an inherently fruity flavor with oak and has a firm tannin finish. **price range:** C

producer: Quelltaler Wines, Ltd.
classification: White table wine
grape variety: Semillon
district: Clare/Watervale Valley
city or village: Watervale

"White Burgundy" is a full-bodied dry white wine made from Semillon grapes grown in primarily red-brown soil over a limestone base. The wine was matured in imported oak casks in century-old cool cellars, and is a consistent gold-medal winner.

Straw-yellow color and a bouquet that displays good fruit with some oak character showing through. The wine is dry and quite full-bodied. **price range:** A

producer: Quelltaler Wines, Ltd.
classification: Fortified wine
grape variety: Various
district: Clare/Watervale Valley
city or village: Watervale

A fine old semi-dry Oloroso Sherry matured in imported oak casks for several years in their century-old cool cellars.

Pale amber color and a complex bouquet with some oak showing through. The wine is mellow and semi-dry.
price range: B

producer: Quelltaler Wines, Ltd.
classification: White table wine
grape variety: Various
district: Clare/Watervale Valley
city or village: Watervale

A delicious medium-sweet white table wine made from grapes grown at Watervale. It is matured in imported oak casks in century-old cool cellars.

Golden color and a bouquet showing full fruit character. The wine is slightly sweet and has a clean finish. **price range:** A

producer: Quelltaler Wines, Ltd.
classification: White varietal table wine
grape variety: Rhine Riesling
district: Clare/Watervale Valley
city or village: Watervale

"Vintage Rhine Riesling" is a young and zestful wine that shows the full fruit character of the Rhine Riesling grape. It was awarded a gold medal at the Royal Sydney Wine Show in 1976.

Green-gold color and a fruity bouquet. The wine is clean and crisp.
price range: A

producer: Quelltaler Wines, Ltd.
classification: White table wine
grape variety: Semillon
district: Clare/Watervale Valley
city or village: Watervale

"Chablis" is a medium-dry and medium-bodied white wine made from Semillon grapes grown at Watervale in mainly red-brown soils over a limestone base. It was matured in imported oak casks in century-old cool cellars.

Pale gold color and a bouquet showing good balance of acid and fruit. The wine is very dry, with a crisp acid finish.

price range: A

producer: Quelltaler Wines, Ltd.
classification: White table wine
grape variety: Pedro Ximenez, Semillon, and Rhine Riesling
district: Clare/Watervale Valley
city or village: Watervale

Pale gold color and a bouquet with delicate fruit. The wine is delicate, with clean acidity and excellent fruit character, and has a clean, acid finish.

price range: A

producer: Quelltaler Wines, Ltd.
classification: White table wine
grape variety: Semillon and Pedro Ximenez, and others
district: Clare/Watervale Valley
city or village: Watervale

"Sauternes" is a luscious golden wine made from grapes grown in the Watervale area. Distinctly sweet in flavor, it is matured in imported oak casks in century-old cool cellars.

Golden color and a full, fruity bouquet. The wine is lusciously sweet.

price range: A

producer: Quelltaler Wines, Ltd.
classification: Red table wine
grape variety: Shiraz and Grenache
district: McLaren Vale
city or village: Watervale

"Vintage Claret" was matured in small wood casks, and the wood character consequently appears in the bouquet as a true oak characteristic.

Bright ruby color and a bouquet showing fruit and oak. The wine is pleasantly fruity, with a tannic finish appearing as a slight astringency.

price range: A

producer: Quelltaler Wines, Ltd.
classification: Fortified wine
grape variety: Pedro Ximenez and Rhine Riesling
district: Clare/Watervale Valley
city or village: Watervale

"Granfiesta Sherry" is blended via the Spanish Solera system, giving it an excellent bouquet and flavor.

Pale gold color and an aromatic oak character showing in the bouquet. The wine displays the traditional flor yeast character, has a slight woody flavor, and finishes dry.

price range: A

producer: Quelltaler Wines, Ltd.
classification: Fortified wine
grape variety: Shiraz
district: Clare/Watervale Valley
city or village: Watervale

"Vintage Port" is made only from grapes grown in exceptional vintages. This exquisite wine, like the Vintage Ports of Portugal, spends only a short time in wood before continuing its development in bottle. It was a champion and gold-medal winner at the 1973 Adelaide show.

Deep red-brown color and a blackberry bouquet. The wine has well-balanced berry flavor, with a good spirit finish.

price range: B

producer: Quelltaler Wines, Ltd.
classification: White table wine
grape variety: Pedro Ximenez and Trebbiano
district: Clare/Watervale Valley
city or village: Watervale

Golden color and a fresh, fruity bouquet. The wine is delicate, slightly sweet, and crisp.

price range: A

producer: B. Seppelt & Sons Ltd.
classification: Red table wine
grape variety: Cabernet Sauvignon and Hermitage
district: Rutherglen, Great Western, Barossa Valley

Seppelt Claret is Australia's most popular dry red table wine, and is popularly priced. Although vintage-dated, it is blended from year to year to maintain a consistent style. It is extensively imported to Southeast Asia, New Zealand, the Pacific, Canada, the United States, and to East and West Africa.

Distinctive Claret color and a bouquet with light grape characteristics. The wine has slight tannin and finishes smoothly.

price range: A

producer: B. Seppelt & Sons Ltd.
classification: Fortified wine
grape variety: Palomino (50%) and Grenache (50%)
district: Barossa Valley and Rutherglen

A medium-dry Sherry, the brand name of which is the most popular of its type. It is exported to many countries in Southeast Asia and to the United States.

price range: A

producer: B. Seppelt & Sons Ltd.
classification: Rosé table wine
grape variety: Grenache and Miquel d'Argo
district: Rutherglen and Barossa Valley

A popular style of Australian rosé, this delicate wine has a slight residual sparkle, or "spritz." The wine is extensively exported to Southeast Asia, the Pacific areas, Canada, the United States, the West Indies, and to East and West Africa.

Light pink color and a fresh, grapey bouquet. The wine is light and fresh, with slight spritz.

price range: A

producer: B. Seppelt & Sons Ltd.
classification: Fortified wine
grape variety: Grenache
district: Barossa Valley
city or village: Seppeltsfield

"Aged Tawny" is made from grapes grown at the Seppeltsfield estate in the Barossa Valley. The wine is matured in wood at the Seppeltsfield Winery, renowned as the producer of the premium fortified wines of Australia.

price range: B

producer: B. Seppelt & Sons Ltd.
classification: White varietal table wine
grape variety: Rhine Riesling
district: Barossa Valley, Clare, and Keppoch

This dry white wine is produced from Rhine Riesling grapes grown in the cooler wine-growing districts of Australia. It is bottled shortly after fermentation to retain its delicate attributes.

Slight yellow-green tinge and a delicate Rhine Riesling bouquet. The wine is dry, with varietal characteristics.

price range: A

producer: S. Smith & Son Pty. Ltd.
classification: White table wine
grape variety: Rhine Riesling
district: Eden Valley

This straw-colored wine has a crisp, dry taste and plenty of fruit character. Its bouquet is very subtle. **price range:** A

"When a man drinks wine at dinner, he begins to be better pleased with himself."
— Plato

producer: S. Smith & Son Pty. Ltd.
classification: White varietal table wine
grape variety: Rhine Riesling
district: Pewsey Vale

This crisp, dry wine has a slight suggestion of the Rhine Riesling grape. Its bouquet is fragrant and its color straw.

Pewsey Vale is the highest-producing commercial vineyard in Australia.
price range: A

AUSTRALIA, VICTORIA

producer: Brown Bros.
classification: White varietal table wine
grape variety: Rhine Riesling
district: North East
city or village: Milawa

This full-flavored Riesling was fermented at very low temperatures over a period of three months. The small amount of residual sugar results from stopping the fermentation by means of refrigeration and filtration.

producer: Tolley Scott & Tolley Ltd.
classification: Red varietal table wine
grape variety: Shiraz and Cabernet Sauvignon
district: Barossa Valley
city or village: Nuriootpa

The 1972 vintage shows excellent development after four years of bottle aging.

Medium-deep red color and a well-developed varietal bouquet with slight oak flavor. **price range:** A

producer: Tolley Scott & Tolley Ltd.
classification: White varietal table wine
grape variety: Rhine Riesling
district: Barossa Valley
city or village: Nuriootpa

1976 vintage.

Pale straw color and a delicate varietal bouquet. On the palate the wine has distinctive fruit flavor, balanced with crisp acidity. **price range:** A

Medium green-gold color and a typical varietal bouquet. The wine is fruity and sprited, with clean acid and a good finish.
price range: B

producer: Brown Bros.
classification: White varietal table wine
grape variety: Rhine Riesling

district: North East
city or village: Milawa

This special wine was made from grapes left on the vine for approximately four weeks after the normal harvest time, during which time the "noble rot" (*Botrytis cinerea*) formed, giving the wine a luscious character.

Deep gold color and a highly aromatic bouquet suggesting the style of a white Graves. The wine is full, luscious and has good acid balance that balances its sweetness; hence, there is no cloying quality. **price range:** B

producer: Brown Bros.
classification: White varietal table wine
grape variety: White Frontignac
district: North East
city or village: Milawa

This wine shows the luscious varietal character of the Frontignac grape, from which the juice is quickly removed after crushing so as to avoid picking up any color. The wine was made under controlled-temperature and atmosphere conditions. It was stored in stainless steel and bottled when very young, allowing the powerful varietal characteristics to be retained.

Pale gold color and a varietal bouquet. The wine has luscious fruit and a dry, acid finish. **price range:** B

producer: Brown Bros.
classification: Red varietal table wine
grape variety: Cabernet Sauvignon and Shiraz
district: North East
city or village: Milawa

The vintage year of 1974 produced red wines well up to the standards of the area. This wine was fermented in closed fermentors under controlled temperatures, and was left to age in small American oak casks. It is typical of the style of the North East region in Victoria, where red wines are characteristically full in color and flavor.

Deep red color and a varietal bouquet with some new oak. The wine is full-flavored, with good oak and tannin, and should age well; the assertiveness of Shiraz is balanced by the Cabernet Sauvignon. **price range:** B

producer: Brown Bros.
classification: Red varietal table wine
grape variety: Shiraz
district: North East
city or village: Milawa

The vintage year of 1974 produced red wines well up to the standards of the area. This wine was fermented in closed fermentors under controlled temperatures and was left to age in small American oak casks. It is typical of the style of the North East region in Victoria, where red wines are characteristically full in color and flavor.

Medium red color and a varietal bouquet showing some oak. The wine is full-flavored and has some tannin from the oak casks. **price range:** B

producer: McWilliam's Wines Pty. Ltd.
classification: White table wine
grape variety: Gordo Blanco (Lexia)
district: Murray River Valley
city or village: Robinvale

This light, fruity white wine was fermented at very cold temperatures, then bottled without any wood aging.

Pale straw color with a touch of green and a scented, grapey aroma. The wine is light and delicate, with a tremendous volume of flavor. **price range:** A

producer: McWilliam's Wines Pty. Ltd.
classification: Fortified wine
grape variety: Gordo Blanco
district: Murray River Valley
city or village: Robinvale

A specially selected sweet Sherry.

Pale straw color and an aroma of Muscat. The wine has a grapey flavor, with a soft finish; it is fruity, mild, and mellow.
price range: A

producer: Quelltaler Wines Ltd.
classification: White sparkling wine
grape variety: White Hermitage
district: North West
city or village: Avoca
   This Brut Champagne was fermented in the bottle by the traditional *méthode champenoise.*
   Pale gold color and a bouquet showing good fruit and yeast balance. The wine is very dry on the palate.   **price range:** C

producer: B. Seppelt & Sons Ltd.
classification: White sparkling wine
grape variety: Irvine's White
district: Great Western
   Australia's premium and most popular sparkling wine, the wine is bottle-fermented at the Great Western Winery in Victoria.
   Slight straw color and a delicate Champagne bouquet. The wine is dry, with a slight yeast flavor and true grape characteristics.   **price range:** C

producer: Tahbilk Proprietary Ltd.
classification: Red table wine
grape variety: Shiraz
district: Goulburn Valley
city or village: Tabilk
   Claret style.
   Deep purple color and a good varietal bouquet with delicate oak overtones. The wine has good acid balance and shows good tannin in the finish.   **price range:** C

producer: Tahbilk Proprietary Ltd.
classification: Rosé table wine
grape variety: Shiraz
district: Goulburn Valley
city or village: Tabilk
   This is a rosé wine produced with a minimum of fermentation on the skins. The grapes in 1976 were higher in sugar than usual; as a result, the wines are bigger and fruitier than normal.
   Pink, light-medium rosé color, and a good varietal bouquet. The wine is clean and dry, with good acidity.
price range: B

producer: Tahbilk Proprietary Ltd.
classification: White table wine
grape variety: Marsanne
district: Goulburn Valley
city or village: Tabilk
   In the hotter climates in northern Victoria, this wine is frequently fortified into a White Port.
   Deep, honey-gold color and a vinous bouquet. The wine is made in a Chablis style—it is clean, soft, and has good acid balance.   **price range:** B

producer: Tahbilk Proprietary Ltd.
classification: White table wine
grape variety: Rhine Riesling
district: Goulburn Valley
city or village: Tabilk
   Very deep gold color and a soft, fruity bouquet. The wine lacks great acidity but has good fruit.   **price range:** B

producer: Tahbilk Proprietary Ltd.
classification: White table wine
grape variety: White Hermitage
   (Trebbiano/Ugni Blanc)
district: Goulburn Valley
city or village: Tabilk
   In northern Victoria the White Hermitage produces wines in a very full-flavored style.
   Green-gold color and a clean, crisp bouquet. The wine is in the Hock style, with delicate fruit and good acidity.
price range: B

producer: Tahbilk Proprietary Ltd.
classification: Red table wine
grape variety: Cabernet Sauvignon
district: Goulburn Valley
city or village: Tabilk
   Deep red color and a good varietal bouquet with delicate oak overtones. The wine is made in the Burgundy style, with soft acidity and good tannin.
price range: C

Growing vines and making wine are activities that have occupied New Zealand's settlers from the beginning. The wine industry in this country stems directly from the Australian success in this fascinating field. Around 1819, the Reverend Samuel Marsden noted in his diary that he had "planted at Keriki about 100 grape vines of different kinds brought from Port Jackson." In 1835 Charles Darwin recorded that he had observed grapes growing at Waimate North. On the South Island, French settlers established vineyards at Akaroa.

The first wine known to have been made in New Zealand was produced in 1840 by James Busby, the Scottish-born viticulturist. It was a light white wine produced from the grapes of his Bay of Islands vineyard as well as from cuttings that he had brought with him from Australia.

Today's main wine-producing regions are located in three areas on the North Island: on the east coast, around Napier and Gisborne; west of Auckland, in the Henderson-Kumeu area; and south of Auckland, in the area around Te Kauwhata.

Some fifty different grape varieties are grown in New Zealand, including a number of classic European wine varieties such as Cabernet Sauvignon, Riesling, Sylvaner, Pinot Noir, Pinot Blanc, Chardonnay, Malbec, Palomino, Chenin Blanc, and Gamay. A trend toward increased planting of classical European varieties for the production of table wines indicates that New Zealand is zealously seeking a superior product, not only for New Zealand consumption, but also for export.

producer: Balic Estate Wines
classification: White table wine
grape variety: Palomino
region: North Island
district: Auckland
city or village: Henderson
This full-bodied sweet wine has a mellow bouquet and rich golden color.
price range: A

producer: Balic Estate Wines
classification: White table wine
grape variety: Siebel 4643
region: North Island
district: Auckland
city or village: Henderson
This full-bodied sweet wine has a moorish bouquet and rich, tawny color.
The wine is aged for three years in oak casks.
price range: A

producer: Balic Estate Wines
classification: White table wine
grape variety: Baco 22A
region: North Island
district: Auckland
city or village: Henderson
This is a crisp, clean white table wine with a delicate, dry bouquet. It has a slightly golden color.
price range: A

producer: Balic Estate Wines
classification: Fortified wine
grape variety: Palomino
region: North Island
district: Auckland
city or village: Henderson
This dry, mellow wine has a distinctive flor bouquet.
price range: B

producer: Balic Estate Wines
classification: White sparkling wine
grape variety: Dro Hogg's Muscat and Niagara
region: North Island
district: Auckland
city or village: Henderson
This sparkling wine is made by the *charmat* (bulk) process, and is similar in all characteristics to the Italian Asti. It is sweet and full-bodied, with a fruity bouquet.
price range: B

producer: Balic Estate Wines
classification: White table wine
grape variety: Müller-Thurgau and Riesling
region: North Island
district: Auckland
city or village: Henderson
This aromatic wine is crisp, with a full, fruity aftertaste. It is quite dry, with a slightly golden color.
price range: A

producer: Balic Estate Wines
classification: White table wine
grape variety: Baco 22A and Bilo Nova
region: North Island
district: Auckland
city or village: Henderson
This is a full-bodied sweet wine with a soft aroma.
price range: A

producer: Balic Estate Wines
classification: Rosé table wine
grape variety: Siebel 5455
region: North Island
district: Auckland
city or village: Henderson
This semi-sweet rosé has a delicate bouquet.
price range: A

producer: Balic Estate Wines
classification: Red table wine
grape variety: Siebel 4643 and 5455
region: North Island
district: Auckland
city or village: Henderson
This burgundy-colored wine is robust, with a full bouquet. It is rich but dry.
price range: A

producer: Balic Estate Wines
classification: White table wine
grape variety: Palomino, Baco 22A, and Gee-Gee
region: North Island
district: Auckland
village: Henderson
The fruity flavor of this clear wine is reminiscent of the Rhine Valley wines. It has a delicate bouquet.
price range: A

producer: Collard Bros. Ltd.
classification: Red varietal table wine
grape variety: Cabernet Sauvignon and Pinotage
region: Auckland
district: Henderson
city or village: Henderson

This very robust red wine ages very well in bottle. It combines softness and color from Pinotage with the firmness and longevity from Cabernet Sauvignon and was the only gold-medal winner in the 1976 February Easter Show. Careful decanting is advised before serving.

Dark red color and a complex, mature oak-fruit bouquet. The wine is full-bodied, with good oak-fruit balance, and has sufficient tannin to age well. **price range:** B

producer: Collard Bros. Ltd.
classification: White varietal table wine
grape variety: Müller-Thurgau (Riesling and Sylvaner)
region: Auckland
district: Henderson
city or village: Henderson

This wine is a good example of a Müller-Thurgau grown in the Henderson area. Pale in color but remarkably fruity, it is low in alcohol and hence has great appeal. Good acidity balances the slight residual sugar; it was the top wine in its class at the Trade & Industry Wine Show in 1974.

Pale color and a fruity, flowery bouquet. The wine is light, crisp, and fruity, with good varietal character, and finishes well. **price range:** B

producer: Collard Bros. Ltd.
classification: White varietal table wine
grape variety: Baco
region: Auckland
district: Henderson
city or village: Henderson

This white wine is made in the white Burgundy style and is a good example of a high-quality wine made from hybrid grapes. Controlled cold fermentation and early bottling results in good acidity and a clean, dry finish; the wine is released when

nine months old, but further bottle aging is recommended.

Pale bright color and a soft, mature bouquet. The wine is full-bodied, soft, and dry. **price range:** A

producer: Collard Bros. Ltd.
classification: White varietal table wine
grape variety: Gewürztraminer
region: Auckland
district: Henderson
village: Henderson

This is possibly the first Gewürztraminer produced in New Zealand from virus-free vines.

Pale bright color and an aromatic, full, and fruity bouquet. The wine combines good body and strong varietal characteristics; it has fine Traminer flavor, the high natural sugar in balance with proper acidity. **price range:** B

producer: Cooks New Zealand Wine Co., Ltd.
classification: White varietal table wine
grape variety: Riesling
region: North Island
district: Waikato
city or village: Te Kauwhata

Unfortunately, this wine is not available outside New Zealand at the present time.

Greenish-yellow color and a young, fruity bouquet. The wine is soft and mild, with outstanding flavor. **price range:** A

producer: Cooks New Zealand Wine Co., Ltd.
classification: White varietal table wine
grape variety: Pinot Gris
region: North Island
district: Waikato
city or village: Te Kauwhata

This full-bodied white wine improves in

bottle with distinct character; unfortunately, it is not available outside New Zealand at the present time.

Clear color with slight pink tinges and a slight spicy bouquet. The wine is quite full-bodied. **price range:** A

producer: Cooks New Zealand Wine Co., Ltd.
classification: White varietal table wine
grape variety: Chasselas
region: North Island
district: Waikato
city or village: Te Kauwhata

This soft, mild white wine improves with bottle age; however, it is unfortunately not available outside New Zealand at the present time.

Greenish-yellow-tinged color and a flowery bouquet. **price range:** A

producer: Cooks New Zealand Wine Co., Ltd.
classification: Red varietal table wine
grape variety: Alicanté
region: North Island
district: Waikato
city or village: Te Kauwhata

This red wine attains added softness with age; unfortunately, it is not available outside New Zealand at the present time.

Ruby-red color and an earthy bouquet characteristic of the varietal. The wine is full-bodied and finishes smooth. **price range:** A

producer: Cooks New Zealand Wine Co., Ltd.
classification: White varietal table wine
grape variety: Chasseur
region: North Island

district: Waikato
city or village: Te Kauwhata

This slightly sweet white wine is made to suit the average palate; unfortunately, it is not available outside New Zealand at the present time.

Golden-tinged color and a sweet, flowery bouquet. On the palate the wine is sweet, with a fruity flavor. **price range:** A

producer: Cooks New Zealand Wine Co., Ltd.
classification: Red varietal table wine
grape variety: Cabernet Sauvignon
region: North Island
district: Waikato
city or village: Te Kauwhata

This outstanding red varietal wine is made from grapes grown to perfect maturity; unfortunately, it is not available outside New Zealand at the present time.

Deep dark red color and a pronounced varietal bouquet. On the palate the wine is full and round, with a slightly tannic finish. **price range:** B

producer: Cooks New Zealand Wine Co., Ltd.
classification: Red table wine
region: North Island
district: Waikato
city or village: Te Kauwhata

This fine red wine mellows and develops with bottle age; however, it is unfortunately not available outside New Zealand at the present time.

Ruby-red color and a slightly woody bouquet. On the palate the wine is light and has a slight tannic finish. **price range:** B

"Fan the flame of hilarity with the wing of friendship; and pass the rosy wine."
—Charles Dickens,
The Old Curiosity Shop

producer: Lombardi Wines, Ltd.
classification: Aromatized wine
grape variety: Palomino blend
region: Hawkes Bay
district: Te Mata
city or village: Havelock North
A fine imitation of an Italian-style vermouth.
Brilliant clear color and a characteristic vermouth aroma and flavor.
price range: A

producer: Lombardi Wines, Ltd.
classification: White table wine
grape variety: Baco 22A
region: Hawkes Bay
district: Te Mata
city or village: Havelock North
A not-too-bland *vin ordinaire*.
Brilliant-hued color and a typical hybrid bouquet. The wine has a light grapey flavor. **price range:** A

producer: Lombardi Wines, Ltd.
classification: White table wine
grape variety: Chasselas
region: Hawkes Bay
district: Te Mata
city or village: Havelock North
A fresh, grapey bouquet and a semi-sweet delicate flavor. It is a fine quality dinner wine with good body and acidity.
price range: A

producer: Lombardi Wines, Ltd.
classification: White sparkling wine
grape variety: Riesling and Sylvaner
region: Hawkes Bay
district: Te Mata
city or village: Havelock North
A characteristic Riesling bouquet and a crisp, fruity, and delicate flavored wine with good Riesling character.
price range: A

producer: Lombardi Wines, Ltd.
classification: Fortified wine
grape variety: Golden Chasselas
region: Hawkes Bay
district: Te Mata
city or village: Havelock North
An estate-bottled medium-sweet Sherry.
Clear, bright golden color and a heady grapey bouquet. The wine has a pronounced grapey flavor. **price range:** A

producer: Lombardi Wines, Ltd.
classification: Fortified wine
grape variety: Muscat blend
region: Hawkes Bay
district: Te Mata
city or village: Havelock North
A Cream Sherry.
Amber color and a spicy, grapey bouquet. The wine is rich, creamy, spicy, and full-bodied. **price range:** A

producer: Lombardi Wines, Ltd.
classification: Rosé varietal table wine

grape variety: Pinotage
region: Hawkes Bay
district: Te Mata
city or village: Havelock North
Brilliant crystal-clear rosé color and a fruity bouquet. The wine is medium dry, crisp, light, and delicate.
price range: A

producer: Lombardi Wines, Ltd.
classification: Fortified wine
grape variety: Muscat
region: Hawkes Bay
district: Te Mata
city or village: Havelock North
Bright amber color and a Muscat bouquet. The wine has a pronounced grapey Muscat flavor and is rich and full-bodied. **price range:** A

producer: Lombardi Wines, Ltd.
classification: Fortified wine
grape variety: Palomino
region: Hawkes Bay
district: Te Mata
city or village: Havelock North
An estate-bottled fine-quality Palomino Sherry aged in wood.
Amber color and a Sherry-like bouquet. A fine-styled Sherry. **price range:** A

producer: Lombardi Wines, Ltd.
classification: Fortified wine
grape variety: Seibel
region: Hawkes Bay
district: Te Mata
city or village: Havelock North
A Port wine aged in oak casks.
Ruby-red color and a fruity bouquet. The wine has a typical Port flavor.
price range: A

producer: McWilliam's Wines Pty. Ltd.
classification: White varietal table wine
grape variety: Riesling and Sylvaner
region: Hawkes Bay
Made only from free-run juice, this wine is made under controlled cold fermentation to preserve its fruity aroma and flavor.
Pale green-gold color and a full, fruity bouquet of flowers. The wine is dry, fruity, and has a clean, crisp finish.
price range: B

producer: McWilliams Wines Pty. Ltd.
classification: Red varietal table wine
grape variety: Cabernet Sauvignon
region: Hawkes Bay
Only one release of this wine is made nationally per year. An optimum production of 20,000 gallons is projected by 1982; the wine was first made in 1962, and has been a consistent gold-medal winner ever since. It is a premium red wine, released after four years of wood aging.
Deep red color and a full grapey bouquet showing some wood. On the palate the wine is rich, dry, and has a tannic finish. **price range:** B

producer: McWilliams Wines Pty. Ltd.
classification: Fortified wine
grape variety: Palomino
region: Hawkes Bay
This Sherry receives five years of aging in wood and is back blended for consistent quality.
Pale gold, reflective and brilliant color, and a bouquet with soft wood tones. The wine is dry, full, fruity, and finishes dry.
price range: A

producer: McWilliam's Wines Pty. Ltd.
classification: Fortified wine
grape variety: Brown Muscat
region: Hawkes Bay

A Muscat wine aged for four to five years in the wood and is fortified to 19% alcohol by volume.

Deep, rich amber-brown color and a nutty bouquet with the characteristic spiciness of Muscat. On the palate the wine is nutty, sweet, and spicy.   **price range:** A

producer: McWilliam's Wines Pty. Ltd.
classification: Red table wine
grape variety: Blend of Baco Noir, Seibel, Pinot Noir, and Gamay
region: Hawkes Bay

Made in the dry Claret style, this wine was first produced in 1956. Vintage dated, it is aged for six months in new oak puncheons, then released after two years' bottle aging. It is available either in pints or in quarts (375 ml. and 750 ml.).

Clear, reflective light red color and a mixed bouquet of grape and wood. The wine is light, grapey, clean, and dry, with a tart finish.   **price range:** A

producer: McWilliam's Wines Pty. Ltd.
classification: White table wine
grape variety: Riesling and Sylvaner/Chasselas
region: Hawkes Bay

This crackling medium-sweet white wine was first released in June 1976. It has a slight residual fermentation and is packaged similar to "Spritzig Rosé."

Straw-gold color and a bouquet with Riesling fruit predominant. On the palate the wine tastes slightly sweet, with a clean acid finish.   **price range:** A

producer: McWilliam's Wines Pty. Ltd.
classification: Rosé table wine
grape variety: Baco and Seibel hybrids
region: Hawkes Bay

A still rosé, not crackling like their other ones.

Light pink color and a distinctive grapey bouquet. The wine is slightly sweet and finishes cleanly.

price range: A

producer: McWilliam's Wines Pty. Ltd.
classification: Fortified wine
grape variety: Pedro Ximenez and Palomino
region: Hawkes Bay

A Sherry-type wine fortified to 19% alcohol by volume and blended with older wines after eight years of wood aging so as to maintain quality and consistency.

Bright reflective amber color and a full grape aroma. The wine is sweet and full.
price range: A

producer: McWilliam's Wines Pty. Ltd.
classification: White varietal table wine
grape variety: Riesling and Sylvaner
region: Hawkes Bay

This light, dry white wine was first made in 1954. It was the first commercially produced white wine made from this variety in New Zealand.

Reflective pale gold color and a very aromatic, definite Riesling "nose" becoming more pronounced with age. The wine is fresh and fruity, with a clean, dry finish.
price range: A

producer: McWilliam's Wines Pty. Ltd.
classification: Fortified wine
grape variety: Grenache and Seibel hybrids
region: Hawkes Bay

A full, sweet Port aged in wood for five years prior to bottling.

Deep bright red color and a full aroma of wood and fortified grapes. On the palate the wine tastes full, sweet, and vigorous.
price range: A

producer: McWilliam's Wines Pty. Ltd.
classification: Fortified wine
grape variety: Palomino
region: Hawkes Bay

This dry Sherry is aged in the wood for three years and back-blended for consistent quality and taste.

Deep gold-amber color and a pronounced varietal bouquet. The wine is dry, fruity, and vigorous.   **price range:** A

producer: McWilliam's Wines Pty. Ltd.
classification: Fortified wine
grape variety: Grenache and Seibel hybrids
region: Hawkes Bay

This rich, wood-aged sweet Port is given eight years of wood aging, is back-blended to maintain quality and consistency, and is fortified to 19% alcohol by volume.

Deep ruby-red to amber color and a distinctive bouquet of grape and wood. On the palate the wine is rich, full, and sweet, in the true Port style.   **price range:** A

producer: McWilliam's Wines Pty. Ltd.
classification: White table wine
grape variety: Chasselas
region: Hawkes Bay

A full, sweet wine made in the Sauternes style.

Medium gold color and a full, fruity bouquet. The flavor is sweet, with full grapiness.   **price range:** A

producer: McWilliam's Wines Pty. Ltd.
classification: Rosé table wine
grape variety: Baco and Seibel hybrids
region: Hawkes Bay

This crackling medium-sweet rosé was first produced in 1969; it is now exported to Australia in quantities of twenty-five hundred cases per year.

Light pink color with small bubbles from residual fermentation and a bouquet displaying mixed grape aromas. On the palate the wine is slightly sweet, clean, with a tart finish.   **price range:** A

producer: McWilliam's Wines Pty. Ltd.
classification: Fortified wine
grape variety: Palomino, Chasselas, and Pedro Ximenez
region: Hawkes Bay

This medium-dry Sherry is aged in wood for three years. It is composed of a blend of dry and sweet Sherry bases.

Amber to mid-amber color and a fruity bouquet. The wine is medium sweet, with full fruit.   **price range:** A

producer: McWilliam's Wines Pty. Ltd.
classification: Fortified wine
grape variety: Chasselas and Pedro Ximenez
region: Hawkes Bay

This full, sweet Sherry is aged in wood for three years and is back-blended for consistent quality.

Deep rich amber color and a full, fruity bouquet. The wine is sweet and full-bodied, with pronounced grape fruitiness.
price range: A

producer: McWilliam's Wines Pty. Ltd.
classification: White sparkling wine
grape variety: Chasselas
region: Hawkes Bay

In 1972 the grapes for this dry white sparkling wine were changed from Palomino to Chasselas. The wine is produced by the *charmat* (bulk) process, and the wines are blended from a two-year-old base.

Pale gold color and a delicately fruity bouquet. The wine is dry, soft, and finishes cleanly. **price range:** A

producer: McWilliam's Wines Pty. Ltd.
classification: White sparkling wine
grape variety: Palomino
region: Hawkes Bay

This medium sweet sparkling wine was first introduced in 1969. The wine is produced by the *charmat* (bulk) process, and the wines are blended from a two-year-old base. They are available in pints, quarts, and magnums.

Clear color and a delicate bouquet. The wine is fruity and medium sweet.
price range: A

producer: McWilliam's Wines Pty. Ltd.
classification: White varietal table wine
grape variety: Pinot Chardonnay
region: Hawkes Bay

This dry white Burgundy-type wine is made from 100% Pinot Chardonnay (vinifera) grapes, and has consistently been awarded gold medals in international competition.

Pale gold, brilliant color, and a full, distinctive grapey aroma. The wine is dry, full of fruit, and finishes cleanly.
price range: B

producer: Mission Vineyards
classification: Red varietal table wine
grape variety: Cabernet Sauvignon
region: North Island
district: Hawkes Bay
city or village: Greenmeadows

A malolactic fermentation softens the tannin and acid levels in this wine.

Medium red color and a soft bouquet with a typical Cabernet nose. The wine has low tannin and a soft acid finish.
price range: A

producer: Mission Vineyards
classification: White sparkling wine
grape variety: Pinot Gris blend
region: North Island
district: Hawkes Bay
city or village: Greenmeadows

This sparkling wine is bottle-fermented and "autolyzed."

Straw-amber color and a bouquet with yeast character. The wine is crisp and dry.
price range: B

producer: Mission Vineyards
classification: Red table wine
grape variety: Pinot Meunier and Cabernet Sauvignon
region: North Island
district: Hawkes Bay
city or village: Greenmeadows

A light wine that is fairly typical of the area.

Light red color and a characteristic Pinot bouquet. The wine is fruity, with light tannin. **price range:** B

producer: Nobilo Vintners, Ltd.
classification: Red varietal table wine
grape variety: Pinot Noir
region: Auckland
district: Huapai Valley
city or village: Huapai

Pinot Noir is new to the Nobilo Classic range, but it shows signs of becoming a new style of red wines previously unexplored in New Zealand.

Light red color and a sweetish Burgundy-style bouquet. The wine has a nice balance of oak and fruit, without too much astringency, and is medium-bodied.
price range: B

producer: Nobilo Vintners, Ltd.
classification: White varietal table wine
grape variety: Gewürztraminer
region: Auckland
district: Huapai Valley
city or village: Huapai

Only a very limited supply of this wine is made, but in good years the wine has great character reminiscent of an Alsatian wine.

Brilliant pale greenish-gold color and an aromatic, fruity bouquet. The wine is full-bodied with plenty of fruit flavor and a hint of honey in the finish. **price range:** B

producer: Nobilo Vintners, Ltd.
classification: Red varietal table wine
grape variety: Pinotage
region: Auckland
district: Huapai Valley
city or village: Huapai

Nobilo has established a reputation with this wine, the 1970 vintage having won the highest award possible in New Zealand. It also won a gold medal in Ljubljana, Yugoslavia. All Nobilo wines carry a vintage date on neck labels.

Medium red color and a subtle Burgundy-type bouquet. The wine shows a pleasant combination of fruit and wood in an easy-drinking style. **price range:** B

producer: Nobilo Vintners, Ltd.
classification: White varietal table wine
grape variety: Müller-Thurgau (Riesling and Sylvaner)
region: Auckland
district: Huapai Valley
city or village: Huapai

This slightly sweet, aromatic, and fruity white wine derives most of its character from back blending the juice into the finished wine. Only free-run juice from Müller-Thurgau grapes ripened fully on the vine is used, which is back-blended and cold-fermented under temperature-controlled conditions.

Pale greenish-gold color and a very fresh, flowery "nose" with some residual carbon dioxide. The wine is crisp and fruity, with good acid balance.
price range: A

producer: Nobilo Vintners, Ltd.
classification: White varietal table wine
grape variety: Pinot Chardonnay
region: Auckland
district: Huapai Valley

city or village: Huapai

This wine is fermented in the traditional French manner, using Limousin oak hogsheads; it is bottled after one year of aging.

Pale straw-gold color and a pleasant bouquet with good fruit-oak balance. The wine is typical of the French white Burgundy style—full, flinty, and crisply dry.
price range: B

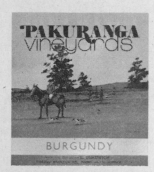

producer: Pakuranga Vineyards
classification: Red table wine
region: North Auckland
city or village: Pakuranga

This full-flavored dark red wine is very nice with meals.

The Pakuranga Hunt is the largest in New Zealand, which is why the vineyard chose a hunt motif for the labels.
price range: A

producer: Pakuranga Vineyards
classification: White table wine
grape variety: Golden Chasselas
region: North Auckland
city or village: Pakuranga

This slightly golden white wine is very smooth and an excellent table wine.
price range: A

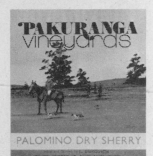

producer: Pakuranga Vineyards
classification: Red table wine
region: North Auckland
city or village: Pakuranga

This dry red wine should be drunk with meals.
price range: A

producer: Soljans Wines
classification: Red table wine
grape variety: Blend of hybrid varieties
region: Auckland
district: Henderson
city or village: Henderson

Ruby-red color and a young, light bouquet. The wine is dry, well-balanced, and shows hybrid character.
price range: A

producer: Soljans Wines
classification: Brandy
grape variety: Black Hamburg and Palomino
region: Auckland
district: Henderson
city or village: Henderson

This is a private-bin Brandy that is at least ten years old prior to sale. During that entire time it is left to age in small oak casks.

Dark amber color and a rich, oaky "nose." The wine is medium sweet, rich, full-bodied, and shows its age.
price range: B

"O thou invisible spirit of wine!"
—Shakespeare, *Othello*

producer: Soljans Wines
classification: White sparkling wine
grape variety: Dr. Hogg and White Muscat
region: Auckland
district: Henderson
city or village: Henderson

This medium-sweet sparkling wine is similar to an Asti Spumante. It was a silver-award winner in 1974 and 1975.

A fruity Muscat "nose"; the wine has fine body, is well-balanced and fruity.
price range: A

producer: Soljans Wines
classification: Red table wine
grape variety: Blend of hybrid varieties
region: Auckland
district: Henderson
city or village: Henderson

The picture of Stari Grad on our labels is the original home of the Soljan family in Yugoslavia.

Ruby color and a quite rich, fruity bouquet with a touch of wood. On the palate the wine is medium sweet and medium-bodied.
price range: A

producer: Soljans Wines
classification: Fortified wine
grape variety: Black Hamburg and Palomino
region: Auckland
district: Henderson
city or village: Henderson

This fine-quality medium-dry Sherry has won silver awards in wine competition.

Amber color and a rich, wood-aged bouquet showing Sherry character. On the palate the wine is smooth, full-bodied, and well balanced.
price range: A

producer: Montana Wines Ltd.
classification: Red table wine
grape variety: Cabernet Sauvignon
district: Gisborne
city or village: Gisborne

A full-bodied dry red wine which has been wood-aged before bottling. The wine exhibits a very distinct varietal character.
price range: B

producer: Montana Wines Ltd.
classification: White table wine
grape variety: Riesling Sylvaner
district: Marlborough
city or village: Blenheim

The Montana Marlborough Vineyards are the largest vineyard area in New Zealand planted entirely with Vinifera grapes, including Cabernet Sauvignon, Rhine Riesling, and Riesling Sauvignon. Marlborough Riesling is a fresh fruity wine, slightly sweet on the palate, with a crisp refreshing finish.
price range: B

producer: Corbans Wines Limited
classification: Dry red table wine
grape variety: A blend, predominantly Cabernet Sauvignon and Pinotage
region: North Island of New Zealand
city or village: Gisborne and Auckland

A full-bodied dry red table wine with some wood aging evident.
price range: B

producer: Corbans Wines Limited
classification: Still white table wine
grape variety: Chenin Blanc
region: North Island of New Zealand
district: Tolaga Bay region of Gisborne
city or village: Gisborne

A medium dry light, fruity wine with a spiciness and delicate bouquet.
price range: B

The first vineyard of Canada was established in 1811 near Toronto, Ontario. Today, about 95 percent of the vineyards are in the Lake Erie, Lake Ontario, and Niagara River areas. The other vineyards are in the Okanagan Valley of British Columbia. The major vine plantings are made with North American varieties. As in the eastern United States, there is great interest in planting European hybrids, which are slowly gaining popularity among Canadian wine makers.

producer: Andrés Wines (B.C.) Ltd.
classification: Red varietal table wine
grape variety: Maréchal Foch
region: British Columbia
district: Okanagan Valley
city or village: Port Moody

This red wine is made from the French hybrid grape Maréchal Foch, one of the major red grapes grown in British Columbia.

Intense red color with purple tinges; the wine is youthful and well-balanced; as it has good tannin, it should age well.
price range: A

producer: Andrés Wines (B.C.) Ltd.
classification: White varietal table wine
grape variety: Verdelet
region: British Columbia
district: Oliver
city or village: Port Moody

This wine is a limited bottling from a specific vineyard in the Oliver district noted for its superior-quality grapes.

Very pale yellow color with hints of green; and a flowery, fragrant, and delicately sweet bouquet. The wine is clean, true to the variety and delicate, with a hint of sweetness.
price range: B

producer: Andrés Wines (B.C.) Ltd.
classification: White varietal table wine
grape variety: Chenin Blanc
region: British Columbia

district: Okanagan Valley
city or village: Port Moody

Made in the German style, this wine is made slightly sweet by adding unfermented juice back into the final blend.

Pale yellow color and a full, fruity bouquet. The wine is crisp, fruity, and full-bodied, with good acid; it is pleasantly sweet but finishes on the dry side.
price range: A

producer: Andrés Wines (B.C.) Ltd.
classification: Red varietal table wine
grape variety: De Chaunac
region: British Columbia
district: Similkameen
city or village: Port Moody

This wine is named for the Similkameen of British Columbia, in which are situated the southernmost vineyards of the province. This region has the most desirable climate for grape growing in British Columbia; the wine is the largest-selling red table wine in the district. It is produced in the Beaujolais style.

Light, delicate bouquet showing the fruity characteristics of the varietal. The wine is fruity, clean, and tart; it has the high acidity characteristic of De Chaunac, turning mellow with age and keeping well.
price range: A

producer: Andrés Wines (B.C.) ltd.
classification Fortified wine
grape variety: Grenache
region: British Columbia
district: Okanagan Valley
city of village: Port Moody

This Sherry is produced by the "baked" method, and is later aged for two to four years in small European oak barrels.

Deep amber color and a fruity bouquet with lots of oak. The wine is balanced, fruity, and well-aged, with vanillalike tones in the background. **price range:** A

producer: Andrés Wines (B.C.) Ltd.
classification: White varietal table wine
grape variety: Okanagan Riesling
region: British Columbia
district: Okanagan Valley
city or village: Port Moody

The origin of the Okanagan Riesling variety is unknown. The grape was introduced in the early 1920s by an immigrant family from Italy and is thought to be the Walschriesling, which is grown in Europe.

Straw-yellow color and a clean, flowery varietal bouquet. The wine is crisp, with medium body, and is dry and fresh tasting; it is quite pleasant. **price range:** A

producer: Andrés Wines (B.C.) Ltd.
classification: White table wine
grape variety: Verdelet, B.C. Riesling, and Diamond
region: British Columbia
district: Okanagan Valley

A pleasing white wine made from a blend of Okanagan Valley grape varieties.

Pale yellow color and a flowery bouquet. The wine is tart and fruity, with a hint of sweetness. **price range:** A

producer: Barnes Wines Ltd.
classification: White table wine
grape variety: Elvira and Diana
region: Niagara Peninsula

The wine is medium dry, with a very fruity bouquet. It is of deep straw color, and bright. **price range:** below A

producer: Barnes Wines Ltd.
classification: Fortified wine
grape variety: Ontario
region: Niagara Peninsula

This rich golden Sherry is medium sweet, with a fruity bouquet.

The wine is aged in small oak casks and blended in the traditional Solera method.
price range: A

producer: Barnes Wines Ltd.
classification: Red table wine
grape variety: Veeport and Seible
region: Niagara Peninsula

The wine is dry, with a hint of sugar, of deep ruby color with a well-balanced bouquet. **price range:** below A

producer: Barnes Wines Ltd.
classification: White table wine
grape variety: Niagara
region: Niagara Peninsula

This medium-sweet wine has a fruity bouquet and a bright, pale golden appearance.

The same wine is produced in New York State, under the Widmer label.
price range: A

producer: Barnes Wines Ltd.
classification: Rosé table wine
grape variety: Niagara and Concord
region: Niagara Peninsula
This is a medium dry rosé with a slight sparkle and a fruity bouquet.
price range: A

producer: T. G. Bright & Co. Ltd.
classification: Red varietal table wine
grape variety: Chelois
region: Ontario
district: Niagara Peninsula
city or village: Niagara Falls
A light, dry red varietal wine sealed with a cork closure.
Clear color and a fine bouquet.
price range: A

producer: T. G. Bright & Co. Ltd.
classification: Red varietal table wine
grape variety: Maréchal Foch
region: Ontario
district: Niagara Peninsula
city or village: Niagara Falls
A French hybrid grown successfully in the Niagara Peninsula. The wine is sealed by a cork closure.
Brilliant red color and a prominent bouquet. **price range:** A

producer: T. G. Bright & Co. Ltd.
classification: Red varietal table wine
grape variety: Villard Noir

region: Ontario
district: Niagara Peninsula
city or village: Niagara Falls
A medium-bodied dry red wine produced from a French hybrid variety. It is sealed via a cork closure.
price range: A

producer: T. G. Bright & Co. Ltd.
classification: White varietal table wine
grape variety: Pinot Chardonnay (100%)
region: Ontario
district: Niagara Peninsula
city or village: Niagara Falls
Sealed via a cork closure.
Brilliant clear color and a prominent bouquet. **price range:** A

producer: T. G. Bright & Co. Ltd.
classification: White table wine
grape variety: Muscat
region: Ontario
district: Niagara Peninsula
city or village: Niagara Falls
Deep, dark amber color and an excellent bouquet. The wine has a full, pronounced Muscat flavor. **price range:** A

producer: T. G. Bright & Co. Ltd.
classification: Red varietal table wine
grape variety: Seibel
region: Ontario
district: Niagara Peninsula
city or village: Niagara Falls
Seibel is a hybrid grape variety of European ancestry that makes an excellent light, dry red wine.
Brilliant clear color; the wine is light and dry. **price range:** A

producer: T. G. Bright & Co. Ltd.
classification: White sparkling wine
grape variety: Blend
region: Ontario
district: Niagara Peninsula
city or village: Niagara Falls
"President" is a superior bottle-fermented Canadian Champagne.
price range: C

producer: T. G. Bright & Co. Ltd.
classification: Red table wine
grape variety: Maréchal Foch
region: Ontario
district: Niagara Peninsula
city or village: Niagara Falls
"President Burgundy" was one of the first Canadian wines made from hybrid grapes introduced around 1955.
Brilliant red color and a prominent bouquet. **price range:** A

producer: T. G. Bright & Co. Ltd.
classification: White table wine
grape variety: Delaware and Seibel
region: Ontario
district: Niagara Peninsula
city or village: Niagara Falls
"President Sauterne" contains 5 degrees residual sugar and is medium-bodied.
Brilliant clear color and a prominent bouquet. **price range:** A

producer: T. G. Bright & Co. Ltd.
classification: Red table wine

grape variety: Hybrid blend
region: Ontario
district: Niagara Peninsula
city or village: Niagara Falls
"Manor St. David's Claret" is a light dry red table wine with practically no residual sugar.
Brilliant red color and a good bouquet.
price range: A

producer: T. G. Bright & Co. Ltd.
classification: White table wine
grape variety: Blend
region: Ontario
district: Niagara Peninsula
city or village: Niagara Falls
"Manor St. David's Sauterne" is a medium-dry white table wine.
Brilliant clear color and a good bouquet. The wine is medium dry. **price range:** A

producer: T. G. Bright & Co. Ltd.
classification: Fortified wine
grape variety: President
region: Ontario
district: Niagara Peninsula
city or village: Niagara Falls
This wine is called "President Port" after the President grape, a hybrid with European and American heritage.
Ruby-red color and a prominent bouquet. **price range:** A

producer: T. G. Bright & Co. Ltd.
classification: Fortified wine
grape variety: Blend
region: Ontario
district: Niagara Peninsula
city or village: Niagara Falls
A dry Sherry aged in barrels three years.
Clear golden-amber color and a good bouquet. **price range:** A

producer: T. G. Bright & Co. Ltd.
classification: Red varietal table wine
grape variety: Baco Noir
region: Ontario
district: Niagara Peninsula
city or village: Niagara Falls

Made from a French hybrid grape and sealed by a cork closure.

Brilliant deep red color and a good bouquet. **price range:** A

producer: Casabello Wines Ltd.
classification: Red varietal table wine
grape variety: Pinot Noir (100%)
region: Washington State
district: Yakima Valley
city or village: Prosser

This Pinot Noir of 1972 was made from grapes grown in the Yakima Valley in Washington State, then processed in Penticton, British Columbia.

Clear red color, a good bouquet; it is a well-balanced red wine that will benefit from further aging in bottle.
price range: B

producer: Casabello Wines Ltd.
classification: White varietal table wine
grape variety: Pinot Chardonnay (100%)
region: Washington State
district: Yakima Valley
city or village: Prosser

This Chardonnay is made from grapes grown near Prosser in the Yakima Valley, Washington State, and processed in Penticton, British Columbia.

Clear amber color and an excellent bouquet. The wine is clean, well-balanced, and characteristic of the Chardonnay grape. **price range:** A

producer: Casabello Wines Ltd.
classification: White varietal table wine
grape variety: Semillon (100%)
region: Washington State
district: Yakima Valley
city or village: Prosser

This Semillon was produced from grapes grown near Prosser in the Yakima Valley, Washington State, and the wine was processed and bottled in Penticton, British Columbia.

Good clear amber color and a good bouquet. The wine is clean and well-balanced, with good flavor and aroma.
price range: A

producer: Casabello Wines Ltd.
classification: Red table wine
grape variety: De Chaunac 9549 and Chelois 10878
region: British Columbia
district: Okanegan Valley
city or village: Osoyoos (produced in Penticton)

A very clean generic red wine made from a blend of hybrid grapes grown in the Okanegan Valley.

Clear red color and a fair bouquet. The wine is well-balanced and clean.
price range: A

producer: Casabello Wines Ltd.
classification: Red varietal table wine
grape variety: Gamay Beaujolais (100%)
region: Washington State
district: Yakima Valley
city or village: Pasco

This Gamay Beaujolais was made from grapes grown near Pasco in the Yakima Valley and processed in Penticton, British Columbia.

Good clear color and a fine bouquet. The wine is clean and well-balanced, very characteristic of the Gamay Beaujolais grape. **price range:** A

producer: Casabello Wines Ltd.
classification: White varietal table wine
grape variety: Okanagan Riesling and others
region: British Columbia
district: Okanagan Valley
city or village: Osoyoos and Summerland (processed in Penticton)

This unusual wine contains 85% Okanagan Riesling, a local variety of unknown origin that gives wines strong in character and flavor.

Clear color and a good bouquet. The wine is clean and well-balanced.
price range: A

producer: Casabello Wines Ltd.
classification: Fortified wine
grape variety: Palomino and Bath
region: British Columbia
district: Okanagan Valley
city or village: Osoyoos (produced in Penticton)

Although classified and taxed as a fortified wine, this light Sherry did not receive any addition of Brandy. It was aged in oak barrels.

Amber-brown color characteristic of Sherry and a fruity aroma and flavor. The wine is very clean. **price range:** B

producer: Casabello Wines Ltd.
classification: Red varietal table wine
grape variety: Zinfandel (100%)
region: Washington State
district: Yakima Valley
city or village: Pasco

This Zinfandel is very light in color but has good body. The grapes were grown in the Yakima Valley, Washington State, and were processed in Penticton, British Columbia.

Clear red color and a fine, traditional bouquet. The wine is very clean and well-balanced. **price range:** A

producer: Casabello Wines Ltd.
classification: Red table wine
grape variety: Carignane, Foch, Rubired, and some Pinot Noir
region: British Columbia
district: Okanagan Valley
city or village: Osoyoos (Penticton)

This generic red "Burgundy" is blended and aged in oak barrels for two years; it is a blend of two- and three-year-old wines processed in Penticton, British Columbia.

Clear red color and a moderate bouquet. The wine is clean and well-balanced.
price range: A

producer: Casabello Wines Ltd.
classification: White varietal table wine
grape variety: Chenin Blanc (100%)
region: Washington State
district: Yakima Valley
city or village: Prosser

This Chenin Blanc was made from grapes grown near Prosser in the Yakima Valley, Washington State, and was processed and bottled in Casabello's cellars in Penticton, British Columbia.

Clear color and a good bouquet. The wine is very clean and well-balanced, with fine aromas. **price range:** A

producer: Casabello Wines Ltd.
classification: White table wine
grape variety: Verdelette 9110, Aurora 5279, and Muscat
region: British Columbia
district: Okanagan Valley
city or village: Penticton

This generic white wine was made from a blend of vinifera and hybrid grapes, and was bottled in a 1-liter souvenir carafe.

Clear color, a good bouquet, and well-balanced with a Muscat flavor.
price range: A

producer: Inniskillin House Wines Inc.
classification: Red varietal table wine
grape variety: Maréchal Foch (Kuhlmann 182)
region: Ontario
district: Niagara Peninsula
city or village: Niagara-on-the-Lake

Maréchal Foch is an Alsatian hybrid derived from Pinot Noir and Gamay. Inniskillin was the first winery to be granted a license in Ontario since 1929.

Deep ruby-red color and a light bouquet. Michael Vaughan calls it "full-bodied, somewhat reminiscent of a red Burgundy."
price range: B

producer: Jordan Valley Wines Ltd.
classification: Red table wine
grape variety: French hybrid blend
region: Ontario
district: Niagara Peninsula
city or village: St. Catharines

"Bin #28" is aged in oak barrels.

Deep, brilliant red color and a pleasing, full bouquet. The wine is dry, well-aged, and full-bodied—excellent at mealtime.
price range: B

"Never think of leaving perfume or wines to your heir. Administer these yourself and let him have the money!"
— Martial

producer: Jordan Valley Wines Ltd.
classification: Red varietal table wine
grape variety: Maréchal Foch
region: Ontario
district: Niagara Peninsula
city or village: St. Catharines

Aged in oak barrels.

Deep, brilliant red color and a clean varietal bouquet. The wine is dry, soft, medium-bodied, and well-aged—excellent at mealtime.　　**price range:** B

producer: Jordan Valley Wines Ltd.
classification: Red table wine
grape variety: French hybrids
region: Ontario
district: Niagara Peninsula
city or village: St. Catharines

Brilliant ruby-red color and a fruity, slightly fragrant bouquet. The wine is dry and robust, excellent with meals.
price range: B

producer: Jordan Valley Wines Ltd.
classification: White table wine
region: Ontario
district: Niagara Peninsula
city or village: St. Catharines

Light green-gold color and a clean, fruity, and slightly fragrant bouquet. The wine is dry, soft, and medium-bodied—excellent with meals.　　**price range:** B

producer: Inniskillin House Wines Inc.
classification: Red varietal table wine
grape variety: De Chaunac
region: Ontario
district: Niagara Peninsula
city or village: Niagara-on-the-Lake

De Chaunac (Seibel 9549) is a French hybrid named for Adhemar de Chaunac, a French-born agronomist who devoted a lifetime to improving Canadian wines.

Brilliant dark red color and a medium-to-light body. The wine does not have the depth and lingering aftertaste of the fuller-bodied Maréchal Foch.
price range: B

producer: Jordan Valley Wines Ltd.
classification: White table wine
region: Ontario
district: Niagara Peninsula
city or village: St. Catharines

Brilliant light gold color and a pleasant, fruity bouquet. The wine is medium sweet, medium-bodied, and delicious—excellent anytime.
price range: B

producer: Jordan Valley Wines Ltd.
classification: Red table wine
grape variety: French hybrids
region: Ontario
district: Niagara Peninsula
city or village: St. Catharines

Brilliant red color and a fragrant bouquet. The wine is full-bodied and slightly sweet—ideal for wine, cheeses, and with meals.　　**price range:** B

producer: Jordan Valley Wines Ltd.
classification: White table wine
region: Ontario
district: Niagara Peninsula
city or village: St. Catharines

Brilliant light green-gold color and a clean, slightly fragrant bouquet. The wine is soft, dry, and light-bodied—excellent with meals.　　**price range:** B

producer: Jordan Valley Wines Ltd.
classification: White table wine
region: Ontario
district: Niagara Peninsula
city or village: St. Catharines

Light gold color and a clean, fruity bouquet. The wine is crisp, semi-dry, and full-bodied—excellent anytime.
price range: B

producer: Jordan Valley Wines Ltd.
classification: Red table wine
grape variety: French hybrids
region: Ontario
district: Niagara Peninsula
city or village: St. Catharines

Brilliant deep red color and a clean, fruity bouquet. The wine is dry, soft, and full-bodied—excellent with meals.
price range: B

producer: Jordan Valley Wines Ltd.
classification: Fortified wine
grape variety: Labrusca varieties
region: Ontario
district: Niagara Peninsula
city or village: St. Catharines

Ruby-red color and a clean, fruity bouquet. The wine is sweet, young, and full-bodied—an ideal dessert wine.
price range: B

producer: Jordan Valley Wines Ltd.
classification: Fortified wine
grape variety: Labrusca varieties
region: Ontario
district: Niagara Peninsula
city or village: St. Catharines

"Classic Cream Port" is a superb blend of Ports aged in oak barrels for five or more years.

Tawny-red color and a rounded, deeply mellow bouquet. The wine is sweet, soft, and well-aged, with robust flavor—excellent dessert wine.
price range: B

producer: Jordan & Ste-Michelle Cellars Ltd.
classification: White table wine
grape variety: Lambrusca
region: Ontario
district: Niagara Peninsula
city or village: St. Catharines

This is a smooth, delicate, medium-dry wine with a fresh, fruity, subtle bouquet. It can be enjoyed by itself or with any type of food. **price range:** below A

producer: Les Vins Andrés du Québec Ltée.
classification: Rosé sparkling wine
grape variety: Grenache and California whites and reds
region: Quebec

A refreshing sparkling rosé to make any occasion something special.

Brilliant sparkling rosé color and a light, fresh and fruity bouquet. The wine is light-bodied and bubbly. **price range:** A

producer: Les Vins Andrés du Québec Ltée.
classification: White sparkling wine
grape variety: California whites and Elvira
region: Quebec

"Chanté Blanc" is a light sparkling wine reminiscent of a Champagne, to accompany any meal.

Brilliant light straw color and a fresh, fruity bouquet. The wine is bubbly, slightly tangy, and off-dry. **price range:** A

producer: Les Vins Andrés du Québec Ltée.
classification: White table wine
grape variety: Chenin Blanc, Riesling, and California whites
region: Quebec

A good dry white table wine made in the Rhine tradition.

Light straw color and a vinous bouquet. The wine is dry, soft in taste, and balanced. **price range:** A

producer: Les Vins Andrés du Québec Ltée.
classification: Red table wine
grape variety: California reds and de Chaunac
region: Quebec

A clean, dry, and tasty red table wine made in the Burgundy fashion, "Moulin Rouge" comes in a cork-finished bottle.

Dark red color and a clean, aged bouquet. The wine is dry, balanced, and vinous. **price range:** A

producer: London Winery Limited
classification: White table wine
grape variety: Delaware and Elvira
region: Ontario
district: Niagara Peninsula
city or village: London

"Buffet Sauterne" is produced from grapes grown in the Niagara Peninsula, Canada.

Brilliant light yellow color and a fruity bouquet. The wine is soft, well-rounded, and pleasant, with a subtle character. **price range:** A

producer: London Winery Limited
classification: Fortified wine
grape variety: Delaware, Elvira, and Niagara
region: Ontario
district: Niagara Peninsula
city or village: London

Produced from grapes grown in the Niagara Peninsula.

Deep amber color and a nutty bouquet. The wine is rich and full-bodied; it is a fine sweet, light-bodied Canadian Sherry, an excellent dessert wine. **price range:** A

producer: London Winery Limited
classification: Fortified wine
grape variety: Fredonia, Chelois, and Van Buren
region: Ontario
district: Niagara Peninsula
city or village: London

"St. Augustine" is a communion wine traditionally made for over one hundred years by the same method. It is produced from grapes grown in the Niagara Peninsula.

Deep ruby-red color and a fruity bouquet. The wine is rich and smooth, an excellent dessert wine. **price range:** A

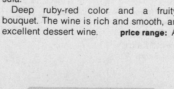

producer: London Winery Limited
classification: White sparkling wine
grape variety: Delaware and Elvira
region: Ontario
district: Niagara Peninsula
city or village: London

Produced from grapes grown in the Niagara Peninsula.

Clear light yellow color and a lively,

brisk bouquet. The wine is full-bodied and is well suited for any occasion.
price range: D

producer: London Winery Limited
classification: Rosé table wine
grape variety: Chelois
region: Ontario
district: Niagara Peninsula
city or village: London

Produced from grapes grown in the Niagara Peninsula.

Clear rosé color and a fruity bouquet. The wine is refreshing, light, and delicate and will enhance any meal.
price range: A

producer: London Winery Limited
classification: Fortified wine
grape variety: Niagara, Concord, and Catawba
region: Ontario
district: Niagara Peninsula
city or village: London

Produced from grapes grown in the Niagara Peninsula. A medium-sweet Canadian Sherry.

Brilliant amber color, and an appealing Sherry bouquet. The wine is medium sweet—excellent either as an aperitif wine or with dessert. **price range:** A

producer: London Winery Limited
classification: Fortified wine
grape variety: Fredonia, de Chaunac, and Van Buren
region: Ontario
district: Niagara Peninsula
city or village: London

This Port-type wine is a top-seller in its category. It is produced from grapes grown in the Niagara Peninsula.

Clear ruby color and a fruity bouquet. The wine is well-balanced—an excellent dessert wine. **price range:** A

producer: London Winery Limited
classification: Fortified wine
grape variety: Agawam
region: Ontario
district: Niagara Peninsula
city or village: London

"Peter London" is a golden dry Sherry produced under the action of flor yeast. After initial fermentation to 11% alcohol by volume, the wine is inoculated with a strain of cultured flor yeast and agitated for three weeks. The wine is later aged in white wood, 45-gallon containers for two years. It is produced from grapes grown in the Niagara Peninsula and has won many medals at international fairs.

Clear golden color and a nutty, strong flor bouquet. The wine is rich and smooth—an excellent dry Sherry.
price range: A

producer: Stoneycroft Cellars
classification: White table wine
grape variety: French Colombard
region: Alberta
district: Calgary
price range: A

producer: Stoneycroft Cellars
classification: White table wine
grape variety: Emerald Riesling
region: Alberta
district: Calgary
price range: A

producer: Stoneycroft Cellars
classification: Red table wine
grape variety: Barbera
region: Alberta
district: Calgary
price range: A

producer: Stoneycroft Cellars
classification: Red table wine
grape variety: Ruby Cabernet
region: Alberta
district: Calgary
price range: A

producer: Stoneycroft Cellars
classification: White table wine
grape variety: Grey Riesling
region: Alberta
district: Calgary
price range: A

producer: Uncle Ben's Industries Ltd., Winery Division
classification: White table wine
grape variety: Diamond
region: British Columbia
district: Okanagan Valley
city or village: Westbank

The Diamond variety is a pioneer grape in the Okanagan Valley. Called "Sauterne," this wine contains 13.3% alcohol by volume.

Pale yellow color and a "North American" bouquet. The wine is fruity, full-bodied, and medium sweet; serve chilled with light meals or as a refreshment at parties and receptions. **price range:** A

producer: Uncle Ben's Industries Ltd., Winery Division
classification: Red table wine
grape variety: Foch and de Chaunac
region: British Columbia
district: Okanagan Valley
city or village: Westbank

Made entirely from Okanagan Valley grapes, this light and dry red dinner wine is aged in oak barrels and contains 13.5% alcohol by volume.

Clear red color and a fully matured bouquet. The wine is dry, light, and pleasant; it is excellent with steaks and other red meats. Chill 45 minutes before serving.
price range: A

producer: Uncle Ben's Industries Ltd., Winery Division
classification: Red varietal table wine
grape variety: Ruby Cabernet
region: British Columbia
district: Okanagan Valley
village: Westbank

This rich, full-bodied dry red wine is a winemaker's pride for its elegance and satisfaction. It contains 12.8% alcohol by volume.

Fine red color and a heavily matured bouquet. The wine is flavorful and full-bodied; chill for 45 minutes before serving with roast beef, venison, and other red meat dishes. **price range:** A

producer: Uncle Ben's Industries Ltd., Winery Division
classification: White table wine
grape variety: Riesling and Burger
region: British Columbia
district: Okanagan Valley
city or village: Westbank

Light gold color and a characteristic bouquet. The wine is light, fine, and full-bodied; it should be served chilled with chicken, seafood, and light meals.
price range: A

producer: Uncle Ben's Industries Ltd., Winery Division
classification: White table wine
grape variety: Chenin Blanc
region: British Columbia
district: Okanagan Valley
city or village: Westbank

The vintner's choice for dinners of seafood, fowl, and light meals.

Light gold color with greenish reflections and a fully balanced bouquet. The wine is smooth and light; delicate, pale dry, and exquisite. Serve chilled.
price range: A

producer: Uncle Ben's Industries Ltd., Winery Division
classification: Fortified wine
grape variety: Tinta Madeira
region: British Columbia
district: Okanagan Valley
city or village: Westbank

A rich, smooth Port wine aged for several years in oak barrels.

Well-matured red color and a full-bodied, smooth bouquet. The wine is pleasantly rounded and sweet; serve with desserts, coffee, or by itself, after a meal.
price range: A

producer: Uncle Ben's Industries Ltd., Winery Division
classification: Fortified wine
grape variety: Palomino
region: British Columbia
district: Okanagan Valley
city or village: Westbank

A sturdy Sherry containing over 19% alcohol by volume.

Full-bodied, well-matured bouquet, and well-balanced flavor, Spanish in style. The wine should be served as a casual refreshment or appetizer or as a social drink with hors d'oeuvres or nuts and cheese.
price range: A

ALGERIA

producer: Office National de Commercialisation des Produits Viti-Vinicoles (ONCV)
classification: Rosé table wine
grape variety: Cinsault, Carignan, and Grenache
region: Northern Algeria
district: Coteaux de Mascara
city or village: Mascara

These wines are the best known in Algeria. As far back as 1859 they received many gold medals in Europe, and their quality has continued to improve.

Deep rosé color and an earthy bouquet. The wine is flinty dry, with a trace of acidity; it has a very distinctive and particular flavor and is easy to drink.
price range: A

"A good party is where you enjoy good people, and they taste even better with Champagne."
—Wilson Mizner

producer: Office National de Commercialisation des Produits Viti-Vinicoles (ONCV)
classification: Red table wine
grape variety: Cinsault, Carignan, Grenache, and Syrah
region: Northern Algeria
district: Coteaux de Mascara
city or village: Mascara

These are the best-known wines of Algeria. As early as 1859 they received many gold medals in Europe, and their quality has continued to improve. They are strong in alcohol: the minimum is 12.5%, but they average 13.5% and sometimes go as high as 14%.

Full red color and an earthy bouquet. The wine is well-knit, strongly flavored, and very full-bodied; a truly classical wine.
price range: A

producer: Office National de Commercialisation des Produits Viti-Vinicoles (ONCV)
classification: White table wine
grape variety: Clairette (over 51%) and Farranah
region: Oranie
district: Oran

A "Blanc de Blancs," this wine is a blend of carefully selected Clairette and Farranah grapes. Various blends each year result in a perfectly balanced white wine of consistent quality.

Clear, brilliant yellow color and a slight fruity bouquet. The wine has a fine, piquant flavor and is very refreshing.
price range: A

producer: Office National de Commercialisation des Produits Viti-Vinicoles (ONCV)
classification: Red table wine
grape variety: Carignan, Cinsault, Grenache, Cabernet, and Pinot Noir
region: Médéa
district: Médéa
city or village: Médéa

At the end of the nineteenth century Médéa was already an important wine-growing center. The wines were later classified by the French as worthy of the V.D.Q.S. appellation. Located south of Algiers, the vineyards are located on marl slopes at an elevation of 4000 meters (13,000 feet). The winter is hard, and the summers are hot and dry; the grapes are picked in early October when fully ripe.

Rich, brilliant ruby color and a pleasant bouquet suggesting violets. The wine is well-rounded, fresh, and fruity, with full body; a fine mountain wine.
price range: A

producer: Office National de Commercialisation des Produits Viti-Vinicoles (ONCV)
classification: White table wine
grape variety: Clairette Egrainée
region: Northern Algeria
district: Médéa
city or village: Médéa

At the end of the nineteenth century Médéa was already an important wine-growing center. Later the wines of this area were classified by the French as worthy of the V.D.Q.S. classification. The vineyards lie south of Algiers at an altitude of 4000 meters (13,000 feet) on marl slopes. White wine production is very small— only a few thousand gallons a year—but the wines have remarkable quality. In Algeria they are collector's items.

Pale gold color and a bouquet "of the morning dew." The wine has a full earthy taste, with a pleasing bitter quality.
price range: A

producer: Office National de Commercialisation des Produits Viti-Vinicoles (ONCV)
classification: Red table wine
grape variety: Carignan, Cinsault, Syrah, and Pinot Noir
region: Dahra
district: Ain Merane
city or village: Tenes

The region of Dahra is made up of four areas: Taoughrite, formerly known as Paul Robert; Ain Merane, formerly known as Rabelais; Mazouna, formerly known as Renault, and Khadra Achaaca, formerly Picard. Different soils, favorable climate, and superior vines give Dahra wines an outstanding quality easily recognized by connoisseurs. The wines have a minimum alcoholic strength of 12.5%.

Deep red color and a full, fruity bouquet. The wine is very harmonious, powerful, and full-bodied.
price range: A

ARGENTINA

producer: Vinos Argentinos S.A.E.
classification: White table wine
grape variety: Pedro Ximenez
region: Northwest
district: San Juan

The only Argentinian medium-dry white wine widely available in the United Kingdom. Early picking of the grapes helps retain proper acidity, required in the hot climate of San Juan province.

Pale golden color and a fresh, clean bouquet. The wine's acidity balances its slight residual sugar, and the taste is well constructed as a result.
price range: A

producer: Vinos Argentinos S.A.E.
classification: White table wine
grape variety: Semillon
region: Northwest
district: San Juan

A well-made sweet white wine, which comes from a country where sweet white wines are not traditional. This is the only Argentinian sweet white wine widely distributed in the United Kingdom.

Deep golden color and a rich, fruity bouquet. The wine has a full, rich flavor, with grapey aromas, and finishes well.
price range: A

producer: Vinos Argentinos S.A.E.
classification: Red table wine
grape variety: Malbeck (Malbec)
region: Northwest
district: Mendoza

This well-made, modestly priced red wine is the only one from Argentina that is widely distributed in the United Kingdom.

Deep red color and a good, fruity bouquet. The wine has a pleasant, round flavor, with good balance and a fine finish.
price range: A

producer: Cooperativa la Consulta Ltda.
classification: Red varietal table wine
grape variety: Malbec
region: Mendoza Province

"Bodega de Oro Gran Reserva Malbec 1967" was aged for three years in wooden casks from Nancy, France, then three years in bottle prior to release. It should be opened at least one hour before serving so as to develop its complex, well-bred finesse. It is made from all natural ingredients, with no chemicals, preservatives, or additives.

Deep red color and a delicate bouquet. The wine has a fine woody flavor with a fine, lingering aftertaste; a light, gracefully elegant wine. **price range:** A

AUSTRIA

producer: Herbert Donner Weinkellerei
classification: White table wine
grape variety: Spätrot-Rotgipfler
region: Eastern Austria
district: Vienna
city or village: Gumpoldskirchen

An authentic Gumpoldskirchner, classified as a *Spitzenwein* (top-quality wine).

Medium yellow color and a rich bouquet. The wine is elegant, well-balanced, and full-bodied. **price range:** B

producer: Herbert Donner Weinkellerei
classification: Red table wine
grape variety: Blaufränkisch
region: Burgenland
district: Neusiedler See
city or village: Rust

An authentic "Ruster Blaufränkisch."

Medium red color and a pleasant bouquet. The wine is dry, full-bodied, and elegant. **price range:** B

producer: Herbert Donner Weinkellerei
classification: Red table wine
grape variety: Blauburgunder
region: Burgenland
district: Neusiedler See
city or village: Oggau-Moerbisch

A typical Burgenland wine.

Medium red color and a very pleasant bouquet. The wine is dry, crisp, and well-rounded, a charming Austrian red wine.
price range: B

producer: Herbert Donner Weinkellerei
classification: White table wine
grape variety: Walschriesling and Weissburgunder
region: Burgenland
district: Neusiedler See
city or village: Oggau-Moerbisch

A typical Burgenland white wine.

Medium light color and a pleasant bouquet. The wine is dry, crisp, and fruity, with a delightfully well-rounded quality.
price range: B

producer: Rudolf Kutschera
classification: White table wine
grape variety: Gewürztraminer and Riesling
region: North-central Austria
district: Wachau
city or village: Krems

Pale straw color and a fruity bouquet. The wine has good flavor, fruit, and acidity in total balance; it is a fine Kremser wine.
price range: B

producer: Rudolf Kutschera
classification: White table wine
grape variety: Gewürztraminer, Veltliner, and Riesling

Clean straw color and a fragrant, fruity bouquet. The wine shows good fruit and acid balance—it is a fine example of a well-made Austrian wine and a pleasure to drink. **price range:** B

producer: Lessner & Kamper
classification: White table wine
grape variety: Riesling
region: Wachau

The house of Lessner & Kamper, recently incorporated as Lessner & Grams, has a history of wine making that encompasses the era of the Austro-Hungarian empire. Although extensively represented throughout Europe for many generations, their wines were not introduced to America until 1972.

Light straw color and a very mild, flowery bouquet. The wine is clean, mellow, light, and dry, with a tart aftertaste; it is delightfully refreshing, lighter, and more delicate than some German wines.
price range: A

producer: Lenz Moser
classification: White table wine

Straw color and a light bouquet. The wine is soft and semi-dry, with a clean flavor. **price range:** A

producer: Lenz Moser
classification: White table wine

grape variety: Walschriesling and Grüner Veltliner
region: Danube valley
district: Wachau
city or village: Krems

The largest-selling Austrian wine on the export market, with worldwide distribution.

Bright clear color and a bouquet with lingering fruit. The wine is fresh, clean, and has good fruit and depth. It is excellent value, suitable as an aperitif or with any meal. **price range:** A

producer: Winzergenossenschaft Krems
classification: Red table wine
grape variety: St. Laurent
region: Danube River valley
district: Wachau
city or village: Krems

Brilliant, deep red color and a fine, fragrant bouquet. The wine is soft and caressing on the palate, and quite refreshing, it is a very mild, light table wine.
price range: B

producer: Winzergenossenschaft Krems
classification: White table wine
grape variety: Veltliner
region: Danube River valley
district: Wachau
city or village: Krems

The label indicates that this wine is an *Auslese*, a selection of specially ripe grape bunches harvested late in the season. This high natural sugar content endows the wine with exceptionally rich body and full taste.

Full bouquet; the wine has a delicate, fruity flavor and exceptionally rich body; it is well bred. **price range:** C

producer: Winzergenossenschaft Krems
classification: White table wine
grape variety: Rosenhügler
region: Danube River valley
district: Wachau
city or village: Krems

A fresh wine whose charming bouquet and crisp, fruity taste allows it to be drunk with pleasure at any stage in a meal, especially with seafood. **price range: B**

producer: Winzergenossenschaft Krems
classification: White table wine
grape variety: Grüner Veltliner
region: Danube River valley
district: Wachau
city or village: Krems

If your preference is for a light, dry, and characteristic Grüner Veltliner that will brighten up and stimulate your mood, while leaving your head clear, then you'll choose this pure and natural vintage wine.

Light color and a fresh bouquet. The wine is medium dry, fruity, and has a spicy flavor. **price range: B**

producer: Winzergenossenschaft Krems
classification: Rosé table wine
region: Danube River valley
district: Wachau
city or village: Krems

"Count George's Kremser Rosé" is an excellent wine for all occasions, very agreeable to the American taste. It was one of the first rosés produced in Austria.

Lovely fresh, light rosé color and a delicate bouquet. The wine is refined, mildly smooth, and pleasant. **price range: B**

producer: Winzergenossenschaft Krems
classification: White table wine
region: Danube River valley
district: Wachau
city or village: Krems

"Count George's Kremser Jungfau" is aptly named, for it means "Maiden of Krems."

Light color and a fragrant, flowery bouquet. The wine is dry and luxurious, with a pleasant aftertaste. **price range: B**

producer: Winzergenossenschaft Dinstlgut Loiben
classification: White table wine
grape variety: Grüner Veltliner
region: Danube River valley
district: Wachau
city or village: Loiben

Full bouquet; the wine is spicy, fruity, and has a pleasant heartiness. **price range: B**

producer: Winzergenossenschaft Gumpoldskirchen
classification: Red table wine
grape variety: Spätrot-Rotgipfler
region: Eastern Austria
district: Vienna
city or village: Gumpoldskirchen

Medium dark red color and a full, flavorful bouquet. An outstanding-quality wine. **price range: B**

producer: Winzergenossenschaft Gumpoldskirchen
classification: White table wine
grape variety: Neuburger
region: Eastern Austria
district: Vienna
city or village: Gumpoldskirchen

Gumpoldskirchner Königswein, "The Wine of Kings—The King of Wines," comes from the beautiful and festive village of Gumpoldskirchen, the wine center of the Baden region south of Vienna. The King label on the bottle is awarded only to the highest quality wine.

Light color and a full bouquet. The wine is pleasant, mild, and very drinkable. **price range: B**

CYPRUS

producer: KEO Ltd.
classification: Fortified wine
grape variety: Mavron (red) and Xinisteri (white)
region: Central Cyprus
district: Limassol
city or village: Kalo Horio, Zoopighi

The Commandarie has the oldest tradition of any individually named wine in the world. KEO "Commandarie St. John" is linked in name and history with the Knights Hospitallers of the Order of St. John.

Bright tawny color; it is a delicious dessert wine of nobility, with an unrivaled bouquet *fruite* of its own, coupled with a luscious honeylike sweetness. **price range: B**

producer: KEO Ltd.
classification: Red table wine
grape variety: Mavron and Ophthalmo
region: Central Cyprus
district: Limassol
city or village: Mallia

"Othello" is a full-bodied red table wine aged in bottle in the underground KEO cellars, protected from temperature fluctuations.

Bright red color and a very rich, fragrant bouquet. The wine is smooth and full-bodied, with a characteristic grapeyness. **price range: B**

producer: KEO Ltd.
classification: White table wine
grape variety: Xinisteri
region: Western Cyprus
district: Paphos
city or village: Kathikas

This wine won a gold medal at the Second International Wine & Spirits Competition held at Yalta in 1970, and a silver medal at the International Wine Fair in Yugoslavia in 1958. It also won a silver medal at the International Wine Competition in Langenlois, Austria, in 1959.

Bright clear color and a rich, fragrant bouquet. The wine is smooth, full-bodied, and well-balanced. **price range: A**

CZECHO-SLOVAKIA

producer: Vinarske Zavody O.P. Bratislava
classification: White table wine
grape variety: Müller-Thurgau
region: Slovakia

This wine was introduced on the English market in August of 1976. It is sold under the Silver Prince label.

Pale gold color and a fragrant, grapey bouquet. The wine is light, crisp, and dry; it has a refreshing crispness and is ideal when drunk on. its own, as an aperitif, or with a biscuit after dinner. Serve well-chilled. **price range: A**

producer: Vinarske Zavody O.P. Bratislava
classification: White table wine
grape variety: Traminer
region: Slovakia

"Silver Prince Traminer" was first introduced to the United Kingdom in August 1976.

Golden color and a fragrant, spicy bouquet. The wine is spicy, medium dry, and has a fruity flavor; it can be drunk with any dish, even the rich-flavored foods of Eastern Europe. It may also be enjoyed on its own and is best served chilled. **price range: A**

producer: Vinarske Zavody O.P. Bratislava
classification: White table wine
grape variety: Walschriesling (Italian Riesling)

region: Slovakia

"Silver Prince Welsch Riesling" was first offered to the English wine trade in August 1976.

Clear, pale gold color and a fresh, fruity bouquet. The wine is medium dry, with a full Riesling flavor; its fruity style allows it to be enjoyed either as an aperitif or as a perfect complement to fish, poultry, and lightly flavored meat dishes. Serve well chilled. **price range:** A

DENMARK

producer: T. Jespersen & Co.
classification: Fruit wine
variety: Cherries
region: Zealand
district: Copenhagen

"Cherry Kirsberry" is a red, semi-sweet dessert wine made from cherries.
price range: B

GREECE

producer: Achaia-Clauss
classification: Red table wine
grape variety: Volitza
region: Peloponnesus
district: Akhaia
city or village: Patras

A private-estate wine.

Ruby-red color and a flowery bouquet. The wine is fruity and soft—a quality Greek wine. **price range:** B

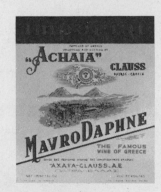

producer: Achaia-Clauss
classification: Red table wine
region: Peloponnesus
district: Akhaia

city or village: Patras

Pine resin is added to the wine to obtain a resiny flavor.

An acquired taste; very popular in Greece. **price range:** B

producer: Achaia-Clauss
classification: White table wine
region: Peloponnese
district: Akhaia
city or village: Patras

This is the proprietary wine of Achaia-Clauss.

This is a light, fruity, pale straw-colored wine. **price range:** B

producer: Achaia-Clauss
classification: Red table wine
region: Peloponnesus
district: Akhaia
city or village: Patras

The most popular red wine in Greek restaurants.

Bright ruby color and an elegant bouquet. The wine is soft, elegant, and easy to drink. **price range:** B

producer: Achaia-Clauss
classification: Red varietal wine
grape variety: Mavroudin
region: Peloponnese
district: Akhaia
city or village: Patras

This is a heavy, sweet, red dessert wine.

This is the famous original Mavrodaphne, which was developed by Gustav Clauss, the founder of Achaia-Clauss, in 1861. **price range:** B

producer: Achaia-Clauss
classification: Rosé wine
region: Peloponnese

This is the rosé version of the very popular resin-flavored wines of Greece.
price range: B

producer: Achaia-Clauss
classification: White table wine
region: Peloponnese
district: Akhaia
city or village: Patras

This is a light, dry white wine with a delicate bouquet. **price range:** B

producer: Achaia-Clauss
classification: White table wine
region: Peloponnesus
district: Akhaia
city or village: Patras

The most popular white wine in Greek restaurants.

Bright golden color and a flowery bouquet. The wine is dry, with a full grape flavor—a high-quality wine.
price range: B

producer: Achaia-Clauss
classification: Rosé wine
region: Peloponnese

This dry rosé wine is the traditional rosé wine of Greece. **price range:** B

producer: Achaia-Clauss
classification: Red table wine
region: Peloponnese
district: Akhaia
city or village: Patras

This is a light, dry, deep-ruby-colored wine. **price range:** B

producer: Achaia-Clauss
classification: Red table wine
region: Peloponnese
district: Akhaia
city or village: Patras

This is a dry, light, pleasant wine of ruby color. **price range:** B

producer: Achaia-Clauss
classification: White wine
region: Peloponnese

This is the traditional resin-flavored white wine of Greece. **price range:** B

producer: Andrew P. Cambas Co., Ltd.
classification: Rosé table wine
grape variety: Roditys
region: Attica
district: Mesogia
city or village Kantza

"Cambas Roditys" is a dry rosé with no additives. It is unblended and made entirely from the Roditys grape.

Fruity bouquet; the wine is full-bodied and well-balanced, pleasant when enjoyed with almost any food providing it is not too highly spiced. Serve well chilled.

price range: A

producer: Andrew P. Cambas Co., Ltd.
classification: White table wine
grape variety: Savatiano
region: Attica
district: Mesogia
city or village: Hymettus

Hymettus wine is named after Mount Hymettus, where the grapes used for this wine are grown. Mesogia in Attica is noted for some of the best wines produced in Greece.

Pale gold color and a fruity bouquet. The wine is well-balanced and may be enjoyed with fish, poultry, and white meat, except highly spiced dishes. Always serve chilled.

price range: A

producer: Andrew P. Cambas Co., Ltd.
classification: Red table wine
grape variety: Mandalaria (Mandalari)
region: Attica
district: Mesogia
city or village: Pendeli

Pendeli wine is named after Mount Pendeli near Mesogia, where the grapes used for this wine are grown. Mesogia in Attica is noted for some of the best wine produced in Greece.

Ruby-red color and a delicate, fruity bouquet. The wine is very well-balanced, not too dry, and can be accepted by new wine drinkers as well as old wine drinkers. Enjoy it with casserole dishes and spicy foods.

price range: A

producer: Andrew P. Cambas Co., Ltd.
classification: White table wine
grape variety: Savatiano
region: Attica
district: Mesogia
city or village: Kantza

"Cava Cambas" is named for the underground cellars of Cambas in Kantza, Mesogia, where the wine is kept for at least twelve years before being sold. The wine has just been introduced on the U.S. market.

Golden color and a fruity bouquet. The wine is well-balanced and is one of the best Greek wines that can compete with many of the world's finest. Enjoy it with fish, poultry, and white meats prepared without too many spices.

price range: C

producer: D. Nicolaou Sons Co.
classification: Red table wine
grape variety: Mavroudia
region: Attica

A hearty red wine with the unique Retsina touch (with pine resin added during fermentation).

This distinct, historic wine is perfect for any Greek dish.

price range: A

producer: D. Nicolaou Sons Co.
classification: White table wine
grape variety: Savatiano
region: Attica

Retsina is made from white wine to which pine resin is added during fermentation, giving a unique flavor that marks this distinctive wine. Retsina is the most popular wine in Greece.

The impeccable bouquet and flavor makes Nicolaou Retsina a perfect companion to all Greek foods.

price range: A

producer: D. Nicolaou Sons Co.
classification: Rosé table wine
grape variety: Roditis
region: Attica, Peloponnesus

Pink color and a fine bouquet. The wine is dry and hearty, perfect when served lightly chilled.

price range: A

producer: D. Nicolaou Sons Co.
classification: Red table wine
grape variety: Kotsifali and Mandilari
region: Attica

Ruby-red color and a unique bouquet of Kotsifali and Mandilari grapes. The wine is reminiscent of a good Bordeaux and, served at room temperature, is a perfect complement to red meats.

price range: A

producer: D. Nicolaou Sons Co.
classification: Fortified wine
grape variety: Muscat
region: Peloponnese
city or village: Patras

This wine is made by adding grape brandy to partially fermented grape juice. This retains natural grape sugar in the wine and keeps the full, luscious flavor and grape aroma during fermentation.

Full, luscious bouquet and flavor; a fine Greek wine that is perfect for dinners and desserts.

price range: A

producer: D. Nicolaou Sons Co.
classification: White table wine
grape variety: Savatiano
region: Attica

Fine, aromatic bouquet; the wine is reminiscent of a French Graves and should be served chilled to accompany fish, fowl, or veal dishes. It has classic proportions.

price range: A

producer: D. Nicolaou Sons Co.
classification: Fortified wine
grape variety: Mavrodaphne
region: Peloponnese
city or village: Patras

Mavrodaphne is made from partially fermented grape juice to which grape brandy has been added. This retains natural grape sugar in the wine.

Luscious, full aroma and flavor of the grape; the wine is a perfect dessert accompaniment.

price range: A

HUNGARY

producer: Monimpex
classification: White table wine
grape variety: Szürkebarát
region: Central Hungary
district: Lake Balaton
city or village: Badacsony

"Badacsonyi Szürkebarát" is one of the most famous white wines of Hungary. It comes from the village of Badacsony on Lake Balaton, and is highly praised in Hungary.

Yellow color and a pleasant, flowery bouquet. The wine is beautifully balanced and subtle, medium dry, and has a round finish.

price range: A

producer: Monimpex
classification: White sparkling wine
region: North and South Hungary
A sweet sparkling wine.
White-yellow color and a rich and fruity bouquet. The wine is very clean and elegant, very suitable for drinking with sweets and rich cakes, and very good for birthday celebrations. **price range:** B

producer: Monimpex
classification: White table wine
grape variety: Hárslevelü
region: Northeast Hungary
district: Matra Mountains
city or village: Debrö
"Debröi Hárslevelü" is the second-best-known white wine of Hungary.
Deep gold color and a beautiful "honeysuckle" bouquet characteristic of the grape variety. The wine is medium dry, full-bodied, and rich. **price range:** A

producer: Monimpex
classification: White table wine
grape variety: Furmint
region: Northeast Hungary
district: Tokay
village: Authorized villages in Tokay zone
Although a true Tokay, this is not a sweet wine as it is made from Furmint grapes not affected by *pourriture noble* (noble mold), producing a drier wine.
Deep golden color and a big, richly fruity bouquet. The wine is medium dry, full-bodied, robust, and has a long-lasting finish; it is suitable for strong-flavored dishes or for those who prefer white wines.
price range: B

producer: Monimpex
classification: White table wine

grape variety: Furmint and Hárslevelü
region: Northeast Hungary
district: Tokay
village: Authorized villages in Tokay zone
Labeled *Aszu* (selection), this lusciously sweet wine is produced from specially selected grapes that have shriveled under the action of the *pourriture noble* (noble mold). The sweetness is indicated by the number of *puttonyos* (putts) of overripe grapes added to the casks at the time of vinification, when the wine ferments in open casks. Three *puttonyos* is the driest *Aszu*, five *puttonyos* the sweetest, and the wines are priced accordingly. The wines are sold only in clear half-liter bottles and are quite expensive.
Deep gold color and a lusciously big, fruity bouquet with a faint "burnt" aroma. The wine is rich, sweet, and full-bodied, with a slight flavor of Botrytis carrying over from the grapes; it can live for decades, and is normally not released for sale until five years after the vintage.
price range: B-C

producer: Monimpex
classification: White table wine
grape variety: Furmint and Hárslevelü
region: Northeast Hungary
district: Tokay
village: Authorized villages in Tokay zone
"Tokaji Szamorodni" is a sweet dessert wine, but not an *Aszu*, which is made from selected overripe grapes. *Szamorodni* means "such as it was grown" in Hungarian, and being sweet, the wine is similar to a Tokay *Aszu* but lacks its concentration. The wine is a Hungarian specialty and has been famous for centuries.
Golden color and a rich bouquet of honey and fruit. The wine is full-bodied and full-flavored, as it is rich in extracts.
price range: A

producer: Monimpex
classification: White table wine
grape variety: Furmint and Hárslevelü
region: Northeastern Hungary
district: Tokay
village: Authorized villages in Tokay zone
"Szamorodni" is a dry Tokay made from grapes not affected by the noble mold (*pourriture noble*). It is not fortified with any Brandy and has its own particular charm.
Golden yellow color and a strong, fruity bouquet. The wine is dry, rich, and has an elegant fragrance; it can be served as an aperitif or with rich food like duck, pork, and smoked salmon. A very interesting wine. **price range:** A

producer: Monimpex
classification: Red table wine
grape variety: Cabernet Franc
region: Düna (Danube River)
district: Alfold
city or village: Hajós
"Hajósi Cabernet" comes from a single property and is made entirely from the Cabernet Franc grape. The wines are matured by small growers in their cellars, giving the wine character as it ages.
Ruby-purple color and a strong, fruity bouquet. The wine is full and rich, with a fruity but mellow flavor; it is interesting to those who like fruity wines with definite breeding. **price range:** A

producer: Monimpex
classification: White table wine
grape variety: Walschriesling (Italian Riesling)
region: Central Hungary
district: Lake Balaton
"Balatoni Riesling" comes from the northern shores of Lake Balaton, where the sunny climate produces fine, rich wines that are very famous, fuller in flavor and bouquet than those grown farther north.
Golden yellow color and an elegant, fruity bouquet. The wine is medium sweet and quite fruity, with strong vinosity and a long finish. **price range:** A

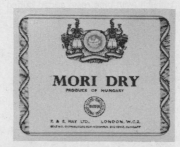

producer: Monimpex
classification: White table wine
grape variety: Ezerjo
region: Northeast Hungary
district: Matras Mountains
city or village: Mór
"Móri Ezerjo" (the thousand goods of Mór), is a famous white wine prized for its dryness and full body. The Ezerjo is a traditional Hungarian grape.
Green-yellow color and a fine, strongly fruity bouquet. The wine is full-bodied but

beautifully dry, with an elegant fragrance; it is drier and more delicate than some other Hungarian whites.
price range: A

producer: Monimpex
classification: White table wine
grape variety: Furmint
region: Central Hungary
district: Lake Balaton
"Balatoni Furmint" comes from the shores of Lake Balaton and is excellent value.
Rich golden color and a big, "honey" bouquet. The wine is fruity, medium dry, and full-bodied, with a round finish; it is excellent for drinking with full-flavored dishes and is also very good with meat.
price range: A

producer: Monimpex
classification: White table wine
grape variety: Olasz-Riesling
region: Southern Hungary
district: Pécs-Villány
Pale straw-lemon color and a light, fruity bouquet characteristic of Riesling. The wine is medium dry, fruity, and well-balanced. **price range:** A

producer: Monimpex
classification: Red table wine
grape variety: Kadarka, Pinot Noir, and Merlot
region: Northeast Hungary
district: Matras Mountains
city or village: Eger
"Egri Bikavér" (Bull's Blood of Eger), the origins of this wine are steeped in Hungary's ancient history. During the siege of the fortress of Eger by the Turks in 1552, the Magyars, led by Istvan Dobo, fought so fiercely that their opponents were led to believe that they had been fortified by drinking bull's blood.

Deep garnet-red color and a lovely bouquet of inviting fruit. The wine is "meaty," with a good depth of flavor.
price range: A

producer: Monimpex
classification: Red table wine
region: Southern Hungary
district: Trolna
city or village: Szekszárd
A light, dry, and sturdy red wine.
price range: B

producer: Monimpex
classification: White table wine
grape variety: Leányka
region: North-Central Hungary
district: Matras Mountains
city or village: Eger
A dry, rich white wine.
price range: B

producer: Monimpex
classification: White table wine
grape variety: Keknyelü (Blue Stalk)
region: Central Hungary-Lake Balaton
district: Badacsonyi
A semi-dry white wine.
price range: B

producer: Monimpex
classification: Rosé table wine
grape variety: Kadarka
"Nemes Kadar" is a slightly effervescent, semi-sweet rosé.
price range: B

producer: Monimpex
classification: White table wine
grape variety: Furmint and Hárslevelü
region: Northeast Hungary
district: Tokay
village: Authorized villages in Tokay zone
This exceedingly rare dessert wine, "Tokaji Essencia" (essence of Tokay), is made from the juice exuded by selected grapes as they wait to be crushed and fermented. It is more of a natural liqueur than a wine, and is suitable for the most special occasions, either alone or with an appropriate dessert.
Rich, golden color and a floral fragrance. The wine is lusciously sweet—a noble dessert wine.
price range: E

producer: Monimpex
classification: Red table wine
grape variety: Pinot Noir
region: Southern Hungary
district: Baranya
city or village: Pécs-Villány
"Villányi Burgundi" (Villány Burgundy) is a soft, dry red wine.
price range: B

ISRAEL

producer: Ankalon Wine Cellars
classification: Red table wine
grape variety: Alicanté Bouschet
district: Plain of Judea
city or village: Ramla
A rich sweet dessert wine; 13% alcohol. It stays in good condition for many months after opening.
Rich, fruity aroma; the wine is sweet, rich, and fruity.
price range: A

producer: Carmel Wine Co., Inc.
classification: Red sparkling wine
price range: C

producer: Carmel Wine Co., Inc.
classification: White
price range: C

producer: Carmel Wine Co., Inc.
classification: Red table wine
price range: B

producer: Carmel Wine Co., Inc.
classification: Red table wine
grape variety: Carignan
price range: A

producer: Carmel Wine Co., Inc.
classification: White table wine
grape variety: Semillon and Sauvignon
price range: A

producer: Carmel Wine Co., Inc.
classification: Red table wine
grape variety: Carignan
price range: A

producer: Carmel Wine Co., Inc.
classification: White table wine
grape variety: Sauvignon Blanc and Clairette
price range: A

producer: Carmel Wine Co., Inc.
classification: Rosé table wine
grape variety: Grenache
region: Mount Carmel and Judan Hills
price range: A

producer: Carmel Wine Co., Inc.
classification: White table wine
grape variety: Semillon
district: Judan Hills entrance to Jerusalem
price range: A

producer: Carmel Wine Co., Inc.
classification: White table wine
grape variety: Sauvignon Blanc
region: Mount Carmel
price range: A

producer: Carmel Wine Co., Inc.
classification: White table wine
grape variety: Chenin Blanc
district: Galilea
price range: A

producer: Carmel Wine Co., Inc.
classification: White table wine
grape variety: French Colombard
district: Galilea
price range: A

producer: Carmel-Zion, Ltd.
classification: Red table wine
grape variety: Carignan
region: Judaea
district: Gadera
A fairly recent addition to Israel's wines. It compares favorably with many European wines of similar price.
Brilliant red color and a round bouquet. The wine is dry, full-bodied, and smooth.
price range: A

producer: Carmel Zion Ltd.
classification: White table wine
grape variety: Sauvignon Blanc
region: Judaea
district: Ascalon
Grown near the old Roman town of Ascalon, where wine was made in the first and second centuries.
Very pale gold color and a fragrant, delicate bouquet. The wine is dry, but smooth and sound, and has a crisp finish. It is a satisfying summer drink if served chilled.
price range: A

producer: Ein Karem Wine Co.
classification: Red table wine
grape variety: Alicanté
region: Samaria
district: Hadera
This wine is made from the type of vine brought to the Holy Land by the Crusaders, who came by sea from southern Spain to the Palestine region in the eleventh century. The grapes were originally grown for raisins and table grapes by the Moslems, who are prohibited by their religion to drink alcohol. The wine industry in Palestine was resuscitated by Jewish immigrants at the end of the nineteenth century.
Light ruby-red color and a typically rich, fruity bouquet. The wine is robust and full-flavored, but has a fresh taste; an ideal wine to enjoy with a sweet biscuit or dessert.
price range: A

producer: Eliaz Wine Cellars
classification: Rosé table wine
grape variety: Malbec
region: Samaria
city or village: Binyamina
Flowery bouquet; the wine is very slightly sweet and full-flavored, very fresh and pleasant if served with pastry. Drink chilled.
price range: A

JAPAN

producer: Godo Shusei Co., Ltd.
classification: Fruit wine
variety: Plums
region: Honshu
district: Tokyo
A sweet plum wine.
Bright golden color and a fruity bouquet. The wine is sweet.
price range: A

producer: Hannah Winery Co.
classification: Fruit wine
variety: Plums
region: Honshu
district: Kobe
price range: A

producer: Kiku-Masamune Sake Brewing Co. Ltd.
classification: Rice wine
variety: Rice
region: Honshu
district: Kobe
A dry rice wine with wood character resulting from aging in cedar barrels.
price range: B

producer: Kiku-Masamune Sake Brewing Co., Ltd.
classification: Rice wine
variety: Rice
region: Honshu
district: Kobe
A semi-dry, bittersweet white rice wine.
price range: B

MEXICO

producer: Casa Madero, S.A.
classification: Red table wine
grape variety: Ruby Cabernet and Grenache
region: Parras
district: Coahuila
city or village: San Lorenzo
price range: B

producer: Casa Madero, S.A.
classification: Rosé table wine
grape variety: Grenache
region: Parras
district: Coahuila
city or village: San Lorenzo
price range: B

producer: Cavas de San Juan, S.A.
classification: Red table wine
grape variety: Cabernet Sauvignon

region: Queretaro
city or village: San Juan del Rio Oro
Fruity bouquet; the wine is good, with light Cabernet flavor. **price range: B**

producer: Cavas de San Juan, S.A.
classification: Red table wine
grape variety: Tempranillo
region: Queretaro
city or village: San Juan del Rio Oro
A dry red wine made from the same variety grown in the celebrated Rioja district of Spain. **price range: A**

producer: Cavas de San Juan, S.A.
classification: Rosé table wine
grape variety: Carignane and Grenache
region: Queretaro
city or village: San Juan del Rio Oro
A good dry rosé. **price range: A**

producer: Cavas de San Juan, S.A.
classification: White table wine
grape variety: Chenin Blanc and Ugni Blanc
region: Queretaro
city or village: San Juan del Rio Oro
A nice dry white wine.
price range: B

producer: Cavas de San Juan, S.A.
classification: Red table wine
grape variety: Pinot Noir

---

region: Queretaro
city or village: San Juan del Rio Oro
A full-bodied red wine.
price range: B

producer: Cavas de San Juan, S.A.
classification: White table wine
grape variety: Feher Zagos and Ugni Blanc
region Queretaro
city or village: San Juan del Rio Oro
A good dry white wine.
price range: A

RUSSIA

producer: Abrau-Dyrso Winery
classification: White sparkling wine
grape variety: Pinot Noir and Pinot Chardonnay
region: Black Sea
district: Krasnodar
city or village: Abrau Dyurso
Nazdorovya Champagne is the only Russian Champagne imported to the United States. It is produced by the *méthode champenoise* and comes in *brut* (dry) and extra *brut* (extra dry) grades of sweetness.
Bright golden color and a light bouquet. The wine is dry. **price range: D**

producer: Abrau-Dyurso Winery
classification: White sparkling wine
grape variety: Pinot Noir and Pinot Chardonnay
region: Black Sea
district: Krasnodar
city or village: Abrau-Dyurso
Nazdorovya is the only Russian Champagne imported to the United States. It is produced via the *méthode champenoise* and comes either in *brut* (dry) or extra *brut* (very dry); the latter is produced only in limited quantities and is more expensive.
Bright golden color and a light bouquet. The wine is very dry. **price range: E**

SOUTH AFRICA

producer: KVW
classification: Fortified wine
grape variety: Blend
region: Cape Province
A typical smooth and satisfying cocktail Sherry matured in oak vats and containing 17.5% alcohol by volume.
Pale golden color and a characteristic bouquet. The wine is round and smooth, with a tangy flavor. **price range: B**

producer: KVW
classification: Fortified wine
grape variety: Semillon and Pedro Ximenez
This Cream Sherry is full and round, a rich, full-bodied wine with a fruity bouquet and deep amber color. The balance and smoothness are attained by blending wines that have matured for at least eight years in wood. This is a luscious wine.
price range: A

producer: KVW
classification: Fortified wine
grape variety: Chenin Blanc
This is a fine dry South African Sherry, where the distinctive flor character is shown to excellent advantage. Its bouquet is clean and refreshing, and its aftertaste nutty.
The average age of this wine in wood is between four and five years. This is considered by some to be the best dry South African Sherry. **price range: A**

producer: KVW
classification: Fortified wine
grape variety: Chenin Blanc
This is a fine-quality South African Sherry that retains all the characteristics of a medium nutty-flavored Sherry with an overlying full body. It has a pleasant, round, medium-to-full bouquet.
The average age in wood of this blend is not less than two years. By fining and cold stabilizing after blending, a fairly full-bodied but smooth wine is attained.
price range: A

producer: Nederburg Wines Pty., Ltd.
classification: White sparkling wine
grape variety: Riesling and Chenin Blanc
region: Cape Province
district: Paarl
city or village: Paarl
"Nederburg Cuvée" is produced from selected grape varieties with high fruit and acid content, naturally fermented by the time-honored *charmat* process using selected yeast cultures. This process yields wines of maximum delicacy, entertaining fruitiness and exquisite character, with the finest and most persistent effervescence. Two types are produced: *brut* (dry) and *doux* (sweet).
Pale yellow color and a crisp, fruity, and elegant bouquet. The wine is appetizing, delicately dry, and tart, with a lingering flavor. **price range: A**

producer: Nederburg Wines Pty., Ltd.
classification: White table wine
grape variety: Chenin Blanc
region: Cape Province
district: Paarl
city or village: Paarl
"Nederburg Paarl Late Harvest" wines are the crowning glory of South African sunshine, clonal (grape) selection, and the wine maker's art. The wines are produced from sun-ripened grapes affected by "noble rot" (Botrytis) that are picked late in the growing season, giving the wines full, rich character. The wines are vinified in contact

with the skins after removal of the stalks, under temperature-controlled conditions.

Pale yellow color and a flowery, nobly fragrant bouquet. The wine is sweet, noble, and has a velvety texture, with a long, lingering finish. **price range:** B

producer: Nederburg Wines Pty., Ltd.
classification: White table wine
grape variety: Muscat de Cannelli and Muscat d'Alexandria
region: Cape Province
district: Paarl
city or village: Paarl

"Nederburg Fonternel" is produced from selected grape varieties that have delectable fruit-acid content and an aromatic Muscat bouquet. The aim of the vinification process is consistency in style and character, where different grape varieties are harvested and crushed together.

Yellow color with greenish tints and a floral, aromatic Muscat bouquet. The wine is off-dry, spicy, and has a tart, lingering finish. **price range:** A

producer: Nederburg Wines Pty., Ltd.
classification: White table wine
grape variety: Riesling
region: Cape Province
district: Paarl
city or village: Paarl

This delicate Riesling wine is made only in limited quantity in order to protect its inherently thoroughbred characteristics.

Pale yellow color with green glints and a delicate, fruity, and fragrant bouquet. The wine is elegantly light and dry, with a tart aftertaste and appetizing flavor. Serve with hors d'oeuvres, seafood, and poultry for an enchanting combination. **price range:** A

producer: Nederburg Wines Pty., Ltd.
classification: White table wine
grape variety: Riesling
region: Cape Province
district: Paarl
city or village: Paarl

This wine is produced from Riesling grapes grown in the renowned district of Paarl. The vine is a shy bearer, and the grapes are grown on withered granitic soils. The vines are trellised so as to protect the grapes from the sun, and the vinification assures maximum delicacy and long shelf life.

Pale yellow color and a delicate, fragrant and floral bouquet. The wine is fruity, tartly dry, and has a lingering flavor; it enhances any occasion and is ideal with hors d'oeuvres, seafood, and poultry.
price range: A

producer: Nederburg Wines Pty., Ltd.
classification: Rosé table wine
grape variety: Cinsault, Shiraz, and Cabernet Sauvignon
region: Cape Province
district: Paarl
city or village: Paarl

Skillful Nederburg blending and noble grapes result in this delectable wine, made by the traditional vinification process native to France: short contact with the skins. The grapes are picked when they are crisp, young, and particularly fruity.

Pale ruby color and a crisp, fruity bouquet. The wine is delicately dry and has light body and elegance; it can be served throughout a meal. **price range:** A

producer: Nederburg Wines Pty., Ltd.
classification: Red table wine
grape variety: Cabernet Sauvignon, Shiraz, and Cinsault
region: Cape Province
district: Paarl
city or village: Paarl

This mature, full-bodied red wine is the result of a proud marriage between some of the Cape's choicest grape varieties, fermented together in enamel-lined pressure tanks under temperature-controlled conditions. Maturation later on in oak casks ensures a mellow, full texture and a lingering aftertaste.

Clean, garnet-red color and a mature, aromatic and velvety bouquet. The wine is smooth, full, and round, with a lingering finish. **price range:** B

producer: Nederburg Wines Pty., Ltd.
classification: Rosé table wine
grape variety: Cinsault, Pinotage, and Chenin Blanc
region: Cape Province
district: Paarl
city or village: Paarl

"Nederburg Rosé" is derived from grapes fermented briefly on their skins and is not a blend of red and white wines. The wine is fermented under temperature-controlled conditions and is semi-dry.

Delicately pale, light red color and a youthfully fruity and aromatic bouquet. The wine is light and delicate, with lingering sweetness; it is generally preferred by the ladies, but is highly regarded by young and old. **price range:** A

producer: Nederburg Wines Pty., Ltd.
classification: Red table wine
grape variety: Cabernet Sauvignon
region: Cape Province
district: Paarl
city or village: Paarl

This thoroughbred grape variety represents a challenge to South African wine makers. The grapes are grown on thin soils, and the vines are trellised so that the grapes receive maximum sunshine. The wine is fermented on the skins in enamel-lined tanks, then matured in oak for eighteen months prior to bottling.

Full garnet-red color; time-honored maturation brings out a full, rich nutty flavor. The wine's noble dignity and lingering aftertaste makes it exquisite with game and roasts, and it is also an ideal companion to fine cheese and nuts. **price range:** B

producer: Oude Meester Group/Die Bergkelder
classification: White table wine

grape variety: Riesling
region: Cape Province
district: Stellenbosch

"Riesling Cultivar" is produced in the western area of Cape Province. At the Monde Selection in Belgium, this wine was awarded a silver medal in its category.

Light clear color and a delicate bouquet. The wine is crisp and dry.
price range: B

producer: Oude Meester Group/Die Bergkelder
classification: Red table wine
grape variety: Cabernet Sauvignon
region: Cape Province
district: Stellenbosch

Fragrant bouquet; a dry, soft, and velvety red wine. **price range:** B

producer: Oude Meester Group/Die Bergkelder
classification: White table wine
grape variety: Chenin Blanc blend
region: Cape Province
district: Stellenbosch

Fresh, fruity bouquet; the wine is delicate, clean, and semi-sweet.
price range: B

producer: Oude Meester Group/Die Bergkelder
classification: Red table wine
grape variety: Pinotage (cross between Pinot Noir and Hermitage)
region: Cape Province
district: Durbanville

Grown on the Meerendal Estate, this is a wine of Superior Origin as outlined in the 1973 South African Wine Law.

Well-rounded bouquet; a delightfully smooth red wine. **price range:** B

SWITZERLAND

producer: J & P Testuz
classification: White table wine
grape variety: Chasselas (Dorin)
region: Vaud
district: Lavaux
city or village: Dezaley
Dezaley is one of the best white wines of Switzerland.
Light, bright gold color and an elegantly fragrant bouquet. The wine is quite dry and well-balanced. **price range:** C

producer: Aloys de Montmollin
classification: White table wine
grape variety: Chasselas
region: Northwestern Switzerland
district: Lake Neuchatel
village: Neuchatel
Light silver-gold color and a light, clean and flowery bouquet. The wine is dry, light, and sprightly. **price range:** C

producer: Henri Badoux
classification: White table wine
grape variety: Chasselas (Dorin)
region: Vaud
district: Chablais
city or village: Aigle
Bright medium-gold color and a lively, clean and flowery bouquet. The wine is dry, medium- to full-bodied, and quite flavorful.
price range: D

producer: Robert Gilliard
classification: Red table wine
grape variety: Gamay and Pinot Noir
region: Valais
Dôle is one of the best red wines of Switzerland.
Light clear ruby color and a fragrant, fruity bouquet. The wine is light-bodied and supple. **price range:** C

producer: Robert Gilliard
classification: White table wine
grape variety: Chasselas (Fendant)
region: Valais
A typical Fendant du Valais.
Shimmering pale straw color and a mild, distinctive bouquet. The wine is soft, fruity, and not overly dry. **price range:** C

YUGOSLAVIA

producer: Adriatica
classification: White varietal table wine
grape variety: Rizling (Riesling)
region: Vojvodina
district: Novi Sad
city or village: Fruska Gora
A charming, fruity white wine with a touch of sweetness. It complements snacks as well as fish and fowl dishes.
price range: A

producer: Adriatica
classification: Red varietal table wine
grape variety: Cabernet
region: Croatia
district: Istrian Peninsula
A dry, sturdy, and full-bodied red wine with a pleasant, earthy quality and sturdy character. It provides the proper accent for steaks, chops, and other red meats, as well as sharp cheeses. Serve at cool room temperature (cellar temperature).
price range: A

producer: Adriatica
classification: Rosé table wine
grape variety: Opol
region: Dalmatia
Dark color; the wine is medium dry, with good fruit and body and an excellent fresh quality. It goes well with most foods and makes an extremely pleasant aperitif.
price range: A

producer: Yugoslav government
classification: White varietal table wine
grape variety: Walschriesling
region: Slovenia
A reasonable *tafelwein* (table wine) made from Walschriesling.
Pale golden color and a spicy bouquet with some fruit. The wine is acidic but has balanced sweetness, with an "earthy" flavor not present in wines made from the true German Riesling.
price range: A

producer: State monopoly
classification: White varietal table wine
grape variety: Talijanski Riesling (Walschriesling)
region: Serbia
A very popular and reasonably priced quality wine.
Bright greenish-yellow color and a fragrant bouquet. The wine is fresh, full-bodied, and medium dry; it is beautifully balanced and very versatile.
price range: A

producer: State monopoly
classification: Red varietal table wine
grape variety: Procupac
region: Serbia
Made from a grape variety indigenous to Yugoslavia, this is a quality red wine made in the European tradition. It is excellent value.
Very attractive dark red color and a fruity bouquet. The wine is full-bodied, not at all harsh, and well-balanced.
price range: A